A Companion to Rationalism

Blackwell Companions to Philosophy

This outstanding student reference series offers a comprehensive and authoritative survey of philosophy as a whole. Written by today's leading philosophers, each volume provides lucid and engaging coverage of the key figures, terms, topics, and problems of the field. Taken together, the volumes provide the ideal basis for course use, representing an unparalleled work of reference for students and specialists alike.

Already published in the series:

The Blackwell Companion to Philosophy,
Second Edition
Edited by Nicholas Bunnin and Eric Tsui-James

A Companion to Ethics
Edited by Peter Singer

A Companion to Aesthetics
Edited by David Cooper

A Companion to Epistemology
Edited by Jonathan Dancy and Ernest Sosa

A Companion to Contemporary Political Philosophy
Edited by Robert E. Goodin and Philip Pettit

A Companion to Philosophy of Mind
Edited by Samuel Guttenplan

A Companion to Metaphysics
Edited by Jaegwon Kim and Ernest Sosa

A Companion to Philosophy of Law and Legal Theory
Edited by Dennis Patterson

A Companion to Philosophy of Religion
Edited by Philip L. Quinn and Charles Taliaferro

A Companion to the Philosophy of Language
Edited by Bob Hale and Crispin Wright

A Companion to World Philosophies
Edited by Eliot Deutsch and Ron Bontekoe

A Companion to Continental Philosophy
Edited by Simon Critchley and William Schroeder

A Companion to Feminist Philosophy
Edited by Alison M. Jaggar and Iris Marion Young

A Companion to Cognitive Science
Edited by William Bechtel and George Graham

A Companion to Bioethics
Edited by Helga Kuhse and Peter Singer

A Companion to the Philosophers
Edited by Robert L. Arrington

A Companion to Business Ethics
Edited by Robert E. Frederick

A Companion to the Philosophy of Science
Edited by W. H. Newton-Smith

A Companion to Environmental Philosophy
Edited by Dale Jamieson

A Companion to Analytic Philosophy
Edited by A. P. Martinich and David Sosa

A Companion to Genethics
Edited by Justine Burley and John Harris

A Companion to Philosophical Logic
Edited by Dale Jacquette

A Companion to Early Modern Philosophy
Edited by Steven Nadler

A Companion to Philosophy in the Middle Ages
Edited by Jorge J. E. Gracia and Timothy B. Noone

A Companion to African-American Philosophy
Edited by Tommy L. Lott and John P. Pittman

A Companion to Applied Ethics
Edited by R. G. Frey and Christopher Heath Wellman

A Companion to the Philosophy of Education
Edited by Randall Curren

A Companion to African Philosophy
Edited by Kwasi Wiredu

A Companion to Heidegger
Edited by Hubert L. Dreyfus and Mark A. Wrathall

A Companion to Rationalism
Edited by Alan Nelson

A Companion to Ancient Philosophy
Edited by Mary Louise Gill and Pierre Pellegrin

A Companion to Pragmatism
Edited by John R. Shook and Joseph Margolis

A Companion to Nietzsche
Edited by Keith Ansell Pearson

A Companion to Rationalism

Edited by
Alan Nelson

Blackwell
Publishing

BLACKWELL PUBLISHING
350 Main Street, Malden, MA 02148-5020, USA
9600 Garsington Road, Oxford OX4 2DQ, UK
550 Swanston Street, Carlton, Victoria 3053, Australia

First published 2005 by Blackwell Publishing Ltd

1   2005

Library of Congress Cataloging-in-Publication Data

A companion to rationalism / edited by Alan Nelson.
  p. cm. – (Blackwell companions to philosophy)
Includes bibliographical references and index.
ISBN-13: 978-1-4051-0909-3 (alk. paper)
ISBN-10: 1-4051-0909-2 (alk. paper)
1. Rationalism. I. Nelson, Alan Jean. II. Series.

B833.C66 2006
149'.7–dc22

2005010996

A catalogue record for this title is available from the British Library.

Set in 10/12.5pt Photina
by Graphicraft Limited, Hong Kong
Printed and bound in the United Kingdom
by TJ International, Padstow, Cornwall

The publisher's policy is to use permanent paper from mills that operate a sustainable forestry policy,
and which has been manufactured from pulp processed using acid-free and elementary chlorine-free
practices. Furthermore, the publisher ensures that the text paper and cover board used have met
acceptable environmental accreditation standards.

For further information on
Blackwell Publishing, visit our website:
www.blackwellpublishing.com

To Linda and Ian with love

Contents

Contributors

Henry E. Allison is Research Professor of Philosophy at the University of California, Davis.

Hugh H. Benson is Professor and Chair of Philosophy at the University of Oklahoma.

Timothy Crockett is Assistant Professor of Philosophy at Marquette University.

David Cunning is Assistant Professor of Philosophy at the University of Iowa

Gary Hatfield is the Adam Seybert Professor in Moral and Intellectual Philosophy at the University of Pennsylvania.

Jonathan Michael Kaplan is Assistant Professor of Philosophy at Oregon State University.

Matthew J. Kisner is Assistant Professor of Philosophy at the University of South Carolina.

Thomas M. Lennon is Professor of Philosophy at the University of Western Ontario.

Paul Livingston is Assistant Professor of Philosophy at Villanova University.

Antonia LoLordo is Assistant Professor of Philosophy at the University of Virginia.

Richard N. Manning is Associate Professor of Philosophy at Carleton University.

Steven Nadler is Professor of Philosophy at the University of Wisconsin-Madison.

Alan Nelson is Professor of Philosophy at the University of California, Irvine.

Lex Newman is Associate Professor of Philosophy at the University of Utah.

Lawrence Nolan is Associate Professor and Chair of Philosophy at California State University, Long Beach.

Dennis L. Sepper is Professor of Philosophy at the University of Dallas.

David Woodruff Smith is Professor of Philosophy at the University of California, Irvine.

Kurt Smith is Assistant Professor of Philosophy at Bloomsburg University of Pennsylvania.

Alice Sowaal is Assistant Professor of Philosophy at San Francisco State University.

David Stump is Associate Professor and Chair of Philosophy at the University of San Francisco.

Mariam Thalos is Professor of Philosophy at the University of Utah.

Andrew Youpa is Assistant Professor of Philosophy at Southern Illinois University, Carbondale.

Acknowledgments

I thank the authors and the editors at Blackwell Publishing for making this volume possible. The final stage of my own editorial contributions was supported by a leave from the University of California, Irvine; and by the hospitality of the Philosophy Department at the University of North Carolina, Chapel Hill, and the Center for Human Science, Chapel Hill.

Abbreviations

Works cited frequently throughout the volume are abbreviated as follows:

A   Leibniz, *Sämtliche Schriften und Briefe* (Deutsche Akademie der Wissenschafter, ed.). Darmstadt: Akademie-Verlag, 1923–. Cited by series, volume, and page.

AG   Leibniz, *Philosophical Essays* (Roger Ariew and Daniel Garber, trans. and eds.). Indianapolis, IN: Hackett, 1989.

AL   Bacon, *The Advancement of Learning*. In Brian Vickers (ed.), *Francis Bacon: A Critical Edition of the Major Works*. Oxford: Oxford University Press, 1996. Cited by page.

Ar   Aristotle, *De Anima* (J. A. Smith, trans.). In J. Barnes (ed.), *Complete Works of Aristotle*, 2 vols. Princeton, NJ: Princeton University Press, 1984. Cited by the standard page and line numbers for Aristotle's works (Bekker numbers).

AT   Descartes, *Oeuvres de Descartes*, 11 vols. (C. Adam and P. Tannery, eds.). Paris: Librairie Philosophique J. Vrin, 1996.

C   Leibniz, *Opuscules et fragments inédits de Leibniz* (L. Couturat, ed.). Paris: Presses Universitaires, 1903.

CSM   Descartes, *Philosophical Writings*, 2 vols. (J. Cottingham, R. Stoothoff, and D. Murdoch, trans.). Cambridge: Cambridge University Press, 1984–5. Cited by volume and page number.

CSMK   Descartes, *Philosophical Writings, Vol. 3: Correspondence* (J. Cottingham, R. Stoothoff, D. Murdoch, and A. Kenny, trans.). Cambridge: Cambridge University Press, 1991.

DG   Descartes, *The World and Other Writings* (S. Gaukroger, trans.). Cambridge: Cambridge University Press, 1998.

DM   Leibniz, *Discourse on Metaphysics*. In C. J. Gerhardt (ed.), *Die philosophischen Schriften von G.W. Leibniz*, 7 vols. Hildescheim: Olms, 1965. Cited by article number.

G   Leibniz, *Nouvelles lettres et opuscules inédits de Leibniz* (Foucher de Careil, ed.). Paris: Auguste Durand, 1857.

GM   Leibniz, *Leibniz' Mathematische Schriften* (C. I. Gerhardt, ed.). Berlin: A. Asher; Halle: H. W. Schmidt, 1849–63. Cited by volume and page.

GP	Leibniz, *Die philosophischen Schriften von Gottfried Wilhelm Leibniz* (C. I. Gerhardt, ed.). Berlin: Weidmann, 1875–90. Cited by volume and page.
JS	Malebranche, *Dialogues on Metaphysics and on Religion* (N. Jolley and D. Scott, trans.). Cambridge: Cambridge University Press, 1997.
Le Grand	Antoine Le Grand, *An Entire Body of Philosophy According to the Principles of the Famous Renate Des Cartes*, 2 vols. (R. Blome, trans.). London: Samuel Roycroft, 1694. (Reprint, New York: Johnson Reprint, 1972.)
LL	Leibniz, *Philosophical Papers and Letters* (L. E. Loemker, trans.). Dordrecht: Reidel, 1969.
LNE	Leibniz, *New Essays on Human Understanding* (P. Remnant and J. Bennett, trans.). Cambridge: Cambridge University Press, 1981.
M	Leibniz, *The Leibniz Arnauld Correspondence* (H. T. Mason, trans. and ed.). Manchester: Manchester University Press, 1967.
Mal	Malebranche, *The Search after Truth* (T. M. Lennon and P. J. Olscamp, trans.). Cambridge: Cambridge University Press, 1997.
NO	Francis Bacon, *Novum Organum*. Cited by section.
OC	Malebranche, *Oeuvres complètes de Malebranche*, 20 vols. (A. Robinet, ed.). Paris: J. Vrin, 1958–67.
P	Leibniz, *Leibniz: Philosophical Writings* (G. H. R. Parkinson, ed., M. Morris and G. H. R. Parkinson, trans.). London: Dent, 1973.
QNS	Francisco Sanchez, *Quod Nihil Scitur* (D. Thomson, trans.; introduction, notes, and bibliography by E. Limbrick). New York: Cambridge University Press, 1988. Cited by page.
RA	Leibniz, *The Labyrinth of the Continuum: Writings on the Continuum Problem, 1672–1686* (R. T. W. Arthur, trans. and ed.). New Haven, CT: Yale University Press, 2001.
RB	Leibniz, *New Essays on Human Understanding* (P. Remnant and J. Bennett, eds. and trans.). Cambridge: Cambridge University Press, 1981.
Régis	Pierre Régis, *Cours entier de philosophie, ou systeme general selon les principes de M. Descartes*, Latest Edition, 3 vols. [Entire Course of Philosophy, or General System According to the Principles of Mr. Descartes]. Amsterdam: Huguetan, 1691. (Reprint, New York: Johnson Reprint, 1970.)
Rohault	Jacques Rohault, *System of Natural Philosophy*, 2nd edn. (J. Clarke, trans.). London: Knapton, 1728–9. (Reprint, New York: Garland, 1987.)
SE	Spinoza, *Ethics*. In E. Curley (ed. and trans.), *Collected Works of Spinoza* (pp. 401–617). Princeton, NJ: Princeton University Press, 1985. Cited by Part, Proposition, and Note.
Search	Malebranche, *The Search After Truth* (T. M. Lennon and P. J. Olscamp, trans.). Columbus: Ohio State University Press, 1980.
TEI	Spinoza, *Treatise on the Emendation of the Intellect*. In S. Feldman (ed.) and S. Shirley (trans.), *Ethics, Treatise on the Emendation of the Intellect and Selected Letters*. Indianapolis, IN: Hackett, 1992. Cited by page and line number.
TTP	Spinoza, *Theological-Political Treatise*. In C. Gebhardt (ed.), *Spinoza Opera*. Heidelberg: Carl Winter, 1925. Cited by volume and page.

Introduction

What is rationalism? Philosophers have learned not to expect detailed, or even fully coherent, answers to this sweeping kind of question. There is, nevertheless, a core of rationalist thinking that can be traced through two millennia of recorded philosophical development. The rationalist insists on the distinction between appearance and reality. Reality is revealed to our rational thought, which might also be called "reason" or "intellect." Since appearance is the way reality appears to *us*, philosophy has two important tasks. The first is to employ rational thought to reveal the truth about the real. The second is to *explain* the appearances in terms of the real. Why do we naturally fasten on apparent truth instead of the real? Why must the real appear as it does when our rationality is not specially applied to it? Most rationalists want the appearances to be explained as *necessary* consequences of the human condition.

The central example of this philosophical attitude is the explanation of sense perception. Our sensing something to be colored red is treated as depending on something that is ultimately not red – not really red – perhaps particles of light affecting our sense organs. This provides a fairly neat and iconic contrast with empiricism, the complement of rationalism. The empiricist takes sensory information as prior to, and providing data for, explanatory *hypotheses*. The role of these hypotheses is to classify, simplify, and interrelate the data. There is no sense in which the hypotheses are more true or real than appearances for the empiricist.

The chapters in part one of this book, "The Core of Rationalism," explore these fundamental features of rationalism. "The Rationalist Impulse" explores the attitudinal differences between rationalist and empiricist philosophy. "The Rationalist Conception of Substance" tracks the development of that crucial element of rationalist reality with a particular focus on Spinoza, who made it central in his philosophy. "Rationalist Theories of Sense Perception and Mind–Body Relation" examines explanations of how appearances come to the mind through the body's sense organs and how this relates the appearances to reality so that they can be used as part of the quest for truth. Finally, the philosopher's path from a childhood immersed in the senses to a sagacious adulthood and how rationalists try to bring their readers along this path is the topic of "Rationalism and Education."

The chapters in part two, "The Historical Background," take us from the beginnings of theoretical rationalism up until the great flowering of rationalist thought in the seventeenth century. Plato is the iconic rationalist, though "Plato's Rationalistic Method" brings out some of the problems in making this characterization precise. An important link between the ancients and Spinoza is forged by focusing on medieval rationalism in the Jewish tradition in "Rationalism in Jewish Philosophy." One of the great critics of early modern rationalism was Pierre Gassendi, who championed an updated understanding of ancient anti-rationalist atomism. The chapter "Early Modern Critiques of Rationalist Psychology" puts Gassendi's critique of rationalist theories of sense perception into the context of the intense debates sparked by Descartes' rationalism. Another aspect of these debates was concerned with the new stress on method in philosophical and scientific thinking. The development of Descartes' canonical statement of the rationalist side of this story is the main topic of "Rationalism and Method." The distinction between passive sensation and active reasoning is central to the history of Rationalism. This distinction is richly elaborated by the consideration of imagination, which is naturally understood as the active combination of elements passively received in sensation. "Cartesian Imaginations: The Method and Passions of Imagining" follows the development of this theme into the seventeenth century and the transformation of the role assigned to imagination in Descartes and his followers.

The chapters in part three, "The Heyday of Rationalism," examine rationalism as it appears in the works of the great canonical figures formerly known as the Continental Rationalists. "Descartes' Rationalist Epistemology" analyzes the distinction between knowledge that is transmitted via the senses and knowledge that is innate to the mind. Because the treatment is in the context of Descartes' philosophy, his famous method of doubt also comes under scrutiny. This critical distinction is developed in the context of the notion of mental representation in "Rationalism and Representation." We return to the delicate issue of imagination in "The Role of the Imagination in Rationalist Philosophies of Mathematics." Much depends on mathematics in Cartesian systems because of the identification of the essence of matter with the subject matter of geometry – extension in length, breadth, and depth. This means that the foundation of physics is geometry; this is one version of scientific mechanism. "Idealism and Cartesian Motion" is devoted to the various conceptual problems inherent to this part of Cartesianism. Leibniz's critique of this conception of matter and his own Rationalistic approach to solving the problems is the subject of "Leibniz on Shape and the Cartesian Conception of Body." His rationalism is considered in a more general framework in "Leibniz on Modality, Cognition, and Expression." The great rationalists insisted that their philosophical thought, even the natural philosophical part of it (what we now call physics) was in the service of the development of moral philosophy. Spinoza's great work was, of course, entitled *Ethics*. "Rationalist Moral Philosophy" addresses some of the most salient considerations. We return to the hybrid faculty of imagination in "Spinoza, Leibniz, and the Rationalist Reconceptions of Imagination," which brings the story up to some of the pressures that lead from Leibniz through Wolff to Kant. Finally, "Kant and the Two Dogmas of Rationalism" is a critical examination of Kant's engagement with rationalist theories of truth and of the contrast between sensory and intellectual knowledge.

The chapters in part four, "Rationalist Themes in Contemporary Philosophy," study how both the core issues and transformations of them remain alive in more recent thought. Indeed, there are some ways in which traditional rationalist themes are very much alive even in contemporary philosophy. All of these chapters, however, also serve to bring out how it is ultimately problematic to distinguish sharply between rationalism and empiricism. "Rationalism in the Phenomenological Tradition" explicitly puts into the historical tradition the phenomenology of Husserl and later phenomenological research in the important Husserlian tradition. "Rationalist Elements of Twentieth-Century Analytic Philosophy" does the same for another, even more dominant twentieth-century philosophical tradition; here we find a particular focus on the development from the early Russell to Carnap. "Proust and the Rationalist Conception of the Self" makes a case that the great novelist represents one culmination of rationalist theorizing about self and identity. Rationalism in its seventeenth-century heyday was animated by the ideal of providing rationalist foundations for modern science. "Rationalism in Science" traces this theme up to the present day. "Rational Decision Making: Descriptive, Prescriptive, or Explanatory?" is an explanation and also an internal critique of contemporary rationalism with respect to action and choice. "What is a Feminist to do with Rational Choice?" is a more external critique that raises important questions about hidden presuppositions. Finally, "Rationalism in the Philosophy of Donald Davidson" shows how the distinction between rationalism and empiricism plays out in one of the most influential systems of philosophical thought in contemporary philosophy.

Part I

THE CORE OF RATIONALISM

1

The Rationalist Impulse

ALAN NELSON

Philosophers are rightly suspicious of the usefulness of broadly conceived labels and "-isms." They are particularly suspicious when the labels mark dichotomies. Rationalism thus qualifies as suspicious if it is taken to be a neatly delineated set of doctrines. The task assumed by this chapter is not to find such a set, but instead to provide an analysis of what I shall call the impulse to philosophize rationalistically. The analysis therefore does not purport to sharply distinguish a set of maxims or propositions characteristic of rationalism from another set proper to its foil, empiricism. Nor does it attempt to delineate specific doctrines to which all "rationalists" adhere. I shall, however, argue that attention to some overarching themes in rationalist systems of philosophy can be of considerable use in understanding the philosophical accomplishments of the great rationalists. Insufficient attention to these themes has often led to interpretations of rationalists that skew the dialectic with their empiricist antagonists in favor of the latter.

I shall draw some examples from Plato, who provides most of the earliest texts clearly articulating rationalist themes. The primary focus will be on the great thinkers from the seventeenth-century heyday of rationalism, but in conclusion some observations will be made about the rationalist impulse in Russell's logical atomism. This should help bring into relief some respects in which the triumph of empiricist sensibilities among historians of philosophy in the twentieth century and beyond has made the rationalist impulse rather alien. Naturally, this is not conducive to recovering the spirit of rationalist projects.

I

The primary and customary sense of the term "rationalism" characterizes a philosophical attitude toward knowledge. Knowledge itself is partly characterized both by the subjects, or possessors, of knowledge and by the objects of knowledge, the things to be known. Rationalism, therefore, bears on ontology since it requires an understanding of the natures of these subjects and objects. There are also characteristically rational processes or techniques for obtaining or developing knowledge, so rationalism bears on method, philosophical education, and the nature of philosophy itself.

The traditional series of contrasts with its foil, empiricism, thus begins with subjects and objects of knowledge. Traditional rationalisms identify the intellect, the mind, or the rational part of the soul (or even the State) as of primary importance in receiving and holding knowledge. The corresponding objects of knowledge are then non-sensory, general, and unchanging or eternal. Traditional empiricisms, by contrast, identify the senses, or common sense, or the sensitive part of the soul as of primary importance. The corresponding objects of knowledge are then the inhabitants of the temporal world in flux. Of course, rationalists have a story to tell about how some kinds of derivative knowledge depend directly on the senses. We can come to know that the senses are reliable indicators of what is beneficial to us and we can then know (as opposed to taking it for granted) that, for example, bread nourishes. Furthermore, absolutely all knowledge depends in some attenuated ways on the sensory because we need to learn more esoteric truths by first hearing or reading things that bring us to understand them. Empiricists similarly have a story to tell about the role of the non-sensory. The clearest example is Locke's essential reliance on innate operations of the mind. This is an extreme case, but all empiricists need to have some account of how abstract, general truths are derived from what is given by the senses.

These points are crucial to appreciating the depth of the chasm between rationalism and empiricism despite the pockets of shared concerns and overlap. It is easy to see that the empiricist has an initial debater's advantage. Because human beings are born helpless, pre-linguistic, and dependent, they first become cognizant of the sensory qualities of objects familiar to common sense. A normal person not having a prior education in rationalist philosophy will cling to thoughts of these familiar things when beginning a philosophical education. Thus the empiricist finds a ready pupil, an ally in fact, in what we now like to call the "untutored common sense" of a "sensible" person or a person of "good sense." Such a person is apt to appreciate an analysis of features of the intangible, vaguely perceived, intellectual objects of rationalist knowledge into commonsensical items and their features. The rationalist teacher cannot display the reward of hard study to the beginning student like candy in a jar. Students are instead told that their opinions, while perhaps of considerable utility, are strictly speaking false and that the truth can be only vaguely characterized until they can see it for themselves. And the goal is to *see* the truth. Not visually, of course, but with the mind's eye, through a "purely mental scrutiny" as Descartes put it.

II

How is the esoteric truth of the rationalist to be accessed? If mere exhortation is the last resort, even open-minded students will be justifiably suspicious. And even those who are somehow moved to appreciate the truth by exhortations might be later persuaded by other, contrary doctrines. What is required is some technique or method for bringing the student from a starting place favoring empiricism to the truth. An effective method must start with easy steps and progressively draw the pupil away from sensory distractions. Let us consider examples with some detail.

A rudimentary development of such a method can be found in Plato's dialogue, *Symposium* (210a–212b). Here, the esoteric truth to be sought is described as a "vision" of Beauty itself, the Platonic form. Love is characterized as desire, ultimately desire for Beauty. The method, then, can be regarded as instruction in the art of loving well. The first step in this form of Platonic education requires that one love a beautiful body. This is ingeniously designed to be an easy step that requires no prior commitment and no special effort from most students. Loving (that is, desiring) a beautiful body comes naturally to humans and can be mostly driven by sensual appetites. The Trojan horse, of course, is that the body is beautiful in a way that connects it, albeit distantly and vaguely, to the final goal of Beauty itself. The next step is to love many beautiful bodies and this is, unbeknownst to the pupil, loving the Beauty in all these bodies. The beginning students' inability to understand fully their intermediate accomplishments is characteristic of rationalist enlightenment. As students progress, they typically will not fully understand the nature of the progress they have made, nor do they need to. It is the final goal that is important. So lovers of many bodies might conceive their achievement as the ability to love different kinds of corporeal beauty, but the already enlightened understand that those at the second step are loving Beauty despite its degradation by various corporeal guises.

In this course of instruction, students next progress to the love of individual souls, and then to what might be regarded as the soul of the State, its laws. This leads to love of various kinds of knowledge and then to the love of knowledge in general – philosophy. The Philosopher, having thus advanced through these stages of love, is prepared to catch glimpses of Beauty itself. One crucial aspect of this method is that those who completed the course of instruction are able to perceive in ways that are unavailable to the uninitiated. Even a generally competent adult immersed in the world of sense will be unable to perceive truth at will. The situation is quite analogous to the development that can be effected in sensory capacities. All wine might taste sour to the neophyte, but a trained wine taster might make very fine discriminations with some reliability. A symphony orchestra might sound like noise to a child or someone trained in another musical tradition and so on. It is to be expected, therefore, that if rationalists begin a lesson or an exposition with a plain statement of Truth, they will meet with skepticism and incomprehension.

An interesting feature of the method described in the *Symposium* is that it is much more than a means of acquiring some abstract doctrines. It also involves learning a way of life. Since the "bringing forth of beautiful ideas" is itself a high form of appreciating Beauty, the advanced philosopher is motivated to teach beginners. It is not expected that pupils go it alone. This makes progress highly contingent on the availability of suitable teachers. It also means that the process of education requires a very long-term, daunting initial commitment of time from the student. The search for a method of discovery with greater generality, reliability, efficiency, and power led Descartes to his infamous method of universal doubt. Descartes himself would, of course, be horrified by later use of the term "Cartesian Skepticism." Universal doubt is meant to lead to "perfect knowledge" of the truth and it is for this reason that he calls it "methodical." The various functions of the doubt include (a) withdrawal from the senses whose particular deliverances are most easily doubted, (b) a preemptive strike against later doubts; if the project begins with, and then overcomes a universal, all-inclusive doubt there is no room for subsequent second guessing of anything that emerges from the doubt, and (c) the imposition of a strict order on the acquisition of knowledge.

Insufficient attention has been given to Descartes' emphasis on the importance of "philosophizing in the correct order." One reason that universal doubt comes first in the order is that it establishes an order for the entire enterprise. The first positive result is the *cogito*, "I think, therefore I am," or simply, "I think, I am." Why is the cogito first? Not because it is the obvious place to begin philosophizing; no one before Descartes chose this point. Nor is the cogito first because of any special, mysterious fecundity to be found in it. In fact, though Descartes moves from the cogito to some very important results, everything beyond the most basic principles of knowledge depends on one's being a human with sensation, memory, and imagination. And the idea that has foundational priority for knowledge is not of the self, it is of God. It is not even the certainty that attaches to the cogito that makes it first in the proper order. The trilaterality of triangles is just as certain as the cogito. The cogito comes first because it is delivered by the universal doubt itself. Doubting is thinking, so given that one doubts, one must exist to doubt. The very fact that one is doubting does not inevitably draw the attention to triangles, squares, or anything else; doubting instead brings to mind that one is doubting.

Once it emerges that one's own existence follows from the idea of oneself present when doubting, there is no way to proceed except to ask whether the existence of anything else at all follows from the ideas of the thinking thing. The pupil, now in the guise of a solitary, independent meditator (independent except for reading Descartes!), is inexorably led to the existence of God, the existence of extension, and finally to the existence of the self as an embodied, thinking thing. This procedure does not enable one to clearly state the Truth to the unenlightened any more than the "steps of love" from the *Symposium*. Descartes' method is, however, designed to be implemented in a number of days rather than a number of years. The method itself is, moreover, something to be employed once in a lifetime of learning with perhaps brief annual checkups or refreshers. And unlike the method described by Plato, it can serve as a foundation for various pursuits.

It is not surprising to the historian that different versions of the Truth are attained by different rationalists. This provides empiricists with a justifiable basis for attacking the general procedures of rationalism notwithstanding the fact that empiricists agree among themselves no more than do rationalists. There are, however, significant generalizations to be made about the sorts of Truth that a rationalist education is supposed to reveal. Perhaps the most striking characteristic of rationalist truth is its simplicity. It is simple in the strict sense that it is undivided and indivisible. In case there are a modest number of separate truths, they are each simple in themselves.

III

The most prominent example of a simple rationalist truth is the idea of infinite being. Empiricists tend to believe that insofar as we can understand infinity at all, our concept of it must be constructed from ideas of finite things. And insofar as we can do that, the result will be complex and unclear relative to the ideas of finite things employed in its construction. Rationalists, by contrast, believe that the idea of the infinite is conceptually prior to ideas of the finite. This does not mean that infants think about the infinite before they think about the finite. The point is that finite things are to be philosophically understood as limitations of the infinite. One does not begin with the truth concerning the finite and work to extend these truths to the infinite. Instead the post-enlightenment beginning, the principle of philosophy proper, is the infinite. The task of philosophy, after the attainment of the simple truth, is discovering the truth about finite things by understanding the respects in which they are limitations of what is infinite.

For example, finite things are limited in their knowledge, their power, their creative activity, their temporal and spatial extent (at least in some rationalist accounts), their goodness, etc. Again, the rationalist will agree with the empiricist that learning to conceive infinity might involve first reflecting on the conceptions of finite things and then imagining the various limitations being removed, perhaps one by one. But once in command of the idea of infinity, the epistemic situation is reversed. The perfect wholeness and simplicity of the idea of the infinite must have limitations imposed upon it in thought to arrive at accurate conceptions of finite things. Spinoza expresses this by saying that finite things "follow" from the infinite and must be "conceived through" it.

A more specific example is provided once more by Descartes' position on the nature of thought. Scholars have long debated whether Descartes is best interpreted as taking consciousness or intentionality as the fundamental core of thought. Others have disputed whether it is the intellect or the will that is more basic to the thinking thing. None of these discussions are Cartesian in spirit. Descartes makes it very clear that the essence of a thinking thing is to think. Thought itself is something as perfectly simple as a finite thing can be. The philosopher's task is to explain the variety of phenomena, the empirical, given the simple idea of thought. This is the opposite of the empiricist's task of searching for deep mysterious essences (often concluded to be inaccessible anyway) using commonsensical building blocks.

The principal theoretical device for explaining the appearance of diversity in what is really simple depends on being able to think identically the same ideas "under different aspects" or "regarding" them in different ways. Doing this is said to produce a distinction of reason, a conceptual distinction, or (especially appropriate in the present context) a *rational distinction*. So a Cartesian philosopher might regard the idea of himself as a finite thinking thing in various ways. He might regard the passive aspect of thought in which it perceives ideas of things, or instead he might regard its active aspect in which it chooses to attend to the apparent good. In this account, will and intellect are only rationally distinct. When one accurately perceives will or intellect one is in each case perceiving the same idea, the idea of finite thought albeit under different aspects. Similarly, perceiving omniscience and omnipotence is to perceive exactly the same thing, infinity, but under different aspects. Yet another example would be the perception of divisibility and quantity, which are both aspects of Cartesian extension. In each case, the simple ideas of infinity, thought, or extension are conceptually prior to the particular, rationally distinct aspects under which they might be regarded.

The notion of rational distinction itself was probably an invention of medieval philosophers attempting to explain the various ways in which the perfect simplicity of God is perceived. The device is particularly important in developing the rationalist impulse, but it is very important to note that empiricists also have occasion to put it to work. The arch empiricist Hume found it necessary to employ a version of the rational distinction to understand the comparisons between, for example, "figure and body figured; motion and the body moved" (*A Treatise of Human Nature*, 1.1.7). The only essential difference between Hume and Descartes on this point is that Hume takes sensory impressions to be prior to the abstract ideas in question, while Descartes would take these ideas to be distinct, "concrete," and prior to their confused representation in the senses.

Although the centrality of the theory of rational distinction has not been much noted by scholars, its importance to rationalist philosophy cannot be overstated. After an education in rationalism has freed the philosopher from the prejudices of the senses and the truth is uncovered, that truth is revealed to be simple. For most rationalists, the truth available to human beings is expressed in a handful of innate ideas. The richness of human experience then needs to be explained as somehow arising from this source. Otherwise, rationalism would be reduced to either the inquiry-halting position of Zeno of Elea who taught that Being is an unintelligible, really undifferentiated unity, or else to a skeptical phenomenalism in which sensation is utterly unconnected with reality. Once it is understood that the appearances or phenomena of unschooled, everyday life are grounded in simple ideas expressing a Truth inaccessible to sensory investigation, the phenomena themselves appear in a new light to the rationalist. The appearances are transformed and reconfigured by the reality of which they are, after all, mere appearances.

IV

The rationalists' reconfiguration of experience brings into sharp relief an important contrast with empiricism. For an empiricist, the ultimate test of the reasonableness, the credibility, and the fruitfulness of a philosophical theory is its conformity with appearances as experienced by common sense. It is fine to be told that the dog down the street is a machine, or an aggregate of monads, or a finite mode of the infinite, so long as one arrives at a deep analysis of what the *dog* really is. And the same holds for cookies, hands, the moral wrongness of taking candy from babies, and so on. A committed, theoretically minded empiricist might be prepared for thoroughgoing analyses, or even reductions, of all these items to esoteric theoretical entities. A cookie might be an aggregate of elementary particles, and the wrongness of an action might even reduce to something that is not intrinsically normative – say, Hume's custom. What a certain kind of empiricist is not prepared to accept is that *dogs, hands, taking candy from babies*, etc. are not the touchstones, the base from which philosophical theorizing begins. For these empiricists, philosophical theories are to be judged according to the fidelity with which their analyses result in the furniture of the commonsense world. The rationalist, by contrast, discovers that the world of common sense is merely an appearance of what is real and true. So it is to be expected that dogs, hands, and the rest are not *really* precisely individuated.

The present point connects with the previous observations about rationalism. We first saw how the proper starting place for philosophical explanation is not ready to hand, but requires careful education. One must unlearn the apparent truths of common sense to gain an appreciation of where philosophy proper begins. Perhaps this is best expressed by saying that philosophy consists of two stages. The first stage is an unlearning of prejudice, a preparation for doing real philosophy. According to a rationalist, the empiricist attempts to do philosophy on the cheap without bothering to put in the requisite training. The empiricist is like the tennis player who wants to be a champion without practicing ground strokes or the pianist who wants to play Chopin without practicing scales. The second stage can only begin once an adequate understanding of the Truth is in place. The rationalist's understanding of the Truth is, therefore, not rightly characterized as a "theory." It is not a hypothesis supported by evidence. What might the evidence be except for the deliverances of the empiricist's common sense? The Truth must instead come to be understood, appreciated, or "seen" by the knower's innate attunement with it. This attunement must, of course, receive some explanation. But – and this is the sticking point – the explanation of attunement must itself proceed from the Truth as explanans.

We also saw that the rationalist's Truth is relatively simple. Infinity, thought, and extension are simple in Descartes' system, for example. And this simplicity means that they are easy to understand for the enlightened sage; a claim that provokes frustration or amusement from the empiricist. But given that the rationalist's Truth is simple, the empiricist's easily understood items – dog, hand, etc. – turn out to be fabulously complex in reality. This is not to deny that empiricists might welcome a theory which maintains that dogs are complexes of cells, or atoms, or impressions, or etc. It is instead characteristic of the empiricist to insist that what are *really* dogs can be given a theoretical analysis into theoretical simples. The theoretical entities cannot be more *real* than commonsensical objects because the latter are what ground the fallible *postulation* of the former.

V

Once the topic of the analysis of appearances has been raised in this way, it is natural to see how it is played out in philosophy that is analytic in a historically strict sense of the term. The issues arise clearly at the very beginning in the twentieth-century analytic philosophy of Russell and Moore. To standardize terminology we can say that this sort of analysis takes the objects of knowledge to be *facts*. Facts are symbolized or expressed by propositions. Analysis then consists in analyzing some propositions into others. For Moore, analysis typically begins with a proposition that we *know* to be true. Some of these propositions also have analyses that are known. We might know, for example, "T is an equilateral triangle" and know that this analyzes into "T is a closed, plane figure with three equal sides." Philosophical analysis most typically involves cases in which we know the analysandum to be true, but do not know its correct analysis. A typical Moorean example is the proposition expressed by the sentence "I now see a hand before me" when one is looking at one's own hand before oneself. Moore regards this as known for certain, but thinks the correct analysis is very hard to come by. At times he thought the first step in the analysis includes the proposition "'This is seen by me' and 'This is part of the surface of a hand,'" but he was never sure of how to proceed. What I wish to stress here is that Moore begins by taking the deliverances of common sense as known for certain. Being in possession of correct analyses would somehow enhance this knowledge though Moore, with characteristic caution, was unsure of the nature of the enhancement. This is very much in the spirit of empiricism. Knowledge in philosophy derives from analyses of what is known for certain by common sense. Moore rejected outright the suggestion that an analysis of common sense could lead to knowledge that revealed common sense as false. That is, propositions expressing commonsensical truisms express *facts*, and these propositions cannot be discovered to be false because these facts are indisputable. This is the foundation of Moore's famous "defense of common sense." We know that any philosopher purporting to undercut common sense by showing propositions expressing commonsensical truisms to be false must have made a mistake in analysis.

Analysis in Russell's logical atomism is different in character. He agrees with Moore that valuable philosophical analyses begin with things that we take for certainly true. Where else would we begin the quest for philosophical enlightenment – with things we regard as highly dubious? Russell believed, however, that sentences in natural language expressing commonsensical truisms are highly misleading in their logical form. Sentences like "Socrates was snub-nosed" or "The cat is on the mat" might appear to the uneducated to express simple facts about Socrates and the cat. We begin the analysis of such sentences by first translating them into a more appropriate symbolism. The full analysis of the sentences into a proposition with an appropriate logical form would reveal vast complexity, perhaps an infinite complexity. This is because the logical atoms which are the goal of the analysis must include names for logically perfect simples, items with no further structure whatsoever. These atoms are manifestly unavailable to common sense. They are, in fact, probably unavailable altogether although logical atomism holds by a kind of transcendental argument that they must be at the "ground floor" as a condition of the possibility of a symbolic system's representing reality.

Russellian analysis thus displays some of the characteristic features of rationalism. Most prominent is its radical reconfiguration of common sense. Propositions that Moore knows to express facts are revealed under Russellian analysis to be vaguely and ambiguously expressed complexes of facts beyond the grasp of human intellect. So "Socrates,'" "snub-nosedness," "the cat," and "Piccadilly" all stand for logical constructions, and apparently well-formed propositions employing these symbols vaguely and ambiguously symbolize complexes of atomic facts. Russell, therefore, was prepared for analysis to reveal that such "things" as dogs, cats, mats, even persons, the "properties" of these things, and their ordinary activities are not fully real. (Or better, that they are not in the end constituents of facts.)

Russell himself does seem to have been inclined to think that the atomic facts contain as constituents something very much like Hume's simple impressions and simple ideas. This reflects his sympathy with empiricism. In other places, he seems to regard it as no more than a hypothesis, or even an example of what the logical atoms might be like. So it seems to be the simplicity and indivisibility of the atoms that impressed Russell most and this is, as we have seen, guided by the rationalist impulse. To be sure, logical atomism results in a great many of the simples; in this respect it is more like Leibniz's Monadology than like the systems of Descartes or Spinoza. Russell diverged from the more empirically minded Moore in laying heavy stress on the inadequacy of ordinary expressions in natural languages. For Russell, learning a system of symbols that reflected the structure of the esoteric atomic facts was a necessary prerequisite to effective philosophy. This might be seen as a version of the first of the three characteristics of rationalist thought discussed above; namely the requirement that the philosopher be trained to transcend the truths of common sense to appreciate an esoteric simple truth.

In short, Russell's analytic philosophy, especially in this period of his development, was in crucial aspects aligned with mainline rationalism. Moore's version of analysis was much more in line with traditional empiricism. It is interesting to observe that much contemporary analytic philosophy is done more in the spirit of Moore than in the spirit of Russell. When an analysis is controlled by, and ultimately answerable to, untutored "intuitions" about the commonsensical observations of "plain" people in Western cultures, that analysis is in an empiricist tradition.

Philosophers trained in these techniques might be in an excellent position to understand what the great, canonical empiricists were trying to do and how they viewed the philosophical enterprise. It might, however, be necessary for them to exercise particular caution when they turn to the interpretation of the rationalist tradition. Rationalist philosophy, like modern science, does not "leave everything as it is." It is instead an adventure that transforms the philosopher's perception of the world.

2

The Rationalist Conception of Substance

THOMAS M. LENNON

Two Philosophical Impulses

Rationalism is often best understood against the foil of empiricism, for these two styles of philosophizing spring from very different philosophical impulses. Empiricists seek to know the way the world *is*. Their goal is to gather data, whether from controlled experiment or from hurly-burly experience, in order to produce a description of the world. The drift among them is away from the ideal of a single description of the world toward the acceptability of a multiplicity of descriptions, constrained only by pure pragmatics, to the point that whether there is one world, many worlds, or none at all answering to their describing makes no difference.

By contrast, rationalists already know the way the world is. Recall Plato and his doctrine of learning as reminiscence, but also Descartes, who, in ruminating on the essence of material things, finds his discovery of the truth he discovers "not so much learning something new as remembering what I knew before" (Descartes 1985b: 44). Rationalists instead seek to know *why* the world *must* be the way it is. Their theories are thus prescriptive instead of descriptive. Descartes, in asserting that existence is inseparable from God, makes clear that the modal terms he employs are based in objective features of the world. "It is not that my thought makes it so, or imposes any necessity on anything." (This sort of imposition by the mind would be what Leibniz called the super-nominalism of Hobbes, whom Descartes summarily dismisses (Descartes 1985b: 135–6), or of Locke, for whom the essences of things, or the kinds to which they belong, depend on our ways of sorting them.) "On the contrary," Descartes continues, "it is the thing itself, namely the existence of God, which determines my thinking in this respect" (Descartes 1985b: 46). Necessity imposes itself on the mind by prescribing the way it must think about the world.

If the underlying impulse of rationalists, prior to all argument, is the visceral conviction that the world could not have been otherwise, the empiricists' conviction is that the world inexplicably just is the way it is. Thus the defining commitment of empiricism to experience as the ultimate source of all knowledge is in fact posterior to its initial impulse. Experience of the world is needed because reason does not tell, or is not told, why it must be as it is. An additional part of the empiricist conviction is that the world is multiple, diverse, and complex. There are many things in the world, they differ in many ways, and it is not clear how they relate to one another. So much is revealed by experience, which then becomes the only basis for dealing with such a world.

The rationalist impulse is in response to a perceived unity, uniformity, and simplicity in the world; to rationalists, the world seems to hang together and form a coherent whole. This simplicity and unity provide the ground for necessity insofar as what is said (or thought) about the world is said (or thought) about a single thing. Truth, as Leibniz insisted, is ultimately a matter of identity, even if the identities that we finite minds are able to demonstrate are limited to those that hold in all possible worlds (such would be the truths of logic and mathematics). Those truths that hold only in this actual world (factual truths such as that Caesar crossed the Rubicon, for example) are also identities; but they are known as such only to God's infinite mind. Leibniz himself thought that these identities are individually true of a multiplicity of objects, but the implicit tendency in his thought, and certainly among the rationalists generally, is toward a single object. A fragment from the ancient Greek poet Archilochus has it that the fox knows many things, but the hedgehog knows one big thing. The empiricists are foxes, the rationalists hedgehogs.

A good model for this initially bizarre view that there is but one object to be known is the fairly intuitive proposition 5 from book 1 of Euclid's *Elements*, namely, that the base angles of an isosceles triangle are equal. Euclid's proof is rather complicated, relying on additional construction. Pappus avoided this complication with a very simple proof: "let us conceive this one [isosceles] triangle as two triangles . . . all the corresponding parts (in the triangles) are equal, including the two equal sides and the angle between them, and therefore [as proven by proposition 4] the angles subtended by the equal sides, which are the base angles of the triangle." But what of the *two* triangles? According to the classic commentary of Thomas Heath, "we may answer we keep to one triangle and merely view it in two aspects. If it were a question of helping a beginner to understand this, we might say that the one triangle is the triangle looked at in front and that the other is the *same* triangle looked at from *behind*; but even this is not really necessary" (Euclid 1956: 254). To put it another way, constructing an isosceles triangle just is to construct a triangle whose base angles are equal, and to think about the one is to think about the other, albeit in a different way, for they are the same thing. What is true of this knowledge of isosceles triangles is true of all the others of Euclid's demonstrations, which from a rationalist perspective are so many dispensable heuristics whose function is to bring us to the perception of the single object. And what is true of geometrical knowledge is, according to this rationalist thinking, true of all our knowledge.

This model for knowledge as rationalists conceive it is very important and will often be referred to below. Reference will be made easier by a name for it: the *sub specie* ("under the aspect of") model. Knowledge is a matter of making necessary connections, which we are able to do because we are viewing the same thing under different aspects. The world must be the way it is for the same sort of reason that the base angles of an isosceles triangle are equal. This is the basis for the putative unity, uniformity, and simplicity of the world.

The principal aim of this chapter is to show how this model might be of use at three interconnected levels: first, in understanding how some of the major rationalists thought about basic issues; secondly, in understanding some of what has been written about

13

what they thought; and thirdly, in understanding some of the apparent differences in how the major rationalists thought. At the first level is rationalist thought about substance; at the second is the dispute in the literature over Spinoza's conception of an attribute and its connection with substance; thirdly, there is the question of how Spinoza differed on this issue from Descartes.

However much the *sub specie* model might be reflected in rationalist thinking, that model is only a model. For the world is not an abstract object like a triangle. What is it about the concrete world that allows application of the model? What is it about the world itself that accommodates the rationalist impulse to know why the world must be the way it is? The answer to these questions, and part of the thesis of this chapter, is that substance is thought by rationalists to ground the *sub specie* model and to secure the necessity they perceive in the world.

Substance

One way to accommodate the rationalist impulse came from Aristotle. He took the universal terms applied in classifying things to refer to real features of the world that in principle tie things into just those classes. Thus, Bucephalus and Citation are tied together as horses by the horseness they share, horses and cows are tied as animals, animals and trees as living things, etc. In the early modern period, this sort of realism with respect to universals had generally fallen into disrepute, universals being identified with "occult qualities" that were empty of explanatory value. The focus therefore shifted from the predicate place to the subject, thus from horseness to Bucephalus, as a way of tying the world together to reflect its simplicity, unity, and intelligibility. This shift to the Aristotelian category of substance might tie the qualities of Bucephalus, but not all qualities can be bundled together unless ultimately they are qualities of a single substance. Rationalists tend to go in this direction, as has already been seen in the monism encountered in the *sub specie* model above.

Throughout the history of the concept, substance was thought to be a bundler, something that ties together otherwise disparate aspects of experience. In particular, substance was thought to bundle qualities, and to do so in two ways, corresponding to the two senses that Aristotle assigned to the term *ousia*, or "being," sometimes translated as "substance" (*Metaphysics*: 1017b10ff). The two senses might be understood as construing substance as a bundler of qualities *at* a time and *over* time. Substance as a bundler at a time is the ultimate subject of predication, something which, unlike horse, for instance, is not predicated of anything else. Substance in this sense is an individuator, distinguishing Bucephalus from Citation. The brownness and strength of the former are tied together by his substance, in contrast to the substance of the latter, which bundles grayness and speed. In this sense, substance also grounds such universal qualities, which for Aristotle, rejecting Plato's theory of separated forms, must always be exemplified as qualities *of* something. Aristotle's term for substance in this sense is *hypokeimenon*, literally "something standing under," which is the Latin etymology of the English term. Substance stands under, or supports, qualities insofar as it is that of which qualities are the qualities. Without substance, qualities like grayness or speed would have nothing to be qualities of, and would not exist. If there is speediness there must be something that is speedy, for example Citation.

The second sense of the term focuses on substance as a continuant, something that exists over time and thus is in a position to tie qualities in such a way as to form kinds of things. Thus an acorn is the kind of thing that eventually becomes an oaktree because of its continuing substance. Aristotle refers to substance in this sense as an *eidos*, that is, a form or an idea, somewhat like Plato's notion of a form except that it is in the thing of which it is the form. Substance in this sense refers to the potential history of a thing. To say of a given thing that it is a substance in this sense is to say what would happen to it if certain conditions were realized (that an acorn will grow into an oaktree if it is nourished).

In the seventeenth century, the concept of substance underwent very considerable revision, especially by the rationalists, and among them by Descartes and those he influenced. According to Descartes, the only substance in the second sense, at least as far as material things are concerned, is extended substance. Roughly, the *eidos* is extension. How an acorn can be understood as essentially its "quantity [or] extension in length, breadth and depth" might not be immediately clear. What is clear, however, is that Descartes retained the basic concept of substance, and especially the relevance to it of the *sub specie* model.

In both of its senses, as a bundler at a time and over time, substance is the ground for necessary connections – in the first sense by serving as the single thing of which apparently independent descriptions are true (in the case of a triangle, two equal angles and subtended equal sides), in the second by endowing a thing with a continuing nature that necessarily includes certain properties (the equality of its internal angles to a straight angle) and excludes others (having four sides).

The Empiricists on Substance

The empiricists' impulse in response to a perceived multiplicity, diversity, and complexity of the world naturally leads them to assign a vanishingly diminished role to substance. For Locke, substance is an "obscure and relative" idea of something we know not what; we know only what it does, viz. support accidents that inhere in it. But even how it supports is something knowledge of which he seems to reject. He ridicules the assumptions of those who claim such knowledge by twice relating the story of the Indian philosopher who, when asked what the earth rested on, replied, an elephant, and, when asked what the elephant rested on, replied, a tortoise, and as to what it rested on, replied, something he knew not what (Locke 1975: 295–6, 174–5).

The putative emptiness of the expressions "substance" and "inherence of accidents" is revealed for Locke by their translation into plain English: standing under or underpropping, and sticking on. Moreover, the doctrine of substance is for him another mischievous instance of mistaking words for things. If the same idea of substance is thought to be had in the three cases of the "substance" of God, finite mind, and body, these latter will be taken, according to Locke, as modifications of a single substance, "which [for religion] will be a very harsh doctrine." The upshot is

15

that for Locke, at least on one reading of him, substance is only a kind of complex idea – the thing idea – in terms of which we make sense of an otherwise unstructured world.

Berkeley, too, ridicules the attempt to make sense of substance as a support. Insofar as substance is a support for qualities, it must be spread under them and thus be extended. But, in a *reductio ad absurdum* at least faintly echoing Locke's Indian philosopher, Berkeley argues that extension is one such quality, which itself thus needs a support *in infinitum*. For Berkeley, too, the notion of substance is inimical to religion. He certainly took it to lead to skepticism, and perhaps to idolatry (in this he might have been inspired by an idea from his rationalist source, Malebranche). Most of all, material substance as the object of our knowledge undermines his conception of experience as the divine language of the author of nature. Not God but things would speak to us if the things of our experience were material substances.

A problem with Berkeley's discussion is that his own notion of the mind as a substance faces the same need for its role as a support to be explicated, even if the mind is a support for what is in it only by perceiving it. Moreover, his omnibus argument against material substance, his so-called Master Argument, is that it as something that exists unconceived is inconceivable and thus impossible. As the recent literature has pointed out, the same argument applies to the mind as a substance, perhaps even leaving him with nothing more than a solipsism of the present moment.

With such instability injected into the concept, it is not surprising that the third great empiricist should find substance to be a "fiction," "an unintelligible chimera," that involves us in evident "contradictions" (Hume 1988: 219–22, 232–3, 240–4). His argument is based on two principles. The first is that "whatever is clearly conceiv'd, after any manner, may exist in that manner." The second principle, which seems to be an application of the first, is that "everything, which is different, is distinguishable, and everything which is distinguishable, is separable in thought and imagination" (Hume 1988: 233). The converses of the pairs of implications in this principle are also true for Hume, so what is separable in imagination is distinguishable and different (i.e., numerically distinct). The whole of his principle was very important to the rationalists, from whom it was derived, so it will be useful to have a name for it: the *conceivability-apart* principle.

Hume's argument is straightforward: qualities and perceptions can be imagined in isolation, therefore they can exist apart from all else and have no need of a support from substance, either material or immaterial. Indeed, every individual quality and perception would itself be a substance, "something which may exist by *itself*" (Hume 1988: 233). We are led to suppose substance as a support not by any sound philosophical reasoning, according to Hume, but only by human psychology as an attempt to structure our experience.

In this account, Hume closely follows Locke with respect to (a) the nature of the idea of substance, (b) the psychological principle leading us to posit an idea, and (c) the rejection of any basis for it in reality. The idea is the complex one of simple ideas found constantly to go together; the principle is that we are led to regard the complex as simple and identical over time because the collection of simple ideas is unchanged or changes imperceptibly; and finally, despite our having to think in terms of substance, there is no such thing independent of the mind.

16

Like Locke and Berkeley, Hume takes the doctrine of substance to be prejudicial to the interests of religion. At least, he takes the doctrine of the soul as an immaterial, simple, and indivisible substance to stand or fall with the "hideous hypothesis" of Spinoza's atheism that there is but one simple and indivisible substance in the world. (Both his interpretation of Spinoza's view and his derogatory term for it come from Bayle's article on Spinoza in the famous *Dictionary*.) Hume argues, for example, that if it is objected against Spinoza's view that every part of his single, extended substance can be conceived apart from every other, and is thus not a mode of substance, but a substance itself, the same is true of every perception which is thus not a mode of the mind, but a substance. Or, if it is objected that Spinoza's view of a single substance entails that it is the subject of contrary modes such as the round and square shapes variously perceived in the world, the same is true of a substantial mind when it perceives such shapes.

Hume's motivation might have been to deflect noisome criticism from his own position, rather than, as in the case of Locke and Berkeley, to protect the precinct of religion, but the logic of his position is very similar to theirs. Moreover, the interpretation Hume offers of Spinoza might not be very wide of the mark; for the rationalist pedigree of his premises is impeccable. He bases both his arguments on the conceivability-apart principle, that two things are conceivable apart just in case they can exist apart. This principle is to be found at the core of the rationalists' thinking about substance, beginning with Descartes.

Descartes on Substance

Descartes appears to give "two very different definitions" of substance (Kemp Smith 1963: 313). In his *Principles* he first defines substance in terms of its independence of all else: "by *substance* we can understand nothing other than a thing which exists in such a way as to depend on no other thing for its existence" (Descartes 1985b: 210). He says that strictly speaking this definition applies only to God, for the existence of everything else depends on God's concurrence. God creates substances not only in bringing them into existence, but also actively keeps them in existence by exercising the same power of creation as long as they exist. (These powers are the same power conceived *sub specie* in the way just indicated.) But aside from this concurrence, the definition can apply to created substances such as minds. He goes on to say, however, that we can first know substance only by an inference from one of its attributes, since every attribute must be the attribute of something. Here Descartes appeals to the notion of substance as an ultimate subject of predication (Aristotle's *hypokeimenon*). Here, too, there is an appeal to the independence of substance: attributes depend on it, but the converse is false. The two definitions are to this extent "closely connected" (Woolhouse 1993: 17).

The two conceptions are not identical, however, since they rest on different conceptions of dependence. Finite substances are *dependent* on divine concurrence, which is to say, on the brute power of creation exercised by the unconstrained will of God, whereas they are *independent* insofar as they can be conceived apart from all else.

17

This is why Descartes does not say that his definition of substance applies fully to God alone and to a finite substance only with the qualification that it is independent of all else but God. Instead, he says that the definition does not apply *univocally* to both. To put it another way, the term, although equivocal, applies without qualification to both God and finite substance. Conceivability apart would seem to be the unique characterization of finite substance.

A difficulty in Descartes' account is that he uses the same notion of conceivability apart to characterize the independence both of one substance from another, and of a substance from certain of its attributes, or in his more technical language, from its modes. To begin, the difficulty of Descartes' terminology must be sorted out. Attributes are of three sorts. First are those that are inessential, such as a particular shape. These he calls *modes*. Second are essential, *principal* attributes. Anything having a principal attribute must have it, and everything has exactly one (Descartes 1985a: 298). There are two such: thought and extension. All the modes, and only the modes of a thing, are "referred" to its principal attribute (i.e., they are explained in terms of it). In this sense, the principal attribute of a thing "constitutes its essence and nature" (Descartes 1985a: 210). One might think of extension as corresponding to the axioms and postulates of geometry, and the mode as corresponding to a theorem deducible from them. So, a triangle's having equal base angles is referred to the axioms and postulates deployed in constructing an isosceles triangle. Finally, there are essential but non-principal attributes, such as duration or existence. Since every substance must have them they might be called generic attributes (Nolan 1998: 165). They do not sort substances into kinds of things, therefore have no modes. Modes, and the two sorts of attributes, are really all the same thing understood *sub specie* in the ways just described. Not every substance can be thought of in these ways, however. Since in God there is no variation, he contains no modes, only attributes (Descartes 1985a: 211).

If two things can be conceived apart from each other, they can exist apart from each other, and are really distinct from each other. Finite substances satisfy the conceivability-apart principle, and are really distinct. Thought and extension also satisfy this principle, and thus are really distinct. It is natural to think of conceivability apart as a symmetrical relation, as it is in the case of two or more substances, but for Descartes it is generally non-symmetrical: if x is conceivable apart from y, nothing follows concerning the y's conceivability apart from x. In the case of a mode, the substance is conceivable apart from the mode, but the mode is inconceivable apart from the substance. If there is a shape, it must be the shape of something. The distinction between a shape and the substance of which it is the mode is not a real distinction, but a modal distinction. Finally, in the case of attributes in the technical sense, for example its duration, it seems that neither can be conceived apart from the other. Substance and attribute thus are conceptually distinct.

In the *Principles* Descartes perhaps leaves open the possibility that some attributes might not stand in this relation of inconceivability apart, for he speaks of this distinction as between "substance and some attribute, without which the substance is inconceivable" (Descartes 1985a: 214, modified). The suggestion is that for some other attribute substance would not be inconceivable without it. In an important piece of correspondence, however, he drops the qualifier "some"; all attributes, including generic attributes, would thus be essential to a thing, although only the principal attribute constitutes its essence (Descartes 1985a: 348–9). It may be that every attribute is essential precisely because it differs only conceptually from the substance of which it is the attribute. *Really* they are the same one thing thought about in different ways (*sub specie*), such that the attribute that we conceptually distinguish from substance is but a mode of our thinking about it. In two important texts, Descartes expresses the status of attributes in just such terms (Descartes 1985a: 214; 1995: 279–80). The status of attribute as a mode of thought is a sensitive issue, however (Nolan 1998: 168–70). It will become more so in the case of Spinoza, below.

Spinoza on Attribute

Spinoza eliminates the equivocation in Descartes' account of substance by rejecting as unintelligible the notion of brute power of creation exercised by the unconstrained will of God. For him, the only notion of dependence is in terms of conceivability apart. At the outset of his *Ethics* Spinoza retains from Descartes the notion of substance as independent of all else, but only insofar as it is conceivable apart from all else: "By substance I mean that which is in itself and is conceived through itself." The argument of the early stages of the *Ethics* is that there is only one substance, and that is God (the hideous hypothesis). He also retains the notion of a mode as inconceivable apart from substance: "by mode I mean the affections of substance, that is, that which is in something else and is conceived through something else," which ultimately is substance. Spinoza's doctrine of how modes are ultimately derived from substance is exceedingly complex. In the end, individual minds and bodies are modes of two different attributes, whose technical sense, too, is carried over from Descartes: "By attribute I mean that which the intellect perceives of substance as [*tanquam*] constituting its essence." It seems that substance has an infinite number of (principal) attributes, of which two, thought and extension, are known to us. But how an attribute should be understood for Spinoza is one of the great exegetical chestnuts of the literature. His definition is "one of the most puzzling passages in the *Ethics*" (Bennett 1984: 62). Moreover, the interpretation of attribute is a test of how closely his view of substance matches the rationalist conception of substance developed above.

There are two schools of thought on how to read this definition of attribute, and between them might lie "the schism that cuts deepest into the interpretation of Spinoza" (Francis S. Haserot, cited by Jarrett 1977: 453). The parties to this exegetical split subscribe to either the "Objective Interpretation" (hereafter OI) or to the "Subjective Interpretation" (hereafter SI) (Wolfson 1958: 146). The parties take, or appear to take, opposite sides on two distinguishable but related questions: what is the relation between attribute and substance? and, what is the relation between attributes?

A component common to all versions of OI is that the distinction between attributes is a real distinction, such that there is a plurality of attributes, the distinction among which is not merely a conceptual distinction that we draw. The principal text for this interpretation is proposition 10 of part one: "Each attribute of a substance must be conceived through itself." If attributes are conceivable apart from each other, indeed if they must be so conceived, then they are really distinct from each other – which is precisely what is asserted in the scholium. An additional and obvious feature of OI is that attributes really do constitute the essence of substance, and do not merely appear to do so. Less clear, or at least not common to all versions of OI, is some account of what it means for an attribute to constitute the essence of substance.

Although this interpretation has come to be regarded as the "consensus view" (Garrett 2003: 23 n.7), there is an immediate problem it must face. If any two items x and y are really distinct, then both cannot be only conceptually distinct from some third item z; if x and y are only conceptually distinct from z, then they are only conceptually distinct from each other. The problem is that if attributes are really distinct from each other, they are also really distinct from substance. Indeed, as Hume would have put it, they appear to be substances themselves. One early commentator, who nonetheless supports OI, takes this to be an insoluble problem for it: "how that essence [which the intellect perceives as constituted by attribute] can be one and self-identical, while its constituents are many, heterogeneous and unrelated, is a question which is hopeless of solution" (Martineau 1895: 185). Nor is this desperation unique. A more recent commentator, who also inclines to OI, thinks that Spinoza failed to see the magnitude of the problem generated by his real distinction between attributes and did not deal with it (Delahunty 1985: 123). At any rate, there appears to be a violation of the monism that appears right at the outset of the *Ethics*: "Except God, no substance can be or be conceived" (Spinoza 1985: 420).

Moreover, if attributes are really distinct from substance, there is no obvious sense in which they might constitute the essence of substance. One natural reading is ruled out by what he says about essence, the term for which, perhaps surprisingly, does not appear with any frequency or prominence in Spinoza's work. He gives something like a definition of it only well into the *Ethics*, at the outset of book 2: "I say that to the essence of anything belongs that which, being given, the thing is necessarily posited and which, being taken away, the thing is necessarily taken away" (Spinoza 1985: 447). At a minimum, it would seem that the relation of constituting is not that of part to whole, for while parts are really distinct from the whole, the converse is generally not true. The rest of Spinoza's would-be definition is important in this regard: "or that without which the thing can neither be nor be conceived, and which can neither be nor be conceived to be without the thing." Clearly, the relation of dependence between essence and attribute, whatever it might be, and however it might bear on the relation of constituting, is symmetrical.

The Subjective Interpretation

These problems are avoided by SI, according to which the distinction between attributes, and between attributes and substance, is not a real distinction, but a conceptual distinction. Attributes are not so many substances, because they are all of them really identical to each other and to the one substance of which they are attributes. Saying that an attribute is not really distinct from substance does not tell us how it constitutes the essence of substance, but it does reflect the symmetrical relation that Spinoza indicates as holding between them.

A clear articulation of SI is not easy, however. Although not the first expression of it, the *locus classicus* of the view is provided by Wolfson (1958). As he distinguishes it from OI, "attributes are only *in* [the mind]," not "outside [the mind]"; they are "*invented* by the mind," not "*discovered* by the mind." In this reading, Wolfson seems to be following the much earlier reading of Erdmann, according to whom "attribute is what our mind sets up in order to constitute a way of perceiving substance" (Martineau 1895: 184). But Wolfson also takes it, according to his version of SI, that attributes are identical to each other and to substance, thus posing a problem for it not unlike the problem for OI above. For if substance is outside the mind, as everyone agrees it is for Spinoza, then how can an attribute, which is in the mind, be identical with substance? It might be better to say, as he does, that "attributes appear to the mind as distinct from each other. In reality, however, they are one" (Jarrett 1977: 450).

SI thus understood seems to be given support by Spinoza's use of psychological language in discussing attributes as "what the intellect perceives," and by the occurrence of the particle "as" in the definition: "by attribute I understand what the intellect perceives of a substance, as [*tanquam*] constituting its essence." The sense of the Latin term is "as if," "as it were," or "so to speak." Wolfson draws on this support, emphasizing the lack of such language in Descartes, who says of a principal attribute, as has been seen above, that it "constitutes the nature and essence of substance" (Wolfson 1958: 153). But so deep an exegetical disagreement is not likely to be resolved on such evidence (Jarrett 1977: 447, 453 n.1).

How much SI is helped by this formulation is questionable; for if SI denies that an attribute truly constitutes the essence of substance, it comes in for some serious text-based criticism. One important defender of OI takes proponents of SI to assert that divine attributes are attributes "only in the sense that they each appear to some finite beings . . . to constitute God's essence, even though they do not constitute it" (Donagan 1996: 346). He takes them to read the phrase "what the intellect perceives" along these lines to mean "what the intellect (possibly) falsely perceives," and he then attacks SI as follows. "Spinoza himself treats his definition as implying that attributes really are what the intellect perceives them to be. For example, [in 1Ep10s] he describes the attributes of a substance as 'hav[ing] always been in it together . . . each express[ing] the reality or being (*esse*) of substance'" (Donagan 1988: 70). Others have read SI in similar fashion as having made the distinction between attributes "merely subjective" (Martineau 1895: 184), "illusory" (Curley, in Spinoza 1985: 409 n.2), with an attribute "mistakenly perceived" as if it constituted the essence of substance (Jarrett 1977: 447). To construe the distinction between attribute and substance as mind-dependent and yet to construe them as really identical in such a way that attributes truly constitute the essence of substance is the main challenge for proponents of SI.

The challenge might not be worth the effort. Some of the best known of recent Spinoza scholars have taken SI to have been "demolished" by Martial Gueroult's monumental work on Spinoza (Donagan 1988: 70). Gueroult is supposed to have "provided us with a definitive refutation of the subjective interpretation" (Curley, in Spinoza 1985: 409 n.2). Indeed, Gueroult's criticism is regarded as so "decisive" that "it is as certain as anything disputed in Spinoza's *Ethics* can be, that Wolfson's interpretation of these passages is mistaken" (Donagan 1973: 171, and n.32; see also Donagan 1996: 379 n.5).

Gueroult mounted two main arguments against SI (Gueroult 1968: 50). First, if attributes were only conceptually distinct, they would depend on the mind; if attributes depended on the mind, the mind would be prior to the attribute of thought. But no mode can be prior to that of which it is only the mode. At a minimum, if "attribute" is to be defined in merely epistemic terms (i.e., in terms of thought), then as Bennett later argued, "one of the attributes [namely, thought] has a special place in the definition of 'attribute,' which creates a lopsidedness in Spinoza's system which he does not mention, could not explain, and should not have tolerated" (Bennett 1984: 62). Second, if attributes were only conceptually distinct, they would be mere concepts; we would therefore not know things as they are in themselves, as Spinoza says we do, but only, in the fashion of Kant, as they are conceptualized. Proponents of OI have taken the Kantian reading as an anachronism; it is unacceptable simply on the ground that Kant was the first to hold the view that SI is supposed to ascribe to Spinoza (Martineau 1895: 184).

In addition, Gueroult gave an argument against what is Wolfson's better formulation of SI, that attributes only appear to the mind as distinct from each other, but are really one. Against taking attributes to be "identical in God," he appeals to the scholium attached to proposition 10 of part one of the *Ethics*, and concludes that attributes "must be conceived in God as distinguished by a real distinction, and not just a conceptual distinction, being diverse realities which together constitute one and the same being" (Gueroult 1968: 430). This scholium is the foundation of Gueroult's three arguments; it is referred to repeatedly by proponents of OI; and on it hangs the difference between OI and SI. We shall return to it below.

The Objective Interpretation

It is remarkable that although Gueroult has been taken to undo SI, his own version of OI has gained no adherents at all. (Bennett 1984 calls it "strange.") In particular, no one seems convinced by his solution to the monism problem, which if unsolved seems in fact to be a *reductio ad absurdum* of OI, or at least of Gueroult's version of it. He accepts as an implication of his interpretation that the multi-attributed substance is a union of substances of one attribute, the model for which is the union that Descartes sees between mind and body in man, magnified to infinity. That this is supposed to explain how a number of substances of one attribute form one substance of many attributes might seem like explaining the obscure by the still more obscure (Woolhouse 1993: 39). In any case, "it is very difficult to see that he really can reconcile his view that Spinoza's *one* really existing substance is constituted by or consists of infinitely many attributes with his further view that *each* attribute satisfies the definition of substance and, therefore, is a substantial being in its own right" (Eisenberg 1990: 4).

Some proponents of OI have, as we have seen, just swallowed the bitter pill, a problem unsolved and insoluble in the system. Some have tried other solutions, though with no obvious success. Donagan, for example, takes the question to be the following: "How can really distinct attributes, which express really distinct essences, constitute the essence of one and the same substance?" (Donagan 1996: 351). He suggests that a "clue" to the answer comes from what is one of the most quoted propositions in the

Ethics: "the order and connection of ideas is the same as the order and connection of things." Donagan takes the connection to consist in a *correspondence* between modes of different attributes that is determined by "transattribute laws of nature" (Donagan 1996: 352). But this "conjecture" of such laws, for which there is no textual warrant here or anywhere else, seems designed to explain what needs no explanation. For in the scholium to the proposition (which appears only in book 2, hardly placed to perform the fundamental role Donagan assigns it), Spinoza takes the metaphysics of substance and attribute as *already* settled in book 1, and in a way, moreover, that appeals to SI as an explanation of modal correspondence across attributes. Here is what he says:

> We must recall here what we showed [in the First Part] that whatever can be perceived by an infinite intellect as constituting an essence of substance pertains to one substance only, and consequently that the thinking substance and the extended substance are one and the same substance, which is now comprehended under this attribute, now under that. So also a mode of extension and the idea of that mode are one and the same thing, but expressed in two ways [*duobis modis*]. (Spinoza 1985: 451)

What needs explanation is not how attributes, and modes, can be the same, but how they can be different.

As to how OI construes the connection between substance and attribute, the only alternative to Gueroult's position seems to be to make it a unique, *sui generis*, primitive notion. Each of substance's attributes "constitutes" or "expresses" the essence of that substance. "A fundamental formal property of this relation would be that two attributes might on the one hand be really distinct, and on the other constitute or express the same essence" (Donagan 1973: 180). How does an attribute constitute or express an essence? It just does. That this interpretation, however unsatisfying it may be, is not without merit is attested to by the debate over how Spinoza's terms for constituting and expressing should be translated into English (Curley, in Spinoza 1985: 416 n.24). The terms might be primitive technical terms without translation. Still, OI would be better off if sense could be reconstructed from Gueroult's part-whole theory of constituting.

Before any attempt at the reconstruction, the foundation of OI must be investigated, namely the text in which Spinoza takes the distinction between attributes to be a real distinction. For it is a foundation full of cracks. The text appears in a letter from De Vries to Spinoza, quoted back to him from a draft of the *Ethics*:

> From these [propositions] it is evident that although two attributes may be conceived to be really distinct (i.e., one may be conceived without the aid of the other), they do not, on that account, constitute two beings or two different substances. The reason is that it is of the nature of a substance that all of its attributes (I mean each of them) should be conceived through themselves, since they have [always] been in it together. (Spinoza 1985: 192)

Attributes are really distinct and in substance prior to any operation of the mind. The worry generated for De Vries seems to be that, from a Cartesian standpoint, Spinoza's position is contradictory. For Descartes had argued that it would be contradictory for there to be two principal attributes of the same substance:

> As for the attributes which constitute the natures of things, it cannot be said that those which are different, and such that the concept of the one is not contained in the other, are present together in one and the same subject; for that would be equivalent to saying that one and the same subject has two different natures – a statement that implies a contradiction, at least when it is a question of a simple subject . . . rather than a composite one. (Descartes 1985a: 298)

For De Vries, since each substance has but one attribute, Spinoza ought to hold that there are as many substances as there are attributes.

In reply, however, Spinoza seems to support SI by arguing in psychological terms that infinite substance must have infinite attributes. We *conceive* being under some attribute, he says, and a being has more being the more attributes that are attributed to it. Moreover, he runs the definitions of substance and attribute together, in a way they might have been in the draft, with only a conceptual distinction between them: "By substance I understand what is in itself and is conceived through itself, i.e., whose concept does not involve the concept of another thing. I understand the same by attribute, except that it is called attribute in relation to the intellect, which attributes such and such a definition to substance" (Spinoza 1985: 195). He goes on to say that this explains what he means by "substance *or* attribute," and gives illustrations of "how one and the same thing can be designated by two names."

The material De Vries quoted to Spinoza appeared essentially intact in the final version of the *Ethics*, in a much longer text attached as a scholium to the crucial proposition 10. The proposition reads: "Each attribute of a substance must be conceived through itself." Spinoza thinks that this follows directly from his definitions of substance and attribute: "For an attribute is what the intellect perceives concerning a substance, as constituting its essence; so it must be conceived through itself."

Unless a substance and its essence are somehow really distinct, it would seem that an attribute is conceived through itself because it is really identical to substance, which is conceived through itself. If this is Spinoza's argument, and substance and attribute are really identical, then the scholium can be read as an acknowledgment that what can be conceived apart, and what in that sense and that sense only is really distinct, need not be capable of existing apart. In short, Spinoza takes the inevitable step of denying the conceivability-apart principle. He does so for the reason that, while some things are conceivable apart, *nothing* can exist apart. To put it another way, real distinction is only an epistemic notion. He concludes the scholium by claiming that neither conceivability-apart, nor any other test, shows existibility apart, for, as he is about to show, there is but one substance. "If someone now asks by what sign we shall be able to distinguish the diversity of substances, let him read the following propositions, which show that in Nature there exists only one substance, and that it is absolutely infinite. So that sign would be sought in vain." Neither conceivability-apart nor anything else shows existibility-apart.

Gueroult

None of these texts is unknown to Gueroult. He attempts to reconcile them to OI with one brilliant move, largely ignored by his critics. He claims that while for Spinoza substance is unique and indivisible, it is not simple. Previously in the tradition, substance was thought to be simple in order that it be immutable. That the soul, for example, is a simple substance and therefore immortal was known throughout the early modern period as the "Achilles of rationalist arguments" (Mijuskovic 1974: chs. 1–2). Not only immortality, but also personal identity and the unity of consciousness were thought to depend on this simplicity (Mijuskovic 1974: chs. 3–4). For even longer it was thought, even more importantly, that God's impassivity required simplicity. Divine simplicity was connected to the even more important notion of monotheism or divine uniqueness, and thus the requirement is found throughout the Judeo-Christian tradition (Wolfson 1958: 113–16). If God is complex, God could be divided; not only could God change, but also there would then be a multiplicity of Gods, or none at all. More generally, the immutability entailed by simplicity seems to be required in order for substance to play the rationalist role sketched at the outset above. Unless substance is the immutable bedrock for bundling qualities at a time and over time, then there is no basis for the perceived necessity in the world. The rationalists may think that the world hangs together, and perhaps it does, but there would be no reason why it should do so.

In denying the simplicity of Spinozan substance, therefore, Gueroult risks undoing all that substance is thought to do. The brilliance of his proposal lies in its locating the unity of substance in precisely what might be thought to undo it, namely its multiplicity of attributes. There is and can be no multiplicity of substances because substance is an *ens realissimum*, an utterly real being, than which nothing could be more real. And since reality of substance is a function of its attributes, substance must have all attributes. The attribute that would constitute or express the nature of some other substance is already possessed by the utterly real substance, which is thus unique. Thus does Spinoza claim in the scholium to proposition 10, "not only is it far from absurd to attribute many attributes to one substance . . . [but] there is also nothing clearer than that a being absolutely infinite must be defined . . . as a being that consists of infinite attributes, each of which expresses a certain eternal and infinite essence." If, as proposition 6 has it, "there cannot be two or more substances of the same nature or attribute," seemingly because two substances with the same attribute would be numerically identical, then there is no room, so to speak, for more than one substance. The one substance has already taken up all the attributes that might constitute the essence of some other substance.

For the same reason that substance cannot gain or lose attributes, it cannot undergo change. It is only the modes of attributes, which unlike substance and attributes, cannot be conceived through themselves, that undergo change. The sort of change that especially concerned the tradition was divisibility in some spatial sense. Although it has the attribute of extension, substance cannot be spatially divided. For extension is itself without parts and thus indivisible. Instead, it is the individual modes of extension, the ordinary material things of the world, that are divisible. Spinoza took these Cartesian positions very early and never departed from them (Spinoza 1985: 70–2).

Not incidentally, the logic of Leibniz's position on substance might be read in very similar fashion. His individual concepts might be understood in terms of Gueroult's notion of attributes for each of infinitely many substances. On both schemes there is a kind for each individual. And, as attributes are bundled because the perfect reality of substance requires all of them as its attributes, so Leibniz's individuals are bundled into possible worlds as maximally compossible sets. The essence of each Leibnizian individual is an "exigency to existence," such that the existent is that which is compossible with more than anything incompossible with it. So unified is the set that it seems to be substance itself that excludes the possibility of any other substance, in its world or any other world.

OI and SI

Does OI prevail, then, over SI? As a rationalist might say, it depends on how you look at it. If the focus is on the status of the distinction between attributes, and between attributes and substance, SI seems to get it right. But if the focus is on what it is that enables us to draw those distinctions, then OI seems to get it right. The suggestion is that the OI–SI confrontation is itself an instance of an issue that can be understood on the *sub specie* model. Such an outcome would be the best explanation of what otherwise is a Mexican standoff between formidable interpretive forces in which it is difficult to imagine either being bested.

To motivate this reading, consider once again the definition of attribute. "By attribute I understand what the intellect perceives of a substance, as constituting its essence." If OI is the correct reading, why doesn't Spinoza say simply that attribute constitutes the essence of substance? On the face of it, OI either leaves the epistemic language unexplained, or it construes it as an idle operator that prefixes every claim of the *Ethics*. That is, whenever Spinoza says that something is the case, he is saying that the intellect perceives that to be the case in what G. E. Moore would have called a pragmatic tautology: p, and I believe p. That is, when I say that p, it goes without saying that I take p as true.

But uttering a pragmatic tautology might, like uttering a logical tautology, have a point. In this case, it draws attention to the subjective point of view, to the conceptual status of attributes, and to their merely conceptual distinction from substance and from each other – whatever the language that Spinoza might use to refer to that status. The point is that if there were no minds such as ours, there would be no such distinctions. This is why Spinoza can claim, as he does, that "outside the intellect there is nothing but substances and their affections [modes]" (Spinoza 1985: 411). As a conceptual being, an attribute is nothing outside the intellect. "For if anyone looks outside the intellect for what is signified by [conceptual being], he will find it to be a mere nothing" (Spinoza 1985: 301). This is the line emphasized by SI. It emphasizes the Cartesian conception of attribute as a mode of thought.

On the other hand, attributes are not mere fictions. "A fictitious being is nothing but two terms connected by a sheer act of the will alone, without any guidance from reason." In the terminology, and example, that Descartes takes over from Suarez, it would be a something arrived at via a distinction of reason *rationantis*, a reasoning conceptual distinction. It would be a distinction without a difference, such as Peter distinguished from himself. Descartes rejects such entities, thus the designation "fictitious," and so does Spinoza, who was familiar both with Descartes, of course, but also with Suarez, who might have been his most important medieval source (Spinoza 1985: 223).

By contrast to a fictitious being, a conceptual being "does not depend on the will alone, nor does it consist of any terms connected with one another" (Spinoza 1985: 302). Spinoza takes a conceptual being to be "nothing but a mode of thinking, which helps us to more easily *retain, explain*, and *imagine* what we have understood" (Spinoza 1985: 299–300). In this sense, an attribute as a conceptual being would not be a mere nothing, but a real being. For inquiry about such a being seeks "nothing but the nature of that mode of thinking, which is really a being and distinguished from another mode of thinking" (Spinoza 1985: 301). Although these modes of thinking are not ideas with proper objects outside the intellect, they arise from the ideas of real beings (and in fact do so with such immediacy that they are confused by the unwary, who then reify them). To this extent they are grounded in real beings. Attributes are not pie in the sky, but ways of retaining, explaining, and imaging the real beings we have understood. This is the line emphasized by OI. It emphasizes the Cartesian conception of attribute as not really distinct from substance. Just because of the real identity, the distinction drawn by abstraction, although not found in the thing itself, has a ground in it. In the terminology that Descartes again takes over from Suarez attribute is something arrived at via a distinction of reason *rationatae*, a reasoned conceptual distinction (Descartes 1995: 280–1).

An approach to the substance–attribute connection along these lines already exists in the literature. Bennett takes Spinoza to be using psychological language to make a logical or conceptual point. Spinoza is "saying that substance differs from attribute only by the difference between a substantival and an adjectival presentation of the very same content." They are the same thing, but substance is the thing conceived of as what has the attribute, and attribute is the thing conceived as what is had by that same thing (Bennett 1984: 62–3). While this approach is friendly, there are problems with it (Eisenberg 1990: 8–9). Chiefly, Bennett's inclination to treat the alternative versions as "a bit of formal apparatus" rather understates the significance of the *sub specie* model in rationalist thinking.

Such is not the case with the similar approach of Collins, who like Donagan takes proposition 7 of part two to be crucial to Spinoza's thinking about attribute. "The intelligibility that we commonly think of as incorporated in representations such as pictures or descriptions is, for Spinoza, simply the reality of what is represented when considered under the attribute of thought. So the possibility that attributes are patterns of intelligibility by which things are representable does not contrast with the idea that attributes are intrinsic features of substance" (Collins 1985: 86). Although the dual conception of attribute is thus an intrinsic feature of the system, according to Collins, he does not think, however, that "the resulting metaphysical unity of being and thought, representation and represented, leaves us with a clear view of things." Yet the putative unclarity might be due to a lack of what in the nature of the case cannot be forthcoming, namely a definitive demonstration of the status of attribute. Instead, we might, in the fashion of Euclid's proposition 5, have the intuition of the single object, for which all demonstrations are but dispensable heuristics.

Descartes and Spinoza

Gueroult would not be happy with this resolution of his difference from Wolfson. For one thing, the texts just cited for Spinoza's views on conceptual being come from the "Cogitata metaphysica," appended to his expository work, *Descartes' Principles*, which, according to Gueroult, expresses not Spinoza's views but Descartes'. Gueroult's reservations are pertinent. In a letter to Oldenburg, Spinoza says he agreed to the publication of the work only on condition that a preface to it indicate that not all the views in it were his own, "since I had written many things in it which were the very opposite of what I held" (Spinoza 1985: 207). Meyer's preface does just that, with a few examples as Spinoza had requested (Spinoza 1985: 229–30).

On the other hand, there is much in this work with which Spinoza undoubtedly agrees. As Meyer also says, Descartes is the "brightest star of our age"; he first brought much of mathematics "from darkness into the light . . . Then he uncovered firm foundations for philosophy, on which a great many theses can be built, with Mathematical order and certainty" (Spinoza 1985: 226). Indeed, the Descartes–Spinoza connection might itself provide an example of a topic amenable to treatment in terms of the rationalist *sub specie* model. Think of Descartes as talking about an isosceles triangle, Spinoza about one with equal base angles.

Much of the case for such an approach to the Descartes–Spinoza connection is obvious, even from the above. There remains one very dramatic difference, of course, and that is the fact, according to Descartes, of the creation *ex nihilo* of a multiplicity of substances by the free and indifferent will of God. To be sure, Spinoza is prepared to speak of a creation, but by it he means the immanent causation which necessarily unfolds what God already contains, not the transeunt causation envisaged by Descartes and the Judeo-Christian tradition.

However, even this difference might appear to be only conceptual, as it were, when the Cartesian theory of modality is considered. Especially as it is developed by Desgabets and Arnauld, that theory has it that possibility is entirely a function of the actual. Prior to creation of substance, there are not any mere possibilities (i.e., essences without existence, or possibles that are not actual) among which God would be constrained to select in the way Leibniz was later to imagine (Nelson 1993: 676, 682). The world becomes possible only upon becoming actual (Desgabets 1983: 65–79). Indeed, as the product of an immutable will, substance upon creation becomes necessary. As on Spinoza's view, all temporality and change have merely modal status. So it is not clear just what would be meant by "prior to creation" (or by the world "becoming" possible) – certainly not temporal priority, but not logical priority, either.

Desgabets expresses the necessary existence of substance by using a theological term, indefectibility (Schmaltz 2002: 94 n.44). It is natural to think of indefectibility, as Desgabets himself does, in terms of substance's permanent duration: there is no point at which it is annihilated. But given its dependence on an immutable will, what is true of a substance's future is true of its past as well: there is no point at which it is first created. (Strictly speaking, of course, substance is not in time at all; only its modes are.) The world is created only in the sense that it depends for its existence on a single act in which only a conceptual distinction is drawn between creation and conservation in existence (Descartes 1985b: 33). In addition, the multiplicity of actual substances, like Spinoza's attributes as Gueroult understands them (and perhaps like Leibnizian monads), exhausts the realm of possibility.

At this point, the difference between the Cartesians and Spinoza seems to mirror the difference between SI and OI (at least on Gueroult's version of it). There is a single view with respect to which we draw distinctions; but Spinoza focuses on the status of the items distinguished, the Cartesians on the basis for the distinction. To put it another way, the hideous hypothesis might be only one way of looking at Spinoza's system; or alternatively, Descartes' hypothesis is no less hideous.

References and Further Reading

Bennett, Jonathan (1984). *A Study of Spinoza's Ethics*. New York: Hackett.

Collins, Arthur W. (1985). *Thought and Nature: Studies in Rationalist Philosophy*. Notre Dame, IN: Notre Dame University Press.

Delahunty, R. J. (1985). *Spinoza*. London: Routledge and Kegan Paul.

Descartes, René (1985a, b). *The Philosophical Writings*, 2 vols. (J. Cottingham, R. Stoothoff, D. Murdoch, trans.). Cambridge: Cambridge University Press.

—— (1995). *The Philosophical Writings: The Correspondence* (J. Cottingham, R. Stoothoff, D. Murdoch, A. Kenny, trans.). Cambridge: Cambridge University Press.

Desgabets, Robert (1983). *Oeuvres philosophiques inédites* (J. Beaude, ed.). Amsterdam: Quadratures.

Donagan, Alan (1973). Essence and distinction of attributes in Spinoza's metaphysics. In M. Grene (ed.), *Spinoza: A Collection of Critical Essays* (pp. 164–81). Garden City, NY: Anchor.

—— (1988). *Spinoza*. Chicago: University of Chicago Press.

—— (1996). Spinoza's theology. In D. Garrett (ed.), *The Cambridge Companion to Spinoza* (pp. 343–82). Cambridge: Cambridge University Press.

Eisenberg, Paul (1990). On the attributes and their alleged independence of one another: A commentary on Spinoza's *Ethics* 1P10. In E. Curley and P.-F. Moreau (eds.). *Spinoza: Issues and Directions* (pp. 1–15). Leiden: E. J. Brill.

Euclid (1956). *The Thirteen Books of Euclid's Elements* (Thomas L. Heath, trans.). New York: Dover.

Garrett, Aaron V. (2003). *Meaning in Spinoza's Method*. Cambridge: Cambridge University Press.

Gueroult, Martial (1968). *Spinoza: Dieu*. Paris: Aubier.

Hume, David (1988). *A Treatise of Human Nature* (L. A. Selby-Bigge, ed.). Oxford: Clarendon Press.

Jarrett, Charles E. (1977). Some remarks on the "objective" and "subjective" interpretations of the attributes. *Inquiry*, 9 (20), 447–56.

Kemp Smith, Norman (1963). *New Studies in the Philosophy of Descartes: Descartes as Pioneer*. London: Macmillan.

Locke, John (1975). *An Essay Concerning Human Understanding* (P. H. Nidditch, ed.). Oxford: Clarendon Press.

Martineau, James (1895). *A Study of Spinoza*. Freeport, NY: Books for Libraries Press.

Mijuskovic, Ben Lazare (1974). *The Achilles of Rationalist Arguments*. The Hague: Martinus Nijhoff.

Nelson, Alan (1993). Cartesian actualism in the Leibniz–Arnauld correspondence. *Canadian Journal of Philosophy*, 23, 675–94.

Nolan, Lawrence (1998). Descartes' theory of universals. *Philosophical Studies*, 89, 161–80.

Schmaltz, Tad M. (2002). *Radical Cartesianism: The French Reception of Descartes*. Cambridge: Cambridge University Press.

Spinoza, B. (1985). *The Collected Works of Spinoza* (E. Curley, ed. and trans.). Princeton, NJ: Princeton University Press.

Wolfson, Harry Austryn (1958). *The Philosophy of Spinoza*, 2 vols. Cleveland, OH: World Publishing.

Woolhouse, R. S. (1993). *Descartes, Spinoza, Leibniz: The Concept of Substance in Seventeenth-Century Metaphysics*. London: Routledge.

3

Rationalist Theories of Sense Perception and Mind–Body Relation

GARY HATFIELD

The theory of perception is a microcosm of the metaphysics, the theories of mind and cognition, and the methodologies of the rationalist philosophers of the seventeenth century. Through sense perception we engage the surrounding world. When this happens, bodily processes occur in the sense organs and brain and there are mental experiences. Since the rationalists held that mind is different from body, the fact of sense perception raised questions about the causal interaction of mind and body (to which they gave differing answers). Sense perception provides us with knowledge. The rationalists knew that the investigation of nature requires some knowledge that must come through the senses. Theories of perception are therefore implicated in accounts of scientific knowledge of nature ("natural philosophy," in seventeenth-century parlance). The role of the senses in acquiring knowledge more generally, and the postulated need (if any) of sensory content for general thought processes, take us into theories of mind and cognition.

The major seventeenth-century rationalists – Descartes, Malebranche, Spinoza, and Leibniz – are so named because they placed emphasis on reason or intellect, by contrast with the senses, for acquiring important truths. Indeed, they agreed that the basic truths of metaphysics are known by the intellect acting alone, independently of the senses. They thus held that the intellect can know the existence of God and the essential attributes of substance through purely intellectual perceptions. They cautioned that sense perception taken by itself presents a confused and misleading picture of the fundamental features of the material world. Thus, under the guidance of sense perception we might conclude from the apparently empty space surrounding the bodies we see that matter moves through empty space that is truly void (a vacuum); or that color in bodies resembles color as we experience it and is a so-called "real quality" (defined below); or from the fact that heavy bodies fall toward the earth we might conclude that there is in those bodies a quality called "weight" that pushes them downward (CSM 1: 125; 216, 285; 182–3, 234).[1] The rationalists typically considered such judgments to be errors that result from the unguided use of the senses and that must be corrected through conceptions that arise from reason or intellect alone.

Nonetheless, seventeenth-century rationalists did not abandon sense perception or consider it to be uniformly faulty. They limited the importance of the senses in metaphysics, while acknowledging that they are essential in at least two other areas. First, the senses are required for gaining knowledge of particular facts and of contingent regularities for the purposes of natural philosophy. Such facts might include the apparent size and position of the sun (as needed in astronomy), the refractive indexes of various media (as required in optics), and the properties of the magnet (as needed in physics). Second, the senses are needed for daily activities. In this regard, the rationalists held that the qualities perceived by the senses, and also the perceptual responses implicated in the emotions (or "passions," which Descartes and others considered to be a subset of the emotions), are attuned to the preservation of the human being (or at least the body). In daily living, the "confused" or "inadequate" perceptions of the senses must and should be trusted, since the intellect usually lacks the clear data, and the time, that would be required if each person were to deliberate carefully before taking each step. In the absence of rational deliberation, sensory impressions and the resultant passions can guide behavior in ways that usually work. Reason still has a role to play in mitigating or overseeing the effects of the passions when they become disruptive, or when, as sometimes happens, their guidance is incorrect.

In this chapter I compare rationalist theories of sense perception to previously held theories of perception (especially of vision) and I examine rationalist accounts of sensory qualities and sensory representation, of the role of the sense-based passions in guiding behavior, of the epistemological benefits and dangers of sense perception, and of mind–body relations. Within each section I begin with Descartes, the first major rationalist of the seventeenth century. The other major rationalists, Malebranche, Spinoza, and Leibniz, and also lesser-known figures such as Pierre Régis, Jacques Rohault, and Antoine Le Grand, were well acquainted with Descartes' work. Indeed, the first three were each deeply influenced by Descartes in their early years before developing their own philosophical systems, and the latter three were all advocates of Descartes' philosophy (perhaps with slight revision). Each of the major rationalists, while sharing some positions in common, developed a distinctive metaphysics of perception and of the mind–body relation. Earlier sections chart these differences and a final section sums up common features and touches on the continuing significance of their views.

For our topic, the best-known differences among the major rationalists pertain to their metaphysical views on the substantial nature of mind and body and the nature of mind–body union and interaction. Descartes held that mind and body are two distinct finite substances (*dualism*) that depend only on the sustaining power of God (an infinite substance) for their existence (CSM 1: 210). His position, also adopted by Malebranche and the lesser Cartesians, was that mind and body have mutually distinct essences, namely, thought and extension (extension in the three spatial dimensions). Critics of Descartes' position asked how distinct substances can interact. Descartes' replies (e.g., CSMK 217–19, 226–8) were unclear or waffling, although we may hope to uncover some coherence through further investigation. His successors adopted various positions. Le Grand (1: 324–5) endorsed a genuine causal interaction between mind and body (*interactionism*). Malebranche (Mal 448) held that God establishes and sustains laws of interaction, so that on every occasion in which the body or mind is in a specified state, God himself causes the appropriate effect in the other substance (*occasionalism*). Régis (1: 109–10, 123–4) rejected Malebranche's talk of occasional causes and described God as a "primary cause" who grants mind and body, as "secondary causes," powers of causal interaction; but he then allowed that secondary causes "do not have causality proper," but serve as "instruments" that God uses "to modify the action through which he produces" all effects (1: 125, 200). Other rationalists adopted different views of the substantial basis of mind and body. Spinoza (SE, Pts. 1–2) held that there is only one substance, the infinite substance that he called "God or nature." This substance has (at least) two wholly different attributes, mind and body. The individual instances of mental and bodily states (called *modes*) do not interact, for they are not separate; rather, they are identical in their substantial basis, being two aspects of the one underlying substance. The states of mind and body occur in parallel because they are identical (*dual-aspect monism*). Leibniz (LL 453–60, 492–7) adopted a third position on the substantial natures of mind and body, arguing that besides God there is an infinity of finite substances that should be conceived by analogy with mind (in that they all have perception, although not all of them have reflective thought). These finite substances do not genuinely interact; rather, their states are coordinated through a grand scheme that God envisions in creating the universe (setting up a *preestablished harmony* among all finite substances).

At various points I compare the positions of the rationalists on these matters with the positions found in other major philosophical traditions. In the seventeenth century, the best-known philosophical traditions were Platonic and Aristotelian (or a mixture of these), but ancient atomism and Stoicism had some influence (Grafton 1988; Menn 1998). These traditions gave various accounts of the physics of sensory qualities, the nature of mind and its relation to body, and the significance of sense perception for human knowledge. The Aristotelian tradition (in one or another variant) dominated university instruction, but Platonism had undergone a revival in the fifteenth and sixteenth centuries ("Platonism" was an amalgam of Plato's positions with various ancient and Renaissance Neoplatonists). Atomist and Stoic positions were available through popular sources, including works by the Roman orator Cicero (first century BCE), the Greek philosopher Plutarch (second century), and the Greek philosophical biographer Diogenes Laertius (third century). The Aristotelian commentaries common in university instruction often surveyed the major non-Aristotelian positions (including Platonism, Stoicism, and atomism) before seeking to refute them. The available interpretations of Aristotle were themselves influenced to varying degrees by Platonic or Neoplatonic factors. The writings of Augustine of Hippo (fourth century) were influential in the seventeenth century. Augustine's basic metaphysics and epistemology were Neoplatonic, though his accounts of sense perception were influenced by the Egyptian physician Galen of Pergamon (second century), and hence also by Aristotle. On the theory of the sense organs and the physical, physiological, and psychological processes of perception, medical writers such as Galen and optical writers such as Ibn al-Haytham (eleventh century), Witelo (thirteenth century), and Johannes Kepler (1571–1630) were important (and their works were widely available). Contemporary empiricist philosophers (including Thomas Hobbes and John Locke) disagreed with the rationalists about the epistemic basis for general principles in philosophy (including natural philosophy). Their positions can be used for comparison, and sometimes the rationalists responded directly to them (as did Descartes to Hobbes, and Leibniz to Locke).

Sense Perception as a Natural Process

Sense perception was regarded as a natural process by all parties involved. In the Aristotelian university curriculum and throughout the seventeenth century, it was studied under several headings. The basic process of perception, including the nature of the external medium in sight and hearing, the nature of sensory qualities, the structure of the sense organs, and the physiology and psychology of perception, were studied in physics. At the time, the term "physics," which derives from the Greek root *physis*, meant the science of nature in general, and it included topics that we would now describe as biological and psychological. Hence, the study of sense perception even in its mental aspect was commonly placed under physics (both before and after Descartes, e.g., Eustache [1609] 1998: 70 and Rohault 1: 248). Indeed, the union of mind and body was sometimes itself described as "physical" (Régis 1: 123),[2] although most authors (including Régis) also considered questions about mind–body union and interaction to fall under metaphysics – a discipline that, in rationalist hands, became an account of substances and their basic properties and causal powers (the chief substances or substantial natures being God, mind, and matter). Despite fundamental disagreements on the metaphysics of mind, body, and mind–body union and interaction, all of the rationalists recognized regularities (sometimes called "laws," Régis 1: 126–7) that describe the relation between brain states and sensory experience.

Sense perception and the attendant phenomena of the passions also were investigated in other contexts. The science of optics had as its subject matter the theory of vision in general, including the physics of light, the physiological processes in the eye and optic nerves, and the psychological processes of perception. Descartes, Malebranche, and Spinoza were well acquainted with optical writings. Optics, as a "mixed-mathematical science," was considered distinct from physics in the Aristotelian scheme (in which "physics" examined qualitative properties). Descartes and his followers incorporated optics into physics (CSMK 28; Le Grand 1: 294–303; Régis 3: 137–292; Rohault 1: 196–285). The sense organs and their physiology were also examined in medical writings, and Descartes, who had a strong interest in anatomy, physiology, and medicine more generally, was familiar with such sources (e.g., Galen [2nd century] 1968; Fernel [1567] 2003). Medical writers discussed the passions of the soul as responses of a healthy organism to its environment and also in contexts in which the passions become unbalanced (as in severe melancholy). Descartes, Malebranche, and Spinoza were deeply interested in the passions, which they examined in connection with sense perception. Descartes to some extent, and Malebranche and Spinoza more strongly, connected the passions with ethics. The senses and the passions were examined in theological writings. Here the questions concerned how the fallibility of sensory cognition and of the passions were connected with the presumed fall of mankind from God's grace, as described in Christian theology. Although some seventeenth-century authors (e.g., Senault) argued that sensory knowledge is confused and that we are subject to passions because of the fall from grace, the rationalists rejected this point of view. To the rationalists, the senses are useful in their proper spheres and the passions tend naturally toward the wellbeing of the whole human being (body and mind). Among the rationalists, Malebranche was especially concerned with such theological issues.

Sense perception, then, was broadly and deeply studied in the seventeenth century. Many divergent theories of its physical, physiological, and psychological conditions were on offer, as were various accounts of the metaphysics of sensory qualities and mind–body interaction.

As a way of managing this complexity and providing us with a common framework for discussion, in the next four subsections I examine the physical, physiological, and psychological components of the process of perception as understood in the seventeenth century (along with some historical background). Then, as now, vision was considered the dominant human sense and received the most attention. The process of visual perception can be viewed as a causal chain, or rather a causal loop, which includes the object, the physical processes affecting the sense organ, subsequent nervous processes, mental events that are caused by or correlated with brain events, and subsequent action by the perceiver that may change the object or the perceiver's relation to it. The components of this loop are best understood in connection with their role in affording sensory contact with the surrounding world. After detailing the process of perception, I turn in subsequent sections to metaphysical, epistemological, and functional themes.

Physical conditions of vision

The sense of vision is remarkable because it allows us to detect and know objects at a distance. (Hearing does this, too, as does smell, Le Grand 1: 290.) There is a red ball across the room. I see it from here, experiencing it as red and round. In normal circumstances, I am thereby able to know that it is red and round. And yet it is there and I am here. Its shape and color, or something that informs my sight of its shape and color, must somehow affect me perceptually.

Our ability to perceive things at a distance by sight cries out for an explanation. In the ancient world, the most common explanation held that, in sight, something proceeds out from the eye to touch the object, sensing its shape and color at the place where they are, across the room. Euclid (fourth century BCE) and Ptolemy (second century) analyzed this outflow mathematically as a sheath of rays that touches the object where it is, with the uppermost rays sensing things higher in the field of view, and lower rays sensing things that are lower. This sheath of rays forms a cone, with the apex in the eye (at least virtually) and the base at the surface of distant objects (figure 3.1). Galen (1978–84: 7.5) provided a physiological analysis of the processes proceeding outward from the eye. He used the notion of *pneuma*, which literally means "breath" or "air," and in this context signifies *psychic pneuma*, which is subtle matter that affects the air that is contiguous to the eye and thereby endows it with a power of sentience. When the air itself becomes sentient, this in effect extends the reach of the visual nerves and makes sight a kind of distant touching by means of transformed air. Such theories are called "extramission" theories of vision. Although Galen acknowledged that light from the sun or other source prepares the ambient air, he required pneuma to render the air into a sentient medium. When we see the moon or the stars, the power of sight would have to extend extremely rapidly to fill the heavens, a consequence that critics of the theory found implausible (Lindberg 1976: 3–6, 9–17, 51–2).

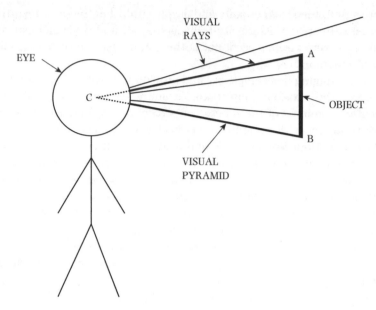

Figure 3.1 The geometry of visual rays and the visual pyramid in extramission theories.

Some ancient theorists accepted an "intromission" theory, according to which something comes from the object to the eyes. The best-known such theory was due to ancient atomists, and is preserved in Lucretius' poem *On the Nature of the Universe* (first century BCE), a work widely available from the fifteenth century on. According to the atomists, objects in the environment are constantly sending off thin skins from their surface, something like the shedding of a snake's skin. These thin skins – called *eidola* in Greek and named *simulacra* ("likenesses" or "replicas") in Lucretius' Latin – retain the order of the parts of things and so are like copies of the surfaces of things (Lucretius 1994: 95–100). On this view, a round (or half-spherical) skin would proceed from the red ball across the room to the eye, carrying a sample of both the shape and the color of the ball's surface. Such skins must proceed through the air in every direction from the ball and enter any eye pointed in the ball's direction. These consequences of the theory raised several problems. Unless the object is very small to start with, the *eidolon* must shrink to fit the pupil of the eye. Thus, when we see a mountain, the skin of the mountain would shrink to enter the eye, and since we can see the mountain from many places, such shrinking skins would need to be arriving constantly at every station a viewer might occupy. Another objection was that the skins would need to pass through one another when two people can see one another at the same time, since we both would be receiving skins that traveled on a straight path from the object to us. It is difficult to see why the skins would not interfere with one another, since the air would have to be filled with them.

The atomist and extramission theories were known and discussed in the seventeenth century, but they were given little credence. By then, the Islamic natural philosopher Ibn al-Haytham, who was born in Basra and later worked in Cairo, had devised a form of the intromission theory that solved the problem of how something could proceed to the eye that preserves the ordering of the parts of a visible object. Al-Haytham's geometrical analysis of intromission guided the theory of vision into the seventeenth century, when Kepler transformed the analysis into its modern form.

Al-Haytham ([eleventh century] 1989, 1: 63–9) understood that in order to explain spatial vision through intromission, he would need to establish a point-for-point correspondence between some part of the eye and the spatial distribution of objects in the visual scene. This problem is difficult. Consider an object bathed in light. If the object were a mirror, each light ray would be reflected at the very angle in which it strikes the mirror's surface (the angle of reflection is equal to the angle of incidence). Most objects, however, are not mirror-like. On most objects, light rays are reflected at various angles, so that light from various surface points (or punctiform areas) scatters in all directions. This means that at the cornea of the eye (the clear coating at the front of the eye), each corneal point receives light from each point in the visual scene. Given just these facts, it follows that no orderly relation has yet been established between the eye and the visual scene, since light from every point in the scene arrives at each point of the cornea.

Al-Haytham realized that the problem of order would be solved if the eye sensed only those rays that impinge on the cornea perpendicularly (at right angles). He thereby established a visual cone that was geometrically similar to that postulated by Euclid and Ptolemy, but with the direction of causation reversed. In al-Haytham's theory, the non-perpendicular rays that reach the cornea at oblique angles (from all points in the scene) can be ignored. The sensitive surface of the eye (located inside the eye at the surface of the "glacial" (ice-like) or "crystalline" body, now known as the lens) would receive a two-dimensional cross-section of the visual cone. Each object would be seen under the angle that it subtended within that cone (figure 3.2).

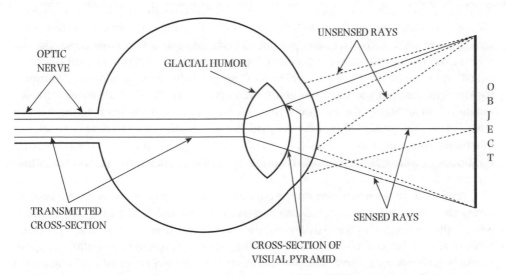

Figure 3.2 The geometry of sight according to Ibn al-Haytham. The cross-section of the visual pyramid, as received at the front surface of the glacial humor, undergoes a quasi-optical transmission through the eye and down the optic nerve.

Early in the seventeenth century, Kepler modified al-Haytham's geometric analysis when he discovered that the retina (at the back of the eye) is the sensitive surface that receives the cross-section of the cone. As is well known, the retinal image that Kepler discovered is formed by the cornea and the crystalline body, which together act as lenses to focus an image on the retina with point-for-point correspondence to the scene (Lindberg 1976: ch. 9). (Each sheath of rays from a single point on the object, arriving at points all across the cornea, is refocused onto a single punctiform area of the retina, as illustrated in figure 3.3, below.)

Kepler's discovery did not alter the fundamental challenge that a geometrically based intromission theory had to meet: to explain perception of the (three-dimensional) distances and sizes of things, given that a two-dimensional pattern is received in the eye (Hatfield and Epstein 1979). On an extramission theory, the visual rays might sense their own lengths, and together they might register the size of a distant object. But in the intromission theory the distance and size of objects would need to be gathered from other aspects of visual stimulation. Al-Haytham (1989, 1: 156) explained that distance might be inferred if the size of the object were known, by using known size and currently sensed visual angle (the angle within the visual cone) to solve for distance (using previously known AB and sensed angle C to solve for AC and BC in figure 3.1). He held that perception of distance is more usually achieved by tacitly recognizing the magnitudes of designated intervals on the ground between object and observer (1989, 1: 152). As we shall see, Descartes devoted careful attention to the perception of distance and size; some of his explanations repeated those of al-Haytham, while others were novel, drawing on Keplerian theory.

Physiology of the eye and optic nerves

Whether the cross-section of the cone is received at the lens or on the retina, it must be conveyed into the brain for perception to occur. Al-Haytham attributed properties to the optic nerves that would make them like lucite tubes (or bundles of lucite fibers), which could convey the two-dimensional pattern into the brain while preserving its order, even though the nerves curve and can move and bend. This account has been called "quasi-optical" (Lindberg 1976: 81), because the transmission is through a transparent medium postulated as filling the nerves. After Kepler's discovery that an image is spread across the opaque retina, a new account of the transmitted pattern was needed. Descartes held that the optic nerves are bundles of small nerve fibers, each of which carries an isolated physical response to the light that falls on the retina into the brain, in a way that (collectively) preserves two-dimensional order on the retina (figure 3.3).

Thus far I have been focusing on the conditions for the perception of spatial properties such as size and distance. We also perceive color by sight. Al-Haytham (1989, 1: 48) adopted a version of the Aristotelian theory. On this theory, color is a "real property" of the surfaces of objects. Descartes and others interpreted the notion of a real property as positing a "resemblance" between color as experienced and color as a property "in" objects (CSM 1: 153–4; Mal 220; Le Grand 1: 284; Régis 1: 174–5; Rohault 1: 7, 12). This characterization has some justice, even if it simplifies. Aristotle and his followers held that like knows like, so that the mind must receive a sample ("similitude") of the color-quality in objects in order to sense it (Simmons 1994). This occurs, they said, by the transmission of a "form without matter" from the object to the eye (Ar 424a19). In Aristotelian doctrine, a "form" united to a formless material substrate gives an object its characteristic essence and also its "accidents" or non-essential properties (such as color). To say that the form of color is conveyed to the eye "without the matter" means that no atomistic material "skin" is transferred, and indeed no material object at all. According to subsequent Aristotelians, the air is trans-formed into a medium that provides material conditions for transmitting the form, but the air does not thereby become the natural "matter" for that form, and hence does not become colored itself. This form, which Aristotle's medieval followers called an "intentional species" (the word "intentional" indicates that it represents the color with-out being a instance of a colored thing), is then received in the eye and conveyed physiologically into the brain (see Hatfield 1998: 956–8).

It was characteristic of the new natural philosophy of the seventeenth century, as elaborated by Galileo and Descartes and later adopted by rationalists and empiricists alike (including Hobbes and Locke), to reject Aristotelian real qualities. This meant rejecting the account of color perception as occurring through the transmission of forms or intentional species, and replacing it with an account that was mechanistic in spirit and similar in some ways to ancient atomism. Their accounts stressed that mat-ter intrinsically possesses only certain kinds of properties, called "primary qualities" by Locke (1975, II.viii.9). Descartes thought of these properties as "modes" or modifica-tions of spatial extension, including size, shape, position, and motion (CSM 1: 208–9). This meant that, whatever the property of color in objects turns out to be, it can be constituted only from such modes (also Le Grand 1: 296; Régis 1: 273–83, 3: 174; Rohault 1: 23–4, 220). Similarly, light, the air, and the eyes, nerves, and brain must all be constituted of matter having only these "mechanical" properties. (On seventeenth-century "mechanism," see Hatfield 2003: 302–12.)

Descartes and others asserted that color in bodies is some property of their surface that affects light in some way (e.g., by imparting a "spin" to particles of light). The reflected and altered light (conceived by Descartes and his followers as pressure in a material medium) is propagated in straight lines to the eyes, which focus it onto the retina, where it affects the nerve endings in a purely mechanical way (e.g., by jiggling them in a certain way that varies depending on the speed of the transmitted spin). It is this jiggling, rather than a "form without matter," that is transmitted into the brain and ultimately gives rise to a color sensation (an experience of color). This color sensa-tion (defined phenomenally as the color in our experience) varies with the physical color properties in the object, but it does not "resemble" the surface properties of objects. Rather, it is a mind-dependent aspect of experience. We will return below to questions about how experienced color "represents" (or not) the color properties of objects, and whether this subjectively based quality should therefore, on the rational-ists' view, be considered as illusory or as epistemically defective in some other way.

Brain physiology and visual psychology

The nerve fibers in the optic nerves, and indeed all nerve fibers, had long been con-sidered to be hollow tubes filled with a subtle matter called "animal spirits" (or psychic pneuma). As conceived by Descartes and other mechanical philosophers, these spirits were denied the power of sentience that both the Aristotelian and Galenic traditions had attributed to them; they were merely a fluid material without intrinsic sentience. Descartes retained the common view, prominent in Galen, that the spirits are distilled out of the blood at the base of the brain and that they fill an inner cavity in the brain. But he reconceived their manner of operation as wholly mechanical, viewing the spirits as a hydraulic fluid filling the brain and nerves and operating through pressure and motion in sensory and motor processes. For example, when the spirits are sent down the nerve tubules to the muscles, they cause the muscles to inflate and hence to contract (DG 106–17; also Le Grand 1: 276; Régis 2: 531; Rohault 2: 273; cf. Mal 88–9).

Descartes conceived the spirits as flowing out from a single source at the center of a large cavity in the brain. He located this source in the pineal gland, which he also considered to be the seat of mind–body interaction. He needed to explain the role of the spirits in sense perception, and also how the spirits could be shunted into the proper tubes to control the motion of the body. He developed a general account of this process for both human and non-human animals. Since he believed that non-human animals lack a mind or soul and are mere machines, this common account had to be entirely mechanistic (CSM 1: 139–41, 2: 161–2; also Mal 98, 324; Spinoza, SE 3p2, 4p37n1; and Leibniz, LL 578, 650–1, treated animal and human bodies as machines, but ascribed feeling to non-human animals).[3] Descartes allowed that the human mind can direct the spirits in willed activities, and that it responds to the spirits in sensation. But let us first consider his purely mechanistic account of sensory and motor functions.

Descartes developed a novel conception of nerve function. He held that inside each spirit-filled nerve tubule there is a filament, like a thin wire or microcable, that serves a sensory function. In the case of vision, each optic nerve is a bundle of ensleeved fibers that proceed from the retina (where they spread across its surface) to the interior surface of the brain cavity, facing the pineal gland. Spirits flow out from the gland and enter whichever tubules are open. Light striking the retina jiggles many of the fibrils, setting up a jerking motion, which causes the fibril to open the central end of the tubule, allowing spirits to flow in. Descartes asserted that the anatomy of the nerve bundles permits the pattern of light-induced activity on the retina to be transmitted, point-for-point, to the interior surface of the brain (figure 3.3). He further assumed that the spirits would flow in a rectilinear pattern from the surface of the pineal into the nerve tubules that had been jiggled open through the effects of retinal stimulation on the microcables. The spatial pattern of spirit outflow from the pineal would then replicate the pattern of the retinal image, with lights of different colors (particles with different spins) causing differing jiggles, different tubule openings, and hence a different character to the outflowing pineal spirits. Depending on the pattern of sensory openings, and also on innate or acquired features of the "plumbing" of the brain, these outflowing spirits might also enter into the nerves that lead to the muscles, thereby controlling the behavior of the machine. Generally similar accounts of spirit or fluid function were given by Malebranche (Mal 49–50, 87–111), Spinoza (SE 2p13), Régis (3: 73–93), Le Grand (1: 300), and Rohault (1: 245–6, 2: 252–4,

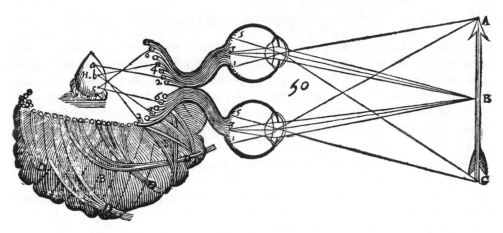

Figure 3.3 The geometry of sight and the physiology of nervous transmission according to Descartes. Object ABC reflects light rays that are focused on the retina at 1-3-5, jiggling the nerve fibrils and leading to tubule openings 2-4-6, which induce spirit-flows a2, b4, and c6, resulting in pineal image abc. Reproduced from the *Traité de l'Homme* (1664). The inversion of the spirit flow is not required by Descartes' text and presumably was introduced by Gerard van Gutschoven (Professor of Medicine at Leiden), who produced the drawing at the request of Claude Clerselier, who prepared *L'Homme* for publication after Descartes' death.

271–3), although Rohault (1: 246, 2: 253) only tentatively endorsed Descartes' pineal physiology, Malebranche and Spinoza did not endorse it, and Régis (3: 89) emphasized fibril vibration over spirit flow in sensory function and did not mention the pineal gland.

According to Descartes and his followers, animal behavior must be produced solely from such mechanisms. Human behavior that occurs without mental intervention, which Descartes believed was frequent (CSM 2: 161), also results from purely mechanistic processes (CSM 1: 139, 2: 58). This meant that Descartes needed to explain how both human and non-human animals could respond to objects at a distance without any mental intervention. He imagined clever mechanisms to carry out such tasks as grasping food that is present (DG 161–4) or fleeing a wolf (which both sheep and humans do), merely because patterns of light reflected from the food or wolf have entered the eyes and affected some brain processes (CSM 2: 161). These mechanisms (DG 169) were to take the place of the cognitive processes that Aristotelians assigned to the so-called sensory soul (common to human and non-human animals). To perform the functions of the sensory soul, Descartes (DG 142–65) imagined mechanisms that would change the brain as the result of previous sensory stimulation and its consequences (mechanistic "learning" through brain "memory"), as well as mechanisms that would make the animal machine respond selectively, for example, turning away from food or gobbling it down, depending on how full its stomach was (mechanical "hunger"). His claims about the extent to which human and animal behavior might be explained purely mechanistically were expanded by subsequent rationalists, including Spinoza and Leibniz.

41

Sensation, perception, and judgment

According to Descartes, in human beings the pattern on the pineal gland can also cause a visual sensation. Such sensations provide us with experiences of light and of color, and they enter into the perception of objects at a distance. Theories of sense perception commonly distinguished between qualities that are proper to each individual sense, and those that can be perceived through more than one sense. For vision, color (or light and color) was called the "proper object" of sight (Ar 418a7–28; CSM 1: 167; also Al-Haytham 1989, 1: 113, 130). This meant that light and color are the only type of sensation that occurs solely through vision (like sounds for hearing, and odors for smelling). And yet we also perceive other properties through vision: spatial properties, including size and distance. Properties such as these, which are perceived through more than one sense (at least through both sight and touch), were called "common sensibles" (Ar 418a18–19).

Several of the rationalists echoed this division by distinguishing between the bare sensations of light and color and the perception of size and distance. They sometimes called the former "sensations," to indicate that they are in a way subjective, in that they depend on the mind of the subject for their phenomenal content (e.g., phenomenal color). They sometimes called the latter "perceptions," partly to indicate that they provide knowledge of objective properties that external things do (or at least can) have. Descartes used this terminology sometimes (CSM 1: 217–19); Malebranche drew an explicit distinction between "sensations" (of color and the like) and purely "perceptual" ideas of modes of extension (Mal 2, 234).

The perception of light and color was distinguished from that of size and shape in another context, pertaining to the type of process by which these sense perceptions arise. The Cartesians treated light and color as bare sensations, caused in the mind according to the laws of the mind–body union (CSM 1: 167; Le Grand 1: 283; Régis 3: 173–4; Rohault 1: 220; also Mal 49–59). They construed the sensation of color as the regular effect in the mind of a certain brain state. Sensations would therefore be correlated with brain states and so with the surface properties of distant objects that affect the light that influences the nerves so as to produce those brain states. Although this regular connection would allow us to distinguish objects according to their color, our color sensations would provide no further information about their causes. Thus, a red object would produce a certain spin in light, which would jiggle the nerves a certain way, ultimately causing a certain type of effect in the brain (a pineal outflow or a vibration), and this would cause a sensation of red. Attention to the sensation itself would not reveal anything about either the brain state or the microproperties of distant things. In particular, the bare sensation of red would in no way reveal that color in objects has to do with an effect on the spin of light particles, or even that light particles have spin. Only a theory of color, derived from natural philosophy, perhaps via metaphysics, could reveal those things about the properties of light and the nature of color in objects.

Perception of spatial properties (common sensibles) is more complicated. Some spatial order is present in the initial sensations of light and color, for these sensations come as a pattern (mimicking the retinal image). Descartes' followers described such sensations as "spiritual" or "immaterial" images that mimic the physical pattern of the brain (Le Grand 1: 300; Régis 3: 221; Rohault 1: 248). Such a pattern in sensation was given a direct physiological explanation: a spatial pattern in the brain causes a (two-dimensional) spatial pattern in sensation (DG 149; CSM 2: 295). As with color sensation, only a theorist would know to infer the shape of the brain state from the shape in the sensations. Using the postulated psychophysiological rule that (some) shaped brain patterns yield sensations of like pattern, the theorist could "read off" the shape of the brain state from the visual sensation. This contrasts with color sensation, where the theorist is able to infer from a certain color sensation only that a jiggle of some sort or other has occurred in the brain. (On conscious access to such sensations according to Descartes, see Hatfield and Epstein 1979.)

Our ordinary visual experience is not a copy of this (two-dimensional) pattern in sensation, for we experience a world of objects in three dimensions, with objects of various sizes at different distances. Various authors gave differing accounts of the processes by which such perceptions arise. Descartes envisioned a direct physiological explanation of distance perception, contending that such perceptions can be caused directly in the mind by brain states that change as the eye (or the lens in the eye) accommodates for near and far vision. Thus, if the states of musculature controlling the lens during accommodation vary continuously with the distance to an object, then the brain state that controls that musculature could also cause in the mind a feeling or perception of distance (DG 155; CSM 1: 170; Descartes held that this can occur only for objects a few feet away; DG 138; CSM 1: 173). This explanation posits a direct psychophysiological law or rule, of the sort also found in the explanation of color sensations. (The need for an accommodating mechanism in the lens system of the eye first arose with Keplerian theory.)

Most rationalist authors, including Descartes, also repeated or adapted the accounts of size and distance perception previously found in al-Haytham. In these accounts, distance may be inferred from known size, and an unknown size may be inferred from visual angle and perceived distance. Neither al-Haytham nor the seventeenth-century theorists held that we make these inferences deliberately; they maintained that the judgments or inferences occur rapidly and by habit.[4] The result is that we simply experience the object at a distance and as being of a certain size, without being aware (again, except by means of theory) that these perceptions have resulted from rapid inferences or judgments. Spinoza did not treat visual perception in great detail, but as a consequence of his dual-aspect monism, he was committed to there being a purely physiological counterpart to such judgments (SE 3p2, 4p37n1), which must be sufficient to explain human behavior but could have no role in producing mental experience (as discussed below). Malebranche called the rapid judgments underlying visual perception "natural judgments." In the first edition of his major work, the *Search after Truth*, he described these judgments as if they might be innate tendencies of the human mind (Malebranche [1674–5] 1962: 96). In later editions (Malebranche 1962: 96–7, 19–20; Mal 34, 46–7), he attributed these "judgments" to God, who directly gives us spatial perceptions that are appropriate to the stimulus information and state of the ocular musculature. Finally, Leibniz adopted something similar to the Cartesian account, ascribing rapid and unnoticed judgments to the individual perceiving soul. Like Spinoza, he was also committed to a wholly mechanistic (but causally isolated) bodily counterpart to such judgments (LL 578, 650–1).

43

With this outline of the physical and psychological conditions of vision in hand, we can now focus on selected questions concerning sensory qualities, sense perception as it guides behavior, perceptual knowledge, and mind–body union and interaction.

Metaphysical, Epistemological, and Functional Aspects of Perception

The physical and physiological topics discussed in the previous section were considered "philosophical" topics in the seventeenth century, and not only because natural science was then called "natural philosophy." The "new science" of the seventeenth century transformed the conceptual foundations of natural science. The conceptual changes often were supported through philosophical argumentation rather than directly by experiments or observations. We might compare the "philosophical" character of those arguments with present-day philosophical discussions of the theory of evolution, the theory of relativity, or theories in cognitive science – that is, with what we now call the philosophy of the special sciences.

Other philosophical topics associated with sense perception in the seventeenth century are more akin to what we now call epistemology and philosophy of mind. Descartes' use of skeptical arguments in the *Meditations* (see "The method of doubt") raised questions concerning the existence of the external world that became part of the Cartesian legacy (Mal 217–19, 572; Le Grand 1: 93; Régis 1: 74–5; Rohault 1: 10–11). But even if we assume (or prove) that there is a world beyond the individual human mind, questions remain about the extent to which sense perception informs us of it. One such question concerned the relationship by which perception is said to "represent" the world. Despite their disagreements over the metaphysics of mind–body union, all our philosophers agreed that sense perception arises, in some way, because of the external world and its relation to us. Setting aside any putative causal relation until later, let us consider questions about the informativeness of sense perception in relation to the doctrine of secondary qualities.

Sensory qualities and sensory representation

Philosophers today sometimes blame seventeenth-century theories of color perception for holding that color experience is "illusory" and unreal (e.g., Hacker 1987). In fact, those theories were more subtle. Like others who accepted the new science, rationalist philosophers sought to replace the Aristotelian theory of "real qualities" with a theory founded upon a new conception of matter. They denied that color was "real" only in the sense that Aristotelians used this term. In their own terms, they denied that color experience "resembles" color in objects. They did not deny that color is (in some sense) a property of objects (e.g., for putting spin on light particles) or that color experience is informative and useful (CSM 2: 56–7; Le Grand 1: 6; Régis 1: 170; Mal 24; LL 547–8). They did deny that one can "read off," from phenomenal experience itself, the nature of the color property in objects. But they also denied that one could find, directly in sensory experience, the nature of magnetism or the cause of gravity.

All the same, Descartes did speak of a way in which color sensations contain a kind of falsity or error. He labeled as "materially false" (CSM 2: 30, 162) the group of sensations that Locke later called the "ideas of secondary qualities" (colors, sounds, tastes, odors, and tactual qualities). This description has perplexed subsequent philosophers. Does it mean that color sensations are inherently "false" in some sense? But how can a bare sensation be false, if it contains no judgment and hence makes no assertion? Descartes and others also described sensations as "obscure and confused." Does this mean that color sensations seem confused to those who have them? Or are they confused by comparison to something else? Or is it that, because "mere" color sensations tacitly contain a judgment within themselves, they are "confused with" that judgment?

Aristotle had remarked that each sense perceives its proper object infallibly or without error (Ar 418a13). Seventeenth-century Aristotelians (e.g., Eustache 1998: 86–7) interpreted this as responding to the question of whether the senses "lead astray" the power of judgment (these philosophers held that error, properly so-called, pertains to judgment, which they distinguished from sense). They held that sight never leads judgment astray about the fact *that* it experiences color, but it may cause error concerning the *specific color* an object has (due to defects in the conditions of observation or in the sense organ). Descartes also held that, in material falsity, our judgment is somehow led astray. Bare sensations simply provide the experience of a color. As bare sensations they contain no judgment about how they relate to the external world, and so, strictly speaking, cannot be false. When Descartes described them as "materially false" or as "obscure," he relied on additional considerations that he sometimes struggled to articulate.

In elaborating the notions of the material falsity and the obscurity and confusion of sensations, we must distinguish at least four points. First, there is the point that the bare sensation is not false because it contains no judgment (but cf. Régis 1: 176). Second, we have a natural tendency, which expresses itself in childhood, to judge that our sensations "resemble" the external world. This judgment is false. Inasmuch as the obscurity of our sensations give us "material" for making such judgments, they give us material for judgmental error and so are "materially false." Third, our sensations are obscure in that we cannot, by scrutinizing them, tell what properties in distant objects cause them, or what properties they represent. Fourth, our sensory experiences are obscure and confused because we cannot, simply by scrutinizing them, discover that they have become infused with our childhood judgment about resemblance.

For many purposes, the obscurity and confusion of sensory experience, and the falsehood of the childhood judgment, would not matter. We can see that an apple is ripe by its red color, independently of whether we know the nature of color in objects or have a proper theory of color sensation. For the purposes of metaphysics, however, such confusion can lead us astray unless we correct it through our theories of matter, mind, and their relation. The rationalists all accepted that matter should be conceived mechanistically, so as to include size, shape, position, and motion, but not color as a "real quality," among its basic properties. They understood this position to entail that color in objects must be explained mechanistically (as the putting of spin on particles of light, or the like).

Although rationalist philosophers agreed on the mechanistic account of physical color, they disagreed on the metaphysics of color sensation itself. The basis for this disagreement is already found in Descartes, who provided grounds for talking about color sensations in two different ways. One such way of talking, found in the *Principles* (CSM 1: 217–19), lets Descartes treat color sensations as bare signs of an unknown surface property. Accordingly, color sensations are nothing but subjective effects in us. They permit us to know that there is a property in objects that causes them, and in this way to tell objects apart or to reidentify objects by their color. Here, phenomenal color would serve as a sign of its cause, but would not specifically represent the microphysical properties of objects. Color sensations would be obscure and confused just because (1) we can't learn the detailed properties of their causes simply by attending to the sensations themselves, and (2) we fall prey to the childhood judgment about resemblance. Malebranche (Mal 51–3, 67), Le Grand (1: 6–7), Régis (1: 188–9), and Rohault (1: 6) echoed this view.

The second way of talking is not so much directly expressed by Descartes as implied by his theoretical framework. Descartes held that there are only two fully distinct faculties in the mind: will and intellect. Accordingly, he held that sense perception is a kind of intellectual activity (CSM 1: 204, 2: 54). He distinguished this activity from "pure intellect," which is the intellect operating on its own, independently of the senses (CSM 2: 50–1). Sensation arises when the body affects the mind (by whatever means that happens). The resultant sensation is a bodily induced act of intellect. Such acts of intellect possess what Descartes called "objective reality": they represent, or purport to represent, the properties of things (CSM 2: 28–9). On this view, a color sensation would have surface microstructure as its objective reality. Its representational content would be fixed by the property in objects that naturally (as "ordained by nature," CSM 1: 167) causes the sensation. Color sensations would be obscure representations of the microfeatures of objects. Phenomenal red would (obscurely) represent one surface structure (a spin-inducing property), phenomenal green another.

One might hold, according to the first way of talking, that the objective or representational reality of sensations is just that they seem to represent a resembling quality in objects; on this way of thinking, sensations would be misrepresentations. But if the "resemblance" view of sensations is ascribed to a childhood judgment, rather than included in the content of the sensation proper, then another source is needed for the representational reality of sensations. In the second way of talking, that source is provided by the microstructure of object surfaces.

This second theory fits much of what Descartes says. A version of it is tacit in Spinoza's theory of perception, according to which the mind has knowledge of external things in virtue of their effects on the human body (SE Pt. 2). For Spinoza, mind is not a separate substance but is a complex idea, the idea of a particular human body. Its content in the first instance arises from its representing that body and its particular states. Being finite, the mind has only limited ideas of those states and their causes. It therefore perceives external bodies only confusedly, as remote causes of effects in the human body. Leibniz also accepted, in his own way, the parallelism between bodily states and sense perceptions. He developed a further explanation of the confusion of sensory states, asserting that color perceptions are confused because they are composed of thousands of "petite perceptions," each of which represents a distinct microstate in the brain that is itself related to an external cause through a mechanistically described causal chain (LNE 55–6, 131–3, 403–4). This view might be seen as a development of Descartes' second way of talking.

The topic of obscure and confused sensations gave rise to a further philosophical disagreement among rationalists. Descartes held that the mind clearly and distinctly knows itself as a thinking substance (CSM 1: 211, 2: 54). Sometimes this is taken to mean that he thought the mind finds its own nature to be introspectively transparent (see Ryle 1949: 11–15). However, from what Descartes has said about obscure and confused sensations, it would be inconsistent for him to hold that their representational nature is transparent to introspection. In the Cartesian view, we do not discover the mind's nature simply by scrutinizing our sensations or other mental operations. Rather, the mind has a direct intellectual perception (through the "pure intellect") of its own nature (Le Grand 1: 9, 324; Régis 1: 70–1, 127, 160). Leibniz also granted the mind direct intellectual apprehension of its substantial nature (LL 549). Spinoza allowed that the mind can have clear knowledge of the attribute of thought (SE 2p47, 5p30). However, he did not think of the mind (either the individual mind or the infinite mind of God or nature) as a separate substance. The human mind, as a finite set of modes associated with a particular body that is itself in complex causal relation to its environment, has only confused knowledge of itself (2p29). Malebranche, by contrast, held that the human mind has only a confused knowledge of the attribute of thought (the essence of thinking substance). He contended that color sensation, about which the mind is initially confused (as regards its nature), shows that the mind does not clearly perceive itself (its own states). Rather, it must learn about itself simply by experiencing its own states (Mal 237–9).

The senses, the passions, and the preservation of the body

Whatever their disagreements over the metaphysics of sensation, all the rationalists agreed that the senses have a positive role to play in preserving the body. Cartesian rationalists understood the function of the mind–body union within the context of preservation of the body (Mal 24) or the mind–body complex (CSM 2: 59; Le Grand 1: 6; Régis 1: 188–9). The outer senses orient perceivers to their environments, warn them of impending dangers, and alert them to beneficial opportunities. Inner sensations such as hunger and thirst inform the mind–body complex about the body's needs. Finally, the passions that arise in the mind as a result of complex brain states are naturally constituted to guide behavior.

The benefits that the senses provide can be readily understood, as can the functions of sensations of hunger, thirst, and so on. The theory of the passions is more complex theoretically.

With their theory that animals are mere machines, devoid of feeling, Descartes and his followers assumed the burden of having to explain all behaviors of non-human animals through mechanistic physiological processes alone. Such explanations would have to cover the functions of the external senses (navigation in the environment) and of the internal senses (conditionally altered behavior after periods without food or drink), as well as such behaviors as responding to dangers by shrinking back or showing ferocity when nests or young are threatened. These explanations would invoke

47

sensory receptivity of a wholly mechanical, unfeeling kind, along with internal plumb-ing to produce the situationally appropriate behavior. The mechanisms were to be mediated by the flow of the animal spirits, in what we might now call a sensory–motor feedback loop.

In human beings, the same physiological mechanisms that set the body in motion, say, to flee from a wolf, also cause the feeling of fear. The function of this feeling is to make the mind want to do what the body is already doing. Fear is a "passion," or a passively caused state in the mind that does not cause any bodily activity but merely affirms what is already happening. The mind can also respond actively, altering the bodily process so as to change the direction of running or to hold the legs still (CSM 1: 338–48; Mal 338–40, 347–52; also, Le Grand 1: 331–5; Régis 3: 338–42).

Other rationalists, such as Spinoza and Leibniz, agreed that animal physiology (human or not) should be explicated mechanistically, but they did not agree that animals are without feeling. Indeed, Spinoza and Leibniz affirmed that *all* human behavior can be explained mechanistically through bodily structures alone (SE 3p2, 3p57n; LL 578, 650–1). Unlike the Cartesians, however, they offered few speculations on the precise mechanisms by which such behavior would be caused. Spinoza engaged the issue most fully, offering generic arguments about the amazing things that the body can do on its own. For him, sleepwalking is human behavior effected by purely bodily mechanisms, presumably because he assumed that the sleepwalker is unconscious and so not guided by thought (SE 3p2). All the same, he held that all material modes have a mode of thought associated with them, and hence that animals have feeling (SE 2p7, 3p57n). Animal consciousness is not capable of the clarity of abstract thought found in humans, but it does include sensations and passions as genuinely mental states.

Leibniz said little about the passions themselves, although as usual he saw them as responses that tend toward preservation of the body (LNE 166, 194–5). Spinoza, by contrast, devoted considerable effort to explicating the emotions, distinguishing life-invigorating active responses from life-diminishing passivity. A consequence of Spinoza's view that thought and extension are two aspects of one underlying substance was that the two domains are causally and explanatorily closed. Hence, his metaphysics led him to affirm that all animal and human behavior can be accounted for in mechan-istic terms. On the same basis, he posited a parallel set of ideas and feelings that con-stitute psychological or mental causal chains (SE 2p7, 3p1–3). One wouldn't explain the bodily effect of running from a wolf by appealing to the feeling of fear (or any other mental state), but by wholly mechanical physiological processes. The ideas of these processes, as constituting a human or animal mind, would include the feeling of fear, which would also induce the desire to run. The bodily and mental aspects agree (they must, as two aspects of one substance). For Spinoza, unlike Descartes, the passions are not effects of body on mind. They are feelings the mind has that coincide with and represent a passive response in the body. There are also active emotions that represent active responses in the body. Spinoza's *Ethics* is an effort to promote appropriate active responses in body and mind (SE Pt. 3–5).

Theories of the passions among the rationalists form a rich area of discussion. Besides Descartes and Spinoza, Malebranche devoted considerable attention to the topic, in both natural philosophical and theological contexts.

Perceptual knowledge and cognition

The major rationalists agreed that the mind has available to it certain purely intellectual cognitions that are independent of particular sensory experiences. Descartes and Malebranche held that these cognitions are independent of bodily states in the strongest sense: they can occur independently of any brain activity, and they do not rely on the senses for their content. They held that even geometrical properties and the essence of matter can be cognized in this sense-independent way.[5] Leibniz allowed such purely intellectual perceptions of God and of immaterial substances (LL 549), and he declared that "the whole of arithmetic and geometry should be regarded as innate" and hence as independent of sensory images (LNE 77). His doctrine of preestablished harmony led him to posit a bodily counterpart even to intellectual thoughts, but such counterparts were not causally implicated in pure intellection, or in any other thought (LL 578). Spinoza described intellectual perception as the highest form of knowledge (SE 2p40n2). His dual-aspect monism required that every mental state has a corresponding bodily state, and his view that the mind is constituted by ideas of bodily states entailed that every thought is in some way related to a bodily state. (With thoughts of thoughts, the first-order thought must be related to a bodily state, and thereby confers that relation onto higher-order thoughts, i.e., to all the others.) He treated the ideas of geometry as representing universal aspects of bodily states (their extension). They are perceptions of what is common to all bodily states and indeed all extended things; they respond to the generic or universal features of such states (SE 2p38).

The rationalists held that these intellectual thoughts are the firmest and most certain kind of knowledge. In their methodological remarks, they encouraged prospective knowers to seek intellectual knowledge apart from the senses. This encouragement, especially as found in Descartes' *Meditations*, has sometimes led interpreters to think that Descartes and his fellow rationalists denigrated sensory knowledge as both dubious and misleading. Such interpretations are themselves faulty. Although Descartes and the other rationalists sought the certainty achieved through full intellectual clarity in areas where it might be attained (in mathematics and in the first principles of metaphysics), they did not require such certainty in all realms. In particular, they allowed that our sensory cognitions may be less than certain, but that we must be guided by them anyway. Moreover, they recognized that sensory perception is required to ascertain particular facts and contingent regularities in natural philosophy.

The various rationalists characterized this less-than-apodictic knowledge in differing terms. Descartes (CSM 1: 289–90) spoke of "moral certainty" – certainty sufficient to guide action – as the best that one can attain for many theses in natural philosophy (those not determined directly from first principles). He described many of his own hypotheses in natural philosophy as possessing only moral certainty. These would include his hypothetical postulation of microstructures to explain magnetism or the actions of minerals, and presumably also included his developmental hypotheses about the formation of the earth and the origin of minerals as specific effects of the swirling vortices of matter. (He may well have regarded his commitment to vortices themselves as following from first principles.) Le Grand (1: 91–2) argued that natural philosophy (both "general" and "special," i.e., pertaining to particular types of bodies) could achieve the status of demonstrative science, therein promoting a stronger claim to certainty than that found in Descartes. Régis (1: 275–6) and Rohault (1: 13–14) allowed that the particular hypotheses (or conjectures) of natural philosophy were known with less than absolute certainty, and encouraged the development of a web of mutually consistent (hence mutually supporting) hypotheses.

Spinoza, although equating falsity with lack of certitude (SE 2p49), acknowledged that in many cases we must be guided by "knowledge of the first kind," which is "knowledge from vague experience" (2p40). Indeed, he allowed that perceptual knowledge of bodies in our vicinity is always "inadequate," since truly adequate knowledge would comprehend the entire causal nexus (a causal chain extending to infinity) required to explain the presence and attributes of the bodies in our environment and their effects on our bodies (1p28, 2p24–31). Recall that Spinoza made our perception of bodies depend on their effects on our own body. In essence, we come to know external bodies by a kind of reverse transitivity, back along the causal chain. He did not explain in detail how our perception comes to focus on, say, the distal surfaces of objects in vision, but one may assume that, because those surfaces are important in the causal process of vision as considered under the attribute of extension, they also figure prominently in our ideas of the bodily states that are caused in our nervous system by light reflected from those surfaces. This explication is supported by Spinoza's dictum that the idea of the cause is implicated in the idea of the effect (2p7). Our visual ideas, then, are immediately of some state of our nervous system, but they reach back along the causal chain responsible for that state. Since we know those causal chains inadequately, our perceptual knowledge is inherently confused. It is still to be relied upon in the day-to-day activities needed to preserve the body and for the observations required in natural philosophy, since it is the only source of knowledge we can have of the particulars in our environments.

For Leibniz, "perception" (in an extended sense) is one of two basic features of all individual substances, or monads, that God created in forming the world. The other is appetite (LL 636, 644). On his view, each monad is "a world apart" (LL 312) such that "the present is great with the future" (645), its present state determining its future state (to infinity), and each monad, as a "living mirror" (648), represents the entire world (more or less clearly) from its point of view. Perceptions in monads succeed one another according to a law of appetite. All monads are soul-like (LL 644), and these soul-like entities provide the basis for everything. Bodies, in his account, are "well-founded phenomena" (Brown 1984: ch. 10; Rutherford 1995: 157, 222–6; Wilson 1989: 190–6), that is, phenomena that are founded in the perceptions of the infinity of monadic substances in the universe. These perceptions represent spatially extended bodies, the reality of which lies in unextended, soul-like entities (LL 311–12, 600–1). They do not represent a separate, monad-independent material stuff: there is no such stuff. Bodies are objects of perceptions, but they are independent of individual souls in that each body is represented by many souls from their various points of view (including points of view within bodies). Some souls (those with sense perception and intellection) represent the world more clearly than other souls (those with the point of view of a bit of rock or a droplet of water). Among animal souls, sensory perceptions are, as with Spinoza, immediately of the state of the body of the perceiver. Through the representation of these states, these perceptions represent bodies in the surrounding environment (LL 649). These representations occur in accordance with mechanical laws that relate external bodies to our sense organs. All individual souls agree in representing these mechanical processes from their various points of view (hence with more or less local clarity), according to a program of perceptions established by God and now proceeding in causal independence of one another, through preestablished harmony. Sense perceptions are inherently confused, but they nonetheless provide guidance for our daily activities and important sources of fact in natural philosophy, such as the empirically derived law of falling bodies that Leibniz (LL 443) used in his famous refutation of Descartes' laws of motion.

The rationalists not only taught that the senses are needed in natural philosophy, they also conducted empirical observations or encouraged others to do so. Descartes made many anatomical observations during the 1630s (CSMK 40, 134). More generally, he recognized (CSM 1: 143–4) the need for experiments (controlled observations) in physics for determining regularities and for testing hypotheses. One such regularity describes the angles at which the bands of a rainbow are seen. Descartes tested this regularity, as used in his explanation of the rainbow, by using water-filled globes to model water droplets (*Meteorology*, ch. 8, in Descartes [1637] 1965). Malebranche, although elevating knowledge of God and self above natural philosophy (Mal 296–7), acknowledged the need for observation in natural philosophy (464). Leibniz (LL 284; LNE 454–5) fully recognized the need for experiment and observation in natural philosophy. Cartesian natural philosophers, including Le Grand (1: xix), Régis (2: xiii–xiv), and Rohault (1: 13–14), endorsed experience and experiment. But they also recognized the importance of purely intellectual truths. Rohault, whose writings least examined such matters, treated such truths as self-evident axioms (a litany of Cartesian metaphysics) for arriving at natural philosophical knowledge (1: 18–20).

Finally, although the rationalists considered sense perception to be an indispensable source of knowledge, they realized that sense perception can lead to error. The most obvious type of error occurs when perceivers conclude something about the external world from their perceptions, and they are wrong. They make an error of judgment, based in perception. Descartes offered examples with respect to both primary and secondary qualities: one might mistakenly conclude, from the way that a square tower looks in the distance, that it is round (CSM 2: 53); or a jaundiced man might conclude that the things he is looking at are yellow, when it is only the yellow matter in his eyes that makes them look yellow (CSM 2: 104). Malebranche provided a detailed analysis of errors with respect to primary qualities, that is, extension and its modes (Mal 25–47); in treating of secondary or "sensible" qualities (48–75), he found the main error to lie in the tacit theory "that our sensations are in objects" (the resemblance thesis). Spinoza gave a general analysis of conditions in which we might think we perceive objects that are not present (SE 2p17), and in any case he stressed the inadequacy of sensory ideas (2p24–6). Leibniz devoted little attention to sensory error.

Philosophers in the first half of the twentieth century were especially concerned with the question of whether we can know with certainty how things appear to us, as opposed to how they are in themselves. In the examples just given, one might suppose that at least the perceiver knows with certainty that the distant tower *looks* round, and that he is *experiencing* an object as yellow. In twentieth-century discussions, some philosophers asserted that the current contents of experience are known incorrigibly, that is, without the possibility of error. This same view of incorrigibility has sometimes been ascribed to the rationalists, especially Descartes. As mentioned above, Gilbert Ryle (1949: 12–14) suggested that Descartes held not only that we know the appearances with certainty but also that the mind is wholly transparent to itself, so that it knows with certainty all of its own contents.

Descartes and other rationalists did make statements that could suggest the incorrigibility and transparency theses (e.g., CSM 2: 34, 171). Nevertheless, Descartes was clear that we can't know everything "in" the mind, including its faculties and dispositions, by direct introspection (CSM 2: 162, 172). And he asserted that on various occasions we are mistaken about the contents of our minds, or else we fail to note what is in our minds. We are sometimes mistaken about whether we do have a "clear and distinct" perception and wrongly believe that we do when we don't (CSM 2: 25). We fail to notice that our sensory experience may include childhood judgments (about resemblance), or habitual judgments that relate size and distance (CSM 2: 295). In these cases, the mind is not fully transparent to itself, even if all of its states are in some sense conscious. Descartes effectively explained this possibility by distinguishing between consciousness itself and reflective awareness. Although all mental states may be states of consciousness, the perceiver is not always reflectively aware of them, and so does not notice or remember them (CSM 2: 171–2). Other Cartesians, with the doctrine that judgments are implicitly confused with sensations (discussed above), acknowledged the lack of full transparency. Leibniz (LL 637) drew a bright line between bare perception and reflective awareness of such perception, calling the latter "apperception" – a term later made prominent by Immanuel Kant.

Mind–body relation

The mind–body relation enters into sense perception in several ways. First, there are the causal questions: Does the body directly cause sensations in the mind? If so, how? If not, how do sensations arise? Second, there are the content questions: Do the bodily states that cause or occasion sensory states contribute aspects of the content of those states? Or is there an arbitrary, but perhaps teleologically instituted, relation between bodily states and sensations?

The possibility of causal influence from bodily states to (at least some) mental states has perplexed philosophers since antiquity. In the Aristotelian (Ar 424a17–b2) and Galenic (1978–84: 7.4–5) traditions, the sense organs and the nerves are infused with a sensory soul or with a power of sentience, which renders the bodily organs sentient. Because body itself takes on vital and sensitive powers, there is no "gap" to traverse between bodily and sentient being. For the intellect, the problem is more difficult. In the Aristotelian tradition, the intellect was considered immaterial (Ar 430a17–18), either as a faculty of a separate immaterial substance (in especially Platonized versions of Aristotle, such as that developed by Albertus Magnus), or as an "immaterial power" of the form of the human being (as in the Thomistic interpretation of Aristotle). In either case, theorists doubted that the intellect could be affected by bodily things. In the Platonic tradition proper, insulating the immaterial intellect from bodily processes caused little problem: the objects of the intellect were considered to be forms or ideas apart from matter that the immaterial intellect grasped directly. Aristotelian philosophy, by contrast, held that human knowers can abstract universals or common natures through sensory experience. Because most Aristotelians agreed that the human mind, as the immaterial power of the form of the human body, operated without an organ and could not be affected by bodily organs, they rejected a direct causal influence on the intellect by sensory forms received into the bodily organs. Aristotelians therefore developed a complex analysis of ways in which images from the senses, as "phantasms" found in the corporeal organs of the brain, could serve or participate in the process of abstracting common natures (or "intelligible species"). While restricting genuine causal agency to the abstracting power of the immaterial intellect itself, they described corporeal phantasms as "material" or "instrumental" or "partial" "causes" (Hatfield 1998: 956–7, 959–61).[6]

Rationalist philosophers, while not adopting Platonic forms, were closer to Plato than to Aristotle on the mind–body causal relation in sense perception. Augustine's discussion of the Platonic theory was widely known in the seventeenth century. Augustine posited a single immaterial human soul with various powers, including sense perception (Bourke 1990; O'Daly 1987). He reasoned that since an immaterial soul has a higher order of being than mere matter, the soul can affect matter but cannot be affected by it. This meant that the human soul inhabits the human body as a pilot or navigator. Sense perception is not effected through the body's causing a passive state in the soul but by the soul's instrumental use of the bodily organs (Augustine [fifth century] 1982, 1: 78, 2: 214). The soul is active in sense perception, causing in itself a sensory state appropriate to the states of the sense organs (which, as material, interact with the surrounding environment). Without being affected by the body, the soul "becomes aware of" or "attends to" or "notices" what has happened in the bodily organs (Augustine [fourth century] 1947: 83–5, 334–8).

One solution to the mind–body union for rationalist dualists would be to accept this Augustinian view that the human mind forms a sensory idea "on the occasion" (as they might put it) of the presence of appropriate activity in the brain. This is an *individual occasionalism*, in which an individual human mind actively forms its own sensory ideas. The mind or soul is not affected, through efficient causality, by the bodily state. Rather, because the mind can affect the body, it possesses the power of responding to the body's states. There is no chain of efficient causation running from body to mind; rather, the mind "turns toward" or "inspects" the bodily state (e.g., CSM 2: 51, 295; CSMK 180) and then, from its own resources, forms a sensory idea that is appropriate to current sensory stimulation (i.e., one that is "of" the distal object). The individual mind is like the God of traditional occasionalism, who can affect both body and mind. The individual mind affects its own body (e.g., during willed action) and it forms sensory images within itself; its power is, however, restricted to itself and its own body. More generally, the mind's production of sensory ideas by "turning toward" the body shares features with Aristotelian accounts of the active causality of the intellect in producing intelligible species when it turns toward the phantasms.

Descartes adopted a conception of mind as immaterial substance like that in the Augustinian and Platonic traditions. However, it is not easy to pin him down on the mind–body relation. In many writings, he seems to describe a direct causal effect of body on mind (CSM 1: 167, 335–41, 2: 59–60). Such passages occur both before and after the early 1640s, when Princess Elisabeth of Bohemia challenged Descartes to explain how mind and body could interact (CSMK 217–20, 226–8). Throughout this period he also employed another way of speaking. He described the mind as actively forming sensations "on the occasion" of brain movements (CSM 1: 304; also 1: 103), and he spoke of it as an active "force" that could affect the body (CSMK 361; also 375). The body does not affect the mind, but the mind of its own power forms a sensation in response to a bodily state (and it can alter a brain state to produce a voluntary motion). In sense perception, one must accept the ability of the mind to "know" the bodily state without being affected by it through efficient causation. Such descriptions suggest an individual occasionalism of the sort just described, rather than the divine occasionalism of Malebranche. This interpretation would allow one to take seriously Descartes' talk of causal occasions, without attributing a God-mediated occasionalism to him (as regards mind–body interaction). Nonetheless, the extent to which Descartes held that even human minds have genuine causal power, as opposed to holding that all agency resides in God, is made vexed by one of his letters to Henry More (CSMK 381).

The other major rationalists each provided a distinctive characterization of the mind–body relation, none of which involved genuine mind–body causal interaction. In Malebranche's God-mediated occasionalism, God creates the appropriate sensation in our mind "on the occasion" of our brain entering a certain state (Mal 3, 448–50). In visual perception, God calculates the appropriate perceptions of size and distance (Mal 34). For Spinoza, the attributes of mind and body constitute distinct explanatory and causal realms. Mental and bodily states are at base identical. They are related in a representational or ideational manner: states of mind are in the first instance nothing but ideas of the body (SE 2p7, 11). Leibniz retained the notion of souls and minds as individual substances. He avoided Malebranche's occasionalism, contending that it was beneath the dignity of God always to be adjusting one substance to another. Instead, God builds a complete program into each substance from the beginning. As a result, mental and bodily states are in preestablished harmony (LL 457–60). Since bodies are well-founded phenomena, this comes down to a harmony among perceptions, including God-arranged relations between monadic perceptions and states of other monads, which states are themselves perceptions.

Beyond interaction, rationalists also considered how mind and body are related so as to constitute individual human beings. In the Aristotelian scheme, the soul was viewed as the "form" of the human body. Its natural state was to be united to matter – although it also had to be theoretically capable of existing after death (Aristotelian philosophers extensively discussed the details of this theoretical desideratum). When Descartes argued that mind and body are each naturally complete as substances, he was then pressed to avoid the conclusion that the human being is an accidental combination of the two. He cleverly responded that the combination is *accidental* with respect to each substance taken by itself, but *essential* with respect to the whole human being (CSM 2: 56–61; CSMK 206, 209). Malebranche faced a similar problem. Spinoza and Leibniz, with their doctrines that states of mind or soul are intrinsically related to the body through an ideational or representational relation, had a suitable means of explaining the union. (But Leibniz faced a challenge to his account from Des Bosses, LL 598–614.)

The Cartesians especially emphasized that the mind–body relation is teleologically ordered. Whether they viewed the mind and body as genuinely interacting or as following God-mediated laws of reciprocal influence, and no matter how they solved the unity question, they regarded the mind–body relation as teleologically adjusted toward preserving the health of the human body and hence toward benefiting the mind–body complex. This problem was slightly altered for Spinoza, since he regarded the body as being able to mechanically produce the appropriate behaviors for preserving its health. The mechanical processes would be reflected *in* the mind (inasmuch as it contains ideas of the body) but are not caused *by* the mind's influencing the body. For Leibniz as well, the preservative behaviors must have a completely mechanical explanation, with a parallel set of confused feelings and perceptions represented in the mind.

Sense, Mind, and Knowledge in Seventeenth-Century Rationalism

The rationalist philosophers, with their emphasis on intellectual cognition, shared some features of Platonic philosophy. They were not strictly Platonist, for they did not accept a domain of ideas or Platonic forms independent of God or human minds. Instead, they all posited the dependence of the eternal truths, in one way or another, on God – whether as his free creations, as in Descartes, or as depending on the being of God, as in Spinoza, or as residing in the divine intellect, as in Malebranche and Leibniz.

It was characteristic of Platonic philosophy to view the senses with suspicion. Although the rationalists expressed reservations about sensory cognition as a source for metaphysical first principles, they did not view the senses as inherently faulty or misleading when functioning in their proper spheres: preserving the body (and the mind–body complex) and ascertaining particular facts. As Descartes observed (CSM 2: 143), it was characteristic of some Platonic philosophers to equate the true person or self with the mind alone and to regard the body as a vessel for or instrument of the mind, which the mind inhabits and directs much as a sailor inhabits and directs his ship. By contrast, rationalists accepted that the person is composed of, or has as essential aspects, both mind and body. As Descartes explained, the "I" of the early *Meditations* is isolated from the body solely for the purpose of attaining knowledge of first principles (CSM 2: 366–83). The human person, as described in the Sixth Meditation, is a composite of mind and body (CSM 2: 160). Through its connection with body, the mind receives external and internal sensations and passions. It cannot know the full nature of these states simply from introspection; by rationalist lights, the mind and its states are not fully transparent in this respect.

All the rationalist philosophers were advocates of the new mechanical philosophy. They did not, however, cede all philosophical authority to natural philosophy: metaphysics remained the arbiter of theories concerning the fundamental nature of reality. Only metaphysics could guide natural philosophers as they developed theories of sensory qualities and of sense perception. Outside this theoretical context, the rationalists accepted that one might successfully navigate the world using sense perception, even without a correct theory of sensory qualities. But they did not mistakenly infer from this possibility that one should simply generalize from "ordinary" beliefs (most likely, in their day, disguised Aristotelian assumptions) to a philosophical account of sense perception. They recognized the need for sophisticated theory in understanding the nature of sense perception, but they did not thereby imply that we need any such theory in order to engage in sense perception for everyday purposes.

It was also characteristic of Aristotelian and Platonic philosophers to assign vital and sensory functions to a lower soul, or to lower powers of the rational soul. As subscribers to the mechanical philosophy, rationalist philosophers sought a basis for these functions in purely mechanistic physiological processes. Descartes and Malebranche held that mental processes must supplement these material mechanisms in order for human beings to guide their behavior rationally. Spinoza and Leibniz, following the metaphysical implications of their two versions of parallelism, affirmed that all human behavior must have a fully mechanical explanation, including reason-guided behavior, and they also posited a parallel set of mental processes that are identical with (for Spinoza) or in harmony with (for Leibniz) the purely mechanical processes.

Kant famously criticized the rationalist tradition, and especially Leibniz, for treating sense perception as confused intellection that might be clarified into intellectual knowledge. In fact, Kant was oversimplifying. The rationalists all distinguished sense perception from intellection in one way or another. Those like Descartes who regarded sense perception as a form of intellectual perception nonetheless distinguished it from pure intellection through its dependence on bodily causes (or "occasions"). Similarly, Malebranche, Spinoza, and Leibniz distinguished the inherently confused knowledge of the senses from adequate knowledge of abstract essences. None of them suggested that, by close introspective attention, one might transform sensory representations into clear intellectual knowledge. For the rationalists, the fact that sense perceptions are confused does not render them in need of clarification. Confused sense perceptions function well enough for their purpose. (If any rationalist is to be understood as requiring "clarifying" activity directed toward sense perceptions themselves, it would be Spinoza, who held that greater knowledge of the causal chains of perception would yield clearer perception.) The truly clear perceptions come in purely intellectual perception. Here is the real difference between the rationalists and Kant: they affirmed and he denied that the mind is able to perceive essences apart from sensory representations. The rationalists claimed that it was possible to know essences (or "common natures") independently of the peculiarities of our sense experience. Kant denied such purely intellectual grasping of essences, and tethered abstract metaphysical knowledge to possible sense experience. The Kantian critique successfully engages rationalist philosophy precisely here, with respect to the use of the pure intellect. The strong apriorism of the rationalists, which allowed for knowledge of essences independent of all sense perception, fell prey to Kant's request for an explanation of how human cognition could possess *a priori* principles or concepts that conformed to things in themselves (as mind-independent objects).

Still, much of the rationalist theory of sense perception remains philosophically valuable, even without its metaphysical basis. Some main functions of rationalist metaphysics were to critique the Aristotelian theory of real qualities and to support the new mechanical philosophy. We now accept descendant versions of this "new science," as in our theories of light, color, and vision, but without a foundation in *a priori* metaphysics. Further, the rationalist insight that a good point of entry into theorizing about the senses begins from their function in guiding our behavior remains viable. The question of how to understand the metaphysics of the sensory qualities has not been settled. The rationalist theory that ties representational aspects of sensory states to

56

body-preserving discriminations remains a good starting point. Although their theories of the intellect may be defunct, their questions about mind–body interaction and union and their functional attitude toward the senses and the passions live on.

Notes

1   In this chapter I use the abbreviations listed at the front of the book to cite the works of the rationalists, some of their followers, and some background sources. I cite other works (including some primary sources) by author and date, in accordance with the References and Further Reading. In comparing authors, I do not attempt to note every similarity and difference but only to indicate those similarities and differences directly relevant to my discussion. Greater detail can be found by consulting the secondary sources listed in the references or by studying the original sources. I treat the major rationalists in their mature periods. For Leibniz, I take this to begin in the mid-1680s (I don't attempt to signal shifts of terminology or uncertainties of doctrine within this period, on which see Wilson 1989). I treat Le Grand, Régis, and Rohault according only to the works cited; all three identified themselves as expositors or defenders of Descartes' doctrines (from which they sometimes departed). Of the other major rationalists, Malebranche is the most Cartesian as regards sense perception and the passions. (Régis, 1: [lxxxi], listed Malebranche, along with Rohault and himself, as among the most "celebrated Cartesians.")

2   The wider notion of "physics" from the seventeenth century (and earlier) did not imply the kind of materialistic reductionism that was associated with early twentieth-century claims that biology and psychology are part of physics. Hence, the word "physical" when used to describe the union of mind and body would have the root sense of "natural." On the concepts of science and natural philosophy in this period, see Hatfield (1996) and Wallace (1988); on the terms "physiology" and "psychology" in the seventeenth century, see Hatfield (1992).

3   Some historians of philosophy today (e.g., Cottingham 1998) contend that Descartes did not deny feeling, or at least genuine cognitive states (e.g., Gaukroger 1995: 278–89), to non-human animals. Descartes admitted that he could not *prove* that animals have no souls (CSMK 365–6). But when he spoke of their blood as a kind of soul (CSMK 230), he might simply have meant that the blood, as the source of animal spirits, is the source of life and activity in animals; and when he attributed "sense" to them (CSMK 366), this term need only extend to their corporeal sense organs and the nervous processes that guide behavior. Neither these nor other passages conclusively attributes feeling or mental representation to animals. In his *Treatise on Man*, which describes his basic physiology of human and non-human animals alike, Descartes used psychological terms to describe the mechanisms underlying behavior, including material "ideas," and mechanistic "memory" and "passions," but he made clear in context that these mechanisms were wholly mechanical in the way that clocks and other automata are (DG 169; CSM 1: 141). Other rationalists read Descartes and the Cartesians as denying feeling to animals, rendering them as mere machines (Mal 324, 493; LL 275, 342, 588, 637). Le Grand (1: 230, 2: 228–9) defended animal mechanism; Régis (2: 506) accepted the animal–machine hypothesis as a dictate of religious faith.

4   Judgment-based accounts are found at: CSM 1: 172, 2: 295; Le Grand 1: 301; Régis 3: 235–8; Rohault 1: 252–3 (he combines physiological linkages and judgments); Mal 34–5, 41–6. Descartes' differing accounts of distance perception, the psychophysiological account and the unnoticed judgment account, are not mutually incompatible. Descartes had developed both by the early 1630s (DG 131–9, 155, 157–60; CSM 1: 170–2). In a summary account

of sense perception in the Replies to the Sixth Objections to the *Meditations*, where he distinguished the raw sensations of vision (his "second grade") from the three-dimensional experiences that are produced by unnoticed judgments (his "third grade"), he did not mention the psychophysiological account of distance perception. One might consider this omission as grounds to infer that he had abandoned it, if one wished to make a clean division between sensations of color (the "second grade" of sense at CSM 2: 295) and judgmentally based perceptions of size, shape, and distance. One might seek further support for the abandonment thesis from his saying there that he had "demonstrated in the *Dioptrics* how size, distance, and shape can be perceived by reasoning alone, which works out any one feature from the other features" (CSM 2: 295). However, this statement does not preclude Descartes from holding that a perception of distance also arises from a direct psychophysiological mechanism, although size perception would still require combining distance with visual angle, presumably via an unnoticed judgment. More generally, in the sixth Replies Descartes was addressing the role of touch in "correcting" vision. His task required that he distinguish pure sensation from judgments in the perceptual act, but it did not require that he mention his elaborate psychophysiological account, which was most fully described in a then-unpublished work from the early 1630s (the *Treatise*). The animal–machine hypothesis required elaborate physiological mechanisms to explain animal behavior, and the same mechanisms served in his psychophysiological descriptions of human beings, which he worked on throughout his life (including in his final published work, *Passions of the Soul*). Hence, Descartes surely remained committed to the existence of a brain state in animals and humans that tracks distance. Finally, as regards the judgmental account, I have suggested that the judgment acts to produce an experience of a three-dimensional world (which would count as a sensory idea distinct from the judgment itself). In an unpublished paper and in correspondence, Tom Vinci has proposed that the judgment might actually act back on the pineal image, to produce a material counterpart to the three-dimensional experience. Vinci's proposal has the virtue of making the sensory idea of a three-dimensional world depend directly on mind–body interaction, while also accounting for the causal role of unnoticed judgments, which cause the mind to act on the pineal image so as to produce the bodily state that underlies the sensory idea of a three-dimensional scene.

5   Descartes held that the pure intellect has clear and distinct perceptions of the essences of both mind and matter (CSM 2: 54). Le Grand (1: 9, 325, 327–8) agreed, stipulating that ideas of particular bodies (as opposed to abstract extension) involve sense and imagination, hence brain activity; he also said that the mind, when united to the body, depends on the body for its thinking, but he restricted that conclusion to thoughts of particular bodies by sense and imagination. Other Cartesians modified this doctrine in various ways. Régis held that the intellect knows spirits (itself, God, and other minds) through itself, using a purely intellectual "faculty of conceiving" (1: 156, 160–2); the mind as spirit (*esprit*, 1: 113, 192–6) provides the content for its ideas of spirit, including that of God. Régis held that God, as first cause, provides the mind with ideas of extension and with sensations. The "secondary cause" of the idea of extension is extension itself, which the mind (as a "soul": *ame*) knows, even abstractly, only because it is united with a body (1: 113, 157–60, 200–1). Malebranche (Mal 236–9) allowed that there is a purely intellectual perception of extension, but not of the essence of mind (or of the essence of God); he indicated that even purely intellectual ideas (revealed to us by God) can become associated with brain traces (Mal 102), but he did not take that to imply that we think using such traces.

6   During this period, the term "cause" was not restricted to efficient causes or what I have called "genuine" causality: Malebranche (Mal 448) called occasional causes "causes," while distinguishing them from "true" causes, and Régis (1: 125) called secondary causes "true secondary causes," though (contrary to Schmaltz 1996: 55) denying them "causality proper."

References and Further Reading

Augustine, Bishop of Hippo (1947). *The Magnitude of the Soul* (J. J. JcMahon, trans.) and *On Music* (R. C. Taliaferro, trans.), in *Writings of Augustine, Vol. 2* (pp. 51–149, 153–379). New York: CIMA (originally written in Latin in the late fourth century).

—— (1982). *The Literal Meaning of Genesis*, 2 vols. (J. H. Taylor, trans.). New York: Newman Press (originally written in Latin in the early fifth century).

Bourke, V. J. (1990). The body–soul relation in the early Augustine. In J. C. Schnaubelt and F. Van Fleteren (eds.), *Collectanea Augustiniana* (pp. 435–50). New York: Peter Lang.

Brown, S. (1984). *Leibniz*. Minneapolis: University of Minnesota Press.

Cottingham, J. (1998). Descartes' treatment of animals. In J. Cottingham (ed.), *Descartes* (pp. 225–33). Oxford: Oxford University Press.

Descartes, R. (1965). *Discourse on Method, Optics, Geometry, and Meteorology* (P. J. Olscamp, trans.). Indianapolis, IN: Bobbs-Merrill (originally published in French in 1637).

Eustache of St. Paul (1998). *A Compendium of Philosophy in Four Parts* (J. Cottingham, trans.). In R. Ariew, J. Cottingham, and T. Sorell (eds.), *Descartes' Meditations: Background Source Materials* (pp. 68–96). Cambridge: Cambridge University Press (originally published in Latin in 1609).

Fernel, J. (2003). *Physiologia* (J. M. Forrester, trans.). Philadelphia, PA: American Philosophical Society (originally published in Latin in 1567).

Galen (1968). *On the Usefulness of the Parts of the Body*, 2 vols. (M. T. May, trans.). Ithaca, NY: Cornell University Press (originally written in Greek in the second century).

—— (1978–84). *On the Doctrines of Hippocrates and Plato*, 3 vols. (P. De Lacy, trans.). Berlin: Akademie Verlag (originally written in Greek in the second century). Cited by Book and Chapter.

Gaukroger, S. (1995). *Descartes: An Intellectual Biography*. Oxford: Clarendon Press.

Grafton, A. (1988). The availability of ancient works. In C. B. Schmitt (ed.), *Cambridge History of Renaissance Philosophy* (pp. 767–91). Cambridge: Cambridge University Press.

Hacker, P. M. S. (1987). *Appearance and Reality: A Philosophical Investigation into Perception and Perceptual Qualities*. Oxford: Blackwell.

Hatfield, G. (1992). Descartes' physiology and its relation to his psychology. In J. Cottingham (ed.), *Cambridge Companion to Descartes* (pp. 335–70). Cambridge: Cambridge University Press.

—— (1996). Was the scientific revolution really a revolution in science? In J. Ragep and S. Ragep (eds.), *Tradition, Transmission, Transformation* (pp. 489–525). Leiden: Brill.

—— (1998). The cognitive faculties. In M. Ayers and D. Garber (eds.), *Cambridge History of Seventeenth Century Philosophy* (pp. 953–1002). Cambridge: Cambridge University Press.

—— (2002). Perception as unconscious inference. In D. Heyer and R. Mausfeld (eds.), *Perception and the Physical World: Psychological and Philosophical Issues in Perception* (pp. 115–43). New York: Wiley.

—— (2003). *Descartes and the Meditations*. London: Routledge.

Hatfield, G., and Epstein, W. (1979). The sensory core and the medieval foundations of early modern perceptual theory. *Isis*, 70, 363–84.

Ibn al-Haytham (1989). *Optics*, 2 vols. (A. I. Sabra, trans.). London: Warburg Institute (originally written in Arabic, eleventh century).

Lindberg, C. (1976). *Theories of Vision from al-Kindi to Kepler*. Chicago: University of Chicago Press.

Locke, J. (1975). *An Essay Concerning Human Understanding* (P. H. Nidditch, ed.). Oxford: Clarendon Press (originally published in 1690). Cited by Book, Chapter, and Article.

Lucretius (1994). *On the Nature of the Universe* [literally, On the Nature of Things] (R. E. Latham and J. Godwin, trans.). London: Penguin Books (originally written in Latin in the first century BCE).

Malebranche, N. (1962). *Oeuvres complètes, Tome I: Recherche de la vérité* (G. Rodis-Lewis, ed.). [Complete Works, Vol. 1: Search after Truth]. Paris: Vrin.

Menn, S. (1998). The intellectual setting. In M. Ayers and D. Garber (eds.), *Cambridge History of Seventeenth Century Philosophy* (pp. 33–86). Cambridge: Cambridge University Press.

O'Daly, G. (1987). *Augustine's Philosophy of Mind*. Berkeley: University of California Press.

Rutherford, D. (1995). *Leibniz and the Rational Order of Nature*. Cambridge: Cambridge University Press.

Ryle, G. (1949). *The Concept of Mind*. London: Hutchinson.

Schmaltz, T. M. (1996). *Malebranche's Theory of the Soul*. New York: Oxford University Press.

Senault, J.-F. (1641). *De L'Usage des passions*. [On the Use of the Passions.] Paris: Veuve Iean Camusat (Modern Edition, Paris: Fayard, 1987).

Simmons, A. (1994). Explaining sense perception: A scholastic challenge. *Philosophical Studies*, 73, 257–75.

Wallace, W. (1988). Traditional natural philosophy. In C. B. Schmitt (ed.), *Cambridge History of Renaissance Philosophy* (pp. 201–35). Cambridge: Cambridge University Press.

Wilson, C. (1989). *Leibniz's Metaphysics: A Historical and Comparative Study*. Princeton, NJ: Princeton University Press.

—— (1993). Constancy, emergence, and illusions: Obstacles to a naturalistic theory of vision. In S. Nadler (ed.), *Causation in Early Modern Philosophy: Cartesianism, Occasionalism, and Pre-established Harmony* (pp. 159–77). University Park: Pennsylvania State University Press.

4

Rationalism and Education

DAVID CUNNING

Early in *An Enquiry Concerning Human Understanding*, David Hume quips that the meta-physician "is a character . . . [who] lives remote from communication with mankind, and is wrapped up in principles and notions equally remote from their comprehension" (Hume 1999: 89). Hume is writing in the context of setting up his view that metaphysics, or the "abstruse philosophy" (88), is remote and abstruse precisely because our minds are not able to conceive its objects. The Humean reaction to the abstruseness of metaphysics is to say that we should not engage in it. Another reaction is to admit that to ordinary ways of thinking metaphysical concepts are slippery and obscure, but to insist that these ways of thinking are to be abandoned. If the metaphysician is going to teach us his view, he must figure out how to bring us from (1) an allegiance to our current commitments and habits to (2) a view that initially we are inclined to reject. If at the start of inquiry things like Platonic forms, numbers (Pythagoras), immaterial monads (Leibniz), or even the divine substance itself (Spinoza) seem to us to be unlikely contenders for the title of fundamental element of reality, the route by which we come to embrace them as such will be circuitous. If at the start of inquiry our minds are not even in a position to conceive these things, we will not understand the arguments of the metaphysician, and if we do not reject them on the basis of our current commitments and conceptions, at best we will hear something other than what the metaphysician is trying to say.

The metaphysician is aware of all of this. Plato realizes that his student will judge the plausibility of Plato's views on the basis of what he already believes. Since his current beliefs incline him to reject Plato's theory of forms, he will have to start some-where else:

> What do you suppose would be his answer if someone told him that what he had seen before was all a cheat and an illusion, but that now, being nearer to reality and turned toward more real things, he saw truly? . . . Do you not think that he would be at a loss and that he would regard what he formerly saw as more real than the things now pointed out to him? . . . Then there would be need of habituation, to enable him to see things higher up. (Plato 515c–516b)

To get a person out of the cave, a special procedure is in order. If Plato talks about non-sensible beauty, for example, a prisoner too well practiced at conceiving of sensible objects will take Plato to be talking about particular bodies that are beautiful. Accordingly, in *Symposium* we are led from an appreciation of the beauty of imperfect particular bodies to an appreciation of beauty in general. When we finally do come to understand Plato, we might still reject his views as absurd if they conflict with our existing commitments. Alternately, we might continue to misconceive Plato's view and then on the basis of our current commitments reject what we *think* is the view rather than the view itself. There are no such things as forms or *nous*, we might conclude, because the idea of sensible objects that are fully perfect is incoherent, or because things that are not spatial are not things at all.

Plato is certainly not the only philosopher who is sensitive to the epistemic position of those who would convert to his view. Lucretius worries that his views are so unusual that his readers will not even allow them to register. He presents his views in verse so that they can more easily get through:

> I sing dark matters into the light, / Spicing all with the grace of poetry. / I have good reason for doing this too: / When doctors try to coax children to take / Foul wormwood, first they brush the rim of the cups / All around with the sweet and golden juice of honey, / To fool their short-sighted years, fool them all the way / Past the lips, so they drink down those bitter drops / Of wormwood and are tricked but not betrayed, / For all the sooner is their health restored. / So I too, since this doctrine seems so harsh / To many who have never sampled it, / Since the mob shrinks back in horror – I have desired / To reveal our doctrine in sweet-throated song, / Touching it with the honey of the Muses, / That I might hold your mind by this device / To attend to my verse, until you grasp the entire / Nature of things – the structure of the world. (Lucretius 1995: 51)

Lucretius holds that the fundamental elements of reality are invisible physical atoms. In case we might be suspicious that invisible things could make up the larger objects with which we are familiar, or that they could constitute human souls, Lucretius has to be extremely careful in how he presents his view. He knows that atoms sometimes collide or scrape against each other, and that only some of the atoms of the soul are smooth. He would anticipate that his metaphysics would not sit well with a number of his readers, and he presents it accordingly.

We find a similar move in the seventeenth-century metaphysician Nicholas Malebranche. In *Elucidations of the Search After Truth*, he argues that in the short term it is sometimes dangerous for the metaphysician to describe things exactly as they are. He asks us to consider for example the author who

> will say in a hundred places that beasts sense, that dogs know their master, that they love and fear him, and in only two or three places will . . . say that beasts do not sense, that dogs are incapable of knowledge, that they neither fear nor love anything. (Malebranche 1997: 672–3)

He then asks us what we should say about this author given the explicit contradictions in his text. One option is to conclude that the author is very confused. Another is to say that the author is aware that his readers would not understand him if he spoke rigorously and thus that much of what he says is in the confused language of common sense. Malebranche opts for the latter:

I realize that the ordinary man will not agree with this observation [that bodies do not resemble our perceptions of them] and that, depending on whether he has too few or too many animal spirits, he will either ridicule or be alarmed at the arguments I have just given, for the imagination cannot endure strange or abstract truths; it views them either as terrifying specters or as ridiculous shadows. (Malebranche 1997: 575)

For Malebranche, a metaphysician often has to employ "manners of speaking [that] agree with prejudice" (673) and "common opinion" (672). Speaking again of the author who puts forward explicit contradictions, he says:

Shall we group all the passages pro and con, and judge his view by the larger number? If so, I do not think there is a man to whom, for example, we can attribute the view that animals do not have a soul: for even the Cartesians always say that a dog senses when struck, and it rarely happens that they say it does not sense. And although I myself attack an infinity of prejudices in this work, several passages can be drawn from it by which it will be proved, unless the rule I am explaining be received, that I uphold them all, and even that I hold the view concerning the efficacy of secondary causes that I am now refuting. (Malebranche 1997: 673)

Part of Malebranche's system is the view that most minds think by means of extremely confused ideas (Malebranche 1997: 539–43, 568, 612). In the process of helping us to arrive at clear and distinct ideas, Malebranche piggybacks on a habit of ours that he hopes eventually we will overcome (Cunning 2003a: 356–7).

The same pedagogical sensitivities are in Leibniz. In *Monadology* 3, he concludes that the fundamental elements of reality are immaterial monads and so have neither shape, divisibility, nor extension. However, he immediately resorts to physical analogies to flesh out a monad's nature. To capture their independence from each other, he says that monads have no windows through which anything can enter or leave (*Monadology* 7). In *Monadology* 21, he marks the distinction between the perceptions of a bare monad and those of a soul monad with the analogous distinction between the perception of a person who is spinning and dizzy and the perception of a person who is not. To elucidate his view that monads perceive all of the same objects but still differ with respect to their point of view, he refers to the way in which perceivers in different spatial locations can have different perspectives on a city (*Monadology* 57). In making clear the plenitude of composites he makes use of a corporeal analogy yet again:

Each portion of matter can be conceived as a garden full of plants, and as a pond full of fish. But each branch of a plant, each limb of an animal, each drop of its humors, is still another such garden or pond. (*Monadology* 67; Leibniz 1989: 222)

For Leibniz, the deepest level of reality is the monadic level. Although every one of us is omniscient, we are also very confused, and Leibniz very appropriately instructs us in terms of the surface beings with which we are familiar.

Spinoza is sensitive to the epistemic position of his reader as well. In *Treatise on the Emendation of the Intellect*, he argues that words are not the best vehicle for arriving at an accurate picture of reality:

> Since words are part of the imagination, i.e., since we feign many concepts in accordance with the random composition of words in the memory from some disposition of the body, it is not to be doubted that words, as much as the imagination, can be the cause of many and great errors, unless we are very wary of them. Moreover, they are established according to the pleasure and power of understanding of ordinary people, so that they are only signs of things as they are in the imagination, but not as they are in the intellect . . . The aim, then, is to have clear and distinct ideas, i.e., such as have been made from the pure mind, and not from fortuitous motions of the body. (Spinoza 2002: 19–20)

In the most egregious kind of case, our ideas are in terms of words that do not represent what we would report them to represent. We might report that we are thinking of God, for example, but not be thinking of God at all:

> Although many say that they doubt the existence of God, they have in mind nothing but a word, or some fictitious idea that they call God. This does not accord with the nature of God, as I shall later demonstrate in its proper place. (Spinoza 2002: 14)

Such a person is not in doubt about the existence of God, but that of course does not mean that he is certain that God exists. He is not in a position to have commitments about God at all.

The idea of God is just one example for Spinoza of an idea that we can merely *seem* to have. A person with a clear and distinct idea of God cannot doubt the existence of God, and a person who clearly and distinctly perceives that something cannot come from nothing cannot think that something can come from nothing. However, a person might entertain the linguistic entity "something can come from nothing" and report that perhaps something can come from nothing after all (Spinoza 2002: 16). Similarly, a person with a clear and distinct idea of mind cannot doubt her own existence, but a person with an idea of "mind" can be in doubt about "I am, I exist." Spinoza says that there are

> some who are not even aware of their own selves . . . Although in matters relating to the usages of life and society necessity has compelled them to suppose their existence, to seek their own good and frequently to affirm and deny things on oath, it is quite impossible to discuss the sciences with them . . . So they must be regarded as automata, completely lacking in mind. (Spinoza 2002: 13)

The completely mindless automaton is at one end of the Spinozistic spectrum of confusion. At the other end is the (equally idealized) person who has clear and distinct perceptions only. Spinoza offers a diagnosis of our situation, and also a proposal for treatment: that we come to notice what an idea is like that *does* refer and then come to have a second-order perspective on our ideas so that we can check them against that standard (Spinoza 2002: 11; also Garrett 2003: 83–6). If we are as confused as Spinoza thinks, what we would count as a paradigm case of an idea that refers is not a good standard, and so we would need some assistance. If we continue to think in terms that are not properly referential, we will sound like philosophers, but we will be very, very confused.

Since most of those who would be converted to Spinoza's system have intellects that are not yet emended, and since they conceive of reality in terms of a not-yet-emended language, the ideas that they have of metaphysical objects will not accurately represent those objects until they have done a lot of philosophy. In one case, we might think that the universe contains numerous corporeal substances. However, Spinoza holds that after sufficient reflection we notice that

> matter is everywhere the same, and [that] there are no distinct parts in it except in so far as we conceive matter as modified in various ways. (*Ethics*; Spinoza 2002: 226)

Because there cannot be two substances of the same attribute, there are no divisions within extended substance, and the thought of multiple individual substances of any kind is absolutely unintelligible. Nonetheless, Spinoza begins his *Ethics* with propositions about the relationships that obtain between multiple substances. These propositions are not the false premises of a *reductio* argument, but are by Spinoza's lights unthinkable. Still, we enter the *Ethics* with thoughts about the "multiple substances" that surround us. Spinoza will have us think our way through these confusions to the point where they implode. In a second kind of case, we might enter the *Ethics* thinking that omnipotence is the ability to do anything and *ipso facto* the ability to bring about possibilities that are not actual. Spinoza of course rejects this conception of omnipotence:

> There must necessarily follow from the necessity of the divine nature an infinity of things in infinite ways (that is, everything that can come within the scope of infinite intellect). (Spinoza 2002: 227)

When he concludes in Propositions 16 and 17 that God is omnipotent, he is not drawing the conclusion that God has the power to bring about things that God never in fact wills or creates, but he expects that many of us will draw this conclusion. If we do, we will have arrived at the result "God is omnipotent" but we will not have arrived at a result about omnipotence at all. Spinoza takes steps to make sure that we draw the right conclusion in offering a scholium that will emend readers' pre-*Ethics* understanding of omnipotence (Cunning 2003b: 85).

The rationalist faces a dilemma in that he cannot communicate his view except in terms that it does not sanction. The problem is clear:

> The truth cannot force its way in when something else is occupying its place. To convince someone of the truth, it is not enough to state it, but one must find the *path* from error to truth. (Wittgenstein 1979: 61)

If a philosopher is also a teacher, he will have to explain his view to us in terms that we already understand; otherwise we will not understand it. However, a rationalist is likely to hold that reality is far different from what we conceive it to be. Historically, the most brilliant attempt to address and overcome the obstacles of teaching a rationalist metaphysics is in Descartes' *Meditations on First Philosophy*. Descartes is the paradigm case of a rationalist who is also a teacher.

Like Plato, Malebranche, and other metaphysicians, Descartes has views on what we are like before we have engaged in (proper) philosophical reflection. For example, he holds that our conceptions of things like color, smell, and taste are inaccurate. Descartes' view is that strictly speaking, pain and color and so on are clearly and distinctly perceived when they are regarded merely as sensations or thoughts. (*Principles* 1: 68; AT 8A: 63; also Nelson 1996: 23–6; 1997: 166; Morris 1995)

However, most of us have very different conceptions of things like color. Descartes has views on what color is like, but he also has views on how we conceive of color pre-philosophically. *Our* conception of color, he thinks, is of something that exists mind-independently:

All of us have, from our early childhood, judged that all the objects of our sense-perception are things existing outside our minds and closely resembling our sensations, i.e., the perceptions that we had of them. Thus, on seeing a color, for example, we supposed we were seeing a thing located outside us which closely resembled the idea of color that we experienced within us at the time. (*Principles* 1: 66; AT 8A: 32)

If we still have this idea of color when we begin to engage in philosophical inquiry, we will not arrive at any true claims about color if the idea is not emended. The idea will be subject matter for error because there is nothing to which it conforms:

Even if I do not refer my ideas to anything outside myself, there is still subject matter for error, since I can make a mistake with regard to the actual nature of the ideas. For example, I may consider the idea of color, and say that it is a thing or quality; or rather I may say that the color itself, which is represented by this idea, is something of the kind. For example, I may say whiteness is a quality; and even if I do not refer this idea to anything outside myself – even if I do not say or suppose that there is any white thing – I may still make a mistake in the abstract, with regard to whiteness itself and its nature or the idea I have of it. (*Conversation with Burman*, AT 5: 152)

Descartes holds that materially false ideas are subject matter for error in the sense that they "provide the . . . subject matter for false judgments" (Fourth Replies, AT 7: 233). Some of the analytic judgments that we make on the basis of our concept of color will be false, and as a result any judgments that we make about color will have no chance of being true. They will simply misfire (Strawson 1950: 330–1).

The paradigm examples of materially false ideas that Descartes offers in the Third Meditation are ideas of sensible qualities like color. Materially false sensory are not clearly and distinctly perceived, according to Descartes, for it is not true that sensible qualities exist mind-independently. However, it is still the case that not a single idea that God implants in us is confused:

If we frequently have ideas containing some falsity, this can happen only because there is something confused and obscure in them, for in that respect they participate in nothingness, that is, they are in us in this confused state only because we are not wholly perfect. And it is evident that it is no less contradictory that falsity or imperfection as such should proceed from God than that truth or perfection should proceed from nothingness. (*Discourse* IV, AT 6: 38–9; also Fourth Replies, AT 7234–5)

Here Descartes says unequivocally that God does not produce falsity. In the Fourth Meditation, he attributes human error to the fact that we are not wholly perfect, and here he attributes material falsity to the same thing (Nelson 1996: 23–6). In the particular case of a materially false idea of color, Descartes offers a detailed account of how we come to amplify our God-given idea of color to the point that nothing answers to it. First, he notes that our sensations of the *extensive* qualities of bodies are presented to us in sensory perception as sensations of mind-independent things. Then he argues that when we do not (have the opportunity or time to) notice that our sensations of qualities like color are not so presented, we run all of our sensations together as sensations of mind-independent things and suppose that colors exist mind-independently as well:

> At the same time [that it perceived tastes, smells, sounds, heat, cold, light, colors, etc.] the mind perceived sizes, shapes, motions and so on, which were presented to it not as sensations but as things, or modes of things, existing (or at least capable of existing) outside thought, although it was not yet aware of the difference between things and sensations. (*Principles* 1: 71; AT 8A: 35)

In the Sixth Meditation, Descartes will argue that we have a strong propensity to believe that corporeal things are the mind-independent occasion of our sensory perceptions (AT 7: 80); here he is saying that we have this propensity in childhood as well, even if to a different degree. In childhood, however, we were not yet aware of the fact that there is a "difference between things and sensations," and we included in the category of mind-independent things what in fact are sensations only:

> [the mind] attributed to [the objects perceived by the senses] not only sizes, shapes, motions and the like, which it perceived as things or modes of things, but also tastes, smells and so on. (*Principles* 1: 71; AT 8A: 35–6)

We end up discovering the difference between sensations and things, but only after sufficient reflection on "what is called 'having a sensory perception'" (AT 7: 29) in the Second Meditation. Descartes thinks that prior to working through the *Meditations* we will think of a mind-independent thing when we think of color, but color is not a mind-dependent thing at all.

One of Descartes' aims in the *Meditations* is to offer us arguments that establish that his metaphysical system is the correct one. A problem is that if he puts forward arguments for the nature of things that we misconceive, we will invariably misunderstand the premises of these arguments. If we draw a conclusion in which we predicate color of something, the conclusion has no chance of being true because the predicate in question is confused. Descartes will offer arguments in the *Meditations*, but any argument that he offers about an x of which we do not yet have an accurate conception will contain premises that are problematic. First he must offer arguments that clear up our confused conceptions, and only then can he offer arguments that are sound. He does not censure us for having generated the confused conceptions in the first place; given our embodiment it would have been difficult for us to have done anything else:

> In our early childhood the mind was so closely tied to the body that it had no leisure for any thoughts except those by means of which it had sensory awareness of what was happening to the body. (*Principles* 1: 71; AT 8A: 35; also *Discourse* II, AT 6: 12–13)

However, in later life he would have us engage in philosophical reflection and restore our idea of color to an idea of something "which do[es] not represent anything located outside our thought" (*Principles* 1: 71; AT 8A: 35; also Morris 1995: 297–305).

Descartes holds that before we do philosophy we are not in a very good position to do philosophy. Another cognitive obstacle that we face is that we have a very poor standard for determining when a perception is indubitable. In childhood, our embodiment is so pronounced that we never stop to evaluate the false judgments that we make about bodies. If we make these judgments into adulthood and continue to do so uncritically, we assume that the reason they have stood the test of time is that they are unimpeachable:

> This [namely, that color exists mind-independently] was something that, because of our habit of making such judgments, we thought we saw clearly and distinctly – so much so that we took it for something certain and indubitable. (*Principles* 1: 66; AT 8A: 32; also *Principles* 1: 70; AT 8A: 35; *Principles* 1: 71; AT 8A: 36)

Descartes' view is not that these judgments are distinct and indubitable, but that they are false. However, we take them to be paradigmatic of certainty. When we enter the *Meditations* with a poor sense of what counts as indubitable, we are not in a position to recognize indubitability, and what we do recognize as indubitable is not indubitable in any strict sense.

A third obstacle that interferes with our ability to do philosophy is that we tend to hold that things are real or substantial to the extent that they can be sensed. Descartes holds that, as a result of our embodiment, our childhood judgments are pegged not to what things are like in their own right but to their usefulness to us. What is relevant to a person when he is attending to his bodily needs is his body and the bodies on which it depends, and when he does not notice what he does not sense, he assumes that there is nothing there:

> Since the mind judged everything in terms of its utility to the body in which it was immersed, it assessed the amount of reality in each object by the extent to which it was effected by it. As a result, it supposed that there was more substance or corporeality in rocks and metals than in water or air, since it felt more hardness and heaviness in them. Indeed, it regarded the air as a mere nothing, so long as it felt no wind or cold or heat in it. (*Principles* 1: 71; AT 8A: 36; also *The World*, AT 11: 17)

Someone who is accomplished in this manner of misconception is certain to encounter cognitive dissonance in attempting to conceive of non-sensible things. Operating on the assumption that a being that is not sensible is not a being at all, such a person will be unlikely to grasp Descartes' positive views. For example, Descartes holds that what we take to be the empty space that surrounds us is actually a plenum:

> There is no real distinction between space, or internal place, and the corporeal substance contained in it; the only difference lies in the way in which we are accustomed to conceive of them. (*Principles* 1: 10; AT 8A: 45)

However, to pre-*Meditations* sensibilities the view that the space between sensible objects has as much being per unit as the objects themselves is absurd. Even more absurd is the idea that non-sensible objects can contain an infinite amount of being. If in pre-*Meditations* circumstances we attempt to think of an object or substance with an infinite amount of being, we will succeed at thinking of an infinitely large body:

> Many people's understanding of substance is still limited to that which is imaginable and corporeal, or even to that which is capable of being perceived by the senses . . . They suppose that nothing can subsist unless it is a body, and that no body can subsist unless it can be perceived by the senses. (*Principles* 1: 73; AT 8A: 37)

According to Descartes, we judge the amount of substantiality in a thing by the effect that we notice it to have on us, and before we do philosophy what we notice to have an effect on us are bodies (*The World*, AT 11: 21). If we attempt to conceive of a being that has more reality than any other being, we will likely attempt to conceive of an immense corporeal being (Fifth Replies, AT 7: 252). If we do think of a being that is not corporeal, we might step back and wonder if we were really thinking anything at all. If we are still in childhood, and "if the mechanism of the body . . . [is] twist[ing] around aimlessly in all directions in attempts to pursue the beneficial and avoid the harmful" (*Principles* 1: 71; AT 8A: 35), our misconceptions are not such a problem. We do not have the leisure to do the philosophical work that will correct them, but philosophical truth is not what we are after. Descartes is instead worried about the ways in which our opinions about the substantiality of the non-sensible manifest themselves in later life:

> Right from infancy our mind was swamped with a thousand such preconceived opinions; and in later childhood, forgetting that they were adopted without sufficient examination, it regarded them as known by the senses or implanted by nature, and accepted them as utterly true and evident. (*Principles* 1: 71; AT 8A: 36)

In later life, we have opinions that we take to be unrevisable but that in fact are false or muddled. If given the opportunity to evaluate the arguments that Descartes offers for his metaphysics, we will either fail to conceive them, or else we will find them extremely implausible. Part of Descartes' metaphysics entails that the conceptions and commitments that we have at the start of philosophical inquiry are going to be incongruous with the ones that we will have when we are done. However, our point of departure is necessarily our current commitments.

Another cognitive obstacle that Descartes thinks we must overcome in order to do philosophy is our penchant for thinking by means of ideas of sensible objects. Descartes holds that in childhood our attention is focused on sensible objects because they are so relevant to the preservation of our bodies. In a way, that we focus on these objects is inevitable. In the Sixth Meditation, Descartes argues that our sensory perceptions compel us to pursue and avoid objects and that because they are will-compelling we can be sure that they are truth-tracking insofar as they "inform the mind of what is beneficial or harmful for the composite of which the mind is a part" (AT 7: 83). The Sixth Meditation result tells us that our sensory perceptions are tracking the benefits and harms of sensible objects *before* we do philosophy as well. Given Descartes' theory of will, sensible objects are things to which we are inclined to pay attention:

69

> A great light in the intellect is followed by a great inclination in the will; so that if we see very clearly that a thing is good for us, it is very difficult – and, on my view, impossible, as long as one continues in the same thought – to stop the course of our desire. (To Mesland, May 2, 1644; AT 4: 116)

At some point in childhood, when our wills are done twisting "aimlessly in all directions," we locate and appropriate the sensible objects that will benefit us, and our wills are compelled to pay attention to them. If in childhood we think exclusively of sensible objects and of how to manipulate them, we will not be proficient at thinking of other kinds of thing:

> Our mind is unable to keep its attention on things without some degree of difficulty and fatigue; and it is hardest of all for it to attend to what is not present to the senses or even to the imagination. (*Principles* 1: 73; AT 8A: 37)

If we become too accustomed to thinking of sensible objects, our approach to thinking of any object will be to think of it as a sensible thing. If the object that we are trying to conceive is in fact not a sensible object, what we end up conceiving will not be that object but something else:

> What does very often give rise to error is that there are many things which we think we perceived in the past; once these things are committed to memory, we give our assent to them just as we would if we had fully perceived them, *whereas in reality we never perceived them at all*. (*Principles* 1: 44; AT 8A: 21, emphasis added)

For example, some people might report themselves to have an idea of God when their idea is instead of an immense corporeal being (Fifth Replies, AT 7: 385; *Discourse* IV, AT 6: 37). Such people might introspect and report that they are theists, but if what it means for them to think of "God" is to think of an immense corporeal being, their belief is not in the existence of God (Appendix to Fifth Replies, AT 9A: 209–10; To Mersenne, July 1641, AT 3: 393–4). Descartes might offer arguments concerning God, souls, and bodies early in the *Meditations*, and these arguments might depend on notions of distinctness and indubitability, but his reader is not yet in a position to think of these in Cartesian terms. A piece of philosophy, the *Meditations* is largely about conceptual analysis, but Descartes holds that at the start of inquiry our concepts are not in order.

Complicating Descartes' task of helping us to overcome our tendencies to pay attention to and to think of sensible things is that these tendencies are fueled by our ever-present embodiment. One of the primary ways that we think of sensible objects, according to Descartes, is by imagining them. Imaginings are "shadows and pictures of" (*The Passions of the Soul* 1: 21; AT 11: 345) the bodies that we sense, and both involve the soul inspecting a figure on the pineal gland:

> It is only the latter figures ["those which are traced in the spirits on the surface of the gland H," the pineal gland] which should be taken to be the forms or images which the rational soul united to this machine will consider directly when it imagines some object or perceives it by the senses. (*Treatise on Man*, AT 11: 176–7)

Our sensations occur independently of our will; the soul inspects figures traced on the pineal gland by bodies that pass through the nerves (*Passions* 1: 23; AT 11: 346). When we imagine something, the figure is traced either by a volition of the soul or, in less intentional cases, by bodies in the brain that as a result of chance trace figures that are similar to the ones normally traced through the nerves (*Passions* 1: 20–1; AT 11: 344–5; *Rules for the Direction of the Mind*, AT 10: 412–18; To Princess Elizabeth, October 6, 1645, AT 4: 310). On Descartes' view, an embodied mind is not well suited to do philosophy. Processes in the body make a person sense and imagine things – in particular, things that he is inclined to desire and to see as good – and these processes occur in our bodies regardless of whether or not our minds will them to occur:

> The reception by the external sense organs of light, sounds, smells, tastes, heat and other such qualities, the imprinting of the ideas of these qualities in the organ of the "common" sense and the imagination, the retention or stamping of these ideas in memory . . . In order to explain these functions, then, it is not necessary to conceive of this machine as having any vegetative or sensitive soul or other principle of movement and life, apart from its blood and its spirits. (*Treatise on Man*, AT 11: 202)

In the time leading up to philosophical inquiry, our will, imagination, and senses are in a way working at odds.

Corporeal memory is a problem as well. Descartes does not have a fully articulated theory of memory, but he does hold that its operation depends on the body. He says that, as with the imagination, "the retention or stamping of these ideas [of sense] in memory" can occur in a purely corporeal machine. When we want to remember something, we have a volition that makes

> the [pineal] gland lean . . . first to one side and then to another, thus driving the spirits towards different regions of the brain until they come upon the one containing the traces of the object we want to remember. (*Passions* 1: 42; AT 11: 360; also Joyce 1997: 375–93)

It is clear how the corporeal aspect of memory can work against us. If, as sometimes occurs in the case of imagination, something other than our will drives the spirits to appropriate traces in the brain, we might recall an opinion that we have habitually affirmed and have assumed is indubitable. In particular, when we do philosophy and so talk and think about things like God, bodies, and the soul, the discussion will lead us to remember our related opinions and conceptions, to ill-effect:

> In later years the mind is no longer a total slave to the body, and does not refer everything to it. Indeed, it inquires into the truth of things considered in themselves, and discovers very many of its previous judgments to be false. But despite this, it is not easy for the mind to erase these false judgments from its memory; and as long as they stick there, they can cause a variety of errors. For example, in our early childhood we imagined stars as being very small; and although astronomical arguments now clearly show us that they are very large indeed, our preconceived opinion is still strong enough to make it very hard for us to imagine them differently from the way we did before. (*Principles* 1: 72; AT 8A: 36–7; also Reiss 1996: 596–602)

If Descartes holds that the physical causes of a particular memory can be in place independently of our will, he would expect that many of his readers would stagger in the process of doing philosophy. When putting forward claims about God, distinctness, or anything else about which he thinks we have confused but entrenched opinions, he would anticipate that we would reject them. Accordingly, it is important not only that we stop paying attention to the objects of the senses but that, while we are engaging in the reflective activity of philosophy, bodily movements that occur independently of our will and that incline us to affirm our false opinions be somehow kept at bay. Corporeal memory and the will work at odds, for Descartes. It will be part of philosophical reflection to adjust them while at the same time having to employ them.

A final problem that Descartes must face in communicating his metaphysics is that (according to him) our thoughts are often in terms of words that do not refer. When we think in terms of such words, we literally have no idea what we are talking about:

> . . . because of the use of language, we tie all our concepts to the words used to express them; and when we store the concepts in our memory we always simultaneously store the corresponding words. Later on we find the words easier to recall than the things; and because of this it is very seldom that our concept of a thing is so distinct that we can separate it totally from our concept of the words involved. The thoughts of almost all people are more concerned with words than with things; and as a result people very often give their assent to words they do not understand, thinking they once understood them, or that they got them from others who did understand them correctly. (*Principles* 1: 74; AT 8A: 37–8)

In the extreme case, we do not understand any more by the words that we (habitually) use than an animal understands if it has been trained to speak. Descartes admits that parrots can mimic human language, and he also allows that much of human behavior takes place without being guided by thought:

> A very large number of the motions occurring inside us do not depend in any way on the mind. These include heartbeat, digestion, nutrition, respiration when we are asleep, and also such waking actions as walking, singing, and the like, when these occur without the mind attending to them. (Fourth Replies, AT 7: 229–30)

The reason why an animal can speak, according to Descartes, is that, without any accompanying mental activity, its animal spirits can cause its body to make the relevant noises. Our animal spirits can cause bodily movements as well, in particular in the case of singing and the use of language more generally (*Passions* 1: 50; AT 11: 368–9; To the Marquess of Newcastle, November 23, 1646, AT 4: 573–5). In the Second Meditation, Descartes suggests that before we do philosophy we have no better understanding of body than does an animal (AT 7: 32). If behaviorism is the right account of significant amount of pre-*Meditations* thinking, and if much of the rest of pre-*Meditations* thinking is a matter of considering strings of imagistic terms as they pass before the conscious mind, the results of pre-*Meditations* conceptual analysis will be garbage. Part of Descartes' philosophical system is a series of views on what we are like before we do philosophy. If we are so constituted that at the start of inquiry we encounter great difficulty attending to what cannot be sensed or imagined; if we misconceive things that we would insist we conceive quite well; if we often are wrong in our reports of what we are thinking; if our wills are inclined to reject data that conflict with our current conceptions and commitments; and if our insurmountable embodiment stokes all of these, Descartes faces a serious pedagogical problem if it is by our minds that we would grasp his larger system.

Descartes realizes that given the multiple ways that an embodied mind can go wrong, not all minds are in the exact same condition at the start of inquiry. He holds that most of us are very attached to our senses and that

> since . . . there is nothing whose true nature we perceive by the senses alone, it turns out that *most* people have nothing but confused perceptions throughout their entire lives. (*Principles* 1: 73; AT 8A: 37)

However, some people are less attached to their senses than others, and so it is only most people who have nothing but confused conceptions. Famously, an atheist geometer can have "perceptions that are clear and distinct" (Second Replies, AT 7: 141–2; Fifth Replies, AT 7: 384). More generally, "the study of mathematics, which exercises mainly the imagination in the consideration of shapes and motions, accustoms us to form very distinct notions of body" (To Elizabeth, June 28, 1643, AT 3: 692; also *Conversation with Burman*, AT 5: 177; *The World*, AT 11: 39).

Descartes also suggests that there are skeptics who have had clear and distinct perceptions. He says famously that the doubt of the First Meditation is not intended to motivate skeptical conclusions: instead, "its greatest benefit lies in freeing us from all our preconceived opinions, and providing the easiest route by which the mind may be led away from the senses" (Synopsis of the *Meditations*, AT 7: 12).

He also says in a number of places that clear and distinct perceptions come easily if preconceived opinions and sensory perceptions are not interfering with our thought (Fifth Replies, AT 7: 375; Second Replies, AT 7: 157; the Fifth Meditation, AT 7: 69). Among skeptics, "such a renunciation [as in the First Meditation] is commonplace" (AT 7: 477), and although they are not skeptical while having a clear and distinct perception, and although they will not achieve metaphysical certainty about any result unless they have a clear and distinct perception of God's existence in particular, they still have clear and distinct perceptions of other things. Descartes says:

> I said that the skeptics would not have doubted the truths of geometry if they had truly recognized God, because since those geometrical truths are very clear, they would have had no occasion to doubt them if they had known that whatever is clearly understood is true. Now this last is contained in a sufficient acquaintance with God, and that is the premise which they do not have ready at hand. (To Hyperaspistes, August 1641, AT 3: 433)

Here Descartes is suggesting that skeptics have clear and distinct perceptions even though they are not in a position to rule out that their clear and distinct perceptions are false. One of the aims of the First Meditation skeptical arguments is to lead us from the senses so that we can have clear and distinct perceptions, but in many cases the skeptic is already sufficiently withdrawn. Descartes holds that *most* people are so

73

occupied with the objects of the senses that they have nothing but confused perceptions their entire lives. He says that "until making [the] renunciation [of belief of the First Meditation], there is virtually no one who ever perceives anything clearly, i.e., with the clarity which is required for metaphysical certainty" (Seventh Replies, AT 7: 476–7). He would be wrong if he thought that nobody thinks abstractly before engaging in philosophical inquiry, or that nobody overcomes at least some of the habits of childhood.

Descartes would also be wrong if he thought that everyone entered the *Meditations* with the same commitments. Many of his readers are Aristotelians: "the majority of those aspiring to be philosophers in the last few centuries have blindly followed Aristotle" (preface to *Principles*, AT 9B: 7). In his correspondence and in replies to objections, Descartes makes clear that, however much he would like them to go away, Aristotelian views are alive and well (To Mersenne, April 5, 1632, AT 1: 243; To Morin, July 13, 1638, AT 2: 200). The remainder of Descartes' readers are non-Aristotelians, and as we have seen these include atheists and skeptics (also Sixth Replies, AT 7: 549). But they also include mechanists like Gassendi and Hobbes. Of course, these would not be *Cartesian* mechanists; they might instead be adherents of the Epicureanism that made its way to Europe in the early seventeenth century. Descartes would emend the intellects of these thinkers as well, for they have at least some of the bad cognitive habits of childhood, and they are committed to views that are false. Although they do not believe in substantial forms, many would posit equally non-existent vacua. They would also affirm Aristotelian principles, even if unwittingly:

> Those who have not followed Aristotle (and this group includes many of the best minds) have nevertheless been saturated with his opinions in their youth (since these are the only opinions taught in the Schools) and this has so dominated their outlook that they have been unable to arrive at knowledge of true principles. (Preface to *Principles*, AT 9B: 7)

Descartes clearly admires some of his non-Aristotelian readers, but he thinks that their views have been infected by Aristotelianism nonetheless. For example, if his mechanist readers are empiricists, they will embrace the principle that whatever is in the intellect first must have been in the senses (Fifth Objections, AT 7: 321–2; To Voetius, May 1643, AT 8B: 26–36).

Another important subset of Descartes' readers would be individuals who have the habits and preconceptions that come with embodiment, but who do not yet have a fully articulated view of reality (Broughton 2002: 26–8; Frankfurt 1970: 15, 32; Rozemond 1996: 22–4). In particular, Descartes presents the *Meditations* as an offering to the faculty at the Sorbonne, and although he does not explicitly request that it be adopted as a textbook, he holds that no one will ever discover better proofs in philosophy than are in the *Meditations*, and he of course knows that philosophy is an important field of study at the Sorbonne ("Dedicatory Letter to the Sorbonne," AT 7: 4). He would go so far as to argue that untrained students have a better chance of grasping his metaphysics than philosophers with a fully articulated metaphysics. Speaking of "the problems caused by preconceived opinions, from which no one is entirely free," he says "those who have studied bad science the most are the greatest victims" (preface to *Principles*, AT 9B: 12–13). Descartes writes the *Meditations* in Latin, and his audience is thereby delimited, but he assumes that with assistance almost anyone can grasp his metaphysics (preface to *Principles*, AT 9B: 12–13). He says of the publication of the French version of the *Principles* that "it make[s] me hope that the work will be more widely read in French than in Latin, and better understood" (preface to *Principles*, AT 9B: 1). It is very possible that he writes the *Meditations* in Latin not because he thinks that it can only be grasped by a certain kind of mind, but at least in part because he is writing it for philosophers and for acceptance at institutions like the Sorbonne and because Latin is the more scholarly language.

Although they have much in common, different readers enter the *Meditations* with different epistemic histories. Descartes writes the *Meditations* accordingly. He offers a variety of explanations and analogies so that as many of his readers as possible can understand him. For example, he says of the Fifth Meditation proof of God's existence that

> it does not differ from anything I have written before, except for the method of explanation adopted. This I have deliberately altered so as to appeal to a variety of different minds. (First Replies, AT 7: 120)

As a teacher, Descartes is aware that an illustration or analogy that helps one reader to understand his views will not necessarily help another. He is also aware that the first-person perspective from which his readers work through the *Meditations* will vary with the differences in their commitments and habits. He speaks in the first person but captures multiple points of view:

> It was not my intention to make a survey of all the views anyone else had ever held on these matters, nor was there any reason why I should have done so. I confined myself to what I had originally believed quite spontaneously and with nature as my guide, *and to the commonly held views of others*. (Seventh Replies, AT 7: 482, emphasis added)

One of the aims of the *Meditations* is to overthrow preconceived opinions. However, in cases where two readers have different commitments, the commitments that one reader doubts on the basis of a given skeptical argument will be different from the commitments that another reader doubts on that same basis, and what remains of a reader's commitments after a given argument will vary as well. In addition, some readers will confront an argument with a preconceived opinion that conflicts with the results of the argument, and they will experience cognitive dissonance; but other readers will not. Descartes will do what any teacher would do when faced with the pedagogical predicament that minds differ in ways that are relevant for their instruction:

> Some Objects had need to be turned on every side; and when the Notion is new, as I confess some of these are to me; or out of the ordinary Road, as I suspect they will appear to others, 'tis not one simple view of it, that will gain it admittance into every Understanding, or fix it there with a clear and lasting Impression. There are few, I believe, who have not observed in themselves or others, That what in one way of proposing was very obscure, another way of expressing it, has made very clear and intelligible: Though afterward the Mind found little difference in the Phrases, and wondered why one failed to be understood more than the other. But every thing does not hit alike upon every Man's Imagination.

75

> We have our Understandings no less than our Palates; and he that thinks the same Truth shall be equally relished by every one in the same dress, may as well hope to feast every one with the same sort of Cookery: The Meat may be the same, and the Nourishment good, yet every one not be able to receive it with that Seasoning; and it must be dressed another way, if you will have it go down with some, even of strong Constitutions. (Locke 1975: 8)

Descartes uses the first-person perspective in the *Meditations*, but he uses it to represent a variety of minds.

Descartes holds that different minds have different commitments and habits, but he also holds that in some ways minds are the same. For example, all have the features shared by minds generally – will, understanding, duration, and also a variety of modes of thought. In addition, all minds are compelled to affirm what they perceive clearly and distinctly: "Admittedly my nature is such that so long as I perceive something very clearly and distinctly I cannot but believe it to be true" (Fifth Meditation, AT 7: 69; also Kenny 1998: 149–52; Larmore 1984; Nelson 1997: 163–4).

Even if Descartes' reader is a disciplined skeptic, he will affirm clear and distinct perceptions while he is having them and so will "surrender" (AT 7: 136) to Descartes' view. The same applies for a reader who begins the *Meditations* thinking by means of extremely confused ideas. The fact that a human will is so compelled will be of tremendous importance for Descartes' project of converting minds that are inclined to affirm confused opinions and to reject what opposes them. At the beginning of inquiry we think that we grasp our commitments very distinctly and vividly, and we will continue to think this unless we come to accept a standard of distinctness according to which they are not grasped distinctly. Descartes will expose us to this standard by way of the clear and distinct perceptions that meet it, and he expects that subsequently we will affirm that our pre-*Meditations* commitments do not compare. When our clear and distinct perceptions and their implications conflict with these commitments, we will revise the less distinct on the basis of the more distinct:

> In order to philosophize seriously and search out the truth about all the things that are capable of being known, we must first lay aside all our preconceived opinions, or at least we must take the greatest care not to put our trust in any of the opinions accepted by us in the past until we have first scrutinized them afresh and confirmed their truth. Next, we must give our attention in an orderly way to the notions that we have within us, and we must judge to be true all and only those whose truth we clearly and distinctly recognize when we attend to them in this way . . . When we contrast all this [clear and distinct] knowledge with the confused thoughts we had before, we will acquire the habit of forming clear and distinct concepts of all the things that can be known. (*Principles* 1: 75; AT 8A: 38–9)

If Descartes is right, we can reverse our cognitive habits by leveraging clear and distinct perceptions against them.

Descartes calls the teaching method that he employs to help us to arrive at philosophical truth the *analytic* method. He says: "Now it is analysis which is the best and truest method of instruction, and it was this method alone which I employed in my *Meditations*" (Second Replies, AT 7: 156). The "synthetic" method – that of starting with premises that are understood and proceeding to a conclusion – is a good method for teaching some subjects, but not for teaching philosophy. A prospective geometer can be taught with such a method:

> The primary notions which are presupposed for the demonstration of geometrical truths are readily accepted by anyone, since they accord with the use of our senses. Hence there is no difficulty there, except in the proper deduction of the consequences. (Second Replies, AT 7: 156–7)

For the prospective metaphysician, things are different:

> In metaphysics by contrast there is nothing which causes so much effort as making our perceptions of the primary notions clear and distinct. Admittedly, they are by their nature as evident as, or even more evident than, the primary notions which the geometers study; but they conflict with many preconceived notions derived from the senses which we have got into the habit of holding from our earliest years, and so only those who really concentrate and meditate and withdraw their minds from corporeal things . . . will achieve perfect knowledge of them. (Second Replies, AT 7: 157)

We do not acquire from our teachers or our sensory experience the confused view that right triangles have four internal angles or that parallel lines intersect. If we did, a teacher's attempt to guide us to the Pythagorean theorem would begin not with proofs about the relevant figures but with a clarification of the concepts of those figures. Descartes thinks that largely because of our embodiment we do acquire such misconceptions in metaphysics. The synthetic method is not appropriate for teaching metaphysics if (as Descartes thinks is likely) the student does not yet understand the terms of the debate.

Commentators have highlighted that although the precise nature of Descartes' teaching method is obscure, it is a method for helping a person to overcome confusions and arrive at truth (especially Garber 1984: 98; Hatfield 1984: 48–55). Here I am not going to attempt to offer a complete account of the method. In part, this is because Descartes says so little about what the method is and about how the *Meditations* is an implementation of it. He says "it was synthesis alone that the ancient geometers usually employed in their writings" and "this was not because they were utterly ignorant of analysis, but because they had such a high regard for it that they kept it to themselves like a sacred mystery" (Second Replies, AT 7: 156).

Descartes does not tell us much, either. Instead of offering a complete account of his analytic method, I want to fix on a single component of that method, one that has to do with Descartes' aim of teaching his metaphysics to minds that (his metaphysics entails) are not in a good position to grasp it.

In Fourth Replies, Descartes makes a connection between the method of analysis and the making of false claims. He says to Arnauld:

> The analytic style of writing that I adopted there [in the *Meditations*] allows us from time to time to make certain assumptions that have not yet been thoroughly examined; and this comes out in the First Meditation where I made many assumptions which I proceeded to refute in the subsequent *Meditations*. (Fourth Replies, AT 7: 249)

77

Descartes' analytic method is in some way a version of the analytic method of ancient geometers, and here he indicates that one aspect of the implementation of his method is to put forward claims that are false. In other passages, Descartes specifically connects geometrical proof with the making of false claims. He says to Morin:

> One could draw very true and certain consequences from [assumptions] even though they were false and uncertain. For the parallax, the obliquity of the ecliptic, and so on cannot be assumed as false or uncertain, but only as true; whereas the equator, the zodiac, the epicycles and other such circles are commonly assumed as false, and the movement of the earth as uncertain, and yet for all that one can derive true consequences from them. (To Morin, July 13, 1638; AT 2: 199)

In Fourth Replies, he notes in demonstrating the properties of a sphere Archimedes would attribute to spheres properties that they cannot possibly have. Rather than criticize that method, Descartes says it was the

> comparison between a sphere (or other curvilinear figure) and a rectilinear figure that enabled Archimedes to demonstrate various properties of the sphere which could scarcely be understood otherwise. (Fourth Replies, AT 7: 241)

Descartes reports that in the Third Meditation he is doing the same thing when he explains God's self-creation in terms of efficient causation, even though talk of God as the efficient cause of himself "involves an evident contradiction" (AT 7: 241). He admits such talk is confused, but

> nonetheless, all the above ways of talking, which are derived by analogy with the notion of efficient causation, are very necessary for guiding the natural light in such a way as to enable us to have a clear awareness of these matters. (AT 7: 241)

Very generally, Descartes' aim in the *Meditations* is to guide us to clear and distinct perceptions (To Mersenne, September 30, 1640, AT 3: 192). Many of us have not had a clear and distinct perception before entering the *Meditations*, and if Descartes is going to offer us analogies and explanations that we can follow, they will have to be in the confused pre-*Meditations* terms that we understand. For the same reason that (for example) the good calculus teacher does not simply throw more and more calculus at the student who finds it completely baffling from the start, Descartes explains his view in terms that we understand and are prepared to affirm, but in Descartes' case almost all of what we understand or affirm is either muddled or false.

Descartes sees himself as having little choice in speaking imprecisely. If he speaks in terms that run counter to the preconceived ideas and opinions that we bring to the *Meditations*, we will reject his argumentation. If he speaks in terms of clear and distinct perception, but our ideas are materially false or even non-referential, his argumentation will be lost on us. Given Descartes' views on the recalcitrance of finite will, the only way that we will get past our confusions is if we reason from within them and watch as they implode. Most of the claims of the *Meditations* are extremely confused. The claims that Descartes would identify as true are preceded by confusion, and are surrounded by confusion. A meditator who is suspicious of a result that she clearly and distinctly perceives will work to get over her suspicion, but to do this she will have to reason through and past the confusions that made her suspicious in the first place. The fictions of the *Meditations* include the false ideas and commitments through which the meditator must sort. They also include fictions that Descartes introduces to facilitate the process of emendation. Descartes sees himself as having little choice in speaking imprecisely, and even as providing a service:

> Take the case of someone who imagines a deceiving god – even the true God, but not yet clearly enough known to himself or to the others for whom he frames his hypothesis. Let us suppose that he does not misuse this fiction for the evil purpose of persuading others to believe something false of the Godhead, but uses it only to enlighten the intellect, and bring greater knowledge of God's nature to himself and to others. Such a person is in no way sinning in order that good may come. There is no malice at all in his action; he does something which is good in itself, and no one can rebuke him for it except slanderously. (To Buitendijck, 1643; AT 4: 64)

If Descartes speaks to us of God in the First Meditation, his larger metaphysics entails that most of us will think a term or corporeal image and will not be thinking of God at all. As a teacher, Descartes wants us to leave the *Meditations* with a grasp of his metaphysics, but if at the end of philosophical inquiry our ideas are what they were at the start of the *Meditations*, we will leave with a grasp of something else. The *Meditations* therefore contains the first successful proof of God's existence, as earlier proofs are not working with a proper conception of God (Seventh Replies, AT 7: 549; Second Replies, AT 7: 130–1).

Commentators have noted that an important component of the analytic method of ancient geometry was the use of constructions for the sake of facilitating demonstrations (Hintikka and Remes 1974: 22–30; Hintikka 1978: 79; Knorr 1983: 125–8). For example, to prove that the adjacent angles of a parallelogram ABCD add to 180 degrees, a geometer might extend line AB to point E and then point out that since angle EBC and angle ABC add to 180 degrees and since angle EBC is equal to angle DCB, angles ABC and DCB add to 180 degrees as well. Descartes considers the false but pedagogically fruitful claims that he makes in the *Meditations* as on a par with such constructions:

> The philosopher knows that it is often useful to assume falsehoods instead of truths in this way in order to shed light on the truth, e.g., when astronomers imagine the equator, the zodiac, or other circles in the sky, or when geometers add new lines to given figures. Philosophers frequently do the same. If someone calls this "having recourse to artifice, sleight of hand and circumlocution" and says it is unworthy of "philosophical honesty and the love of truth" then he certainly shows that he himself, so far from being philosophically honest or being prepared to employ any argument at all, simply wants to indulge in rhetorical display. (Fifth Replies, AT 7: 349)

The false claims of the *Meditations* are not the exact same sort of thing as the equator, the zodiac, or a geometrical construction. However, they are similar in that (1) they are falsehoods, (2) the teacher knows they are falsehoods, (3) at the time of instruction the student may or may not know that they are falsehoods, (4) they are posited for the sake of facilitating instruction, and (5) they are successful at facilitating instruction only if the student understands them. Descartes thinks that in some cases what it means to be philosophically honest is to employ whatever explanations and illustrations are necessary to help a student arrive at philosophical truth. Otherwise he would not arrive at it:

> A philosopher would be no more surprised at such suppositions of falsity than he would be if, in order to straighten out a curved stick, we bent it round in the opposite direction. (Fifth Replies, AT 7: 349)

One of Descartes' aims is to show us what can be clearly and distinctly perceived, but his views on what we are like before we do philosophy entail that he cannot achieve this aim by lobbing up clear and distinct perceptions. An important component of Descartes' analytic method is the use of fictions to facilitate his student's grasp of the Cartesian system. The implications of all of this for interpreting the *Meditations* are tremendous. A natural way to proceed in interpreting a philosopher's system is to extrapolate it from the claims that he makes. The *Meditations* is Descartes' "treatise on metaphysics" (To Mersenne, September 30, 1640; AT 3: 183), yet we will go astray if our interpretation of his metaphysics is an extrapolation from the claims put forward in it.

An important component of the method of the *Meditations* is the use of fictions to help us to neutralize our pre-*Meditations* opinions and habits. According to Descartes, most of us have a confused understanding of things like color, taste, and sounds. Most of us have a confused understanding of substance and think that something is substantial to the extent that it can be sensed. Probably all of us hold that there is a distinction between space and the bodies that it separates. We encounter great difficulty thinking abstractly; instead, our attention is kept by the objects of sense and imagination. All of us are inclined to reject what conflicts with our current commitments: even if we are convinced of a new position, we are inclined by our embodiment to remember and then affirm our former opinion straightaway. In spite of all of this, Descartes is committed to teaching us his philosophical system. To communicate his view, he will have to speak in terms that his view does not endorse. He begins at our state of confusion, resistance, and inattention, and forges a route to (what he takes to be) the clear and distinct perceptions of metaphysics.

References and Further Reading

Broughton, Janet (2002). *Descartes's Method of Doubt*. Princeton, NJ: Princeton University Press.

Cottingham, John (ed.) (1986). *Descartes*. Oxford: Blackwell.

Cottingham, John, Stoothoff, Robert, and Murdoch, Dugald (eds.) (1984). *The Philosophical Writings of Descartes, Volume 1*. Cambridge: Cambridge University Press.

—— (1985). *The Philosophical Writings of Descartes, Volume 2*. Cambridge: Cambridge University Press.

Cottingham, John, Stoothoff, Robert, Murdoch, Dugald, and Kenny, Anthony (eds.) (1991). *The Philosophical Writings of Descartes, Volume 3*. Cambridge: Cambridge University Press.

Cunning, David (2003a). Systematic divergences in Malebranche and Cudworth. *Journal of the History of Philosophy*, 41 (3), 343–63.

—— (2003b). Descartes on the immutability of the divine will. *Religious Studies*, 39, 79–92.

Frankfurt, Harry (1970). *Demons, Dreamers, and Madmen*. New York: Bobbs-Merrill.

Garber, Daniel (1984). Semel in vita: The scientific background to Descartes' *Meditations*. In Amelie Oksenberg Rorty (ed.), *Essays on Descartes' Meditations* (pp. 81–116). Berkeley: University of California Press.

Garrett, Aaron V. (2003). *Meaning in Spinoza's Method*. Cambridge: Cambridge University Press.

Hatfield, Gary (1984). The senses and the fleshless eye: The *Meditations* as cognitive exercises. In Amelie Oksenberg Rorty (ed.), *Essays on Descartes' Meditations* (pp. 45–79). Berkeley: University of California Press.

Hintikka, Jaako (1978). A discourse on Descartes's method. In Michael Hooker (ed.), *Descartes: Critical and Interpretive Essays* (pp. 74–88). Baltimore: Johns Hopkins University Press.

Hintikka, Jaako, and Unto Remes (1974). *The Method of Analysis: Its Geometrical Origin and its General Significance*. Boston, MA: D. Reidel.

Hume, David (1999). *An Enquiry Concerning Human Understanding* (Tom L. Beauchamp, ed.). Oxford: Oxford University Press.

Joyce, Richard (1997). Cartesian memory. *Journal of the History of Philosophy*, 35, 375–93.

Kenny, Anthony (1968). *Descartes: A Study of His Philosophy*. Bristol: Thoemmes Press.

—— (1998). Descartes on the will. In John Cottingham (ed.), *Descartes* (pp. 132–59). Oxford: Oxford University Press.

Knorr, Wilbur (1983). Construction as existence proof in ancient geometry. *Ancient Philosophy*, 3, 125–48.

Larmore, Charles (1984). Descartes' psychologistic theory of assent. *History of Philosophy Quarterly*, 1, 61–74.

Leibniz, G. W. (1989). *G. W. Leibniz: Philosophical Essays* (Daniel Garber and Roger Ariew, trans. and eds.). Indianapolis, IN: Hackett.

Locke, John (1975). *An Essay Concerning Human Understanding* (P. H. Nidditch, ed.). Oxford: Clarendon Press.

Lucretius (1995). *On the Nature of Things* (A. Esolen, trans. and ed.). Baltimore, MD: Johns Hopkins University Press.

Malebranche, Nicholas (1997). *The Search After Truth* (Thomas M. Lennon and Paul J. Oscamp, trans. and eds.). Cambridge: Cambridge University Press.

Morris, Katherine J. (1995). Intermingling and confusion. *International Journal of Philosophical Studies*, 3, 290–7.

Nelson, Alan (1996). The falsity in sensory ideas: Descartes and Arnauld. In E. Kremer (ed.), *Interpreting Arnauld*. Toronto: University of Toronto Press.

—— (1997). Descartes' ontology of thought. *Topoi*, 16, 163–78.

Plato (1921). *Republic* (H. N. Fowler, trans. and ed.). *Plato*, Vol. 7. Cambridge, MA: Harvard University Press.

Reiss, Timothy J. (1996). Denying the body? Memory and the dilemmas of history in Descartes. *Journal of the History of Ideas*, 57, 587–607.

Rozemond, Marleen (1996). The First Meditation and the senses. *British Journal of the History of Philosophy*, 4, 21–52.

Spinoza, Baruch (2002). *Spinoza: Complete Works* (Samuel Shirley, trans., Michael L. Morgan, ed.). Indianapolis, IN: Hackett.

Strawson, P. F. (1950). On referring. *Mind*, 59, 320–44.

Williams, Bernard (1978). *Descartes: The Project of Pure Enquiry*. London: Penguin Books.

Wilson, Margaret (1978). *Descartes*. New York: Routledge.

Wittgenstein, Ludwig (1979). Remarks on Frazer's *Golden Bough* (John Beversluis, trans.). In C. G. Luckhardt (ed.), *Wittgenstein: Sources and Perspectives*. Ithaca, NY: Cornell University Press.

Part II

THE HISTORICAL BACKGROUND

5

Plato's Rationalistic Method

HUGH H. BENSON

It is a commonplace that the two greatest Greek philosophers – Plato and Aristotle – split along the rationalist/empiricist divide. Plato is the rationalist, it is thought, and Aristotle the empiricist. According to this commonplace, Plato's fundamental ontological items are immortal, immutable, hyperborean universals known as *forms* – like the form of the Good and the form of Justice – to which we have epistemological access through some sort of prenatal noetic vision. Aristotle's fundamental entities, on the other hand are commonsense everyday things – like horses, and trees, and statues – to which we have epistemological access through our physical senses of sight, hearing, touch, etc. Like all commonplaces, there is much that is true about this picture, but it is also rife with caricature, distortion, and inaccuracy. To sort out the truth from the falsehoods in this commonplace is a monumental task well beyond the scope of this chapter. A great deal depends upon not only what one thinks Plato and Aristotle are up to, but also upon what rationalism and empiricism amount to. Consequently, my goal instead will be to focus in on one side of the commonplace – Plato's alleged rationalism, and specifically on his alleged rationalistic method. I will not argue that Plato's method is rationalistic, although we will bump up against features of the commonplace that may sound familiar to readers of Descartes, and other philosophers of a rationalist stripe. Nor will I argue that Plato's method is not rationalistic. Rather, I will describe in a generally programmatic manner Plato's mature philosophical method. My focus is on Plato and his philosophical method. I leave it to the reader to decide whether it is rationalistic, and to another time to address the Aristotelian half of the commonplace.

Preliminaries

Let me begin by turning to the notion of philosophical method. Much has been written on this issue to little consensus. Both what makes a way of behaving methodological and what makes a way of behaving philosophical are controversial matters. Consequently, I should say what I mean by "philosophical method" in the present context. By Plato's "mature philosophical method" I mean the systematic (purposive and repeatable) strategy Plato recommends (and may employ himself) in his classical dialogues in order to acquire the knowledge one lacks. For Plato, philosophy is the love of wisdom. Philosophy is not restricted to a particular kind of wisdom or subject matter. It is the desire for and attempt to acquire all knowledge or wisdom (see, for example, *Republic* 474c8–475c8; following Plato, I will be using "knowledge," "wisdom," and "expertise" interchangeably). Philosophy may engage in other activities. It may attempt to teach others what one has come to know oneself. It may attempt to explain or justify further what one already knows or believes. But, for Plato, it is first and foremost the attempt to acquire the knowledge one does not yet have.

Plato recognizes two ways in which this attempt to acquire knowledge can be made. One can learn it from another who already possesses knowledge or one can discover it on one's own (see, for example, *Laches* 186a6–187a1). Moreover, Plato may allow two ways in which one can acquire knowledge on one's own – through oracles, dreams, and other forms of divination (see, for example, *Apology* 33b9–c8) and through a systematic strategy. However, Plato would not take these distinctions to be sharp. He does not think that one with knowledge can simply hand over what one knows to the student, nor that genuine knowledge is simply the result of hearing an oracle or having a dream. In order to acquire genuine knowledge in either of these ways one must engage in a strategy of examination much like the systematic strategy of discovering on one's own. It is this systematic strategy of acquiring knowledge, whether aided by one who knows (human or divine) or not, with which I will be concerned in this chapter.

Of course, to say that Plato recommends a systematic strategy of knowledge acquisition is hardly remarkable. The question is "What is the nature of Plato's systematic strategy of knowledge acquisition?" What, that is, is the nature of Plato's philosophical method? I will argue that Plato's mature philosophical method has three components: the method of refutation or *elenchos*, the method of hypothesis, and the method of dialectic. Each component builds on the other. Plato proceeds not by abandoning one method in favor of a new one, nor by revising an inadequate method. Rather, he retains each component for what it does well and adds components to address inadequacies. Plato highlights each of these components in different dialogues. The method of *elenchos* is highlighted in the so-called Socratic dialogues (in alphabetical order *Apology*, *Charmides*, *Crito*, *Euthyphro*, *Euthydemus*, *Gorgias*, *Hippias Major*, *Hippias Minor*, *Ion*, *Laches*, *Lysis*, and *Protagoras*), the method of hypothesis in the *Meno* and the *Phaedo*, and dialectic in the *Republic*. So understood, Plato's mature philosophical method appears in the *Republic* as a philosophical development of the virtues and vices of the methods depicted in other dialogues. Whether this development reflects Plato's own philosophical development (whether at the time each dialogue was composed or not) or instead Plato's pedagogical judgment concerning how his views about philosophical method may best be presented remains an open question for the purposes of this chapter. The key is that the method is presented in components – with each new component offered not as a rejection or revision of other components, but as an addition to those other components.

Finally, I should mention an additional method Plato discusses but not one that I will be examining here: the method of collection and division. This method is not explicitly mentioned in any of the dialogues we will be discussing, but does get explicitly discussed in the *Phaedrus*. It becomes considerably more prevalent in a group of dialogues traditionally thought to have been written last in Plato's philosophical career (in alphabetical order *Critias, Laws, Philebus, Politicus, Statesman*, and *Timaeus*). To include even a programmatic account of the method of collection and division and the dialogues in which it predominates would require an essay of twice the current length.

The *Elenchos*

In Plato's *Apology* Socrates explains the motivations for his prosecution. He claims that he is not being prosecuted because he is actually thought guilty of the official charges leveled against him in the sworn deposition. Nor does he appear to think that he is being prosecuted because of the unofficial or informal charges leveled against him on the streets or in the theaters. Rather, he tells the jurors that he is being prosecuted because of a certain practice he has engaged in ever since his friend Chaerephon received from the Delphic oracle the answer that no one was wiser than Socrates.

Socrates was at a loss at what the oracle could mean. For he was aware of being "not wise at all" (21b4–5; all translations are from Cooper 1997) and yet the god could not lie. In order to understand the oracle, Socrates sought out those reputed to be wise either by themselves or others, thinking that he could thereby refute the oracle – saying "this man is wiser than I am, but you said I was wiser" (21c2). However, after going through the politicians, poets, and craftsmen, Socrates discovered that he was unable to refute the oracle in the manner he had anticipated. Instead, he discovered that all of those whose reputed wisdom he examined suffered the same fault. They all thought they knew (or perhaps were reputed to know) certain things that they did not. Consequently, his investigation led him to conclude that the oracle meant that "This man among you, mortals, is wisest who, like Socrates, understands that his wisdom is worthless" (23b2–4), thereby commanding Socrates to "go around seeking out anyone, citizen or stranger, whom I think wise. Then if I do not think he is, I come to the assistance of the god and show him that he is not wise" (23b4–7).

In describing this practice that Socrates takes to be responsible for his prosecution two features become immediately apparent. First, Socrates examines the reputed wisdom of anyone he happens to meet. Second, Socrates performs this examination not only to come to understand the oracle, but also to persuade those reputed to be wise of their ignorance, if they are not wise (*Apology* 23b7), and to learn from them, if they are wise (*Apology* 22b5). Using these features as identity conditions we can see that Socrates engages in this practice throughout much of the Socratic dialogues. He does not, however, *only* engage in this practice. He is not always examining the reputed wisdom of interlocutors. Socrates is not examining anyone's wisdom in the *Apology* (except, perhaps, at *Apology* 24c4–28a4), during the speech of the Laws in the *Crito*, during the myth at the end of the *Gorgias*, or in the first half of the *Laches* leading up to the "What is courage?" question at *Laches* 190d7–e3, to mention just four examples. Nevertheless, of the 34 interlocutors in the Socratic dialogues, 21 have some claim to wisdom that Socrates does go on to examine. In nearly every case, Socrates indicates that he is prepared to learn from them should their wisdom be confirmed and he attempts to persuade them of their ignorance once Socrates recognizes it.

87

In these examinations a pattern begins to emerge. Socrates begins by asking the interlocutor a question, the answer to which is an indication of the interlocutor's reputed wisdom. This is often, though not always, a question like "What is holiness?" or "What is courage?" Following the interlocutor's answer to this initial question, a series of other questions elicit answers from the interlocutor that are used by Socrates to derive the negation of the original answer. At this point either the interlocutor changes his initial answer by revising it or offering an entirely new one, or the dialogue with that interlocutor comes to an end. Consequently, typical Socratic *elenchoi* have roughly the following formal structure:

1   Socrates asks the interlocutor a question the answer to which is meant to exhibit the interlocutor's wisdom: usually, but not always, Socrates' "What is F-ness?" question. (I will refer to this initial answer, *p*, as the apparent refutand.)
2   The interlocutor provides answers, *q*, *r*, and *s* to a series of other Socratic questions. (I will refer to these answers as the premises of the *elenchos*.)
3   Socrates goes on to show that these answers entail the negation of the original answer.
4   Thus, the conjunction *p* & *q* & *r* & *s* is false.

Here then we have something like a systematic strategy – a method – but is it philosophical? Is it a strategy for knowledge acquisition – a method of philosophical inquiry? The two leading interpretations of the *elenchos* appear to split on this question. According to one, it is. According to the other, it is not, or at least not straightforwardly.

According to the constructivist interpretation of the *elenchos* – made famous in Vlastos' classic paper "The Socratic elenchus" (1983) – Socrates takes and is justified in taking his *elenchos* to establish the truth of individual beliefs. Thus, according to the constructivist interpretation, the *elenchos* does not end at step (4) above, but Socrates goes on to conclude:

5   Thus, *p* is false and not-*p* is true

and he is justified in doing so. Thus, according to this interpretation, the *elenchos* is a systematic strategy for acquiring knowledge. It is a method that proves or establishes the truth of individual beliefs like that piety is not (at least by definition) what is dear to the gods (*Euthyphro* 6e7–8b6) or that doing injustice is worse than suffering it (*Gorgias* 469b8–475e6).

According to the non-constructivist interpretation, Socrates neither takes nor would be justified in taking his *elenchos* to establish the truth of individual beliefs. Thus, according to the non-constructivist interpretation, Socrates takes the *elenchos* to end at step (4) above, and wisely so. The *elenchos* can do no more than establish the falsehood of the conjunction. It can only establish an inconsistency among the premises of the *elenchos* and the apparent refutand. Understood in this way, however, the *elenchos* looks to be a dismal failure as a method of knowledge acquisition. By practicing the *elenchos* one can only acquire knowledge that a particular set of beliefs is inconsistent. One cannot come to know which of those beliefs is true and which false.

The utter failure of the *elenchos* as a method of knowledge acquisition on the non-constructivist account has led many to reject this account. Although, as I mentioned above, the *elenchos* is not the only method Socrates practices in the Socratic dialogues, it is the only method of *knowledge acquisition* Socrates recommends or practices in those dialogues. And so, if the non-constructivist account is accepted, then the Socratic *elenchos* as a systematic method of knowledge acquisition is a dismal failure. To reject the non-constructivist account for this reason, however, is to misunderstand the *elenchos* and Socrates' systematic method of knowledge acquisition in the Socratic dialogues.

First, the *elenchos'* inability to establish the falsehood of one of the conjuncts in step (4) is not a result of the form of the *elenchos*, but a result of the constraints Socrates places on acceptable premises and apparent refutands. Throughout the Socratic dialogues Socrates suggests that the only requirement that the premises of an *elenchos* must meet is that they are believed by the interlocutor. There is no appeal to perception, expert opinion, or common sense, but only to the beliefs of the interlocutor. But being believed by the interlocutor is also a requirement of the apparent refutand. Consequently, in the Socratic dialogues, Socrates recognizes no epistemic distinction between the conjuncts in (4). They are all equally credible. They are all believed by the interlocutor and Socrates does not suggest that any other feature of the conjuncts is relevant. Consequently, with no distinction in the credibility of the conjuncts in (4) – or at least none that Socrates indicates is relevant – the *elenchos* can do no more than establish the falsehood of the conjunction at (4), whatever the consequences for his only method of knowledge acquisition.

Second, while such a result may appear inadequate as a method of knowledge acquisition, the *elenchos* so understood provides the necessary first step for philosophical inquiry – or the systematic pursuit of knowledge. According to Socrates, philosophical inquiry cannot begin until one recognizes that one lacks the knowledge one seeks to acquire. The interlocutors whom Socrates elencticly engages in the Socratic dialogues begin by already thinking they have the knowledge Socrates is pursuing. By requiring that the premises and the apparent refutand are all believed by the interlocutor, Socrates can disabuse them of this conceit as long as Socrates and his interlocutors think that consistency of belief is a necessary condition of knowledge. Of course, to think that knowledge requires consistent beliefs is to be committed to a rather robust conception of knowledge, but there are a variety of indications throughout the entire Platonic corpus for thinking that Plato was so committed. The *elenchos*, then, on the non-constructivist account is exactly the right method to use to begin the method of knowledge acquisition for those who do not yet recognize the need to employ it. Recall that one of the aims of his method that Socrates mentions in the *Apology* is to persuade those reputed to be wise of their ignorance.

Third, while Socrates does indeed take the *elenchos* as his method of knowledge acquisition, he does not – at least explicitly – understand it as his method of acquiring knowledge by discovering it on one's own. Rather, his explicit recommendation is to employ the *elenchos* in order to learn from those who already have this knowledge. (Recall the second aim mentioned in the *Apology*.) But the non-constructivist account of the *elenchos* need not rule out the possibility of acquiring knowledge from another who already has it by practicing the *elenchos*. We need to be cautious here. Frankly, the Socratic dialogues provide little evidence one way or the other on this issue. Socrates never uncovers someone who has the knowledge he is seeking in order to learn from him (except the craftsmen at *Apology* 22d2–4 whose knowledge he apparently does not attempt to learn). So we can only speculate how Socrates thinks the *elenchos* would enable him to learn from such an individual if such an individual were to be found. Moreover, the Socratic dialogues may indicate that Plato is concerned about the *elenchos*' ability to uncover one with knowledge if it is being employed by one who does not yet know (*Protagoras* 313c4–314b4 and *Charmides* 167b10–172c3). Nevertheless, we should remember that Plato fails to testify very enthusiastically about the success of the *elenchos* as a method of knowledge acquisition. Even near the end of Socrates' life, Plato has him profess to not being "wise at all" despite having practiced the *elenchos* at least since Chaerephon reported back the answer from the oracle.

In the Socratic dialogues, then, Plato presents us with a philosophical method that is largely unsuccessful. Plato has Socrates describe and practice in the Socratic dialogues a systematic strategy for knowledge acquisition. The strategy is to examine the knowledge or wisdom of those with some claim to it, and then to elicit from them a series of answers to questions in order to test the consistency of their beliefs. He does this in order to learn from those he examines, if they are discovered to have the knowledge they claim – as none are, and in order to persuade them of their lack of knowledge, if indeed they are discovered to lack it – as they all are. He persuades these latter of their ignorance, so that they may join him in the pursuit of the knowledge they lack. The method is very successful in determining the ignorance of those who lack knowledge (at least given a robust conception of knowledge) – again, as indeed everyone he engages does. It is somewhat less successful in persuading those who lack knowledge of their ignorance. And it is a dismal failure at acquiring the knowledge Socrates is seeking. We will see in the next two sections that Plato recognizes the inadequacies of the *elenchos* as a method of knowledge acquisition, but he does not abandon it. Rather, he supplements it with additional methods once the *elenchos* has achieved its goal of leading the interlocutor to recognize the need to join Socrates in the pursuit of the knowledge he lacks.

The Method of Hypothesis

Plato's *Meno* begins like a Socratic dialogue. Meno professes to know what virtue is and Socrates seeks to learn this from him by asking him the "What is virtue?" question and then a series of other questions. Meno's answers, however, turn out to be inconsistent, just like the interlocutors of the Socratic dialogues, so that by 80a8–b1 Meno has come to recognize his ignorance, saying: "both my mind and tongue are numb, and I have no answer to give you." At this point, however, the similarity between the *Meno* and the Socratic dialogues comes to an end. For rather than bringing the dialogue to a close or having Socrates turn to another interlocutor, Plato has Socrates say to Meno: "So now I do not know what virtue is; . . . Nevertheless, I want to examine and seek together with you what it may be" (80d1–4). Rather than continuing the inquiry, however, the reader is presented with the following paradox: *Meno*'s paradox.

1   Either one knows what one is inquiring into (one has the knowledge one is systematically attempting to acquire) or one does not.
2   If one knows what one is inquiring into, then one does not need to inquire into it.
3   If one does not know what one is inquiring into, then one does not know how to begin the inquiry or when the inquiry has been completed.
4   If one does not know how to begin the inquiry or when the inquiry has been completed, then one cannot inquire.
5   So, if one does not know what one is inquiring into, then one cannot inquire.
6   So inquiry (i.e., the systematic attempt to acquire knowledge) is either unnecessary or impossible (80d5–e5).

Here Plato has Socrates and Meno raise a more generalized version of the problem we faced at the end of the last section. There we worried whether the *elenchos* could be a successful systematic strategy for knowledge acquisition. Here the worry is whether *any* method could be successful. Plato has Socrates proffer the theory of recollection as a solution to this more generalized worry. Yes, a successful systematic strategy for knowledge acquisition is possible because humans previously possessed the knowledge they are seeking to acquire and a systematic strategy for reacquiring knowledge is not generally problematic. Now, one might be skeptical concerning the plausibility of such a solution – both concerning the plausibility of an appeal to something like innate or prenatal knowledge in general, and concerning the plausibility of such an appeal being able to resolve *Meno*'s paradox, but I want to focus on a further question. Even if we grant that something like the theory of recollection is true and that it resolves the paradox, the *elenchos* continues to be a dismal failure at acquiring this previously possessed knowledge. It is a failure because as Plato understands the method in the Socratic dialogues, it depends on finding someone who has already recovered the prepossessed knowledge. It is a method of acquiring knowledge by learning from someone who already knows. Even granting the theory of recollection and what it is supposed to do, Plato still owes us a systematic strategy of acquiring (or reacquiring) knowledge when no one who has already reacquired it can be found. Plato meets this obligation following the conversation with the slave-boy offered to illustrate the theory of recollection.

At 86c Socrates and Meno agree to resume the inquiry that was interrupted by Meno's presentation of the paradox. Meno, however, insists that they return to the original question of the dialogue ("Can virtue be taught?") rather than the question which they had been pursuing just before the paradox ("What is virtue?"). Socrates yields to Meno's insistence on the condition that Meno permit Socrates to use a new method – a method with which he suggests Meno will be familiar as a result of his knowledge of geometry. Socrates illustrates this new method by appealing to a complex geometrical problem and then uses it on the question Meno wants to pursue – whether virtue can be taught. While the details of these passages are obscure, the general structure of the method Socrates appears to be recommending is not. It begins by first reducing the target question to a secondary question which it is supposed will be easier to answer. One brings about this reduction by identifying a property such that it is true of the subject of the primary question just in case the property of the primary question is true of that subject. For example, when the primary question is

"Is *a* F?," one seeks to identify a property G, such that *a* is G just in case *a* if F. So the primary question in the case of the *Meno* – "Is virtue teachable?" – is reduced to the question "Is virtue a kind of knowledge?" in virtue of the fact that a thing is teachable just in case it is a kind of knowledge. Once this reduction is accomplished, the next step in the new method of the *Meno* is to seek to acquire knowledge of the answer to the secondary question. So far this is hardly an improvement on the *elenchos*. It has only pushed the problem back to the secondary question. If all Plato has to offer as a systematic strategy for acquiring the knowledge of the answer to the secondary question is to examine someone who has a claim to know it, persuade him of his ignorance if it turns out that he does not, and learn from him if it turns out that he does, we have made no progress. Fortunately, Plato has more to offer.

The new systematic strategy Plato recommends is described in the *Phaedo*. If we assume that a positive answer to the secondary question is the hypothesis, Socrates is made to recommend two complementary procedures for acquiring the knowledge of its truth. The first is that one "examine the consequences that follow from [the hypothesis to see whether they] agree with one another or contradict one another" (*Phaedo* 101d4–5). The second is to "assume another hypothesis, the one which seems to you best of the higher ones until you come to something acceptable" (101d6–e1). To better understand this description we can watch Socrates practicing the method in the *Meno*. Socrates first takes up the second procedure described in the *Phaedo* and derives a positive answer to the secondary question – that virtue is a kind of knowledge – from the "higher" hypothesis that virtue is good, which Socrates takes to be adequate on the grounds that it will "stand firm for us." Next, Socrates takes up the second procedure examining the consequences of the hypothesis that virtue is a kind of knowledge. It turns out that the consequences do not agree with each other but contradict one another. According to Socrates it follows from the hypothesis that virtue is a kind of knowledge that there are teachers of virtue. But as a matter of fact there are no teachers of virtue.

Here then we have described in the *Phaedo* and depicted in the *Meno* a systematic strategy for knowledge acquisition distinct from the *elenchos*. First, one reduces the question the answer to which one seeks to know to another question. We might call this the reduction stage. One then assumes the answer to the secondary question to be positive and attempts to derive this positive answer from other positive answers until one reaches something "adequate" – perhaps something with a high degree of antecedent probability. We might call this procedure the upward path, since Socrates describes the process as proceeding through "higher" hypotheses until one reaches something adequate. We might also think of this procedure as a continuation of the reduction stage, except that the reduction requires an equivalence between the two questions while the upward path appears only to require that a positive answer to the higher question (together with other perhaps subsidiary premises) entails a positive answer to the lower question. The upward path, however, is distinct from a second procedure which we might call the downward path.

The downward path consists in deriving the consequences of the positive answer to the secondary question (one of which will, of course, be a positive answer to the primary question) and testing their consistency. The evidence from the *Meno* suggests that this consistency test is not meant to be merely a self-consistency test (despite the language of the *Phaedo*). Presumably, few positive answers to the secondary question will be self-contradictory. Rather, the *Meno* depicts Socrates as testing the consequences of the hypothesis that virtue is a kind of knowledge against its consistency with other logically independent propositions (e.g., that there are in fact no teachers of virtue). The status of these independent propositions is far from clear, but they appear to be roughly the phenomena – contingent matters of fact, perceptual evidence, expert opinion, common sense – or conclusions of arguments with premises that are themselves the phenomena.

The method of hypothesis so understood is, of course, subject to a variety of inadequacies. First, and perhaps most obviously, the adequacy of the "highest" hypothesis from which the positive answers to the secondary and primary questions are ultimately derived is suspect. As a method of knowledge acquisition, one's knowledge of the answer to the primary question can be no more secure than one's knowledge of the "adequate" hypothesis and one's knowledge of this hypothesis appears at best provisional. Plato seems to be aware of the provisionality of the upward procedure since he supplements it with an additional check – the downward procedure – but this procedure too is problematic in ways reminiscent of the *elenchos*. We saw that Plato did not think that the downward path consisted simply in examining whether the answer to the secondary question was self-contradictory, but in examining whether its consequences were consistent with the phenomena – contingent matters of fact, perceptual evidence, expert opinion, common sense. But consistency with the phenomena does not suffice for establishing the truth of the positive answer to the secondary question even if the phenomena are credible. Moreover, like the *elenchos*, inconsistency with the phenomena does not suffice for establishing the positive answer's falsity either. For Plato nowhere indicates a distinction in the credibility of the higher hypothesis and the phenomena. The truth of the phenomena appears no more secure than the truth of the positive answer to the secondary question. Finally, Plato provides little guidance concerning how to go on when the results of the two procedures conflict, as they do for example in the *Meno*. The upward path in the *Meno* suggests that virtue is indeed a kind of knowledge and so teachable, while the downward path suggests that it is not a kind of knowledge and so not teachable. In the *Meno*, Socrates goes on to reconsider the upward path and suggests that one of the premises used in deriving the positive answer that virtue is a kind of knowledge from the "adequate" hypothesis that virtue is good, viz. the premise that the only good things are kinds of knowledge, is false. In fact, some good things are true beliefs. But Plato's commitment to this final argument in the *Meno*, according to which virtue is true belief and so acquirable by divine dispensation, has been subject to considerable doubt. So we cannot be confident that the procedure Plato has Socrates adopt when these two procedures conflict is the procedure Plato means to recommend.

Despite these inadequacies – as formidable as they are – we should not think that Plato has failed to make progress. Recall the difficulty at this point in the *Meno*. Both Socrates and Meno have become aware of their lack of knowledge of what virtue is and so whether virtue is teachable. Nevertheless, Socrates encourages Meno to join him in the pursuit of this knowledge. Meno wonders whether any systematic strategy for acquiring this knowledge is possible and puts forward the paradox to drive this worry home. Socrates responds to this general worry by proposing the theory of recollection, according to which it is possible to engage in a systematic strategy for acquiring knowledge because we all have already possessed the knowledge we are seeking to acquire. Nevertheless the specific systematic strategy to employ in this pursuit is yet to be addressed. The *elenchos* cannot be employed in this pursuit because as a systematic strategy of knowledge acquisition it aims to learn from those who know, but both Meno and Socrates have admitted they do not know. Thus, Plato proposes the method of hypothesis as the specific strategy to employ. Besides being a method of discovery as opposed to a method of learning from another, the method of hypothesis differs from the *elenchos* in that (1) the *elenchos* contains no obvious counterpart to the upward path of the hypothetical method; (2) the positive answer to the secondary question (unlike the apparent refutand of the *elenchos*) need not be believed by any of the participants at the beginning of the method, let alone by the interlocutor whom Socrates is engaging; and (3) the phenomena of the downward path must possess epistemic credibility besides being merely believed by the interlocutor (although, to repeat, their credibility is no more secure than the credibility of the positive answer to the secondary question). Nevertheless, the *Meno* makes clear that the *elenchos* is not abandoned in favor of the method of hypothesis, nor transformed into the method of hypothesis. The method of hypothesis is employed only after the *elenchos* has accomplished all that it can. It is only after the *elenchos* has exposed the ignorance of both Meno at 80a8–b2 and the slave-boy at 84a1–2 – so that they can no longer be reliably learned from and so that they will join Socrates in the pursuit of the knowledge they now recognize that they lack – that Socrates turns to the method of hypothesis as a strategy for going on. Thus, progress has been made despite the inadequacies of the method of hypothesis. We will see in the next section that Plato tries to respond to some of these inadequacies in the *Republic*.

The Method of Dialectic

In the middle books (V–VII) of Plato's *Republic*, Plato has Socrates turn to the question of the nature of the philosopher-rulers. We have already seen that for Plato philosophy is the love of all wisdom and philosophers for Plato are those who love and seek to acquire all wisdom. I want to focus on two passages in the course of this discussion in which Plato appears to have in view yet a third component of his philosophical method. These two passages are the analogy of the line at *Republic* 509c–511d and Plato's description of the education of the philosopher at *Republic* 521b–540c. The first passage introduces explicitly for the first time a new method distinct from the method of hypothesis, which Plato calls dialectic. The second passage makes clear that dialectic is not introduced as a rejection of or revision to the method of hypothesis, but rather as a continuation and completion of his systematic strategy for knowledge acquisition.

In the second of his analogies aimed at explaining the nature of the good, Socrates imagines a line cut into two unequal portions. The smaller portion represents the things that share in forms (e.g., the beautiful things) and the larger portion the forms themselves (e.g., the Beautiful itself). Each of these two portions of the line is similarly divided into two unequal subsections. The smaller subsection of the portion of the line representing the beautiful things represents images of the beautiful things (shadows, reflections in pools of water, etc.), while the larger subsection represents the originals of the things imaged in the smaller subsection. Turning to the subsections of the portion representing the forms, Socrates says concerning the smaller subsection that the soul uses as images the originals of the previous subsection, is forced to investigate from hypotheses, and proceeds to conclusions, not to a first principle (510b4–6). In the larger subsection the soul makes "its way to a first principle that is not a hypothesis, proceeding from a hypothesis but without images used in the previous subsection, using forms themselves and making its investigation through them" (510b6–9). Notice that Plato has Socrates distinguish the subsections of the first portion in ontological terms, while he distinguishes the subsections of the second portion in methodological terms. Why he does so has been a matter of considerable controversy, but since I am concerned with methodological issues I will sidestep much of this controversy and simply focus on the nature of the methodological distinction.

The first subsection of the larger portion describes the method of hypothesis from the *Meno* and the *Phaedo*. The method of the first subsection is the method of "geometry, calculation and the like" (510c2–3), just as the method of hypothesis is described as the method of the geometers in the *Meno*. The practitioners of the first subsection's method employ hypotheses "as if they were known," not thinking "it necessary to give any account of them, either to themselves or to others, as if they were clear to everyone" (510c6–d1). Here Plato refers to the higher hypotheses of the *Meno* and *Phaedo*, which are described as "standing firm for us" and "adequate," respectively. Having arrived at adequate hypotheses, the practitioners of the first subsection's method then proceed to ends or conclusions (the Greek is *teleuten*), rather than to beginnings or first principles (*archen*), referring to the downward path of the method of hypothesis. Finally, Socrates explains that the practitioners of the first subsection's method "use visible figures and talk about them, [though] their thought isn't directed at" those visible figures but at the things their visible figures are like (510d5–7). This appeal to perception is easy enough to explain in the case of geometry given its frequent appeal to constructions, but why think that an appeal to perception applies to the method of hypothesis generally? Recall that the *Meno* suggested that the downward path consisted not simply in testing the self-consistency of the higher hypothesis, but also in testing its consistency with the phenomena. It was because the hypotheses that all good things are instances of knowledge and that virtue is good were inconsistent with the quasi-perceptual contingent fact that there are (in fifth-century BCE Athens) no teachers of virtue that led to the rejection of the claim that virtue was teachable. According to Plato, in pursuing the downward path in the *Meno* Socrates and Meno were employing images of virtue through thinking about virtue itself. In all these ways, then, the method of the first subsection alludes to the method of hypothesis.

Since Plato is referring to the method of hypothesis in the first subsection of the upper portion of the line, one should expect that the method in the second subsection with which it is contrasted will seek to resolve some of the inadequacies of the method of hypothesis which we mentioned earlier. And indeed, this is precisely what the method of dialectic appears aimed at doing. While Plato does not have Socrates explicitly call the method of this second subsection the method of dialectic until 533c7, he has dialectic in mind when he uses the phrase "the power of dialoguing" at 511b4. Socrates tells Glaucon that the "power of dialoguing" "does not consider these hypotheses as first principles but as stepping stones to take off from, enabling it to reach the unhypothetical first principle of everything. Having grasped this principle, it reverses itself and, keeping hold of what follows from it, comes down to a conclusion without making use of anything visible at all, but only of forms themselves, moving on from forms to forms, and ending in forms" (511b5–c2). Dialectic is here described as consisting of both an upward path and downward path like the method of hypothesis, but the differences go directly to addressing the inadequacies of the method of hypothesis we discussed earlier.

The upward path of dialectic does not stop when it reaches an "adequate" hypothesis or one that merely "stands firm for us." It does not treat what is provisional (hypothetical) as though it were a first principle. Rather, it continues on its upward path until it reaches what is no longer provisional, what is not merely adequate or firm for us, but what is an "unhypothetical first principle of everything." Plato explicitly recognizes the failure of the method of hypothesis to acquire knowledge precisely because it fails to go beyond its provisional higher hypothesis to the "unhypothetical first principle" a little later in the *Republic*, when he fills out his description of dialectic. He has Socrates say: "What mechanism could possibly turn any agreement into knowledge when it begins with something unknown and puts together the conclusion and the steps in between from what is unknown?" (533c3–5). Now that the upward path is no longer provisional, the role of the downward path of dialectic is importantly different from the role of the downward path in the method of hypothesis. Recall that in the latter method the downward path provided an additional check on the truth of the higher hypothesis given its provisionality. But in dialectic the end of the upward path is no longer provisional, but secure. Consequently, the downward path in dialectic does not provide a further check on the "unhypothetical first principle" but, rather, simply becomes the procedure by which one derives the results or consequences of that first principle, much like the procedure of a deductive science whose first principles are taken to be necessary and self-evident. (See, for example, Aristotle's *Posterior Analytics* or Euclid's *Elements*.)

This novel role for the downward path in dialectic may avoid some of the inadequacies of the downward path of the method of hypothesis, but it leads directly to dialectic's own inadequacies. For if the downward path is really meant to be simply drawing the deductive consequences of the "unhypothetical first principle," one cannot expect to get very far on the basis of a single "unhypothetical first principle." Deductive sciences of the sort mentioned above employ a plurality of first principles to even begin to appear substantive. Nevertheless, nothing in the middle books of the *Republic* would suggest that Plato allows a plurality of "unhypothetical first principles." Indeed, Plato appears to identify the "unhypothetical first principle" with a single form – the form of the Good. Plato may fail to see a difficulty here if he thinks of the "unhypothetical first principle" as less like an axiom and more like an entire completed deductive theory. The form of the Good, on this account, is not a single axiom acquired at the end of the upward path of dialectic from which one is supposed to derive the theory via the downward path, but rather it is the complete theory "of everything" acquired via the long arduous upward path from which implicit theorems are relatively easily derived via the downward path. Of course, understanding the form of the Good or "the unhypothetical first principle" in this way has its own difficulties, not the least of which is the allegedly self-certifying or non-provisionality of this principle. In the typical case one seeks epistemic security or credibility by stripping away content, while in the case of dialectic so understood one packs content in. One continues on the upward path – packing in content, so to speak – "until one can survive all refutation, as if in a battle, striving to judge things not in accordance with opinion but in accordance with being, and come through all of this with his account still intact" (534c1–3). It is as if the upward and downward paths of the hypothetical method have been absorbed into the upward path of dialectic. Perhaps Plato has in mind something more like the experience that chess masters are said to have when they "see" the board and hundreds of moves ahead, than the experience of the Cartesian indubitable belief that I exist. Nevertheless, however Plato ultimately thinks the inadequacies of dialectic are to be met, his analogy of the line makes it clear that he sees dialectic as an advance beyond the method of hypothesis of the *Meno* and *Phaedo*.

Having said this, however, we should not think that Plato has abandoned the method of hypothesis in favor of dialectic. Rather, the method of hypothesis is a preliminary step in his systematic strategy of knowledge acquisition, as is made clear later in the *Republic* when he describes the education of the philosopher-rulers. According to Plato, following their compulsory physical education around the age of 20, the future philosopher-rulers embark upon a ten-year education, first in number and calculation, then plane geometry, next solid geometry, then astronomy, and finally harmonics – disciplines according to the divided line passage that employ the method of hypothesis. Following this ten-year immersion in mathematics, the future philosopher-rulers will be introduced to arguments (*logoi*) – a kind of preliminary dialectic – for five years. Plato has Socrates stress the importance of withholding this education in "arguments" until the future philosopher-rulers have achieved a mature age and have completed their mathematical studies. For when this is not done, "young people getting their first taste of arguments . . . misuse it by treating it as a kind of game of contradiction. They imitate those who've refuted them by refuting others themselves, and, like puppies, they enjoy dragging and tearing those around them with their arguments" (539b3–7). Plato here alludes to the elenctic method of the Socratic dialogues. Following this five-year immersion in "arguments," the future philosopher-rulers must engage in a 15-year practicum of politics, military affairs, and administration. It is only then at the age of 50 that the systematic strategy of knowledge acquisition known as dialectic can come to completion.

> Then at the age of 50, those who have survived the tests and been successful both in practical matters and in the sciences must be led to the goal and compelled to lift up the radiant light of their souls to what itself provides light for everything [the upward path of dialectic]. And once they've seen the good itself, they must each in turn put the city, its citizens, and themselves in order, using it as their model [the downward path of dialectic]. (540a–b)

Notice that Plato abandons neither the *elenchos* nor the method of hypothesis. Both are incorporated into the mature method as propaedeutic preliminaries to the final ascent to the form of the Good (however it is to be understood) and the derivations therefrom (however they are to be understood).

97

Exactly how the *elenchos* and the method of hypothesis are incorporated is only hinted at in these passages, but the idea seems to be the following. The *elenchos* maintains its function of eliminating the interlocutor's false conceit of knowledge – a conceit that must be eliminated before the interlocutor will willingly begin the arduous task of dialectic. But the elimination of the interlocutor's false conceit of knowledge – at least of what is called "the most important things" in the *Apology* (22d7) or what is called the form of the Good in the *Republic* – should not be attempted until the interlocutor is in a position to know that systematic knowledge acquisition is possible as a result of one's experience in successfully employing the method of hypothesis in the mathematical disciplines and until the interlocutor is sufficiently mature to have the courage to pursue knowledge acquisition in face of numerous setbacks, rather than opt for skepticism or relativism (see *Laches* 193e8–194b6). The *elenchos* will presumably still have this role to play even in the mathematical disciplines, but it is less dangerous and less difficult to accomplish in those disciplines (see *Meno* 82e14–84a1).

The role of the method of hypothesis is at least threefold. First, like the *elenchos*, it prepares the interlocutor cognitively both as a kind of mental gymnastics, making the interlocutor agile in the use of sophisticated inferences, and as a reassurance that a systematic strategy of knowledge acquisition can make progress. Second, the hypotheses arrived at by the mathematical disciplines will be used "as stepping stones to take off from" as dialectic employs the upward and downward paths of the hypothetical method in ascending to the "unhypothetical first principle." Third, the method of hypothesis remains Plato's preferred method of acquiring knowledge when one does not have 50-plus years to spare (see *Phaedo* 100b1–c2 and *Republic* 435c9–d5). Even so, it remains a second-best method to the complete method of dialectic as described in the *Republic*.

Conclusion

Let me summarize Plato's mature systematic strategy for knowledge acquisition as it is ultimately laid out in the *Republic*. It begins with a method designed to bring home to us the need to pursue such a strategy to begin with. It begins by making us aware of our lack of knowledge. It continues with a method arduously learned through years of immersion in the mathematical disciplines. It culminates in the "vision" of the "unhypothetical first principle of everything" from which everything that is knowable can be derived. It has little use for perception, except as a provisional form of verification and falsification. And it presupposes a robust conception of knowledge or wisdom – the complete theory of everything which must be grasped before anything else can be genuinely known. Such a method contains traces of the Platonic half of the commonplace with which we began this chapter – the noetic vision as the culmination of the years of arduous training in the mathematical disciplines, prenatal access as the theory of recollection offered as part of the solution to *Meno*'s paradox, immortal, immutable, hyperborean universals as the "unhypothetical first principle of everything." But those traces are now seen in the context of some fairly sophisticated and rigorous theorizing concerning the nature of a systematic strategy of knowledge acquisition and the nature of philosophical inquiry itself. In the end, of course, the plausibility of such a systematic strategy of knowledge acquisition remains open to question, but its influence – for better or worse – in the history of thought does not.

References and Further Reading

Annas, Julia (1981). *An Introduction to Plato's Republic*. Oxford: Clarendon Press.

—— (1986). Plato, *Republic* V–VII. *Philosophy*, 20, 3–18.

Benson, Hugh H. (2000). *Socratic Wisdom: The Model of Knowledge in Plato's Early Dialogues*. New York: Oxford University Press.

—— (2003). The method of hypothesis in the *Meno. Proceedings of the Boston Area Colloquium in Ancient Philosophy*, 18, 95–126.

Burnyeat, M. F. (1987). Platonism and mathematics: A prelude to discussion. In A. Graeser (ed.), *Mathematics and Metaphysics in Aristotle*. Berne: Paul Haupt.

—— (2000). Plato on why mathematics is good for the soul. In Timothy Smiley (ed.), *Mathematics and Necessity*. Oxford: Clarendon Press.

Cooper, John (ed.) (1997). *Plato: Complete Works*. Indianapolis, IN: Hackett.

Gentzler, Jyl (ed.) (1998). *Method in Ancient Philosophy*. Oxford: Clarendon Press.

Gonzalez, Francisco J. (1998). *Dialectic and Dialogue: Plato's Practice of Philosophical Inquiry*. Evanston, IL: Northwestern University Press.

Irwin, Terence (1995). *Plato's Ethics*. Oxford: Oxford University Press.

Kahn, Charles H. (1996). *Plato and the Socratic Dialogue*. Cambridge: Cambridge University Press.

Menn, Stephen (2002). Plato and the method of analysis. *Phronesis*, 47, 193–223.

Mueller, Ian (1992). Mathematical method and philosophical truth. In Richard Kraut (ed.), *The Cambridge Companion to Plato*. Cambridge: Cambridge University Press.

Reeve, C. D. C. (1988). *Philosopher-Kings: The Argument of Plato's Republic*. Princeton, NJ: Princeton University Press.

Robinson, Richard (1953). *Plato's Earlier Dialectic*. Oxford: Clarendon Press.

Scott, Dominic (1995). *Recollection and Experience: Plato's Theory of Learning and Its Successors*. Cambridge: Cambridge University Press.

Scott, Gary Alan (2002). *Does Socrates Have a Method? Rethinking the Elenchus in Plato's Dialogues and Beyond*. University Park: Pennsylvania State University Press.

Vlastos, G. (1983). The Socratic elenchus. *Oxford Studies in Ancient Philosophy*, 1, 27–58.

—— (1991). *Socrates, Ironist and Moral Philosopher*. Ithaca, NY: Cornell University Press.

—— (1994). *Socratic Studies* (M. F. Burnyeat, ed.). Cambridge: Cambridge University Press.

6

Rationalism in Jewish Philosophy

STEVEN NADLER

The topic of rationalism in Jewish philosophy is a potentially enormous one, something that could not possibly be adequately treated in a single essay. After all, it has been argued (with good reason) that the defining feature of Jewish philosophy in general (and perhaps any religious philosophy) is the project of harmonizing faith and reason, or bringing together what one believes as a matter of religious tradition and what one believes as a rational knower. "One can say that the history of Jewish philosophy in the Middle Ages is the history of the effort of the Jews to reconcile philosophy (or a system of rationalist thought) and scripture" (Sirat 1985: 5). On this view, Jewish philosophy is essentially a rationalistic enterprise. This would make the study of rationalism in Jewish philosophy the study of Jewish philosophy itself.

And yet, even putting aside the mysticist tradition within Jewish philosophy – a strong and heterogeneous tradition that extends from Philo of Alexandria up through medieval and Renaissance kabbalah and on into the modern period – it is certainly possible to distinguish within Jewish philosophy several different attitudes toward rationalism, ranging from dogmatic devotion to outright hostility. One can find, between the ninth century, when medieval Jewish philosophy really begins, and the seventeenth century, when it reaches its logical culmination in the heretical thought of Spinoza, radical rationalists, moderate rationalists, and arch anti-rationalists. The twelfth-century philosopher and physician Maimonides, for one, had great confidence in the ability of the human intellect to provide a rationalization of revealed truths and to come to an understanding of the deepest metaphysical principles about God and nature, an intellectual condition that for him constituted human perfection and blessedness. Like the rationalist thinkers of the Kalam, or Muslim religious philosophy, by which he and many other early medieval Jewish philosophers were influenced, Maimonides believed that not only was there no conflict between what could be discovered by reason and what was received by revelation, but also that the former could be used to explain and justify the latter. Indeed, Bahya ibn Paquda, a generation older than Maimonides, insisted that Jews have a religious obligation to rationally understand the principles of their religion and even to prove their truth. By contrast, Hasdai Crescas, in the late fourteenth and early fifteenth centuries, attacked the pretensions of Jewish Aristotelianism and argued that philosophy had gone too far in trying to rationalize the principles of the faith and intellectualize the path to felicity; rather,

Crescas insisted, human perfection lay in the performance of the Torah's commandments and the love of God. Still other philosophers sought a safe middle ground and offered moderate alternatives to the radical rationalism of the Aristotelians and the hostility to philosophy of their opponents.

In this chapter, I will focus on radical rationalism within medieval Jewish philosophy. This represents the philosophically most interesting and influential variety of rationalism in the Jewish intellectual tradition. And within that radical rationalist camp I will concentrate on three seminal figures: Saadya ben Joseph, or Saadya Gaon (b. 882, Egypt; d. 942, Babylonia), Maimonides, or Moses ben Maimon (b. 1135, Cordova; d. 1204, Egypt), and, in Provence, Gersonides, or Levi ben Gershom (1288–1344). These philosophers basically define the arch-rationalist trend in Jewish philosophy, with the intellectualism of Maimonides and Gersonides laying the groundwork for the notoriously reductive rationalism of Baruch Spinoza (b. 1632, Amsterdam; d. 1677, The Hague).

To provide some definition for my discussion and bring out a number of important themes within Jewish rationalism, I have organized this chapter into three main topics. The first section considers the question of the interpretation of scripture. In the second section, I turn to the justification of the Law (that is, Jewish law, *halachah*). The subject of the third section is the relationship between reason, happiness, and divine providence. Finally, in the fourth section, I examine Spinoza's complex rationalist response to medieval Jewish rationalism.

The Interpretation of Scripture

Most religious philosophy in the Western tradition at some point addresses the question of the reconciliation of religious or revealed truth and philosophical or rational truth. The need for a reconciliation, or at least for an explanation of the lack thereof, arises when certain claims made by a revealed source (for example, a prophetic writing) appear, at least prima facie, to be inconsistent with principles that natural reason regards as certain. For example, Christian faith speaks of an individual being both one person and three persons, while reason insists that something cannot be both one and three. And the Bible proclaims that the world was created, while philosophy (at least of the Aristotelian variety, which dominated Latin, Arabic, and Hebrew thought in the twelfth through fourteenth centuries) purports to demonstrate that the world is eternal. What is one to do in the face of such conflict?

One can, of course, conclude that a reconciliation is not, in fact, possible. On this view, it is conceded that truths of faith and truths of reason will often be inconsistent with each other and incapable of being brought into harmony, either because they speak of different things or because they speak about the same things but in different ways. This is the doctrine of double-truth. Rationalists, on the other hand, believe that truth can never conflict with truth. They have full confidence that what reason proclaims to be true will, despite what may be first appearances, not conflict with, and perhaps ultimately harmonize with, the propositions of revelation. This is the doctrine of single-truth. And the reconciliation will come not because reason submits to revelation and concedes that there are certain things which it cannot understand (the skeptical path), but rather because revelation and reason are both legitimate, authoritative, and complementary means of discovering what is true. For the radical rationalist, in fact, revealed truths are in principle rational truths, and reason offers the key to a true understanding of their content, although in many cases it may take a little work to see that this is the case.

Another way to put this is to say that the defining feature of rationalism in religious philosophy is the idea that reason is the touchstone of faith. Now there is a fairly weak way of understanding this claim. It could mean that if a proposition is contrary to reason, then it cannot be something that ought to be accepted even on faith. This minimal position claims that the articles of faith will never conflict with or be contrary to what is rational – that is, they will never be logically inconsistent with a demonstrated truth – but does not go so far as to insist that revealed truths can either be rationally supported or discovered by reason alone. For example, it might be held that while the creation of the world by God cannot be demonstrated with rational argument, it is not an irrational thing to believe since its contrary, the eternity of the world, has not been conclusively proven.

But radical rationalism goes beyond this and argues that what is revealed and is to be accepted as a religious truth or as the word of God is necessarily something that is rational to believe. Radical rationalists adopt one of two more robust positions. First, they may believe that while revelation is indeed necessary for the *discovery* of certain truths, all truths so discovered can be rationally *justified*. Thus, scripture says that God created the world, and some philosophers believe that this can also be confirmed (to some degree) by reason. Second, there is the even stronger position that, while the religious truths in question have as a matter of fact been discovered by revelation, they could just as well have been discovered independently by reason alone, in which they find their justification. For example, even if God through scripture had not proclaimed that certain laws are binding upon us, we would have come to discover those laws by ourselves.

The rationalist intuition behind all three of these positions gave rise within Jewish philosophy to a distinctive approach to the interpretation of scripture. The default position in almost all Jewish philosophy is to interpret the words of the Bible literally. However, when the Bible asserts things that, if taken literally, contradict reason, then according to the rationalists the statement should be read figuratively or metaphorically. Although, as the Talmud says, "the Torah speaks in the language of human beings" (*Babylonian Talmud*, Yebamot 71a), the word of God is always reasonable. Thus, some passages in scripture use highly concrete and even anthropomorphic imagery that, while well suited for conveying their messages, seem to conflict with some foundational principles established by reason. A literal reading of such passages would lead one to beliefs that, according to reason, are unacceptable. For example, scripture speaks of the hand of God, or of God sitting on a throne. But it can be demonstrated rationally that God is an incorporeal being and thus does not have a body. Therefore, such passages must be read figuratively, as speaking "in human terms" of God's governance or power.

This theory of the interpretation of scripture is found in a particularly clear form in some early Jewish thinkers in the Karaite tradition. Thus, Jacob al-Kirkisani (fl. ca. 930–40 in Mesopotamia), in his *Book of Lights*, insists:

102

Scripture as a whole is to be interpreted literally, except where literal interpretation may involve something objectionable or imply a contradiction . . . Thus we are compelled to say that the verse, "And they saw the God of Israel . . ." (Exodus 24: 10), must not be understood literally, and does not signify seeing with one's eyes, since it is contrary to reason to assume that the Creator may be perceived by man's senses. (Nemoy 1932: 60)

It is clear that the criterion for what is "objectionable" is reason itself. Similarly, Japheth ben Ali ha-Levi (fl. second half of the tenth century) writes:

We are not justified in setting aside the literal meaning of the word of God or of His prophets except where that literal meaning is hindered or precluded as being contradicted by reason or by a clear idea. (Sirat 1985: 47)

This approach to the interpretation of scripture finds perhaps its earliest systematic expression not in a Karaite text, however, but in *The Book of Beliefs and Opinions*, by Saadya ben Joseph, the *gaon* or head of the rabbinical academy in Sura. Saadya first approaches the issue when he asks how one is to know whether a person is a true prophet and what he proclaims is indeed divine prophecy. In the first place, he answers, prophetic messages are accompanied by "certain signs and wondrous miracles." Just as important, however, is the fact that *what* is communicated by the prophetic message is rational, acceptable to, and confirmed by reason:

The basis of our belief in the mission of Moses is not solely the miracles and marvels that he performed. The reason for our believing in him, and in every other prophet, is rather the fact that he first called upon us to do what is proper. Then, when we had heard his appeal and we saw that it was proper, we demanded from him miracles in support of it and, when he performed them, we believed in him. If, however, we had felt that the appeal that he made at the beginning was not proper, we would not have demanded any miracles from him, because miracles are of no account in supporting the unacceptable. (Saadya 1948: 163; 1969: 113)

The criterion for what is "proper" and "acceptable" is what is rational. Reason, in fact, has absolute authority here, and cannot be overruled even by the performance of a miracle.

The same procedure is to be followed in the case of every claimant of prophecy. If he says to us, "My Lord commands you to fast today," we ask him for a sign in support of his mission, and when he shows it to us, we accept it and fast. If, however, he were to say to us, "My Lord commands you to commit adultery and steal," or "He informs you that He is about to bring a flood of water upon the world," or "He makes it known to you that He created heaven and earth thoughtlessly while He was asleep," we would not ask him for any sign, since what he called upon us to do is not sanctioned by either reason or tradition. (Saadya 1948: 164; 1969: 114)

While Saadya's mention of "tradition" in this passage seems to offer a second, non-rational criterion, it is clear from his discussion of scripture that tradition is itself informed by reason.

103

Saadya insists that every statement found in the Bible is to be understood in its literal sense unless one of four conditions obtain. First, a literal reading might contradict what is clearly known from sense experience. Thus, Eve could not literally have been "the mother of all living beings," since it is obvious that oxen and lions are not the offspring of a woman. Second, sometimes a literal reading is "rendered impossible" by another, non-negotiable text elsewhere in scripture that is explicitly inconsistent with it. Third, if rabbinic tradition has attached a certain interpretation to the text in question, then it should be interpreted according to that tradition and not literally. Although scripture says "Forty stripes he may give him" (Deuteronomy 25:3), the rabbis have laid it down that only 39 stripes are to be administered, and thus the biblical text represents just a rough way of saying that there should be 39 stripes. Fourth, and most important for our purposes, a figurative reading of scripture is justified, even required, if a literal reading is contrary to something that is known for certain by reason. Saadya notes that

> the literal sense may be negated by reason, such as that of the statement: "For the Lord thy God is a devouring fire, a jealous God" (Deuteronomy 4:24). Now fire is something created and defective, for it is subject to extinction. Hence it is logically inadmissible that God resemble it. We must, therefore, impute to this statement the meaning that God's punishment is like a consuming fire. (Saadya 1948: 266; 1969: 157)

When we turn to Maimonides, arguably the greatest of all Jewish philosophers, we find an equally forthright embrace of this hermeneutic principle. In the *Guide of the Perplexed*, Maimonides devotes a good deal of his discussion to refuting a materialist or corporeal conception of God and to reinterpreting the anthropomorphic language in scripture on which it tends to be grounded. The Bible's talk of God's "head," "hands," "face," and other bodily elements is all equivocal, and should not be read literally. This is because, as we know from reason, God cannot possibly have a body. The principle "God is one" is the most important principle in all of Judaism. And it can be rationally demonstrated that a being that is essentially one cannot be corporeal. "There is no profession of unity unless the doctrine of God's corporeality is denied. For a body cannot be one, but is composed of matter and form, which by definition are two; it is also divisible, subject to partition" (Maimonides 1963: 81). Thus, a reading of a scriptural passage that involves attributing corporeal parts to God runs up against a demonstrated truth and, for that reason, must be rejected. Any mention of God's "eye" is to be read as referring to his watchfulness, his providence, or his intellectual apprehension; while talk of God's "heart" is to be understood as referring to his thought or his opinion.

More generally, whenever a literal reading of a word or passage in the Bible would carry a meaning that is inconsistent with a rationally demonstrated truth, the word or passage must be read figuratively or metaphorically. On the other hand, when a literal reading does not contradict any demonstrated truth, it should be adopted. Thus, Maimonides insists that although some philosophers believe that the world is eternal and necessary, no one – and, he insists, certainly not Aristotle – has yet offered a conclusive proof of this. Therefore, there is no justification for reading the Bible's account of creation figuratively.

That the deity is not a body has been demonstrated; from this it follows necessarily that everything that in its external meaning disagrees with this demonstration must be interpreted figuratively . . . However, the eternity of the world has not been demonstrated. Consequently in this case the texts ought not to be rejected and figuratively interpreted in order to make prevail an opinion whose contrary can be made to prevail by means of various sorts of arguments. (Maimonides 1963: 328)

Maimonides is committed to this principle of interpretation because he believes that prophecy, biblical or otherwise, is essentially the communication of scientific, metaphysical, and moral truths in concrete and imaginative form. The prophet is like the philosopher in that the content of what he proclaims comes to him as an "intellectual overflow" or emanation from the higher intellects of the cosmos and, ultimately, from God. Thus, there is a sense in which prophetic utterances are of the same nature and have the same epistemological stature as philosophical or rational statements. The prophet, like the philosopher, has achieved perfection in his speculative or rational faculties (the difference between the two is that the prophet has also achieved perfection in his imaginative faculty). Thus, what the prophet communicates is, in its substance, rational knowledge, and reason will therefore be the key to interpreting prophetic writings.

The same radical rationalism, both in theory and in practice, appears in Gersonides' philosophical writings and Bible commentaries. The purpose of prophecy is to convey truth, and so what better tool for interpreting scripture than reason? It is evident, he says (explicitly citing Maimonides as his mentor on this point), that

if reason causes us to affirm doctrines that are incompatible with the literal sense of scripture, we are not prohibited by the Torah to pronounce the truth on these matters, for reason is not incompatible with the true understanding of the Torah. The Torah is not a law that forces us to believe false ideas; rather, it leads us to the truth to the extent that it is possible. (Gersonides 1984: 98)

Gersonides insists that we must believe what reason has determined to be true. "If the literal sense of the Torah differs from reason, it is necessary to interpret those passages in accordance with the demands of reason" (Gersonides 1984: 98).

It must be emphasized that what unites these rationalist thinkers is not merely the idea that the words of scripture are open to allegorical readings. After all, the mystically inclined Philo was devoted to the allegorical interpretation of biblical texts. Rather, it is the justification they offer for when a figurative reading is called for, as well as the source of their confidence in that justification, that defines rationalism. Behind that confidence lies a simple argument that one can find, explicitly or tacitly, among radical rationalists of many religious persuasions: scripture is divine revelation. God is supremely perfect, all-knowing, and necessarily veracious. Therefore, what God puts forth in revelation must be true knowledge. Thus, the message conveyed by scripture must also be the truth. It is an argument about which Spinoza will have much to say.

Reason and the Law

There has always been, from the beginning of the Talmudic period, a kind of semi-rationalism at the heart of Jewish law. Traditionally, rabbinic Judaism recognizes among the *mitzvot*, or commandments, of the Torah a distinction between *mishpatim*, judgments or ordinances, and *huqqim*, ritual laws or edicts (see, for example, *Babylonian Talmud*, Yoma 67b). *Mishpatim* are divine commandments for which reasons independent of divine authority can be given; among these are ranked the commandments not to kill, not to commit adultery, and not to steal. The evident rationality of such rules provides them with a kind of additional normativity. *Huqqim*, on the other hand, are commanded for no reason other than God's will, and are to be obeyed solely on the basis of divine authority; examples of *huqqim* are the commandments not to eat certain foods and not to wear certain kinds of garments, as well as a wide variety of ceremonial laws.

Radical rationalism takes the Talmudic doctrine of *ta'amei ha-mitzvot*, or providing reasons for the commandments, to an extreme degree and insists that *all* of the commandments are reasonable, at least in their generalities if not also in their specifics. Moreover, the reasonableness of any commandment is not a matter of citing its divine origin or tracing its ancestry back to an authoritative textual source, as the issue is sometimes framed among the sages of the Talmud, but rather lies in some accessible standard (e.g., personal wellbeing, social utility) that provides an intellectually satisfying justification for it.

Another way to put this point is to consider the age-old question, most famously raised in Plato's dialogue *Euthyphro*, whether something is good because God loves it or God loves it because it is good (for Euthyphro, the question is whether something is pious because the gods love it, or the gods love it because it is pious). The rationalist, when speaking of the laws God has laid down, will respond that the law is chosen by God *because* it is just and useful and conforms to wisdom.

Once again, Saadya sets the standard for this aspect of Jewish rationalism. He begins by distinguishing between two classes of law. The first class comprises those laws that are discoverable by reason alone, although God has commanded them; the second class are those laws that are discovered only by divine revelation.

Included in the first class, which Saadya calls the "rational laws," are the most important moral commandments that govern our direct behavior toward God and toward other human beings. Reason or speculation confirms as necessary the following principles: (a) that a benefactor should be respected by having his kindness returned or by being thanked; (b) that a wise person (and even more so the Creator) should not allow himself to be vilified and treated with contempt; (c) that human beings should be forbidden from trespassing upon one another's rights by aggression; and (d) a wise person should be permitted to employ a worker and pay him wages (Saadya 1948: 138–9; 1969: 95–6). A number of the Torah's commandments fall under one or another of these general ethical principles "dictated by reason." Thus, the commandment to know God and serve him with a sincere heart is an instantiation of the first principle; the commandment not to take God's name in vain is an example of the second; the prohibitions against stealing and dealing falsely with others represent applications of the third; and so on. While these are, of course, things that God commands us to do or not to do, Saadya insists that God has also "implanted approval of them in our reason." In a somewhat Kantian vein, Saadya notes:

> Wisdom imposes the prohibition of theft; for if it were permitted some people would rely
> on their ability to steal some other people's property, and would not do any productive

work nor amass wealth. But if everyone relied on this sort of subsistence, theft itself would
be rendered impossible by the abolition of property since nothing at all would be found to
steal. (Saadya 1948: 141–2; 1969: 98–9)

The laws of the second class ("the revelational laws") concern "matters regarding
which reason passes no judgment in the way either of approval or disapproval so far as
their essence is concerned . . . The second class of laws concerns such matters as are of
a neutral character from the point of view of reason." Strictly speaking, then, they are
distinct from the rational laws. Among the "acts which from the standpoint of reason
are optional" are those related to the consecration of days and seasons, the cleanliness
and uncleanliness of foods and materials, and ritual purity. And yet, Saadya insists,
even these commandments have a reason and purpose. "Our Lord has given us an
abundance of such commandments and prohibitions in order to increase our reward
and happiness through them." While the revelational laws, especially in their specific
and detailed individuality, may not have any immediate rational justification by way
of the principles outlined above – why, for example, are Jews supposed to refrain from
certain foods but not others? – nonetheless, they too, like the rational laws, have a
kind of utility. "Thus the second [class of laws] is joined to the first class . . . one cannot
fail, upon closer examination, to find in them some slender moral benefits as well as a
certain slight justification from the point of view of reason, just as those belonging to
the first class have important uses and great justification from the point of view of
reason" (Saadya 1948: 141; 1969: 98). Speaking of the ceremonial and other non-
moral laws – distinguishing the Sabbath from the other days of the week, the selection
of certain individuals to be leaders and prophets, the avoidance of sexual intercourse
with certain people – Saadya insists that while "the great motive for the observance of
these principles and the laws derived and branching out from them is, of course, the
command of our Lord and the promotion of our happiness resulting from it . . . I find
for most of them also some minor and partial motives of a useful character" (Saadya
1948: 143; 1969: 100). Thus, the sanctification of the Sabbath day and the prohibi-
tion against work on it affords us the important opportunity to rest and relax and take
time for study.

All of the commandments, therefore, are ultimately rational, in either a strong or
a weak sense. While the normative force of the second class of laws derives from
God's authority rather than the approval of reason, they too are not without their
utilitarian reasonableness. There is apparently no law that God commands arbitrarily
and capriciously.

But why, then, is revelation even necessary? In the case of the second class of laws,
revelation is absolutely necessary for their discovery. Reason alone could never have
come up with these commandments and prohibitions. But, Saadya insists, revelation
is required also for the first class of laws, the rational laws. Even though reason by
itself might discover the general principles they represent – such as the need to refrain
from theft or adultery – revelation is needed to specify the particular manner in which
the commandments are to be carried out. "Their practice cannot be complete unless
the prophets show us how to perform them" (Saadya 1948: 145; 1969: 103). Thus,
while reason commands us to respect God and show gratitude toward him, it does not,
by itself, tell us in what manner and at what times we are to do so. And while reason

107

disapproves of adultery, it does not provide any guidance as to how a man and a woman become legally united as husband and wife.

Moreover, revelation serves an important purpose even with respect to the general features of the rational commandments. If left to its own devices, reason would probably have discovered these rules by itself, but it might have taken a long time; in some cases, in fact – either because of distraction, incapacity, laziness, or other impediments – they might never have been discovered at all. And these moral commandments and prohibitions are much too important for individual and social wellbeing to have their implementation delayed or left to chance.

> Inasmuch as all matters of religious belief, as imparted to us by our Master, can be attained by means of research and correct speculation, what was the reason that prompted [divine] wisdom to transmit them to us by way of prophecy and support them by means of visible proofs and miracles rather than intellectual demonstrations? . . . We say, then, that the All-Wise knew that the conclusions reached by means of the art of speculation could be attained only in the course of a certain measure of time. If, therefore, He had referred us for our acquaintance with His religion to that art alone, we would have remained without religious guidance whatever for a while, until the process of reasoning was completed by us so that we could make use of its conclusions.

Thanks to revelation, however, "even if it should take a long time for one of us who indulges in speculation to complete his speculation, he is without worry" (Saadya 1948: 31–2; 1969: 45–6).

Maimonides is not content to speak in such general terms about the purposes of the Law. He devotes 25 chapters of the *Guide* to a closely argued and detailed examination of the rationality and utility of the laws of the Torah. Just as his monumental *Mishneh Torah* offers a categorization and distilled summary of the rabbinic code, simplified and without all the disputes and extraneous material found in the Talmud, so these sections of the *Guide* present an equally systematic series of rationalist justifications of the various classes of law.

Maimonides insists that "all the Laws have a cause" and "conform to wisdom"; that is, they all serve a useful purpose that reason can apprehend. This is because the Law has been instituted by God, who is governed by goodness and wisdom in all that he does and who is incapable of doing anything that is "vain, futile, or frivolous," that is, incapable of acting for the sake of no end.

> Any particular commandment or prohibition has a useful end. In the case of some of them, it is clear to us in what way they are useful – as in the case of the prohibition of killing and stealing. In the case of others, their utility is not clear – as in the case of the interdiction of the first products [of trees] and of [sowing] the vineyard with diverse seeds. Those commandments whose utility is clear to the multitude are called *mishpatim* [judgments], and those whose utility is not clear to the multitude are called *huqqim* [statutes]. (Maimonides 1963: 507)

Notice that what distinguishes the *huqqim* from the *mishpatim* is not the lack of any reasons, but rather the accessibility of such reasons to the multitude.

Like Saadya, Maimonides says that the reasonableness of any law is most easily seen in its generality. But, he insists, even the particularities of the laws often have a clear utility. Should one ask, for example, why animals should be killed in one way rather than another – such as cutting the throat in a certain manner – the answer would be that this insures a quicker and more humane death. He concedes, however, that in the case of the particular details of many laws, a cause or a reason cannot be found. But even this lack of a cause is not without its own reason: "No cause will ever be found for the fact that one particular sacrifice consists in a lamb and another in a ram . . . Know that wisdom rendered it necessary that there should be particulars for which no cause can be found" (Maimonides 1963: 509).

In general, for Maimonides, the Law serves two main purposes. First, it fosters the wellbeing of the body. Through its wealth of moral, communal, and ceremonial regulations – "Do not steal," "Do not kill," "Do not commit adultery," etc. – the commandments seek to abolish "reciprocal wrongdoing" and establish a stable and supportive domestic, social, and political environment, a necessary condition for individual flourishing.

> Man has two perfections: a first perfection, which is the perfection of the body, and an ultimate perfection, which is the perfection of the soul. The first perfection consists in being healthy and in the very best bodily state, and this is only possible through his finding the things necessary for him whenever he seeks them. These are his food and all the other things needed for the governance of his body, such as a shelter, bathing, and so forth. (Maimonides 1963: 511)

Moreover, following these ethical commandments through habitual practice leads an individual to acquire excellence of character, the most important step on the way to ultimate perfection.

Second, the Law fosters the welfare of the soul. This it accomplishes by communicating true beliefs, either directly ("God is one," "God rewards the good and punishes the wicked," "God is the creator and ought to be worshiped and loved and feared") or through parables. The individual who, through a study of the "speculative opinions" embodied in the Law, acquires an understanding of natural science and metaphysical truths – and, above all, a knowledge of God – has become truly rational *in actu*. He has developed his intellect to the highest degree and has thereby perfected himself. This is the supreme aim of the Law, and its ultimate reason.

> Every commandment from among these six hundred and thirteen commandments exists either with a view to communicating a correct opinion, or to putting an end to an unhealthy opinion, or to communicating a rule of justice, or to warding off an injustice, or to endowing men with a noble moral quality, or to warning them against an evil moral quality. Thus all [the commandments] are bound up with three things: opinions, moral qualities, and political civic actions . . . Therefore we have limited ourselves here in giving reasons for every law to these three classes. (Maimonides 1963: 524)

The Law, for Maimonides no less than for Saadya, is not a non-rational body of *mitzvot* that find their only validation in the inscrutable will of God. There is no commandment, Maimonides insists, that cannot find its approval and even demonstration in reason. The Law is first received through revelation and tradition. But this does not abrogate the obligation to seek the "verification" of the Law in a rational science and "correct speculation" on its foundations. "Man is first required to obtain knowledge of the Torah, then to obtain wisdom . . . The opinions in question should first be known as being received through tradition; then they should be demonstrated" (Maimonides 1963: 633–4).

Reason and Happiness

In the domain of moral philosophy, and particularly with regard to the question of individual perfection, happiness, and wellbeing, rationalism is distinguished by two theses. First, there is the claim that the supreme human condition consists in the perfecting of the rational faculty through the attainment of intellectual knowledge. Second, rationalists argue that this perfection of reason is at least a necessary condition for human happiness (*eudaimonia*); one cannot possibly enjoy true felicity unless one has achieved the proper cognitive state. Some even argue that rational perfection is also a sufficient condition for happiness, and that all one need do to secure a well-being that is immune to the onslaughts of the external world and the slings and arrows of outrageous fortune is to refine the intellect in the appropriate manner; a few go so far as to equate happiness with rational perfection.

Both of these general theses are found in Jewish rationalism. What is particularly striking is the way in which medieval Jewish rationalists identify the securing of well-being through reason as the working of divine providence. Eschewing the anthropomorphic picture of an intentional agent-like God watching over certain individuals, taking special care for them and rewarding them for their virtue, Maimonides and Gersonides explain providence as the protection that naturally (albeit through God's ordination) comes to one who has perfected his intellect through the pursuit of rational knowledge.

Maimonides distinguishes between four different kinds of human perfection. Material perfection, the lowest species, consists in acquiring external goods (wealth, possessions, honors, etc.). The perfection thereby acquired is only relational (and transitory), and does not affect the individual's nature. Then there is the physical perfection of a person's body and temperament, an intrinsic condition that, while valuable, is common to all species of animals. Moral perfection is the attainment of excellence in ethical habits, or the acquisition of the virtues and proper character. Yet even these, Maimonides insists, are merely of instrumental value, both because they are meant only to govern our relations with others and because they are worthwhile as a means towards the highest excellence of the human being: the perfection of reason.

> The fourth species is the true human perfection; it consists in the acquisition of the rational virtues – I refer to the conception of intelligibles, which teach true opinions concerning the divine things. This is in true reality the ultimate end; this is what gives the individual true perfection, a perfection belonging to him alone; and it gives him permanent perdurance; through it man is man. (Maimonides 1963: 635)

Knowledge is the supreme good, the highest purpose of the Law, and the bond between human beings and God. Through the acquisition of true speculative opinions about the cosmos and about God – what Maimonides calls "natural science" and "divine science" – a human being attains his ultimate perfection. This is wisdom (*hokhmah*), and it is accompanied by joy (in its possession) and love (of its object). "Love is proportionate to apprehension," Maimonides insists, and he makes it clear that he is always referring to abstract intellectual apprehension of necessary truths, not sensory or imaginative perception.

Moreover, the person who reaches this condition is, *ipso facto*, benefiting from divine providence. The individual who lacks wisdom ("the wicked and imperfect person") is, because of his ignorance, subject to the vicissitudes of nature and abandoned to chance; his wellbeing is at the mercy of the elements, of which he has no understanding and over which he has no control. The perfected individual, on the other hand, enjoys – through his wisdom itself, through his knowledge of nature and God – a kind of protection from nature's forces. He can successfully navigate the obstacles to wellbeing that nature constantly puts in his way.

> If a man's thought is free from distraction, if he apprehends Him, may He be exalted, in the right way and rejoices in what he apprehends, that individual can never be afflicted with evil of any kind . . . When, however, he abandons Him, may He be exalted, and is thus separated from God and God separated from him, he becomes in consequence of this a target for every evil that may happen to befall him. For the thing that necessarily brings about providence and deliverance from the sea of chance consists in that intellectual overflow . . . the reason for a human individual's being abandoned to chance so that he is permitted to be devoured like the beasts is his being separated from God. (Maimonides 1963: 625–6)

An even more explicit exposition of the close relationship between rational perfection, *eudaimonia*, and divine providence is provided by Gersonides in his philosophical magnum opus, *The Wars of the Lord*.

Gersonides is concerned with two species of providence. First, there is what he calls "special" or "individual" providence (*hashgachah perati*). This is the protection that comes only to a certain class of human beings, namely, those who, through the use of their intellects, achieve a union with the Active or Agent Intellect – the separate intellect of the sublunar realm that embodies a full knowledge of the world it rules, a kind of quasi-divine governing spirit – and a consequent insight into the ways of nature. Second, there is a general providence (*hashgachah kelali*) that extends across all of nature and, thereby, to all human beings. Let us look at these more closely in turn.

The source of evil, Gersonides says, is never God. Nor does it come from the (immaterial) forms of things. Rather, evil has its origins either in matter or in chance. By "matter" he means the mixture of elements in material nature (including human bodies) and the human choices that may be influenced by this. By "chance" Gersonides understands the unfortunate effects upon human beings of occurrences of nature ("land upheavals, earthquakes, fires from the heavens, and so forth"). These occurrences are as causally ordered as anything else in the sublunar realm: they are "the evils that befall man from the patterns determined by the arrangements of the heavenly bodies." What is "accidental" and a matter of "chance" is the *evilness* of their results relative to human beings and their ends; it is an evil that is unforeseen and unintended by the natural causes of such things. As Gersonides notes, it is the "*evil* resulting from these events [for human beings] that is due to chance" (Gersonides 1987: 168–9).

111

Now nature has provided in a general way for all creatures through the endow-
ments of the species. Each type of animal has been given the appropriate means
necessary for its survival. And the more noble the creature, the greater its capacities
for self-preservation.

> Induction shows that the Agent Intellect provides for existing things in giving them either
> bodily organs or instinctual powers, by virtue of which the possessors of these faculties
> can preserve their individual existence and ward off or avoid harm. For example, it
> endows some animals with horns, cloven hooves, or beaks to keep them from harm or to
> enable predatory animals to obtain prey. In some animals the Agent Intellect bestows
> only instinctual desires or skills. An example of an instinctual desire is the natural instinct
> of a lamb to run away from a wolf upon seeing it, even though it does not know that the
> wolf will harm it, and [indeed] it has not even seen a wolf previously. Similarly, many
> birds flee from predatory birds, although they have never seen them previously . . . This
> kind of providence is exhibited in man in a much more perfect form. For man is endowed
> with a practical intellect from which many kinds of useful arts are derived for his preser-
> vation. He is also given an intellect from which are derived the tendencies to flee from
> harmful things and to obtain advantageous things. (Gersonides 1987: 166–7)

This "general providence" derives, like all the determined aspects of nature, from
the ordinary causal course of nature as this is driven by celestial bodies and through
the Agent Intellect. All individual human beings are thus endowed by nature with the
faculties and instincts that they need for survival in a world governed by laws which
themselves derive from the same celestial influences. The heavenly spheres provide us
with desires, thoughts, and intentions for action that are to our benefit. The general
celestial providence thus takes care of all individuals *qua* members of the human species, but not *qua* particulars. It extends to all humans as humans in their interactions
both with material nature and with each other, without taking any account of their
particularities, especially their moral differences, their virtues and vices. Of course,
although this general ordering of nature aims for the best, and generally results in
good, sometimes it brings about evil. "Sometimes there necessarily results from these
patterns some accidental misfortunes." Although we have, by general providence, the
wherewithal to deal for the most part with what fortune brings our way, we are not,
by nature alone, prepared to deal with all the threats to our wellbeing. Nature is still a
risky environment, full of potential harm and obstacles to our flourishing.

This is where special providence comes in. Although God has not ordered the patterns (*ha-siddurim*) of the heavens such that no evil is to occur, nonetheless "he has
given man an instrument whereby these evils can be avoided – reason [*ha-sekhel*]"
(Gersonides 1987: 184). Thus, in addition to the astral-based (general) providence,
there is also an intellect-based providence available to human beings, through the
achievement of which they can escape (or at least limit) the occasional unfortunate
effects of general providence.

Because the Agent Intellect is an intelligent cause, it possesses full knowledge – the
"maker's knowledge" – of the order it imposes on the world.

> Since the agent responsible for the [existence] of all beings in the sublunar world must
> possess the knowledge of the order [obtaining in this world] – just as the craftsman must

have an idea of the order obtaining among the things he is to create – and since . . . this agent is the Agent Intellect . . . it follows that the Agent Intellect possesses the knowledge of the order obtaining in the sublunary world. (Gersonides 1984: 151)

By generating the natural sublunar forms, the Agent Intellect is the cause of substances; and because it emanates from even higher intellects and ultimately from God, it knows fully the plan it is thereby carrying out.

The separate agent responsible for all these things [substances] should know the law, order and rightness inherent in these sublunar phenomena, since these things acquire their very existence from the intelligible order of them in the soul of this separate agent. (Gersonides 1987: 135)

The Agent Intellect contains the concepts of all beings, organized comprehensively and systematically, such that the totality of what the Agent Intellect knows constitutes an exhaustive body of science. Its knowledge is thus a kind of complete and archetypal blueprint for the world it governs. "The Agent Intellect . . . possesses [the knowledge] of the plan and order [of the terrestrial domain]." Gersonides, in fact, calls it "the rational order of the terrestrial world," although its science also includes knowledge of all celestial phenomena. It is an eternal and incorruptible order, in contrast to the changing, corruptible, and temporal procession of things and events in the world that instantiates and dynamically exemplifies it. This knowledge in the Agent Intellect exists in "a perfect and unified manner" (Gersonides 1984: 13).

Through the proper use of his intellect, an individual human being perfects himself and becomes "closer" to the Agent Intellect, discerns that Intellect's "maker's knowledge" of the essences of things and of the patterns and laws of nature, and thereby attains a higher degree of "protection" from nature's vicissitudes. The person enjoying special providence is a person who, through the actualization of his intellect and the acquisition of higher knowledge, is better equipped to obtain what is good and avoid any evils impending from the ordinary course of nature. As the human mind comes to an understanding of the true order of the world, its knowledge grows, in fact, to mirror (as much as possible for human beings) the knowledge that is in the Agent Intellect itself. One thereby becomes "enlightened." Unlike the general run of people, "who are not within the scope of divine providence except in a general way as members of the human species," this person knows how nature operates; he can predict what, according to nature's laws, the future will bring and generally be able to put nature's ways to his own use.

This kind of "communication" between the Agent Intellect (and ultimately God, from whom its knowledge derives) and a particular human being does not require any knowledge of or action upon particulars *as* particulars on God's or the Agent Intellect's part. The knowledge acquired by the person who has developed his intellect is neither itself particular nor aimed at anyone in particular. It is general information – perhaps best captured by a system of conditional propositions (if x occurs, then y occurs) – that is there for anyone to pursue and tap into. Still, as a matter of fact, only the truly righteous – those who are guided by reason – will attain it.

> Our theory is compatible with the admission that God (may he be blessed) does not know particulars as particulars. For the kind of providence that guides the righteous by means of the communication given them concerning the benefits or evils that are to befall them can occur even though the giver of this communication does not know the particular individual receiving this communication, and despite the fact that the giver of this communication does not know the particular events, concerning which this communication is given, as particulars. (Gersonides 1987: 180)

If virtue is the pursuit of intellectual perfection – as Gersonides believes – then this special providence is the natural product and reward of virtue. The truly righteous person will, for the most part and just *because* of his intellectual achievements, obtain the goods that this world has to offer and avoid its evils. Sinners, on the other hand, will in general be punished – not directly, through some particular directive from God (since God cannot be the cause of evil, nor can he know particulars *as* particulars), but by being left out in the cold. Those who do not pursue virtue, who do not perfect their intellects, will be subject to the vicissitudes of nature.

> When the Torah warns men of evil because of their great sins, it states clearly that this evil will be that God will not look upon them and that He will abandon them to the contingencies of time . . . The punishment of sinners consists in God's hiding and indifference. God leaves them to the contingencies of time, and whatever happens to them is determined by the patterns of the heavenly bodies. Nor does God save them from the evil that is to befall them. (Gersonides 1987: 173)

> [Sinners] are left and abandoned to those accidents that are ordered by the heavenly bodies and . . . are not protected by God from the evils that are to befall them, for they are not at the level of perfection such that this kind of divine providence could extend to them. (Gersonides 1987: 181)

Without the knowledge possessed by the virtuous, sinners cannot properly navigate their way through nature and protect themselves accordingly.

Gersonides concedes that in this life no one, not even the most virtuous, can completely escape nature's inconveniences. The perfection of reason affords the righteous a relatively high degree of wellbeing in this world, but true happiness is attained only in the world to come, the afterlife wherein the intellect enjoys pure spiritual joy unencumbered by the inconveniences of the body.

The Spinozistic Denouement

Spinoza stands in a fascinatingly complex relationship to the Jewish rationalist tradition that precedes him. On the one hand, he was that tradition's most systematic critic, especially on the issue of the interpretation of scripture. On the other hand, there can be no question that, despite the many other influences on Spinoza's thought – Cartesian, Stoic, and otherwise – his moral philosophy stands as the apex of the rationalist/eudaimonist trend best represented in Jewish philosophy by Maimonides and Gersonides.

In the *Theological-Political Treatise*, Spinoza rejects the idea that the Bible was literally authored by God; it was, rather, the work of human beings in very concrete historical circumstances. Thus, he concludes, scripture, like any work of human literature, must be interpreted on its own terms and not by reference to any absolute standards outside the text. In particular, the type of exegesis proposed by Saadya and Maimonides is, for Spinoza, illegitimate insofar as it goes beyond scripture itself – to an external canon of rationality or truth – in order to interpret scripture. "The question as to whether Moses did or did not believe that God is fire must in no wise be decided by the rationality or irrationality of the belief, but solely from other pronouncements of Moses" (Spinoza 2001: 89). There must, in other words, be a distinction between the meaning of scripture, which is what one is after when interpreting any text, and what is philosophically or historically true.

> The point at issue is merely the meaning of the texts, not their truth. I would go further: in seeking the meaning of scripture we should take every precaution against the undue influence, not only of our own prejudices, but of our faculty of reason insofar as that is based on the principles of natural cognition. In order to avoid confusion between true meaning and truth of fact, the former must be sought simply from linguistic usage, or from a process of reasoning that looks to no other basis than scripture. (Spinoza 2001: 88–9)

Much of what scripture relates is not, in fact, true, no more so than what is related by any other work of human literature. And if what scripture states does happen to be true, it is not, *pace* Maimonides, *necessarily* the case that what it states is true. In one of his typically bold statements, Spinoza insists that "to understand scripture and the mind of the prophets is by no means the same thing as to understand the mind of God, that is, to understand truth itself" (Spinoza 2001: 149). Scripture is not by its nature a source of knowledge, least of all true knowledge about God, the heavens, or even human nature (although it *is* a source of knowledge about what its writers believed on these matters). It is not, in other words, philosophy or science, and therefore the principles of reason, the touchstone of truth, must not serve as our guide in interpreting scripture. The moral message of scripture – that one should love God above all, and one's neighbor as oneself – does, indeed, agree with reason in the sense that our rational faculties approve of it. But *that* scripture teaches such a message can be discovered only through the "historical" method.

When, then, is a figurative or metaphorical reading of a passage from scripture called for, if not when that passage conflicts with rationally demonstrated truth? Only when a literal reading is in clear violation of "the basic principles derived from the study of scripture," that is, only when a literal reading stands in the way of clarifying the intentions or beliefs of the author. The question, then, is not whether God is, in metaphysical truth, fire or susceptible to passions such as anger and jealousy, but whether or not a particular prophet believed these things and intended to convey that message through his writings. And we can only answer this question by examining those writings themselves, as well as the circumstances of their composition. Thus, Moses (assuming him to be the author) proclaims in the Torah that God has no resemblance to visible things, and yet he also likens God to fire. One needs to inquire, then, as to which of these passages needs to be read metaphorically, regardless of the

115

rationality or irrationality of the belief that would consequently be attributed to the prophet. If linguistic usage in biblical Hebrew suggests that the word "fire" does not have anything besides a literal meaning, then the other passages that say that God has no resemblance to things in heaven or on the earth need to be read figuratively.

Spinoza says that one needs to keep in mind that the purpose of scripture is not to communicate speculative truth, but to compel obedience. The narratives of the Torah and other writings of the Hebrew Bible – the events they relate about God, human beings, and nature – are a reflection of the beliefs, values, preconceptions, and purposes of their authors and especially what they presumed would most appeal to their audience. The prophets, distinguished from ordinary people by their particularly active and vivid imaginations, adopted various literary devices to convey a simple moral and religious message and to inspire readers to obey it. The truth of the resulting propositions and stories is irrelevant to this goal, and indeed to the value of scripture itself. Thus, he concludes, "the method of Maimonides is plainly of no value." Moreover, because that method deprives common people (who presumably have little knowledge of philosophy and therefore of demonstrated truths) of any direct approach to the meaning of scripture, he insists that "we can dismiss Maimonides' view as harmful, unprofitable, and absurd" (Spinoza 2001: 102).

Despite this direct attack on Maimonides on the question of biblical hermeneutics, there can be no question that Spinoza's views on the relationship between rational knowledge and happiness are deeply Maimonidean (and Gersonidean), and represent the logical culmination of the intellectualism found in his Jewish rationalist ancestors.

When human beings are acting rationally in their pursuit of self-preservation, Spinoza says in his philosophical masterpiece, the *Ethics*, they strive for knowledge. Since we are, among all creatures, uniquely endowed with reason and the capacity for understanding – that is, with intelligent minds – we recognize that our own proper good, our ultimate perfection and wellbeing, consists in the pursuit of what benefits this our highest part. But what else could benefit our highest intellectual faculties except knowledge? Thus, if virtue is the pursuit of what is in one's own self-interest, as Spinoza believes; and if the acquisition of knowledge is what is in our own self-interest, then (as he shows in propositions 20–6 of part four of the *Ethics*) (or, to use the standard convention for referring to the parts of this work, IVp20–26) human virtue consists in the pursuit of knowledge.

But Spinoza is not concerned here with the pursuit of just any ordinary kind of knowledge. He does not think that what is in our best interest as rational beings is sensory or imaginative knowledge. Rather, what is most beneficial to a being endowed with reason is a particular sort of deep understanding of the universal principles of God or Nature (*Deus sive Natura*, the two are identical for him) and of the individual things that are governed by them. He calls this understanding "intuitive knowledge (*scientia intuitiva*)" and "the third kind of knowledge" (to distinguish it from sensation and imagination, "the first kind of knowledge"; and Reason, "the second kind of knowledge," whose content is closely related to that of Intuition). It is an absolutely certain, purely intellectual apprehension of the eternal essences of individual things. The essence of a thing captures that thing's relations to higher causes, to the infinite and eternal aspects of Nature, and shows how it is necessarily determined by them. It shows how a body relates to Extension in general and its laws; and how an idea or mental event relates to Thought and its laws. Intuitive knowledge represents the highest form of knowledge available to us. To perceive things through Reason and, ultimately, through Intuition is to perceive them through "adequate ideas" and from a timeless perspective (what Spinoza calls *sub specie aeternitatis*). It is to see how things ultimately relate to God or Nature as God or Nature itself sees this.

Spinoza's conception of adequate knowledge reveals an unrivaled optimism in the cognitive powers of the human being. Not even Descartes, so often cited as the paradigmatic rationalist, believed that we could know all of nature and its innermost secrets with the degree of depth and certainty that Spinoza thought possible. Most remarkably, because Spinoza thought that the adequate knowledge of any object involves a thorough knowledge of God (Nature) and of how the object relates to God/Nature and its attributes, he also had no scruples about claiming that we can, at least in principle, know God itself.

IIp45:	Each idea of each body, or of each singular thing which actually exists, necessarily involves an eternal and infinite essence of God.
Demonstration:	The idea of a singular thing which actually exists necessarily involves both the essence of the thing and its existence. But singular things cannot be conceived without God – on the contrary, because they have God for a cause insofar as he is considered under the attribute of which the things are modes, their ideas must involve the concept of their attribute, that is, must involve an eternal and infinite essence of God.

As we come to a greater understanding of nature, we necessarily come to a greater understanding of God. "The more we understand singular things, the more we understand God" (Vp24). There is a particularly fine expression of this idea in the *Theological-Political Treatise*:

> Since all our knowledge, and the certainty that banishes every possible doubt, depend solely on the knowledge of God – because, firstly, without God nothing can be or be conceived, and secondly, everything can be called into doubt as long as we have no clear and distinct idea of God – it follows that our supreme good and perfection depends solely on the knowledge of God. Again, since nothing can be or be conceived without God, it is clear that everything in Nature involves and expresses the conception of God in proportion to its essence and perfection; and therefore we acquire a greater and more perfect knowledge of God as we gain more knowledge of natural phenomena. To put it another way, since the knowledge of an effect through its cause is nothing other than the knowledge of a property of that cause, the greater our knowledge of natural phenomena, the more perfect is our knowledge of God's essence, which is the cause of all things. (Spinoza 2001: 50)

As it is for Maimonides and Gersonides, human perfection for Spinoza consists in the actualization of our highest cognitive faculty, reason, through the attainment of intellectual understanding. This is the rationalist way to wisdom, joy, and blessedness (*beatitudo*). "Blessedness consists in Love of God, a Love which arises from the third kind of knowledge. So this Love must be related to the Mind insofar as it acts. Therefore, it

117

is virtue itself" (Vp42). Spinoza's Love of God is not a passion but an intellectual love in which the mind takes cognizance of the eternal object of its understanding.

Spinoza's bold move, however – a move that constitutes his transformation of Jewish rationalism into a secular or naturalistic rationalism – is twofold. First, he identifies God with Nature, and thereby explicitly makes Nature itself the supreme object of our cognitive quest. Reason is no longer what binds us to a transcendent deity but rather is what provides our intellectual connection to the cosmos of which we are a part. Second, he argues much more explicitly than either Maimonides or Gersonides that, while the pursuit of rational knowledge constitutes our supreme perfection and the true path to happiness, its "rewards" and benefits (to return to the question of "divine providence") are merely the natural effects that such understanding brings to a person and are limited solely to this life. Maimonides and Gersonides laid the philosophical groundwork for both of these conclusions, but it took a thinker as audacious as Spinoza to bring it all to a stunning logical conclusion.

References and Further Reading

Fox, Marvin (1990). *Interpreting Maimonides*. Chicago: University of Chicago Press.

Frank, Daniel H., and Leaman, Oliver (eds.) (1997). *History of Jewish Philosophy*. New York: Routledge.

—— (eds.) (2003). *The Cambridge Companion to Medieval Jewish Philosophy*. New York: Cambridge University Press.

Freudenthal, Gad (ed.) (1992). *Studies on Gersonides*. Leiden: Brill.

Gersonides [Levi ben Gershom] (1984). *The Wars of the Lord, Volume 1* (Seymour Feldman, trans.). Philadelphia, PA: Jewish Publication Society.

—— (1987). *The Wars of the Lord, Volume 2* (Seymour Feldman, trans.). Philadelphia, PA: Jewish Publication Society.

Hartman, David (1976). *Maimonides: Torah and Philosophic Quest*. Philadelphia, PA: Jewish Publication Society.

Kraemer, Joel L. (ed.) (1991). *Perspectives on Maimonides*. Oxford: Oxford University Press.

Maimonides (1963). *The Guide of the Perplexed*. 2 vols. (Shlomo Pines, trans.). Chicago: University of Chicago Press.

Nadler, Steven (2002). *Spinoza's Heresy*. Oxford: Oxford University Press.

Nadler, Steven, and Rudavsky, Tamar (in preparation). *The Cambridge History of Jewish Philosophy: From Antiquity Through the Seventeenth Century*. New York: Cambridge University Press.

Nemoy, L. (1932). *Karaite Anthology*. New Haven, CT: Yale University Press.

Saadya ben Joseph (1948). *The Book of Beliefs and Opinions* (Samuel Rosenblatt, trans.). New Haven, CT: Yale University Press.

—— (1969). *Three Jewish Philosophers* (Hans Lewy, Alexander Altmann, Isaak Heinemann, eds.). New York: Atheneum.

Sirat, Colette (1985). *A History of Jewish Philosophy in the Middle Ages*. Cambridge: Cambridge University Press.

Spinoza, Baruch (1984). *The Collected Works of Spinoza, Volume 1* (Edwin Curley, trans.). Princeton, NJ: Princeton University Press.

—— (2001). *Theological-Political Treatise* (Samuel Shirley, trans.). Indianapolis, IN: Hackett.

Touati, Charles (1973). *La Pensée philosophique et théologique de Gersonide*. Paris: Les Editions de Minuit.

Wolfson, Harry (1934). *The Philosophy of Spinoza*. Cambridge, MA: Harvard University Press.

7

Early Modern Critiques of Rationalist Psychology

ANTONIA LOLORDO

The terms "rationalism" and "empiricism" were first used in ancient Greek medicine. Roughly, empiricists held that medical knowledge is simply a matter of having had the appropriate experiences and having remembered them correctly. Knowing that a drug cures a disease requires nothing more than having observed and remembered that an improvement in the disease occurred when the drug was administered. Rationalists, by contrast, assumed that something more than experience was required – typically a proof or inference of some sort, for instance an inference to the underlying state of the diseased body and an account of the action of the drug.

Neither term, as used today, had much currency in the early modern period. Bacon draws a comparison between the "Empirical Philosophers" (who are "mere pismires") and the "Rationalists," recommending a middle path, but the context does not make clear what precisely he takes the terms to convey (*Apopthegms* 3.21). The one use Locke makes of the relevant terms and their cognates is still very close to the ancient meaning: he talks of swallowing down opinions "as silly people do empirics pills, without knowing what they are made of, or how they will work" (*Essay* 4.20.4). Clearly, neither Bacon nor Locke counts themselves as empiricists. The pejorative connotation the term sometimes has for early moderns is even clearer in the claim, reported by Hume concerning a civil suit against one James Fraser, apothecary, that he prescribed a regimen concerning which "none but Quacks & Empirics, who had never taken their Degrees, will agree with him" (*Letters* 2.342). The empiric is not one who abjures theory as a matter of principle, but rather one who is simply ignorant of theory.

Kant (A855/B883) uses the terms "empiricist" (or "sensualist") and "rationalist" (or "intellectualist") in something closer to the twentieth-century sense, delineating by them two opposed schools of philosophy: the school of Aristotle, Locke, and most consistently Epicurus, and the school of Plato and Leibniz. The terms became institutionalized in English in the nineteenth century, and are used to organize the curriculum. Philosophy departments in the English-speaking world often teach classes called "Rationalism" and "Empiricism," or the "Continental Rationalists" and the "British Empiricists."

The usefulness and appropriateness of the terms has been questioned. One problem is that the common association of empiricism with England, Scotland, and Ireland, and rationalism with the Continent, fails to take into account such figures as Voltaire,

Etienne de Condillac, Jean D'Alembert, and other French *philosophes*. Nor can it account for English Platonists like Henry More and Anne Conway. Perhaps more seriously from the point of view of the canon, although Berkeley has traditionally been counted as one of the three British Empiricists (along with Locke and Hume), his system has much more in common with the metaphysical system of Nicolas Malebranche than with the epistemological and psychological concerns of someone like Locke, Gassendi, Hobbes, or Hume.

Even setting aside the geographical associations of the terms "empiricism" and "rationalism," use of the terms can obscure differences between the various philosophers assigned to each camp. Thus reliance on the terms may mistakenly suggest that all those thinkers we count as empiricists would identify themselves as engaged in a common project or that they agree on a set of crucial doctrines. But the various doctrines commonly identified as empiricist are not necessarily connected. The example of Locke shows that one can deny the existence of innate ideas without rejecting the possibility of *a priori* knowledge. And the example of Descartes shows that one can believe in innate ideas exhibiting the essences of things, and still hold that the progress of science depends on empirical work. We do not even need to go beyond the canonical list of early moderns to see this: there is no one crucial doctrine which Locke, Berkeley, and Hume all accept and Descartes, Spinoza, and Leibniz all reject – nor can the situation be remedied simply by recategorizing Berkeley.

Nevertheless, the different elements traditionally associated with the categories "rationalism" and "empiricism" can each be made to do useful work. I shall focus on the psychological element of the traditional distinction. On this way of understanding the terms, the rationalist holds that there are ideas innate in the human mind and typically postulates an independent faculty, the intellect, to contain such ideas. Paradigm innate ideas are the ideas of mathematical entities, the ideas of broad metaphysical categories like substance and accident, and the idea of God. The empiricist denies that there are innate ideas and provides alternate accounts of cognition which depend only on content acquired from the world through sense perception (and, in most cases, certain natural faculties of the mind). Typically, this is done in such a way that no independent intellect is necessary, so the empiricist rejects the existence of a distinct intellect. This way of drawing the distinction leaves out a number of figures: for instance, Malebranche, who locates ideas in God's mind as the eternal archetypes of things and downgrades the power of the intellect while accepting its existence; and Berkeley, who seems to accept innate ideas but denies that intellect and imagination are distinct faculties. But this is as it should be.

Accepting or denying innate ideas has epistemological ramifications. Indeed, it was entirely standard in the early modern period to treat psychological and epistemological theses as very closely entwined, in a way that some twentieth-century philosophers would have labeled pejoratively as "psychologistic." Thus, those who accepted the existence of innate ideas typically assumed that those ideas were true and provided grounds for knowledge of the world. This assumption was backed up by the claim that our cognitive faculties are created by a benevolent God – a claim which Descartes explicitly defended and which most writers accepted. Twentieth-century empiricists have criticized the assumption that innate ideas are thereby knowledge conducive, but, with the exception of one Samuel Parker, it was almost universally granted in the early modern period. Instead of attacking the link between innateness and truth, empiricists proceeded by trying to undermine the claim that we have innate ideas. However, it is important to notice that while pretty much all advocates of innate ideas took them to ground *a priori* knowledge, the deniers of innate ideas did not thereby always reject *a priori* knowledge. The case of Locke, discussed below, will show this very clearly.

There are two classic early modern texts for the conflict between proponents and opponents of innate ideas: first, Descartes' *Meditations* and the *Objections* he solicited, particularly those of Thomas Hobbes and Pierre Gassendi; and second, Locke's *Essay Concerning Human Understanding* and Leibniz's chapter-by-chapter commentary and objections in the *New Essays*. I begin with Descartes, for the influence of Cartesianism, not only as a positive philosophy but also as a target and goad for empiricist accounts of human cognition, can scarcely be overestimated. We see objections to Descartes and Cartesianism in Locke and Hume, as well as many others.

Both Locke and Hume drew inspiration from the work – or at least the myth – of Francis Bacon (1561–1626). Bacon's calls for a natural philosophy based solely on observations compiled into exhaustive, tabular "histories" constituted a radically sense-based response to both the Aristotelian methodology dominant in his time and its main competitor, the Neoplatonism revived by fifteenth- and sixteenth-century humanists. Bacon's name and rhetoric were also crucial for the Royal Society of England – a group whose members and associates included, in addition to Locke, such notables as Robert Boyle (1627–91) and Isaac Newton (1642–1727). The allegedly Baconian methodology of the Royal Society is sometimes what people have in mind when using the term "empiricism," and indeed there may be something particularly Baconian in Locke and Hume's appeal to natural histories. However, it is better to downplay the Baconian aspects of the term "empiricism," for if this is what the term means then virtually *all* early modern natural philosophers were empiricists. Philosophers traditionally counted as rationalists, as well as those considered empiricists, use a rhetoric of observation and experience which is primarily directed at a moribund and in any case somewhat caricatured methodology, the methodology of Aristotelian scholasticism.

The Aristotelianism taught in the schools and universities of the sixteenth and seventeenth centuries was an enlargement, revision, and interpretation of Aristotle by centuries of Arabic and Latin commentators. This Aristotelianism, which came in many varieties, is one of the major sources and influences in the background during early modern debates about rationalist psychology. I provide a sketch of Aristotelian psychology. First, however, I want to look at one of the main sources of early modern empiricism, the Epicurean philosophy which flourished in the Hellenistic period and was revived by French and Italian humanists in the sixteenth and seventeenth centuries.

Epicurean Empiricism

Epicurus and his school are perhaps most famous for their ethics, which centers around the pursuit of happiness through bodily and intellectual pleasures, withdrawal from civic life and the disturbances it causes, and the elimination of fears induced by religion. However, Epicurus' account of the nature and sources of human cognition casts an equally long shadow over early modern philosophy.

Epicurus takes as his starting point the fact of human sensory experience, and argues that the entire human cognitive endowment can be explained on this basis. Sense impressions leave behind traces, and repeated traces form what Epicurus called *preconceptions* – mental items that allow us to recognize, discuss, and reason about the things which caused them. These preconceptions suffice to explain cognition of absent objects, imaginative thought, and theoretical reasoning (to the extent that such reasoning is legitimate).

Epicurus asserts, against the skeptic, that human sensory experience must have some external cause. He also made the apparently much stronger assertion that all sensations are true, although it is disputed whether he in fact intended anything more than the claim that whenever I have a sensation there is truly something which is its cause. However, Epicurus' modern reviver, Gassendi, understood this claim in its strong sense and derived epistemological consequences from it, beginning with the claim that the senses provide the first criterion of truth.

In order to deal with problems of perceptual inconsistency and error, Epicurus instituted a sharp distinction between sensory impressions on the one hand, and the judgments constructed on their basis on the other. While all sensations are true, judgments are capable of either truth or falsity. False judgments are typically made when we hastily form conclusions on the basis of sensations which are not "evident." An example of an evident perception is the perception of a familiar man from a few feet away in good light, as opposed to the perception of him in a distant crowd. Epicurus seems, at least in early modern accounts of his work, to have assumed that just those sensations that compel judgment lead to true judgment.

A number of issues concerning how sensation leads to judgment that arise in interpreting the Epicurean theory of cognition remain in play in the early modern period. These issues concern the move from psychological to epistemological claims, and thus are centrally involved in empiricist accounts of human cognition and their critiques. I formulate these issues as they originally arise in Gassendi's reconstruction of Epicurean accounts of cognition and as they are played out later in the century.

One issue is identifying exactly what is the content of sensation. Early moderns often held that in perception we are directly aware of our ideas and only indirectly aware of real things, although some direct realists like Gassendi insisted that sensations present things in the world. But if the sensory given is a mental entity like an idea, how can it license belief about an external world? Indirect realists are typically forced to say that our knowledge of the world proceeds via inference from sense impressions to external objects; one famous way to characterize the inference is found in Descartes' Sixth Meditation. This claim is often thought to open the door for "veil-of-ideas" skeptical worries, and indeed, Hume famously argues that although we do form beliefs about an external world on the basis of our sensations, there is no rational basis for doing so.

Second, does what is given in sensation resemble the real constitution of things, and if not, how can we come to have knowledge of the real constitution of things? Epicurus, who held that the ultimate constituents of things are atoms possessing only the properties of size, shape, and weight, must deny that the sensory given resembles the real constitution of things. This denial is repeated by many early moderns, most famously in the terminology of Locke's distinction between primary and secondary qualities. Many empiricists took the skeptical line that we are unable to know the real constitutions of things. This line weakens the anti-rationalist claim that no recourse to innate ideas is necessary to explain our actual cognitive endowment, although certain of its adherents would claim that they have merely accurately described the current state of scientific knowledge. Others held that some process of inference and reasoning was sufficient to get us from our sensory experience to the real constitution of things. This point highlights one important difference between "empiricism" as it refers to a view typified by Locke, Bacon, or Hume and "empiricism" as a school of Greek medicine. No early modern denied that humans have the power of reason (although they argued about whether that power was distinct from imagination and how wide its scope was) or that the power of reason contributed significantly to our knowledge.

A third issue is closely related. How can an Epicurean account of cognition that denies any non-sensory source of content license belief in unobservable entities? And how can it explain *certain* and *necessary* beliefs such as beliefs about mathematics? Typically, writers argued that ideas of unobservable things are formed by analogy with things we have already experienced, and that we come to believe in these unobservables by construing our experiences as effects of a cause which is either the only possible explanation of them or at least the best explanation of them. It is somewhat more difficult to explain how ideas of God and the immaterial soul can be formed by analogy with things we have sensed, since the former are immaterial and the latter are material. But the existence of God and the immaterial human soul were widely (although not universally) accepted as fundamental entities for philosophy by seventeenth- and eighteenth-century philosophers. The accounts of Epicurus and his most famous follower Lucretius incline towards naturalism and materialism, but this was deliberately rebutted or downplayed by most of the early moderns influenced by them.

Epicurus and his followers dealt with the purported certainty and necessity of mathematical knowledge by denying it. Thus they were led to a form of skepticism about mathematics that few in the seventeenth and eighteenth centuries could accept, impressed as they were by the successes of the mathematical image of the natural world that emerged through the work of such figures as Galileo, Descartes, Huygens, Newton, and Leibniz. The difficulties inherent in this claim come out very clearly in Leibniz's *New Essays*.

The transmission of Epicurean texts to the early modern period is somewhat indirect. One important vehicle is Lucretius' great poem *De Rerum Natura* or *On the Nature of Things*. Further information about Epicurean philosophy is given in some of the Ciceronian dialogues (albeit not terribly sympathetically) and in Book X of Diogenes Laertius' *Lives of the Eminent Philosophers*. Just as various fifteenth- and sixteenth-century writers had attempted to promulgate revised versions of Platonism and Stoicism, Gassendi put forth a revised and Christianized version of Epicureanism in his *Syntagma Philosophicum* and other works. These became better known in England through the partial translations provided in the *Physiologia Epicuro-Gassendo-Charletonia* of Walter Charleton (1620–1707) and Thomas Stanley (1625–78).

Gassendi was for a long time cited as an important influence on Locke, but it is unclear whether Locke actually knew any of Gassendi's work save the Fifth Objections to the *Meditations*. Those philosophical similarities that do exist between the two may be the result of a common cause rather than direct influence. In any case, a taxonomy of the early moderns into their Epicurean and Platonist influences is at least as useful as a taxonomy of empiricists and rationalists, and perhaps would serve to make clearer that the fundamental point at issue is one of the source and content of cognition. Indeed, Kant describes the contrast between "intellectualists" or rationalists and "sensualists" or empiricists as "the contrast between the teaching of Epicurus and that of Plato" (A471/B499; cf. A853/B881).

Sensory and intellectual cognition in scholastic writers

It is worth looking briefly at how a roughly Epicurean view differs from that of scholastic Aristotelians. The Aristotelianism of the sixteenth- and seventeenth-century European universities encompasses a great diversity of views. I center my account not on any of the views of more sophisticated thinkers such as Francisco Suarez or the Coimbra commentators, but rather on a somewhat simplified account provided in the textbooks read by Descartes and Gassendi, such as the *Summa Philosophiae Quadripartita* or *Summary of Philosophy in Four Parts* of Eustachius a Sancto Paolo.

One of the most famous Aristotelian slogans is *nihil in intellectu quod prius non fuerit in sensu* (there is nothing in the intellect which was not previously in sense). It is easy to read this as an empiricist claim in our sense of the term, and to some extent this reading is correct, as the slogan does imply a denial of innate ideas. However, at the same time, Aristotelians typically rejected the Epicurean claim that all mental content is derived entirely from the senses.

On this account of cognition, sensation occurs when the faculty of sense, located in the brain and connected to the sense organs, receives *sensible species* that convey information about the surface characteristics of the thing sensed. Sensible species inhering in the brain trigger the formation of an immaterial *intelligible species* in the immaterial intellect. Intelligible species, unlike the sensible species that occasion them, contain the essence of the sensed object. This grasp of essences goes beyond the sensory information required to bring it about, so that there is both an empiricist and an anti-empiricist element to the theory of cognition. Even this very limited empiricism, however, raised certain difficulties in understanding the possibility of cognition of immaterial entities like God or the human soul, and Aristotelians also had to place a great deal of weight on the notion of analogical cognition. Indeed, the ease with which roughly Platonist theories could explain cognition of God and the immaterial soul was often adduced in their favor by Christian Platonists, both ancient and early modern.

Scholastic Aristotelianism is also sometimes thought of as non-empiricist or anti-empiricist in virtue of a reliance on tradition and the authority of Aristotle in place of direct experience and observation. This conception of scholasticism is in large part a triumph of the rhetoric of early modern anti-Aristotelians. Both Arabic and, later, European Aristotelianism contain a strong tradition of optics which has nothing to do with Aristotle himself, and the physics of fourteenth-century Paris is often cited as the

124

beginning of a tradition and methodology which Galileo continued. Moreover, the Aristotelian tradition that was taught in medical schools and philosophy sources was mixed with other, more experientially oriented methodologies. Two well-known examples are the anatomical work most notable in the Italian medical schools of the sixteenth century and the strand of alchemy which focused on the production of effects and phenomena in the laboratory.

Nevertheless, writers such as Bacon attacked scholasticism for being insufficiently sensitive to experience. Bacon denied the existence of innate ideas or an independent intellect; however, he was less than optimistic about the ability of the human sensory and intellectual powers to achieve knowledge of the world. He argued that a highly structured method was necessary to attain knowledge, and in his *New Organon* – his replacement for Aristotle's logical works – he provides such a method, explaining how one goes about collecting systematic natural histories, arranging them into table form, and using a version of induction to make reliable generalizations. Although Bacon's critiques of Aristotelianism were by no means entirely original, his critical rhetoric and, to a lesser extent, his emphasis on structured observation were widely praised by later early moderns – empiricist and rationalist alike – although his specific recommendations were almost never followed. In his *Preliminary Discourse to the Encyclopedia of Diderot*, for instance, D'Alembert portrays Bacon as a hero and model, despite Bacon's manifest lack of sympathy for the mathematics D'Alembert relied on in his work on mechanics. Epicurean and Baconian critiques of reliance on mathematics did not last very far into the seventeenth century, although attendant worries about mathematical ontology lingered.

Critiques of Cartesianism

Scholastic accounts of human cognition lie in the background of Descartes' *Meditations* and the empiricist objections of Gassendi and Hobbes. The scholastics adduced four cognitive faculties (or four ways of thinking about the human cognitive endowment): sense, imagination, memory, and a fourth variously called intellect, understanding, or reason. The first three faculties were understood as corporeal. Intellect was understood as incorporeal, but depended on the deliverances of the corporeal faculties for its operation; as we have seen, intellectual grasp of essences is triggered by, but not derivative from, sensory content.

Descartes accepts the four faculties and, like the scholastics, understands intellect as an immaterial faculty operating over essences. However, he arrives at a rather different account of how many essences there are. While scholastics took there to be a distinct essence for every distinct type of thing, so that every kind of plant, for instance, has its own essence, Descartes grants only the two essences thought and extension. He also differs from the scholastic account in holding that the intellect can operate independently of the corporeal faculties on the basis of the innate ideas it finds within itself – a claim which is central to his meditative method. In accepting the autonomy of the intellect, Descartes has more in common with St. Augustine and such Renaissance Platonists as Marsilio Ficino and Giovanni Pico della Mirandola than the Aristotelianism of his education.

125

Three of Descartes' central theses – that there are ideas innate in the human intellect, that the immaterial intellect operates independently of the corporeal faculties, and that we have intellectual grasp of essences – are targets in both Hobbes' and Gassendi's objections to the *Meditations*. Both Hobbes and Gassendi deny that there are innate ideas and deny that there is an immaterial intellect operating independently of body. Indeed, in their *Objections* they deny that there is any immaterial intellect at all. Thus they also deny that we have the direct cognitive grasp of essences which Descartes and the scholastics relied on, and ultimately reject any mind-independent essences. It is important to see that no early modern, empiricist or rationalist, thought that *sensory* terms gained their meaning by reference to essences or that sensory ideas provided a direct grasp of essences. Thus rejections of the intellect tended to go hand in hand with rejections of essences, or at least with rejections of the possibility of human knowledge of essences.

Hobbes' chief line of attack is that Descartes has provided an ontologically inflationary account of the difference between imagining and understanding. There is no need, he argues, to posit a separate intellectual faculty to explain reasoning. Rather, "reasoning is simply the joining together and linking of names or labels by means of the verb *is*," so that "the inferences in our reasoning tell us nothing at all about the nature of things, but merely tell us about the labels applied to them" (CSM 2.130). This view of reasoning, together with the related conception of ideas as images, leads him to deny that we can have ideas of God, the human soul, or substance.

Hobbes deals with abstract or general terms by treating them as words connected in the imagination to images of various individual things. This radical account of abstract ideas was never widely accepted, perhaps because of the convincing nature of Descartes' dismissive reply that if Hobbes were right then a Frenchman and a German could never have an idea of the same thing. However, explaining the nature and content of abstract ideas without appealing to an essence they refer to became a central issue for many later empiricists.

Hobbes' *Objection* and Descartes' *Reply* provide a clear temperamental and doctrinal contrast. Unfortunately, there is very little genuine philosophical engagement between the two. Hobbes tends simply to assert that Descartes' view is wrong and that his own view is the correct one, without offering direct argument against Descartes. Some of Hobbes' objections about cognition can be read as claims that a simpler, materialist hypothesis can take the place of Descartes' metaphysically loaded theory of cognition. However, since Descartes, in company with most philosophers of the time, thought that a fundamental task of philosophy was to prove the immortality of the soul, it is unsurprising that he was unsympathetic.

There is somewhat more argumentation in Gassendi's *Objections* and Descartes' *Reply*. Gassendi thinks that Descartes' meditative method is supposed to establish the existence of innate ideas and an immaterial intellect operating over them. He objects that we cannot really uncover our innate ideas by withdrawing the mind from the senses, since the evidence of sense is, at least in certain cases, entirely compelling. He then offers alternative accounts of how the ideas of God, the immaterial soul, and mathematical entities could be constructed from material provided by sense – accounts of the sort later found in more detail in Locke and Hume. He objects also that Descartes has failed to explain "why a man born blind has no idea of color, or a man born deaf has no idea of sound" (CSM 2.197). One might expect Descartes to reply simply that he does not think all ideas are innate and could grant that ideas of colors and sounds must be acquired through sense. However, Descartes instead replies that for all Gassendi knows, the blind man is blind because his mind lacks the faculty for forming ideas of color and the like, rather than lacking the ideas because he is blind. This nicely illustrates a tendency of innatists to end up claiming that *all* content is innate. For denying that empiricist accounts of the acquisition of content of ideas of immaterial and mathematical entities can succeed often suggests that *no* content could be acquired from sense. This goes along with the tendency to downgrade apparent sensory content to mere qualia which we see in some, although by no means all, Cartesian texts.

Gassendi also rejects Cartesian essentialism, viz. the claim that cognition of essence precedes cognition of existence so that one cannot have an idea of *x* without grasping the essence of *x*. This partly reflects Gassendi's agreement with Hobbes that there are no extra-mental essences (although he differs from Hobbes in aligning essences with concepts rather than words). He denies extra-mental essences both because of worries about their ontology and because he thinks that we would have no cognitive grasp of them even if they did exist. Gassendi's rejection of essentialism is also grounded in his argument that Cartesian essentialism requires that ideas are acquired all at once, while we observe that ideas are acquired gradually. The child's idea of God is the same idea as the adult's, merely less complete; and similarly for the idea of a triangle, which becomes more complete when the thinker learns the Pythagorean theorem. This raises issues about the individuation of ideas which both rationalists and empiricists must face. In normal cases, everyone agrees that ideas are individuated by their objects, although they disagree about whether objects are extra-mental essences, objects existing in the external world, or some third possibility. Platonists can apply this claim to mathematical cognition as well, but it is more problematic for those who try to give a purely empiricist account of mathematical cognition.

It is clear from the denial of innate ideas and extra-mental essences that Gassendi cannot accept either the Cartesian or the scholastic account of the function of the intellect. Hence it is unsurprising that, at least in his *Objections* to Descartes, Gassendi rejects any distinction between intellect and imagination. He identifies Descartes' two main reasons for drawing such a distinction as the piece of wax example and its conclusion that we know the wax through intellect rather than sense or imagination, and the argument that although we can only form a confused image of a chiliagon we nevertheless have a clear and distinct idea of it. Against the first, Gassendi argues that one cannot conceive the wax "apart from any extension, shape, or color," that is, without forming a perfectly determinate idea of it. (This point recurs, to somewhat different effect, in Berkeley's attack on abstract ideas.) Against the second, Gassendi objects that we have no clear and distinct idea of a chiliagon, but merely perceive that the word 'chiliagon' signifies a thousand-sided figure. Mathematical cognition no more requires appeal to mind-independent essences than cognition of immaterial entities like God and the human soul; it too can be built up out of sensory material. Gassendi's account invites the Leibnizian objection that the certainty and necessity of mathematical cognition cannot be derived purely from sensory material, and to the extent that he would reply by denying any such necessity, his answer would not be convincing to many later empiricists.

Locke

It is easy for readers encountering Locke's *Essay* in the context of other canonical early modern works to think of Locke's arguments as directed against the Cartesian doctrine of innate ideas. However, a little attention to Locke's focus on *moral* principles rather than theoretical ones, and innate *principles* rather than innate ideas, will show that this is false. In fact, Locke is arguing against the English tradition adducing innate moral principles of writers like Herbert of Cherbury (1583–1648) and William Chillingworth (1602–44); and although he objects to Descartes on a number of points, his account of knowledge owes a great deal to Descartes.

One of Locke's most serious worries about innatism is that it has pernicious social and political consequences. For, Locke suggests, innatists hold their innate principles to be true and immune from challenge, thus making critical scrutiny of their doctrines illegitimate. However, Locke does not argue against innatism on the basis of its social consequences. Rather, his general strategy is this. He attempts to show that innatism is either trivial in virtue of reducing to the claim that the mind has certain capacities, or obviously false in virtue of requiring that we consciously have certain principles or ideas in mind from birth. He mounts this argument by focusing on such principles as *whatever is, is*; *it is impossible for the same thing to be and not to be*; and *parents should preserve and cherish their children*; as well as ideas such as God, substance, and identity – all of which had been taken as paradigms of the innate.

Locke considers three common justifications for innatism and rebuts them all. First is the *argument from universal consent*, which holds that all men accept a certain principle *p* and that *p* is therefore innate. Locke argues that the inference is invalid, since there may be other reasons all men believe *p* – sheer obviousness, for one. Thus, while universal consent is a necessary condition for innateness, it is not a sufficient one. Moreover, Locke argues, there are no principles which all men can be shown to accept. Children, the uneducated, and "idiots" have no knowledge of maxims like *it is impossible for the same thing to be and not to be*, and different societies use different fundamental moral principles. Locke's argument relies on the premise that it is "near a contradiction, to say that there are truths imprinted on the soul, which it perceives or understands not" (*Essay* 1.2.5). For if we give up the notion that we are or have once been aware of all the truths we know, then we may as well say that *every* principle which is later assented to is innate.

The second argument Locke considers is the *argument from the use of reason*, which holds that all men know and assent to *p* when they come to the use of reason and that *p* is thus innate. Locke replies that the premise is ambiguous. If the innatist means that *p can be known by the use of reason*, then the inference is invalid. Reason is simply the faculty of deducing unknown truths from the principles already known. If the innatist's argument is read in this way, then again everything we know or can know is innate, which Locke takes to be absurd and which was not in any case the conclusion Herbert and Chillingworth were aiming at. But if the innatist means that everyone knows *p* as soon as they are able to use reason, then the premise is false. Children use reason long before they know that *it is impossible for the same thing to be and not to be*, and many uneducated people reason perfectly well without knowing such general maxims. In any case, the inference would be invalid even if the premise were true: that we acquire certain principles at a fixed point in our development cannot by itself show that they are innate.

Finally, Locke considers the *argument from assenting as soon as proposed*: all men assent to *p* as soon as *p* is proposed to them, and thus *p* is innate. Locke objects that the inference must be invalid, since if it succeeded then every obvious or self-evident principle would be innate. Again, Locke's argument relies on a rejection of the possibility of merely implicit knowledge.

Locke's denial of innate ideas has been alternately read as the grounds for his concept-empiricism and as one of its conclusions, one which implicitly relies on the positive theory of cognition developed later in the *Essay*. Indeed, Locke offers two very different sorts of arguments against innate ideas. One line of argument suggests that we need not suppose any innate ideas to explain the phenomena of human cognition. Another combines the claim that it is "near a contradiction to suppose that there are ideas in the mind which the mind perceives not" with the claim, granted by all sophisticated innatists, that the mind is not actually aware of its innate ideas from birth. The second line of argument falls victim to the more sophisticated understandings of consciousness and attention offered by Condillac and others, but the first remains the preeminent empiricist line of attack.

It is important to notice that although Locke rejects innate ideas and uses the metaphor of the mind as a blank slate, he allows that a substantial portion of the human cognitive endowment is innate. For Locke, like Gassendi, accepts that the mind has an "innate faculty of knowing," which allows it to receive simple ideas from sense, correlate ideas arriving from different sense modalities, and combine and rearrange simple ideas. At a general level, any sophisticated empiricist must agree with Locke on this point, although we shall see that later figures like Condillac worry that Locke leaves far too much work to the innate faculties. At the same time, rationalists such as Descartes often allow that some sense experience is necessary to "trigger" awareness of the ideas innate in the mind. This claim goes back to Plato. Indeed, one of Leibniz's concerns in the *New Essays* is to defend against Locke's anti-innatism the claim that the senses occasion awareness of innate ideas without producing their content. Because sophisticated nativists and sophisticated empiricists agree that awareness of content requires both some sensory stimulus and some innate cognitive endowment, one might worry that debates over innatism are more verbal than substantive. The claim that mathematical ideas have a necessity and certainty which could not be empirically derived is often introduced, as it is by Leibniz, to show that there is indeed a difference between content being acquired through sense and merely being occasioned by sense. This claim becomes central in Kant's doctrine of the synthetic *a priori*.

However, it can be questioned whether necessity and certainty belong to mathematical *ideas* or rather to mathematical *judgments*. Although Locke holds that all ideas are acquired from sense, he also holds that knowledge is "the perception of . . . agreement, or disagreement . . . of our ideas" (*Essay* 4.1.2). In other words, he holds that knowledge is *a priori* in the sense that it requires no experience beyond that needed to acquire the relevant ideas. Thus Locke could hold that the certainty and necessity of mathematical judgments comes from their being the result of a perception of agreement between two ideas, regardless of how the ideas are acquired. This may go some way towards answering the Leibnizian objection, but it pushes the problem back to the relation between ideas and the things they purport to represent. If mathematics is merely a system of relations among ideas, then we gain its certainty and necessity at the cost of rendering it uncertain that it applies to all possible objects of experience.

Locke's account of knowledge shows very clearly that there is a gap between the psychological claim of empiricism that all content derives from sensory content, and the epistemological claim, sometimes thought to accompany it, that all knowledge is *a posteriori*. Thus Locke's account of knowledge is worth looking at in more detail. Locke delineates four ways in which ideas can be perceived as agreeing or disagreeing: identity or diversity; necessary connection, as when the yellow color of gold always accompanies having a certain specific gravity; relation, most saliently the part–whole relation; and finally the "real existence" of the self, of God, and of external objects.

The most interesting case of real existence is a subset of the last, "sensitive knowledge of real existence" of objects external to the mind. It is often pointed out that this cannot be accommodated within Locke's official definition of knowledge as the perception of agreement or disagreement among *ideas*, but this need not concern us; Locke recognizes it himself and explains that sensitive knowledge counts as knowledge because of its certainty. The interesting issue is the scope and justification of Lockean sensitive knowledge. Sensitive knowledge extends only to "the existence of things actually present to the senses" and not to their nature, causes, or continuing existence. When I perceive a tomato, I thereby know that something exists which is such as to cause my ideas of redness, sweetness, roundness, and so on. (Locke seems simply to assume that our natural tendency to group qualities together into bundles is truth-conducive, i.e., that my natural assumption that the same thing causes the idea of redness and the idea of sweetness is reliable.) But I do not know that the tomato is itself red or sweet, nor that it existed before I sensed it or that it will continue to exist afterwards. These claims – and indeed most of what we ordinarily count as knowledge – constitute probability rather than knowledge on Locke's account. Probability is a matter of the varying degrees of confidence we have in a certain claim as a result of its conformity with our own experience and with the properly assessed testimony of others.

Is Locke merely restricting use of the term "knowledge"? Or does he have a substantive philosophical point to make? Locke infers a relatively sweeping recommendation of tolerance from his sharp restriction of knowledge. Since we should recognize that the vast majority of our opinions are merely probable, we should not impose them on others. Thus Locke draws a close connection between his epistemology and his Latitudinarian tendencies, which strictly limit the number of articles of Christian faith and accept a wide range of practices and beliefs. But Locke also has in mind a rather sweeping downgrading of the status of scientific knowledge claims. Although he was a member of the Royal Society, strongly influenced by the corpuscularianism of people like Robert Boyle, Locke is somewhat skeptical about the certainty and metaphysical import of the natural philosophy of his day. This is less surprising than it may seem, as the Royal Society itself tended to stress probability over Aristotelian *scientia* (i.e., deduction of knowledge from first principles and essences). However, Locke is not merely recategorizing the epistemic status of claims in natural philosophy. He is also concerned to point out their lack of certainty relative to the truths of religion and morality crucial for everyday life.

Locke's claim that we have sensitive knowledge of the real existence of bodies and his response to skepticism about knowledge of the external world is consonant with this emphasis on the relative importance of the knowledge-claims of everyday life. His response to skepticism contains three main claims. First, that we have nothing beyond perception to go on, so that we must take at least *some* perceptions as veridical in order to make any progress and, indeed, in order to make life possible. Second – and here Locke is using an argument going back to ancient Greek critiques of skepticism – that since the skeptic cannot live or believe her doubts, we need not take them seriously. Third, he objects that the sort of skepticism about the external world embodied in Descartes' First Meditation doubts does not have the salutary effects on our mental equilibrium that ancient skepticism was generally intended to have. It is worth noting that these are not all responses to the same *sort* of skepticism. An ancient skeptic who thought that withholding assent was the best way to attain tranquillity would not worry that his skepticism made epistemic progress impossible.

Locke's response to skepticism about the external world relies heavily on his claim that all simple ideas are real, true and adequate (i.e., that they all do conform to some real existence as an effect to its cause). Thus Locke holds that simple ideas provide us with information about patterns of causes in the world. Locke does not grant to the skeptic that there are no stable, law-governed connections between how things appear and what they are really like. He merely grants – indeed, argues – that the connection is not always one of resemblance. In thus splitting the difference between the commonsense realist and a skeptic motivated by worries about perceptual variability and error, Locke in effect grants that perceptual variability poses a challenge to commonsense realism, but denies that this challenge needs to be solved by skeptical suspension of judgment. For instance, Locke could tell us, the fact that the same glass of water feels hot to one hand and cool to another provides us with no reason to suspend judgment about what the water is really like in itself. It merely shows that the water is such as to produce the idea of warmth in sense organs disposed one way and the idea of coolness in sense organs disposed another way.

This claim allows Locke to reconcile the mechanist claim that the world is not as we experience it (since qualities such as colors, tastes, etc. will not appear in fundamental descriptions of the world) with his insistence on perception as a genuine – indeed, the only – source of information about the world. However, it is unclear that Locke has any real justification to offer for his claim that all simple ideas are real, true, and adequate beyond the insistence that if we do not assume this, no philosophical progress can be made. He sometimes adds that if we do not assume the veracity and adequacy of simple ideas then everyday life would be impossible. But this line of objection did not fare well in ancient Greek debates about skepticism, since the skeptic can accept the appearances for the purposes of everyday life without making any theoretical claims or ascribing such attributes as adequacy to any of her ideas. It seems that Locke does not really think we need to worry about the reality, truth, and adequacy of simple ideas of perception, given that we cannot help relying on them and given that their deliverances are largely consistent. This is perhaps unsurprising in someone who thinks that there are no sources of content beyond the senses, but it does not by itself constitute an argument.

The innate powers of the mind

Locke seems to accept as unproblematic that there are innate faculties of knowing and that there is a significant difference between allowing innate faculties and allowing innate ideas. However, theories of cognition in the next few generations were centrally concerned with working out what the mind's innate powers were. One such theory was provided in Berkeley's early *New Theory of Vision*, which is much more crucial to the development of empiricist psychology than any of his later metaphysical works.

The *New Theory* has two overarching projects. One is to provide an explanation of how the human visual system perceives size and distance. Descartes had argued that visual perception of distance depends on an innate "natural geometry": the mind unconsciously calculates the distance of objects from the eye on the basis of knowledge of the distance between the two eyes and the angle at which rays of light from the object strike the eyes. Berkeley argued against the psychological reality of this natural geometry, and offered a new account of judgments of distance as dependent on learned associations between tactile ideas and visual cues like the sensation of the eyes converging and the lenses changing shape.

Berkeley's other chief project in the *New Theory* is to explain the relationship between the ideas of the various senses. This is most easily grasped by comparison with the Molyneux problem discussed in Locke's *Essay*. Molyneux proposed the following situation. Take a blind man who can easily distinguish a cube from a sphere by touch and who has newly become able to see. Will he be able immediately to distinguish the cube and the sphere by vision? Or do we need to learn from experience how to correlate impressions of different sense modalities? This question is often thought to be the same as asking whether the visual and tactile ideas of a sphere can be recognized as similar on purely internal grounds or whether they must be associated for some extrinsic reason. Berkeley argued that no ideas are common to more than one sense. Our association of certain visual ideas with tangible ideas results from our learning to take visual ideas as signs of tactile ideas. So does our belief that what we see exists without the mind, at a certain distance from us: nothing in the visual idea of a sphere tells us that it (or something corresponding to it) exists outside the mind. Here Berkeley expands the sphere of what must be acquired from sense and correspondingly reduces the extent of the innate faculties of the mind.

For Berkeley, the *New Theory* also served as a step on the way towards immaterialism by suggesting idealistic conclusions about the ideas of vision while leaving our normal conception of the ideas of touch alone. In later works, Berkeley attacks an indirect realist opponent, one who accepts that the immediate objects of human knowledge are ideas. His arguments are largely metaphysical, although he also argues that indirect realism relies on an abstract idea of matter which we cannot possess. Berkeley's metaphysical conclusions were never widely accepted, and they are in no way implied by the empiricist account of size and distance perception given in the *New Theory*. However, the *New Theory*'s focus on the relations we construct between ideas of various senses sets the stage for later empiricist accounts of cognition. By drawing out the real issues underlying Molyneux's problem, Berkeley lays out issues that became central for theories of vision, and thus theories of cognition more generally. Both Condillac and Diderot, for instance, wrote about the Molyneux problem as Berkeley interpreted it.

A rather different attack on the innate powers of the mind is provided in Hume's *Treatise*, one of whose overarching arguments is that there is no distinct faculty of reason and that the powers traditionally ascribed to reason in fact result from learned habits of association. Let us approach this somewhat indirectly. One of Hume's most fundamental principles is what has come to be known as the *copy principle*: every simple idea is a copy of a simple impression, and every complex idea is composed of simple ideas. Thus there are no innate ideas and all content is derived from the senses. Hume is clearer than earlier writers about what justifies this. All known phenomena are consistent with it and no exceptions have been found; no one has come up with a complex idea not reducible to simple impressions. Moreover, the copy principle provides the best available explanation for facts like the (alleged) fact that a blind man has no idea of colors.

Empiricism has been variously seen as the cure for skepticism about the external world and as its main cause. Epicurean accounts, with their insistence on the truth of the appearances, can easily be read as anti-skeptical; and Gassendi and Locke's answers to skepticism about the external world both depend heavily on Epicurean elements in their theories of cognition. However, the sort of "veil of ideas" worries introduced by Berkeley delineate a path by which any indirect realist, empiricist or not, can easily be led to skeptical conclusions.

Hume's discussion in the *Treatise* of the "single-existence" and "double-existence" views, that is, direct and indirect realism, takes its starting point from this dialectic. Direct realism, which Hume assumes to be the view of common sense, cannot be maintained. The fact of perceptual relativity and perceptual error forces us to accept that perception involves real psychological intermediaries. At the same time, however, Hume argues that the philosophical view, indirect realism, also fails. For neither sensation nor reason are sufficient to explain how we can infer from our sensations to the existence of external objects which continue existing even when unperceived. Hume's second claim, that reason does not generate belief in continuing, distinct objects, is directed towards a Cartesian account which takes knowledge of external objects to be inferential. It is important to see that Hume's first claim, that sensation is not good enough, is not the claim that sensations do not *cause* our belief in continued, distinct objects. Rather, it is the claim that sensation does not *justify* that belief. For in the end Hume will conclude that sensation, together with the mind's innate powers of association, does give rise to belief in an external world which cannot be justified on any but a pragmatic basis.

Many have read Hume's argument as a skeptical one, but it is best, at least in this context, to emphasize the naturalism of Hume's story over its skepticism. We accept the existence of external objects with continuing existence on the basis of custom or habit, which Hume ultimately explains in terms of associationistic learning. This grounds no recommendation to alter our customary beliefs in external continuing objects. Indeed, Hume thinks no philosophical recommendation could convince us to do so. However, Hume does think his overarching argument that our practices of belief derive more from association than from reason, understood in a Cartesian or Lockean sense, has important implications for intellectual life. Thus, Hume not only attacks innate ideas and thus argues that there are no special entities for the faculty of reason to operate over; he has also threatened the ability of the faculty of reason as understood by Descartes and Locke to produce belief or guide action in any way. Even our belief that the data of the senses represents an enduring, mind-independent world is acquired as the result of the associations of information received in sense. By separating the *justification* of our beliefs from its *genesis*, Hume draws a separation between epistemology and psychology which would have been entirely unacceptable to theistic philosophers like Descartes, Gassendi, and Locke. In the course of doing this, he offers an account of human cognition which requires nothing innate beyond the three laws of association.

Empiricism understood as the denial of innate ideas and the claim that all content is constructed out of sensory materials is not tightly connected with empiricism understood as the methodology which favors observation and experimentation over hypothesis construction. (Someone who holds that it is the ideas of logic and morality which are innate could easily accept an empiricist methodology in science.) However, the two sorts of empiricism are often found together, and one of the most noteworthy examples of this is Hume's comparison between the principles of association and Newton's gravity – phenomena whose existence and effects we are sure of by observation, but whose nature or underlying causes we should remain silent about.

Another salient example is to be found in the work of the French Encyclopedists, who endorsed both a psychological principle of empiricism and a Newtonianism in scientific methodology. In his "Preliminary Discourse" to the *Encyclopedia*, D'Alembert writes that "in order to prove that [sensations] are the principle of all our knowledge, it suffices to show that they can be" – for "why suppose that we have purely intellectual notions at the outset, if all we need do in order to form them is to reflect upon our sensations?" (p. 7). D'Alembert's argument proceeds in the familiar form of giving an account of how the Cartesian "innate ideas" could be constructed from materials acquired in sense. The interest of his claim lies in the clarity with which he states that refuting innatism does not require showing that innate ideas cannot or do not exist. Rather, it merely requires showing that we need not give such an inflationary hypothesis to explain the phenomena. The language is reminiscent of Newton's *hypotheses non fingo*, and indeed D'Alembert goes on to praise Newton for seeing "that it was time to banish conjectures and vague hypotheses from physics" (p. 81). It is important to note how strictly D'Alembert intends this. He writes that "physics is therefore confined solely to observations and to calculations, medicine to the history of the human body . . . all the sciences are confined, as much as possible, to facts and to consequences deduced from them" (pp. 95–6). While the empiricist critique of Gassendi took as its starting point a psychological principle and inferred in large part from this a denial of the mind-independent natures grounding rationalist apriorism, by the mid-eighteenth century the methodological thesis of abstaining from hypotheses and merely exhibiting regularities among the phenomena is taken as providing grounds for psychological empiricism.

The line-up of empiricists which became canonical in the twentieth century begins to emerge in Condillac's writing. Condillac identifies the principle "that all our knowledge is derived from the senses" as one that the scholastics accepted without understanding, Bacon fully grasped, and Locke demonstrated. However, Locke mistakenly thought that this principle only applied to ideas, when it should be applied to the operations of the mind as well. Condillac takes "the design of explaining the origin of the operations of the mind by deriving them from a simple perception" as his original contribution. Just as Berkeley attempted to give an empiricist and, very roughly, associationist account of the mental operations Descartes ascribed to the mind's innate geometry, and Hume gave a reinterpretation in terms of association of what had been assumed to come from a roughly Cartesian innate faculty of reason, Condillac offers an empiricist account of what Locke held to be the mind's "innate faculty of knowing."

Condillac gives a list of the canonical "rationalists" – Descartes, Leibniz, Malebranche, and Spinoza – in the course of his argument that metaphysical system-building derives from a failure to understand the nature and function of human language. We find this emphasis on language as a source of error in Epicurus' division of inquiry into inquiries about things and trivial inquiries into "mere utterance," in Gassendi's recommendation that we use common words linked to clear ideas, and in Hume's insistence that we only use statements whose terms can be traced back to simple impressions. All these suggestions are accompanied, more or less explicitly, by the claim that the way to resolve metaphysical difficulties is by tracing word-meaning and linguistic ability back to the information provided by sensation. It is thus ironic that nativism resurfaces in the twentieth century in large part as a result of Noam Chomsky's *Cartesian Linguistics*, which argues that knowledge of the structure of language is innate in humans.

Conclusion

Any theory is empiricist, in my sense of the term, which denies the existence of innate ideas and argues that all the mental content we actually possess can be acquired from sensation and "inner sense" or reflection. I have considered empiricist accounts of cognition as they develop, in opposition to theories relying on innate content and with successive reformulations of what innate faculties can be appealed to, through the seventeenth and eighteenth centuries until the generation before Kant. The overarching empiricist line of objection is similar to one found in Epicurus, and indeed the categories of rationalism and empiricism, construed psychologically, could equally well be called Platonism and Epicureanism. Both Plato and the early modern rationalists who are his heirs tend to assume that innate ideas are thereby true and knowledge conducive, and empiricists tend to assume the same thing about basic sensory ideas. This easy derivation of epistemological conclusions from psychological premises is characteristic of early modern philosophy, and it is perhaps the most important way in which contemporary nativism in psychology differs from the nativism of early modern writers such as Descartes.

References and Further Reading

Bacon, Francis (1860). *Apopthegms*. In his *Works, Volume 13*. Brown and Taggart.
Condillac, Etienne de (1756). *An Essay on the Origin of Human Knowledge* (Thomas Nugent, trans.). J. Nourse.

D'Alembert, Jean Le Rond (1963). *Preliminary Discourse to the Encyclopedia of Diderot* (Richard Schwab, trans.). New York: Bobbs-Merrill.

Descartes, René (1984). *Collected Writings, Volume 2*. John Cottingham, Robert Stoothoff, and Dugald Murdoch, eds. and trans.). Cambridge: Cambridge University Press.

Grieg, J. Y. T. (ed.) (1932). *The Letters of David Hume*. Oxford: Clarendon Press.

Hume, David (2000). *Treatise of Human Nature* (David Norton and Mary Norton, eds.). Oxford: Oxford University Press.

Kant, Immanuel (1965). *Critique of Pure Reason* (Norman Kemp-Smith, trans.). New York: St. Martin's Press.

Locke, John (1979). *An Essay Concerning Human Understanding* (Peter H. Nidditch, ed.). Oxford: Clarendon Press.

8

Rationalism and Method

MATTHEW J. KISNER

The seventeenth century witnessed a dramatic transformation in the notion of method. Scholastic Aristotelians regarded method (*methodus*) as a branch of logic, in particular, the branch explaining the acquisition or discovery of knowledge. For these philosophers, method consisted of a formal procedure for arriving at the conclusions of demonstrative syllogisms. This view drew criticism from proponents of the emerging "new science." They pointed to the practical shortcomings of scholastic Aristotelianism, most notably its failure to provide either genuine explanations or new knowledge. In place of Aristotelian natural philosophy, followers of the new science conceived of the natural world as extended matter in motion. Consequently, its disciples turned to mathematics, rather than logic, as offering the tools of science. Furthermore, followers of the new science tended to view their findings as probable, the best conclusions given the available evidence. Consequently, they distanced themselves from the scholastic notion that our knowledge of the natural world follows from premises with logical necessity, as in demonstrative syllogisms. Although these philosophers continued to discuss method, they conceived of it more broadly as practices for discovering knowledge.

On the basis of the foregoing discussion, one might imagine that modern empiricist philosophers would receive the lion's share of the credit for extricating method from its scholastic Aristotelian roots. After all, the changes mentioned above are motivated by views we tend to associate with empiricists; for instance, that the certainty of scientific knowledge is limited by the available evidence or that knowledge is acquired by testing hypotheses against observed phenomena. Yet rationalists, led by Descartes, played a pioneering role in reinventing method. Descartes took issue with the scholastic notion that Aristotelian logic describes proper reasoning. He argued that sound reasoning is actually hindered by the systems of formal logic developed by Aristotle and his followers. Rather, Descartes characterized the proper function of reason as primitive, intellectual perception, what he described as "intuition" (*intuitus*). This account was derived largely from mathematics or, at least, Descartes' interpretation of it. He offered his own method for cultivating and employing this sort of reasoning. After surveying method at the beginning of the seventeenth century, this chapter will examine Descartes' method and its influence on the methods of Malebranche and Spinoza.

The Philosophical Background to Method

Method was one of the most extensively debated topics of the seventeenth century, largely because it offered scholastic institutions a venue for debating the success of Aristotelian science. By the mid-sixteenth century, before the emergence of the new science, there was already a vocal and growing dissatisfaction with received Aristotelianism. One source of dissatisfaction was the desire for a more practical science. Philosophers grew increasingly interested in knowledge that would be useful for manipulating and intervening in natural processes. This is evident, for instance, from the growing interest in alchemy and astrology, as well as the rise of the Italian medical schools. The philosophers of Padua and Bologna sought practical solutions to medical problems (for instance, treatments for disease), as well as procedures for acquiring such knowledge. In other words, there was a strong interest in the intersection of *scientia* and *techne*, the connection between demonstrated knowledge of the natural world, and the practical arts of doctors, surgeons, anatomists, and so forth.

This interest is demonstrated by the rise of Galenism, particularly in the great Italian universities. Galen remains today the most renowned Roman doctor, attending to the emperor Marcus Aurelius, as well as other Roman elites and even gladiators. Galen insisted on the importance of scientific knowledge for medical practice, arguing famously "the best doctor is also a philosopher" (Galen 1997: 30). He left a large body of philosophical and medical work, much of it procedures for scientific investigation, the proper demonstration of conclusions and practical medical advice (e.g., how best to take and interpret a pulse). Perhaps most interesting to fifteenth- and sixteenth-century scholars, he also offered commentaries to Aristotle. In general, Aristotle was a thoroughly theoretical philosopher, offering little guidance on the practical questions that concerned late medieval philosophers. Galen offered these later scholars the groundwork for a more practical Aristotelianism. Much of the interest in method arises in this context, as part of a project to recover such a science from ancient texts.

The interest in method also spoke to the apparent failure of Aristotle's philosophy to provide genuine explanations of the natural world. Aristotelianism holds that an explanation amounts to an account of the causes that bring about natural change. According to the most prevalent Thomist interpretation, this amounts to an account of phenomena in terms of forms and qualities. This interpretation leads to particularly weak explanations, arguing, for instance, that a swan is white because it possesses the quality of whiteness. Consequently, scholastic Aristotelianism was criticized on the grounds that it failed to produce conclusions which were previously unknown. This criticism is expressed in the context of the demonstrative syllogism. Although Aristotle maintained that a demonstration is distinguished from other syllogisms by its explanatory power, critics challenged that it is actually a *petitio principii*, circular or question begging (e.g., Sextus Empiricus, *Outlines of Pyrrhonism*, II: 134–244; *Adversus Mathematicos*, II: 300–481; Cicero, *Academica*, II: xiv–xxx). It was believed that in order to correct this problem philosophy required a systematic procedure, or method, for moving from what is known, the premises of a demonstration, to what is genuinely unknown, new conclusions. Consequently, the explanation problem was addressed obliquely by calls for a method of discovery. In this respect, the focus on method opened up space for considering problems with Aristotelianism, providing a voice for growing dissatisfaction with the tradition.

Given the close relationship between anti-Aristotelianism and the rise of method, there is an important distinction between two kinds of work on method at the dawn of the seventeenth century. The first aimed to devise a method to supplement and reform scholastic Aristotelianism. The second, more radical, used method as a platform for rejecting Aristotelianism altogether. The latter would become more popular with the rise of the new science in the mid-seventeenth century. By 1619, however, it was advanced only by a few, though highly visible philosophers, most notably Sanchez and Bacon. In order to understand the issues at stake between these groups, we should first examine the reformed Aristotelian method in closer detail. The popular Paduan method is derived from Aristotle's account of the demonstrative syllogism. The demonstration was central to scholastic science for several reasons. Most importantly, it provided an account of *scientia* and thus a standard for scientific knowledge. According to Aristotelian method, the demonstration also directs scientific inquiry by providing a procedure for acquiring knowledge. This claim was supported by an unusual interpretation of *Posterior Analytics*. In chapter 13 Aristotle emphasizes the demonstration's explanatory powers by providing two examples of syllogisms:

Q The planets do not twinkle.
R What does not twinkle is near the earth.
P Therefore, the planets are near the earth.

R What is near the earth does not twinkle.
Q The planets are near the earth.
P Therefore, the planets do not twinkle.

According to Aristotle, both syllogisms are deductively sound; however, only the latter demonstrative syllogism provides an explanation because it proceeds from the cause. "It is not because they do not twinkle that they are near, but because they are near they do not twinkle" (Aristotle 1975: 40). Consequently, the former kind of syllogism was known as *demonstratio quia* and the latter *demonstratio propter quid*. The Paduan school, best represented by Zabarella, read these examples as complementary steps in a method. The *demonstratio propter quid* was taken to represent a compositive step, which demonstrates that an effect or phenomenon follows from a cause. This step is necessary for the presentation of scientific conclusions and as evidence of their validity. Zabarella addresses the call for a method of discovery by arguing that there is an additional prior step indicated by the *demonstratio quia*: resolution.

> Since because of the weakness of our mind and powers the principles from which demonstration is to be made are unknown to us, and since we cannot set out from the unknown, we are of necessity forced to resort to a kind of secondary procedure, which is the resolutive method that leads to the discovery of principles, so that once they are found we can demonstrate the natural effects from them. (Zabarella, *De Methodis*, III, xviii; in Randall 1961: 52)

The notion that method consists of this "double process" was originally derived from Galen's interpretation of Aristotle by prominent Paduans such as Hugo of Siena, Jacopa

139

da Forli, and Pietro Pomponazzi. The addition of the resolutive or regress step adds the element of discovery because it explains how to arrive at the general principle that serves as the premise of a demonstration – in other words, the cause. The Paduans did not accept that these general principles were obvious or could be established by simple observation. Rather, they could only be discovered through the process of resolution or regress. The resolutive step begins from what is known, usually the observation of a natural phenomenon (e.g., the non-twinkling of the planets), and proceeds to what is unknown, the causal mechanism that explains the phenomena. It consists of three stages: (1) observe the effects (phenomena); (2) resolve the complex fact into component parts and conditions; (3) analyze these to determine the cause. Although the procedure appears arcane, it is predicated on an insightful way of approaching scientific discovery: discovery consists of both the observation and *analysis* of natural phenomena in order to determine the general causal forces at work. Once this has been accomplished, the practitioner of method is in a position to demonstrate his knowledge by showing how the various effects, the natural phenomena, are a consequence of the causal principle. Thus, the *demonstratio quia* represents the first step of scientific investigation, whereby causal principles are determined or "discovered" and the *demonstratio propter quid* represents the second, whereby the effects are demonstrated.

Although Zabarella supplemented Aristotle's theory with a new method of discovery, he left intact the notion that Aristotle's logic describes proper reasoning. The Paduan method held that a conclusion is demonstrated by showing how the effects are properly inferred by means of a syllogism. The method even treated the regress as the inference of a general causal principle from particulars more or less consistent with Aristotelian theories of inference. Anti-Aristotelian methods, however, rejected Aristotelian logic as a description of sound reasoning. This claim is most clearly articulated in the work of Francisco Sanchez. He served on the faculty at the University of Toulouse from 1575 to 1623, first as a professor of arts and then of medicine. Sanchez was educated within the same Galenist medical tradition as Zabarella. His close association with this tradition is sometimes obscured by his commitment to skepticism. Sanchez's most famous work, *Quod Nihil Scitur* or *That Nothing Is Known* (1581), upholds the Pyrronhian position that even the claim of its title cannot be proven with certainty. Sanchez, however, should be distinguished from other Renaissance skeptics such as Montaigne, because his views arose from consideration of scholastic Aristotelianism, rather than rediscovered ancient skepticism. Sanchez echoed the criticisms of Vives and Ramus in arguing that scholastic science traps its students in a labyrinth of terms and distinctions, which serve only to obscure its subject:

> Even if the sky should exist, it at once ceases to be anything at all if it has not found a place in some categorical proposition! In short, this leads those philosophers into endless quibbles. Manufacturing still more words to explain words, they plunge themselves and their unfortunate audience utterly into a deep abyss of chaotic folly. (QNS 179)

This rhetoric was supported by a deeper criticism than those offered by his predecessors. Sanchez targeted logic or dialectic, charging that its formal system of inference lays no special claim to true conclusions.

What, now, is this thing called a "demonstration"? You will define it afresh as follows: "a syllogism that gives birth to knowledge." You have been guilty of a circular argument, and have deceived me just as you have deceived yourself. But – what is a syllogism? This is marvelous – prick up your ears! Strain your imagination! – for perhaps it will not be large enough to contain so many words. How subtle, how long, and how difficult is the science of syllogisms! In fact it is futile, long and difficult, and there is no science of syllogisms. (QNS 181)

Sanchez's writing is highly polemical and often the arguments themselves are difficult to reconstruct. However, the main thrust of his attack is clear: against scholastic method, Sanchez argues that demonstrative syllogism is powerless to reveal genuine natural causes. "Whereas they ought to investigate the natures of things and their causes, and do in fact claim to do so, they invent *new* things" (QNS 180). Indeed, Sanchez's skepticism arose largely from this line of reasoning. Following the Pyrrhonist's classic *ad hominem* strategy, Sanchez attacked Aristotelianism with its own account of *scientia*, arguing that the demonstration cannot, according to its own standards, claim knowledge of anything. In doing so, Sanchez rejected the notion that Aristotelian logic is the means by which we recognize *scientia*, the vehicle of sound reasoning.

Although Sanchez concluded that true knowledge is, strictly speaking, unattainable, he remained optimistic about the prospects for science. Sanchez proposed an alternative method that aims to attain the closest possible approximation to perfect knowledge. In place of formal inference, "the science of syllogism," he emphasized the importance of observation, offering a more genuinely empirical method than scholasticism. This stands in stark contrast to the Zabarellan method, which still looked to Aristotelianism for an account of metaphysics, theories of forms, qualities, causes, and so forth. Sanchez extricated method from this Aristotelian machinery, providing an alternative framework for conceiving of knowledge, its proof and acquisition.

> My purpose is to establish, as far as I am able, a kind of scientific knowledge that is both sound and as easy as possible to attain; but not a science that is full of those chimeras and fictions, unconnected with factual truth, which are put together, not to teach facts, but solely to show off the writer's intellectual subtlety. (QNS 290)

Bacon similarly argued against the notion that dialectic serves as the basis for the method by which we acquire and demonstrate knowledge. This view arose, foremost, as a criticism of the imagination, evident in Bacon's discussion of poesy:

> *Poesy* is a part of learning in measure of words for the most part restrained, but in all other points extremely licensed, and doth truly refer to the Imagination; which, being not tied to the laws of matter, may at pleasure join that which nature hath severed, and sever that which nature hath joined, and so make unlawful matches and divorces of things. (AL 186)

The danger is that the imagination may sometimes interfere in the natural function of reason to "buckle and bow the mind unto the nature of things" (AL 187). Thus, the danger of poesy and, to a certain extent, language in general is that it has a tendency to employ a kind of flawed reasoning which misrepresents nature. This argument is

141

part of a general criticism of similitude, reasoning in which one mistakenly attributes human ways of representing and understanding things to nature itself. Bacon took issue with Aristotelianism by directing this criticism at the syllogism. The premises of syllogisms import concepts that are foreign to nature.

> Allow some Principles or Axioms were rightly induced, yet nevertheless certain it is that Middle Propositions cannot be deduced from them in subject of nature by Syllogism, that is, by touch and reduction of them to principles in a middle term . . . The subtlety of nature and its operations will not be enchained in those bonds: for Arguments consist of Propositions, and Propositions of Words; and Words are but the current tokens or marks of Popular Notions of things, which notions if they be grossly and variably collected out of particulars, it is not the laborious examination either of consequences of arguments or of the truth of propositions, that can ever correct that error. (AL 222)

Bacon's reasoning is nicely illustrated by his theory of the idols. The idols of the human mind are contrasted to the ideas of the divine. "The former are nothing more than arbitrary abstractions; the latter are the creator's own stamp upon creation, impressed and defined in matter by true and exquisite lines" (NO 1: 124). Bacon's view is that our human way of understanding things – the idols of the mind – colors our understanding of nature, obscuring the divine ideas that shape it. Syllogism perpetuates the idols of the mind, false understandings of things that are reified in popular notions of things and language. The antidote to this problem is Bacon's method of true induction. This is a process by which the real causes of things are revealed by considering all possible causes and then systematically ruling out candidates by means of careful observation. It is only through this procedure that the true natures of things are revealed and God's creation is understood, at least, to the best of our ability. Although Bacon occasionally resorts to dialectic he holds that it is powerless to see beyond the idols.

Descartes' Method

Given the nature of Descartes' studies at La Flèche, he most likely had a general idea of the major themes and issues at stake in discussions of method. Descartes' main published claims about the method are contained in the *Discourse on Method*. There he argues that there is a single method, which is applicable to all scientific questions – what he sometimes called a "universal science" (CSMK 51). The *Discourse* situates the project of method within a larger, far more ambitious philosophical program. Descartes was a member of a circle of philosophers, working primarily in Paris, outside the academic establishment. They held that scholastic Aristotelianism was incapable of generating scientific progress. They took this failure to be symptomatic of a misconceived philosophical system. To revive philosophy, they would have to devise a system that overcame its problems. Hobbes articulates the main features of this project:

> They who reject, or not much regard philosophy, are commonly esteemed, and are, indeed, men of sounder judgment than those who, from opinions, though not vulgar, yet full of uncertainty, and carelessly received, do nothing but dispute and wrangle, like men

that are not well in their wits. I confess, indeed, that that part of philosophy by which magnitudes and figures are computed, is highly improved. But because I have not observed the like advancement in the other parts of it, my purpose is, as far forth as I am able, to lay open the few and first Elements of Philosophy in general, as so many seeds from which pure and true Philosophy may hereafter spring up by little and little. (Hobbes 1656: 2)

Descartes' account in the *Discourse* reflects Hobbes' diagnosis – and prognosis – for philosophy. Although Descartes took issue with almost every facet of Aristotelianism, his various criticisms sprang from the fundamental conviction that it failed to provide an adequate platform for scientific progress: "regarding philosophy, it had been cultivated for many centuries by the most excellent minds and yet there is still no point in it which is not disputed and hence doubtful" (CSM 1: 114–15). The *Discourse* served as an introduction to a set of treatises in natural philosophy, which Descartes saw as the makings of a new science. These treatises do not rest upon Aristotelian metaphysics or natural philosophy; except for the occasional jibe, there is no reference to forms, intelligible species, elements, or other scholastic terminology. The *Discourse* aims to situate this work within an alternative conception of science. Consequently, this text offers a sketch of the main features of Descartes' philosophical system: an overview of his natural philosophy (part five), a preview of his metaphysics (parts three and four), and an account of the method.

Given Descartes' aims in the *Discourse*, this final point concerning method was the most important. Descartes' account of the method explains how to attain certain knowledge and, consequently, how he was entitled to his conclusions, even though they are presented without the benefit of the usual Aristotelian justificatory machinery. In the service of this aim, Descartes presented his method as an alternative way of identifying and attaining certain knowledge.

I thought I had to seek some other method comprising the advantages of these three subjects [logic, algebra, and geometry] but free from their defects. I thought, in place of the large number of rules that make up logic, I would find the following four to be sufficient, provided that I made a strong and unswerving resolution never to fail to observe them. (CSM 1: 120)

In short, the four rules are:

1 Reach judgments only on the basis of clear and distinct perception.
2 Resolve problems into their simplest parts.
3 Proceed from simple to complex matters.
4 Reach answers only through complete enumeration.

The call for resolution (rule 2) and composition (rule 3) should not be confused with the popular scholastic method to which it bears some similarity. Remember, scholastic methods are parasitic on an Aristotelian philosophical system, in which resolution and composition are employed to produce demonstrations. Perhaps in order to avoid such confusion, Descartes explicitly rejects methods which merely reform scholasticism. "It would be unreasonable for an individual to plan to reform a state by changing it from the foundations up and overturning it in order to set it up again; or again for him to plan to reform the body of the sciences or the established order of teaching them in the schools" (CSM 1: 117). Thus, like Bacon and Sanchez, Descartes offered his method as an alternative to, rather than a reform of, Aristotelian philosophy. In this respect, the *Discourse* treats method as the cornerstone of an anti-Aristotelian philosophical program.

Descartes justified his method on the basis that it properly employs our cognitive faculties, namely reason. At first glance, it is not clear how this sets Descartes apart from Aristotelians. As Descartes admits in the *Regulae*, dialecticians provide precepts, which they suppose

> govern human reason. They prescribe certain forms of reasoning in which the conclusions follow with such irresistible necessity that if our reason relies on them, even though it takes, as it were, a rest from considering a particular inference clearly and attentively, it can nevertheless draw a conclusion which is certain simply in virtue of the form. (CSM 1: 36)

In other words, scholastic Aristotelians claim that their method properly employs reason. Descartes disagrees. His denigration of the Aristotelian account of reason is illustrated nicely by his use of the term *bon sens*. This term is calculated, for rhetorical effect, to undermine the scholastic conception of reason, by contrasting it to good sense or, as we might say, common sense. Indeed, Descartes treated scholastic dialectic as the paradigm of poor reasoning, reading its historical failure as evidence of this point. In contrast, when reason is used correctly, Descartes claimed it produces conclusions which are as certain and uncontroversial as mathematical proofs. In other words, Descartes held that the method possesses all the certainty afforded by proper reasoning. "What pleased me most about this method was that by following it I was sure in every case to use my reason, if not perfectly, at least as well as was in my power" (CSM 1: 121).

By rejecting the notion that Aristotelian logic describes the proper exercise of reason, Descartes echoed the criticisms of Bacon and Sanchez. This point is made explicit in the early unpublished *Regulae*. In a section of the text dating as early as 1620, Descartes directed his criticism of Aristotle at the demonstrative syllogism. The text advances two claims. First, syllogism does not lead to the discovery of new knowledge; "dialecticians are unable to formulate a syllogism with a true conclusion unless they are already in possession of the substance of the conclusion, i.e., unless they have previous knowledge of the very truth deduced in the syllogism" (CSM 1: 36–7). Second, the demonstrative syllogism admits false conclusions. "As we have often noticed, truth often slips through these fetters, while those who employ them are left entrapped in them" (CSM 1: 36). The former is the usual criticism of scholastic Aristotelianism, that it is a *petitio principii*; the Paduan method is intended to address this worry. The latter, a much stronger charge, raises the more general criticism that Aristotelian dialectic leads us away from real knowledge. Descartes likens the syllogism to a trap, which commits one to false conclusions. This rhetorical device is not original to Descartes. In a previously quoted passage, Bacon refers to the syllogism as a "bond" which truth resists. Sanchez similarly argues that Aristotle taught "how to lay snares for" the ignorant "by means of which they may be forced to abandon the truth" (QNS 273).

Despite their common ground, Descartes' optimism in the power of reason set him apart from Bacon and Sanchez. Sanchez's low opinion of reason is evident in his skeptical leanings. Bacon similarly argued that our faculties are, by their nature, highly fallible. He belonged to a tradition which focused on the machinery of human cognition in order to explain error.

> The human understanding on account of its own nature readily supposes a greater order and uniformity in things than it finds. And though there are many things in Nature which are unique and unlike anything else, it devises parallels and correspondences and relations which are not there. (NO 1: 45)

Consequently, Bacon emphasized the role that the faculties play in hindering science and obscuring truth. For Bacon, like Glanvill and others, this view is supported by the theology of the fall, according to which original sin corrupts the faculties and distorts the mirror of human understanding. The method of true induction is a rigid procedure that is intended to rein in – indeed, to supplant – the natural operation of the faculties. Bacon balked at the notion that reason alone, in other words, without the discipline of a method, is a capable instrument of science:

> The earlier Greeks, whose writings have been lost, were more careful to steer a course between a boasting certainty and despairing Acatalepsy; and though more often indignantly complaining of the difficulty of inquiry and the obscurity of things, and fairly champing at the bit, they still press on with their object and engaged with Nature, thinking, it seems that it is best not to argue that nothing can be known, but rather to try and find out. Even they, however, trusted in the power of their intellect and applied no rule, but based everything on keen meditation and perpetual turning and twisting of mind. (NO: preface)

In contrast, Descartes identified the natural function of reason, rather than a rigid procedure, as the way to avoid error. He focused on the proper function of the faculties: how they provide us with knowledge, rather than keep us from it. Descartes' account of cognition is most developed in the *Regulae*. In the second rule, Descartes argues that the best strategy for examining reason is to focus on domains in which science has attained certain knowledge. "Of all the sciences so far discovered, arithmetic and geometry alone are, as we said above, free from any taint of falsity and uncertainty" (CSM 1: 12). Descartes privileges arithmetic and geometry because:

> they are alone concerned with an object so pure and simple that they make no assumptions that experience might render uncertain; they consist entirely in deducing conclusions by means of rational arguments. They are therefore the easiest and clearest of all the sciences and have just the sort of object we are looking for. (CSM 1: 12)

In other words, Descartes champions mathematics because it reasons about its objects independently of experience. This is what it means for them to be "pure" and "simple." Descartes' conclusion is the prescription of the second rule: science should cultivate this kind of reasoning by attending "only to those objects of which our minds seem capable of having certain and indubitable cognition" (CSM 1: 10). In pursuing this line of reasoning, Descartes took a rather controversial position in a longstanding feud. In the previous century, mathematics had undergone a serious attack. Beginning with the publication of Piccolimin's *Commentarium de Certitudine Mathematicarum Disciplinarum* in 1547, it was argued that mathematical demonstrations did not qualify as *scientia* because they did not traffic in causes. Debate over this question continued well into the seventeenth century; Giusepe Blancana's *De Mathematicarum Natura* was published in 1615, just a few years before Descartes began work on the *Regulae*. Descartes' defense of mathematics was likely influenced by Clavius, the author of the mathematics textbook used at La Flèche, who defended mathematics as the paradigm of certain reasoning:

> Truly, if the nobility and preeminence of a science is to be judged by the certainty of the demonstrations that it uses, there is no doubt that the mathematical disciplines will have the first place among all the rest. For they demonstrate and confirm everything concerning which they undertake disputation by the firmest reasons, so that they truly produce knowledge in the soul of the hearers and, in short, remove all doubt. (Clavius 1611: 5)

The centerpiece of Descartes' account of mathematics and reason in general is intuition, the paradigm case of proper reasoning. Intuition is characterized foremost by its immediacy. It is a single cognitive act in which the mind grasps or apprehends its object directly. Descartes probably had in mind geometry, in which fundamental concepts, such as line or angle, appear to be understood, not by analyzing definitions, but through a more primitive cognitive act: we know these things by "seeing" them with our mind. For this reason, Descartes compares intuition to visual perception, calling it "mental vision" or "intellectual vision." This metaphor is central to Descartes' account of intuition. He makes it explicit in rule 9:

> We can best learn how mental intuition is to be employed by comparing it with ordinary vision. If one tries to look at many objects at one glance, one sees none of them distinctly. Likewise, if one is inclined to attend to many things at the same time in a single act of thought, one does so with a confused mind. Yet craftsmen who engage in delicate operations, and are used to fixing their eyes on a single point, acquire through practice the ability to make perfect distinctions between things, however minute and delicate. The same is true of those who never let their thinking be distracted by many different objects at the same time, but always devote their whole attention to the simplest and easiest of matters; they become perspicacious. (CSM 1: 33)

This metaphor pervades all of Descartes' thinking about intuition. It is implied by the binary opposition of "clarity" and "obscurity." In the same vein, he describes our intellectual faculties as "the mind's eye" (CSM 1: 20) or "a light innate in us" (CSM 1: 22). The term "natural light" is specifically equated with intuition in a letter to Mersenne of 1639: "la lumiere naturelle ou intuitus mentis" (CSMK 140).

It is significant that Descartes describes this vision as "intellectual." As early as 1620 Descartes had already arrived at his tripartite division of the faculties: intellect, imagination, and sensation. Descartes argues that intuition derives its truth-revealing power from its close association with the intellect:

146

By "intuition" I do not mean the fluctuating testimony of the senses or the deceptive judgment of the imagination as it botches things together, but the conception of a clear and attentive mind, which is so easy and distinct that there can be no room for doubt about what we are understanding. Alternatively, and this comes to the same thing, intuition is the indubitable conception of a clear and attentive mind which proceeds solely from the light of reason. (CSM 1: 14)

We should be careful, however, not to identify intuition exclusively with the intellect. Intuitions can occur through the cooperation of the imagination, which furnishes the intellect with images of its objects. As Descartes makes explicit in the later *Regulae*, this is the case with intuitions of quantities and extended figures – bodies and pure geometrical objects (CSM 1: 43, 56). It is for this reason that Descartes later claims the imagination is necessary for all mathematics (CSMK 227). In this respect, Descartes left an important role for the imagination in intuition. This claim is easily reconciled with the criticism of imagination raised in the passage above. Descartes' concern that the imagination may interfere in proper judgments is familiar from earlier thinkers such as Bacon. Descartes tended to conceive of the imagination as playing either an active or passive role with respect to the intellect: "The intellect can either be stimulated by the imagination or act upon it" (CSM 1: 43). As long as the imagination is passive, constrained by the intellect to provide images as directed, it plays an important role in reasoning. Imagination only leads to error when it becomes active, by misrepresenting matters so as to force a deceptive judgment. It is because the imagination can play a critical role in intuition that so many of Descartes' examples from the late *Regulae* (in particular rules 14–16) involve the imagination.

The most perplexing aspect of Descartes' account is his insistence that intuitions are self-evident; they leave "no room for doubt" about their object. This remark presupposes two important claims. The first is one of the central presuppositions of Descartes' method, that it is the nature of reason to reveal the truth. It follows that, by using reason correctly – as we do in the case of intuition – we are guaranteed to perceive the truth. The second is that truth, in general, is primitive. To bring this point into relief, it is helpful to compare a scholastic Aristotelian conception of truth to Descartes'. Scholastics agree with Descartes that the truth is grasped by a particular mental operation, though on the scholastic account the conclusions of all syllogisms are reached through inference, as opposed to intuition. Furthermore, scholastics agree that the truth of these conclusions is, in a sense, self-evident: in performing a deduction it becomes obvious that the conclusion necessarily follows from the premises. The scholastic view, however, parts company with Descartes in supposing that the conclusion of a syllogism is true in virtue of its form. Scholastics claim to "draw a conclusion which is certain simply in virtue of its form" (CSM 1: 36). To Descartes this suggests that argument forms, rules of inference, and so forth, are required to define and identify the truth. His hostility to this claim is best demonstrated by the most important intuition of Descartes' mature philosophy: the *cogito*. Descartes bristles at the suggestion that the conclusion "I am" follows from the premise "I think" as in a syllogism (CSM 2: 100). Although Descartes may concede that a valid argument form sets forth conditions for the conclusion's being true, he rejects the notion that truth can be defined by recourse to any such system.

147

Descartes suggests an argument for this view in a letter to Mersenne of October 16, 1639:

> I have never had any doubts about truth, because it seems a notion so transcendentally clear that nobody can be ignorant of it. There are many ways of examining a balance before using it, but there is no way to learn what truth is, if one does not know it by nature. What reason would we have for accepting anything which could teach us the nature of truth if we did not know that it was true, that is to say, if we did not know truth? (CSMK 139)

The argument asserts that any definition of truth would be circular. This is because we could only arrive at such a definition by examining examples of the truth, which we could not identify unless we already knew what truth was. An implicit target of this criticism is the scholastic notion that truth can be explained by appealing to argument forms. This is impossible, the argument goes, because we could not judge an argument form to be truth preserving in the first place, without presupposing an understanding of what truth is. Without such a prior understanding of truth, we would have no way of distinguishing the truth-preserving inferences that characterize a valid argument form like Barbara from fallacious inferences. Descartes concludes that truth is indefinable; in other words, primitive. Although this passage is written much later than the *Regulae*, this kind of reasoning clearly influences Descartes' claim that intuitions are self-evident: because truth cannot be defined, we know it only when we see it. Thus, we know the truth only through intuition, the cognitive act by which we "see" it.

Descartes' Successors: Malebranche and Spinoza on Method

The central claims of Descartes' method reverberate in the subsequent rationalists Malebranche and Spinoza. Malebranche's method, methodically laid out in the *Search after Truth*, is particularly indebted to Descartes. Like Descartes, Malebranche held that method entails cultivating proper reasoning. In this respect, he presents the method as offering a kind of mental training. "The aim of this final book [on method] is to render the mind as perfect as it can naturally be, by supplying the help necessary to extend its scope and make it more attentive" (*Search* Vi.i.i, 408). Malebranche's remark about extending the scope of the mind should be read quite literally. Malebranche argues that because the method consists in proper reasoning, it should be applicable to all disciplines and questions. For this reason his method follows Descartes' in aspiring to the mantle "universal science." "If I fulfilled this aim perfectly, which I do not pretend to do since this is but an attempt thereat, I could be said to have produced a universal science" (*Search* VI.i.i, 408).

When it comes to characterizing the proper direction of reason, Malebranche was wary of Aristotelian logic. He writes that Aristotle's logic "contains nothing of worth other than a few definitions so vague and a few terms so general that they can be used in all sorts of philosophies" (*Search* III.ii.viii, 243). Book III, Part I, chapter 3 of the *Search* is devoted entirely to a criticism of Aristotelian logic. It concludes:

This alone shows that the ordinary sorts of logic are more suited for diminishing rather than increasing the mind's capacity, because clearly, if in the search after a given truth one wishes to use the rules these logics give us, the mind's capacity will be so divided up that it will have less capacity for carefully understanding the full extent of the subject under consideration. (p. 210)

Thus Malebranche felt that Aristotelian logic actually did more harm than good in the pursuit of knowledge. In order to understand proper reasoning, Malebranche turned, not to dialectics, but rather to mathematics. A subheading in the aforementioned chapter reads: "the method of geometers increases the mind's capacity, whereas Aristotle's diminishes it."

To understand how Malebranche favored mathematics and more generally how he conceived of proper reasoning, we must first consider his account of cognition. Malebranche's account is premised on the distinction between the understanding and the will. The former is a faculty for receiving ideas and the latter a faculty for volition by means of which we (among other things) assent to or deny the truth of things perceived by the understanding (*Search* I.i.i, 8). Since the mind is neither extended nor divisible, Malebranche is clear that these are merely different faculties, not different "parts" of the mind. The understanding operates either in conjunction with the corporeal faculties (senses and imagination) or in isolation from the body. In both cases, the understanding performs no activity other than passive perception. Although Malebranche may not use the term "intuition," he conceives of intellectual activity in the same terms.

> Just as the faculty of receiving different figures and configurations in bodies is entirely passive and contains no action, so the faculty of receiving different ideas and modifications in the mind is entirely passive and contains no action. (*Search* I.i.i, 3)

As with Descartes, this characterization of the understanding is sweeping. It extends not only to the perception of ideas but also to the understanding's role in inference, deduction, and judgment. In each of these, Malebranche claims that the activity of the understanding is nothing more than the perception of the relationship between things.

> I say, then, that there is no difference on the part of the understanding between a simple perception, a judgment, and an inference, other than that the understanding by a simple perception perceives a simple thing without any relation to anything else whatsoever, that in judgments it perceives the relations between two or more things, and that in inferences it perceives the relations among the relations of things. Consequently, all the operations of the understanding are nothing but pure perceptions. (*Search* I.ii.vii).

This account of cognition gives rise to the two main directives of Malebranche's method. First, it exhorts us to rein in our will by assenting to the truth of something only when doing so is justified by the appropriate perceptions. This reflects a concern to train and focus our attention properly – a natural consequence of conceiving of proper cognitive activity as perception. In pursuit of this aim, Malebranche's method, like Descartes', directs us to focus on what is self-evident. The first rule of Malebranche's method is to "never give complete consent except to propositions which seem so evidently true that we cannot refuse it of them without feeling an inward pain and the secret reproaches of reason" (*Search* I.ii.iv, 10). In other words, Malebranche recommends that we reason "only on the basis of clear ideas," or to use Descartes' language, that we accept as true only what we can clearly and distinctly perceive (*Search* VI.ii.ii, 440). He argues that Aristotelian science had met with failure precisely because it neglected to observe this rule.

Although this focus on self-evident cognition resembles Descartes' method, Malebranche's was shaped by a greater concern with the role corporeal faculties play in error. Descartes expounded his method early in his career, before he developed his criticism of sensation as unreliable and prone to error (evident in the skeptical arguments of the First Meditation). In fact, Descartes' work on method never advanced a hallmark view of his mature philosophy, that pure perceptions of the intellect possess greater certainty than those of the imagination. On the contrary, the method takes mathematics, which exercises the corporeal faculty of imagination, as the standard of the most perfect knowledge. In fact, much of Descartes' work on method, particularly the late *Regulae*, is concerned with harnessing the image-making powers of the imagination.

Malebranche's method is clearly influenced by Descartes' *mature* work, where he came to regard the imagination as less certain than pure intellect. In this respect, Malebranche's method gives us some idea of how Descartes' might have looked, had he (Descartes) devised it in the 1640s. For Malebranche, the body's influence on the mind is usually deceptive. The better part of Books I and II is an effort to catalogue and stave off "the infinite errors and very great miseries" arising from the influence of the body (*Search* II.iii.vi, 195). For instance, the close relationship between parents and children, necessary for biological survival, inclines children to accept the truth of whatever they are told by their elders, thereby leading them into error. When Malebranche finally turns in Book III to the understanding, he apologizes that there is so little to say about errors involving the understanding alone: "The imagination and the senses are fertile and inexhaustible sources of error and illusions, but the mind acting by itself is not so liable to err" (*Search* III.i.i, 197).

Malebranche's denigration of the corporeal faculties is supported by deep theological commitments, the sort that motivated Bacon's criticisms of our faculties. Malebranche lays these out in the first lines of the *Search*:

> The mind of man is by its nature situated, as it were, between its Creator and corporeal creatures, for, according to Saint Augustine, there is nothing but God above it and nothing but bodies below it. (*Search*, preface: xix)

From its creator "the mind receives its life, its light, and its entire felicity"; "the mind's union with the body, on the contrary, infinitely debases man and is today the main cause of all his errors and miseries." This view dovetails with Malebranche's Platonic epistemological commitments as well. According to Malebranche, the ideas of the intellect exist independently of us, in a third realm, distinct from both bodies and minds. Malebranche identifies this third realm with God. Proper perception, on this view, famously means perceiving ideas in God. Malebranche's aim is both to avoid error and to create a closer relationship with God by perceiving true ideas in him.

Despite this damning picture of our corporeal cognitive faculties, Malebranche nevertheless recognized that they play an important heuristic role in understanding. This is expressed in the second directive of Malebranche's method. Because the mind is mired in bodily things and more accustomed to examining them, Malebranche recommends using the imagination for representation. "We cannot learn anything if we do not give it our attention, and . . . we can hardly be attentive to something if we do not imagine it and do not represent it vividly in our brain" (*Search* II.ii.i, 132). There is a deep reason for Malebranche admitting the imagination as a heuristic device. Malebranche conceives of truth as the relationships which obtain between ideas and things. "Truth is nothing else but a real relation" (*Search* VI.i.v, 433). Malebranche believes that these relationships can be represented to us as magnitudes. "As every relation is a magnitude, we can clearly express all relations by numbers and represent them to the imagination with lines" (*Search* VI.i.v, 434). Thus, Malebranche turns to mathematics as providing a model for his method, in part because mathematics provides a way of representing magnitude and relationships of magnitude.

> It is clear that man's mind is so meager, his memory so unfaithful, and his imagination of so little scope, that without using numbers and written symbols, and without the skill employed in arithmetic, it would be impossible to perform the operations necessary for knowing the precise inequality of magnitudes and their relations. (*Search* VI.i.v, 435)

It is important to note that the relationships among ideas are not relationships of magnitude; ideas are not material or extended. Malebranche's suggestion is merely that we represent them as such in order to grasp them.

The general Cartesian tendencies of Malebranche's method are also reflected in the work of Spinoza. Spinoza's method is usually most closely associated with Bacon's (Savan 1986). In the *Theological-Political Treatise*, Spinoza suggests that one should begin interpreting nature by compiling natural histories, in other words by cataloguing observed phenomena. In this vein, Spinoza compares interpreting nature to interpreting scripture.

> For just as the method of interpreting nature consists above all in compiling a natural history from which, as from established facts, we infer definitions of natural things; so also to interpret scripture we must prepare a sound scriptural history, and from that, as from established facts and principles, to reach legitimate conclusions about the intentions of the authors of scripture. (TTP III 98; trans. Gabbey 1996: 170)

This resembles Bacon's method for interpreting nature by applying the method of true induction to compiled natural histories. At first glance, this description of Spinoza's method might seem too empiricist to be considered under the same heading as Descartes' method of intuition. However, we should not make too much of these Baconian tendencies. Bacon claimed that the work of true induction and compiling histories reveals the true natures of things. In the previously cited passage, Spinoza claims only that this method provides us with "definitions." Spinoza maintains that the true natures of things are grasped through the direct perception of essences and their causes, in short, through the natural light. He argues that the Baconian interpretive method is only

151

called for in those instances where such perceptions are not available. Following the passage previously cited, Spinoza continues:

> Scripture very often deals with matters that cannot be deduced from principles known to the natural light, for it comprises for the most part historical accounts and revelations ... therefore the knowledge of ... nearly everything contained in scripture must be sought only from scripture itself, just as the knowledge of nature is sought from nature itself.

Here Spinoza relies upon a distinction, implicit in rationalists like Descartes, between the certain, general knowledge acquired through intuition (the sort found in metaphysics) and particular, probabilistic empirical knowledge, common to the particular sciences. Spinoza's Baconian method applies to the latter, but not the former.

Spinoza expounds the true method for grasping the natures of things in the uncompleted *Treatise on the Emendation of the Intellect*. As its title indicates, Spinoza, like Descartes, saw his method as cultivating the best kind of reasoning, in other words, offering a kind of mental training. "Our first consideration must be to devise a method of emending the intellect and of purifying it, as far as is feasible at the outset, so that it may succeed in understanding things without error and as well as possible" (TEI 236, 16). Spinoza identifies the best kind of reasoning as the direct perception of essences, "the perception we have when a thing is perceived through its essence alone, or through knowledge of its proximate cause" (TEI 237, 20). Using a tool-making analogy, Spinoza identifies these perceptions as the basis of all reasoning: in order to construct a reliable set of tools, we first require more primitive tools; in turn, the construction of such primitive tools requires even more primitive tools. Spinoza argues that at bottom humans are equipped with certain innate skills from which all such tools are ultimately constructed. The analogy follows that

> in just the same way, the intellect by its inborn power makes intellectual tools for itself by which it acquires other powers for other intellectual works, and from these works still other tools – or capacity for further investigation – and thus makes steady progress until it reaches the summit of wisdom. (TEI 240, 31)

The inborn power in the analogy is the perception of true ideas, from which all other intellectual tools are constructed. As this discussion suggests, Spinoza – like Descartes – treated the perception of the truth as primitive. Spinoza claims that to achieve certainty of the truth "no other sign is needed but to have a true idea" (TEI 241, 35). Relatedly, Spinoza claims that the perception of the truth is infallible. Spinoza distinguishes four modes of knowing: (1) from hearsay or convention, (2) from wandering (vaga) or casual experience, (3) from inference, and (4) from perception of essences. Spinoza claims that "only the fourth mode comprehends the adequate essence of the thing, and is without danger of error" (TEI 239, 29).

Despite their similarities, Spinoza's method also departed significantly from Descartes'. Most notably, Spinoza saw his method as closely connected to an ethical project. Spinoza is ultimately concerned to achieve the highest good or happiness. He sets out this aim at the beginning of the treatise:

I resolved at length to enquire whether there existed a true good, one which was capable of communicating itself and could alone affect the mind to the exclusion of all else, whether, in fact, there was something whose discovery and acquisition would afford me a continuous and supreme joy to all eternity. (TEI 233, 1)

In this respect, Spinoza followed in the footsteps of an ancient ethical tradition, including the Stoics, Epicureans, and Aristotle. Spinoza identifies the highest good as "knowledge of the union which the mind has with the whole of Nature" (TEI 235, 13). Consequently, Spinoza saw his method, not purely as an instrument of science, but rather as an activity of self-discovery central to the attainment of happiness. Furthermore, it is a central tenet of Spinoza's philosophy that humans achieve happiness through the proper use of reason. Thus, he does not see his method as instrumental for achieving happiness, but rather as constitutive of happiness itself.

Spinoza's method also diverged from Descartes in emphasizing proper definitions and derivation thereof. Spinoza's motivation for this practice is Baconian in origin. Spinoza worried that language tends to reify mistakes in reasoning. These mistakes come from common notions enshrined in language, as well as an unbridled imagination.

Since words are part of the imagination — that is, since many of our concepts are formed according to the haphazard composition of words in memory from some disposition of the body – there can be no doubt that words no less than imagination can bring about many grave errors unless we exercise great caution in that respect. Add to this that words owe their formation to the whim and understanding of the common people, so that they are merely symbols of things as they are in the imagination not the intellect. (TEI 256, 88)

Spinoza's solution is to establish strict definitions supported only by the appropriate perception of essences. To protect from errors in reasoning, Spinoza insists that all conclusions be reached entirely by deduction from these definitions. The best example of this method is the *Ethics*, which sets forth axioms and definitions from which all of Spinoza's conclusions follow. The model here is not dialectic, for which Spinoza has no particular fondness, but rather Descartes' favorite: mathematics, in particular geometry. Spinoza's method mirrors the method of Euclid, which proceeds from strict definitions of terms: point, line, and so forth. Spinoza's emulation of this method is supported by a Cartesian philosophy of mathematics. Spinoza supposes that his definitions follow from perceptions of the essences of the things themselves, in other words, the deliverances of the natural light or clear and distinct perception.

It is not initially clear how Spinoza understood the activity of deriving conclusions from definitions and axioms. Descartes and Malebranche clearly conceived of inference, deduction, and so forth as forms of intellectual perception or intuition. At first glance, it is not clear that this is true of Spinoza. As indicated earlier, he set aside inference as the third mode of knowing, distinct from the perception of essences. Let us examine that passage more closely:

3. There is the perception we have when the essence of a thing is inferred from another thing, but not adequately. This happens either when we infer a cause from some effect or when an inference is made from some universal which is always accompanied by some property. (TEI 237, 19)

153

Interestingly, Spinoza suggests that only inadequate inference belongs to this third mode of knowing. The examples he gives appear to be probabilistic inferences. In the first case, one infers the cause of some effect; for instance, that water turns to steam because it is heated. In the second case, one infers that something possesses some property on the basis that the said property always accompanies a universal which obtains. For instance, one might infer that Socrates is mortal because he is human, which is always accompanied by mortality. Spinoza calls these inferences inadequate because the conclusion is not revealed by the direct perception of an essence. In the second case, one does not perceive that the property (mortality) belongs to the essence of that thing under consideration (either Socrates or humans). Rather, the inference is justified by concurrence: humans are always mortal. In other words, one infers that Socrates is mortal simply because all humans are mortal, not because one perceives that mortality belongs to the essence of humans. If such a conclusion were based on the direct perception of essences, Spinoza indicates that this would be an example of the fourth mode of knowing. Thus, Spinoza allows that some inferences are instances of the fourth mode of knowing, namely those instances where the inference is based on direct perception of essences. It follows that all of the propositions of the *Ethics* are inferences of this sort, since they are purportedly based on perceptions of essences, as offered in the definitions and axioms. Thus Spinoza, like Descartes and Malebranche, treats the primary inferences of his philosophical system as a species of intuition.

References and Further Reading

Aristotle (1975). *Aristotle's Posterior Analytics* (Jonathan Barnes, ed. and trans.). Oxford: Clarendon Press.

Clavius, Christoph (1611). *Operum mathematicorum tomus primus.* Mainz: Reinhardus Eltz.

Copenhaver, Brian (1998). The occultist tradition and its critics. In D. Garber and M. Ayers (eds.), *The Cambridge History of Seventeenth-Century Philosophy* (pp. 454–512). Cambridge: Cambridge University Press.

Gabbey, Alan (1996). Spinoza's natural science and methodology. In D. Garrett (ed.), *The Cambridge Companion to Spinoza* (pp. 142–91). Cambridge: Cambridge University Press.

Galen (1997). *Selected Works* (P. N. Singer, trans.). Oxford: Oxford University Press.

Gaukroger, Stephen (1989). *Cartesian Logic.* Oxford: Clarendon Press.

—— (1995). *Descartes: An Intellectual Biography.* Oxford: Clarendon Press.

Hobbes, Thomas (1656). *De Corpore.* London: R. and W. Leyboune.

Jolley, Nicholas (1990). *The Light of the Soul: Theories of Ideas in Leibniz, Malebranche, and Descartes.* Oxford: Clarendon Press.

Lennon, Thomas M. (2000). Malebranche and method. In S. Nadler (ed.), *The Cambridge Companion to Malebranche* (pp. 8–30). Cambridge: Cambridge University Press.

Mancosu, Paulo (1996). *Philosophy of Mathematics and Mathematical Practice in the Seventeenth Century.* New York: Oxford University Press.

Nadler, Stephen (1998). Doctrines of explanation in late scholasticism and in the mechanical philosophy. In D. Garber and M. Ayers (eds.), *The Cambridge History of Seventeenth-Century Philosophy* (pp. 513–52). Cambridge: Cambridge University Press.

Popkin, Richard (1979). *The History of Skepticism from Erasmus to Descartes.* Los Angeles: University of California Press.

Randall, J. H. (1961). *The School of Padua and the Emergence of Modern Science*. Padua: Antenore.

Savan, David (1986). Spinoza: Scientist and theorist of scientific method. In M. Grene and D. Nails (eds.), *Spinoza and the Sciences* (pp. 95–123). Dordrecht: Reidel.

Sepper, Dennis L. (1996). *Descartes' Imagination: Proportion, Images, and the Activity of Thinking*. Los Angeles: University of California Press.

Wallace, William A. (1984). *Galileo and His Sources: The Heritage of the Collegio Romano in Galileo's Science*. Princeton, NJ: Princeton University Press.

155

9

Cartesian Imaginations: The Method and Passions of Imagining

DENNIS L. SEPPER

"Rationalist imagination" may seem like a contradiction in terms. The argument goes like this. Rationalists, in contrast to empiricists, understand reason to be the definitive source of knowledge. Human experience is crowned by intellect and its accomplishments. Although factually most of what we encounter day by day is sensory, sensation is no more than raw material for producing knowledge. Intellect governs the cognitive forms and standards, and the highest and most universal truths do not depend on sense at all. Imagination, however, is nothing more than a pale remnant or continuation of sense, and it deals more in fantasy than in truth. At its best, imagination pleases; at its worst, it falsifies things; it is always arbitrary. Nothing serves the purposes of knowledge less than imagination.

Standard accounts of the history of imagination (e.g., Engell 1981; Brann 1991; Kearney 1988) further discourage the notion that there might be a positive history of rationalist imagination. Consider some of these well-known facts. Descartes argues that imagination composes things badly and that it cannot achieve the clear and distinct conception of anything so simple as a heptagon, much less a chiliagon. By intellect, however, we can with equal ease conceive a seven-sided and a thousand-sided figure. Leibniz affirms the same difference between intellect and imagination, and he thinks of images as at best confused and indistinct ideas. Spinoza classifies imagination as a kind of knowledge, but it is the lowest, least dependable kind. Malebranche devotes one of the longest books of *The Search after Truth* to narrating the deceptive ways of imagination. For Pascal, imagination is what attaches us to low, mortal, fleshly things. One might easily conclude, then, that rationalist thinkers would agree with Marcus Aurelius' injunction: "Wipe out the imagination!" (*Meditations*, VII, 29). It seems that their conceptions of imagination's faults and limits place them worlds apart from the theories that would arise at the end of the eighteenth and the beginning of the nineteenth century: for example, Kant's notion of imagination synthesizing the manifold of sensory appearances into a unified, space-time field populated with determinate objects of sense; or Schelling and the Romantics' conception of an imagination that produces not just art but the universe itself.

It would be a mistake, however, to think that there is no significant rationalist imagination. This chapter will show that things are far more complicated than they first appear. We will find different conceptions of imagination and quite different

156

conceptions of its importance among the rationalists, but we will also find innovations and basic themes that distinguish them from empiricists and set the stage for later developments in Kant and Romanticism.

As with so much else in the history of rationalism, the starting point is Descartes; as with so much else in the history of imagination, the starting point is the status of the image.

The Status of the Rationalist Image

Philosophy in the early modern period is now often portrayed by historians as following the "way of ideas," because the idea-concept and its equivalents so decisively shaped the entire period. The way of ideas, in turn, was shaped by debates about what, precisely, ideas were, how and from where they originated, and what part they played in knowing. Thus, if for no other reason, it is the relationship of "image" to "idea" that assures the historical importance of imagination for understanding early modern thought.

Consider one of the most influential books of the second half of the seventeenth century: *Logic, or the Art of Thinking*, known more familiarly as the *Port-Royal Logic*. It was first published, anonymously, in 1662. It issued from followers of Cornelius Jansen's strict Augustinianism, who assembled at Port-Royal, a former convent about 20 miles west of Paris. The principal author was the theologian and philosopher Antoine Arnauld (1612–94), assisted by Pierre Nicole (1625–95). Arnauld had been one of the earliest correspondent-critics of Descartes' *Meditations*, and by the time of the *Logic* he was considered a leading representative of Cartesian philosophy. The book is a classic not just in the rationalist tradition but also for the entire period. It is therefore a good place to look for a first approximation to the early modern understanding of the "idea" and its connection to the traditional concept of "image."

The introduction starts by defining logic as "the art of directing reason to a knowledge of things for the instruction of both ourselves and others" and says that this art "consists in man's reflecting on the mind's four principal operations – conceiving, judging, reasoning, and ordering" (Arnauld and Nicole 1964: 29). The first three had been accepted for centuries as the basic "matter" of logic; the last, ordering (also called method), is a modern concern. All four begin with and depend on the first, conception.

> To conceive a thing is simply to view that thing as it presents itself to the mind . . . For example, we are conceiving when we represent to ourselves a sun, an earth, a tree, thought, being, a circle, or a square but form no explicit judgment about the thing. The form by which we represent a thing to ourselves is called an idea. (Arnauld and Nicole 1964: 29)

Ideas are thus the most basic, the most fundamental "matter" of logic; they are the forms of the representations of things to the mind. The basic presentations in consciousness are single ideas (horse, mammal); when we expressly put two together in an affirmation or a negation we make a judgment ("Horses are mammals"); in reasoning we conclude new judgments from several judgments already given; and by method we "arrange the various ideas, judgments, and reasonings we have on a certain subject" so as to understand. Logic, then, is the general theory of forming, using, and organizing ideas in order to know.

The section that follows takes pains to show that ideas are not to be confused with images. By "images" are meant the *corporeal* forms of things that we perceive when we imagine (or sense, or remember). In making this distinction the *Logic* follows the track of the *Meditations*: it uses the example of the thousand-sided figure that Descartes had cited at the beginning of the Sixth Meditation to distinguish the very limited power of imagination from the expansive power of intellect. It then proceeds to defend the thesis that ideas are not (necessarily) images by criticizing the theories of two materialist critics of Descartes, Thomas Hobbes (1588–1679) and Pierre Gassendi (1592–1655), who had argued that thinking is nothing more than having sequences of corporeal images.

So far the evidence seems mostly negative: ideas are *not* (always, in general) images. But the reason for insisting on the difference was that materialists and empiricists tended to equate the two – in fact to understand the entire process of thinking as nothing more than having and controlling sequences of images. The empiricist tendency in early modern philosophy was to understand thinking as a form of imagination. The senses receive (or produce) images of things – later, in Locke, these will be called ideas – and the mind thinks by comparing, classifying, and altering the images and their sequences. Rationalist thinkers did not deny that there are image-ideas, but they repudiated the notion that there is nothing more than these and that knowledge is just a special way of "having images."

But the origin of the early modern "idea" is more convoluted than at first appears. The clearest evidence occurs in an exchange that took place over the nature of ideas between Descartes and Hobbes, when in 1640 the latter was asked to comment on the *Meditations*. Hobbes had just composed a work the content of which was not published till a decade later, in 1650: *The Elements of Law, Natural and Politic. The Elements* sets out the basics of his theory of human nature, beginning with the "cognitive or imaginative or conceptive" powers of the human mind (*Elements*, pt. 1, ch. 1, para. 7). Cognition depends on sensation, says Hobbes. Sensation is produced by motions that originate in external objects; these motions are communicated to the sense organ and from there along nerves to the brain. From the brain this motion "reboundeth back into the nerves outward," a rebound that gives rise to the seemings or apparition of light, sound, smell, etc., out in the world (*Elements*, 1.2.9). Taking vision as the prototypical sense, Hobbes says "the said image or colour is but an apparition unto us of that motion, agitation, or alteration, which the object worketh in the brain or spirits, or some internal substance of the head" (*Elements*, 1.2.4).

Even after the rebound that produces sensory appearances, the motion begun by sensation actually continues to vibrate in the nerves and decays only very slowly. Dreaming shows that these sensation-producing motions persist, since when sensation is in abeyance the images in dreams seem as vivid as sensed images.

> Though the sense be past, the image or conception remaineth; but more obscurely while
> we are awake, because some object or other continually plieth and soliciteth our eyes,

and ears, keeping the mind in a stronger motion, whereby the weaker doth not easily appear. And this obscure conception is that we call PHANTASY or IMAGINATION: imagination being (to define it) conception remaining, and by little and little decaying from and after the act of sense. (*Elements*, 1.3.1)

Remembrance is an aspect of imagination: when we encounter again the same conception, "we take notice also some way or other of our conceptions" and recognize that we have had the conception before.

Animals other than the human one are slaves to the contingencies of sense experience and nerve vibrations. But because we humans can attend to our conceptions as well as to what they represent we can make marks – for example, words – that allow us to break out of any one sequence of motions and enter another. That is, we can move from image to image according to our will rather than according to the accidents of how our previous experience occurred. This power of will eventually leads to science, which is the knowledge of the truth of propositions. Propositions connect words, and words refer in complex ways to the images produced by nerve motions. Science or cognition is nothing more than the well-ordering of images according to the mind's power of indicating them by signs, either words or some other kind of mark, that are themselves images.

When Hobbes read in Descartes' *Meditations* that a piece of wax "is in no way revealed by my imagination, but is perceived by the mind alone," he agrees that there is a difference here, but that Descartes has failed to grasp it. Imagining is *having an idea of the thing*; conceiving in the mind is using a process of reasoning to infer that something is or exists, and the latter is a question of linking names, so that, says Hobbes,

reasoning will depend on names, names will depend on the imagination, and imagination will depend (as I believe it does) merely on the motions of our bodily organs; and so the mind will be nothing more than motion occurring in various parts of an organic body. (AT 7: 178)

Where Descartes says the ideas of angels and God are not imaginable, Hobbes responds that "the idea by means of which I imagine an angel is composed of the ideas of visible things"; God has no idea or image whatsoever corresponding to "his sacred name"; there is no *idea* of God in us, only the *name* (AT 7: 180).

Descartes responds that his critic wants "idea" to refer only to material images "depicted in the corporeal imagination (*phantasia*)"; in this sense Hobbes is right that there is no idea of God. Then Descartes produces a highly suggestive yet ultimately baffling analogy to explain what he means by the term "idea." Everywhere in the *Meditations*, but especially here in the Third Meditation, he

takes the name "idea" for everything that is immediately perceived by the mind, so that, when I want and I fear, because at the same time I perceive that I want and I fear, this volition and this fear are numbered by me among ideas. And I have used this name because it was already commonplace among Philosophers for signifying the forms of perception of the divine mind, although we acknowledge no phantasia [corporeal organ of imagination] in God; and I had none apter. (AT 7: 181)

159

Thus "idea" as Descartes uses the word is to the human mind as "idea" in the language of philosophers (and theologians) is to the corporeal perception and imagination of God – but of course God doesn't have such perception or imagination, because he is pure spirit and thus his being has nothing material or temporal about it.

Descartes is the historical figure who more than any other initiated both the way of ideas and European rationalism. We therefore have to attend very carefully to what he says here. On the one hand, he is rejecting the notion that ideas and images are the same. An idea is whatever is immediately perceived by the mind; in the second Replies to Objections he says that the idea is the form of a thought, and that the immediate perception of this form makes me conscious of the thought (AT 7: 160), the definition later taken up in the Port-Royal *Logic*. On the other hand, Descartes agrees with Hobbes' theory that the nerves convey motions to the brain. In his early work Descartes called the place where all the nerve and nerve motions converge in the brain the phantasia, and later the pineal gland. He thought that the motions, really a kind of push or pressure, traced out a shape or figure on this organ. This trace of a figure on the organ is a corporeal image (to be distinguished from the image in consciousness). In the twelfth rule of the early *Rules for the Direction of the Mind* Descartes says that the thinking power can direct itself to this image, an act that is called *sensing* if the object is currently affecting the sense organs, *remembering* if the traces are produced from the effects of memory locations in the brain, or *imagining* if the mind is producing these traces itself, for example in producing a fiction or solving a geometry problem (AT 10: 415).

For Descartes, the crucial point is this: the tracing on the organ is a physical impression, it is not the idea conceived by the mind. The mind does not "see" the tracing as such when it "directs its attention" to it; instead, the pressure on the organ stimulates a psychological effect in consciousness that in principle may or may not correspond to the way a thing exists in the world. The mind can induce motions of the pineal gland that will produce nerve and spirit effects in the body. Some of these can activate brain locations in remembering and active imagining; others play a role in translating thoughts into actions of various parts of the body.

Descartes cannot agree with Hobbes' assertion that the mind is nothing more than motion occurring in parts of the body, that images/ideas are in essence the motions in the nerves. For Descartes, these motions are not the images/ideas but only stimulate certain kinds of ideas; but there are many ideas (like ideas of volition, fear, angels, God) that correspond to no bodily motion whatsoever. They are purely intellectual or rational.

Once again the rationalist distinction between images and ideas comes to the fore. But if we look again at the last part of the response to Hobbes quoted above, we see something odd, even paradoxical. Descartes chose "ideas" for what is perceived immediately by the mind because philosophers used it for the forms of perception of the divine mind – despite the fact that God has no phantasia, or organ of corporeal imagining. This is in effect Descartes' paraphrase and fusion of doctrines going back to Augustine (that the divine ideas are the exemplars of all things, according to which God both created them and also knows and understands them) and to Aristotle (that there are bodily locations or organs where the images acquired by the five senses are united into the image of the common sense). Descartes seems to be indicating that ideas as the basic forms of what presents to mind in human beings correspond to divine ideas in God. God, according to the standard theological interpretation, does not perceive things through bodily organs and powers such as phantasia and imagination; properly speaking he does not perceive things in time or according to the physiological processes of human knowing, because he is pure spirit and unchanging. Yet the very mention of the (denied) possibility of God having phantasia evokes the Augustinian teaching that divine ideas are the patterns and intelligible forms of created things, and thus divine ideas are also the likenesses of created things. The human being is said to be created in both the image and likeness not of any single one of the divine ideas but of God himself. The very passage that by the appeal to God's "perceptions" suggests that some human ideas are not images is also a tacit reminder that in another sense all ideas are likenesses (of created things) and thus image-like.

The Deeper Background

If Hobbes and Descartes belong to different sides in the "debate" between empiricists and rationalists, we see that they broadly agree on the chief elements of what is involved in having images and imagining. They share an emphasis on the importance of the physiology of the sense organs, nerves, and brain in the processes of sensation, imagination, and memory. Although in the early twenty-first century we would talk of nerve photoreceptors stimulated by photons, cascades of ions crossing synapses, and cortical and subcortical brain functions, the seventeenth-century physiological theories of Descartes and Hobbes are recognizable ancestors to our own. We see another similarity to our situation as well: Hobbes maintains that psychological events are nothing more than nerve and brain activities, whereas Descartes insists that psychology or consciousness is associated with but not fully reducible to them.

The understanding of imagination that prevailed at the dawn of early modern thought regarded it as a fundamental cognitive power of the soul among other cognitive powers. This conception, which ultimately derives from Aristotle, deals in (1) the familiar five *external senses*; (2) three or more *internal senses*, beginning with (a) the common sense that combines the information from the five external senses into a unified field of sense experience, (b) the imagination that allows us to vary and recombine the sensory forms first provided by the external senses, and (c) the memory that enables us to recall previous mental experiences as they actually occurred; and (3) *intellect*. This theory was widely accepted because it had also been taken up and incorporated into medical knowledge since late Greek antiquity (see Harvey 1975). Many thought that intellect itself did not have a specific organ or bodily location, but each of the other powers of sense and cognition was considered to have an organ or organic place – imagination and the other internal senses were typically located in the ventricles of the brain. This theory had many variants, but the basic scheme was almost universally accepted in the sources Descartes and Hobbes would have known. It was also often amplified by a Stoic-influenced theory that the nerves and other sensitive parts of the body contained a fluid called animal spirits that were thought to play a role in nerve transmissions, either from the sense organs to the brain or from the brain to the muscles (or both).

The single most authoritative philosophical source on imagination before 1600 was Aristotle. In *On the Soul* he explained how the things of the world activated the sense

161

organs to give rise to *proper* sensibles. These were proper to the individual organ: only the eye could see color, only the ear could hear tone, etc. The proper sensibles were brought together in the internal sense called common sense, like five channels of information flowing into a unified experience of the world. The common sense, which itself had a physiological location, allowed *common* sensibles to be perceived – spatial dimension, position, motion, unity, and the like.

The basic phenomenon in sensation, whether proper or common, is that our mind or consciousness "lights up" (to use a visual metaphor) in various ways when physical objects are present to the senses. Moreover, it is possible to have a similar lighting up of consciousness even when an object is not present. This is where imagination begins. Aristotle defines *phantasia* as a "motion coming about as the result of the being-at-work of sense perception, and corresponding to it" (*On the Soul*, bk. 3, ch. 3). This suggests that the activity involved in sensation is in some unexplained way preserved and passed on beyond sensation. Thus, even without expressly discussing memory in *On the Soul*, Aristotle immediately draws the conclusion that imagination and memory can account for purposive animal behavior and also human behavior when reason is obscured or weak. As he explains a little later, the retention of the image of a thing can guide animal and human actions when the object of sense is not immediately present. So a dog can retrieve a piece of meat that is out of view because the imagination of it continues to be effective; a human being can stumble to breakfast while half-asleep in a similar way.

It is easy to see that Hobbes' notion that appearance is the continuing motion of sensations in the nerves might be simply a mechanical-materialist interpretation of Aristotle's definition of *phantasia*. But, as the philosopher-historian-psychoanalyst Cornelius Castoriadis has argued, Aristotle's conception of imagination would never have had such lasting influence if he had not also immediately radicalized it. This radical conception is summarized in the statement that "there is no thinking without phantasm," or, as we would say, no thinking without images (Castoriadis 1997: 220–3).

It is clear that Aristotle believed a phantasm was necessary for intellect to have effect. The active part of intellect he believed acted like a light illuminating the phantasm and searching out its intelligible form; this illumination yielded the intelligible species, which was then received into the passive or receptive part of intellect. For more than two thousand years no Aristotelian teaching has been more variously interpreted, but if one needs a comprehensible account that was accepted at the threshold of the early modern period it would go something like this. Before a human being has sense experience there is really nothing that the person knows. What sensation gives us is sensible forms that are retained in memory and freely reproducible in imagination. Accumulated experience allows us, by what is mostly an unconscious natural process, to form evermore accurate, sophisticated, and interrelated phantasms. This means that all of what the medievals called the internal or inward senses – the common sense, imagination, memory, and estimation/cogitation – contribute to the "perfection" of phantasms. The better formed or more perfect a phantasm is, the more apt it is to yield a fully intelligible species – also called a concept – when it is illuminated by active intellect. It is *through* or *by means of* this intelligible species or concept that we understand things we have experienced.

162

When Aristotle says that there is no thinking without phantasm, this does not mean that phantasms are the direct object of our thinking or that thinking takes place only as the appearance and variation of phantasms. Rather, what the assertion means is that all thinking takes place *stimulated by* phantasms, *in the presence of* phantasms, *with respect to* phantasms. Phantasms are the beginning of abstraction, because they have been "drawn away" from or out of actual physical material, yet they retain the appearances of real-world beings. In a sense this means that there cannot be any direct contemplation of "eternal truths" or "abstract essences" without some remnant of material appearance being present to our consciousness in the phantasm.

Whatever the current state of philosophical, psychological, and neurological research implies, there seems to be little doubt that early modern philosophers thought that imagination and memory presupposed the power of the mind to hold before it the same kind of appearance that is produced by the body in original sensation, only usually less vivid (except in dreams and hallucinations). The nature of imagination is not at all exhausted in simply "having" or "retaining" an image, however. For an Aristotelian imagination was the continuing motion of the sense-form. Since, for Aristotelians, motions always imply some sort of goal, the crucial issue was not the having of the phantasm or image but what became of it and where it led. As we saw earlier, it led ultimately to the formation of more perfect phantasms that would allow the agent intellect to abstract from it, by intellectual illumination, an intelligible species. More generally, all theories of imagination take having images for granted. Their most central concern is where images lead. This concern is in turn always embedded in, or takes for granted, a physical-physiological explanation of the persistence and processing of images, and a comprehensive psychological theory of the cognitive powers of the soul that explains how imagination functions intermediately between sensation and intellect. That is, imagination is understood as a continuation of sense that is based in the body and serves the purposes of cognition.

Since the late eighteenth century, imagination has been primarily and fundamentally associated with creativity and art. It is important to understand that this is a very recent conception. Before the eighteenth century, imagination was regarded as having only accessory importance in art. What came first was the cognition of a model object or event; only thereafter did artistic imagination figure in the process of varying or embellishing it. Imagination, understood as the formation of phantasms through experience that could then be illuminated by intellect so that an intelligible meaning-structure could be grasped, was of course originally at work in recognizing the model object or event. But creativity as originality was not a central concern. We shall see, however, that Descartes took several important steps toward the notion of imagination as creatively productive. The surprise to us will be that this happened above all in his mathematics.

Descartes: The Directed Imagination of Mathematics, and Passions as Nascent Images

Most accounts of imagination in René Descartes (1596–1650) do not look any further than the *Meditations*, where imagination is portrayed as weak (in comparison

163

to intellect) and prone to error. That is a mistake. If you look forward to the 1649 *Passions of the Soul*, or backward to the *Discourse on the Method* and the scientific essays to which it served as preface, you find that imagination plays a much more pervasive and central role in human life and human knowing than the *Meditations* suggests. And if you look into even earlier writings unpublished during his lifetime you discover that imagination is fundamental to Descartes' philosophizing and method.

It is fundamental precisely insofar as Descartes thought through and radicalized the problem-situation of imagination that he inherited. He was interested in the question not just of how we have images, but even more of what we do with and to them. What we do with and to them serves cognitive purposes and in fact provides the model for human thinking. His conception of idea and thinking were radicalizations of image and imagining, respectively, though in thinking through the problem of imagining he also recognized the limitations of images and imagination. And in thinking beyond human cognitive psychology to the deeper questions of human living, Descartes found a fundamental place for imagination in the field of feeling and emotion, which he did not believe we must flee for the sake of rationalist truth but rather must cultivate so that we can "taste as much as possible the sweetness of this life" (AT 11: 488). And by reconceiving, centralizing, and radicalizing imagination as central to human exist-ence, Descartes set the stage for later rationalist thinkers.

The specific kind of imagining that Descartes carefully delimits in the *Meditations* occurs when the intellect attends to the figures traced by the physical effect of animal spirits in the nerve system on the center of that system, the pineal gland. His interest in this problem goes back to some of his earliest work. Ancient and medieval medical theory had long portrayed the nerves as operating by means of a system of very fine and active fluids or gases called spirits. Descartes modernized and adapted the theory to fit the phenomena as understood by seventeenth-century science. The pineal gland – which in his earlier writings was identified as the phantasia, the organ of imagina-tion – was an adaptation of the ancient Stoic brain organ called the *hegemonikon*, the "master organ," where all the nerve and spirit activity was concentrated and where the actions, reactions, and decisions of the person were centered.

The *Meditations* shows that imagination has limits, in particular that by it alone we cannot determine what fundamentally exists (extended matter, immortal soul, and God). This does not imply that imagination is powerless, however, or that it is not deeply embedded in and characteristic of human being. It is often said that Descartes mathematized thought, or that he took mathematical knowledge as the paradigm of knowledge. Few who make this claim recognize that they are thereby placing imagi-nation at the center of Descartes' philosophizing. To put it as bluntly as possible, the highest achievement of Descartes' mathematical and physical thought, what we call analytic geometry, is the most rigorous conception and application of imagination ever developed. Descartes did not develop this rigorous imagination accidentally: it was what he primarily and essentially intended.

Students of elementary algebra are familiar with the method of dividing a problem into elements; organizing and reorganizing them until the solution becomes clear; reviewing the problem, elements, and steps to make sure that the solution is correct and comprehensive; and all the time accepting as certain only what we clearly and distinctly see to be true. These are in essence the four rules of method that Descartes presented in the second part of the *Discourse on the Method*. Immediately after stating those four rules, Descartes says he discovered that the best technique for applying these rules involved representing the parts and relations of problems by lines,

> because I did not find anything simpler, nor anything that I could represent more distinctly to my imagination and senses; but, in order to retain them or to understand several together, it was necessary for me to explicate them by certain symbols, as short as possible; and, in this way, I would borrow all the best of geometrical analysis and of algebra, and would correct all the defects of each by the other. (AT 6: 20)

A simple example illustrates what this means. Suppose we are asked to solve this problem: two trucks set out at the same moment along a road between two cities, each headed in the opposite direction and starting from the opposite city, with one truck's average speed being twice the other's. Where on the road do they pass one another?

Often, we start analyzing by drawing figures. We can draw a line segment AB to represent the distance between the towns and label the length of that line segment as *d*. Though we do not know the numerical value of *d*, it exists. In addition, whether the road is straight, as a line-segment representation shows it, or curved, does not really matter: all that matters is that the distance be represented clearly. We mark with an X the point where they will pass – though we do not know yet exactly where this should be, we know there will be such a point. We can draw two vectors (directed line segments) to represent the velocity of each truck, one twice as long as the other, and we can use the symbols V_A and V_B to stand for the respective speeds (the first for the truck starting out from A, the second from B). A quick assessment of the problem-situation lets us realize that when the paths cross the trucks will have been traveling for the same amount of time, which we can call *t*. After this elapsed time *t*, we reason further, the truck setting out from A will have traveled the segment AX, the other truck the segment BX, which together add up to *d*, the length of the whole segment AB. Since the distance traveled in a certain time is that time multiplied by the average speed, we know further that $AX = V_A * t$ and that $BX = V_B * t$, so that $d = AB = AX + BX = V_A * t + V_B * t = (V_A + V_B) * t$, and thus $t = d/(V_A + V_B)$.

Unfortunately, we do not know the absolute value of any of these numbers. But we can still solve the problem! In fact we do not even need to take the time *t* explicitly into consideration. One thing we have neglected to exploit adequately is that the average speed of one of the trucks (let us assume it is the truck from A) is twice that of the other. We represented it by drawing one directed line segment twice as long as the other, but we did not represent it in symbols. We can correct this omission by writing: $V_A/V_B = 2$. We also failed to reason from this that at any moment the distance traveled by the truck from A will be twice the distance traveled by the truck from B, since its average speed is twice as great: this means, in particular, that $AX/BX = 2$. That fact by itself is enough to solve the problem, since it implies that $AX = 2 * BX$, which means that at the point where they pass the truck from A will have traveled exactly twice as far as the truck from B. So AX is two thirds of the whole length AB, and BX is one third.

This is with only slight simplification the method advocated, and in an important sense invented, by Descartes. We conceive the problem in as much detail as we can, representing the data with figures like line segments to help make clear and distinct

165

the things we are reckoning and their relationships. We use simple letters and algebraic symbols to stand for things like lengths, times, and speeds; we treat unknowns as though they were knowns and designate them by symbols that make them easily recognizable. We formulate simple equations and proportions in terms of the symbols and refer them back to the figures we have drawn. We complicate the formulas by substituting equals for equals in these formulas and performing algebraic manipulations to solve for what is unknown, and finally we correlate the results with the figures we drew and with the original terms of the problem in order to verify that we have found the correct answer and have not left anything out.

If we think of this as primarily rational activity we are sadly mistaken, in Descartes' view. This kind of problem solving is a complex activity involving sensation, imagination, memory, and intellect. It is true that the intellect notices what is or is not the case in problem solving, but the objects to which it attends are not pure ideas but rather the elements of problems represented by images and symbols. Intellect guides the whole procedure by shifting its attention from one thing to another and noticing the proportions that hold between elements – beginning with the simplest question, whether one element is larger than, smaller than, or equal to another – but it can do very little without the images and symbols. There is no problem solving without images, so to speak. Descartes began developing this kind of technique in his very earliest extant notes and writings, going back at least to 1618, when he was a 22-year-old traveling soldier-scholar (for details, see Sepper 1996).

As we know from the *Geometry*, one of the three essays that accompanied the *Discourse*, the heart of this algebraic geometry – analytic geometry as we call it – is that the rigidly interrelated motions of existing points, curves, and lines generate new curves and lines. These motions of points and lines can be expressed by algebraic symbols and equations and can be used to solve any problems based on mathematical proportions. The mathematical figures and motions, in their turn, can be used to represent the motions of actual bodies in space.

It was in the very earliest part of his career (around 1620) that Descartes began working out the principles of this representational mathematics. He did this in large part by imagining complex physical instruments; for example, rulers linked by pivots and grooves so that the rulers could turn or slide as the instrument was opened or closed. He realized that the points where the rulers crossed marked lengths that stood in complex proportions to the lengths on other rulers, and that these proportions could be expressed algebraically. Similarly, the curves traced out by fixed points on the rulers (for instance, if pencils were attached at those points) could also be expressed by algebraic equations. He sought ways in which problems, mathematical and physical, could be represented in relatively simple images, and then imagined how those simple images could be manipulated or interlinked so that solutions could be generated by the motions. In general, whatever could be imagined in geometric figures could be translated into algebra, and vice versa.

What this means, in its ultimate development, is that all mathematics and all physics can be represented by rigorously imaginable figures and their motions, and these motions can be correlated with algebraic formulas. There is an intertranslatability of the geometrical and the algebraic. This mathematical realm is the *res extensa*, the "extended thing" that he described at the end of the Fifth Meditation as "the whole of that corporeal nature which is the subject matter of pure mathematics" (AT 7: 71) and that nearly a decade earlier in *Le Monde* he had presented as existing in imaginary spaces (AT 11: 31–2).

In the *Rules for the Direction of the Mind* (or *Native Wit*), an unfinished precursor to the *Discourse* that Descartes worked on in the decade 1619–29, Descartes presented the art of problem solving he was devising as especially well adapted to the human being's psychological capacities. The senses, memory, and especially imagination were to be deployed in aid of the intellect. In Rule 14 Descartes claimed that most errors were due to the intellect, especially when it makes judgments without reference to an imaginable object. Moreover, Descartes not only simplified the internal senses (common sense, memory, and imagination), a tendency not uncommon in the period, but also reduced all of them to imagination (in Rule 12). And the *ingenium*, the "mind" or "native wit" that is to be directed by rules, is defined in Rule 12 as the knowing force "when it at one moment forms new ideas in phantasia, at another applies itself to those already made" (AT 10: 416). But ideas in phantasia are images; and thus *ingenium* is the power of conceiving, varying, and developing images.

His first work of any significant length, the *Compendium of Music*, which he composed in 1618, had already exploited the insight that figures and images can be used to express complex information. In one very suggestive passage he also claimed that it is imagination that is responsible for *projecting* the unity of a whole song from whatever parts we have already experienced at a given moment of listening. In listening to a song we constantly, recursively, and self-correctingly project from what we have heard how the rhythm and melody are developing, and at every moment this produces a new, projective synthesis that aims to grasp the song as a whole before it is finished. Thus, even in his earliest attempts at coherent philosophizing, the function of imagination issued not just in "having images" but even more fundamentally in our ability to portray proportions, to produce new representations, and thereby to gain insight into and reorganize the data given us by sensation.

As should be evident by now, for Descartes, imagination cannot be disentangled from the other powers of mind, least of all from intellect, or, as he calls it in the *Rules*, the knowing force (*vis cognoscens*; AT 10: 415). Imagination is, properly speaking, the knowing force at work in the organ of imagination, producing and modifying images. From the beginning to the end of his career, Descartes thought that imagination is the knowing force or intellect directing its attention to the organ where the corporeal forms of the world are present, in the phantasia or pineal gland. What the intellect does best is notice the answer to simple questions such as whether one image or representation is like or unlike another, and whether two of them are equal with respect to a certain characteristic, or if not equal which is greater, which less, and by how much. The answers to these questions in turn can and should be expressed in images and marks that are then combined, developed, and reexamined. The chief work of intellect is to deal with things that are presented to it by sense, imagination, and memory – and all of these involve having, varying, projecting, and comparing image-ideas in consciousness. Descartes thus comes quite close to agreeing with Aristotle that there is no thinking without phantasms.

To summarize: the embodied intellect works in and through the organ of imagination. Intellect is the power of perceiving; what is perceived, chiefly, are the sensed,

167

remembered, and creatively imagined products in phantasia. In the imagination, intellect presents space, divides and figures it, puts the figures into relations and motion, and constantly orders and measures them. Analytic geometry allows intellect to track all these effects in imagination more precisely by using symbols and formulas, and the basic laws of physical motion can be presented in the space of phantasia and tracked exactly by algebra. Science and mathematics are directed imaginings, the well ordered working of intellect in phantasia. Mathematics and physics are thus the chief product and invention of rationalist imagination.

This is already a surprising amount of imagination in Descartes, but there is more. As we noted earlier, Descartes' use of "ideas" is not accidentally but intrinsically related to imagination. If the *Meditations* establishes the boundary between what requires imagination and what does not, it accomplishes this only by thinking what is imaginable through to its ultimate limit. Yet it would be rash simply to conclude that the *Meditations* thereby teaches us to think pure intellectual ideas. The end of the Second Meditation shows that when a piece of wax is heated and melts, so that all the sensible and imaginable qualities have changed, it is intellect alone that perceives the substantiality of the wax. This is not to say that it thinks the wax purely intellectually, however, but rather to recognize that intellect perceives the unity of substance *through* all the variety of its sensible and imaginable changes. Without the changing sensible qualities there would be no wax to perceive. Similarly, the self whose existence is proved in the self-evidencing truth of "I think" is present not just in a pure act of intellection but rather in every conscious act. But the only way this becomes evident to mind itself is by calling before the mind the total variety of what appears to sense, memory, and imagination. It is *against the background* of this activity that the presence and distinctness of intellect can be perceived by intellect. This is to achieve a relative, not an absolute, division of intellect from the body. In human beings this appearance of intellect as transcending imagination is atypical and transient. We do not experience the thinking apart from body, only that it is distinct from body. This experience does not disembody us, but it does mean that afterward we see our embodiment differently than before.

The last work Descartes published during his lifetime further deepens our insight into Cartesian imagination. *The Passions of the Soul* investigates the nature and role of the passional or emotional life. The passions are understood, in the first instance, as a consequence of the nerve–spirit–brain physiology and its effects on consciousness. The phantasia or pineal gland is suspended in the middle of the brain, in a sea of animal spirits. In sensation the nerves convey quite determinate impressions to the gland. The powers of memory and imagination produce determinate images in these spirits by the interaction of pineal gland, memory locations in the brain, and the directive activity of intellect. But the spirits also undergo far less determinate flows, eddies, and perturbations; and many of these correspond to conscious effects that are less determinate than ordinary ideas and images. These conscious effects are the passions, moods, emotions, and feelings. They are associated with physiological effects in other parts of the body, like the heart, brain, stomach, skin, and face, that further define, produce, and express the passion. Thus the passions are part of the same nerve–spirit–brain system that is responsible for sensation, imagination, and remembering.

Imagination therefore can play a deep and active role in the passions, since imagination is the most controlled way in which the nerve–spirit–brain system produces spirit flows (in the act of portraying image-ideas in the pineal gland). Intellect has no ability to affect spirit flows by itself. We cannot control passions and moods simply by recognizing them and desiring to stop, continue, or change them. But since sensation and imagination do have direct and determinate effects in the nerve–spirit–brain system, they can affect the passions directly. In trying to manage the emotions we may often think of firm intellectual principles, of course, but they cannot affect the spirit flows constituting the emotions unless they take imaginative form – for example, when we imagine a concrete situation exemplifying one of the principles. It is not enough for a depressed person to reflect on a principle claiming that cheerfulness is superior to melancholy: to make a difference she has to imagine a joyful scene, remember a happy event, or read a cheerful story.

In his later writing Descartes no longer speaks of *intellect* and *will* as the two fundamental acts of the thinking being, the *res cogitans*, but rather of *perception* and *volition*. A thing is better understood, he says, according to its activities than its passivities. Intellect is a form of perception, and perception is basically a passive function simply registering what is presented to it. It is the passive side of a willed act. So the true act is the corresponding volition, and thus volition is more truly characteristic of the thinking thing than intellection. How this affects imagination becomes clear from section 20 of *Passions*, where Descartes says that our directed imaginings are chiefly acts of volition. This is an uncomfortable position for conventional rationalism: intellect is subordinated to will, and imagination is raised to the level of a fundamentally directive act of the embodied thinking thing.

To summarize historically: in Descartes' career imagination began as the knowing force acting in the phantasia-gland; in the classic works around 1640 imagination was more sharply distinguished from intellect but still deployed in manifold ways, especially in mathematics and the sciences; and in the final work, volition displaced intellect as what is most typical of the human being, and by the connection of directed imagination with will and its role in controlling the passions it acquired a central role not just in solving problems but in living life well. Yet "controlling" passions is perhaps a misleading locution, since at the end of the *Passions* Descartes expresses a very unstoic (and uncartesian) thought: that the best life is one in which we enjoy the passions and the sweetness they lend to our existence.

Malebranche

If later historians lost sight of the positive and comprehensive role of imagination in Descartes, this was not true of the other leading rationalist philosophers. Malebranche, Spinoza, and Leibniz each in his own way further developed Descartes' radical reassessment of this psychological power. That these further developments in the other major rationalists have been relatively unapparent is itself something of a mystery. Standard accounts of theories of imagination rush past the rationalists as negative critics of imagination and look to the British empiricists for positive developments. Yet if only because of the recently recognized influence of Malebranche on the British

169

"way of ideas" (see McCracken 1983) it is important to reconsider the adequacy of these accounts. Malebranche in fact elaborated the major themes of Descartes' conception while adding distinctive inflections and limitations that made his theory more like what is portrayed in conventional accounts of rationalism and Cartesianism.

It is commonly said of Nicolas Malebranche (1638–1715) that there were two fundamental influences in his intellectual life: Augustine and Descartes. Malebranche read the latter's newly published *Treatise on Man* in the year he was ordained as a priest (1664) and it revolutionized his thinking. He immediately began adapting its nerve–spirit–brain account of human sensation, memory, and imagination to his philosophical and theological purposes.

Malebranche's philosophical masterwork, *The Search after Truth*, was first published in 1677. The general tone may be gathered from two sentences of the preface: "We have such close ties with our body and depend on it so much that we do well to be apprehensive about not always having distinguished the cacophony with which the body fills the imagination from the pure voice of the truth that speaks to the mind." "The mind must judge all things according to its inner lights, paying no heed to the false and confused testimony of its senses and imagination." His aim in the *Search* is to "combat several errors and especially those most universally received or those that cause a greater disorder of the mind, and I show that these errors are almost all consequences of the mind's union with the body." The search after truth begins with the elucidation of the causes of error, to which the preponderance of this long work is dedicated. The fundamental fact from which it proceeds is an Augustinian one: the mind of man is situated between Creator and corporeal creatures; it is naturally drawn toward the latter, but its true destination is the former.

The imaginative relationship between the soul and the body is of fundamental importance for Malebranche, and it even has theological implications. For example, in the seventh chapter of the first part of book 2, the book devoted to imagination, Malebranche adapts Cartesian physiology to an old theme in imagination studies: how events in the life of a pregnant woman could affect the fetus. Because the nerves and flesh of a fetus are much more susceptible to impression than those of children and adults, very strong impressions or imagining experienced by the mother can cause lasting effects on, and even damage, the fetus. In the case of a pregnant woman who attended too closely to a portrait of Saint Pius on his feast day, the child was born looking exactly like the portrait (*Search* II.i.vii, sect. 3). A woman who strongly imagines and desires a pear will stir that same imagination and desire in the fetus; because of the softness of its tissues, "these unfortunate infants thus become like the things they desire too ardently." Malebranche goes on to argue that this kind of physiological effect on the fetus provides a mechanism for the transmission of original sin, because thereby "men retain in their brains even today the traces and impressions of their first parents," Adam and Eve (*Search* II.i.vii, sect. 4). In the *Elucidations to The Search after Truth* (which were added to the *Search* in the edition of 1678), Malebranche explains a consequence: Adam before sinning had the power to "suspend the natural law of the communication of motion" in his nerve–spirit system, but this was forfeited by sin (*Search*, elucidation 8, sect. 8). The result is that concupiscence, an excessive attachment to corporeal things, is passed down quite literally from Adam to all his descendants by psychophysiological impression.

170

Thus Malebranche uses "imagination" in a very broad sense to apply to the funda-mental characteristics of image formation in the human being, whether those images come to us directly through the senses or are formed mediately in memory and pro-ductive imagination. The chief characteristics and effects of image formation are a product of the nerve–spirit–brain system. The difference between sensation and imagi-nation is in fact one of degree only (*Search* II.i.i). Yet, in the last analysis, Malebranche also makes a strong assertion of the unity of the cognitive faculties that is reminiscent of Descartes. "Men are capable of sensation and imagination only because they are capable of pure intellection, since the senses and the imagination are inseparable from the mind; yet no one finds anything amiss in treating these two faculties of the soul separately, though they are by nature inseparable" (*Search* V.i).

Malebranche's use of the term "idea" is, like the later Descartes', not a synonym of image, although its meaning throughout book 3, part 2 is governed at least in part by a contrast to images. There Malebranche determines that the soul can perceive only what it is immediately joined with. "The immediate object of our mind when it sees the sun, for example, is not the sun, but is something intimately united to our soul, and this is what I call an *idea*" (*Search* III.ii.i, sect. 1). Ideas have to be present to the soul for us to perceive the corresponding object, but there need not be anything in the world similar to the idea (e.g., when we imagine a golden mountain). The soul perceives *things*, both in the soul and outside it; ideas are not needed for things perceived in the soul by the soul's internal sensation (Descartes, of course, disagreed and called these ideas, too); things outside the soul require ideas as a medium. The regularity of the connection between traces in the nerve–spirit–brain system and ideas in the mind has three causes: nature, or rather the constant and immutable will of the Creator; the simultaneous appearance of ideas alongside one another; and the will of men. It is the last that, combined with the natural inclination of human beings to agree to attach their ideas to sensible signs, produces language (*Search* II.i.v, sect. 1). The pursuit of the nature and source of external ideas leads Malebranche ultimately to the notion that the soul knows, properly speaking, only by being united to a completely perfect being who contains all intelligible perfections and all the ideas of created beings; that is, ultimately the soul knows ideas *in God* (*Search* III.ii.vi).

In his brief summary conclusion of the first three books of the *Search*, Malebranche describes the complicated interrelationship between (1) the senses, (2) imagination and memory, and (3) pure mind or understanding. In sense we receive ideas from God mixed with sensation, on the occasion of certain movements taking place in our sense organs in the presence of objects. In imagination and memory we receive "from God ideas mixed with images, which are a kind of weak and languid sensation the mind receives only because of certain traces being produced or aroused in the brain by the flow of spirits." Pure mind or pure understanding occurs when the mind

> receives from God entirely pure ideas of the truth, with no admixture of sensations or images, through its union not with the body but with the Word, or the Wisdom, of God . . . not in order to know mutable things suited to the preservation of the life of the body, but to enter into immutable truths, which preserve in us the life of the mind.

Yet, after offering a glimpse of perfectly disembodied truth in this life, Malebranche warns against expecting too much of pure ideas. Sense and imagination enable us to

171

know the relation of external bodies to our own and are entirely for the benefit of the body. Because they bind us to our bodies and to sensible things, we cannot trust to them for knowledge. "No truth whatever can be clearly discovered through the idea of the senses or the imagination" (*Search* III, conclusion). But one cannot deduce the relations between bodies (including our own) from pure ideas; without the senses the mind knows these things only "in a confused way." In describing how the faculties function when a person tries to decide whether it is better to be just or rich, Malebranche points out that the idea of justice does not present many images for the senses or the imagination to work with, but the idea of riches fills them with abundant imagining. Imagination not only repeats the testimony of the senses, "it will also represent these things in an entirely different way than do the senses, for the imagination always increases the ideas of things that we love and that are related to the body." "It will soon lead me into an enchanted palace like those so wonderfully described by poets and novelists"; and thus imagination enhances and strengthens the attractions of the senses to the point I become convinced that only luxury can make me happy (*Search* III, conclusion).

Though imagination is typically prone to error and temptations, Malebranche does allow a major exception: the use of mathematics in understanding material things clearly and distinctly. He points out that mathematics, especially as practiced by Descartes, is a method of pursuing truth that enables us to avoid error and to see clearly true ideas of things. Malebranche notes that most people would be incredulous were he to claim that

> in applying itself to these sciences [metaphysics, pure mathematics, and all the universal sciences that determine and contain the particular sciences] the mind applies itself to God in the purest and most perfect way of which it is capable, and that it is in perceiving the intelligible world that these sciences have as their object that God Himself knows and produces the sensible world that bodies depend on for their life as minds depend on the intelligible. (*Search* V.v)

Moreover:

> Geometry . . . should be regarded as a kind of universal science that opens the mind, makes it attentive, and gives it the skill to control the imagination and to draw from it all the help it can give; for with the help of geometry the mind controls the imagination, and a controlled imagination sustains the mind's perception and attention. (*Search* VI.i.iv)

Malebranche, who was up to date on the progress of mathematical analysis and so not simply a Cartesian on the question, nevertheless understands arithmetic, algebra, and the analysis that within a few years culminated in the calculus as having to do with magnitudes and their relations. Thus, although he does not explicitly name the imagination as the faculty engaged in these mathematical sciences, they seem (just like geometry) to require the use of imagination ordered by the understanding. As one rises to higher levels of abstractness, with figures representing objects and formulas representing figures, there is an attrition but not an elimination of imaginative concreteness.

There is one more feature of Malebranche's conception of imagination that deserves notice. It is what we might call the social uses of imagination, the social imaginary. It is an extension of his theory of the organic power of the imagination. Malebranche remarks that "it is absolutely necessary to be reminded that we imagine objects only by forming images of them, and that these images are nothing other than the traces the animal spirits make in the brain" (*Search* II.ii.ii). Imagination always works through the medium of animal spirits. The habits that this produces are "the most ordinary cause of the confusion and falsity of our own ideas." The nature of people (for instance, if they are very young or female) and their life practices lead to differences in habits. Malebranche mentioned earlier those due to the softness of the brain. Here he analyzes the effects of select ways of life, beginning with the scholar; proceeding to innovators, the effeminate, and the superficial; and concluding with those who have very powerful imaginations.

All character types depend on the power of receiving and forming images, and of receiving them in a certain manner. The scholar becomes accustomed to not thinking for himself but simply forming his mind according to the opinions of others without clearly thinking what they do. There is thus a tendency for a scholar to end up as a skeptic for lack of exercising his own judgment. Innovators, by contrast, have the tendency to set themselves up as authorities in opposition to what others say. They usually have strong imaginations, with brain fibers capable of retaining traces for a very long time. It is nearly impossible to disabuse them of what they have once thought. Aesthetes and others with very sensitive constitutions, by further contrast, have "fine minds" with respect to sensible things, whereby they notice very slight differences in what appears to the senses but have difficulty with matters of logic.

Human speech makes evident that even people with weak imaginations can engrave traces of what is in their minds in the minds of others. Because a strong imagination can communicate itself to other people most easily of all, it can be contagious to and dominate weaker ones. The problem with this is that those with strong imaginations are typically inflexible. "Since those who have a strong and vigorous imagination are completely unreasonable, there are very few more general causes of men's errors than this dangerous communication of the imagination" (*Search* II.iii.i, sect. 1).

The positive side of the imaginative influence people have on one another is that God established it to bind together human beings, so that they would have need for one another. We are naturally inclined to imitate one another both because of the soul's inclination "for grandeur and high position" and because of the body's predisposition to accept the impressions of the imaginations of others. Fortunately, random or disordered imaginings, as in the insane, have only a slight power of making lasting impressions on other people. Genuine authority must know how to counter the persuasiveness of very powerful and vivid sensible images.

For Malebranche, one cannot live without imagination, but it is possible to bring imagination under the direction of reason. On the surface, then, it seems that he arrives at the same conclusion as Descartes. Yet the tonality of his theory is, as we have seen, quite different. Descartes conceives full human nature as a gift. As thinking beings we could have been combined with bodies (or not!) in many different ways, but God has given us the nature we have, and our duty is to use all our talents well. In

173

order to do so we must above all grow in knowledge. Understanding what we are facing enables us to use our powers well; when we have insufficient knowledge we cannot fully understand what we are doing but must nevertheless act as well as circumstances allow. In either case, we should aim to enjoy all the sweetness that life offers – a sweetness that is due more than anything to the enjoyment of the human passions. Malebranche more resolutely keeps in mind our heavenly destination. According to his conception of how we know, we are at moments of knowledge knowing things through God, more exactly through the ideas in God. Our ultimate destination is to spend eternity with God, so our sojourn in the sensible realm is only temporary. Our principal task in the meantime is to avoid error and to live toward that eternal destination; along the way we take account of the sensible realm only as necessary. If in the last analysis Descartes urges us to live comfortably with our human nature, Malebranche counsels instead that we constantly be ready to turn away from the bodily part of it. Descartes urges us to enjoy our sensible and imaginational nature while we have it, Malebranche constantly urges its restriction.

Conclusion

We have identified two tonalities to Cartesian imagination. What is common to Descartes and Malebranche is a resolutely psychophysiological basis for all sensitive, imaginative, and memorative functions. The states and actions of the nerves, the animal spirits, and the brain are closely correlated with the experience of sensations, images, past–present–future, pleasure and pain, and emotion.

For Descartes, the imaginative functions are expansive, though not unlimited, in their consequences for the mental and spiritual life of human beings. Human being is not just a union of thinking thing and extended thing, it is even more the knowing force intimately joined to the body in a system of nerves, spirits, and brain. This intimate embodiment allows for sensitive responses to the environing world and for a conscious experience that is progressively exploratory, pleasurable, and self-illuminating. The physiology of the animal spirits is the realm where will, imagination, and passion are the fundamental forms, and where perception passively registers intellectual, imaginal, and passional moments of awareness that become starting points for new willed responses. Imagination, as an exploratory and projective capacity to form and refigure the spirit medium, is not capable of arriving at ultimate insight into its own nature. Human beings must nevertheless exercise imagination fully so that its limits and its difference from intellect can appear. The I, as it turns out, is not so much intellectual as volitional; and the imagination, from the perspective of the *Passions of the Soul*, is more volitional than intellectual, more embedded in the whole being of soul and body than in a bodiless abstraction. This is imagination in a major key, a major tonality. Our principal task as human beings is not to be metaphysicians or even physicist-mathematicians but to learn how to be at home in our bodies through the guidance of the sensitive powers (see especially AT 3: 691–3; 10: 203).

Malebranche fully affirms the psychophysiological apparatus of nerve, spirits, and brain and the necessity for human beings to learn how to live with it. But the intellect transcends the body; even more, its destiny belongs to the incorporeal realm of the Christian conception of the afterlife. Even in this world the intellect is directed not toward the sensitive powers or embodiment but to the perception of ideas in God. The realm of sensation, imagination, and memory is fundamentally prone to error. On earth we are biding our time; we need to keep our intellectual eye on the transcendent prize. This is Cartesianism in a minor key.

It is nevertheless too simple to conclude that Descartes represents secular immanentism, Malebranche Christian transcendence. All the medieval philosophies cultivated under the dual influences of Aristotle and monotheism, whether Jewish, Muslim, or Christian, had raised the question of whether human beings are more fully and adequately characterized as knowing beings or as willing ones, and they all wondered about the relations of intellect to will. In this perspective Malebranche is closer to the view that human beings have a fundamentally distorted will but a relatively unimpaired capability of recognizing the truth in God – a position that would be similar to certain stock characterizations of modern rationalism. Descartes, on the other hand, always seems to have considered human intellect to be finite and limited. For example, we do have an idea of God as perfect and infinite, but this idea is a medium that allows us to "see" or "touch" God rather than to comprehend him (AT 7: 46; 1: 152). In the Fourth Meditation he even asserts that it is more with respect to will than intellect that human beings resemble this idea of God: our intellects are limited and error-prone, whereas our wills are perfect in their kind (AT 7: 56–7). In the last analysis it is will that characterizes human being, culminating in the will to truth. Intellect can do its job of noting similarities and differences only when it is motivated by the will to truth; and seeing the truth has to be completed by willing or affirming it. Through our will to truth we keep rearranging, simplifying, and recombining questions until the intellect can clearly and distinctly assess how things stand. The act of measuring the more, the less, and the equal that is characteristic of imagination is merely the embodied form of the cooperation of intellection and volition. For the most part human beings cannot know and live well unless they fully exploit the information yielded by sense, imagination, and memory, by actively manipulating it in the act of productive imagining.

Malebranche recognized the power of Descartes' imagination and restricted it. The other great rationalists recognized and elaborated it (see chapter 17, this volume). But for most later thinkers and historians it fell beneath the threshold of consciousness. This led to distortions in and fundamental misapprehensions of both Cartesianism and rationalism, which in turn made it even more difficult to perceive Cartesian and rationalist imagination. Not the least distortion was the notion that in Descartes and the rationalists intellect possesses overweening power.

Descartes would have an explanation of this. The psychological powers function, indeed exist, in interrelation and interdependence. To diminish one leads to exaggerating another, and vice versa. If imagination, the traditional mediator between sense and intellect, declines, its functions will not vanish: they will simply be reassigned to the other powers. But how we group these powers and functions is not a matter of indifference. What is at stake is nothing less than the fundamental conception of the what and the how of being human.

References and Further Reading

Aristotle (2001). *On the Soul and On Memory and Recollection* (J. Sachs, trans.). Santa Fe, NM: Green Lion Press.

Arnauld, A., and Nicole, P. (1964). *The Art of Thinking: Port-Royal Logic* (J. Dickoff and P. James, trans.). Indianapolis, IN: Bobbs-Merrill.

Brann, E. T. H. (1991). *The World of the Imagination: Sum and Substance*. Savage, MD: Rowman and Littlefield.

Castoriadis, C. (1997). *A World in Fragments: Writings on Politics, Society, Psychoanalysis, and the Imagination* (D. A. Curtis, trans.). Stanford, CA: Stanford University Press.

Descartes, R. (1984–91). *The Philosophical Writings of Descartes*, 3 vols. (J. Cottingham, R. Stoothoff, D. Murdoch, and A. Kenny, trans.). Cambridge: Cambridge University Press.

Engell, J. (1981). *The Creative Imagination: Enlightenment to Romanticism*. Cambridge, MA: Harvard University Press.

Harvey, E. R. (1975). *The Inward Wits: Psychological Theory in the Middle Ages and the Renaissance*. London: Warburg Institute.

Hatfield, G. (1998). The cognitive faculties. In D. Garber and M. Ayers (eds.), *The Cambridge History of Seventeenth-Century Philosophy* (pp. 953–1002). Cambridge: Cambridge University Press.

Hobbes, T. (1994). *The Elements of Law, Natural and Politic* (J. C. A. Gaskin, ed.). Oxford: Oxford University Press.

Kearney, R. (1988). *The Wake of Imagination: Toward a Postmodern Culture*. Minneapolis, MN: University of Minneapolis Press.

McCracken, C. J. (1983). *Malebranche and British Philosophy*. Oxford: Clarendon Press.

Park, K. (1988). The organic soul. In C. B. Schmitt et al. (eds.), *The Cambridge History of Renaissance Philosophy* (pp. 464–84). Cambridge: Cambridge University Press.

Sepper, D. L. (1996). *Descartes' Imagination: Proportion, Images, and the Activity of Thinking*. Los Angeles: University of California Press.

Part III

THE HEYDAY OF RATIONALISM

10

Descartes' Rationalist Epistemology

LEX NEWMAN

Doubtless Descartes belongs in the rationalist tradition. Stating why is not so easy. He nowhere characterizes the view we call "rationalism," nor does he describe himself *as* a rationalist. His express commitment to a doctrine of innateness is suggestive though not sufficient, for some philosophers (e.g., Kant) accept such a doctrine while rejecting rationalism. Further suggestive is that he links innateness with the achievement of knowledge:

> We come to know them [innate truths] by the power of our own native intelligence, without any sensory experience. All geometrical truths are of this sort – not just the most obvious ones, but all the others, however abstruse they may appear. Hence, according to Plato, Socrates asks a slave-boy about the elements of geometry and thereby makes the boy able to dig out certain truths from his own mind which he had not previously recognized were there, thus attempting to establish the doctrine of reminiscence. Our knowledge of God is of this sort. (CSMK 222–3; AT 8b: 166–7)

Clarifying a precise account of rationalism is not the aim of this chapter. I shall instead assume that we're on the rationalist track and attempt to develop central rationalist themes that figure prominently in Descartes' epistemology. The themes I develop center on methodist concerns. Distinguish two sorts of epistemological questions for which one might identify characteristic responses, including rationalist responses:

What-questions (e.g., What particular propositions can be known?)
How-questions (e.g., How are such propositions known?)

Exemplary what-questions concern whether we can know, for example, the nature of being itself, or know necessary truths, or the nature of identity, causality, and so on. Exemplary how-questions concern the nature of knowledge itself, including how it differs from opinion, the origin of our ideas, the reliability of our ideas as a basis for judgment, and so on. Opinions vary about the proper direction of inquiry – about which sort of question should take precedence over the other in the process of discovery. Two broad camps have emerged. (Note that these camps do not map onto the rationalism–empiricism distinction.) According to the *particularist* camp, answers to what-questions take precedence. Proper inquiry begins by identifying exemplary cases of particular propositions that we know. What counts as exemplary? According to G. E. Moore, "Here is a hand" is exemplary (while holding up your hand and looking at it). These exemplary cases are then used to help sort out better and worse answers to how-questions – the better answers will have it that the exemplary cases count *as* knowledge. The *methodist* camp reverses the order of inquiry. How-questions take precedence. Accordingly, we can only correctly identify a knowledge claim as exemplary if we have already sorted out answers to how-questions. A proper such sorting might indeed reveal that Moore's celebrated knowledge claim is not well founded.

Descartes is a methodist *par excellence*. His methodist orientation is perhaps best explained in historical context. The early seventeenth century is entrenched in dogma. Centuries of Aristotelianism having prevailed, the philosophical world is captivated by ancient authorities and longstanding traditions. If the new mechanist philosophy is to supplant Aristotelianism, a strategy is needed to effectively call into question venerated authorities and traditions, but – importantly – without directly impugning their credibility. In a stroke of genius, Descartes devises a broader methodist strategy to accomplish this. As part of the strategy, we're to carry out a once-in-a-lifetime epistemological *audit* – a thorough examination of the books, as it were, scrutinizing our beliefs and their basis. The opening lines of the *Meditations* present a simple and compelling rationale for the audit:

> Some years ago I was struck by the large number of falsehoods that I had accepted as true in my childhood, and by the highly doubtful nature of the whole edifice that I had subsequently based on them. I realized that it was necessary, once in the course of my life, to demolish everything completely and start again right from the foundations if I wanted to establish anything at all in the sciences [*scientiis*] that was stable and likely to last. (CSM 2: 12; AT 7: 17)

The stated rationale in no way impugns venerated Aristotelian institutions. Moreover, the architectural allusions play well to Aristotelian readers, for they already accept a foundationist approach to rigorous knowledge (i.e., *scientia*). Accordingly, knowledge is modeled on an architectural analogy. A structurally sound edifice – one that's "stable and likely to last" – is founded on a solid base that firmly anchors all superstructure. By analogy, an *epistemic* edifice should be founded on a base of evident principles that provide for a deduction of all further knowledge claims. The audit strategy calls for a complete demolition and reconstruction of the edifice, from the very foundations. Because not even Aristotelians accept authority or tradition as *basic* epistemic sources, they would understand the implications of the audit: they should put to the side the very authority of Aristotle, identifying the basic principles to which he would appeal. Descartes' strategy turns out highly influential. His methodist approach (broadly speaking) signals a historical sea-change in the way philosophers approach philosophical inquiry – a change helping move the philosophical world towards modernism.

Because Descartes' approach is strongly methodist in orientation, so is the present chapter. Our focus will be on Descartes' rationalism from the vantage point of how-questions. His answers to what-questions will be of only secondary interest. The remainder of this chapter is organized as follows. It first explains Descartes' account of innateness. It then develops two rationalist doctrines in Descartes – methodist doctrines concerning the proper foundations of knowledge. It then addresses how Descartes' famed method of doubt figures in his treatment of the two doctrines.

Descartes on Innateness

The how-question most characteristic of the rationalism–empiricism debate concerns the origin of mental content. Rationalism standardly affirms a doctrine of innate mental content. Talk of innateness may be applied to a variety of items, including ideas (both sensations and concepts), truths, and knowledge. Ideas are at the center of much of the early modern debate.[1] A near litmus test of one's camp is a commitment to, or against, innate ideas – specifically, innate concepts. Our focus will be on *concepts*, by which I mean general ideas – those with general content. (Innate truths also come into play, where truths and concepts amount to distinct ways of regarding eternal essences – more on this below.) Below, I develop three aspects of Descartes' account: the criterion of innateness, the innateness of sensations, and the dispositional element of innateness.

The criterion of innateness

What, according to Descartes, makes ideas *innate* rather than non-innate? Descartes introduces a threefold distinction of ideas by way of his *meditator* – the inquiring spokesperson of the *Meditations*:

> Among my ideas, some appear to be innate, some to be adventitious, and others to have been invented by me. (CSM 2: 26; AT 7: 37–8)

This text offers a partial answer to our question, by contrasting innateness with two other sorts of ideas: *adventitious* and *invented*. Though the threefold distinction is supposed to be exhaustive (this is presupposed by various arguments that Descartes later puts forward; cf. AT 7: 51), it is not exclusive. Whatever else is true of *invented* ideas, their content draws ultimately on preexisting innate or adventitious ideas (i.e., invention is not a basic ideational source). Presumably, invented ideas can draw on *both* native and sensory resources. I suggest therefore that the threefold taxonomy is consistent with an official doctrine of two ultimate (i.e., basic) ideational sources: the *intellect*, which exemplifies the category of innateness, and the *senses*, which exemplify the category of adventitiousness.

Further help on the category Descartes calls "innate" comes from an important passage in the *Comments on a Certain Broadsheet*:

> I did, however, observe that there were certain thoughts within me which neither came to me from external objects nor were determined by my will, but which *came solely from the power of thinking within me* [*sed à solâ cogitandi facultate*]; so I applied the term "innate" [*innatas*] to the ideas or notions which are the forms of these thoughts in order to

distinguish them from others, which I called "adventitious" or "made up." (CSM 1: 303, AT 8b: 357–8, emphasis added)

I suggest we parse the text, distinguishing its implications for "innateness"-*talk* and its implications for the very notion of *innateness*. Evidently, Descartes thinks it helps avoid confusion to reserve the term "innate" for just those ideas that derive "solely" from the faculty of thinking. The notion of innateness is another matter. On one reading of the passage, innateness admits of degrees (even if the terminology does not): if some ideas exemplify innateness because of deriving *solely* from the mind, other ideas might qualify as partly innate because of deriving *partly* from the mind. I take the official doctrine to be that ideas are innate insofar as their content derives from the nature of the mind alone. Neither of the above passages expressly says this, though both are consistent with it. And this formulation allows us to explain a variety of other texts and doctrinal considerations, so I'll argue. Let's consider further Descartes' two basic categories of ideas – innate and adventitious – in relation to this official doctrine.

Consider the so-called "innate" category. Descartes' examples include various concepts in mathematics (e.g., number, line, triangle, etc.), logic (e.g., contradiction, necessity, etc.), and metaphysics (e.g., identity, substance, causality, etc.). To Mersenne, he notes that our innate concepts include "the idea of God, mind, body, triangle," and others (CSMK 183; AT 3: 383). These ideas are supposed to be exemplary of innateness because of deriving solely from the nature of the mind. The senses play *no* role in their formation. Descartes refers to them as ideas of the pure intellect/understanding (*intellectus*), their purity consisting in an absence of any sensory component. The Sixth Meditation illustrates the difference between thinking of geometric figures using sensory images and using pure intellection:

> I will first examine the difference between imagination and pure understanding. When I imagine a triangle, for example, I do not merely understand that it is a figure bounded by three lines, but at the same time I also see the three lines with my mind's eye as if they were present before me; and this is what I call imagining. But if I want to think of a chiliagon, although I understand that it is a figure consisting of a thousand sides just as well as I understand the triangle to be a three-sided figure, I do not in the same way imagine the thousand sides or see them as if they were present before me. It is true that since I am in the habit of imagining something whenever I think of a corporeal thing, I may construct in my mind a confused representation of some figure; but it is clear that this is not a chiliagon. For it differs in no way from the representation I should form if I were thinking of a myriagon, or any figure with very many sides. Moreover, such a representation is useless for recognizing the properties which distinguish a chiliagon from other polygons. (CSM 2: 50; AT 7: 72)

Because there is no relevant difference between the confused sensory image of a chiliagon and that of a myriagon, Descartes concludes that the sensory images contribute nothing to the *distinct* conception of these geometric figures.[2]

Though Descartes denies sensory images are *constitutive* of a purely intellectual idea, there are ways they may be involved. One way, as in the above passage, is that a sensory element might *accompany* the intellectual idea. This confused image, however, forms a separate idea. Another way is that sensory ideas might help activate a (preexisting) purely intellectual idea. Descartes describes such a case:

[W]hen in our childhood we first happened to see a triangular figure drawn on paper, it cannot have been this figure that showed us how we should conceive of the true triangle studied by geometers, since the true triangle is contained in the figure only in the way in which a statue of Mercury is contained in a rough block of wood. But since the idea of the true triangle was already in us, and could be conceived by our mind more easily than the more composite figure of the triangle drawn on paper, when we saw the composite figure we did not apprehend the figure we saw, but rather the true triangle . . . Thus we could not recognize the geometrical triangle from the diagram on the paper unless our mind already possessed the idea of it from some other source. (CSM 2: 262; AT 7: 382)

Of such cases, the *Comments on a Certain Broadsheet* adds:

[S]trictly speaking, sight in itself presents nothing but pictures, and hearing nothing but utterances and sounds. So everything over and above these utterances and pictures which we think of as being signified by them is represented to us by means of ideas which come to us from no other source than our own faculty of thinking. (CSM 1: 305; AT 8b: 360–1)

Descartes thinks that sensation functions as a "merely accidental cause, which gives the primary cause occasion to produce its effect at one moment rather than another" (CSM 1: 305; AT 8b: 360–1). Purely intellectual concepts may therefore *depend* on the senses, but the conceptual dependence is one of activation, not formation. Something similar holds for any dependence on the will. Strictly, we play no willing role in forming purely intellectual ideas, but only in actualizing/realizing them. Their formation, as part of the mind, derives ultimately from the divine will.

Descartes' notion of intellect marks a clear contrast with empiricism. Philosophers from each camp allow that the mind is equipped with an intellect, or understanding. Only rationalists can consistently dissociate this faculty from the mind's sensory faculties. Devoid of any sensuous element, Descartes' purely intellectual ideas have literally abstract content that is in no way determined by particular imagery. The intellectual conception of a triangle equally well represents right triangles, equilateral triangles, or any other. Early modern empiricist accounts do also employ *abstraction*-talk, designating concepts "abstract ideas." On these accounts, however, the idea's abstract content *is* determined by particular imagery. Idea content is abstract in roughly the manner of so-called abstract art. The minimalism of a sensory image (or of what the mind selectively attends to) enables it to resemble a whole *sort* of particulars and thus to represent each of the particulars of the sort. Cases like the triangle pose notorious difficulties for such accounts. Because every triangular image is already minimal, it is unclear how abstraction is supposed to achieve general representation of what is "neither oblique, nor rectangle, neither equilateral, equicrural, nor scalenon; but all and none of these at once," writes Locke (*Essay* IV.vii.9).

Consider the so-called "adventitious" category of ideas. Descartes cites, as examples, such sensory ideas as hearing a noise, seeing the sun, and feeling heat (AT 7: 38). Prima facie, the ideas in this category derive entirely from the senses – *if* any ideas do. They appear to be utterly *non*-innate, seeming to derive entirely from outside the mind, not from within. The Aristotelian account of sensation accords well with this prima facie character. The account models their formation after the manner in which a seal is impressed in a wax tablet. The mind is utterly passive, contributing nothing to the content of the images, except insofar as it must have the capacity to receive such images via the senses. On such an account, the character of an idea is owed entirely to what impresses it on the mind – its form is quite literally transported into the mind from without.

Descartes' treatment of adventitious ideas may seem confusing, notably on two counts. First, in the unfolding of the *Meditations*, the meditator undergoes anti-skeptical progress. In the context in which the threefold distinction of ideas is first introduced (an early Third Meditation context), the meditator remains in doubt about whether there *is* an external world, and thus about whether any ideas are actually adventitious in the way they appear. Assuming solipsism is correct, such ideas would derive from an innate source – a scenario the meditator takes seriously.[3] Importantly, therefore, the threefold distinction is introduced by the meditator in terms of how his ideas *appear* to arise – "among my ideas, some appear (*videntur*) to be innate, some to be adventitious, and others to have been invented by me." (Note that talk of sensory ideas need not presuppose physical sense organs as opposed merely to sensory faculties. Referring to cases in which we "*seem* to see, to hear, and to be warmed," Descartes writes that "what is called 'having a sensory perception' is strictly just this, and in this restricted sense of the term it is simply thinking" (CSM 2: 19; AT 7: 29).)

Second, Descartes holds in the final analysis that sensations *are* in some manner adventitious, though not fully so. By the Sixth Meditation, the meditator purports to resolve his external-world doubts, demonstrating that his sensations are caused by external things, indeed by "corporeal things" (CSM 2: 55; AT 7: 79–80).[4] Contra the Aristotelian account, however, these sensory ideas are not literally transported into the mind, from without. Sensory stimulation serves merely to *occasion* the mind's sensory content. Taking this seriously implies that the occasioned sensory content is in some manner *innate* – a topic to which I want now to turn.

Sensations and innateness

Though I have been focusing on concepts, our attention turns to sensations – the images produced by individual sense impressions, not the general conception of them. Strictly, these "sensation ideas" (as I'll call them) include only the most immediate, conscious result of the stimulation of each sense. Thus "light and color," writes Descartes, are "the only qualities belonging properly to the sense of sight" (CSM 1: 167; AT 6: 130). Many commentators find puzzling Descartes' claims that even sensation ideas are innate. Our account suggests not this puzzle, but instead a puzzle as to how Descartes can avoid putting sensation ideas on a par with intellectual ideas in terms of their innateness. Let's consider both of these puzzles.

In a famous remark, Descartes claims that sensation ideas are innate. I earlier proposed that, on his official doctrine, ideas are innate insofar as their content derives from the nature of the mind alone, where "insofar" talk allows for degrees of innateness. Far from puzzling, the claim that sensation ideas are innate is explained by Descartes' understanding of mechanism. Accordingly, the real properties of bodies

include size, shape, and motion (what would later come to be called "primary qualities"), but nothing resembling ideas of pain, colors, sounds, tastes, or the like (the
qualities producing these ideas would come to be called "secondary"). Sensation
ideas arise not from exactly resembling qualities in sensibly large external objects,
but from the size, shape, and motion of the insensibly small corporeal bodies reaching the sense organs. For the case of secondary-quality sensation ideas, therefore, it
is especially clear that their content must derive, in part, from innate resources. If
nothing in the corporeal world resembles the sensation idea of *red*, then, contra the
Aristotelian theory, the content of that idea is not transported into the mind from
without.[5] This is what Descartes' famous remark comes to – a remark made in the
Comments on a Certain Broadsheet:

> If we bear well in mind the scope of our senses and what it is exactly that reaches our
> faculty of thinking by way of them, we must admit that in no case are the ideas of things
> presented to us by the senses just as we form them in our thinking. So much so that there
> is nothing in our ideas which is not innate to the mind or the faculty of thinking, with the
> sole exception of those circumstances which relate to experience, such as the fact that we
> judge that this or that idea which we now have immediately before our mind refers to a
> certain thing situated outside us. We make such a judgement not because these things
> transmit the ideas to our mind through the sense organs, but because they transmit
> something which, at exactly that moment, gives the mind occasion to form these ideas by
> means of the faculty innate to it. Nothing reaches our mind from external objects through
> the sense organs except certain corporeal motions . . . Hence it follows that the very ideas
> of the motions themselves and of the figures are innate in us. The ideas of pain, colors,
> sounds and the like must be all the more [evidently][6] innate if, on the occasion of certain
> corporeal motions, our mind is to be capable of representing them to itself, for there is no
> similarity between these ideas and the corporeal motions. (CSM 1: 304; AT 8b: 358–9)

Sensation ideas, therefore, are at least partly innate. Their ideational content derives
from the mind's own faculties, not from qualities in external corporeal things – a point
that, as Descartes notes, is all the more evident for the case of secondary-quality sensation ideas.

The harder puzzle concerns why Descartes does not treat the innateness of sensation ideas on a par with purely intellectual concepts – why he does not regard both
kinds of ideas as fully innate. In both cases, Descartes denies that their content is
transported in from external things; and he allows that they may be activated by
stimulation of the physical sense organs. It might therefore seem that *both* kinds
of ideas are equally innate – viz., fully innate – and thus deserving of the official
designation "innate."

The resolution of this puzzle lies in Descartes' unique views of the ontology of
sensations.[7] Strictly, sensation ideas do not arise from the nature of the mind *alone*,
but from the nature of the mind–body *union* – "the close and intimate union of our
mind with the body" (CSM 1: 209; AT 8a: 23). Though "the faculties of sensation
and imagination belong to the soul," writes Descartes, they belong to it "only insofar
as it is joined to the body" (CSMK 203; AT 3: 479). This understanding of sensation
is anticipated in the chiliagon/myriagon passage discussed above. While working
out differences in imagination and pure intellect, the meditator observes:

185

> This power of imagining which is in me, differing as it does from the power of understanding, is not a necessary constituent of my own essence, that is, of the essence of my mind. For if I lacked it, I should undoubtedly remain the same individual as I now am; from which it seems to follow that it depends on something distinct from myself. (CSM 2: 51; AT 7: 73)

The mental aspect of sensation *is* entirely mental. In a curious way, however, its very *being* depends on more than just the mental. Unlike the content of the purely intellectual idea of a triangle – idea content which *can* be activated by sensation – the content of sensation ideas can *only* be activated in sensation. Sensation ideas, therefore, are not fully innate in the manner of intellectual concepts.

Descartes' view of sensation ideas as partly innate accords well with his mechanist commitments. Can a consistent empiricist hold such an account of sensation ideas (≠ concepts)? Arguably, Locke consistently holds as much, though this is not the place to make the argument. With the onset of the new mechanical physics, rationalists and empiricists alike would abandon the Aristotelian view of sensation, holding instead that the content of sensation ideas derives from the mind's abilities. The debate between rationalism and empiricism would center around the origin not of sensation ideas, but of concepts.

The dispositional element of the account

Not only are fully innate concepts not formed with the help of the senses, but Descartes also denies that they are formed at all – not formed by *our* wills, at any rate. Their formation predates our abilities at concept formation. They're in our minds from birth, whether we notice them or not. An important role of philosophical reflection is to help us to *discover* these ideas, not to form them.

This suggests an objection. By definition, ideas are items of conscious awareness,[8] namely the immediate objects of perception or thinking (cf. AT 7: 160ff.).[9] But no ideas are items of uninterrupted awareness. It seems to follow that no ideas are always *in* the mind, much less in it from birth. As Hobbes objects: "It follows that no idea is innate; for what is innate is always present" (CSM 2: 132; AT 7: 188–9).

Descartes claims to avoid the objection with a dispositional account. Though only occurrent thoughts count as *ideas* strictly speaking, we can regard ideas either in their occurrent state as items of actual awareness, or their state as potential items of awareness. Even in the potential state, ideas are *in* the mind in that the mind is wired with the ability to perceive them – "they always exist within us potentially" (CSM 1: 305; AT 8b: 361). The key to avoiding the Hobbes style of objection is that, in their dispositional state, ideas may be in the mind without our being aware of them – the things "said to be naturally implanted in us are not for that reason expressly known by us" (CSMK 222; AT 8b: 166). It is in this dispositional sense that Descartes refers to ideas in terms of capacities or faculties (cf. AT 7: 246ff.; 8b: 357ff.), including in his reply to Hobbes:

> [W]hen we say that an idea is innate in us, we do not mean that it is always there before us. This would mean that no idea was innate. We simply mean that we have within ourselves the faculty of summoning up the idea. (CSM 2: 132; AT 7: 189)

186

In the case of the idea of God, adds Descartes, "some people will perhaps not notice it even after reading my *Meditations* a thousand times" (CSMK 194; AT 3: 430; cf. AT 4: 187). Descartes, indeed, maintains "there are many things which can be known . . . which *no one* has yet reflected on" (CSMK 139; AT 2: 598, emphasis added). If and when we notice our innate ideas, thinks Descartes, it is apt to occur to us that these ideas have always been with us, a position aligning him with Plato's metaphor of recollection:

> [O]n first discovering [innate ideas] it seems that I am not so much learning something new as remembering what I knew before; or it seems like noticing for the first time things which were long present within me although I had never turned my mental gaze on them before. (CSM 2: 44; AT 7: 64)

Bear in mind that Descartes' appeal to dispositions does not purport to provide an analysis of innateness. It purports only to explain how innateness is compatible with non-awareness. As I have been arguing, Descartes' official analysis of innateness has it that ideas are innate insofar as their content derives from the nature of the mind alone – an analysis that does not, per se, rule out that innate ideas are (contrary to fact) items of uninterrupted awareness.

Descartes' appeal to dispositions invites an objection that would be raised by Locke. The appeal to dispositions appears to trivialize the very notion of an innate idea. For suppose the mind were a quite literal *tabula rasa*. It would nonetheless be *disposed* to have various sense impressions – even an entirely smooth tablet has the capacity to take on whatever form imprints it. Thus, there would seem to be something wrong in Descartes' account, if it implies that even *tabula rasa* impressions come out innate. As Locke complains, the account implies that our ideas "must all be innate, or all adventitious: In vain shall a Man go about to distinguish them" (*Essay* I.ii.5).[10]

Though the problem looks devastating, Leibniz would later clarify a distinction that solves it – a distinction that might plausibly be read into Descartes. In his *New Essays*, Leibniz distinguishes two sorts of dispositions via an analogy to a sculptor's block of marble:

> I have also used the analogy of a veined block of marble, as opposed to an entirely homogeneous block of marble, or to a blank tablet – what the philosophers call a *tabula rasa*. For if the soul were like such a blank tablet then truths would be in us as the shape of Hercules is in a piece of marble when the marble is entirely neutral as to whether it assumes this shape or some other. However, if there were veins in the block which marked out the shape of Hercules rather than other shapes, then that block would be more determined to that shape and Hercules would be innate in it, in a way, even though labor would be required to expose the veins and to polish them into clarity, removing everything that prevents their being seen. This is how ideas and truths are innate in us – as inclinations, dispositions, tendencies, or natural potentialities. (LNE 51–2)

The appeal to dispositions would be insignificant, were the view simply that the mind has "the mere capacity to receive those items of knowledge – a passive power to do so, as indeterminate as the power of wax to receive shapes or of a blank page to receive words" (LNE 79). But this is not Leibniz's view:

> It is not a bare faculty, consisting in a mere possibility of understanding those truths: it is rather a disposition, an aptitude, a preformation, which determines our soul and brings it about that they are derivable from it. (LNE 80)

Both blocks of marble have the bare capacity to be sculpted into the bust of Hercules. Only the veined block is *preformed* to take on this shape. I will mark this difference using the terms 'disposition' and '*pre*disposition' (my terminology, not Leibniz's). The form of Hercules is innate to the veined block in the sense of being *pre*disposed to take on that form. The smooth block – like the empiricist's *tabula rasa* mind – is no more predisposed towards any one form than another.

Borrowing Leibniz's sculptor analogy helps make sense of Descartes' view. The nativist mind is *pre*disposed to having some ideas – hardwired with intellectual concepts – while merely disposed to having others. I have proposed that, on Descartes' official doctrine, ideas are innate insofar as their content derives from the nature of the mind alone. Descartes can maintain that the only ideas for which the mind is predisposed are those that derive *solely* from the mind alone – unlike those requiring union with a body, or deriving from the mind's inventive abilities.

Will the texts sustain this reading? Are Descartes' statements best read in terms of Leibniz's *pre*dispositions, or the *mere* dispositions criticized by Locke? The mere disposition reading is suggested by Descartes' repeated use of the language of faculties – he even clarifies that "the term 'faculty' denotes *nothing but* a potentiality" (CSM 1: 305; AT 8b: 361, emphasis added). This language suggests the mistake of which Locke accuses him. On the other hand, there are texts strongly suggesting the *pre*disposition reading – including texts using "faculty" talk. For example, Descartes makes an analogy to the sense in which diseases are said to be innate:

> This is the same sense as that in which we say that generosity is "innate" in certain families, or that certain diseases such as gout or stones are innate in others: it is not so much that the babies of such families suffer from these diseases in their mother's womb, but simply that they are born with a certain "faculty" or tendency to contract them. (CSM 1: 303–4; AT 8b: 358)

Here, the suggestion is of an inherited disease – one for which there is a predisposition – in contrast with those diseases to which everyone is equally disposed. Note too that the predisposition reading helps make sense of numerous texts entailing that the initial cognition of innate concepts involves the discovery of preexisting (preformed), determinate content – even immutably determinate content (a point I return to below). The mere disposition account is inadequate to explain these texts, because it implies that the mind is innately disposed only for determin*able* content.

Even granting the predisposition reading, problems remain – or at least wrinkles to be ironed out. As some commentators have worried, the suggestion of innate dispositions of which we're unaware is incompatible with Descartes' doctrine of the transparency of mind.[11] There is not sufficient space to develop these issues carefully. I'll note briefly, however, that in important texts Descartes makes clear that the transparency doctrine extends only to the operation or activity of the mind's faculties – that is, to occurrent thoughts – not to unactualized, or inoperative faculties:[12]

As to the fact that there can be nothing in the mind, insofar as it is a thinking thing, of which it is not aware . . . we cannot have any thought of which we are not aware at the very moment when it is in us . . . But it must be noted that, although we are always actually aware of the acts or operations of our minds, we are not always aware of the mind's faculties or powers, except potentially. (CSM 2: 171–2; AT 7: 246)

Difficulties remain, though perhaps this qualification provides Descartes with some room to work.

Two Rationalist Doctrines

Plato's allegory of the cave illustrates well the rationalist themes of the cognitive inferiority of the senses in contrast with the superiority of the intellect. Plato likens what the senses reveal to shadows on the wall of a poorly lit cave – to wit, shadows of mere figurine beings; he likens what the intellect reveals to fully real beings illuminated by bright sunshine. Descartes revives the underlying themes, synthesizing them with a longstanding tradition that characterizes our most evident perceptual states in terms of *clarity* and *distinctness*. Where others had associated these phenomenal markers with sensory apprehension, Descartes identifies them principally with the intellect's luminance. On his account, the senses provide *obscure* (i.e., non-clear) and *confused* (i.e., non-distinct) perception of the world. The sensory view is indeed supposed to be cave-like in ways brought out by Plato's allegory: not only are the senses ill-equipped to illuminate the nature of reality, but they also have mere images as their perceptual objects, not real beings. In contrast, Descartes' references to the intellect are suggestive of the vision enjoyed by supra-cave sunbathers. Making an analogy to physiological vision, he likens the mind's *clear* perception to what "is present to the [physical] eye's gaze" (CSM 1: 207; AT 8a: 22). He characterizes exemplary cases of clear and distinct perception in terms of what we "see" (*intueri*) with the "mind's eye" (*mentis oculis*) (CSM 2: 25; AT 7: 36), and what is "revealed to [us] by the natural light" (CSM 2: 27; AT 7: 38).[13]

We may press the analogy to Plato even further, thereby elucidating a central feature of Descartes' normative epistemology. In contexts of practical importance, the prudent person will prefer to make judgments about visually sensible objects in the bright light of the sun, not a dim cave. In this vein, Descartes develops his doctrine about the proper use of our judgment faculties. In contexts of strict knowledge (*scientia*), the inquirer should make judgments only in the brightness of the "natural light" – the cognitive luminance shed by clear and distinct perception: if I "refrain from making a judgement in cases where I do not perceive the truth with sufficient clarity and distinctness, then it is clear that I am behaving correctly and avoiding error" – otherwise, "I am not using my free will correctly" (CSM 2: 41; AT 7: 59).

Below, I develop Descartes' doctrinal commitments to the two underlying rationalist themes: the doctrine related to the inferiority of the senses and the doctrine related to the superiority of the intellect.

The senses are ill-suited to illuminate the nature of reality

The specific thesis about the senses that I attribute to Descartes is this:

> *Sensation Unreliability Thesis*: The senses are an unreliable basis for judgments about the nature of reality.

The thesis is not that the senses always result in false judgments about the nature of reality, but that they are an unreliable basis. They never illuminate the mind with clear and distinct perception of the nature of reality. Where such judgments *are* true, writes Descartes, "it is by pure chance that I arrive at the truth" (CSM 2: 41; AT 7: 59–60). The texts suggest that unreliability issues are greater for the *external* senses – sight, sound, smell, taste, and touch – but Descartes is clear that they extend "not just to the external senses but to the internal senses as well" (CSM 2: 53; AT 7: 76). A significant aim of the *Meditations* is to teach us how to withdraw from the senses as a step in becoming knowers. In the dedicatory letter to the *Meditations*, Descartes writes that to comprehend his arguments one must have a mind "which can easily detach itself from involvement with the senses" (CSM 2: 5; AT 7: 5). In the preface, he urges his readers "to withdraw their minds from the senses" (CSM 2: 8; AT 7: 9). Elsewhere he adds that if the mind "were released from the prison of the body, it would find them [innate truths] within itself" (CSMK 190; AT 3: 425).

A casual reading of the exhortations to *withdraw from the senses* might suggest shutting-off entirely the mind's sensory awareness. But this is not Descartes' intent, nor does he think it cognitively possible. In properly functioning minds sensory awareness is passively received, an inevitable result of being united with a body. Officially, we're to withdraw not from the senses, but from sense-based *judgments* – the senses don't err, strictly speaking:

> Now as far as ideas are concerned, provided they are considered solely in themselves and I do not refer them to anything else, they cannot strictly speaking be false; for whether it is a goat or a chimera that I am imagining, it is just as true that I imagine the former as the latter . . . [the] thoughts where I must be on my guard against making a mistake are judgements. And the chief and most common mistake which is to be found here consists in my judging that the ideas which are in me resemble, or conform to, things located outside me. (CSM 2: 26; AT 7: 37)

The doctrine is reinforced in Descartes' distinction of "three grades of sensory response":

> The first [grade] is limited to the immediate stimulation of the bodily organs by external objects . . . The second grade comprises all the immediate effects produced in the mind as a result of its being united with a bodily organ which is affected in this way. Such effects include the perceptions of pain, pleasure, thirst, hunger, colors, sound, taste, smell, heat, cold and the like . . . The third grade includes all the judgements about things outside us which we have been accustomed to make from our earliest years. (CSM 2: 294–5; AT 7: 436–7)

Referring to the first two grades, Descartes clarifies that "nothing more than this should be referred to the sensory faculty, if we wish to distinguish it carefully from the intellect"

(CSM 2: 295; AT 7: 437). In the case of a miscalculation about sensible objects, we're apt to blame the senses; yet, thinks Descartes, "it is clear" that the error "depends solely on the intellect" (CSM 2: 295; AT 7: 437–8). Descartes is sometimes careful in his statements to refer the error to the judgment. More often he uses elliptical references that misleadingly incriminate the senses. In any case, his considered view is that we cannot shut-off the senses, nor are they strictly responsible for error. Interestingly, the Third Meditation opens with the meditator expressly misstating the withdrawal doctrine, followed by an immediate correction:

> I will now shut my eyes, stop my ears, and withdraw all my senses. I will eliminate from my thoughts all images of bodily things, or rather, *since this is hardly possible*, I will regard all such images as vacuous, false and worthless. (CSM 2: 24; AT 7: 34, emphasis added)

Though the claimed unreliability lies with sense-based judgments, not all manner of sense-based judgments are unreliable. The Sensation Unreliability Thesis concerns judgments *about the nature of reality* – judgments about "things located outside me," about "things outside us," as noted in the above cited texts. For ease of reference, I'll hereafter refer to these as *metaphysical* judgments. Though the senses are ill-suited for metaphysical judgments, they may contribute well to judgments about the present contents of consciousness. As already noted, the problems associated with the senses can be avoided, if we consider the ideas "without referring them to anything else." Indeed, Descartes allows that sensory ideas may be clearly and distinctly perceived, "provided we take great care in our judgements concerning them to include no more than what is strictly contained in our perception – no more than that of which we have inner awareness" (CSM 1: 216; AT 8a: 32; cf. 8a: 33).

A related interpretive mistake has Descartes holding that *all* judgments about the present contents of consciousness are well founded. Some such doctrine is commonly attributed to him – whether in terms of the *infallibility* of the mental, or merely its *indubitability*. The attribution is a mistake. For Descartes, the sole marker of infallibility, or even indubitability, is the conjunction of clarity and distinctness. Introspective judgments may fall short of this marker – even those involving sincere efforts to represent the present contents of consciousness. Suppose that, upon introspecting my idea of a speckled hen, I judge that it has at least 20 speckles. If what the idea presents is a *confused* array of speckles, then my judgment will be founded on a guess – albeit perhaps a good guess – rather than on what I clearly and distinctly perceive. Though the judgment *is* about the present contents of consciousness, it rests not on a reliable basis but on guesswork.

Interestingly, Descartes concludes not merely that the senses provide unreliable information about the nature of reality, but that they do not even *purport* to do so. The Sixth Meditation meditator observes:

> I misuse them [the senses] by treating them as reliable touchstones for immediate judgements about the essential nature of the bodies located outside us; yet this is an area where they provide only very obscure information. (CSM 2: 57–8; AT 7: 83)

Obscurity is the contrast of *clarity*. According to Descartes, every perception that lacks clarity also lacks distinctness (cf. *Principles* 1: 45–6).

What then are the senses *for*, if not to inform us about the world? Descartes holds that the senses do inform us about the world, but their information is intended for *practical* purposes, not metaphysical inquiry.[14] God designed our senses to convey information about the objects "in the vicinity," e.g., that "some of these are to be sought out and others avoided" (CSM 2: 56; AT 7: 81):

> For the proper purpose of the sensory perceptions given me by nature is simply to inform the mind of what is beneficial or harmful for the composite of which the mind is a part; and to this extent they are sufficiently clear and distinct. (CSM 2: 57; AT 7: 83)

To achieve clarity and distinctness about metaphysics, God intends that we use our intellect: we're not "to draw any conclusions from these sensory perceptions about things located outside us without waiting until the intellect has examined the matter" (CSM 2: 57; AT 7: 82).

From a post-Descartes vantage point, it might appear puzzling that I have treated the Sensation Unreliability Thesis as a *rationalist* doctrine. For empiricists as varied as Locke and Hume do also affirm some such thesis. In significant ways, however, early modern empiricism marks a revolutionary departure from premodern empiricism – a departure owed in large measure to the philosophical revolution Descartes helps bring about. From the vantage point of his pre-revolution audience, the Sensation Unreliability Thesis marks a direct challenge to their empiricism.

The intellect is well-suited to illuminate the nature of reality

The specific thesis about the intellect that I attribute to Descartes is this:

> *Intellection Reliability Thesis*: The intellect is a reliable basis for judgments about the nature of reality.

For Descartes, the reliability of intellect-based judgments is owed to the divine design of our cognitive faculties. Upon properly accessing our innate, intellectual concepts, we discover that our minds are designed to represent perfectly the nature of being. In the *Discourse* Descartes writes:

> I have noticed certain laws which God has so established in nature, and of which he has implanted such notions in our minds, that after adequate reflection we cannot doubt that they are exactly observed in everything which exists or occurs in the world. (CSM 1: 131; AT 6: 41)

Elsewhere, Descartes notes that by means of the eternal truths, "God himself has taught us" how he "has arranged all things," adding:

> The knowledge of these truths is so natural to our souls that we cannot but judge them infallible when we conceive them distinctly, nor doubt that if God had created many worlds, they would be as true in each of them as in this one. (CSM 1: 97; AT 11: 47)

In the final analysis, the mind's treasure house of innate ideas provides the meta-physician's holy grail (as it were): cognitive access to ultimate truths about the nature of reality.

Descartes variously refers to the innate, intellectual items in terms of *ideas* or *truths*. In letters to Mersenne, he writes that the eternal truths are "inborn in our minds" (CSMK 23; AT 1: 145); that the "essence of created things . . . is nothing other than the eternal truths" (CSMK 25; AT 1: 152); and that innate ideas "represent true, immutable and eternal essences" (CSMK 183; AT 3: 383). The Fifth Meditation meditator's thoughts about triangles and God are variously expressed in terms of his ideas of them, or truths about them. Either way, our clear and distinct thoughts apprehend the very nature of being.

In connection with the intellectual apprehension of eternal essences, Descartes emphasizes a *cognitive immutability* (my term) arising in our clear and distinct thoughts of them. Says the Fifth Meditation meditator:

> But I think the most important consideration at this point is that I find within me count-less ideas of things which . . . have their own true and immutable natures. When, for example, I imagine a triangle, even if perhaps no such figure exists, or has ever existed, anywhere outside my thought, there is still a determinate nature, or essence, or form of the triangle which is immutable and eternal, and not invented by me or dependent on my mind. This is clear from the fact that various properties can be demonstrated of the triangle, for example that its three angles equal two right angles, that its greatest side subtends its greatest angle, and the like; and since these properties are ones which I now clearly recognize whether I want to or not, even if I never thought of them at all when I previously imagined the triangle, it follows that they cannot have been invented by me. (CSM 2: 44–5; AT 7: 64)

Descartes develops the cognitive immutability theme in dual ways – one that we might call *epistemic* and the other *psychological*. On the epistemic side, the immutability is manifested in a form of rational insight that is supposed to illuminate truths that are *conceptually unalterable*. When thinking clearly and distinctly with the intellect, the mind apprehends what must be the case, on pain of conceptual repugnance:

> [Regarding] those matters which I think I see utterly clearly with my mind's eye . . . when I turn to the things themselves which I think I perceive very clearly, I am so convinced by them that I spontaneously declare: let whoever can do so deceive me, he will never bring it about that I am nothing, so long as I continue to think I am something; or make it true at some future time that I have never existed, since it is now true that I exist; or bring it about that two and three added together are more or less than five, or anything of this kind in which I see a manifest contradiction [*repugnantiam*]. (CSM 2: 25; AT 7: 36)

According to Descartes, this conceptual immutability of the intellect marks a contrast with the senses. Consider any complex empirical idea – your idea of a cherry, a cow, a tree, or the like. Descartes maintains that the various parts of the complex are concep-tually separable. You can conceive a cherry without the sweet taste; a cow without a mooing sound; a tree without green color; and so on. None of this is conceptually repugnant. In each case, the complex parts are conceptually mutable. Of "ideas which

193

do not contain true and immutable natures," writes Descartes, they "can always be split up" (CSM 2: 83; AT 7: 117). Contrast this with the concept of a triangle. It too has complexity, in that multiple truths express its essence, but its complex nature is conceptually *im*mutable:

> For even if I can understand what a triangle is if I abstract the fact that its three angles are equal to two right angles, I cannot deny that this property applies to the triangle by a clear and distinct intellectual operation – that is, while at the same time understanding what I mean by my denial. (CSM 2: 84; AT 7: 117–18)

On the psychological side, the cognitive immutability of innate truths is manifested in their *indubitability*. When thinking clearly and distinctly, our minds are incapable of doubting the truths we perceive:

> The nature of my mind is such that I cannot but assent to these things, at least so long as I clearly perceive them. (CSM 2: 45; AT 7: 65)[15]

Again, the claimed immutability is supposed to mark a contrast with the senses. As discussed in detail below, Descartes employs methodical doubt as a tool for revealing indubitable essences.

The upshot is a twofold cognitive immutability: we *cannot understand* how these truths could be otherwise and we *cannot doubt* them. The meditator observes: "I could not but judge that something which I understood so clearly was true"; adding, "a great light in the intellect was followed by a great inclination in the will" (CSM 2: 41; AT 7: 58–9). That the claimed cognitive immutability is manifest only *during* moments of clear and distinct perception is significant. Moments of cognitive distraction or confusion explain how we're able to ignore or to misconceive what is innate.

Is it a sufficient condition of *knowledge* that one's judgment is based in innate, clearly and distinctly perceived, intellectual ideas? The answer seems to depend on context.[16] In the *Meditations*, Descartes' goal is the achievement of fully indefeasible knowledge. (Typically, he reserves the term *scientia* for this brand of knowledge.) He also recognizes knowledge of a weaker sort – one appropriate to contexts for which defeasibility issues do not normally arise. (In such contexts, he regularly uses *cognitio* and its cognates – terminology that translators routinely render into the English 'knowledge' and its cognates.) Assume the context involves *scientia* – the goal of the *Meditations*. In that case, it is not a sufficient condition of knowledge that one's judgment is based in innate, clearly and distinctly perceived, intellectual ideas. For this condition might arise in a mind that has been hardwired for error: perhaps an evil genius has so constituted the mind that it clearly and distinctly perceives innate propositions that are in fact false.[17]

Achieving *scientia*, therefore, requires two very different kinds of epistemological moves, both of which Descartes makes in his *Meditations*. Call the one kind of move *intellect identifying moves*. A necessary condition for *scientia* of metaphysical truths is learning how to identify intellectual ideas so as to form judgments on their basis. A further necessary condition is to establish that the intellect is perfectly reliable, thereby ruling out that the mind is hardwired for error. Call this second kind of move *intellect validating moves*. Descartes' intellect validating moves incorporate his well-known effort to demonstrate that clear and distinct perception is a divinely guaranteed, infallible criterion of truth.

The Methodical Case for the Two Rationalist Doctrines

I have attempted to clarify how the two rationalist doctrines fit with Descartes' broader philosophical commitments. I will now focus narrowly on how, in the context of the *Meditations*, Descartes makes a case for the two doctrines. I shall argue that Descartes' primary methodical tool in making his case is the so-called method of doubt (hereafter, MOD).

MOD incorporates various skeptical hypotheses in the service of various ends. Our interest is in how skeptical doubts help distinguish the senses and the intellect. Descartes writes to Hobbes (in a context in which "corporeal things" are regarded as *sensible* objects):

> I wanted to prepare my readers' minds for the study of the things which are related to the intellect, and help them to distinguish these things from corporeal things; and such [doubt-ing] arguments seem to be wholly necessary for this purpose. (CSM 2: 121; AT 7: 171)

Descartes' two most famous doubting arguments will serve our purposes: the Dream Doubt and the Evil Genius Doubt. The Dream Doubt hypothesizes that your present sensory ideas are produced by a vivid dream, not waking sensation. The Evil Genius Doubt hypothesizes that an ingenious deceiver hardwired your mind for error – you go wrong even when your perception is clear and distinct. As we'll see, the senses are undermined by each of these doubts; the intellect is undermined only by the Evil Genius Doubt. This contrast turns out significant to how the meditator is supposed to discover what is innate. Let's consider how Descartes employs MOD in making his case for each doctrine.

The case that the senses are ill-suited to illuminate the nature of reality

The case to be made is for the Sensation Unreliability Thesis – the claim that the senses are an unreliable basis for judgments about the nature of reality. MOD is supposed to show that all metaphysical judgments based in the senses are straightforwardly dubitable. Of course, it does not follow from "*p* is dubitable" that "*p* is false." Nor does it follow from "*p* is dubitable" that "*p* does not draw on innate concepts." It does follow, thinks Descartes, that we can make no positive case for the ability of the senses to illuminate the nature of reality – unlike the intellect. The case to be made, therefore, is negative and epistemological. The conclusions expressly drawn in the *Meditations* do ultimately entail that whole classes of sensory judgments are false, including judg-ments affirming a resemblance between secondary-quality ideas and external things. Yet nowhere in the *Meditations* does Descartes expressly argue for this result. The strongest conclusions expressly drawn are that such judgments are not well founded, and that "it is therefore quite possible that these are false" (CSM 2: 56; AT 7: 82).

195

How exactly is MOD employed in support of the Sensation Unreliability Thesis? Our focus in on the Dream Doubt. Suppose you are now dreaming. In that case, any sense-based judgments about reality that you are now making are unfounded. It might appear that there's a table to your right. But if you're dreaming, then even if there *is* a table to your right (say, a bedside table), the dream image is not a reliable basis for the judgment. Let's now alter the initial supposition. Suppose not that you *are* dreaming, but simply that you are *uncertain of being awake*. In that case too, the sensory image of a table to your right is not a reliable basis of judgment – it *might* be mere dream imagery, for all you know. Some will object to both initial suppositions, contending that they *are* certain of being awake, an objection the meditator considers:

> Yet at the moment my eyes are certainly wide awake when I look at this piece of paper; I shake my head and it is not asleep; as I stretch out and feel my hand I do so deliberately, and I know what I am doing. All this would not happen with such distinctness to someone asleep. (CSM 2: 13; AT 7: 19)

Descartes thinks the objection shows a lack of reflection. For a vivid, realistic dream would induce the same feeling of confidence. The meditator continues:

> As if I did not remember other occasions when I have been tricked by exactly similar thoughts while asleep! As I think about this more carefully, I see plainly that there are never any sure signs by means of which being awake can be distinguished from being asleep. (CSM 2: 13; AT 7: 19)

Because "there are never any sure signs" – no *indubitably* sure signs – sense-based judgments about reality are not well founded.

Not everyone is convinced. Many philosophers insist that there are indeed sure signs of being awake. We'll not settle this debate here, though we can at least clarify it. Descartes' claim is not about whether it is *true* that you are now dreaming, nor about whether you *believe* it, but instead about your *justification*. His contention is that you cannot with certainty rule out that you are dreaming.

Recognizing this uncertainty is supposed to help readers appreciate that the senses are an unreliable basis for metaphysical judgments. Recognizing his own uncertainty, the meditator comes to appreciate that his sensory ideas lack the clarity and distinctness he had formerly supposed:

> Yet I previously accepted as wholly certain and evident many things which I afterwards realized were doubtful. What were these? The earth, sky, stars, and everything else that I apprehended with the senses. But what was it about them that I perceived clearly? Just that the ideas, or thoughts, of such things appeared before my mind. Yet even now I am not denying that these ideas occur within me. But there was something else which I used to assert, and which through habitual belief I thought I perceived clearly, although I did not in fact do so. This was that there were things outside me which were the sources of my ideas and which resembled them in all respects. Here was my mistake; or at any rate, if my judgement was true, it was not thanks to the strength of my perception. (CSM 2: 24–5; AT 7: 35)

By repeated practice with doubt, we are supposed to learn that insofar as our sensory ideas are referred to real things, they are never clear and distinct.

In the closing lines of the Sixth Meditation, Descartes purports to lay the groundwork for overcoming the Dream Doubt, detailing how it is possible, in principle, for theistic meditators to know they are awake.[18] It nonetheless remains the case that the senses are ill-equipped to illuminate the nature of reality – whether or not one achieves knowledge of being awake.

The case that the intellect is well-suited to illuminate the nature of reality

The case to be made is for the Intellection Reliability Thesis – the claim that the intellect is a reliable basis for judgments about the nature of reality. Unlike for the Sensation Unreliability Thesis, the case to be made is for a constructive result. Recall that we distinguished two broad kinds of moves that Descartes makes: *intellect identifying moves* and *intellect validating moves*. Both are integral to achieving the intended constructive result. Without a procedure for reliably distinguishing ideas of the senses and ideas of the intellect, the fact of our being hardwired with innate concepts is of little consequence. But even if we can reliably identify what is native to the intellect, we will lack indefeasible knowledge unless we overcome the Evil Genius Doubt. Thus, Descartes makes his notorious intellect validating moves – his efforts to prove that the nature of his mind derives not from an evil genius, but from a benevolent, omnipotent deity who would never deceive. Though I'll not argue the point here, the intellect validating moves do also employ MOD, and do also depend on innate concepts. For our purposes, the intellect identifying moves are of more central interest. They are more specifically *rationalist*. They will be the focus of our discussion.[19]

I shall develop the issues along three main fronts. First, I address how doubt – an intrinsically destructive tool – is supposed to achieve a constructive result. Second, I discuss how the interpretation helps explain a feature of the Evil Genius Doubt that commentators have found puzzling: its indirect and hyperbolic character. Third, I offer a case study that illustrates the broader account for the concept of mind.

How MOD purports to achieve a constructive result

Descartes' intellect identifying moves must establish a constructive result. They must somehow shed light, not darkness. How *could* doubt – an intrinsically destructive tool – achieve a constructive result?

Descartes' own foundationist metaphors illustrate the intended answer. The setup of the analogy is familiar: making judgments on a sensory basis is supposed to be the analogue of constructing a building on a loose foundation of sand; an intellectual basis, the analogue of an unshakable foundation of bedrock; skeptical doubts are supposed to be the analogues of ground-clearing bulldozers. If the aim is to found an unshakable edifice, ground-clearing bulldozers can be used for both destructive and constructive purposes. On the destructive side, a bulldozer can effectively strip away loose sand, or even moderately firm ground. On the constructive side, a bulldozer can identify bedrock, by confronting ground that it cannot dislodge. Descartes uses skeptical doubts as epistemic bulldozers, for both destructive and constructive purposes:

> Throughout my writings I have made it clear that my method imitates that of the architect. When an architect wants to build a house which is stable on ground where there is a sandy topsoil over underlying rock, or clay, or some other firm base, he begins by digging out a set of trenches from which he removes the sand, and anything resting on or mixed in with the sand, so that he can lay his foundations on firm soil. In the same way, I began by taking everything that was doubtful and throwing it out, like sand; and then, when I noticed that it is impossible to doubt that a doubting or thinking substance exists, I took this as the bedrock on which I could lay the foundations of my philosophy. (CSM 2: 366; AT 7: 536–57)

Doubt is used to identify unshakable epistemic ground, precisely by its inability to undermine that ground.

The epistemic analogue of the unshakability of bedrock is *indubitability* – a form of what I have been calling cognitive immutability. The psychological immutability of innate, intellectual propositions is manifest in our inability to doubt them. Our minds are hardwired such that we cannot but assent to the propositions we clearly and distinctly perceive (cf. above and note 15). For the *tabula rasa* mind (think of Leibniz's veinless block of marble), there is no such hardwiring for epistemic bulldozers to expose. For the nativist mind (think of the veined block of marble), there is.

Of the numerous propositions that Descartes thinks exhibit this sort of cognitive immutability, his most famous example arises from the *cogito*. Leading up to the *cogito*, the meditator articulates MOD's constructive strategy:

> Anything which admits of the slightest doubt I will set aside just as if I had found it to be wholly false; and I will proceed in this way until I recognize something certain, or, if nothing else, until I at least recognize for certain that there is no certainty. Archimedes used to demand just one firm and immovable point in order to shift the entire earth; so I too can hope for great things if I manage to find just one thing, however slight, that is certain and unshakable. (CSM 2: 16; AT 7: 24)

The *cogito* passage immediately follows. Using his most powerful bulldozer, the Evil Genius Doubt, the meditator attempts to undermine the proposition, *I exist*, thereby discovering its impressive doubt resistance: "let him [the evil genius] deceive me as much as he can, he will never bring it about that I am nothing so long as I think that I am something" (CSM 2: 17; AT 7: 25). Descartes goes on to treat the *cogito*'s doubt resistance as the prototype of "being certain about anything," serving also to epitomize clarity and distinctness (CSM 2: 24; AT 7: 35). Elsewhere, Descartes lists "*He who thinks cannot but exist while he thinks*" as an "eternal truth which resides within our mind" (CSM 1: 209; AT 8a: 23–4).

There is much of philosophical and interpretive interest in the *cogito*, much more than can be explored here. Of present interest is that it is supposed to draw on innate cognitive resources, and that its status as epistemic bedrock is supposed to be revealed by subjecting it to doubt.

The hyperbolic and indirect character of the Evil Genius Doubt

The interpretation we have been developing helps explain two aspects of MOD that many commentators find puzzling. One puzzling feature concerns the hyperbolic character of the Evil Genius Doubt. Prima facie, the doubt is gratuitously excessive – sheer hyperbole. Why then does Descartes employ such doubt? Gassendi is perhaps the first to articulate the complaint:

> There is just one point I am not clear about, namely why you did not make a simple and brief statement to the effect that you were regarding your previous knowledge as uncertain so that you could later single out what you found to be true . . . This strategy made it necessary for you to convince yourself by imagining a deceiving God or some evil demon who tricks us, whereas it would surely have been sufficient to cite the darkness of the human mind or the weakness of our nature. (CSM 2: 180; AT 7: 257–8)

In view of MOD's nativist aims (among others), Gassendi's criticism misses the point. The point is not to arrive at *difficult*-to-doubt propositions. The point is to reveal propositions that are cognitively immutable – propositions that the constitution of our minds renders psychologically *impossible* to doubt. Consider again the architectural analogy. Suppose you are an architect laying the foundation for an edifice that will stand the test of time. Your aim is to find unshakable ground. Your tool is a bulldozer. Your problem: how will your bulldozer distinguish (a) unshak*able* ground, and (b) unshak*en* ground that would be shaken by a bigger bulldozer? Clearly, the bigger the bulldozer, the better. A medium-duty bulldozer may be unable to undermine ground that a heavier-duty bulldozer would easily dislodge. The implication is clear. *The bigger the bulldozer, the better* translates into *the more hyperbolic the doubt, the better*. Arguably, the architectural analogy breaks down in a manner that serves Descartes well. For, presumably, there is no *most*-power-bulldozer. In that case, no literal bulldozer could reveal ground that is truly unshak*able*. Perhaps epistemic bulldozing is not subject to this limitation. Perhaps there is a *most*-powerful-doubt – a doubt than which none more hyperbolic can be conceived. Descartes seems to think the Evil Genius Doubt fits the bill. Only a doubt this powerful *could* distinguish (a) unshakable epistemic ground, and (b) ground that is simply not yet shaken. It is therefore essential to Descartes' rationalist aims that MOD employs doubt that is hyperbolic.

The other puzzling feature of Descartes' doubts concerns the indirect character of the Evil Genius Doubt in contrast with the direct character of the Dream Doubt. Distinguish two kinds of ways in which a doubt might operate. In a direct doubt, the skeptical hypothesis induces occurrent doubt while the mind *directly attends* to the undermined proposition. In an indirect doubt, the skeptical hypothesis can induce occurrent doubt only when the mind is *not* directly attending to the undermined proposition. The distinction turns out to be important.

Descartes holds that sense-based judgments about the world are subject to a direct doubt. The Dream Doubt does indeed operate as a direct doubt. Attend carefully and *directly* to your favorite empirical proposition about external things, say, Moore's "Here is a hand." Descartes contends that the hypothesis that you are now having a vivid dream allows you to make rational sense of how the proposition might be false. The First Meditation meditator doubts such propositions while thinking directly about them:

> Suppose then that I am dreaming, and that these particulars – that my eyes are open, that I am moving my head and stretching out my hands – are not true. Perhaps, indeed, I do not even have such hands or such a body at all. (CSM 2: 13; AT 7: 19)

199

The constitution of our minds does not require us to assent to such propositions. While thinking directly about them we can make rational sense of denying them, even if we believe them to be true.

Intellect-based judgments are supposed to be subject only to an indirect doubt. Think carefully and *directly* about the proposition "1 + 1 = 2" and attempt to doubt it. I confess that I cannot directly doubt this proposition. *While* attending to it, I cannot make rational sense of how it could be false. Descartes' explanation of this psychological indubitability is that the proposition is hardwired in my mind. Notwithstanding this hardwiring, he maintains that such propositions are subject to an indirect doubt. Descartes uses the Evil Genius Doubt as an indirect doubt. On occasions when I am not directly attending to the proposition, I can consider the possibility that my mind has been hardwired for error – that my mind is so constituted that it is incapable of doubting some propositions (even false propositions) while attending to them clearly and distinctly. In the two clearest passages of the *Meditations* concerning the operation of the Evil Genius Doubt, its indirect character is unmistakable. These texts clarify that the inability to directly doubt such propositions is owed to our cognitive nature, and that our ability at indirect doubt arises only while redirecting attention towards the possibility that our cognitive nature is deceptive:

> But what about when I was considering something very simple and straightforward in arithmetic or geometry, for example that two and three added together make five, and so on? Did I not see at least these things clearly enough to affirm their truth? Indeed, the only reason for my later judgement that they were open to doubt was that it occurred to me that perhaps some God could have given me a nature such that I was deceived even in matters which seemed most evident. (Third Meditation, 2: 25; AT 7: 35–6)

> Admittedly my nature is such that so long as I perceive something very clearly and distinctly I cannot but believe it to be true. But my nature is also such that I cannot fix my mental vision continually on the same thing, so as to keep perceiving it clearly; and often the memory of a previously made judgement may come back, when I am no longer attending to the arguments which led me to make it . . . so long as I attend to the proof, I cannot but believe this to be true. But as soon as I turn my mind's eye away from the proof, then in spite of still remembering that I perceived it very clearly, I can easily fall into doubt about its truth, if I am unaware of God. For I can convince myself that I have a natural disposition to go wrong from time to time in matters which I think I perceive as evidently as can be. (Fifth Meditation, 2: 48; AT 7: 69–70)

The indirect doubt is, in some sense, a *faculty* doubt: I attend not to the particular proposition (e.g., "1 + 1 = 2") but to my cognitive faculties, casting doubt on *them*; this indirectly undermines *en masse* all such propositions as my faculties are used to apprehend – namely, the "matters which I think I perceive as evidently as can be."

That intellect-based judgments are vulnerable only to a hyperbolic and indirect doubt emerges as an essential aspect of Descartes' intellect identifying moves. He needs a way to distinguish what derives from the senses and what is native to the intellect. The cognitive immutability of the intellect provides the way. Doubt must be hyperbolic and indirect if it is to succeed in revealing the claimed cognitive immutability.

One might object that the hyperbolic and indirect character of the Evil Genius Doubt shows that it is not a doubt in any *real* sense. By way of reply, note that if a "real" doubt is one that dislodges *belief*, then Descartes would agree. Neither the Dream Doubt nor the Evil Genius Doubt is intended to defeat knowledge by undermining belief; they are intended to undermine the *basis* of belief. Even Descartes characterizes the Evil Genius Doubt as a "very slight and, so to speak, metaphysical" doubt (CSM 2: 25; AT 7: 36). While characterizing his reasons for employing such doubts, Descartes writes: "I wanted to show the firmness of the truths which I propound later on, in the light of the fact that they cannot be shaken by these metaphysical doubts" (CSM 2: 121; AT 7: 171). The highly contrived character of his metaphysical doubts is very much to the point. That a class of propositions can be undermined only in such a contrived manner is supposed to help us to identify them as innate – as deriving from the nature of our minds.

A case study

Immediately on the heals of the *cogito*, the meditator employs MOD to help discover the essence of mind – more specifically the *self*, the thinking subject of the *cogito*. An examination of the case will help to clarify the interpretation I have been defending.

Descartes contends that the whole essence of mind is *thought* and that this essence is innate to our intellects. How is MOD supposed to reveal this? The meditator's procedure involves considering his prereflective conception of himself and then subjecting it to doubting arguments: "I will then subtract anything capable of being weakened, even minimally, by the arguments now introduced, so that what is left at the end may be exactly and only what is certain and unshakable" (CSM 2: 17; AT 7: 25). The point of the procedure is twofold: introducing the doubts is supposed to achieve the *destructive* result of stripping away the sensory features of his conception; introducing hyperbolic doubt is supposed to achieve a *constructive* result by revealing what resists any direct doubt.

Implementing the procedure, the meditator recounts his own previous conception – one centering on sensible features:

> Well, the first thought to come to mind was that I had a face, hands, arms and the whole mechanical structure of limbs which can be seen in a corpse, and which I called the body. (CSM 2: 17; AT 7: 25)

MOD helps to call all such features into doubt:

> But what shall I now say that I am, when I am supposing that there is some supremely powerful and, if it is permissible to say so, malicious deceiver, who is deliberately trying to trick me in every way he can? Can I now assert that I possess even the most insignificant of all the attributes which I have just said belong to the nature of a body? (CSM 2: 18; AT 7: 26)

All the while, however, the meditator cannot doubt the existence of himself, nor that the self has a thinking nature. For *thought* is the one feature of his conception that resists direct doubt:

> At last I have discovered it – thought; this alone is inseparable from me. I am, I exist – that is certain. But for how long? For as long as I am thinking. For it could be that were I totally to cease from thinking, I should totally cease to exist . . . I am a thing which is real and which truly exists. But what kind of a thing? As I have just said – a thinking thing. (CSM 2: 18; AT 7: 27)

Of course, the meditator's work is not complete. At best, the procedure thus far implemented will have activated the innate concept of mind. Since the innate concept of body has yet to be activated, the meditator is in no position to draw conclusions about the mind–body relation. Thus the meditator remarks, in the very next paragraph:

> And yet may it not perhaps be the case that these very things which I am supposing to be nothing, because they are unknown to me, are in reality identical with the "I" of which I am aware? I do not know, and for the moment I shall not argue the point. (CSM 2: 18; AT 7: 27)

Moreover, the procedure under consideration involves *intellect identifying moves*. At this early stage of the *Meditations* the aim is to discover innate essences, but not yet to establish them as perfect representations of the nature of reality. For the latter, the meditator will need to engage *intellect validating moves* – moves intended to overcome the indirect doubt posed by the Evil Genius Doubt. Thus Descartes writes of his Second Meditation results:

> Had I not been looking for greater than ordinary certainty, I should have been content to have shown in the Second Meditation that the mind can be understood as a subsisting thing despite the fact that nothing belonging to the body is attributed to it . . . since we commonly judge that the order in which things are mutually related in our perception of them corresponds to the order in which they are related in actual reality. But one of the exaggerated doubts which I put forward in the First Meditation went so far as to make it impossible for me to be certain of this very point (namely whether things do in reality correspond to our perception of them), so long as I was supposing myself to be ignorant of the author of my being. And this is why everything I wrote on the subject of God and truth in the Third, Fourth and Fifth Meditations contributes to the conclusion. (CSM 2: 159; AT 7: 226)

Descartes goes on to characterize the foregoing procedure as the "correct," indeed "unique," method by which "to understand metaphysical matters" (CSM 2: 94; AT 7: 130–1). In the *Meditations*, every claimed discovery of an innate, intellectual truth purports to be clearly and distinctly perceived. And in all such cases, Descartes claims that we "cannot but assent to these things." Being hardwired in our minds, we're supposed to be able to identify them by their cognitive immutability – with MOD providing the tool of choice. Having identified such truths, thinks Descartes, it remains only to be shown that our intellectual nature ultimately derives from an all-perfect deity who would never deceive us.

Acknowledgments

I would like to thank Ron Mallon and Alan Nelson for helpful feedback on the ideas in this chapter.

Notes

1   Descartes uses 'idea' with dual reference, sometimes referring to perceptual *acts* and other times to perceptual *objects*. I take the issues of debate in this chapter to center around ideas *qua* perceptual objects. To avoid confusion, therefore, I use 'idea' exclusively to refer to perceptual objects (unless otherwise noted). Some commentators hold, to the contrary, that Descartes' claims about innate ideas refer to ideas as perceptual *acts*, not perceptual *objects* (cf. Chappell 1986: 178–9; Jolley 1990: 33). Among the considerations supporting my view is a remark coming in the same Third Meditation passage in which Descartes first introduces his threefold distinction of ideas (*innateness* being one of the categories): "Insofar as the ideas are simply modes of thought, there is no recognizable inequality among them: they all appear to come from within me in the same fashion. But insofar as different ideas represent different things, it is clear that they differ widely" (CSM 2: 27–8; AT 7: 40). The implication is that insofar as we regard ideas as perceptual acts, the threefold distinction does not apply.

2   This is one of many passages in which Descartes puts forward some version of a poverty-of-stimulus argument – roughly: I have a concept that cannot derive from sensory resources; therefore, the concept derives from innate resources. Descartes invokes some version of this argument in many places, including the famed wax passage of the Second Meditation.

3   In the same passage introducing the threefold distinction, the meditator concedes of his apparently adventitious ideas: "there may be some other faculty [of my mind] not yet fully known to me, which produces these ideas without any assistance from external things" (CSM 2: 27; AT 7: 39). In interesting ways, the early Third Meditation meditator's external-world doubts parallel Hume's considered views – while in his study, at any rate. In the *Treatise*, Hume maintains that we cannot rule out "with certainty" the hypothesis that sense impressions are produced by nothing external, but instead "by the creative power of the mind" (1.3.5). The doubt is preserved in the *Enquiry*, where he concedes that we cannot prove that impressions are "caused by external objects" instead of arising "from the energy of the mind itself" (sect. 12). I take it that these considerations help motivate him to allow that sense impressions might properly be called innate (see the footnote at the end of *Enquiry* 2).

4   See Newman (1994) for a detailed discussion of how Descartes develops the problem of the external world in terms of hidden faculties of the mind (cf. note 3), and how he purports to refute it.

5   Adams (1975: 77) correctly notes: "If an adventitious idea is an idea that comes into the mind from outside in sensation, Descartes does not believe that we have any adventitious ideas. But he calls some ideas adventitious, meaning that their occurrence in our minds is occasioned (or that we judge it to be occasioned) by the action, on our sense organs, of bodies that we perceive."

6   The CSM rendering of *ac tantò magis innatæ esse debent ideæ* as "the ideas . . . must be all the more innate" suggests that secondary-quality sensation ideas are *more innate* than primary-quality sensation ideas. But Descartes does not hold this. I take the Latin to convey instead

an epistemic claim: that what is all the more the case is not their *innateness* per se, but that they *must be* innate. It is all the more evident.

7 See Rozemond (1998: ch. 6) for a careful treatment of the relevant doctrinal issues in Descartes.

8 There are exceptions in Descartes' early writings in which he refers to corporeal images as "ideas" (cf. *The Rules* AT 10: 419).

9 Descartes uses "perceive"/"perception" (*percipio/perceptio*) with much wider scope than is the current practice in philosophy: for Descartes, to perceive *x* is, roughly, to think of, or to be aware of, *x*.

10 Kenny (1968: 102ff.) and Jolley (1990: 39ff.) provide useful discussions of this problem.

11 Wilson (1978: 164) concludes "that Descartes does not provide a coherent account of how we are both 'conscious of all that is in us' and possibly ignorant of mathematics and metaphysics." Bennett (2001: 40ff.) makes the point that in Leibniz the predispositional account of innateness is parasitic on his doctrine of subconscious perception – a doctrine anathema to Descartes given his own doctrine of the transparency of the mental.

12 I discuss related issues in Newman (1994).

13 For a helpful analysis of Descartes on clarity and distinctness, see Nelson (1997).

14 Simmons (1999) offers a compelling interpretation of Descartes' account here.

15 Later in the Fifth Meditation, Descartes adds: "Admittedly my nature is such that so long as I perceive something very clearly and distinctly I cannot but believe it to be true" (CSM 2: 48; AT 7: 69). In a letter to Regius, he writes: "In your second objection you say: 'the truth of axioms which are clearly and distinctly understood is self-evident.' This too, I agree, is true, during the time they are clearly and distinctly understood; for our mind is of such a nature that it cannot help assenting to what it clearly understands" (CSMK 147; AT 3: 64).

16 I develop the case for this contextualist reading of Descartes more fully in Newman (2004).

17 Roughly this same point is developed by Cowie (1999: 7ff.), namely, that mere innateness is not sufficient for epistemic justification. Surprisingly, Cowie thinks Descartes didn't fully appreciate this point, even claiming that he "waffles shamelessly" on the issues (pp. 11ff.).

18 In Newman (1999) I reconstruct how Descartes' strategy for overcoming the Dream Doubt is supposed to derive from God's benevolence in conjunction with principles argued in the Fourth Meditation.

19 For a comprehensive interpretation of Descartes' intellect validating moves that is continuous with the interpretation of the present chapter, see Newman (1999) and Newman and Nelson (1999).

References and Further Reading

Adams, Robert (1975). Where do our ideas come from? – Descartes *vs.* Locke. In Stephen P. Stich (ed.), *Innate Ideas* (pp. 71–87). Berkeley: University of California Press.

Bennett, Jonathan (2001). *Learning from Six Philosophers: Descartes, Spinoza, Leibniz, Locke, Berkeley, Hume*, Vol. 2. Oxford: Oxford University Press.

Chappell, Vere (1986). The theory of ideas. In A. Rorty (ed.), *Essays on Descartes's Meditations* (pp. 177–98). Berkeley: University of California Press.

Cowie, Fiona (1999). *What's Within? Nativism Reconsidered*. Oxford: Oxford University Press.

Jolley, Nicholas (1990). *The Light of the Soul: Theories of Ideas in Leibniz, Malebranche, and Descartes*. Oxford: Oxford University Press.

Kenny, Anthony (1968). *Descartes: A Study of his Philosophy*. New York: Random House.

Nelson, Alan (1997). Descartes's ontology of thought. *Topoi*, 16: 163–78.

Newman, Lex (1994). Descartes on unknown faculties and our knowledge of the external world. *Philosophical Review*, 103, 489–531.

—— (1999). The Fourth Meditation. *Philosophy and Phenomenological Research*, 59, 559–91.

—— (2004). Rocking the foundations of Cartesian knowledge: Critical notice of Janet Broughton, *Descartes's Method of Doubt*. *Philosophical Review*, 113, 101–25.

Newman, Lex, and Nelson, Alan (1999). Circumventing Cartesian circles. *Noûs*, 33, 370–404.

Rozemond, Marleen (1998). *Descartes's Dualism*. Cambridge, MA: Harvard University Press.

Simmons, Alison (1999). Are Cartesian sensations representational? *Noûs*, 33, 347–69.

Williams, Bernard (1978). *Descartes: The Project of Pure Enquiry*. New Jersey: Humanities Press.

Wilson, Margaret Dauler (1978). *Descartes*. New York: Routledge and Kegan Paul.

11

Rationalism and Representation

KURT SMITH

Traditionally, Aristotle is taken to have held that qualities such as colors, sounds, tastes, odors, and tactile qualities such as hot, cold, wet, and dry are qualities or properties of mind-independent objects. Our perceptions of such qualities reveal to us the mind-independent world as it is. This sort of view has been called "direct realism." Many seventeenth-century theories of perception can be best understood as challenges to direct realism. Galileo (1564–1642), for example, argues:

> I say that upon conceiving of a material or corporeal substance, I immediately feel the need to conceive simultaneously that it is bounded and has this or that shape; that it is in this place or that at any given time; that it moves or stays still; that it does or does not touch another body; and that it is one, few, or many. I cannot separate it from these conditions by any stretch of my imagination. But that it must be white or red, bitter or sweet, noisy or silent, of sweet or foul odor, my mind feels no compulsion to understand as necessary accompaniments. Indeed, without the senses to guide us, reason or imagination alone would perhaps never arrive as such qualities. (Galileo 1960: 309)

On this view, the very concept of body (corporeal substance) compels us to conceive of shape, size, motion, position, and so on. In fact, we cannot intelligibly separate these from the concept of body. By contrast, the concept of body does not compel us to conceive of colors, sounds, tastes, or odors. Not only can we intelligibly separate these from the concept of body, but if we did not have sensory faculties, we may never conceive of such qualities or associate them with body. The distinction between the first group of qualities (size, shape, motion, and position) and the second (colors, sounds, tastes, and odors) is brought to light by way of an analysis of the conceptual landscape inherent in the mind. A view that holds that such an analysis is necessary and sufficient for laying the groundwork for what we can know is a form of rationalism. The division of the above qualities into the two groups, then, is established by way of Galileo's commitment to a form of rationalism.

Galileo believes that his analysis of the concept of body leads to the conclusion that "if the living creature were removed, all these qualities [that is, colors, sounds, odors, and tastes] would be removed and annihilated" (Galileo 1960: 309). He goes further and says:

I do not believe that for exciting in us tastes, odors, and sounds there are required in external bodies anything but sizes, shapes, numbers, and slow or fast movements; and I think that if ears, tongues, and noses were taken away, shapes and numbers and motions would remain but not odors or tastes or sounds. (Galileo 1960: 311)

The mind-independent world is a world of shaped, sized, and moving bodies. With the proper sensory organs, a variety of bodies (the variety defined by differing shapes, sizes, and motions) can "excite" in the mind a variety of perceptions of colors, sounds, odors, and so on. Even so, the very *possibility* of colors, sounds, tastes, odors, and tactile qualities such as hot, cold, wet, and dry is for Galileo ultimately rooted in the mind – the perceiver. They are mind-dependent qualities. This is very different from Aristotle's view.

Rationalists of the seventeenth century followed along Galilean lines, holding that the only properties of bodies were those that demonstrated a conceptually necessary connection to the idea of body. Such qualities as we know are size, shape, motion, and so on – qualities or properties that they knew were subject in all the right ways to mathematics. These qualities were taken to be mind-independent. And they held that the other qualities we sense – for example, colors, sounds, tastes, odors, and qualities of touch – were not properties of bodies. And, again in line with Galileo, these latter qualities were taken to be mind-dependent. Even so, there can be found a wide range of disagreement between seventeenth-century rationalists. For instance, René Descartes (1596–1650) held that although the color blue was a mind-dependent quality, he did not hold that the mind itself was blue.[1] Nicolas Malebranche (1638–1715), on the other hand, held that the color blue was both mind-dependent and that when perceiving blue the mind itself was blue (Malebranche 1992: 86–7). Another disagreement centered around the question of whether such qualities as blue or cold were representational. That is, even though such qualities did not exist independent of a mind, the question was whether they *represented* to us some corresponding modification in the physical or corporeal, mind-independent world.

Descartes answered this question in the affirmative. The sort of theory of perception that we find in his work may be taken to be a representational (or representative) theory of perception. This has been traditionally opposed to the direct realism associated with Aristotle. Generally speaking, a representational theory of perception tells us that our mental states (our ideas) are representational in nature. One version of this theory has it that our ideas stand as intermediaries between our "mind's eye," so to speak, and the objects being represented. And so, I do not *directly* perceive the sun, but rather I am directly presented with a sensory idea that represents the sun. The idea stands between the sun existing in the heavens and me (my mind). My ideas, as some scholars say, form a *veil of perception*. An obvious question arises: if I can never directly perceive the sun, but only have access to my idea that represents it, how can I be certain that the sun, assuming that it exists, is as my idea represents it? The rationalists, as we know, have an answer. The size, shape, and motion as they are represented in my idea resemble the properties (size, shape, and motion) that the sun actually has, for I cannot even conceive of a body that lacked *these* qualities or properties. But, since colors, sounds, tastes, and so on, are not actual properties of bodies (I can conceive of a body lacking them), I can be certain that the yellow and heat that are included in my idea do not resemble properties of the sun – though they may *represent* some of its properties. Descartes seems to have taken the mental qualities yellow and heat, for example, included in the sensory idea of the sun to represent the motions of the particles that constituted the mind-independent sun.

In what follows, we will look carefully at Descartes' view that there is a kind of "falsity" inherent in our sensory ideas – and in particular those ideas that include or contain the qualities of color, sound, taste, odor, heat, cold, and so on. A close examination of his view will reveal a connection between the form of rationalism he adopted and his theory of perception. Although our focus will be fairly narrow, we can take from it a lesson about the bigger picture. For, in understanding the connection between Descartes' epistemological (and ontological) commitments and his theory of perception, we can better understand how the elements of a philosophical system hang together.

The Falsity Inherent in Sensory Ideas

Materially false ideas, Descartes says, are not false in the strict sense, but are false in the sense that they represent non-things as things (AT 7: 43; CSM 2: 30). The "strict" sense of falsity, or formal falsity as he calls it, is attributed to judgments (AT 7: 43; CSM 2: 30). And so, if I judge that the stove is cold, and it turns out that the stove is not, then my judgment about the stove's being cold is false in the strict sense. It is formally false. By contrast, material falsity is attributed to ideas, not to judgments. And so, as Descartes tells us, if my idea represents cold as a positive quality, and it turns out that cold is really the absence of heat (that is, it is not anything at all), then the idea is materially false (AT 7: 44; CSM 2: 30). And it is so even prior to judgment. And so, even though materially false ideas can lead me to make false judgments, since they are not judgments themselves, they are not formally false.

In the Fourth Objection, Antoine Arnauld (1612–94) argues that the notion of material falsity is incompatible with certain fundamental principles underlying Descartes' theory of ideas. Descartes offers a defense of the notion in the Fourth Replies, but as has been noted by commentators, it is very brief and not very clear (e.g., see Wilson 1978; Grene 1983; Kenny 1995). Some have tried their hand at expanding and clarifying the defense, but as we will see, none of them succeeds in getting it just right. Our aim here will be to work up the best philosophical account of the notion. To do this, we will look at Descartes' introduction of the notion of material falsity in the *Meditations*, along with Arnauld's objection, and Descartes' subsequent reply. We will then examine a number of the leading interpretations and show where they seem to go wrong. Then, avoiding the problems of the views examined, we will work up what seems to be the best philosophical take on the notion.

Descartes, Arnauld, and the Notion of Material Falsity

In the Third Meditation Descartes revisits his earlier Second Meditation examination of a piece of wax (AT 7: 43; CSM 2: 29–30). In this context, Descartes – or the meditator, to be more precise – is considering whether there are any ideas of which he cannot be the cause. The concern here is not one about whether there are any modes of which he *qua* finite substance cannot be the cause. For, since the formal reality or being of a mode is less than that of a finite substance, he *qua* finite substance can in principle be the cause of any of his modes (AT 7: 40–5; CSM 2: 28–31). Rather, the concern is one about whether there are any ideas whose objective reality is so great that he *qua* finite substance cannot be the cause (AT 7: 42; CSM 2: 29).[2] In his consideration of ideas that represent finite substances or modes, whether representing minds or bodies, Descartes argues that he *qua* finite substance can in principle be the cause of the objective reality they contain (AT 7: 44–5; CSM 2: 30–1).

As is well known, Descartes does land upon an idea whose objective reality is so great that he cannot be its cause: the idea of God (AT 7: 45–52; CSM 2: 31–5). Descartes argues that since the objective reality contained in an idea is not nothing, and thus requires a cause (AT 7: 41; CSM 2: 28–9), and he cannot be the cause of the objective reality contained in the idea of God (an idea of an infinite substance) (AT 7: 49–51; CSM 2: 34–5), it follows that there exists a being whose formal reality is great enough to cause this level or degree of objective reality. And this being is God – the infinite substance.

However, before he lands upon this idea and is able to make this argument, he works carefully through his ideas related to that piece of wax. Here, he discovers that some of his ideas about the wax appear to be good candidates for being clear and distinct (AT 7: 43; CSM 2: 29–30). These are his ideas of extension, shape, position, and motion, ideas that have a logically or conceptually necessary connection to the idea of body. But there are a number of ideas that are obscure and confused. These are his ideas of colors, sounds, smells, tastes, and touch (AT 7: 43; CSM 2: 30). He finds them so obscure and confused, in fact, that he is unable to tell "whether they are true or false, that is, whether the ideas I have of them are ideas of real things or of non-things" (AT 7: 43; CSM 2: 30). And if it turns out that the qualities white or cold, for example, do not exist, and yet my ideas represent them to me as existent qualities of, say, that piece of wax, then they ought to be called "false" (AT 7: 44; CSM 2: 30) – and in the sense described earlier, "materially false."

Arnauld examines the notion of material falsity in the Fourth Objection, in a section titled "Concerning God" (AT 7: 206–8; CSM 2: 145–6). That he does so in this section is revealing. Here, he argues that if the objective reality of an idea must have a cause, and in the case of sensory ideas, a cause that possesses some level of formal reality, then there can be no materially false ideas – ever (AT 7: 206; CSM 2: 145). The argument takes as foundational a principle underlying Descartes' theory of ideas, namely, *ex nihilo*: something cannot come from nothing.[3]

Arnauld appears to suppose that ideas, or at least those that Descartes calls "primary," represent their objects by way of a causal relation.[4] He also appears to suppose that a primary idea represents the object that it does only if the formal reality of that object causes the objective reality in the idea. Thus the idea represents the sun, for example, only if the formal reality of the sun is the cause of the idea's objective reality. That Descartes holds this himself is not perfectly clear (Wilson 1990). Even so, Arnauld appears to base his suppositions on a number of things: first, on Descartes' claim that "for just as the objective mode of being belongs to ideas by their very nature, so the formal mode of being belongs to the causes of ideas" (AT 7: 42; CSM 2: 29); secondly, on the claim that the idea of God is "of" or "represents" God because the formal reality of God is the cause of the objective reality contained in the idea (AT 7: 45; CSM 2: 31);[5] and, thirdly, on the Sixth Meditation proof for the existence of corporeal substance. For there, Descartes argues that if the formal reality of body is not the cause of his ideas that represent corporeal substance, that is, it is not the cause of the objective reality they contain, then God is a deceiver (AT 7: 80; CSM 2: 55).

Arnauld argues that the materially false idea of cold, which Descartes had introduced in the Third Meditation, is impossible. The argument assumes – in line with Descartes' Third Meditation discussion – that cold is the absence of heat, while at the same time that the idea of cold represents to him cold as though it were a real and positive quality. The idea represents a non-existent quality as though it were an existent quality. His objection unfolds as follows. If cold is the *absence* of heat, that is, it is nothing at all, then it lacks formal reality. And if the idea represents anything at all, it contains some level of objective reality. And so, in representing cold, the idea contains some level of objective reality. Now, supposing that a primary idea represents the object that it does only if the formal reality of the object is the cause of the idea's objective reality, it follows that if the idea represents cold, then the formal reality of cold is the cause of the idea's objective reality. But cold is taken in this case to be an absence, something that lacks formal reality. And so, the idea *cannot* represent cold (AT 7: 207; CSM 2: 145). However, if Descartes will insist that it does, then the objective reality contained in the idea comes from nothing, which, Arnauld concludes, "violates the author's most important principles"(AT 7: 207; CSM 2: 146) – the relevant one here being *ex nihilo*.

As was mentioned earlier, Arnauld makes this objection in the section "Concerning God." Although he does not make it explicit, the larger concern over material falsity seems to be that if the objective reality contained in the materially false idea of cold can come from nothing, there is no reason to deny that an infinite level of objective reality can, too. And if an infinite level of objective reality can come from nothing, there need not exist a being whose formal reality is great enough to cause the objective reality contained in the idea of God. And so, if materially false ideas are possible, Descartes loses the Third Meditation proof for God's existence. Since this is something that Descartes cannot afford to lose, Arnauld argues that Descartes should give up the notion of material falsity.

In his reply to Arnauld, Descartes offers a short defense of the notion, which has been the source of much criticism (AT 7: 232–5; CSM 2: 162–4). Descartes says, for example, that Arnauld's criticism of the notion fails because he wrongly takes ideas in the "formal" sense. Had he taken them in the "material" sense, he would not have made the criticism that he did (AT 7: 232; CSM 2: 162–3). To take an idea "formally," he says, is to take it as representing this or that, whereas to take it "materially" is to take it as an operation of the intellect (AT 7: 232; CSM 2: 163). Additionally, he says that "since ideas are forms of a kind, and are not composed of any matter, when we think of them as representing something we are taking them not materially but formally" (AT 7: 232; CSM 2: 163). Here, it appears that he was appealing to something like the scholastic distinction between formal and material species. Even so, given what he says elsewhere, it is very unlikely that he was doing so. For example, to

Arnauld, he attributes the theory of species to other philosophers, and contrasts this to his own view (AT 7: 249; CSM 2: 174). To Gassendi, he says that the semblances located in the brain are certainly corporeal, and the mind can apply itself to them, which happens when we sense objects, but he clearly rejects the view that the mind receives or in any way possesses the material (corporeal) species (AT 7: 387; CSM 2: 265). Thus, when Descartes says that in taking an idea in the material sense we take it as an operation of the intellect, he simply cannot be understood to be taking his ideas, that is, operations of his own mind, as material species.

In the preface to the reader, which very likely was written after the *Meditations* and his replies to his critics, Descartes introduces the term:

> "Idea" can be taken materially, as an operation of the intellect, in which case it cannot be said to be more perfect than me. Alternatively, it can be taken objectively, as the thing represented by that operation; and this thing, even if it is not regarded as existing outside the intellect, can still, in virtue of its essence, be more perfect than myself. (AT 7: 8; CSM 2: 7)

Supposing, then, that we want to examine an idea, Descartes says, we can consider or regard it in at least two different senses. First, we can think of it as an operation of the intellect. This is to take the idea materially. Secondly, we can think of it in terms of the object represented. This is not to say that we consider the idea as though it were the object existing external to the mind. For, as he says in this passage, we can regard the objects represented as not existing outside the intellect. What he seems to have in mind here is the idea's *content*. So, if we have this right, to take the idea in terms of its content is to take it objectively.

The prima facie reading of the preface's material–objective distinction, it seems, is to read it as being identical to the Third Meditation's formal–objective distinction, which draws the distinction between ideas taken in terms of their formal reality and ideas taken in terms of their objective reality.

> Insofar as the ideas are [considered] simply [as] modes of thought, there is no recognizable inequality among them: they all appear to come from within me in the same fashion. But insofar as different ideas [are considered as images which] represent different things, it is clear that they differ widely. Undoubtedly, the ideas which represent substances to me amount to something more and, so to speak, contain within themselves more objective reality than the ideas which merely represent modes or accidents. (AT 7: 40; CSM 2: 28).

When considering ideas simply as modes of thought, we are considering them solely in terms of their formal being – the being they possess in virtue of their being existent modifications of the mind (AT 7: 40–1; CSM 2: 28). This is to take ideas formally. By contrast, when considering or regarding ideas in terms of what they represent, we are considering them in terms of their objective reality or being – the being they possess in virtue of their representing things. This is to take them objectively. Therefore, this seems to be the same as the preface's material–objective distinction. However, if this is right, "material" and "formal" are synonymous (Grene 1983: 177). Thus, we have to wonder what sort of distinction Descartes took himself to be making when he told

Arnauld that his criticism of the notion of material falsity failed because he mistook ideas in the formal sense instead of rightly taking them in the material sense.

If Descartes' defense of the notion of material falsity is to hold any water at all, it must turn out that there really is a distinction between taking ideas formally and materially. This is what we need to find. Thus, now that Descartes' introduction, Arnauld's criticism, and Descartes' defense of the notion are on the table, we will now look briefly at a number of leading interpretations, including those of Norman Wells, Margaret Wilson, J. M. Beyssade, and Richard Field. What we want to see is how they make sense of the notion of material falsity.

Some Leading Interpretations

Wells traces the regarding of ideas in the formal sense to a theory of representation held by certain Jesuits (Wells 1984: 27, 29). Given Descartes' connection to the Jesuits, he argues, Descartes in all likelihood adopted the theory. According to this theory, when we regard an idea formally we are regarding it in terms of a certain feature it has that accounts for its capacity to represent, namely, its capacity to *conform* to an object (Wells 1984: 31–2). Wells holds that all ideas are conformers. Simply put, he holds that "idea X represents object Y" entails "idea X conforms to object Y." Conformity is a necessary condition for representation. And so, were idea X to fail to conform to object Y, it would follow that idea X does not represent object Y. He takes the regarding of ideas in the material sense to be importantly connected to the phrase *materia errandi*, that is, "material for error" (Wells 1984: 37, 40). This is in line with what Descartes says in his reply to Arnauld, namely, that materially false ideas provide subject matter, or material, for error in judgment (AT 7: 235; CSM 2: 164). Material falsity, says Wells, must be understood not in terms of the pre-judgmental level, which is the level of ideational representation, but solely in terms of the *relation* that holds between the pre-judgmental and judgmental levels (Wells 1984: 45). And so, on Wells' view, had Arnauld not taken the idea of cold as a conformer, but as the material the idea presents in relation to judgment, he would not have made the criticism he did.

There are some troubles here. For example, Descartes draws a distinction between representation and resemblance or conformity. "The chief and most common mistake which is to be found," he says, "consists in my judging that the ideas which are in me resemble, or conform to, things located outside me" (AT 7: 37; CSM 2: 26). In other words, Descartes seems prepared to reject the claim that "idea X represents object Y" entails "idea X conforms to object Y." And so he seems ready to deny, contrary to Wells' view, that conformity is a necessary condition for representation. To be charitable here, it is possible to work up two senses of conformity. For instance, one sense might point out the relationship an idea has to the object it is presenting or exhibiting directly to the mind. This would be *internal* to the idea (say, the relation of intentionality), and in this sense an idea could never fail to conform to the thing it is presenting (Wells 1984: 33–4). For lack of a better name, I will call this "internal" conformity. Another sense might point out the relationship an idea has to an object that exists *external* to thought. I will call this "external" conformity.[6] Thus, when Descartes says "whether it is a goat or a chimera that I am imagining, it is just as true that I imagine the former as the latter" (AT 7: 37; CSM 2: 26), he could be taken to have the internal sense of conformity in mind. Both ideas are "of" their objects, the idea of the chimera being as much "of" the chimera as the idea of the goat is "of" the goat. These ideas are internal conformers. However, only the idea of the goat is an external conformer, or, at least, it is the only one of the two that has a shot at being an external conformer. For, since there is no chimera outside of thought, the idea of the chimera has nothing to which it can externally conform. And it may be that the chief and most common mistake that Descartes mentions is made in judging that our ideas always *externally* conform to their objects. If this is right, then even though Descartes will reject the claim that "idea X represents object Y" entails "idea X *externally* conforms to object Y," he may be friendly to holding that "idea X represents object Y" entails "idea X *internally* conforms to object Y." And so, whereas external conformity is not a necessary condition for representation, internal conformity is.

If internal conformity is what Wells has in mind, then he would appear to be right in holding that all ideas, insofar as they are intentional, for example, are conformers. But if the materially false idea of cold is an internal conformer, and it cannot fail as a conformer, in what sense is it false? As was just entertained above, one possibility is that it is not an *external* conformer. Trouble arises because even though it is not, it nevertheless purports to be one. That is, to the one having the idea, the idea represents its object as though the object existed external to thought. But although this seems to be Wilson (1990), Beyssade (1992), and Field's (1993) view, it is not in the end Wells'. Wells seems to hold that the materially false idea of cold is an idea that "falsely represents" a sensory operation or sensory state – it does not represent anything external to the mind. However, because this messy representation occurs *while* sensing, the one having the idea is led to judge that the object being represented to him or her is a property of a body – in this case, an ice cube – which is the thing responsible for causing the sensation. So, on Wells' view, the idea does not represent cold *as though it were* an existent quality. Rather, the idea represents a sensory operation and the mistake is made by the perceiver in judging that what is being represented to the mind is a property of the ice cube. The difficulty here, of course, is that Descartes says that material falsity is *not* the sort of falsity that arises from judgment. It is a falsity that is inherent in certain kinds of *ideas*. So, if we have Wells' view right, it does not help us to understand Descartes'.

Field (1993) argues that the materially false idea of cold represents a sensible quality (the cold) as though it were a mode of a body (the ice cube, say). On his view, the idea is a bit more misleading than it was for Wells, for it goes one step further and actually represents the quality cold *as though it were* a mode of the ice cube. In judging that the cold is a property of the ice cube, Field's view implies that the judgment is a correct though false one. The one having the idea is *correctly* judging what the idea represents to him or her, but it just so happens that in this case the idea is representing a false state of affairs. The only way to keep from making such a false judgment is to understand that the quality cold, though represented as though it were a mode of the ice cube, is really a mode of the mind.

On Field's view, the proper conceptual or logical subject of size and shape, for example, is extension (body). And the conceptual or logical subject of ideas, judgments, and sensible qualities (like colors, sounds, hot, and cold) is thought (mind). The materially

213

false idea of cold in representing the sensible quality cold as though it were a mode of the ice cube represents a mode of mind as though it were a mode of body. On Field's view, this amounts to the representation of a conceptually or logically impossible state of affairs (Field 1993: 320, 329). But two difficulties arise here. First, in what sense *can* our ideas represent impossible objects or states of affairs? Do I have an idea that *represents* a square-circle, for example? The characterization of the content of the materially false idea of cold as being conceptually or logically impossible seems too strong. Secondly, if it is granted that the materially false idea of cold represents an impossible state of affairs, it certainly cannot be said to represent anything *external* to thought. For, as Descartes says, "self-contradictoriness or impossibility . . . cannot occur in anything which is outside the intellect" (AT 7: 152; CSM 2: 108). And so, in line with Wells, Wilson, and Beyssade, Field holds that the materially false idea of cold does not represent anything external to thought. As we will see below, the sensory (materially false) idea of cold does represent something going on outside of thought – namely, in the case of the sensory idea of the ice cube, it represents the motions of the particles that constitute the ice cube. The idea does *not* represent the quality cold. The quality cold, it will be argued, is a feature of the idea that is *doing* the representing. It is the *medium* of representation. If this is right, then where Wells, Wilson, Beyssade, and Field go wrong (in addition to the other problems mentioned with Wells and Field's views) is in their holding that materially false ideas do not represent anything external to the mind.

A New Interpretation

To get things off the ground, consider for sake of discussion a photograph that sits on my desk. It is a 5×7 inch black and white photograph of Jim (my father), who is posing in his turquoise colored, J. C. Penny leisure suit, while dancing the night away at a swanky Los Angeles disco. The year is 1979. Now, there are many things we can say about this photograph, and one of them seems immediately relevant, namely, that a necessary condition for the photograph's being "of" or its "representing" Jim is that he played a causal role in its production. Based upon this fact, independent of what we take to be causally going on between Jim and the photograph, we are at the very least *conceptually* committed to holding that "The photograph is of Jim" entails "Jim plays a significant causal role in the photograph's production." This sort of conceptual commitment is not found, for example, in such claims as "The painting is of Jim" or "The statue is of Jim." For, there can be paintings or statues of Jim, though Jim never existed – and so he could not have played a causal role in their production.

Other things of course play significant causal roles in the production of the photograph – the Kodak paper company and the Polaroid camera used to take the photograph, to name two. But, clearly, we do not want to say that the photograph is of *them* simply because they are causes. And so, although we are committed to holding that "The photograph is of X" entails "X plays a significant causal role in the photograph's production," we will not be committed to holding that "X plays a significant causal role in the photograph's production" entails "The photograph is of X." Something similar is going on in Descartes' theory of ideas, or, at least, in that part connected to

214

primary ideas. "The idea is of God," for example, entails "God plays a significant causal role in the idea's production." We get a similar view in the Sixth Meditation, where Descartes' proof for the existence of corporeal substance seems to require that "The idea is of corporeal substance" entails "Corporeal substance plays a significant causal role in the idea's production." For, if this were not the case, Descartes says, God would be a deceiver (AT 7: 80; CSM 2: 55). In Cartesian terms, we might say that the formal reality of God (or body, in the other example) plays a significant causal role in the production of the idea's objective reality. This at the very least commits us conceptually to holding that "The idea is of X" entails "The formal reality of X causes the idea's objective reality." The entailment, as in the case of the photograph, does not go the other way (or at least we will not be *conceptually* committed to it). The mind, for instance, also plays a significant causal role in the production of the idea of God. However, "My mind plays a causal role in the production of the idea" does not entail "The idea is of (represents) my mind." And, although we are committed to holding this only for primary ideas, the similarity to the photograph case is strong enough to justify using it as a guiding analogy in the present discussion of ideas. So I will continue using it.

There are properties of the photograph that have nothing at all to do with the photograph's representing anything. Being 5 × 7 inches is such a property. And there are properties of the photograph that do have something to do with the photograph's representing something. In the case of black and white photographs, the various patches of black, for example, found on their surfaces are such properties. Now, being 5 × 7 is a property that is not causally connected to Jim, but is connected to the manufacturer of this particular piece of Polaroid film. By contrast, having certain patches of black, white, or gray on the photograph's surface is, in addition to the manufacturer, causally connected to Jim. Had Jim worn a different colored suit, for example, given all other things remained the same, the gray patches located on that region of the surface of the photograph that represent his suit would have been different shades of gray from those now occupying that region. We might say, then, that there are two sorts of properties of the photograph:

1   Properties causally connected (solely) to the manufacturer.
2   Properties causally connected to the manufacturer and to Jim.

Since properties falling under (1) are not connected to the photograph's representing anything, I will call them "non-representational" properties. And, since properties falling under (2) are connected to the photograph's representing something, I will call them "representational" properties.

Something like this seems to be going on in Descartes' theory of ideas. There are features, we might call them, that ideas possess that have nothing at all to do with representing things. Having a certain level of formal reality is such a feature. And there are features that ideas possess that do have something to do with representing things. Having a certain level of objective reality is such a feature. Descartes says, "the nature of an idea is such that of itself it requires no formal reality except what it derives from my thought" (AT 7: 41; CSM 2: 28). In light of the analogy, I want to read this as suggesting that the formal reality possessed by the idea is caused by the mind of which it is a mode, where the mind here is the analog to the manufacturer. Descartes also says that the objective reality must have a cause "which contains as much formal reality as there is objective reality in the idea" (AT 7: 41; CSM 2: 28–9). Now, insofar as the objective reality is attributed to the idea, and the idea is a mode of the mind, we are not in an obvious position to deny that the mind is playing *some* causal role in producing or maintaining the objective reality contained in the idea. However, the theory of representation that we are assuming here tells us that "The idea is of X" entails "The formal reality of X is the cause of the idea's objective reality." We are not committed to holding that X is the total and efficient cause, of course, but we are committed to holding that X plays *some* causal role. And so, concerning the representational aspect of the idea of an ice cube, say, we play it safe in interpreting Descartes if we say that the idea's objective reality has important, though distinct, causal connections to the formal reality of the mind and to the formal reality of the ice cube. If this is right, then, along the lines of the photograph, there appear to be two sorts of features of the idea of the ice cube:

1′ Features causally connected (solely) to the mind.
2′ Features causally connected to the mind and to the ice cube.

Since the features falling under (1′) are not connected to the idea's representing anything, in line with the photograph case, I will call them "non-representational" features. And since the features falling under (2′) do have something to do with the idea's representing something (its having a certain level of objective reality, for instance), I will call them "representational" features. The distinction being drawn between (1′) and (2′), I want to suggest, is closely aligned with the Third Meditation's formal–objective distinction.

The preface's material–objective distinction, which I take to be *different* from the Third Meditation's formal–objective distinction, is brought to light by way of a further analysis of representational features, those features falling under (2′). My denying the identity of the two distinctions runs counter to the prima facie reading mentioned earlier. But, in my view, the prima facie reading is simply wrong. I want to look now more carefully at (2′) features by way of our analogy.

The representational properties of the photograph, recall, have their causal origin in both the manufacturer and in Jim. Consider the particular region of the photograph's surface that represents Jim's turquoise colored leisure suit. Although the photograph "represents" the turquoise of the leisure suit, it "presents" shades of gray. That it presents these particular shades of gray, as we already know, is in part causally connected to the color of Jim's leisure suit. Had he worn a different colored suit, and yet everything else remained the same (the lighting, the Polaroid camera, and so on), the resulting shades of gray would have been different from those that now occupy that region of the photograph's surface. However, the gray is also causally connected to the manufacturer, for had the film been designed and made differently, the resulting shades of gray would have been different from those that now occupy that region of the photograph's surface.

Suppose that we ask a child or someone not greatly familiar with photographs for their take on the color of Jim's suit. One answer, I think, can be, and perhaps will be,

"It is gray." What has happened here is the child, say, has mistaken the color of the photographic surface for the color of Jim's suit. By contrast, someone familiar with photographs, and who perhaps knew Jim, could point at the photograph and ask if what Jim is wearing is his turquoise suit. That she could point at the gray on the surface of the photograph and ask whether *that* was turquoise is important. She is not crazy or color blind. Rather, she understands that the color "presented" on the photograph's surface "represents" some other color, and in this case, possibly turquoise. If we confine ourselves to the "presented" color, we are right in calling it gray. What I want to suggest, though it may seem a bit strange, is that we are entitled to look at the *photograph* and say that the color of Jim's suit, there in the photograph, is turquoise. But, in this case, we are taking the color on the photograph's surface as a "represented" color. We are considering the photograph's content.

There is, then, an inherent ambiguity in representational properties. In the case of the photograph, taken one way, as the medium or operation of representation, the color is taken to be gray. Taken another way, as the thing represented, which in this case is the color of Jim's suit, the color is taken to be turquoise. And a failure to disambiguate this sort of property can lead a child, for example, to mistakenly judge that Jim's suit is gray. And so the representational property that represents the color of Jim's suit should either be:

2a   A property regarded in terms of the representational operation.
2b   A property regarded in terms of Jim's suit.

Something similar is found in Descartes' material–objective distinction introduced in the preface to the reader of the *Meditations*. Returning to the example of the idea of the ice cube, Descartes holds that coldness is not a mode of the ice cube (AT 7: 75–6, 81; CSM 2: 52–3, 56; AT 8A: 318; CSM 1: 281–2). The cold that is presented in the idea is itself a quality found only in the mind. As is well known, it is Descartes' view that the motions of the particles constituting the ice cube are affecting my sensory organs, which in turn are affecting my brain, which in turn is occasioning the idea that represents to me the ice cube (AT 7: 86–9; CSM 2: 59–61; AT 8A: 318–23; CSM 1: 281–5). A constituent idea of the more complex sensory idea of the ice cube, which we have thus far been calling "the idea of cold," represents the motions of its particles, and is doing so by way of the presentation of the quality cold. Strictly speaking, the idea is not "of" or does not "represent" the quality, but instead represents the motions of the particles constituting the ice cube. The cold here is analogous to the gray of the photograph. As the gray which is presented represents the turquoise, the quality cold which is presented represents these motions. The gray is that property of the photograph *by way of which* the turquoise is being represented. It is taken to be *gray* only in light of our regarding this property of the photograph in terms of its being the representational medium or operation. Likewise, I want to suggest, the cold is that feature of the idea *by way of which* the motions are being represented. It is taken to be *cold* (a quality) only in light of our regarding the idea in terms of its being the representational medium or operation.

As in the photograph case, ideational representational features are ambiguous. For it seems to be Descartes' view that someone who has not undertaken a rigorous

217

philosophical examination, like that worked out in the *Meditations*, can be led to wrongly judge that the cold is a property of the ice cube. To keep from making this mistake, one needs to disambiguate representational features. This can be done by understanding that the representational feature of the idea that represents the motions of the particles constituting the ice cube should either be:

2′a   A feature regarded in terms of the representational operation.
2′b   A feature regarded in terms of the ice cube.

These are two ways of regarding (2′), or representational, properties. Considering the idea in terms of that *by way of which* the particles are represented is to take it in terms of its being a representational medium or operation – which takes the feature as a (2′a) feature. This is to take the idea materially. Considering the idea in terms of the ice cube is to take the idea in terms of what it represents, that is, in terms of its content – which takes the feature as a (2′b) feature. This, as we know, is to take the idea objectively.

Enough has been said for us to draw some important conclusions. First, the "formal" in the Third Meditation's formal–objective distinction emphasizes a relation that holds between the idea *qua* mode and the mind which is its substance. By contrast, the "material" in the preface's material–objective distinction emphasizes a relation that holds between the idea *qua* representational operation and the very same idea *qua* representational content. Thus, "formal" and "material" are not identical.

Even so, the sense of "formal" in the Third Meditation's formal–objective distinction is not identical to that of the Fourth Replies' formal–material distinction. And so, in pointing out the difference between "formal" and "material," as we did above, we still are not finished. What could Descartes mean by "formal" in the Fourth Replies? I believe that the answer has been staring us in the face all along. If "the idea is of X" entails "the formal reality of X is the cause of the idea's objective reality," then in considering *what* an idea represents we are *ipso facto* considering the idea in light of the formal reality of some object. We are not considering the idea in terms of *its own* formal reality, but we are necessarily considering *something's* formal reality, for the latter is a necessary condition for the idea's being "of" anything at all. And so, when specifically looking at what an idea is of, or at what it represents, we could be said to be considering it in a "formal" sense, a sense which emphasizes the relation between the objective reality of the idea and the formal reality of some object (the object that the idea is of). This sense of "formal" is clearly different from that of the Third Meditation's formal–objective distinction. So when Descartes says to Arnauld that when we consider ideas formally, we take them as representing something, we now have a sense that fits.[7] In light of this difference between the terms "formal" found in the Third Meditation and Fourth Replies, I will tag the latter with an asterisk.

Moving forward, then, in the Replies' formal*–material distinction, Descartes connects taking ideas formally* with our making "reference to the truth and falsity of their objects" (AT 7: 232; CSM 2: 163). Truth and falsity in this context are related to existence and non-existence (Wells 1984: 26–30). A true object exists, whereas a false object does not. If saying that X has formal reality is coextensive with saying that X exists, then if "the idea is of X" conceptually commits us to X's having formal reality (which is the cause of the idea's objective reality), we are in turn committed to claiming that X exists. Recall that in our hypothetical case of cold, cold was said to be an absence of heat, that is, it lacked formal reality. What this amounted to on this analysis was our asserting that cold does not exist; it is, in the scholastic sense, a false object.

What got Arnauld so worried, I think, was Descartes' claiming that cold could be nothing and yet we could have an idea that represented it to us. For, if "the idea is of cold" entails "the formal reality of cold is the cause of the idea's objective reality," and cold has no formal reality, Arnauld rightly concludes that the idea cannot be of cold. And Descartes agrees (AT 7: 234; CSM 2: 164). This, I think, shows that Descartes does not take the idea to be of, or to represent, *cold*, that is, the mental quality. By *representare* here, he must mean that the idea *presents* cold, a possibility that other commentators have already noted (Wells 1984; Wilson 1978; Chappell 1986). The sensory or primary idea of cold is really an idea of a mode of the ice cube – in this case, the motions of the particles that constitute it. What the idea presents is the quality cold. It is that feature of the idea by way of which the motions are being represented. Descartes says: "it often happens in the case of obscure and confused ideas – and the ideas of heat and cold fall into this category – that an idea is referred to something other than that of which it is in fact the idea" (AT 7: 233; CSM 2: 163). What I am suggesting here is that in having the sorts of sensory ideas that I have, I can wrongly refer the idea to the quality cold, the thing being presented, instead of rightly referring the idea to the motions of the particles, the thing(s) being represented. This is precisely what happened when the child wrongly took Jim's suit to be gray. She wrongly took the reference of the photograph to be the gray, the color being presented, instead of rightly taking it to be the turquoise, the color being represented.

In taking the idea formally*, the sense that requires us to look for the *cause* of the idea's objective reality, Arnauld is led to the conclusion that there can be no idea that represents cold as a positive and real quality. This is so because in lacking formal reality, cold cannot be the cause of the idea's objective reality. As Descartes appears to be contending, had Arnauld taken the idea materially, he would have taken the representational feature of the idea (the quality cold) in light of the idea's being a *medium* or *operation* of representation, namely, as that mental operation by way of which some mode of the ice cube was being represented. Taken materially, he would not have taken it to be something that exists outside of thought, that is, as a thing requiring some level of formal reality. This seems to be the point of Descartes' defense in the Fourth Replies.

Arnauld certainly cannot be to blame, of course, for the term "materially" appeared nowhere in the body of the *Meditations*, and he would not have had available to him the preface, for, as I mentioned earlier, this appears to have been written after the Objections and Replies.[8] Moreover, Descartes seems to be treating cold in the Third Meditation discussion of material falsity as though the problem was one about the extra-mental status of cold. For example, he says "the ideas of heat and cold contain so little clarity and distinctness that they do not enable me to tell whether cold is merely the absence of heat or vice versa, or whether both of them are real qualities, or neither is" (AT 7: 44; CSM 2: 30). So is he concerned about whether cold is a property of the ice cube, a property that exists external to thought? Perhaps. But there is a way of reading him here so that this turns out not to be his concern.

Consider what he says in the Fourth Replies: "whether cold is a positive thing or an absence does not affect the idea I have of it, which remains the same as it always was" (AT 7: 232; CSM 2: 163). Here it would appear that he is saying something like "whether Pegasus exists or not does not affect the idea I have of Pegasus." But, I contend, this is not what he is saying. Although a bit rough, one possible translation of the Latin is: "whether [the quality] cold is a positive thing or a privation, [the idea] on account of this itself is not other from the idea I have, but remains in me the same [idea] which I have always had." I read this as telling us that the idea would be *of*, or would *represent*, the motions of the particles constituting the ice cube regardless of the ontological status of the quality cold. And, it seems to me, that in the Third Meditation he is raising a similar point, albeit clumsily, by considering whether the ideas he has which present such qualities provide any clues to their representing objects in an extra-mental world.

There is a palpable discussion running throughout the Cartesian corpus concerning the deceptiveness of sensory ideas, and how this is related to their representing bodies and modes of bodies by way of various mental qualities such as sounds and colors. Once located, it is easy to see that the Third Meditation discussion of material falsity is simply a part of this larger discussion. In *The World*, for instance, written roughly ten years before the *Meditations*, Descartes examines a sensory idea of sound. He asks: "Do you think the idea of this sound, as it is formed in our mind, is anything like the object which is its cause?" (AT 11: 5; CSM 1: 82). The cause is a "certain vibration of air which strikes our ears" (AT 11: 5; CSM 1: 82). Here, the idea is caused by the vibration of air particles. The idea represents these particles, and presents the quality sound by way of which the idea is doing the representing. "If the sense of hearing transmitted to our mind the true image of its object," he says, "then, instead of making us conceive the sound, it would have to make us conceive the motion of the parts of the air which is then vibrating against our ears" (AT 11: 5; CSM 1: 82). If our sensory idea presented motions, then it would be a "true image," he says. But, in presenting instead the sound, the implication is that it is a false image – and, arguably, a materially false idea.

In *Description of a Human Body*, written roughly seven years after the *Meditations*, he says "we have sensory awareness of two kinds of motion" (AT 11: 255; CSM 1: 323). What he has in mind is a system of minute balls filling the plenum. As these balls approach my eyes in a straight line, they will produce in me "the sensation of light." And depending on how fast they spin around their centers, as they contact my eyes, they can produce in me a variety of sensations of colors. For instance, "if the speed at which they turn is much smaller than that of their rectilinear motion, the body appears *blue* to us; while if the turning speed is much greater than that of their rectilinear motion, the body appears *red* to us" (AT 11: 255–6; CSM 1: 323). Our ideas, insofar as these motions are their causes, are of, or represent, these motions. However, Descartes tells us that what "appears" to us is a color. Like the idea of sound in *The World* and the idea of cold in the *Meditations*, Descartes says that what the sensory idea represents (its cause) and what it presents are two very different things – though the *same* property (a (2′) property) is being both presented and is doing the representing. And it is because of this inherent ambiguity with representational properties that they can be a source of error in judgment.

The notion of material falsity seems to be an important component of Descartes' theory of ideas. In the *Meditations*, however, he does not make its importance known. But, arguably, this was by design. In a letter to Mersenne he writes:

> Between ourselves . . . these six Meditations contain all the foundations of my physics. But please do not tell people, for that might make it harder for supporters of Aristotle to approve them. I hope that readers will gradually get used to my principles, and recognize their truth, before they notice that they destroy the principles of Aristotle. (AT 3: 297–8; CSMK 3: 172–3)

The principles to which Descartes is referring are the elements earth, air, fire, and water, which are understood in terms of the qualities hot, cold, wet, and dry. Aristotle bases his entire physics on them. If our ideas of such things (hot and cold, for instance) are inherently materially false, Descartes' view seems to be that the whole of Aristotle's physics is based on false ideas. To be sure, he does not come out and say this, but as he tells Mersenne in the letter just quoted, not saying this was an important part of his overall strategy in making out his position in the *Meditations*.

In taking "material" in the way suggested here, we can make some sense of why Descartes calls this sort of falsity "material falsity." To help point the way, consider two remarks Descartes makes in his correspondence. To Reneri, he says "the soul can think without a body, even though, when it is joined to it, it can have its operation disturbed by the bad disposition of the bodily organs" (AT 2: 38; CSMK 3: 99, see also AT 7: 375; CSM 2: 258). And to Regius, he says: "For if an angel were in a human body, he would not have sensations as we do, but would simply perceive the motions which are caused by external objects, and in this way would differ from a real man" (AT 3: 493; CSMK 3: 206). Since the angel is not *essentially* united to a body, it will not have its mental representational operation disturbed, even if it is "occupying" a human body. Consequently, the angel's ideas of bodies, which we must assume are occasioned by some process going on in the man's body, will make completely intelligible the motions of the bodies affecting the man's sensory organs. For the angel's ideas will clearly represent motions. However, this will not be the case for the man. In being essentially united to a body, the man will have his representational operation disturbed, which apparently results in the presentation (manifestation) of such qualities as colors and sounds. Because of this, they do not make intelligible the objects – for example, the motions of the ice cube's particles – which are directly affecting the bodily organs. This aligns itself nicely with what Descartes says in the *Principles*, when he says that there is absolutely no intelligible connection between the mental qualities found in our sensory ideas and the motions of the bodies affecting our sensory organs (AT 8A: 322–3; CSM 1: 285). So the kind of falsity inherent in our sensory ideas has its source in the operation of representation. Understanding our ideas in terms of their being operations of representation is to take them in the material sense. Hence, Descartes calls this sort of falsity "material" falsity.

Conclusion

If the above is right, we now know what "formal," "formal*," "objective," and "material" mean in the preface's material–objective distinction, the Third Meditation's

221

formal–objective distinction, and the Fourth Replies' formal*–material distinction. Taking "material" in the sense argued for above gives us some idea as to why Descartes calls this sort of falsity inherent in our sensory ideas "material falsity." Further, the view developed in this chapter not only shows how the notion of material falsity fits into Descartes' theory of ideas, but also how it is in part generated by his epistemological commitment to rationalism. Finally, we see why the notion is an important component of the theory, for it is shown to be a component that covertly helps him in his attempt to overthrow the very principles underlying Aristotle's physics.

Acknowledgments

The first presentable version of this chapter goes back to 1997, and was presented at a session of the Eastern Division meetings of the APA in Philadelphia. I am indebted to Tad Schmaltz who commented on the paper, and who has graciously commented on subsequent drafts. I am also indebted to Ken Brown, Jill Buroker, David Cunning, Patricia Easton, Richard Field, Paul Hoffman, Nick Jolley, Amy Kind, Ed McCann, Alan Nelson, Lex Newman, Larry Nolan, Calvin Normore, Alison Simmons, Margaret Wilson, and Charles Young – each contributing to this project through helpful (and often multiple) discussions, a number of them commenting on drafts going back before 1997. Lastly, I wish to express special thanks to Nelson Pike who met with me at his hacienda, over several years, and brought a clarity to the project that I could not bring on my own.

Notes

1 In the Fifth Replies, Descartes argues that simply because the mind can have an idea of parts it does not follow that the mind has parts. Likewise, simply because the mind has an idea of the magnitude of the earth, it does not follow that the mind is extended, or is as large as the magnitude of the earth. The same argument will hold for colors: simply because the mind has an idea of blue, it does not follow that the mind is blue.

2 The objective reality of an idea is that reality it contains (or possesses) in virtue of which it represents something to the mind (AT 7: 102–3; CSM 2: 74–5).

3 Although in the Third Meditation (AT 7: 40; CSM 2: 28) Descartes characterizes the principle as being derived from another, in the Second Replies he characterizes *ex nihilo* as "self-evident" (AT 7: 162; CSM 2: 115).

4 A primary idea is one whose objective reality is traceable to the formal reality of an object (see AT 7: 42; CSM 2: 29).

5 This appears to put the entailment the other way. The Third Meditation proof for God's existence, however, requires only the more moderate view that "the idea is of God" entails "God's formal reality causes the idea's objective reality," which is what I will suppose here.

6 Both Wilson and Beyssade work up a similar distinction (Wilson 1990; Beyssade 1992).

7 Though admittedly there is little (if no) textual evidence for thinking that this is what Descartes actually meant outside of the single sentence found in the Fourth Replies.

8 As is well known, Descartes claims to have borrowed the term *materialiter falsitas* from Suarez (AT 7: 235; CSM 2: 164), but a careful study shows that Descartes' *notion* of material falsity is not Suarez's.

References and Further Reading

Aristotle (1906). *De Sensu*. In G. R. T. Ross (trans.), *Aristotle: De Sensu and De Memoria*. Cambridge: Cambridge University Press.

—— (1947). *De Anima*. In Richard McKeon (trans.), *Introduction to Aristotle*. New York: Modern Library.

Beyssade, J. M. (1992). Descartes on material falsity. In Phillip D. Cummins and Guenter Zoeller (eds.), *Minds, Ideas, and Objects: Essays on the Theory of Representation in Modern Philosophy*. Atascadero, CA: Ridgeview Publishing.

Chappell, Vere (1986). The theory of ideas. In Amélie Oksenberg Rorty (ed.), *Essays on Descartes' Meditations*. Los Angeles: University of California Press.

Field, Richard (1993). Descartes on the material falsity of ideas. *Philosophical Review*, 102 (3), 309–34.

Galileo (1960). *The Assayer*. In Stillman Drake and C. D. O. O'Malley (trans.), *The Controversy On the Comets of 1618*. Philadelphia: University of Pennsylvania Press.

Grene, Marjorie (1983). *Descartes*. Minneapolis: University of Minnesota Press.

Kenny, Anthony (1995). *Descartes: A Study of His Philosophy*. Bristol: Thoemmes Press.

Malebranche, Nicolas (1992). *The Search after Truth* (Thomas Lennon and Paul Olscamp trans., Steven Nadler ed.). Indianapolis, IN: Hackett.

Wells, Norman (1984). Material falsity in Descartes, Arnauld, and Suarez. *Journal of the History of Philosophy*, 22 (1), 25.

Wilson, Margaret (1978). *Descartes*. London: Routledge and Kegan Paul.

—— (1990). Descartes on the representationality of sensation. In M. Kulstad and J. Cover (eds.), *Central Themes in Early Modern Philosophy*. Indianapolis, IN: Hackett.

12

The Role of the Imagination in Rationalist Philosophies of Mathematics

LAWRENCE NOLAN

Introduction

Traditional rationalists from Plato onward tend to condemn the imagination as a source of deception and confusion, and oppose the imagination to reason or the pure intellect, which they treat as the sole source of knowledge or wisdom. In the words of one such thinker, Nicolas Malebranche, the imagination is "in revolt against Reason" (OC 12: 126; JS: 85). Alongside such pejorative comments, however, rationalists tend also to say tantalizing things about the important role the imagination plays in attaining mathematical knowledge. This is remarkable, and seemingly inconsistent, as most rationalists glorify mathematics as the paradigm of certainty and truth, and as the model of methodology and logical demonstration. How can they entertain such divergent positions? And what role exactly do they conceive the imagination as serving in mathematics? This chapter is an attempt to answer these questions, with an emphasis on the latter.

I shall focus on the views of René Descartes and Malebranche, two seventeenth-century rationalists who typically diverge on the nature of cognition but who come together in surprising ways in the philosophy of mathematics and on the role of the imagination in conceiving geometrical figures and truths. But I'll start with some suggestive remarks by Plato who, in his famous metaphor of the Divided Line, attempts to distinguish mathematical cognition from other forms of cognition and to explain why it falls short of the highest form of knowledge. Plato's discussion raises certain questions and problems that the Cartesians struggled with themselves and, in some cases, solved. But we shall find Descartes and Malebranche also being guided by one central Platonic insight, namely that mathematical cognition is a stepping stone to a higher form of cognition, to the cognition of a first principle of knowledge.

Plato's Divided Line and Mathematical Cognition

In the *Republic*, Plato famously appeals to the metaphor of a Divided Line in an attempt to characterize mathematical thinking and to distinguish it from other forms of human cognition. For rationalists like Plato, mathematics represents one of the paradigms of

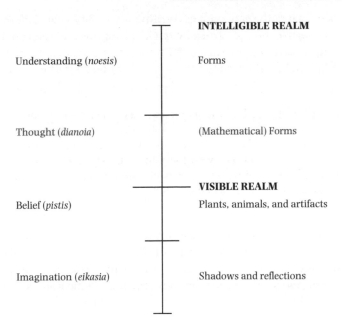

Figure 12.1

human knowledge, but the primary aim of the line metaphor is to relegate it to a lower status than "understanding" – which he exalts as the highest form of knowledge – and to explain mathematics' subordinate status. Unpacking this metaphor and coming to terms with Plato's criticisms of the mathematicians of his day will provide a useful context for investigating Descartes and Malebranche's accounts of mathematical cognition, as there are several important parallels.

The divided line introduces a fourfold division within human cognition. Plato asks us to imagine a line divided into two unequal segments, and then those segments further divided into the same unequal proportions (see figure 12.1). The first (major) division represents the distinction between knowledge and opinion, and, with respect to their objects, the distinction between the intelligible and the visible. One of the hallmarks of Plato's epistemology is that the objects of knowledge lie outside the visible, material realm. We can form beliefs or opinions about the ever-changing objects in this world, but we cannot know them. Knowledge is reserved for what Plato calls the "Forms," immutable and eternal exemplars that subsist in an intelligible realm independent of the mind and of the material world.

Within the visible realm, Plato draws a further division between physical objects (i.e., plants, animals, and manufactured things) and their shadows or reflections. The latter are images of physical objects and, indeed, Plato holds that we cognize these shadows and reflections through the imagination. Although Plato is not completely clear about this, he appears to hold that there is just one type of object in the intelligible realm, namely Forms, though we can distinguish mathematical Forms from others. Thus, the final division on the Line is between two different ways of cognizing Forms – "thinking" and "understanding." Thinking constitutes the third form of cognition,

225

and Plato associates it with mathematics. Writing about fifty years before Euclid wrote his *Elements of Geometry*, he was struck by the fact that the geometers of his day relied on diagrams and constructions to demonstrate their conclusions. Does this mean that geometers are focused on the wrong things – visible objects rather than forms? Plato thinks not.

> Although they [geometers] use visible figures and make claims about them, their thought isn't directed to them but to those other things that they are like. They make their claims for the sake of the [Form of] Square itself and the [Form of] Diagonal itself, not the diagonal they draw, and similarly with the others. These figures that they make and draw, of which shadows and reflections in water are images, they now in turn use as images, in seeking to see those others themselves that one cannot see except by means of thought. (*Republic* 510d–511a)

So just as shadows and reflections serve as images of something higher, namely physical objects, so likewise diagrams (which are themselves physical objects) serve as images of something higher still – namely, the Forms. This analogy provides Plato with a cognitive bridge between the visible and the intelligible realms. Such a bridge is necessary to ascend from a state of opinion to a state of knowledge.

This discussion brings us to Plato's criticism of the mathematicians of his day, and to his reasons for demoting mathematical thinking to a level lower than understanding. Plato says that the divisions within the Line indicate different degrees of clarity and obscurity. Understanding is the clearest form of cognition and imagining is the most obscure. So why is mathematical cognition more obscure than understanding? And what is involved in understanding? How does it grasp forms differently?

One might suppose that mathematical thinking is more obscure because it uses visual aids or imagery. But that is only part of the story. Plato's specific complaint is that geometers ordinarily draw conclusions from unproven assumptions or "hypotheses," and do not even think it necessary to give an account of these assumptions, but take them as self-evident. The hypotheses in question would appear to be the definitions and postulates that later became associated with Euclidean geometry, though the text is too thin to say definitively. In any case, Plato suggests that there is some connection between this appeal to unproven assumptions and the mathematician's reliance on imagery. Perhaps the point is that someone who is relying on visual aids will not even think to demand a proof of a definition or postulate, for it will seem obvious to the eye. For example, Euclidean geometry postulates that from any center and any radius a circle may be drawn. Would anyone who has constructed figures on flat surfaces doubt that or demand a proof? It seems unlikely. But Plato thought that mathematicians were overlooking the fact that even such apparently self-evident truths must be derived from something more basic (viz., the Forms). Thus, he places mathematical thinking at a lower level than understanding.

Plato calls the method by which we achieve understanding "dialectic." He explains that dialectic proceeds in a directly opposite manner than the method of the geometers. Rather than reasoning down to a conclusion from some unproven hypothesis, understanding "reasons up" to a first principle of knowledge, where the first principle in question is one of the Forms. The literal meaning of the Greek term for "hypotheses" is "things set down in front of you." Plato exploits this literal sense when he says that the "hypotheses" of mathematics are only so many "stepping stones" (or springboards) from which to reach first principles. His claim then is that mathematical thinking aims at something higher, that it serves as a stepping stone to the highest form of cognition – dialectical understanding of the Forms.

The Cartesians and the Problem of Pure Thought

Whether or not they had the metaphor of the Divided Line in their sights, Descartes and Malebranche both develop Plato's position on the role played by the imagination in our cognition of geometrical objects, and treat the study of geometry as a stepping stone to a higher form of cognition. We shall turn to their specific accounts in the last two sections of this chapter. But as a prelude to that discussion, let us first investigate how their conception of the human being differs from Plato's. This investigation will illustrate why the imagination plays an even greater role in mathematical cognition among the Cartesians than it does in Plato. It will also explain why I have chosen to focus on the Cartesian rationalists.

Plato, Descartes, and Malebranche are all mind-body dualists insofar as they maintain that the only things that exist in this world are minds (or souls) and bodies (or physical objects). But they have different conceptions of where human beings fit into this ontological scheme. Plato conceives the human being as nothing more than an immaterial soul or mind. He conceives the human body, in turn, as an instrument of the soul; the soul uses the body to investigate matters involving the senses, for mobility, etc. Descartes seems at times to endorse this understanding of the human being. Anyone familiar with the epistemological project in the *Meditations* knows that Descartes thinks of himself as a purely thinking thing (i.e., a thing whose whole essence is to think). But here one must be careful, for when he makes this assertion he is speaking of what he is *qua* mind. As a dualist, Descartes maintains that his mind can exist apart from his body; in his terms, these two substances are "really distinct." This is crucial to his efforts to find a place for the Christian doctrine of the immortality of the soul. But he also holds that a human being is something more than a mind, that it is a union of mind and body. In an attempt to characterize this union in the Sixth Meditation, Descartes invokes an age-old analogy of a sailor and a ship.

> I am not merely present in my body as a sailor is present in a ship, but ... I am very closely joined and, as it were, intermingled with it, so that I and the body form a unit. If this were not so, I, who am nothing but a thinking thing, would not feel pain when the body was hurt, but would perceive the damage purely by the intellect, just as a sailor perceives by sight if anything in his ship is broken. Similarly, when the body needed food or drink, I should have an explicit understanding of the fact, instead of having confused sensations of hunger and thirst. For these sensations of hunger, thirst, pain and so on are nothing but confused modes of thinking which arise from the union and, as it were, intermingling of the mind with the body. (AT 7: 81; CSM 2: 56)

The sailor and ship analogy provides a useful way of characterizing the difference between Plato and Descartes on the nature of the human being. Plato never actually employs this analogy himself, though it is sometimes attributed to him by later philosophers and in some ways befits his description of the body as the instrument of the soul. Descartes, in contrast, rejects this analogy on the ground that it does not do proper justice to the close and intimate nature of the mind-body union: if I were present in my body as a sailor in a ship then I would have to inspect my body in order to detect damage. But of course I do not have to do that, for I feel the effects of this damage immediately in the form of pain. Likewise, when my body is in need of food or drink, I feel hunger or thirst. Although Descartes does not say so here, he thinks that the interaction between mind and body is mutual. Not only does my body causally produce effects in my mind, but my mind also produces effects in my body in the form of voluntary movement, etc. This is the doctrine of mind–body interactionism. Some commentators, however, have thought that in saying that the mind and the body form a "substantial union," Descartes intends something more than their mutual interaction. According to them, he also intends to say that these two radically distinct substances form a single, unified entity in its own right. Whether this is the proper way to interpret Descartes goes beyond the aims of this chapter. However, it does highlight one point that is important for our purposes: in spite of his view that mind and body are really distinct, Descartes lays great stress on the fact that we are embodied creatures, and this has important consequences for the possibility of pure thought, as we shall see below.

Malebranche famously rejects Descartes' view that mind and body causally interact, on the grounds that God is the only true cause and that created beings lack causal powers of their own. But he does follow Descartes' lead in thinking that the mind of human beings is joined to the body in a close and intimate way. Indeed, Malebranche thinks that the mind partakes in two separate unions: one with God "above it" and another with body "below it." This doctrine plays such a foundational role in Malebranche's philosophy that he begins his great work, the *Search after Truth*, by introducing it. Whereas the union with God elevates and enlightens the mind, the union with body "infinitely debases man and is today the main cause of all his errors and miseries" (OC 1: 9; Mal: xxxiii). When one of these unions waxes, the other wanes. The goal of philosophy is to strengthen the mind's union with God and thus decrease its dependence on the body, while recognizing that the union with the body can never be fully severed in this life.

> The . . . mind's union with our body . . . diminishes as our union with God increases, but it is entirely broken only by our death. For even if we were as enlightened and as detached from all sensible things as were the Apostles, there is still the necessity stemming from Original Sin that our mind should depend on our body, and that we should feel the law of our flesh resisting and constantly opposing the law of our mind. (OC 1: 15; Mal: xxxvi–xxxvii)

In supposing that the body debases the soul, the Cartesians are not so far from Plato, who sometimes describes the body as the "prison-house" of the soul. But, as I have indicated, they regard the soul and body as being more intimately related than their rationalist forebear. The reason I stress this point is that it shows why the body and, more specifically, the corporeal imagination is called upon by the Cartesians to play an even greater role in cognition than it is by Plato. This runs counter to the traditional interpretation of the rationalists. According to textbook accounts, one achieves knowledge by withdrawing from the senses, the imagination, and the corporeal images associated with them. Knowledge falls under the sole provenance of reason or the pure intellect, which is devoid of sensory imagery and completely independent from the body. But while making detachment from the body a professed goal, and devising a method to achieve it, the Cartesians tend to stress our state of embodiment as something ineluctable, at least in this life. This is important to remember, for we often entertain a false picture of the rationalist sage as an ascetic who lives in utter detachment from the body, contemplating eternal and immutable truths, and who is unaffected by this world's goings on. But according to the Cartesian rationalists, moments of pure intellection are rare even for the sage. Indeed, given their emphasis on embodiment, Descartes and Malebranche owe us an explanation of how pure intellection and "detachment" from the body is even possible.

One way to escape this difficulty would be to deny the possibility of pure thought. Indeed, two of Descartes' followers take this very path. Robert Desgabets and Pierre-Sylvain Régis argue that all cognition includes a sensory component. Descartes cannot adopt this solution himself, however, for his epistemological project in the *Meditations* depends on the possibility of pure intellections of the soul, body, and God. Only pure intellections can provide the foundations for his new system of knowledge, for only they are fully clear and distinct in the technical sense that allows him to conclude that his perceptions correspond to reality. So, Descartes does allow pure intellections but, because of his views about embodiment, he also thinks that dwelling on them can be harmful to us. Fortunately, the latter position does not conflict with his epistemological project, for it suffices to understand the first principles of metaphysics "once in a lifetime."

> I believe that it is very necessary to have properly understood, once in a lifetime, the principles of metaphysics, since they are what give us the knowledge of God and of our soul. But I think also that it would be very harmful to occupy one's intellect frequently in meditating upon [such principles], since this would impede it from devoting itself to the functions of the imagination and senses. I think the best thing is to content oneself with keeping in one's memory and one's belief the conclusions which one has once drawn from them, and then employ the rest of one's study time to thoughts in which the intellect cooperates with the imagination and the senses. (AT 3: 695; CSMK 3: 228)

Descartes is forced to walk a fine line between denying the possibility of pure intellections and denying the mind-body union. His compromise is to say that pure intellections are rare and need only be cultivated once in a lifetime. This is not completely satisfying, however, for the reason suggested above: given his emphasis on embodiment, absolutely pure intellections should not be possible.

As I show below, Malebranche does better here, for while he sometimes speaks of "pure perceptions," purity for him is a matter of degree and does not admit of a maximal level. For Malebranche, as for Desgabets and Régis, all cognition includes a sensory or imaginative component and is thus confused to some degree. Malebranche can consistently hold such a view for, unlike Descartes, he does not seek metaphysical foundations for knowledge. It suffices for him to show how knowledge is possible, and he achieves this by locating ideas in God, where they serve as archetypes or models for creation. Knowledge is possible because in thinking of the idea of extension, for example, we are grasping the very blueprint that God used to create the world. Hence, Malebranche holds that things in the created world must conform to ideas, rather than the other way around, as on Descartes' theory of cognition. For Malebranche, ideas are inherently pure and distinct because they reside in God, but because of our mind's embodiment, our perceptions of those ideas fall short of absolute purity and perfect distinctness.

Despite this important difference between Descartes and Malebranche, their shared view of the human condition has at least two important consequences for how knowledge is achieved, the second of which is often neglected by textbook accounts of rationalism. First, the road to truth begins in confusion and error. As embodied creatures whose natural state is one of confusion, we are able to glimpse the truth only by ascending out of such a state. And even after achieving an instance of (relatively or absolutely) pure intellection, we typically must descend back into confusion before daring such lofty intellectual heights again. Second, and more importantly, although reason is the means by which truth is apprehended, the fact of our embodiment requires us to enlist the mind's other faculties – even those that depend in some way on the body – as aids to reason. The senses, imagination, and memory are the faculties most often employed here; of these, some will of course serve reason better than others. Interestingly, the Cartesians identify the imagination as the faculty capable of rendering the greatest service to reason, especially when it comes to mathematics and to forming a distinct idea of corporeal nature.

Descartes on the Role of the Imagination in Forming a Distinct Idea of Corporeal Nature

In his early unpublished writings, Descartes envisages a very expansive role for the imagination in human cognition. One can see this point most clearly in his early notion of "ideas." Throughout the corpus, Descartes maintains that all cognition is mediated by ideas or thoughts. In his mature philosophy, ideas fall under the provenance of the intellect, but in his early work, all ideas are formed by, and stored in, the imagination. In these early writings, he also does not draw a fine distinction between the mind's various faculties: he speaks of the mind as a single power that is variously called "pure intellect," "imagination," "memory," or "sense perception" depending on what function it is performing (AT 10: 416; CSM 1: 42). This seems far removed from the mature philosophy, where we find Descartes drawing a sharp distinction between the pure intellect and the imagination, and placing severe limits on the scope of our imaginative powers. Descartes now stresses that the intellect is the sole faculty capable of understanding the truth and that the imagination, along with the sensory images it employs, is the source of confusion and error. He is especially keen to emphasize that the imagination is not capable of cognizing immaterial beings such as the soul and God. Indeed, he thinks that one of the main obstacles to forming distinct ideas of these immaterial beings is the habit, formed in childhood as a result of our reliance on the senses, of attempting to conceive all things in corporeal terms.

Despite these radical shifts in Descartes' view of the imagination, he thinks it continues to play a crucial role as an aid to the intellect in geometry and in our cognition

230

of corporeal nature. Textbook accounts of Descartes' philosophy often fail to appreciate this fact, but there are two crucial passages among his later writings in which he affirms the imagination's role as an aid to the intellect. These passages suggest a greater continuity with Descartes' early views on the imagination, though now the imagination is charged with the more specific task of helping us to form clear and distinct conceptions of corporeal nature. Let us begin by examining these passages.

The most explicit of these passages occurs in an important letter, written in between the publication of Descartes' two great works, the *Meditations* and the *Principles of Philosophy*. This letter is part of a series of exchanges with a distinguished acquaintance named Princess Elizabeth on the union of the soul with the body. In his previous letter, Descartes introduced the claim that there are three "primitive notions," or kinds of notions, upon which all other notions are patterned: the notions of the soul, of the body, and of the union between the soul and the body (AT 3: 665; CSMK 3: 218). Part of what it means to call these notions "primitive" is that "each can be understood only through itself" (AT 3: 666; CSMK 3: 218), and to each there also belongs a unique and proper method of conceiving. Picking up on the latter point in his subsequent letter, Descartes writes:

> First of all then, I observe one great difference between these three kinds of notions. The soul is conceived only by the pure intellect; *body (i.e., extension, shapes and motions) can likewise be known by the intellect alone, but much better by the intellect aided by the imagination*; and finally what belongs to the union of the soul and the body is known only obscurely by the intellect alone or even by the intellect aided by the imagination, but it is known very clearly by the senses . . . Metaphysical thoughts, which exercise the pure intellect, help to familiarize us with the notion of the soul; and *the study of mathematics, which exercises mainly the imagination in the consideration of shapes and motions, accustoms us to form very distinct notions of body*. (AT 3: 691–2; CSM 3: 226–7, emphasis added)

Descartes explicitly affirms here that the imagination aids the intellect in forming distinct ideas of body. Indeed, body is known through the imagination, just as the soul is known through the intellect alone or the union of soul and body is known through the senses. But he appears to say that while the imagination is a useful aid, it is not a necessary one, for such notions can also be known "by the intellect alone." When it comes to the idea of extension, or of body in general, this is indeed Descartes' final position, and he is committed to this position for the reason given in the previous section. But what the passage leaves open, and what requires further investigation, is whether the imagination is a necessary aid in mathematics. To anticipate, Descartes thinks the imagination *is* necessary for forming distinct ideas of geometrical figures and for demonstrating theorems concerning them, for reasons that will become apparent below. Suffice to note here that Descartes thinks there is an important relation between the distinct idea of extension and the ideas of mathematical objects that we form using the imagination. The latter are instrumental in our efforts to attain the former. The study of mathematics, insofar as it exercises the imagination, can aid us in forming a clear and distinct idea of body or corporeal nature. As we shall see, this is very similar to the view expressed in Plato's metaphor of the divided line, that mathematical thinking provides a stepping stone to a first principle of knowledge.

231

The other main text on the relation between mathematics and the imagination is the Fifth Meditation. Whereas in the letter to Elizabeth Descartes explicitly affirms the role of the imagination in forming distinct ideas of corporeal nature, in the Fifth Meditation we see him taking this assumption for granted and using it to enlighten his meditator. The beginning of this meditation is devoted to further clarifying our innate idea of body. Descartes had announced in the Synopsis that we would develop a distinct concept of body in stages, and that this would occur in the Second, Fifth, and Sixth Meditations (AT 7: 13; CSM 2: 9). The main achievement of this stage is the discovery that the essence of body is to be understood in purely geometrical terms as extension in three dimensions or what geometers call "continuous quantity." What is remarkable, especially to a meditator who has learned to withdraw from the senses and the sensory images they elicit, is that Descartes presents this discovery using the language of the imagination: "Quantity, for example, or 'continuous' quantity as the philosophers commonly call it, is something I *distinctly imagine*. That is, I *distinctly imagine* the extension of the quantity (or rather of the thing which is quantified) in length, breadth and depth" (AT 7: 63; CSM 2: 44, emphasis added). The locution "distinctly imagine" (*distincte imaginor*) is quite striking, and casts Descartes' official doctrine of clear and distinct perception in a new light. On standard readings of Cartesian epistemology, such perceptions fall under the sole purview of the pure intellect, but here, only a few paragraphs after enunciating this doctrine in the Fourth Meditation, Descartes allows that the imagination is capable of distinct cognitions as well.

Descartes' appeal to the imagination does not end with this last citation. In the next two paragraphs of this passage he introduces a theory of "true and immutable natures or essences" that makes further reference to the imagination in relation to our ability to conceive mathematical figures. Using language that is clearly designed to invoke the Platonic theory of recollection, he claims to discover within his mind various truths that are "so much in harmony with my nature, that . . . it seems that I am not so much learning something new as remembering what I knew before; or it seems like noticing for the first time things which were long present within me although I had never turned my mental gaze on them before" (AT 7: 63–4; CSM 2: 44). As a Christian, Descartes could not abide Plato's view that the soul existed prior to being incarnated in this body, but he does accept Plato's doctrine of innate ideas, and this passage contains one of his most eloquent affirmations of it. The problem, as we shall see, is that we tend to think of Cartesian innate ideas as purely intellectual in character. The reader is thus unprepared for what Descartes proceeds to say next. Among the items he "recollects" are ideas of things such as a triangle, which are not invented but have their own "true and immutable natures":

> When, for example, I *imagine* a triangle, even if perhaps no such figure exists, or has ever existed, anywhere outside my thought, there is still a determinate nature, or essence, or form of the triangle which is immutable and eternal, and not invented by me or dependent on my mind. This is clear from the fact that various properties can be demonstrated of the triangle, for example that its three angles equal two right angles, that its greatest side subtends its greatest angle, and the like; and since these properties are ones which I now clearly recognize whether I want to or not, even if I never thought of them at all when I previously *imagined* the triangle, it follows that they cannot have been invented by me. (AT 7: 64; CSM 2: 44–5, emphasis added)

This is an especially rich passage, but I would like to focus on one main aspect of it: Descartes speaks twice here of "imagining" a triangle. He is using the language of the imagination self-consciously in the context of distinct ideas – ideas of geometrical figures no less, which he typically upholds as paradigmatically distinct. This is remarkable, since he (and the rationalist tradition generally) often treats the imagination as a faculty of invention, and yet one of the points he stresses here is that a triangle is not something invented. Rather than inventing geometrical figures and their properties, the imagination appears to play an essential role in their discovery. Moreover, Descartes would seem to hold not only that we do, as a matter of fact, use the imagination to contemplate mathematical figures, but that we *must* if we are to cogitate them distinctly. The imagination is presented as a necessary aid to the intellect, rather than merely an incidental or dispensable one.

One does not have to speculate very hard to understand why Descartes thinks that the imagination is necessary in geometry. Euclidean geometry in particular relies heavily on diagrams, constructions, symbols, and other sorts of devices that require sensible things or their imaginary counterparts. One might try to dismiss these as mere aids to the intellect that geometry could do without. But this is likely because one is accustomed to thinking of geometry in terms of contemporary axiomatic systems, which are purely formal. Despite appearances, Euclidean geometry is not such a system. Indeed, the eighteenth-century philosopher Immanuel Kant argues that the constructions that Euclidean geometers use to demonstrate their theorems are not just aids but constitutive of the demonstrations themselves. In other words, the proof of a theorem is contained in the construction itself (see Friedman 1985). Kant's reasons for thinking this are subtle and a full exposition of them here would take us too far afield. Fortunately, we need not go that far to appreciate his insight, for the imagination is necessary not only for demonstrating Euclidean theorems but also for representing them. To take Descartes' favorite example, it is difficult to see how one could represent to oneself the theorem that the sum of the angles of a triangle is equal to two right angles without employing mental imagery of angles and lines. The theorems of geometry can of course be expressed algebraically, but even here one is relying on symbols inscribed on paper or depicted in the imagination, and if one thinks about what those symbols represent, such as in the case of the Pythagorean theorem, one must resort once again to images of mathematical objects.

It might be objected here that Euclid's geometry is not Descartes' own, and so even if the imagination were necessary to the former, it need not be necessary to the latter. It is of course true that analytic geometry, which Descartes invented, is very different from ancient geometry. Whereas Euclid is concerned with static truths and with deriving theorems from axioms and postulates that are taken as given, Descartes' geometry is dynamic and concerned with solving problems. But, as it turns out, diagrams are just as essential to analytic geometry, as Descartes conceived it, as they and other such items are to Euclidean geometry. Descartes solves mathematical problems by using geometric lines drawn on paper (using complex compasses and other instruments that he designed for this purpose) to represent abstract magnitudes. Moreover, despite the revolutionary character of his own geometry, Descartes tends in his metaphysical writings to appeal to Euclidean examples, likely because those were the ones most familiar to his readers.

233

So, again, it is not difficult to see why Descartes found the imagination necessary in geometry. What is more difficult to grasp, and what is more important to get to the bottom of, is why, as he tells Elizabeth, "the study of mathematics, which exercises mainly the imagination in the consideration of shapes and motions, accustoms us to form very distinct notions of body." How exactly can the study of mathematics, insofar as it involves the imagination, help us to form a distinct notion of body, especially since Descartes tends to regard the imagination as a hindrance to distinct perception? As we have seen, Descartes is prepared to say that some of our imaginings in mathematics are already distinct, at least to a degree. How can those in turn enable us to attain an even more distinct notion of body? Unfortunately, Descartes does not address these questions directly and we have exhausted all of the main passages among his mature writings on the role of the imagination in mathematics. But he does leave one important clue.

Descartes closes the Fifth Meditation and begins the Sixth with a refrain that is often ignored but provides the key to his philosophy of mathematics. He asserts that the object or subject matter of pure mathematics is corporeal nature or the material universe as a whole (AT 7: 71; CSM 2: 50). This means that whenever we are engaged in pure mathematics, most notably geometry, the intentional object of our thought is always extension. Descartes later amplifies on this theme in response to a question about the *Meditations*. He reportedly tells a former student that physics and mathematics share the same object, but regard this object in different ways: whereas physics regards extension as actual, mathematics regards it as merely possible (AT 5: 160; CSMK 3: 343). If we put these remarks together with the claim to Elizabeth just cited, we find that Descartes is committed to a position highly reminiscent of Plato's in the Divided Line. Recall that Plato maintains that mathematics and understanding have the same objects, but regard these objects in different ways and with varying degrees of clarity. Mathematics qualifies as a form of knowledge but insofar as it involves the imagination (and relies on unproven hypotheses) it constitutes a lower form of cognition than understanding. Nevertheless, mathematics can serve as a stepping stone to understanding. Similarly, Descartes thinks that physics and mathematics share the same object, but regard this object in different ways. Mathematical cognition is distinct, but insofar as it involves the imagination, it is less distinct than a purely intellectual apprehension of extension. Nevertheless, the distinct imaginings that are possible in mathematics can serve as stepping stones to this higher form of cognition. The similarities here are striking and promise to provide answers to the questions raised in the previous paragraph. Before pursuing those questions further, however, let us first say more about the object of Cartesian geometry and about the status of geometrical objects. This will clarify the similarities between Descartes and Plato's philosophies of mathematics, but also will reveal one important respect in which they diverge.

What does it mean to say that pure mathematics, most notably geometry, takes extension as its intentional object? And why does Descartes hold this view? In answering these questions one must start from the fact that as a physicist, Descartes is famous for having "geometricized" nature (i.e., for introducing a revolutionary conception of matter in terms of geometrical extension alone). As he asserts in the passage cited above from the beginning of the Fifth Meditation, matter is nothing more than extension in three dimensions: length, breadth, and depth. So the reason Descartes maintains that geometry takes corporeal nature or matter as its object is because he conceives matter as geometrical extension.

This point immediately raises a further issue about the ontological status of geometrical objects. If matter is to be understood in geometrical terms, does this mean that there are triangles, planes, and spheres existing in nature? Surprisingly, the answer is no. Indeed, all three rationalists addressed in this chapter deny that there are any perfect geometrical objects in the world. Plato does so on the grounds that things in the sensible, material world are fleeting and in a constant state of flux, whereas mathematics objects are eternal and immutable. Descartes' reasons for banishing geometrical objects from nature are more complicated. He sometimes appeals to empirical considerations, noting, for example, that there are no two-dimensional objects in the world (which rules out plane figures) and also no objects with perfectly straight lines (ruling out solid figures too), at least among the macroscopic objects of our everyday experience (AT 7: 381–2; CSM 2: 262). But Descartes also has deeper motivations stemming from his radically new conception of corporeal nature. One of the most important consequences of this view is that all physical objects, regardless of their sensible and accidental differences, have the same essence, namely extension. Contrary to the traditional Aristotelian conception of the universe, this means that there are no natural kinds: a tiger, for example, does not have a distinct essence from, say, a dandelion. Similarly, a triangular-shaped body does not have an essence that is distinct in kind from that of a square-shaped body. They are all purely extended things whose differences are to be cashed out mechanically (i.e., in terms of differences in size, shape, position, etc.) and not essentially. The irony of Descartes' geometrical conception of matter is that it precludes the possibility of there being any true geometrical objects in nature.

One might object at this point by noting that in the passage from the Fifth Meditation Descartes does say that a triangle has its own "true and immutable nature, essence, or form." But what does this mean exactly? It cannot mean that triangles exist in the world and have their own essence, for the reasons already given. Indeed, in the same passage, Descartes says that geometrical objects have true and immutable natures "even though they may not exist anywhere outside me." Given the Platonic language of this passage, some commentators have taken Descartes to be endorsing a species of Platonic realism: on this view, geometrical figures subsist in a third realm, beyond the mind and beyond the physical world (see Kenny 1970). But this cannot be right either, given Descartes' assertion that extension is the object of pure mathematics. When contemplating a triangle, the intentional object of our thought is the extended universe, not third-realm entities that subsist outside the extended universe.

To say something more positive about Descartes' assertion in the Fifth Meditation, we must return to our initial query: what does it mean to say that extension is the object of geometry? As we have seen, it does not mean that there are genuine geometrical objects in nature to serve as the intentional objects of our ideas. Although we often speak of the idea *of* a triangle as opposed, say, to the idea *of* square, we should not be misled by these genitive expressions to suppose that there is a distinct object in each case. The so-called ideas of triangle and square are both ideas *of* the extended universe. Descartes is not always clear about how to count or individuate ideas, but if we use the

235

intentional object as our guide – counting something as a discrete idea if and only if it takes a discrete object – then there is only one idea in geometry, again, the idea of extension. However, by using the imagination, this one idea can be ramified in various ways, which is just to say that we can associate different corporeal images with it. When we use one sort of image we call it the "idea of square," whereas when we use another we call it the "idea of triangle." But again there is only one idea here, strictly speaking. This idea can be more or less distinct. Whenever we use the imagination to apprehend extension then this idea is to some degree confused, but Descartes thinks this idea can also be perceived perfectly distinctly through the intellect alone.

Given this setup, the claim that a triangle has its own true and immutable nature or essence must be analyzed very carefully. Part of what this means, as Descartes tells us explicitly, is that we can demonstrate various "properties" or theorems of a triangle, such as that the sum of its angles is equal to two right angles. These properties differ from the ones that can be demonstrated of, say, a square. But what is it to "demonstrate" properties of a geometrical figure? As already discussed, a geometrical demonstration for Descartes is not a formal proof but a construction that one produces either by using the imagination, or by manipulating compasses and physical diagrams in the world. But this notion of demonstration is perfectly compatible with the view that there is only one object or essence here – viz., material extension – that is being regarded in different ways via the imagination. A triangle is not a real entity in the world nor even in Platonic Heaven. It is simply material extension itself regarded in a certain way. This means that the truths demonstrated in geometry are all truths *about* the whole of material extension. Although such demonstrations involve the imagination, and thus are not perfectly distinct, they are grounded in a perfectly distinct conception of body as pure extension.

Let us return now to the question of how mathematical cognition, with its use of the imagination, can serve as a stepping stone to a perfectly distinct perception of body. The main point is that when studying geometry we are already regarding extension in a very distinct manner. Pure mathematics takes as its object corporeal nature, which it "distinctly imagines." So it is only a short cognitive step from this way of perceiving extension to a perfectly distinct perception. Like Plato, Descartes wants mathematical cognition to qualify as one of the paradigms of certainty and knowledge, even if it falls short of perfect certainty or the highest form of knowledge. Insofar as it relies on the imagination, mathematical cognition can never be perfectly distinct, but it can come very close. We should think of clarity and distinctness as admitting of degrees on a continuous scale, with our ordinary sense perceptions on the lowest end of the scale and the ideas of God, soul, and body at the highest end, constituting perfectly distinct perceptions. Mathematical cognition would then fall just below this high water mark within a range that can be more or less distinct. If mathematical cognition is as close to perfect distinctness as I claim, while still falling short, it would seem that there must be a way of recognizing the difference. Descartes has the resources for doing this. In the Fourth Meditation and elsewhere, he says that clear and distinct perceptions – and here I take him to mean *perfectly* distinct perceptions – compel our assent (AT 7: 58–9; CSM 2: 41). Inasmuch as they involve the imagination, acts of mathematical cognition would not compel our assent in this way, though they would incline it very strongly.

This explanation answers the main questions that concerned us above, though one still might wonder what specific role the imagination plays in enabling us to form a distinct perception of corporeal nature. Keep in mind, however, that it is not the imagination per se that aids us but, as Descartes tells Elizabeth, the study of mathematics. Nevertheless, we can still speak meaningfully of the role of the imagination here, so long as we think of the imagination as being controlled and purified by the study of mathematics. As Malebranche says, geometry gives the mind "the skill to control the imagination and to draw from it all the help it can give; . . . a controlled imagination sustains the mind's perception and attention" (OC 2: 278; Mal: 429). To understand the imagination's role, recall some of the main points above. We noted that absolutely pure perceptions are rare and fleeting. As embodied creatures, we spend the bulk of our cognitive life trafficking in sensory images. Thus, to attain a purely intellectual conception of body (or, similarly, of mind and God), we must start from a state of confusion and work upwards. This is where the imagination comes into play. The imagination is normally a source of confusion, which explains why rationalists like Descartes typically disparage it. But in geometry the imagination can be controlled and to some extent "purified." To see how this works, let's consider an example. Suppose that one sees a plastic beach ball on a sandy stretch of coastline. Our sensory grasp of such a scene of course does not divide neatly into discrete representations: we do not have one sensation of the beach ball, another of the sand beneath it, yet another of the sound of the waves, etc. Our sensory experience typically is just one "blooming, buzzing confusion," to use William James' choice phrase. We see the color and shape of the beach ball, feel the heat of the sun, smell the misty brine in the air, etc. – *all at the same time*. The imagination sometimes mimics the senses such that what we imagine is just as confused as what we sense, but it can also be more selectively focused. The imagination is subject to the will and thus can be directed to form images that suit the mind's own purposes. This requires effort. Indeed, Descartes sometimes distinguishes the imagination from the intellect proper by noting that the former "requires a peculiar effort of mind" (AT 7: 72–3; CSM 2: 51). But the payoff of this effort is an imagination that is better able to aid the intellect. In the example just discussed, the will can direct the imagination to produce an image of the beach ball in which its size and shape are accentuated, and in which the qualitative features of our sensory experience are largely eliminated. By its very nature, the imagination tends to favor the visual sense, at the expense of the other four senses, which is one reason it is so useful in geometry. All of the geometric properties of bodies – size, shape, and position – can be represented visually but cannot be tasted, smelled, or heard (though they are amenable to the sense of touch). Although color and shading are necessary for delineating shapes even in the imagination, one can represent geometric figures in the imagination using very thin lines against a contrasting background. In this way, the imagination can be "purified" of most, if not all, of the purely qualitative properties present in sense experience, and this process brings us closer to a purely intellectual perception of extension.

We have seen now how the imagination, as employed in geometry, provides a stepping stone to a clear and distinct idea of extension, but how does it provide a stepping stone to a *first principle*? Can the analogy with Plato be consummated on this last point? I think it can, once one appreciates what first principles are for Descartes. Plato thinks there are many first principles, that is, many forms: the Form of triangle, the Form of pyramid, etc. (though he sometimes privileges the Form of the Good). But Descartes rejects Platonic Forms both because they are ontologically extravagant and, as we have seen, because he thinks that all of geometry takes a single object – the extended universe. The first principles of Descartes' system are not Forms but clear and distinct ideas, to wit, the clear and distinct ideas of mind (or thought), body (or extension), and God. These ideas serve as first principles in the sense that they give us knowledge of the essences of things that exist in the Cartesian universe. The clear and distinct idea of body as pure extension, in particular, grounds Descartes' revolutionary anti-Aristotelian physics. This idea enables him to reject the scholastico-Aristotelian appeal to teleology and to various occult qualities, and to explain all physical phenomena solely in terms of differences in motion among the parts of matter.

Like Plato, Descartes devises a special method for attaining the first principles of knowledge – a method he calls "analysis." One commentator has noted an interesting similarity between Descartes' analytic method and Platonic dialectic: in both cases, one begins with a conjecture, considers objections to that conjecture, and then revises the conjecture in the manner suggested by the objections (Curley 1986: 157). Perhaps even more striking, Descartes contrasts analysis with the Euclidean method of starting from axioms, definitions, and postulates, and then deriving theorems from them. He says that the latter is ill-suited to metaphysics, where the first principles or "primary notions" (*primae notions*) cannot be taken for granted but are discovered last (AT 7: 156–7; CSM 2: 111). In keeping with Platonic dialectic, then, Cartesian analysis involves "reasoning up" to a first principle. Once we attain knowledge of first principles, however, Descartes thinks we can, as Plato maintains, reason back down from them in the manner of a geometrical demonstration (*Republic* 511bc).

Let us complete our discussion of Descartes by addressing a couple of closely related objections to the claims above. These objections find their source in a sharp distinction that Descartes draws in his later work between imagination and "pure intellection." It is often assumed that because of this distinction, the imagination cannot play any role in achieving clear and distinct perceptions, which of course runs contrary to my main thesis. In setting forth this distinction in a passage from the Sixth Meditation, Descartes also makes a few remarks about mathematical cognition that are often taken to mean that we can clearly and distinctly understand a geometrical figure such as a triangle without the aid of the imagination. I think this reading is mistaken, and in what follows I defend an alternative interpretation of the passage in question.

Descartes opens the Sixth Meditation by announcing that one of the remaining tasks of his epistemological project is to determine whether the material universe exists. He has already discovered that the nature of matter is pure extension, but he has yet to establish its existence. He claims to know that it is at least capable of existing, for he clearly and distinctly perceives that corporeal nature is the object of pure mathematics, and whatever he clearly and distinctly perceives can be created by God. But Descartes also wonders whether our manner of studying mathematics and corporeal nature might reveal something further. Doesn't the fact that we use our faculty of imagination to contemplate material things demonstrate that they exist? For what is the imagination if not the power of the mind to apply itself to the body or, as he specifies elsewhere, to images depicted on the brain? (AT 7: 71–2; CSM 2: 50).

To answer these questions, Descartes proposes to examine the difference between the imagination and the pure understanding, the goal being to determine whether the faculty of imagination does require something corporeal for its operation. This brings us to the main passage of interest for our purposes. Descartes begins to explain the difference between imagination and pure intellection by using geometrical examples:

> When I imagine a triangle, for example, I do not merely understand that it is a figure bounded by three lines, but at the same time I also see the three lines with my mind's eye as if they were present before me; and this is what I call imagining. But if I want to think of a chiliagon, although I understand that it is a figure consisting of a thousand sides just as well as I understand the triangle to be a three-sided figure, I do not in the same way imagine the thousand sides or see them as if they were present before me. It is true that since I am in the habit of imagining something whenever I think of a corporeal thing, I may construct in my mind a confused representation of some figure; but it is clear that this is not a chiliagon. For it differs in no way from the representation I should form if I were thinking of a myriagon, or any figure with very many sides. Moreover, such a representation is useless for recognizing the properties that distinguish a chiliagon from other polygons. But suppose I am dealing with a pentagon: I can of course understand the figure of a pentagon, just as I can the figure of a chiliagon, without the help of the imagination; but I can also imagine a pentagon, by applying my mind's eye to its five sides and the area contained within them. And in doing this I notice quite clearly that imagination requires a peculiar effort of mind that is not required for understanding; this additional effort of mind clearly shows the difference between imagination and pure understanding. (AT 7: 72–3; CSM 2: 50–1)

This passage is often taken to show that we can clearly and distinctly understand geometrical objects such as a chiliagon without the use of the imagination. Indeed, Descartes appears to say that some figures, such as a chiliagon, cannot be represented by the imagination precisely because of their complex nature. Thus, to represent the difference between two complex figures, such as a chiliagon and a myriagon, we must resort to the pure intellect.

While this surface reading is tempting, we must be careful not to read too much into the passage. As one commentator has noted, Descartes is not necessarily saying that the imagination is inessential to the cognition of geometrical objects (Sepper 1996: 249–50). On the contrary, he says that even in the case of a chiliagon one may construct a confused representation in the imagination. The "habit of imagining something whenever I think of a corporeal thing" may be one that cannot be relinquished, at least when it comes to mathematics. It also helps to consider here that this entire discussion is part of a larger investigation of whether "the distinct idea of corporeal nature *which I find in my imagination* can provide any basis for a necessary inference that some body exists" (AT 7: 73; CSM 2: 51, emphasis added). This is important because it suggests that Descartes may not be distinguishing a pure intellection of a chiliagon from an imagistic representation of the same figure. Rather, he may be distinguishing two aspects of a single *distinct imagining* – an intellectual aspect and an imagistic aspect. This reading is supported by the first line of the passage, where Descartes distinguishes what he clearly and distinctly "understands" with his intellect when he "imagines a triangle" from the imagistic aspect of this same act of cognition. Of course, he wants to draw an important contrast between the case of the triangle

239

and that of a chiliagon, but the contrast is just this: in the latter case, we are unable to represent all of the sides of a chiliagon imagistically. But again this is not to deny the necessity of the imagination in cognizing a chiliagon or any other figure.

It is also important to keep in mind that, in contrasting these two cases, Descartes is focusing on one very narrow dimension of the imagination: the ability to represent all the sides of a figure. But there are other ways to imagine geometrical objects. In thinking about a chiliagon, for example, one might imagine an algebraic formula or, more crudely, the words "thousand-sided polygon." Indeed, it is difficult to see how one could think about a geometric figure without employing at least one of these forms of imagination. Descartes says that, in the case of a chiliagon, the confused representation that we form with our imagination of a multi-sided figure is "useless for recognizing the properties" that distinguish it from other polygons such as a myriagon – the suggestion being that we might use the same confused representation in both cases. But notice that the other forms of imagination just mentioned would not be useless; on the contrary, they would allow us to distinguish the properties of different figures and thus the figures themselves.

Perhaps the most important consideration here concerns what the words "chiliagon," "triangle," "pentagon," and "myriagon" refer to in the passage. If, as I argued earlier, all of geometry takes corporeal nature as its object, then the so-called "idea of chiliagon" just is the idea of extension, and likewise for the "idea of myriagon," etc. Again, geometrical objects are not discrete objects of thought distinct from extension. Rather, they just are the material universe itself, regarded in different ways. Thus, when Descartes says in this passage that we can understand the figure of a chiliagon without the help of the imagination, he might just be referring to a perfectly distinct idea of extension to which mathematical cognition serves as a stepping stone. He calls this the idea of "chiliagon" rather than, say, the idea of "myriagon," because he is presuming that we arrived at our first principle in this instance by imagining the words "thousand-sided closed plane figure." This is a simplification, of course. The cognitive process by which we arrive at a perfectly distinct idea of extension would typically be more complex. We might start by imagining polygons with various sizes and shapes, and with various numbers of sides and angles. We might progress from there to imagining one or more of the properties of these various polygons and, then, if we seize upon some particular figure, to an algebraic formula. As compared with earlier stages in this process, this imagined formula would be largely purified of sensory imagery and thus be very distinct – just shy of the perfect distinctness of a purely intellectual perception of extension, to which it would provide an easy stepping stone. Once we reach this first principle, the cognitive processes that enabled us to achieve it could be discarded. Still, it would be natural to designate this first principle "the idea of chiliagon" or "idea of myriagon," etc., depending on the particular distinct imaginings that led us there.

Malebranche on the Role of the Imagination in Mathematical Cognition

As a strategy for uncovering Descartes' account of mathematical cognition and the role played by the imagination, we first looked to two other related issues: (1) the object of geometry and (2) the ontological status of geometrical objects. Let us employ the same strategy with Malebranche. Malebranche appears to diverge from Descartes on both of these issues and, on the second, to move closer to Plato. His "official position" also seems to be that the imagination is merely an aid to the intellect in mathematics and is not constitutive of mathematical thinking. But when examined closely, and pushed to its limits, Malebranche's position comes very close to Descartes'. The gap between them reduces to different accounts of the ontology of ideas, not in any basic disagreement about the nature of geometrical cognition or the status of geometrical objects.

Malebranche maintains that the object of geometry is not actual extension, as on Descartes' view, but the *idea* of extension (OC 6: 68–9, 201; 9: 930, 942, 1058). The explanation for this shift is that Malebranche has a very different account of the ontology of ideas. Whereas Cartesian ideas are modes of human minds, Malebranche locates ideas in the mind of God. This is one of the main tenets of "Vision in God" (i.e., his theory that we see all material things in the mind of God by means of the idea of extension that he contains and that serves as the model or archetype for the creation of the extended universe). Although Malebranche has a very different account of the locus of ideas, the difference between him and Descartes on the object of geometry may be only verbal. After all, both Descartes and Malebranche embrace representationalism, which holds that all cognition is mediated through ideas. So the immediate object of thought for both philosophers is always an idea. Given this, Descartes could agree with Malebranche that the *immediate* object of geometry is the idea of extension. On the other hand, ideas give us knowledge of things, not immediately but mediately. So the idea of extension gives us knowledge of the nature of the extended universe. Given this, Malebranche could agree with Descartes that the (mediate) object of geometry is material extension. I suspect that he has two reasons for *not* saying this, even though it is consistent with his view. First, he wants to emphasize the priority of the idea of extension over material extension. Malebranche maintains that God consults this idea or archetype in creating the world; thus material things must conform to it, rather than the other way around. Second, and more importantly, he is keen to stress that bodies cannot be the objects of thought in the sense of being "present" to the mind. Malebranche affirms that in order for something to be known it must be cognitively present. In his later philosophy, this notion of presence is analyzed causally. As noted earlier, Malebranche holds that God is the only genuine cause. Indeed, in virtue of being in God, ideas cause our perceptions of them. Cartesian bodies cannot be present to the mind in this sense because they are inert and without causal efficacy. They are therefore "unintelligible" in themselves. In contrast, the idea of extension, or what Malebranche sometimes calls "intelligible extension," can be present to the mind because it acts on the mind, affecting it in different ways.

If the object of geometry is intelligible extension, what consequences does this have for the ontological status of geometrical figures? Like Plato and Descartes before him, Malebranche must deny that there are perfect geometrical figures in nature, and he must do so for the same reason as Descartes. The whole essence of matter is extension. There are not individual essences for pyramids and cubes, as would be required if there were such perfect objects in nature. But where does Malebranche stand on the issue of whether geometrical figures enjoy third-realm status? As we have seen, Descartes and

Plato differ on this important question. Malebranche is certainly more sympathetic to Plato's ontology of Forms than Descartes. Indeed, by putting ideas in God, and regarding them as the essences of things, Malebranche saw himself as resurrecting a type of Platonism, or Neoplatonism, over and against Descartes' view that ideas are modes of finite minds. The important question is whether he thought there were discrete ideas of geometrical figures in God, or whether he countenanced a single idea of extension.

Malebranche certainly flirts with the former, and many commentators have taken it for granted that the divine intellect is populated with an infinite number of mathematical ideas. For one thing, he is happy to speak at times of the general idea of a circle or square, etc., or of the "intelligible triangle" (OC 3: 130; Mal: 614). At one place, he even says that there are "as many infinite numbers of ideas as there are different figures; consequently, since there is an infinite number of different figures, [there must be] an infinity of infinite numbers of ideas" (OC 1: 430; Mal: 227). Since all ideas are in God, if there were discrete mathematical ideas, they would reside there too. Malebranche also holds a very powerful principle of intentionality, which states that if I can think of something it must exist, not necessarily as an object in the world, but at least as an idea. So, if I can think of triangle, then it would seem to follow from the principle of intentionality that it exists as a discrete idea in the divine intellect. Malebranche sometimes puts this point by saying that he "perceives realities," and if these realities were nothing, then he would not be thinking:

> I am thinking of a variety of things: of a number, of a circle, of a house, of such and such beings, of being. Thus, all these things exist, at least while I think of them. Certainly, when I think of a circle, of a number, of being or of infinity, of a particular finite being, I perceive realities. For if the circle I perceived were nothing, in thinking of it I would be thinking of nothing. Thus, I would be thinking and not thinking at the same time. Yet the circle I perceive has properties that no other figure has. Therefore this circle exists while I am thinking of it, because nothingness has no properties and one nothingness cannot be different from another nothingness. (OC 12: 35; JS: 8)

The assertion that the circle one conceives has properties which no other figure has is very similar to Descartes' claim in the Fifth Meditation that a triangle has a true and immutable nature, as is shown by the fact that various properties can be demonstrated of it. The important question, however, is whether he will draw a conclusion here that I argued Descartes would not, namely that geometrical objects are extra-mental entities – specifically, ideas in the divine intellect.

Although Malebranche toys with allowing multiple ideas of figures, I do not think this can constitute his final position. One reason for this is that he is committed to holding that the object of geometry is "nothing other . . . than intelligible extension" (OC 6: 69), a claim he repeats in several places (see OC 6: 201; 9: 930, 942, 1058). How then can there be discrete ideas of geometrical figures in God that serve as intentional objects? If that were true, he should say that the objects of geometry are diverse – indeed, infinitely many. But, in fact, he wants the object of geometry to be singular – the *whole* of intelligible extension, just as it is the whole of material extension for Descartes. Notice that this assertion is completely consistent with the principle of intentionality. All thought takes an object; in the case of geometry it happens to take a single object.

242

Nevertheless, if this position is philosophical bedrock, then he owes us an explanation of the relation between the idea of extension and the so-called "ideas" of geometrical figures of which he sometimes speaks. One place to look for an answer is in his discussion of content-containment. He says that ideas generally are "contained" in one another, with the less general nested in the more general. So, for example, the idea of God, or what he calls the idea of "being in general," contains all other ideas "in one" (OC 1: 441; Mal: 232). The general idea of extension would, in turn, contain the ideas of various geometrical figures. But how should we understand this containment metaphor? Moreover, doesn't this view still commit Malebranche to the position that there are multiple geometrical ideas in God?

Some commentators have conceived this containment relation on the model of an axiomatic system. On this view, intelligible extension serves as the "ground" for the axioms and postulates of Euclidean geometry, and ideas of geometrical figures are the theorems that can be derived from these axioms (Lennon 1980: 787). But there are several difficulties with this view. First, it violates Malebranche's assertion that intelligible extension as a whole is the intentional object of geometry. If the idea of triangle were theorematic, one could cognize it without thinking of intelligible extension and even without understanding how it can be derived from the axioms that take intelligible extension as their ground. What Malebranche needs is an analysis of the containment relation that shows how thinking of triangle just is a certain way of thinking about intelligible extension. Second, as was already noted when discussing Descartes, Cartesian geometry is concerned with solving problems using geometric constructions, not with deriving theorems from axioms. To conceive a geometrical figure, then, is to construct one within a coordinate system (see Lachterman 1989; Radner 1994: 67). Third, Malebranche enlists ideas in God to serve two different functions: to give accounts of (1) mathematical cognition and (2) sense perception. This means that intelligible extension is the object both of geometry *and* of sense perception. But as one commentator has noted, if the axiomatic interpretation were correct, then in seeing an object in nature, such as a tree, the immediate object of my thought would be a theorem, a linguistic entity. Surely, this is absurd (Radner 1994: 66).

In light of such difficulties, I would like to develop a different account of the relation between intelligible extension and the ideas of geometrical figures, one that uncovers the role of the imagination in the cognition of geometrical objects. Let us begin by considering an analogy. The problem that we are concerned with is very similar to another difficulty that Malebranche confronts more directly. As noted in the previous paragraph, Vision in God is intended as a general theory of cognition, including both mathematical thought and sense perception. This means that we not only see geometrical figures in intelligible extension but also sensible objects such as dogs and trees. But Malebranche maintained that intelligible extension is a general idea and "pure" in the sense of non-sensuous. How then are particular sensible objects "contained" in it or, to phrase it differently, how do we see particular sensible objects in intelligible extension? The answer is to be found in Malebranche's distinction between ideas and sensations, and in his account of the relation between them. As previously discussed, ideas are general entities in God and serve as the immediate objects of thought. Sensations of colors, sounds, odors, heat, pleasure, etc., on the other hand, are particular modifications of finite minds. Ideas and sensations, then, are very different kinds of entities, but Malebranche maintains that sense perception combines elements of each.

> When we perceive something sensible, two things are found in our perception: *sensation* and pure *idea*. The sensation is a modification of our soul, and it is God who causes it in us. As for the idea found in conjunction with the sensation, it is in God, and we see it because it pleases God to reveal it to us. (OC 1: 445; Mal: 234, Malebranche's emphasis)

Malebranche's view that any given sense perception is a composite of a pure idea and a sensation explains how we see particular sensible objects in God. Although the ideational component of our sense perceptions is general, the sensory component is not. It is this sensory component – specifically, color sensations – that "particularizes" and "sensualizes" intelligible extension.

> Intelligible extension becomes visible and represents a certain body in particular only by means of color, because it is only by the variety of colors that we judge the difference between the objects we see . . . If I distinguish your hand from your coat and both from the air surrounding them, this is because the sensations of light or color that I have of them are very different. (OC 12: 46–7; JS: 17)

Intelligible extension represents the whole of material extension, but it can be made to represent the size, shape, and extension of particular bodies when, as he says elsewhere, color is "projected" onto it. Color differences enable us to perceive intelligible extension as differentiated into distinct parts, with boundaries between them, just like bodies in the material world. Of course, intelligible extension itself, as it resides in God, is not really affected one way or the other by our perceptions of it. It remains general and "pure." But our sensations can lead us to perceive it in different ways.

At one point in his career, Malebranche realized that invoking color sensations to explain how we perceive sensible objects in intelligible extension presented him with a problem. Sensations are modifications of our soul, and, as he says repeatedly throughout his work, the soul itself and all of its modalities are "pure darkness" and therefore cannot enlighten us. Indeed, the underlying motivation of the theory of Vision in God is to show that the soul lacks cognitive resources of its own and utterly depends on God, via divine ideas, for its enlightenment. How then can Malebranche consistently maintain that sensations play any role in the representation of particular bodies? The answer is that in later years he modifies the theory of Vision in God by endowing ideas with causal properties. Ideas are not only the immediate objects of perception but also cause our perceptions of them. This is the doctrine of efficacious ideas, which he typically expresses by saying that intelligible extension "touches," "affects," or "modifies" the soul in different ways. The introduction of this doctrine marks a twofold shift. In addition to imbuing ideas with causal properties, Malebranche broadens the scope of his original theory of Vision in God. On the original theory, ideas figured exclusively in the intellectual side of sense perception. But on the new version, ideas are causally responsible both for the intellectual aspect of our perceptions *and* for their sensory character. This latter shift enables Malebranche to explain how sensations can play a role in the cognition of individual bodies.

It is only color that renders objects visible. It is only by the variety of colors that we see and that we distinguish the diversity of objects. Now when we see bodies, *it is the idea of extension that modifies us with diverse sensations of color*, and you remain in agreement that this idea is found only in God. *Therefore it is evident that we see in God all this variety of bodies, of which we have sensations so different*; since it is certain that we do not see objects in themselves . . . God teaches us nothing except by the efficacious application of his ideas on our souls, which find themselves penetrated, modified, and illuminated in several ways. (OC 4: 75–6, emphasis added)

We see all things in God through the efficacy of His substance, and particularly sensible things, through God's applying intelligible extension to our minds in a thousand different ways, and that thus intelligible extension contains all the perfections, or rather, all the differences of bodies due to the different sensations that the soul projects on the ideas affecting it. (OC 3: 154; Mal: 628)

Malebranche thinks it makes sense to say that we see sensible objects in intelligible extension because the latter causes our sensations, which in turn leads us to perceive intelligible extension as individuated into discrete objects.

I propose that we use Malebranche's account of how sensible objects are contained in intelligible extension as an analogy for how geometrical figures, or the so-called "ideas" of them, are contained in intelligible extension. Some such analogy is necessary for, as Malebranche makes clear in one crucial text, intelligible figures are not literally contained in intelligible extension. Rather, they are there only "potentially."

It is not that there are literally [*proprement*] intelligible figures in the intelligible spaces that we know, any more than there are *material* figures in material spaces that are entirely immobile. But, as in a block of marble, all possible figures are there potentially, and can be drawn from it by the movement or action of a chisel; likewise, all *intelligible* figures are potentially [*en puissance*] in *intelligible* extension, and are discovered there according to how this extension represents itself diversely to the soul in consequence of the general laws that God has established, and according to which he acts in us without cease. (OC 6: 208, Malebranche's emphasis)

To say that intelligible figures such as the idea of triangle are "potentially" contained in intelligible extension means that we can come to perceive intelligible extension *as* a triangle when it causally acts on our mind in a certain law-like manner. This is very similar to the way in which sensible objects are contained in intelligible extension: we perceive intelligible extension as individuated into distinct bodies when it "touches" our mind in different ways. Indeed, I would like to suggest that, in both cases, what leads us to cognize intelligible extension as a particular body or as one geometrical figure rather than another are the color sensations or color images, respectively, that it produces in us. Malebranche does not speak explicitly of the imagination in this passage, but he does invoke a provocative metaphor that is suggestive of it. At first glance, one might think that the comparison of intelligible extension to a block of marble is misleading, for he clearly wishes to deny that intelligible extension is modified in any way when we perceive it. If anything, it is the soul that is "chiseled" or modified so as to produce a perception of intelligible extension as one figure or another, in keeping with the doctrine of efficacious ideas. But the sculpture metaphor makes

245

the most sense if we view it as Malebranche's attempt to describe the *manner* in which we cognize intelligible extension when studying geometry. Geometrical cognition requires the use of the imagination and involves imagining extension *as* something that can be molded or sculpted into different shapes. The object of our thought is intelligible extension, which again is absolutely pure and general, but our perception of it is something less than absolutely pure inasmuch as it involves the imagination. This means that mathematical cognition, like sense perception, is a composite of sensory (or imaginative) and ideational components, where the idea in question is always intelligible extension. Despite this important analogy between sense perception and geometrical cognition, there is room for Malebranche to say that the latter is more distinct. As we saw in Descartes, the imagination can be refined and controlled in a way that sense perception cannot be, such that the sensory or imaginative component of our cognition recedes progressively into the background as the ideational component becomes ascendant. Indeed, Malebranche speaks at times like Descartes of imagining geometrical figures "distinctly" (OC 2: 279; Mal: 429–30).

So there is really only one idea of extended things in God, namely intelligible extension. To speak of the "ideas" of various kinds of geometrical figures, or to say that these ideas are contained in God, just means that intelligible extension can affect our mind with distinct imaginings of itself. When it affects us with one type of imagining, we call it the "idea of square"; when it affects us in a different way, we call it the "idea of circle," and so on. But again there is only one idea, one immediate object of thought. This account of how the "ideas" of figures are "contained in" intelligible extension (or in God) has several philosophical, textual, and systematic attractions.

First, I noted earlier that there can be no perfect figures in nature as this would require them to have essences distinct from extension. This also provides a reason for thinking that ideas of figures cannot be contained in intelligible extension in any but a metaphorical sense. Malebranche regards ideas in God as essences. So if there were an idea of triangle then this would mean that triangles have an essence distinct from extension. But this runs completely counter to the Cartesian dictum that all bodies have the same essence. In contrast, the view that intelligible extension is unique, and that what Malebranche calls the "ideas" of figures are simply different ways of imagining this single idea of body, preserves the Cartesian dictum.

Second, another part of my thesis, that intelligible extension produces all of our perceptions of geometrical figures by affecting the mind in different ways, squares with a more general trend in Malebranche's thought that makes intelligible extension the sole idea in God to which we have access in this life. The Augustinian theory that divine creation requires archetypes of models entails that the idea of the soul or "intelligible thought" resides in God too, but Malebranche holds that we lack access to this idea prior to shedding our mortal coil. This means that we do not have the kind of self-knowledge to which Descartes subscribed. We can know that we exist and have various perceptions, but we cannot know the nature or essence of the mind. What else is there to be known in the Cartesian universe? God, of course, and sometimes Malebranche allows himself to speak as Descartes does of an "idea of God." But strictly speaking there is no such idea, for as being in general or indeterminate being God cannot be represented by an idea. As archetypes, ideas are also of possible creatures, but God is necessary and uncreated. Malebranche maintains that we know God only through our union with him, a union that consists in him acting on us to enlighten our mind (OC 1: 449; Mal: 237). As it turns out, the only way in which he enlightens us in this life is by producing perceptions of intelligible extension. We know God not in his essential nature but in the material things that he can produce (OC 12: 51; JS: 21). Intelligible extension, then, is the object not only of geometry but also of all human cognition. Malebranche, however, wants to add the important addendum that in knowing this idea we also know God, considered in a certain way. We know God indirectly through his works or, at least, his possible works (OC 1: 442; Mal: 233).

Finally, and most significantly, my claim that geometrical cognition involves the imagination, and is therefore to some degree confused, finds strong support in remarks about the nature of human cognition generally toward the end of the *Search*. There, Malebranche suggests that all human cognition has a composite character, not just sense perception, and that this is a function of our status as embodied creatures. These remarks appear in a context in which he is outlining various aids of which the mind can make use to become more "attentive" to the truth. Although ideas in God are always present to us, in the sense of acting on our mind, the mental component of our perception distracts us from them. Indeed, our sensations, passions, and imaginings are often so strong and lively that they consume our attention, leaving no share of attention for ideas in God.

> The soul's modifications have three causes: the senses, the imagination, and the passions. Everyone knows from his own experience that instances of pleasure and pain and generally all the sensations of a rather strong nature, lively imaginings, and the stronger passions, so occupy the mind that it is incapable of attentiveness while these things are affecting it because its capacity or faculty of perceiving is then entirely exhausted by them . . .
>
> We must therefore draw this important conclusion: that all those who seriously wish to apply themselves to the search after truth must be careful to avoid as best they can all sensations that are too strong, such as loud noise, strong light, pleasure, pain, and so on; they must continuously *guard the purity of their imagination* and prevent deep traces, which continually disturb and dissipate the mind, from being formed in the brain. Finally, they must above all halt the impulses of the passions that form impressions in the body and soul so powerful that it is ordinarily next to impossible for the mind to think about anything but the objects exciting these impulses. For though *the pure ideas of truth are always present to us*, we are unable to consider them when our capacity for thought is filled by these modifications that so affect us.
>
> Nonetheless, as the soul cannot be without passions, sensation, or some other particular modification, we must make a virtue of necessity and draw even from these modifications assistance in making ourselves more attentive. But much skill and care is required in the use of these aids if they are to be of any help. Our need for them must be carefully examined, and we must use them only to the extent to which we are forced to do so by the necessity for becoming more attentive. (OC 2: 252–3; Mal: 413, emphasis added)

Malebranche begins here by noting that the mind is capable of only three kinds of modifications: sensations, passions, and imaginings. This is extremely important because in his later philosophy he uses the term "pure perceptions" to refer to our cognitions of intelligible extension and mathematical truths. But given what he says in this passage, this term must be understood very carefully. If all of our perceptions are composite in character and have as one of their constituents a sensation, passion, or imagining, then no perception can be absolutely pure or absolutely distinct. Every act of cognition is going to be confused to some degree by this mental constituent. Notwithstanding, Malebranche thinks there are measures that we can take to make our perceptions more distinct. For one, we can avoid strong sensations and passions, and "guard the purity of our imagination" – a phrase that further suggests that the imagination can provide us with cognitions that are relatively pure or relatively distinct. In the final paragraph, he notes that we can also use the mind's own modifications as aids. This seems surprising, for these are the source of the problem. But Malebranche's point is that necessity is the mother of invention: the mind cannot be without some particular sensation, passion, imagining, or other. So if the mind is to increase its attention to ideas in God, and thus render its perceptions clearer and more distinct, it must start from one of these modifications. He elaborates this last point later, noting that some of the mind's modifications are more helpful than others. Whereas our passions and senses "affect us too much and so occupy the mind's capacity that it often sees only its own sensations when it thinks it is discovering things in themselves," the imagination makes the mind "more attentive without a wasteful division of its capacity and is thus remarkably aided in clearly and distinctly perceiving objects, with the result that it is almost always to our advantage to avail ourselves of its help" (OC 2: 262; Mal: 419). To put it in Platonic terms, the imagination provides a stepping stone to intelligible extension and the various truths that can be known about it.

Conclusion

Rationalist philosophers often condemn the imagination as a source of error and confusion, and urge us to detach ourselves from it in order to attain knowledge. Notwithstanding these criticisms, rationalists as varied as Plato, Descartes, and Malebranche maintain that the imagination is necessary in mathematics. The claim here is not simply that the imagination provides a useful – albeit ultimately dispensable – aid to the intellect in mathematics, but that it is constitutive of mathematical thinking. They also hold that mathematical thinking provides a stepping stone to a higher form of cognition, to the cognition of a first principle of knowledge.

The bulk of this chapter has been devoted to showing how, according to the Cartesian rationalists, the imagination is constitutive of mathematical thinking and how such thinking provides a stepping stone to a first principle. Concerning the first issue, both Descartes and Malebranche hold that mathematics takes a single object – extension or intelligible extension. But they maintain that the imagination provides different ways of conceiving this single object (i.e., different distinct imaginings). The imagination serves to delimit (intelligible) extension in our thought, so that we cognize it as some figure or other. The imagination also plays an essential role in the conception of the properties or truths that pertain to geometrical figures.

As for the second issue, both Descartes and Malebranche recognize what many philosophers today take as self-evident, that it is extremely difficult to form a non-imagistic representation of extension. Descartes thinks that such perceptions are possible but rare, and attained only after great effort, whereas Malebranche denies that we even are capable of absolutely pure cognitions of intelligible extension. They concur, however, in thinking that the imagination, as controlled and purified by geometry, provides a stepping stone to a (relatively) pure cognition of extension. The imagination can serve this function precisely because in mathematics we are already conceiving (intelligible) extension in a very distinct manner, especially as compared with our everyday thoughts. Malebranche also holds that, unlike the mind's other modifications, the imagination leaves a greater share of attention for ideas in God. These ideas are intrinsically pure and distinct. The more attention that we can devote to them, the purer our perceptions will be.

References and Further Reading

Burnyeat, M. F. (1987). Platonism and mathematics: A prelude to discussion. In Andreas Graeser (ed.), *Mathematics and Metaphysics in Aristotle* (pp. 213–40). Bern: Paul Haupt.

Curley, Edwin (1986). Analysis in the *Meditations*: The quest for clear and distinct ideas. In Amélie Rorty (ed.), *Essays on Descartes' Meditations* (pp. 153–76). Los Angeles: University of California Press.

Friedman, Michael (1985). Kant's theory of geometry. *Philosophical Review*, 94 (4), 455–506.

Kenny, Anthony (1970). The Cartesian circle and the eternal truths. *Journal of Philosophy*, 67, 685–700.

Lachterman, David (1989). *Ethics of Geometry: A Genealogy of Modernity*. New York: Routledge.

Lennon, Thomas (1980). Philosophical Commentary. In Mal (1980).

Nolan, Lawrence (1997). The ontological status of Cartesian natures. *Pacific Philosophical Quarterly*, 78, 169–94.

—— (1998). Descartes' theory of universals. *Philosophical Studies*, 89, 161–80.

Pappas, Nickolas (1998). *Plato and the Republic*. New York: Routledge.

Plato (1992). *Republic* (G. M. A. Grube, trans., C. D. C. Reeve, ed.). Indianapolis, IN: Hackett.

Radner, Daisie (1994). Malebranche and the individuation of perceptual objects. In Kenneth F. Barber and Jorge J. E. Gracia (eds.), *Individuation and Identity in Early Modern Philosophy: Descartes to Kant* (pp. 59–72). New York: State University of New York Press.

Sepper, D. L. (1996). *Descartes's Imagination: Proportion, Images, and the Activity of Thinking*. Los Angeles: University of California Press.

13

Idealism and Cartesian Motion

ALICE SOWAAL

Descartes famously claimed that he could explain the world in terms of matter in motion:

> All the properties which we clearly perceive in [the matter existing in the entire universe] are reducible to its divisibility and consequent mobility in respect of its parts, and its resulting capacity to be affected in all the ways which we perceive as being derivable from the movement of the parts. (*Principles* 2: 23; AT 8A: 52–3; CSM 1: 232)

With this, he repeats the mantra of seventeenth-century science. Like others in the period inspired by a renewed interest in Plato's *Timaeus*, he sought to interpret the world in a purely quantitative manner. Mathematics was understood to be the language of the universe, thus the tool that should be employed when describing all physical change. The fundamental questions and answers altered: instead of "Why does *x* happen?" natural philosophers asked "How does *x* happen?" Answers to this new question would no longer be given in terms of real qualities, hylomorphic unities of substantial forms and prime matter, or "natural tendencies" of such beings, entities embedded in scholastic theories. In their place, the new natural philosophers appealed to pieces of matter in motion to explain changes, like those involved in acceleration, collision, and the paths of projectiles. With this shift, theories of matter and its affections took center stage in metaphysical explanations of the world, and were to be completely separate from theories about or involving that which was qualitative and mentalistic (Burtt 1924: 72–4).

The task of the metaphysician, then, was to give an ontology of matter that was as "really distinct" from an ontology of mind as the two substances – matter and mind – were themselves understood to be. Thus, Descartes developed his theory of material substance, which mirrored his theory of mental substance in that both accounts involve an ontology of substances, attributes, and modes. On this view, the attributes of matter and mind are extension and thinking, respectively. The modes of body are size, shape, surface, position, and motion, all of which can be accounted for mathematically; the modes of mind are individual thoughts. All change in the universe must be explained in terms of the modes of body, the new explanatory tools. Of all the modes, the early modern natural scientists focused their attention on motion. It is evident that

Descartes' account of motion played an important role in this movement, for it was closely attended to by the students of his work, most notably, Leibniz, Spinoza, and Newton, all of whom wrote detailed analyses of it (Ariew and Garber 1989; Hall and Hall 1962; Curley 1985).

Descartes' enthusiasm about this new science has been appreciated and is well documented. However, the details of his contribution are generally considered to be riddled with problems. A review of these problems, as well as the range of solutions to them that have been proposed, suggests that, if Descartes is read as a kind of idealist about both the reality of motion and the substantiality of bodies, his views on these issues not only cohere with those of the early modern rationalist tradition, but also these problems are resolved.

Cartesian Motion

Descartes moves away from the Aristotelian theory of motion, according to which there are as many kinds of motion as there are kinds of change, to discuss both the local motion of individual bodies and the quantity of motion in the universe. The quantity of motion is kept constant by God, who is its ultimate cause:

> In the beginning [in his omnipotence] [God] created matter, along with its motion and rest; and now, merely by his regular concurrence, he preserves the same amount of motion and rest in the material universe as he put there in the beginning. (*Principles* 2: 36; AT 8A: 61; CSM 1: 240)

Descartes defines "local motion" as

> the transfer of one piece of matter, or one body, from the vicinity of the other bodies which are in immediate contact with it, and which are regarded as being at rest, to the vicinity of other bodies. By "one body" or "one piece of matter" I mean whatever is transferred at a given time, even though this may in fact consist of many parts which have different motions relative to each other. (*Principles* 2: 25; AT 8A: 56; CSM 2: 53–4)

Here, Descartes gives a purely kinematic definition, that is, one that does not appeal to forces of any kind. Indeed, Descartes is attempting to capture the nature of local motion separately from its causes, a distinction he understood the scholastics to have collapsed. For this reason, he defines "local motion" geometrically: a body is in motion when it is transferred from one neighborhood, which is regarded as being at rest, to another neighborhood (Gabbey 1980; Garber 1992: 160; Gueroult 1983). This definition of motion can be represented diagramatically, at T_1 and T_2 (figure 13.1).

Consider the body F. Given Descartes' definition of "motion," it is in motion from T_1 to T_2 because when we regard its neighborhood – bodies A, B, C, G, K, J, I, and E – as being at rest, we find that F changes its neighborhood over that time, for at T_2 F is no longer surrounded by A or I, but by new bodies, D and L, in addition to bodies from the previous neighborhood, B, C, G, K, and E. Of course, given the way the definition reads, we can regard F as being at rest and arrive at a very different result: each of the

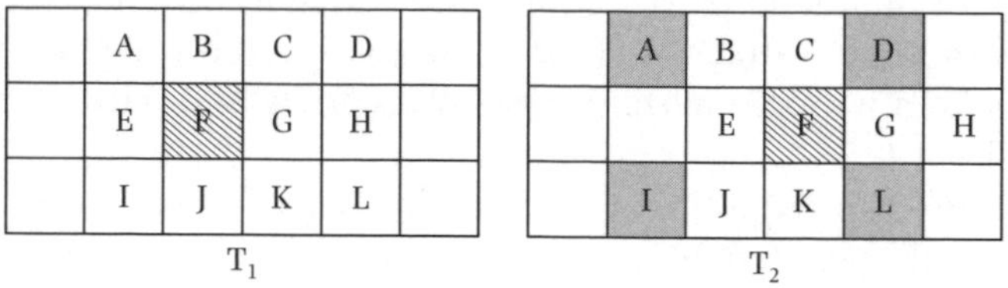

Figure 13.1

bodies that surround F at T_1 are in motion from T_1 to T_2 because they change their neighborhoods.

There are similarities between the kind of motion Descartes defines here and Newton's "relative motion," the motion bodies are in with respect to each other (Cohen and Whitman 1999: 408–9). However, Newton also held that bodies have absolute motions in addition to relative ones. In *Principia*, Scholium to Part 1, Newton characterizes absolute and relative motion along with absolute and relative space and place.

> Absolute space, of its own nature without reference to anything external, always remains homogeneous and immovable. Relative space is any movable measure or dimension of this absolute space; such a measure or dimension is determined by our senses from the situation of the space with respect to bodies and is popularly used for immovable space . . . Place is the part of space that a body occupies, and it is, depending on the space, either absolute or relative . . . and positions, properly speaking, are not so much places as attributes of places . . . Absolute motion is the change of position of a body from one absolute place to another; relative motion is change of position from one relative place to another. (Cohen and Whitman 1999: 408–9)

For Newton, absolute motion is independent of our thought of it; relative motion is dependent on our thought of it, and, in particular, on our sense perception. Thus, absolute space is unchanging and immobile; absolute places are portions of absolute space that bodies occupy; absolute positions are properties of absolute places; and absolute motions are the changes bodies make in position with respect to absolute places. In contrast, relative spaces are portions of absolute space that we differentiate through our sense perceptions of how bodies stand in relation to each other; relative places are portions of relative space that bodies occupy; relative positions are properties of relative places; and relative motions are changes bodies make in relative position.

Thus, unlike Descartes, Newton also accounts for "absolute motion," the kind of motion a body is in when it changes its absolute place. When Descartes defines "local motion" he does not appeal to absolute places and bodies in them, but to bodies that perceivers regard as being at rest. Indeed, given Descartes' metaphysics, the very notion of absolute place is incoherent. The metaphysical difference between the two views is that Newton holds an account of body that is ontologically more complicated. On his view, there is a duality in the nature of matter: absolute space and bodies that reside in it are two different kinds of things. On Descartes' view, this distinction rests on a mistake. He maintains that sometimes we think of matter generally, and thus form an abstract notion of "space," and sometimes we think of it particularly, and thus

252

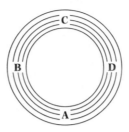

Figure 13.2

form ideas of individual bodies. On his view, it is erroneous to think that these different ways of regarding matter match ontologically different things. Matter is simple, though we can regard it as being diverse. Thus, strictly speaking, bodies cannot "occupy places," and certainly do not "occupy" one "place" at one time and another later; instead, there are no absolute "places," only the relative positions among bodies (*Principles* 2: 10–15; AT 8A: 45–9; CSM 1: 227–9).

Another innovation involved in Descartes' theory of motion – his famous account of vortices – can also be understood as the result of his attempt to distance himself from another dualist theory of matter, that constructed by the scholastics. Descartes understood his predecessors as maintaining an ontological distinction between space and bodies, which they used to account for the origin of motion: some places in space are not occupied by bodies, but vacuums; because nature abhors a vacuum, bodies rush in to fill unoccupied places, and in this way the bodies are pulled into motion. But Descartes cannot account for the possibility of motion by appealing to vacuums because they don't exist, given his ontology. His argument against vacuums is quite simple: the essence of matter is extension in length, breadth, and depth; if a vacuum were to exist, it would have an extension of some length, breadth, and depth; but, thus extended, the vacuum would just be a piece of matter (*Principles* 2: 16–18; AT 8A: 49–50; CSM 1: 229–31). Without vacuums, the world is a plenum: because it is without gaps, it is maximally full of bodies. At first, it may seem that it is impossible for motion to exist in such a situation, for when a body is displaced it cannot move into a place that another has vacated. But, as Descartes explains, another view is available: for one body in the universe to be in motion, other parts must also be in motion. He maintains that all motion occurs in rings, one body pushing another, that one pushing another, ultimately the last one pushing the first, as in figure 13.2.

This circular motion produces effects: bodies are continually moving circularly, and therefore are continually dividing. When circles are irregular, like those in figure 13.3, there are some places in which they have a lot of room to go through, such as G, and there are other places through which they must squeeze, such as E. When a piece of matter that fits easily through G makes it to H and then to E, the piece of matter has to change its shape to fit through the smaller space. Descartes calls these changes in shape "true cases of division":

> For what happens is an infinite, or indefinite, division of the various particles of matter; and the resulting subdivisions are so numerous that however small we make a particle in

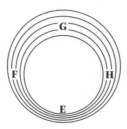

Figure 13.3

our thought, we always understand that it is in fact divided into other still smaller particles . . . This minute shifting of position is a true case of division. (*Principles* 2: 34; AT 8A: 59– 60; CSM 1: 239)

It is because of this kind of motion that bodies divide into particles of different sizes. He maintains that there are three basic sizes of these particles, these "three elements":

> The first is that of the matter which has so much force of agitation that, by colliding with other bodies, it is divided into particles of indefinite smallness, and which adapts its shapes to fill all the narrow parts of the little angles left by the others. The second is that of the matter which is divided into spherical particles, admittedly very small if compared with those bodies which our eyes can discern; yet of a certain and determined quantity and divisible into others much smaller. And, in a short while, we shall discover the third, which is composed of parts which are either much bulkier or have shapes less suited to movement. (*Principles* 3: 52; Miller and Miller 1983: 110; AT 8A: 105)

Descartes' account of the three elements is the basis of his astronomy and chemistry, for he seeks to describe all visible difference in the world in terms of these elements and their characteristic shapes and motions.

Classical Problems

Perhaps the most obvious problem with Descartes' definition of local motion is that it involves a serious logical flaw: it is circular. "Motion" is defined in terms of a body's changes with respect to neighboring bodies, and "one body" is defined in terms of that which is in motion. This circularity derives from the ill-begotten metaphysical parallels of the epistemological "Cartesian Circle" of the *Meditations*, along with other puzzles that arise from Descartes' theory of motion.

This circularity, coupled with other problems that stem from the account of motion, played a pivotal role in early modern rationalist philosophies. For instance, it is evident in section 13 of On Nature Itself: because of the problems in Cartesian theories of matter and motion, Leibniz resolved to "ground" his philosophical system in monads, indivisible mental entities. When he directly addresses ideas of the Cartesian philosopher J. C. Sturm, he argues that a view according to which there are no intrinsic differences among bodies cannot account for extrinsic changes among bodies (i.e., their motions) either. By beginning with metaphysical atoms that are mental, all of which are intrinsically different and inherently indivisible, Leibniz doesn't have a problem grounding his explanation of perceived variations: such changes are real in that they are the real perceptions of real individuals (Ariew and Garber 1989: 162–5).

Twentieth-century critics have also constructed puzzles that arise from Descartes' definition. For instance, Anthony Kenny argues that, given Descartes' account of motion and his view that any pieces of matter would have the same essence, he ultimately cannot account for the motion of individual bodies; rather, he is only committed to maintain that *res extensa* is one block, undifferentiated, and at rest. His argument involves two points, one about motion, the other about matter. First, motion is not possible because of implications that result from the combination of Descartes' definitions of "motion" and "a body" on the one hand, and his theory of circular motion on the other. According to his definition of "a body," all bodies moving together make up one body; according to the account of circular motion, all bodies move together in rings. When these two views are combined, one must conclude that all bodies are ring-shaped. However, given the definition of "motion," the rings themselves can't be in motion: motion is supposed to be the transfer of a body from the vicinity of one body that is at rest to the vicinity of another body that is at rest. But there is no sense in which rings, which are not themselves internally divided into parts that could be in the vicinity of one resting body at one time and another resting body at another time, can be in motion according to this definition. Coupling this impossibility with Kenny's second point, about the Cartesian definition of "matter," the conclusion is devastating: given that individuation cannot come about by "non-geometrical properties" (like motion, according to Kenny), then it must come about by "geometrical properties." But, because extension is homogeneous, there aren't any inherent geometrical properties. Thus, extension is without division, without motion, without the variable change that we perceive (Kenny 1968: 214). (For other twentieth-century treatments of Cartesian motion, see Von Leyden 1968: 271; Westfall 1971: 57–8, 151; Prendergast 1972: 67.)

Focusing on the sense in which Descartes is describing a kind of relative motion, Thomas Prendergast describes two further problems: inconsistencies that arise when relative motion is coupled with the Cartesian ontology. First, if God creates and conserves matter with a certain quantity of motion – as Descartes claims that he does in *Principles of Philosophy* (2: 36) – then it would seem that local motion must be absolute, not relative; but, according to Descartes' account of local motion, all motion is relative (Prendergast 1972: 168–9; Westfall 1971: 151).

Second, in Prendergast's analysis, how can motion be both relative *and* a mode of a body? According to the Cartesian ontology, motion, as a mode of a body, should be a "fact" about it, and thus independent of perceivers or the modes of other bodies (Garber 1992: 168–9; Prendergast 1972: 172–3; Von Leyden 1968: 271; Westfall 1971: 57–8). This, Prendergast argues, reveals asymmetries between motion and shape, both modes: (1) whereas the shape of a body is not relative to how perceivers regard it, the motion of a body *is* relative to how perceivers regard it; (2) whereas there seems to be a real difference between two different shapes that a body can have, there does *not* seem to be a real difference between two different motions that a body can have. As

255

Prendergast points out, the mode of a body is something that a body either has or doesn't have; it should not be relative to how a perceiver regards the body, and it should not be relative to the modes of other bodies. That is, a motion, like a shape, should be an inherent property of the body, and descriptions of the motion of a body should be "facts." Descartes is explicit that motion and size are modes in the same sense: "the motion of something that moves is, like the lack of motion in a thing which is at rest, a mere mode of that thing and not itself a subsistent thing, just as shape is a mere mode of the thing which has shape" (*Principles* 2: 25; AT 8A: 54; CSM 1: 233).

Further, there are two related problems concerning the status of the mode of rest, on the one hand, and the individuation of bodies, on the other. Descartes describes bodies as those that are in motion, which precludes the possibility of resting bodies that are individuated from each other (Garber 1992: 178). Bodies cannot be at rest because they cease to be individual bodies when they cease to move. So what can it mean to say that bodies are at rest? How are resting bodies individuated? This consequence, namely that there are no resting bodies, not only jars our commonsense ideas about rest and motion, but also is problematic because Descartes' physics accounts for how bodies change their rest and motion on impact, an account that requires the existence of individual bodies.

One could also make the case that the definition is metaphysically untenable: it makes the unity of a body dependent on its mode. That is, as the body's mode changes from motion to rest, the body comes into and out of being as it gains and loses its unity. This result is in tension with the Cartesian ontology, according to which modes depend on substances, not the other way around. If Descartes does intend motion to be the individuator of bodies, then his physics, which accounts for interactions among bodies and, thus, presupposes the existence of bodies, encounters what appear to be insurmountable difficulties. How, for instance, would Descartes' third law of motion be read?

> When a moving body collides with another, if its power of continuing in a straight line is less than the resistance of the other body, it is deflected so that, while the quantity of motion is retained, the direction is altered; but if its power of continuing is greater than the resistance of the other body, it carries that body along with it, and loses a quantity of motion equal to that which it imparts to the other body. (*Principles* 2: 40; AT 8A: 65; CSM 1: 242)

According to this law, there are different outcomes when a body collides with another body that is at rest versus one that is in motion. The same point can be made for the laws that govern collision, for they, too, appear to presuppose an ontology of individual bodies with modes of rest and motion (*Principles* 2: 46–52; AT 8A: 68–70; Miller and Miller 1983: 61–9).

It is not only Descartes' physics that is affected by his account of motion. The issue of Cartesian motion, and the closely related issue of the individuation of bodies, have far-ranging consequences for how we understand the rest of his philosophy. First, there are direct implications for how we understand his dualism. Descartes often writes as if there is symmetry between thinking and extended substance. For instance, both have principal attributes, both can be clearly and distinctly perceived as really distinct from each other, and both have modes. The vast majority of commentators on Descartes have thought that, by ."thinking substance," Descartes refers to a finite mind. Therefore, if by "extended substance" he refers to a finite body, the symmetry is preserved; however, if he refers to the whole extended universe, and finite bodies are only modes of that substance, then the symmetry is partly broken.

Second, the interpretation of Cartesian bodies must fit with an account of the Cartesian mind–body union, which itself must involve an explanation of what is united. There are several options: (1) minds could be united with bodies that are much like human bodies, and are somehow individuated prior to the union; (2) minds could be united with individual corpuscles that only cohere as a larger individual after the union; or (3) minds could be united with the whole extended universe (Hoffman 1986).

Third, the interpretation of Cartesian bodies has implications for the account of God's creation. God could have created many corpuscles and then set them in motion, as Descartes seems to suggest in *Le Monde* (AT 11: 34–5; CSM 1: 91), or he could have created things like stones, mountains, and human bodies as individuals. Yet another option is that he created only one individual – the whole extended universe.

In these ways, questions about the ontological status of individual bodies turn out to be at the crux of other issues throughout Descartes' system. The question that began as one about his account of corporeal substantiality becomes one about the whole of his physics and metaphysics.

Realist and Idealist Resolutions

Daniel Garber (1992) does considerable work to resolve the kinds of issues Prendergast raises about the relative aspects of motion, and in doing so suggests a realist interpretation of Descartes' ontology. According to Garber, the issue of the relative status of motion is significant because motion plays an explanatory role in Descartes' physics: the physics hinges on motion being an inherent property of bodies. According to Garber, if something is to be explanatory, then it must really exist: "If all the properties bodies have are ultimately to be explained in terms of motion, then motion must *really be* in body, as a mode" (Garber 1992: 163). If motion and rest are merely relative, and thus depend on how we happen to regard bodies, then motion and rest are not really in bodies as "facts"; but they should be so in order for Descartes' physics to be coherent.

Garber works to resolve this problem by reconsidering Descartes' definition of "local motion." He argues that we should understand local motion not as relative motion, but as mutual transference. On this reading, a body is in motion whenever its surface separates from the surface of another body. Thus, the motion of a body never depends on how we regard it, but on something about the body and its neighborhood. Garber rescues Cartesian local motion by accounting for it as an objective "fact" about the real status of bodies (Garber 1992: 168–9).

However, Garber's resolution remains incomplete: in giving his account of motion as a non-relative state, he refrains from providing a reading of how bodies are individuated when they are at rest. This is not just an oversight, for Garber is convinced by Leibnizian arguments that an account of the individuation of Cartesian bodies cannot be given:

> I shall continue to talk as if Descartes is dealing with a world of individual bodies, collid-
> ing with one another, at motion and at rest with respect of one another. But, in the end,
> I suspect that this is something that he is not entitled to, and this is something that, if
> true, would seriously undermine his whole program. (Garber 1992: 181)

With this statement, Garber throws up his hands. Thus, his reformulation of Descartes'
characterization of motion ultimately is not systematically helpful, for the problems
surrounding individuation remain confounding.

Can the Cartesian ontology of both material and thinking substance be retained,
while also accounting for the individuality of bodies? There are realist and idealist
resolutions.

The realists have two options available. First, they can appeal to God to be the
individuating agent who gives each body its own essence: he could create hylomorphic
unities of matter and essences, or he could individuate bodies in some incomprehensible way. Neither of these is satisfactory, however. Although Descartes may be committed to some sort of hylomorphism for the human mind–body union (Hoffman 1986:
347–9), thereby retaining some scholastic tendencies, he is adamant that his project is
to give an account of the physical world that does not involve form-like entities in its
explanations (*Principles* 2: 64; AT 8A: 78–9; CSM 2: 247). The other explanation is ad
hoc: we should not simply appeal to God's incomprehensibility whenever there is a
difficult interpretive question. Furthermore, Descartes never states that God individuates
bodies in either of these ways.

The second realist account of the individuation of Cartesian bodies maintains that
bodies get their individuality from their determinate quantities of matter. For reasons
discussed above, Descartes' account of vortices forestalls such an account: at the cor-
puscular level, bodies are continually moving in rings, so they are continually dividing. Given this division, there simply is not a determinate quantity of corpuscles that
compose a body (Nelson 1995: 385–91).

One may think that the individuality of a body, say a piece of wax, can be accounted
for in terms of its volume, which is revealed by a simple experiment: put the piece of
wax in a tube of water, and then measure its volume in terms of the amount of water
that the wax displaces. But this is problematic: first, it supposes that Waxiness is a
discrete category that will allow us to decide which corpuscles actually compose the
piece of wax and which are merely foreign bodies lodged in it, and thus that there is a
discrete volume to be measured. Second, practically speaking, we will not be able to
extract the foreign bodies – air corpuscles, granules of sand – from the piece of wax, so
they will contribute to the displacement of water and so will be counted as part of the
wax's volume. Therefore, the individuality of a body cannot be accounted for in terms
of its volume.

Of course, even if there were some third way realists could account for the individuality of bodies, they would still have to confront all of the problems with Descartes'
account of motion discussed above, for these problems arise only if one takes seriously
the substantiality of bodies.

Though most commentators simply suppose that Descartes is a realist, only to
find his ontology to be riddled with problems, there are others who have taken the

problems discussed above seriously enough to develop idealist interpretations of Descartes' metaphysics of body. These lines of interpretation have been developed by Gueroult, Lennon, and myself. All of these readings involve interpreting Cartesian bodies as phenomenally individuated modes of *res extensa*.

According to Gueroult, individual bodies are modes of the one corporeal substance, though they themselves can also be thought of as substances in a "third-order" sense, and thus as phenomenally individuated substances. Ultimately, the unity of bodies is grounded because the bodies are aggregates of unchanging corpuscles held together by cohesion, a kind of force established by God (Gueroult 1983: 297–8 n.165; 1980: 212). Because Gueroult grounds the individuality of bodies in the corpuscles that compose them, his reading is the most realist of the three idealist readings.

Lennon's view, on the other hand, is perhaps the most idealist. According to Lennon, individual bodies are modes of the one corporeal substance. Unlike Gueroult's interpretation, however, individual bodies are not grounded in any changes that take place in the one corporeal substance. According to Lennon, corporeal substance has extension as its essence, and, like the Platonic forms, this essence is apprehended through the intellect. Though it is not apprehended by either the senses or the imagination, through the senses, one "sees extension colored" or "sees extension colorly." On this view, both sensible qualities and all determinate geometrical qualities – size, shape, position, motion, and surface – are purely ideal. One implication of this position is that the one corporeal substance is motionless (Lennon 1988; forthcoming).

On the reading I have developed, there are three kinds of substances – the primary substance (God), secondary substances (minds and *res extensa*), and tertiary substances (individual bodies) – each of which has a different degree of reality, God having the most and bodies having the least. Given that the degree of precision one can attain about an entity tracks the degree of reality of the entity, one can only achieve metaphysical rigor when describing the primary and secondary substances, for, strictly speaking, the tertiary substances are not substances at all but modes of *res extensa*. Though they are dependent on *res extensa* for their extension, they are also dependent on minds for their precise delimitations; thus their individuality is mind-dependent. However, bodies differ from qualities, which are wholly mind-dependent, for bodies are not merely mind-dependent, but are also delimitations of *res extensa*, and thus have an essence that is not mind-dependent. As such delimitations, bodies have "tertiary" attributes that mirror the "secondary" attributes of *res extensa*. For example, as *res extensa* has indefinite size as one of its secondary attributes, bodies have some finite size or other as one of their tertiary attributes; further, as *res extensa* has its quantity of motion as one of its secondary attributes, bodies have some local motion or other as one of their tertiary attributes. Thus, while the particular unities and motions of individual bodies are mind-dependent, that there are bodies in motion is dependent on how God has created *res extensa*, namely, as a substance with a quantity of motion. Given this reading, I argue that the puzzles and problems discussed above either do not arise, or turn out to be virtuous, not vicious, implications of Descartes' general ontology (Sowaal, forthcoming).

As with Gueroult's interpretation, my account affords an interpretation of the many passages in which Descartes refers to bodies with the term "substances." It also gives an account of the degree of reality and mind-independence that bodies have, and distinguishes them from qualities. Unlike Gueroult's reading, tertiary substances are individuated *only* in the phenomenal sense, and so are *not* grounded in a determinate number of corpuscles. Further, my reading avoids the Leibnizian regress arguments, to which Gueroult is committed, insofar as it appeals to a discrete number of corpuscles that compose bodies.

My view also differs significantly from Lennon's, according to which *res extensa* is motionless. *Res extensa* (the "secondary substance") has a quantity of motion as one of its attributes (one of its "secondary attributes") and this attribute grounds the bodies' tertiary attribute of having some motion or other.

The commonality among these idealist interpretations – according to which bodies are to be most strictly classified as modes – is their Spinozistic flavor. Perhaps this is surprising. Spinoza was dissatisfied with the way that Descartes used the term "substance" to stretch over everything – from God's being, to *res extensa*, and to individual things, like pieces of wax. This prompted him to reserve the term "substance" only for God, the term "attributes" for mind and *res extensa*, and the term "modes" for individual bodies.

I should note, however, that though Spinoza recategorized the Cartesian ontology, his account does not escape a number of the problems to which Descartes' view is purportedly subject. For one, Spinoza defines "a body" in terms of "simplest bodies" that make up larger bodies, and, in particular, in reference to the maintenance of the ratio of motion and rest among those simplest bodies (Curley 1985: 460). However, he omits a story of what unites the simplest bodies. Second, given Spinoza's interpretation of attributes and modes, the problem of the individuation of bodies runs parallel to a problem concerning the individuation of ideas: given that each body *just is* its corresponding idea, and given that there is no story to tell about the individuation of bodies, then explanatory weight depends on an account of the individuation of ideas.

Conclusion

The realist will find unsettling the idealist interpretations of Descartes' metaphysics, especially those on which nothing outside of the Cartesian mind grounds the unities of bodies. The complaint will be that Descartes' physics is not about "real" bodies that are rooted in unities that exist independently of Cartesian perceptions of them. One must remember, however, how prevalent the theme of the mind-dependence of bodies was for the early modern rationalists. In Leibniz, for instance, physical objects are "well grounded," but only in monadic perceptions, that is, in mentalistic entities. Further, in Spinoza, as discussed above, there is no physical mechanism that ultimately gives unity to the simplest bodies that compose larger bodies; the only entity that can individuate the simplest bodies are the ideas that correspond to them. If anything, according to the idealist reading of Descartes that I propose, Descartes is the *most* realist of the three best-known of the early modern rationalists: on this interpretation, there is a material substance – *res extensa* – that is "really distinct" from the mind, and, thus, completely mind-independent.

Acknowledgments

Versions of this chapter were presented at the University of Colorado-Boulder, Grinnell College, Texas Tech University, the 1998 Pacific American Philosophical Association, and the 1997 Descartes, Cartesianism, and Anti-Cartesianism Conference at the University of California, Irvine. I am also grateful for the discussions at many meetings of the Southern California Cartesian Circle, and especially to Alan Nelson, Paul Hoffman, Patricia Easton, Tom Lennon, Nick Jolley, Larry Nolan, and Alison Simmons, who commented on earlier drafts.

References and Further Reading

Ariew, R., and Garber, D. (trans. and eds.) (1989). On Nature Itself. In *Philosophical Essays* (pp. 155–66). Indianapolis, IN: Hackett.

Burtt, E. A. (1924). *The Metaphysical Foundations of Modern Science*. Garden City, NY: Doubleday.

Cohen, B., and Whitman, A. (trans and eds.) (1999). *The Principia. Mathematical Principles of Natural Philosophy*. Berkeley: University of California Press.

Curley, E. (trans. and ed.) (1985). Parts I and II of Descartes' Principles of Philosophy: Demonstrated in the geometrical manner. In *The Collected Works of Spinoza* (pp. 224–346). Princeton, NJ: Princeton University Press.

Gabbey, A. (1980). Force and inertia in the seventeenth century: Descartes to Newton. In S. Gaukgroger (ed.), *Descartes: Philosophy, Mathematics and Physics* (pp. 230–320). Brighton: Harvester.

Garber, D. (1992). *Descartes' Metaphysical Physics*. Chicago: University of Chicago Press.

Gueroult, M. (1980). The metaphysics and physics of force in Descartes. In S. Gaukgroger (ed.), *Descartes: Philosophy, Mathematics and Physics* (pp. 196–229). Brighton: Harvester.

—— (1983). *Descartes' Philosophy Interpreted according to the Order of Reasons*. Minneapolis: University of Minnesota Press.

Hall, A. R., and Hall, M. B. (trans. and eds.) (1962). De gravitatione et aequipondio fluidorium. In *Unpublished Scientific Papers of Issac Newton* (pp. 89–156). Cambridge: Cambridge University Press.

Hoffman, P. (1986). The unity of Descartes' man. *Philosophical Review*, 95 (3), 339–70.

Kenny, A. (1968). *Descartes: A Study of His Philosophy*. New York: Random House.

Lennon, T. (1988). Descartes's Idealism. In Cauchy and Venant (eds.), *Philosophy and Culture*, V4, *Proceedings of the XVII World Congress of Philosophy* (pp. 53–6). Montreal: Editions Montmorency.

—— (1993). *The Battle of the Gods and Giants: The Legacy of Descartes and Gassendi*. Princeton, NJ: Princeton University Press.

—— (1994). The problem of individuation among the Cartesians. In K. F. Barber and J. J. E. Gracia (eds.), *Individuation in Early Modern Philosophy: Descartes to Kant* (pp. 13–39). Albany: State University of New York Press.

—— (forthcoming). The Eleatic Descartes.

Miller, V. R., and Miller, R. P. (1983). *René Descartes: Principles of Philosophy*. Boston, MA: Reidel.

Nelson, A. (1995). Micro-chaos and idealization in Cartesian physics. *Philosophical Studies*, 77, 377–91.

Prendergast, T. (1972). Descartes and the relativity of motion. *Modern Schoolman*, 49, 64–72.

Sowaal, A. (forthcoming). Cartesian Bodies.

Von Leyden, W. (1968). *Seventeenth-Century Metaphysics*. London: Garden City Press.

Westfall, R. S. (1971). *Force in Newton's Physics*. New York: Neale Watson Academic.

14

Leibniz on Shape and the Cartesian Conception of Body

TIMOTHY CROCKETT

Descartes' philosophy represents an extraordinary attempt to achieve the rationalist goal of acquiring substantive knowledge about the world by employing reason and *a priori* methods. According to Descartes, human beings have the capacity to acquire knowledge of a broad range of metaphysical facts using only the innate conceptual resources with which we are born. We can, for example, come to possess knowledge of the nature and existence of God, mind, and the corporeal world, and we can discover the laws that govern change in nature, without any appeal to experience. In fact, even natural science is *a priori* in the sense that it should proceed in the same way that mathematical reasoning does, namely, by deducing truths from axioms and by employing algebraic reasoning.

There are two aspects of Descartes' system that make such a wide breadth of *a priori* knowledge possible. The first is the existence in human beings of a rational faculty that comes well stocked with a variety of ideas that have been implanted in us by an infinitely benevolent, and thus non-deceiving, God. This cache of ideas, and the ability to perceive in a clear and distinct way what is contained within them, allows us to draw inferences about physics and metaphysics that are presumed to be every bit as transparent as those drawn in mathematics or geometry. The second aspect, which is just as important, is the existence of a world of objects and events that is accurately represented by those ideas – a world that can be understood *a priori* in virtue of its having an intrinsically rational structure.

This commitment to intelligibility can be found in Descartes' thinking about a variety of issues, but clearly the centerpiece of his rationalist efforts is his conception of corporeal reality. The objects of the corporeal world, he argues, are every bit as intelligible as the objects studied in geometry and mathematics because bodies are in essence nothing more than geometrical objects. Knowledge of the essence and properties of geometrical figures is, therefore, also knowledge of the essence and properties of bodies; and geometrical reasoning, which has long been considered to be the paradigm of intelligibility, is nothing less than reasoning about the properties of corporeal things. Of course, there is an important difference between the realm of geometrical space and the created corporeal world: there is motion in the corporeal world. In fact, Cartesian bodies are necessarily in motion relative to one another because motion is responsible for individuating one part of spatial extension from another; what it is to be one body, as distinct from others, is to be a parcel of matter whose parts are moving in concert. Thus, in addition to the purely geometrical properties of size and shape, bodies also have the property of being in motion relative to other bodies. Accordingly, physics and geometry differ insofar as geometry is concerned only with resting forms of space whereas physics is concerned with forms of space in motion relative to one another. But, for Descartes, this difference does not imply that physics is any less an *a priori* science than geometry. The world of bodies in motion can still be exhaustively characterized in quantitative terms. And facts about body can be derived from axioms established *a priori*. The only difference is that the axioms of physics are not derivable from our idea of spatial extension alone but are additionally dependent upon our innate idea of God.

This conception of matter was quite influential and was still widely accepted by philosophers when Leibniz began his own thinking about physics and the nature of body. Early in his career, Leibniz had been charmed by the elegant explanations of natural phenomena offered by the Cartesians, and he continued to countenance such explanations throughout his life. But he soon realized that Descartes' conception of corporeal substance is not sufficient to account for the reality or substantiality of matter. Having stripped body of sensible qualities, forms, forces, strivings, etc., Descartes was left with something that could at best be an abstraction from our phenomenal experiences. To be sure, Leibniz believed, explanations of corporeal phenomena in terms of size, shape, and motion are sufficient in physics because physics is a science that makes extensive use of abstraction. But if bodies are real they must be more than the mere abstractions employed in our thought about them: they must be substantial.

This general criticism brings out something important about efforts to understand corporeal reality in purely quantitative terms: although the complete mathematization of nature would be ideal from the perspective of a rationalist epistemology, there are limitations to mathematization that undermine the possibility that such a characterization could be exhaustive. Mathematics is the science of ideal spaces and entities, such as numbers and geometrical forms. So the more we push in the direction of purely quantitative accounts of nature, the more we move in the direction of abstraction and idealization, and away from the concrete reality we purport to be characterizing. Pushing too hard in the direction of abstraction, then, inevitably results in characterizations of ideal, rather than substantial, entities. Certainly, if we are doing physics it is legitimate to focus solely upon quantitative aspects of body, such as kinematic and geometrical properties. But we run into problems when we succumb to the urge to reduce body to those characteristics. Thus, a tension seems to exist between a desire to maintain a realist conception of body and a rationalist urge to characterize body purely quantitatively. Descartes' mistake, according to Leibniz, was his failure to come to terms with this tension.

In this chapter, I offer a detailed account of one of Leibniz's central objections to the geometrical conception of body. According to this objection, Descartes' theory cannot account for the reality of matter because one of its central explanatory resources, the mode of shape, is imaginary in some way. Leibniz's reasoning about shape is important for two reasons. First, since his arguments purport to show that shapes are at best mere abstractions, they highlight the tension Leibniz sees between realism about body and the mathematization of nature. Second, the arguments play a central role in

263

Leibniz's early thinking about the possibility of extended substance more generally. As I hope to make clear in this chapter, Leibniz's movement towards an immaterialist metaphysics is at least partially motivated by his sensitivity to the tension between realism and mathematization that Descartes fails to recognize.

The Imaginary Status of Shape: The "Diachronic" Argument

Leibniz first suggests that there is something imaginary about Cartesian extension and its modes in an untitled fragment from the late 1670s (ca. 1678–9):

> That matter and motion are only phenomena, or contain in themselves something imaginary, can be understood from the fact that different and contradictory hypotheses can be made about them, all of which nevertheless satisfy the phenomena perfectly, so that no reason can be devised for determining which of them should be preferred. (A VI, iv, 277; RA 257)

The context of this fragment suggests he is thinking specifically about the relativity of motion, that is, the fact that motion is nothing more than change of position relative to other bodies. His point is that although it may be natural for us, when we see bodies changing position relative to one another, to think that certain bodies have an "absolute motion," this is a mistake because there are other possible frames of reference in which the very same bodies we took to have an absolute motion are at rest. As he says in an essay from 1677:

> The absolute motion we imagine to ourselves, however, is nothing but an affection of our soul while we consider ourselves or other things as immobile, since we are able to understand everything more easily when these things are considered as immobile. (A VI, iv, 360; RA 229)

There are two points here that are analogous to the points he will eventually bring out about shape. The first is a point about metaphysics: there is no absolute motion; there is no reason in the nature of things themselves for saying that one thing is in motion rather than another. The second is a point about the perceiving subject: the apparent (or conceived) absolute motion is merely imagined – it is an affection of the soul, not the world. Although he is not explicit about this, the reason absolute motion must be imaginary seems to be that it does not exist in the nature of things outside of the mind. His justification for the ideality of this quality is thus metaphysical rather than epistemological.

Leibniz makes the analogous metaphysical point about shape in a 1683 essay entitled the "Wonders Concerning the Nature of Corporeal Substance." In this piece, Leibniz argues that although extension and motion are less confused than other qualities, they cannot really be distinctly understood at all. The reason is that

> on the one hand we are always embroiled in the difficulties concerning the composition of the continuum and the infinite, and on the other, because there are in fact no precise shapes in the nature of things, and consequently, no precise motions. (A VI, iv, 279; RA 263)

Unfortunately, Leibniz does not offer any reason for thinking that there are no precise shapes. But the text is worth noting for a couple of reasons. First, Leibniz says explicitly that the mode of shape has a kind of priority over motion, such that showing there are no shapes is sufficient for showing there are no motions. So even if concerns about the relativity of motion can be overcome, there is still a problem for motion that results from the fact that there are no shapes. Second, although it looks as if he is saying something merely about our ability to understand these qualities distinctly, he goes on to make the stronger claim that these modes of extension are phenomena "just as color and sound are phenomena, rather than attributes of things containing a certain absolute nature without relation to us" (A VI, iv, 1465; RA 263). The modes of extension, he suggests, are like secondary qualities in that both are dependent upon the mind in much the same way.

Leibniz begins to present explicit reasons for the claim that there are no determinate shapes in things in the mid-1680s. Many of the arguments look quite similar, and so it is difficult to determine how many arguments there are and how they should be individuated from one another. Some commentators, however, have noted that Leibniz seems to present two distinct lines of reasoning: a "diachronically based" argument and a synchronic argument (Adams 1994: 229–32; Levey forthcoming (a); Sleigh 1990: 211). Roughly, this is correct; one argument explicitly contains diachronic considerations and the other (which I will call the "dominant synchronic argument") does not. However, there are two ways in which contrasting the arguments in terms of a diachronic/synchronic distinction is misleading. First, the argument commentators refer to as diachronic actually contains both diachronic and synchronic considerations. Second, the most interesting difference between the two arguments has to do with the ways in which they purport to demonstrate the impossibility of momentary shapes, rather than with the presence or absence of diachronic considerations. As we will see, the diachronically based argument is quite important to our understanding of Leibniz's thinking in this period because it makes explicit the overall structure of Leibniz's attack on the reality of shape. It is also important, however, because thinking about the strength of the diachronic element of the argument helps us see something important about Leibniz's intentions with respect to the scope of his attack: he intends to show that the reality of shape is inconsistent with any intelligible plenum conception of the world.

Leibniz presents the "diachronically based" argument in only one place, an essay from the mid-1680s entitled "There Is No Perfect Shape in Bodies." The central premise in this argument, as in all the arguments concerning determinate shape, is that matter, which Leibniz believes is a plenum, is actually infinitely divided. These divisions are the result of differing motions of the various parts of matter. So, infinite division of any part of matter implies infinite variety in the motions of its parts. Given this:

> It is true that it will always be possible to draw an imaginary line at each instant; but that line will endure in the same parts only for that instant, because each part has a motion different from every other, since it expresses the whole universe differently. Thus there is no body that has any shape for a definite time, however short it might be. Now I believe that what exists only at a moment has no existence, since it starts and finishes at the same time. (A VI, iv, 1630; RA 297)

265

We can formulate this argument (hereafter, the NPS argument) in the following way. Assume there is some determinate shape in the plenum (or a body with some determinate shape); either this shape endures for some period of time or it exists for a moment; it cannot exist for some period of time (however short), because every part of the shape has a motion that is different from every other and this change is continuous; but it cannot exist for a moment either, since nothing can exist for only a moment; thus the assumption is false.

The first thing to note about the argument is that it involves a dilemma. This is significant because it makes it clear that in order to show that shape is impossible one must rule out two possibilities, namely, that shape could exist over time and that shape could exist at a moment. Any argument against the reality of shape, therefore, is dependent upon some argument against the possibility of temporally enduring shapes, whether or not it appeals explicitly to diachronic considerations. This makes the diachronic part of the NPS argument of central importance to Leibniz's overall critique, since it is the only explicit diachronic argument to be found in Leibniz's writings. Fortunately, the argument is quite strong. In fact, it would very likely have been acceptable to a Cartesian. After all, Descartes would agree that motion in a plenum requires infinite (or, as he puts it, indefinite) divisions in matter, and he would also agree that in order for bodies to exist there must be motion. Leibniz simply draws the obvious conclusion from these premises, namely, that each and every part of the plenum must be in a continual state of modal alteration. (I discuss the justification for the first assumption in the next section.)

The synchronic aspect of the argument, however, is not so obviously sound. The central assumption of the argument is that "what exists only at a moment has no existence" (hereafter, the NME claim); and clearly, this claim is far from being obviously true. Nevertheless, I think Leibniz does have the resources to defend it. In fact, he offers an explicit justification in the text we are considering. The NME claim is true, he says, because what exists at a moment "starts and finishes at the same time." As Samuel Levey has pointed out, it may be that Leibniz is implicitly assuming that anything that exists must have a distinct beginning and end (Levey forthcoming (a)). If this is what Leibniz has in mind, then it would simply be contradictory to say that something exists only at a moment, since such a thing would not have a distinct beginning and end. Further argumentation would, of course, be needed to justify this implicit assumption, since without some justification the argument seems to beg the question quite egregiously; but it is certainly not a wildly implausible principle.

But even if we are skeptical about the soundness of his explicit justification, Leibniz could still justify the NME claim by appealing to his view on entities such as points, instants, lines, etc. According to Leibniz, such entities are not parts of things, nor are they entities out of which things could be composed. Rather, they are *extrema*, *termini* or limits of things (RB II, xiv, 10). As modes of (spatially or temporally) extended things, their existence is entirely dependent upon the extended things they bound. So, considered apart from that which they bound, they have no existence – they are mere abstractions. Of course, we might be able to conceptualize the end-point of a line segment or the first moment of a temporal interval; but apart from the extended things from which they were abstracted these points and instants are nothing more than mere mental entities. If Leibniz understands points and instants as mere abstractions, could he conceive of momentary states in the same way? There are two things that entities such as points, instants, and lines have in common: they are un-extended (at least along one dimension) and they can be conceived of as limiting something. For example, a line, which can be thought of as limiting an area of space, has no breadth; and an instant, which can be thought of as limiting a temporal sequence, has no temporal extension. If Leibniz thinks these entities are abstractions in virtue of these two features, then it seems he could quite easily assimilate momentary states to the same model. Momentary states, after all, are not temporally extended, and they can be conceived of as limiting an extended quantity such as a continuous flow of such states. Of course, there may be some relevant respect in which they are not analogous to limit entities such as points and instants. But it at least seems open to Leibniz to treat momentary states in the same way he treats other limit entities.

So far, I have been arguing that Leibniz has the resources to defend the NME claim. Other commentators, however, have been less convinced of its plausibility. Robert Adams, for example, has called it "a large and dubious assumption." But Adams' central worry is not that it is unmotivated but rather that it seems inconsistent with other things Leibniz either does or should hold. As Adams points out, "Leibniz himself must probably ascribe to monads perceptual states that do not endure, unchanged, beyond an instant" (Adams 1994: 231–2). And in fact, in his 1695 essay "A Specimen of Dynamics," Leibniz seems to say explicitly that forces or strivings exist at a moment: "there is nothing real in motion but a momentary something which must consist in a force striving [*nitente*] towards change" (GM VI 235; AG 118). Despite this apparent textual evidence, I am not convinced that Leibniz is committed to the existence of momentary states. For any textual reference to momentary states is consistent with an ontology in which such states are mere abstractions from the continuous flow of perceptions, forces, etc. Furthermore, I see no reason why Leibniz might need to ascribe such states to monads, nor do I see any reason that he should. If he were committed to a sort of temporal atomism with respect to states, he would need to have some account of the metaphysical individuation of those states (that is, some account of why something counts as one state as opposed to many); and I do not think he has such an account. But, of course, he would not need one if he simply denied the existence of such states.

If I am correct about Leibniz's views on momentary existence, he has the resources to defend the NPS argument; and since he does not express any worries about the argument, there is thus no real reason to doubt his commitment to its soundness. But this raises an important question: why, if he thinks the NPS argument is sound, does he develop an alternative synchronic argument that becomes dominant in his thinking about shape in the mid-1680s? After all, if he thinks the NPS argument is successful, why would he not simply rehearse this argument in his other discussions of shape from this period? Adams' interpretation would seem to provide a ready answer: Leibniz saw that the NME assumption is implausible or inconsistent with other metaphysical facts to which he is more firmly committed. But as ready as this answer may be, I think there is a more subtle explanation, one that is consistent with Leibniz's commitment to the soundness of the NPS argument: Leibniz eventually came to suspect that the Cartesians are committed to the existence of momentary states, and thus to the denial

267

of the NME claim. Whether or not Leibniz's suspicions were correct, there is at least the suggestion of such a commitment to momentary states in Descartes' discussions of the divine preservation of created things. In the *Meditations*, for example, Descartes says that "the same power and action are needed to preserve anything at *each individual moment of its duration* as would be required to create that thing anew if it were not yet in existence" (CSM 2: 33, emphasis added). Assuming that Descartes' metaphysics is one of the central targets of Leibniz's attack, if Leibniz took such statements as indicative of a commitment to momentary states, the appeal to the NME premise would likely have struck him as a huge weakness in his argument. Of course, it is also consistent with my assessment of the NPS argument that Leibniz developed an alternative argument simply because he wanted to present as many good arguments as possible. But I think my explanation gets some support from the fact that later in the text in which the NPS argument is presented, Leibniz offers a different argument against the possibility of momentary shapes, one that is restricted to shapes in a Cartesian plenum. In the last paragraph of the text he says:

> In an instant, with motion not being considered, it is as if the mass were all united; and thus one can give it any shape as one wants. But also, all variety in bodies ceases; and, consequently, all bodies are destroyed. (A VI, iv, 1614; RA 299)

No shape could exist for only a moment, according to this argument, because shape is dependent upon motion and motion requires some period of time. Insofar as motion is necessary for the individuation and qualitative differences among bodies, as it is for a plenum physics of the sort the Cartesians endorsed, the material world at any moment is a completely homogenous mass and is thus without bodies – much less shapes.

This argument, which is similar to an argument Leibniz presents in a text from 1698 (G IV, 512–14; AG 164), is devastating to the possibility of momentary shapes, at least in a Cartesian plenum, and it does not appear to suffer from any of the problems Adams associates with the NME claim. And if Descartes is the primary target of the NPS argument, this is all he would need to rule out the synchronic horn of the dilemma. But this raises a further question, the answer to which reveals something important: why does Leibniz not simply appeal to this line of reasoning in ruling out the synchronic horn of the dilemma in the NPS argument? One possible answer is that Leibniz does not see a distinction between this line of reasoning and his justification for the NME premise, and so in stating the NME premise Leibniz means to be making the more limited claim that in a Cartesian plenum physics, nothing exists at a moment (or, at least, there is no individuation in the plenum). But I have strong doubts about this interpretation. Most importantly, the immediate justification given for the NME claim, namely, that at a moment a thing would start and finish at the same time, is quite general. In fact, it would seem to rule out the momentary existence of anything, whereas the latter argument is effective only against a Cartesian conception of body. I think it is much more likely that Leibniz appeals to the NME principle in the NPS argument because he wants an argument that rules out the existence of shape in any intelligible plenum conception of the world, not just the Cartesian conception, and he thinks the NME principle adequately accomplishes this. As we will see, the alternative synchronic argument that becomes dominant in Leibniz's thought in the mid-1680s has the same broad scope the NPS argument is intended to have. And this, I think, lends some support to the idea that Leibniz wants to rule out the existence of shapes in any type of plenum.

The Dominant Synchronic Argument

As we saw in the previous section, Leibniz has convincing reasons that there can be no shapes in a Cartesian metaphysics. And if I am right about the defensibility of the NME claim, the NPS argument shows something much stronger, namely that shape is impossible in any sort of plenum physics. Nevertheless, Leibniz develops an alternative synchronic argument that becomes dominant in his critique of shape. He offers a clear statement of this argument in a 1687 letter to Arnauld:

> Shape itself, which is of the essence of finite extended mass, is never exact and specific in nature, because of the actual division *ad infinitum* of the parts of matter. There is never a shape without inequalities, nor a straight line without curves intermingled, nor a curve of a certain finite nature unmixed with some other, and in small parts as well as large, with the result that shape, far from being constitutive of bodies, is not even a wholly real and specific quality outside of thought, and one will never be able to fix upon a certain precise surface in a body as one might be able to do if there were atoms. (G II 119; M 152)

Leibniz repeats the central argument of this passage at several places in the correspondence: the parts of body are actually divided to infinity; therefore, there is no fixed and precise shape (or surface) in body. And he presents a similar argument in a 1686 paper entitled "A Specimen of Discoveries About Marvelous Secrets":

> From the fact that no body is so small that it is not actually divided into parts which are excited by various motions, it follows that no determinate shape can be assigned to any body, nor is an exact straight line, nor a circle, nor any assignable figure of body found in the nature of things, though in the derivation of an infinite series certain rules are observed by nature. And so shape involves something imaginary, and no other sword can cut the knots we weave for ourselves by our imperfect understanding of the composition of the continuum. (A VI, iv, 312; P 81)

Diachronic considerations are clearly absent from these arguments. Leibniz is not concerned to point out that shapes are imaginary as a result of their always changing. Also absent are any references to the NME premise, the premise in the NPS argument that ruled out shapes at an instant. Instead, we find a synchronic argument in which the central premise is that the plenum is actually infinitely divided.

A slightly different formulation of the argument is found in "Primary Truths," an essay from around the same period. Here, the reason he gives for there being no determinate shape in actual things is that

> none can be appropriate for an infinite number of impressions. And so neither a circle, nor an ellipse, nor any other line we can define exists except in the intellect, nor do lines exist before they are drawn, nor parts before they are separated. Extension, motion, and

269

> bodies themselves . . . are not substances, but true phenomena like rainbows and parhelia. For there are no shapes in things. (C 522; AG 34)

Again, there is no suggestion in this text that Leibniz is appealing to diachronic considerations. But the argument is interesting in that Leibniz employs an additional premise that he does not mention in the other texts we have looked at so far, namely, that no shape "can be appropriate for an infinite number of impressions." Despite this difference, however, these versions of the argument have something very important in common: they both depend on the idea that determinate shape in body is precluded by the infinite complexity or infinite division of the plenum.

Before considering in more detail the relation Leibniz sees between shape and infinite division, there are two preliminary questions that must be addressed. First, in beginning the argument with the assumption that matter is infinitely divided, is Leibniz assuming from the outset that matter exists? And if he is, does this undermine my claim that these remarks are part of a general critique of realism about extended substance? Second, why does Leibniz think that matter must be actually infinitely divided in the first place?

The answer to the first question is that he is in fact assuming the existence of body and matter. But he is assuming this for the sake of *reductio*. Most of the statements of the shape arguments emerge in a dialectic in which Leibniz is trying to convince Arnauld that there is something incoherent about Cartesian extended substance. So it would be no surprise if Leibniz assumed the view that he is trying to show is incoherent, namely, that extended substance exists. We can answer the second question by considering what Leibniz thinks would have to be true if extended substance did exist. His thinking about this can be drawn from a variety of different contexts. Very briefly, it could be formulated as follows: if there is matter, it must be a plenum (that is, the world must be completely filled with matter in such a way that there can be no void); motion in a plenum requires infinite division; so, on the assumption that there is motion, matter must be infinitely divided.

Let us focus for a moment on the first two premises of this short argument. Leibniz has at least two reasons for thinking that the world must be completely full. The first is based on a principle that has been called the "Principle of Plenitude," which is in turn grounded in a more fundamental principle, the "Principle of Perfection." According to the Principle of Perfection, in his decision to create this world, God acted so as to maximize perfection or goodness. Perfection, in turn, "is nothing but quantity of essence." From this, Leibniz derives the Principle of Plenitude: "Out of the infinite combinations of possibles and possible series, that one exists through which the most essence or possibility is brought into existence" (G VII 303; LL 487). And the possible series that contains the most essence is one that is completely full (Rescher 1979: 27–30, 50–1; Rutherford 1995: 22–3). The second reason he believes the world is a plenum is that he rejects the existence of a vacuum in nature. One argument that he presents for this is based on the Principle of the Identity of Indiscernibles. Roughly, this principle says that two things cannot "resemble each other completely and differ in number alone [*solo numero*]" (G IV 433; AG 41–2). The argument, then, is that if there were a vacuum, there would be parts of space that differ only in number, which is impossible since it violates the principle.

The second premise is that motion in a plenum requires infinite division. Leibniz's central reason for believing this is that he agrees with Descartes' view that in a plenum all motion involves circuits and that in order for any parcel of matter to move through the irregular circuits that exist in the plenum, that parcel of matter must be infinitely divided into smaller parcels of matter. The reason infinite division is required could be summed up as follows: in order for a parcel of matter to pass through a narrow part of a circuit, it must alter its shape; and for this to happen it is necessary that each of its innumerable parts move with respect to its neighboring bodies; since bodies are individuated by their motions, any motion of a body is a real division of that body from the bodies that surround it; thus movement through irregular channels involves innumerable divisions (G IV 370; LL 393).

If we add one more premise to the two premises we have been considering, we get a formulation that reflects the general structure of Leibniz's reasoning about shape in the texts we have been considering in this section:

The infinite division argument
1 Assume: There is body/matter.
2 There is a plenum. (1)
3 Motion in a plenum requires infinite division. (premise)
4 So, matter is infinitely divided. (2), (3)
5 If matter is infinitely divided, then shape is an imaginary, non-objective property of things.
6 So, shape is an imaginary, non-objective property. (4), (5)

This formulation makes it clear that an account of the reasoning behind the conditional in step (5) is crucial to our understanding of the argument. Of course, the inference from infinite division to the impossibility of enduring shapes has already been explained in the NPS argument. But we still need an explanation of why infinite division makes momentary shapes impossible. Unfortunately, Leibniz is not very helpful on this point. In fact, in most presentations of the argument he says nothing about why we should accept it. He does, however, make one remark that I believe is intended to help clarify his thinking about the premise. Recall that in "Primary Truths" Leibniz appeals to a premise we do not find in any other text:

PT Principle: No shape can be appropriate for an infinite number of impressions.

Although this principle is somewhat obscure, it is at least the sort of claim that could be of some help in clarifying premise (5), for Leibniz very likely thinks infinite impressions are the result of infinite division. If this is right, then the conditional in (5) can be justified by the following argument: if there is infinite division, there are infinite impressions; and if there are infinite impressions, then there is no shape; thus, if there is infinite division, there is no shape. Of course, without an understanding of the PT Principle, we will be no better off than we were before, since the principle seems no less obscure than premise (5). It is thus extremely important that we look more carefully at what Leibniz might mean by the principle.

271

The first thing to note about the principle is that in the context in which Leibniz states it, the term "impression" has a physical rather than a perceptual sense. It might refer to a physical effect on something, such as a mark or dent on the surface of a body; or it might refer to that which brings about a physical effect. In either case, a natural way to understand the principle, and the way most commentators interpret it, is as claiming that no shape could have the degree of complexity it would have to have if it suffered infinite physical impressions. Put more simply: no shape could be infinitely dented or variegated. If this interpretation is correct, then the way Leibniz moves from the infinite division of matter to the lack of shape is via the PT Principle and the following premise: (7) if matter is infinitely divided, then if something has a shape, its shape must be infinitely complex. But what might be the relation between infinite division and shape (or lack thereof)? The idea would seem to be the following. Consider a body and its shape (either conceived or perceived). Because of the infinite division of the plenum, the body bounded by that shape is at any moment suffering the impressions of the motions of infinitely many surrounding bodies, and this would have to be reflected or expressed in the complexity of the shape. Furthermore, the same thing will be true for any part of the surface, since contiguous with any part of the surface there will be infinite bodies in motion relative to one another, bodies that are impressing themselves on that surface. And it is not just external bodies that impress themselves on the surface of the body; there are also motions of bodies within the bounds of the surface that would have an effect on the shape, since the body itself is infinitely divided. This is because, according to Leibniz, fluidity is the "fundamental condition" of the material continuum (RB II, xiii, 23), and so we must conceive of all bodies as composites of smaller parcels of matter that are in motion relative to one another, and we must think of each of those smaller parcels of matter as composites of yet smaller parcels of matter that are in motion relative to one another, and so on *ad infinitum*. The idea is thus that since any purported surface would suffer the impressions of an infinitude of internal and external bodies, the surface itself would have to be infinitely complex.

If this is the way Leibniz is thinking about the relation between infinite division and shape, then the remaining interpretive issue is to explain why is it impossible for a shape to be infinitely complex. There are two explanations that have been offered by commentators. The first, by Samuel Levey, is that in the early modern period something counts as a shape only if it can be described by traditional, finite geometry, and so an infinitely complex surface would, by definition, not be a shape. According to Levey, Leibniz's case against Descartes could be summed up as follows: an infinitely complex shape cannot be described by traditional geometry; if something cannot be described by traditional geometry, then that thing is not a shape; given the infinite impressions on the surface of any body, that surface could not be described in terms of traditional geometry; thus, Descartes is wrong: bodies have no shape (Levey forthcoming (b)). The second explanation, offered by Robert Adams, is simply that Leibniz would have thought that an infinitely complex shape is "an absurd and impossible monstrosity" (Adams 1994: 230). Adams does not provide any support for this claim, but it is possible he thinks there is some justification for it lurking in Leibniz's complex views about the infinite. For various reasons, I find both of these ways of understanding Leibniz's thinking about shape inadequate; furthermore, I do not believe Leibniz's discussions of the infinite provide sufficient resources to rule out the possibility of infinite shapes (Crockett 2004). Rather than discuss these interpretations here, however, I will instead lay out an alternative interpretation of the Infinite Division Argument that I believe makes better sense of the texts and makes a stronger case against the reality of shape.

An Alternative Interpretation

The central interpretive difficulty with the Infinite Division Argument is that it is hard to know how Leibniz understands the relation between the infinite division of the plenum and the impossibility of shape. The PT Principle, at least as it is commonly understood, suggests an interpretive direction, but it leaves us with a further puzzle that Leibniz never explicitly addresses, namely, the question of what justifies the principle. There is, however, an alternative way to understand the work this principle is doing that does not leave us with this question. On this interpretation, the upshot of the principle is not that given infinite impressions, any purported shape would have to be too complex to count as a shape or to be real. Rather, it is that given infinite impressions, there is nothing, metaphysically speaking, that we could characterize as the surface of a body. That is, any purported shape will at some level of analysis literally disappear, rather than merely reveal greater complexity than it did at the previous level. This is a subtle distinction, but I think it is significant for our understanding of Leibniz's critique of shape. The rest of this section will thus be devoted to explicating the distinction between these two ways of thinking about infinite impressions and shape.

To begin, it is worth noting that on both interpretations the PT Principle adds something new to the resources we have for understanding the move from the infinite division of the plenum to the impossibility of shape: the notion of physical impressions. In an infinitely divided plenum, any body that we consider (however it is individuated) is going to be impressed upon by infinitely many surrounding bodies. But there are different ways of conceptualizing this state of affairs, and these differences are important. On one way of conceptualizing matters, a way that I think is natural if we think the PT Principle is meant to rule out shapes of infinite complexity, we are to take for granted the intelligibility of a continuous, determinate surface, and then ask whether "it" could have the structure it would have to have in an infinitely divided plenum. We might conceive of this by thinking about the inside and the outside of a body as determinately separated by a metaphysical film, the integrity of which is taken as constant as we consider what would have to be true of it given infinite impressions. (Crudely, it might be helpful to imagine a balloon that is both filled with and buried in extremely fine sand.) This way of conceiving of a body in a plenum seems perfectly natural; and the result of thinking about the plenum in this way is that we are left with some conception of an extremely (in fact, infinitely) complex shape, and with the question of why such a shape could not exist.

One thing that makes this way of thinking about the complexity of a plenum so natural is that we have all had sense experiences in which we took a closer look at one part of the surface of some object, such as a billiard ball, only to find that the shape of that part was much more jagged or complex than it appeared with the naked eye. In such cases, our sensory examination did not, of course, reveal infinite complexity. But it did reveal substantially more complexity than was evident to the naked eye. And we can easily imagine that increasing the magnification on a part of the part we just examined would reveal that it is even more complex than it appeared. In fact, we can imagine that this would be true no matter how great the increase in magnification, or how many times we engage in this process of reexamination. It is not hard to see that this imaginative exercise assumes the "metaphysical film" conception of surfaces in a plenum. For no matter how detailed our analysis becomes we never lose track of the original surface. Certainly, at deeper levels of analysis the surface is going to be more complex than it appeared. But it is assumed that at each level we are noticing more detail about the same surface we considered at the previous level; and this is a way of assuming the determinate individuation of the body with which we started.

There is, however, another way we might conceptualize an infinitely divided plenum that does not assume determinate individuation at every level of analysis. According to this way of thinking about a surface in a plenum, no shape is appropriate for infinite impressions in the sense that being subject to infinite impressions undermines the metaphysical individuation of surfaces; shape is impossible because any purported shape will literally disappear at some level of analysis rather than simply revealing greater complexity. To see this, let us again start by thinking about a body and considering the fact that in an infinitely divided plenum, there are infinitely many bodies impressing themselves along its surface. But this time, rather than focus on a surface that we assume is metaphysically determinate and ask what would have to be true of "it" at any level of analysis, let us think more carefully about the very idea of a surface in an infinitely divided plenum. Let us again consider a billiard ball, and for the time being let us think about that object as abstracted from the plenum. We might grant that on closer analysis what we would find is greater and greater complexity of the apparent shape. But at some point in the analysis we would start to lose a conceptual grip on the surface we are considering. This is because a body in an infinitely divided plenum is really an aggregate of bodies that are individuated from one another by their motions. So eventually this picture of greater and greater complexity in "the shape" of the ball must give way to a picture of a surface as consisting of an aggregate of surfaces.

What follows from the fact that what appeared to be a relatively continuous surface is actually (at this level of analysis) an aggregate of surfaces? We might think it does nothing to undermine the object's having a continuous and determinate shape at all. After all, it seems we could simply draw a line along the exposed surfaces and take that as the shape. But, as I mentioned above, Leibniz thinks that fluidity is the fundamental condition of the plenum. So the (relatively solid) corpuscles that compose the macro-object (the billiard ball) cannot be perfectly hard, nor will they be perfectly contiguous with one another (i.e., perfectly packed together). Rather, they will themselves be aggregates of smaller bodies and will thus be separated from one another by some relatively fluid matter.

Given this micro-complexity, it becomes very difficult to answer the question: where is the shape of the body? One possible answer is that it is wherever there is an interface between matter and void; after all, we are at this point considering the "object" in abstraction from the plenum (say, in a vacuum). But this raises the further question of what it is we in fact abstracted from the plenum. At the time, we really did not pay much attention to the details of the abstraction; and now it seems crucially important. In saying, "Let us consider the billiard ball in abstraction from the rest of the plenum" did we mean, "Let us consider the corpuscles which compose the ball," or did we mean to abstract everything that is contained within some geometrical bound? There seem to be problems with either answer. If we meant the latter, then the abstraction had to involve some decision on our part about what the geometrical bound is, and how much complexity is to be accounted for in that geometrical bound. Given this, it is clear that we were responsible for delineating the shape, rather than the nature of reality. But if we meant the former, then even if there were some determinate set of corpuscles that constitute the body, the object would have no more a shape than a swarm of bees.

We can think about our abstraction on the following analogy. Imagine a glass jar filled with marbles. Now imagine that very spatial arrangement of marbles without the jar. This is in some ways an appropriate model for our billiard ball (as it is for each individual marble): the marbles are the corpuscles that compose the billiard ball, and the air is the relatively fluid matter that surrounds those corpuscles. Now in abstracting our billiard ball from the plenum, were we abstracting merely the corpuscles that compose the body (the marbles)? Or did we mean to also include the relatively fluid matter surrounding the corpuscles (the air around the marbles)? If we were abstracting only the corpuscles (or marbles), it seems clear that the aggregate has no determinate shape at all. And this becomes even more clear when we are careful to bear in mind that each corpuscle (or marble) is fluid too, and so is like the collection of corpuscles (or marbles) in all relevant respects. If, on the other hand, we were abstracting the corpuscles with the fluid matter, then there is a question about what determined the geometrical bounds (where the jar would be) in the first place. To a certain extent, this decision starts to look somewhat (though perhaps not entirely) arbitrary. One thing that is clear, though, is that in this case, we are the ones doing the carving: the boundaries are not metaphysically prescribed. And this only becomes more evident when we finally consider the body as part of the entire plenum, rather than abstracted from it, since the fluid matter that surrounds the corpuscles will be relatively continuous with the fluid matter that is moving between the corpuscles.

Finally, we must keep in mind that it will not help to say that what should be included as part of the body are the corpuscles plus whatever fluid matter is responsible for the corpuscles' bearing the relations they do to one another, and their having the properties they do individually. For in a plenum, there is a real sense in which every part of the plenum is at least partially causally responsible for the states of, and relations among, every other part. Of course, this might show that the sort of abstraction we considered is deeply unintelligible. But even if it is, this does not undermine the point that infinite complexity in the plenum entails that surfaces are illusory rather than real properties of things.

On this interpretation of Leibniz's reasoning, therefore, we are to see that the infinite division of the plenum precludes the existence of shape by focusing on the possibility of individuating surfaces in a plenum physics, not by focusing on the amount of complexity it is possible for a determinate surface to express. In other words, the problem caused by infinite impressions is not that they result in an infinitely messy surface; rather, it is that they make metaphysically individuated surfaces impossible. Of course, on both readings any particular shape is shown to be an abstraction from the infinite complexity of the plenum. But on this alternative interpretation, it is not an abstraction from a surface that is actually more complex than it seems. Rather, it is an abstraction from something that has no real existence. This is the sense, then, in which no shape is appropriate for infinite impressions: there are no surfaces that could do the work of demarcating or individuating bodies in a plenum in which every parcel of matter is being impressed upon by the infinite bodies that compose that body and the infinite bodies that surround it. Put more simply, no infinitely divided plenum, including the Cartesian variety, has the resources to make sense of the real individuation of bodies from one another.

Shape and Idealism

Leibniz's arguments against the reality of shape are clearly intended to undermine the intelligibility of a Cartesian plenum theory; and to this extent I think the arguments are successful. Furthermore, I think the arguments are sufficient to show that shape cannot exist in any type of plenum theory. But do they show anything stronger? That is, do they undermine the intelligibility of realism about matter more generally? I do not think they do, at least on their own. Certainly, showing that shape is impossible is not sufficient for establishing immaterialism. However, if these considerations about shape are conjoined with other assumptions, assumptions which are clearly Leibnizian, we do get something that begins to resemble an argument for immaterialism. In this section, I shall sketch the way such an argument would go.

In section XII of the "Discourse," Leibniz draws an explicit conclusion from his arguments against the reality of the modes of extension: shape (and the other Cartesian modes) "cannot constitute any substance" (AG 44). This clearly undermines the Cartesian conception of extended substance, since Cartesian bodies are nothing more than extension in length, breadth, and depth. But the arguments against the possibility of shape, at least as I interpret them, also get us a slightly stronger conclusion, namely, that shape cannot be a real property of anything. For the arguments against the reality of shape depend on assumptions to which Leibniz is firmly committed: if there is matter it is a plenum, and if there is a plenum it is actually infinitely divided. And if shape cannot be a genuine property of anything, it is certainly true that it cannot be a property of a substance. This, of course, does not show there can be no extended continuum, since we can conceive of an extended continuum in which there are bodies that are not determinately individuated from one another, or that have fuzzy, indeterminate shapes. But there is a central Leibnizian thesis that seems to raise problems for this conception of the plenum: the aggregate thesis.

According to the aggregate thesis, beings by aggregation are only as real as the entities out of which they are aggregated. In other words, the reality an aggregate has is a function of the reality of the ultimate constituents out of which it is aggregated. Leibniz appeals to this principle at many points throughout his career. One of the best statements of it can be found in a letter to Arnauld: "entities made up by aggregation have only as much reality as exists in their constituent parts" (G II, 72; M 88). A direct implication of this thesis is that if an aggregate is real or substantial, the elements which constitute the aggregate must be real or substantial; that is, they must satisfy the conditions on being a substance. With this thesis in hand, it is possible to formulate a *reductio* of any genuinely (mind-independently) extended continuum:

1 Assume: There is a metaphysically real, extended continuum (i.e., a plenum of matter, however constituted).
2 There must be some account of the composition of any real continuum.

This is a principle that Leibniz takes to be fundamental (G II 98, 119; M 123, 153).

3 If a continuum is composed, it is an aggregate.
4 The reality of an aggregate depends on the elements out of which it is aggregated. (Aggregate Thesis)
5 Something that is genuinely extended cannot be composed of unextended entities.

Although early in his career Leibniz flirted with the idea that a continuum could be composed of extensionless points, he had given up this idea by the period in which we find the arguments against the reality of shape.

6 So the elements of the continuum must be extended. (1)–(5)
7 And the elements must not be aggregates; they must be simple and substantial. (1)–(4)
8 So there must be extended substances. (6), (7)
9 If there are extended substances, these entities must be metaphysically individuated from one another in the plenum; that is, there must be a fact of the matter about where one substance ends and another begins.

According to Leibniz, substances are completely determinate, self-contained, and independent of every other substance. It would seem to follow from this that there would need to be absolutely determinate boundaries or surfaces in virtue of which extended substances are individuated from one another.

10 But there is no fact of the matter about the individuation of extended things in a plenum. (The arguments against the reality of shape)

So, on the assumption that there is genuine, mind-independent extension, the aggregate thesis demands there be extended substances that ground its reality. But extended substances would need to be metaphysically individuated from one another, since it could not share a part with any other substance. Thus, the assumption (that an extended continuum exists) is false.

If this argument is sound, then Leibniz's arguments against the reality of shape have at least the potential to play a central role in an argument for immaterialism. And I think it is likely that he did see the connections between the ideality of the modes of extension and impossibility of genuinely (mind-independently) extended substance.

But if he was aware of the strength of his arguments against the modes of extension, a puzzle arises about how we are supposed to understand a second conclusion that he mentions in section XII of the "Discourse." After claiming that the modes of extension are imaginary, he goes on to say that "we must necessarily recognize in body something related to souls, something we commonly call substantial form" (G IV, 436; AG 44). This sounds as if Leibniz is suggesting we need to add something to the Cartesian theory of matter to get an adequate account of body, rather than that we should conclude that there is no matter at all. As paradoxical as it might sound, I believe the truth lies somewhere in between these two options. That is, I think the correct interpretation is that there is a sense in which Leibniz wants to deny the reality of matter and a sense in which he wants to show that something needs to be added to the Cartesian conception to render natural philosophy intelligible.

There are two ways of thinking about what it is that needs to be "recognized in body." In the "Discourse" Leibniz says that we need to recognize something related to souls or substantial forms, yet it is clear from other passages in the "Discourse" that he is concerned to show that an intelligible physics must be one in which dynamical forces play a central role. In the end, I think there is nothing inconsistent in thinking that Leibniz wants to make both of these points. But this depends on a careful interpretation of what Leibniz is arguing for.

Let us begin by thinking about the conclusion that we need to recognize something like soul or substantial form in body. This could mean at least two different things. Commentators who read Leibniz as having an immaterialist metaphysics in this period think he is claiming, roughly, that what we need to recognize is that body is the phenomenal result of an aggregate of simple, immaterial substances, what he calls "monads." This is the sense in which souls or forms are "in" body. However, other commentators have argued that, at least in this period, form is to be understood as one aspect of a hylomorphic composite of form and matter. So what we need to recognize is that without form, the material continuum is completely homogenous, with no individuation or identity over time of its parts, but with form, the idea of a genuinely extended, material continuum is perfectly intelligible. A thorough assessment of this general line of interpretation is not possible here. But I think a brief comment about it is in order. The leading proponent of this view, Daniel Garber, seems to think that Leibniz's arguments against the reality of shape are intended to show only that shapes are not real unless there are "quasi-Aristotelian" substantial forms; after forms have been added to extension there is no problem with completely determinate shapes in the plenum (Garber 1985). In fact, according to Garber, form plays the critical role of marking out metaphysical distinctions in matter; it plays the role of a metaphysical cookie-cutter (albeit one that is always changing its shape). But how can we square this with Leibniz's arguments against the reality of shape? As I have already mentioned, the basic premises of the arguments are claims to which Leibniz remains firmly committed throughout his career. So if Garber is right, there must be some way of understanding the conclusion that would make it consistent with the cookie-cutter account of form. But if there are no metaphysically determinate shapes, it would seem there could be no fact of the matter about where one body ends and another begins.

In the "Discourse," it is clear that Leibniz also wants to point out that force, a physical or dynamical property, must be appealed to in any intelligible physics. Is it possible that this is what he means when he says in Discourse XII that we need to recognize something akin to substantial forms in body? I think it is unlikely. To be sure, Leibniz thinks that a central problem with Cartesian physics is that it does not appeal to forces, and as a result gets the rules of motion and impact wrong. But this is a point about physics, not ground-floor metaphysics. And having a well-developed physics, as Leibniz does, is perfectly consistent with having an immaterialist ontology. In fact, one of the points of showing the Cartesians that the true physics requires forces is that it also shows them that their metaphysics of matter is too austere to account for the dynamical properties of bodies, since physical forces must be grounded in something metaphysical (G IV, 444; AG 51).

Let us consider, nevertheless, whether force is the sort of property that could turn homogenous, unindividuated matter into something real. This way of putting it, of course, is not ideal. For, as Robert Sleigh says, "No one is likely to think that with the injection of force or form into shapeless mass, it literally 'shapes up'" (Sleigh 1990: 112). But there might be a different way of construing matters. In his forthcoming analysis of the shape texts, Samuel Levey offers a different way of stating the point about the relation between shape and force. According to Levey, force is the source of particular shapes in things:

> What it is for there to be matter arranged in a certain way is for there to be a certain nexus of forces acting in a given space . . . Extension itself is to be understood as a diffusion of resistance, and thus the specific diffusion of it into a given space constitutes a body of a given shape. (Levey forthcoming (b))

This may well be the best way of filling out a realist ontology on Leibniz's behalf. Nevertheless, I do not find it convincing as an interpretation. I think it is doubtful that the texts Levey cites in support of it are meant to spell out Leibniz's fundamental metaphysics. In fact, I think it is much more likely that Leibniz's claim that force "fixes shapes in matter" (G IV, 397), or his claim that extension is diffused resistance, is meant to be a piece of physics, rather than a piece of ground-floor metaphysics. Furthermore, Leibniz states explicitly in a text dated from this period that forces are reducible to the perceptual properties of simple substances: "Substances have metaphysical matter or passive power insofar as they express something confusedly, active, insofar as they express it distinctly" (G VII, 322; LL 365). (For Leibniz, "expression" is a technical term; but when it is applied to substances, such as minds, the term is (very roughly) synonymous with "perception.") This text, then, suggests that any talk of the diffusion of forces and the fixing of shape is to be understood as applying at the level of physics, rather than the level of deepest metaphysics.

In the end, there is a sense in which Leibniz wants to deny the reality of matter and a sense in which he wants to show that something needs to be added to the Cartesian ontology to render natural philosophy intelligible. His ultimate view is that the world as it is in itself consists solely in unextended, active, simple substances that bear neither causal nor spatial relations to one another. Nevertheless, he also believes physics is central to our understanding of the natural world, and that it is therefore important that we have the explanatory resources to make the phenomena intelligible. What Cartesian physics lacks, he argues, is a notion of physical force. But he does not think that we can retain a realist conception of body by simply adding a notion of force to Descartes' geometrical conception of matter as extension. Certainly, we can offer explanations of natural phenomena that are sufficient in physics by appealing to the properties of extension and dynamical properties. But there must be a deeper story about what grounds, metaphysically speaking, the dynamical properties of bodies that are essential to corporeal phenomena. And this is the story of the Monadology (G VI 607–23; AG 213–25). Leibniz's ultimate metaphysics is thus immaterialist, rather than realist. Nevertheless, there is an important sense, for Leibniz, in which matter is real. Our perceptions of bodies are not like mere dreams, states of mind that do not represent real things outside the mind. Rather, our perceptions of a world outside the mind represent a real world – a world of monadic reality. To this extent, then, bodies are real. But this only makes sense if we see them as "well-founded" in monadic reality; and this is what Leibniz means when he says we need to recognize something like souls or substantial forms in body.

Acknowledgments

Some of the ideas in this chapter were presented at Marquette University and California State University-Long Beach. I am also grateful for discussions of these ideas with Randall Amano, Richard Arthur, Janet Broughton, Samuel Levey, and Alan Nelson.

References and Further Reading

Adams, Robert M. (1994). *Leibniz: Determinist, Theist, Idealist*. New York: Oxford University Press.

Arthur, Richard (1998). Infinite aggregates and phenomenal wholes: Leibniz's theory of substance as a solution to the continuum problem. *Leibniz Society Review*, 8.

—— (1999). Infinite number and the world soul. *Leibniz Society Review*, 9.

Carlin, L. (1997). Infinite accumulations and pantheistic implications: Leibniz and the "Anima Mundi." *Leibniz Society Review*, 7.

Crockett, Timothy (2004). Leibniz on shape and the reality of body (doctoral dissertation). Berkeley: University of California.

Garber, Daniel (1985). Leibniz and the foundations of physics: The middle years. In K. Okruhlik and J. R. Brown (eds.), *The Natural Philosophy of Leibniz* (pp. 27–130). Dordrecht: D. Reidel.

—— (1992). *Descartes' Metaphysical Physics*. Chicago: University of Chicago Press.

Hartz, G., and Cover, J. (1988). Space and time in the Leibnizian metaphysic. *Nous*, 22, 493–519.

Lamarra, Antonio (1986). Leibniz on Locke on infinity. In *L'infinito in Leibniz: problemi e Terminologia* (pp. 173–91). Rome: Edizioni dell'Ateneo; Hannover: G. W.-Leibniz-Gesellschaft.

Levey, Samuel (1998). Leibniz on mathematics and the actually infinite division of matter. *Philosophical Review*, 107.

—— (forthcoming (a)). Dans les Corps il n'y a point de figure parfaite: Leibniz on time, change and corporeal substance. In M. Mugnai and E. Pasini (eds.), *Leibniz on Corporeal Substance and the Labyrinth of the Continuum* (Studia Leibnitianna Supplement). Stuttgart: Franz Steiner Verlag.

—— (forthcoming (b)). Leibniz on precise shapes and the corporeal world. In Cover and Rutherford (eds.), *Leibniz: Nature and Freedom*. Oxford: Oxford University Press.

McRae, Robert (1976). *Leibniz: Perception, Apperception and Thought*. Toronto: University of Toronto Press.

Mates, Benson (1986). *The Philosophy of Leibniz: Metaphysics and Language*. New York: Oxford University Press.

Rescher, Nicholas (1979). *Leibniz: An Introduction to His Philosophy*. APQ Library of Philosophy. Totowa, NJ: Rowman and Littlefield.

Russell, Bertrand (1937). *A Critical Exposition of the Philosophy of Leibniz*. London: George Allen and Unwin.

Rutherford, Donald (1995). *Leibniz and the Rational Order of Nature*. Cambridge: Cambridge University Press.

Sleigh, Robert C. (1990). *Leibniz and Arnauld: A Commentary on their Correspondence*. New Haven, CT: Yale University Press.

15

Leibniz on Modality, Cognition, and Expression

ALAN NELSON

Leibniz was fond of stressing the importance of the principles of non-contradiction and of sufficient reason in his philosophy. In the *Monadology*, for example, he says that our reasonings (*raisonnemens*) are based or founded upon (*fondés*) these great principles (*Monadology* 31, 32). This is often taken to mean that all the substantive doctrines in Leibniz's philosophy are meant to follow logically from the principles. Because the conclusion of a valid argument cannot contain more than what is in the premises, it is hard to understand the two principles as strong enough to do the job. Mindful of this, Russell (1900: 4) reconstructs Leibniz's system as meant to depend on five principles instead of two. Naturally, Russell concludes that the attempt is a failure, albeit an impressive one. We might, however, understand Leibniz to be saying that the reasonings we employ proceed according to the two great principles, leaving it open what we are reasoning *about*. This chapter proposes that Leibniz be understood as beginning with a more substantive basis for his reasonings. The leading idea is perhaps best introduced by a comparison with Spinoza. In Spinoza's mature thought, God conceived as the infinite mode of intellect obviously contains, or comprises, all the adequate ideas there are. Since nothing exists apart from Spinoza's God and its attributes and affections, and the ideas that are adequate in God are the existing things (considered under either thought or extension), Spinoza's metaphysics is strongly actualistic; merely possible things have no existence whatsoever. Spinoza scholars disagree about the extent to which this is properly called a necessitarian metaphysics, but it was certainly understood by Leibniz as strongly and unacceptably necessitarian.

One crucial metaphysical contrast between the systems of Spinoza and Leibniz concerns the status of possibles in the divine intellect. Leibniz's God knows what other worlds are possible, so that he can exercise his power and goodness by freely creating the best among the possibles. I shall express this familiar idea by saying that the divine intellect contains the possible worlds as well as the actual world (that is, it contains ideas or concepts of the worlds as possible). Now the student of Leibniz has some options for proceeding, though we shall see that the results are the same regardless of where we begin. A full understanding of any point of Leibniz's doctrine depends on all the rest.

The point of departure chosen here is a doctrine that Leibniz affirms consistently and frequently. It is that the foundation of the necessary and eternal truths resides in God. In what follows, the distinction between the "foundation" and the "truths" themselves will be clarified, and the operative sense of "necessary" will be specified. It suffices for now to follow Russell in noting that God knows all the possibles, so it is necessary that the possibles are what they are. God further knows what the possibles are from eternity. This doctrine about divine knowledge ought to be tightly connected with Leibniz's position on the knowledge of the eternal truths that is enjoyed by finite rational monads or "spirits."[1] Leibniz does in fact connect them via his deep commitment to the doctrine that apperceiving, rational spirits, in contrast to other monads, are created in God's image. It is important for understanding this aspect of Leibniz's system to accommodate rational philosophy to the greatest possible degree with the doctrine (required by faith) that spirits are created as images of God.[2] Part of the thesis of this chapter depends on a closer than usual reading of the texts relevant to the "God's image" requirement (as I shall call it) and a correlative emphasis on its centrality in Leibniz's thought. Let us consider, for example:

> The excellence of spirits and that God considers them preferable to other creatures. That spirits express God rather than the world, but that the other substances express the world rather than God. (DM 35, title)

> But the knowledge of necessary and eternal truths is what distinguishes us from simple animals and furnishes us with reason and the sciences, elevating us to a knowledge of ourselves and God. And that is what we call the rational soul, or spirit in ourselves. (*Monadology* 29)

> Among other differences between ordinary souls and spirits, some of which I have already noted, there are also the following: that souls, in general, are living mirrors of images of the universe of creatures, but that minds are also images of the divinity itself, or of the author of nature, capable of knowing the system of the universe, and imitating something of it through their schematic representations of it, each mind being like a little divinity in its own realm. (*Monadology* 83)

What is particularly important about these texts and others like them is that they connect the idea that spirits are created in God's image with their expressing God, and in particular with their being able to know the eternal truths, which are grounded in God's intellect. Leibniz puts this connection to work in two main ways. One furnishes a proof of God's existence. Granting that something is possible (as we must on pain of Spinozism), there is a ground for that possibility: God's knowledge of the possibles, or the "essences." These are the foundation for the eternal truths known by spirits. The second use of the doctrine, already present in the texts above, is in classifying monads according to their expressive capacities. Animal souls, unlike bare monads, express their universe in virtue of sensing it. But spirits, in virtue of being images of God, express the universe still more perfectly than animals. Knowledge of the eternal truths is reflective knowledge, and reflection is required for apperception, rationality, scientific knowledge, and ultimately for status as moral beings. Even stupefied monads are imperfectly omniscient insofar as they very confusedly express everything in their world, but the omniscience of spirits entitles them to a special relationship with God (DM 36, 37). And this relationship derives, in part, from the sense in which spirits'

283

knowledge or the structure of their intellect (which I take to be the same thing) is an image of God's knowledge or the divine intellect.[3]

In light of these texts (others will be discussed below), I think the reasons are already quite clear for Leibniz's wanting to say that spirits express God in virtue of being able to know eternal truths. What is not so clear is exactly how the doctrine itself is to be understood. Russell, characteristically, thought that the doctrine was ultimately logically incoherent and that Leibniz allowed theological pressures to overcome his philosophical good sense, or at least the written expression of that good sense. The task at hand is to construct an alternate interpretation of Leibniz's doctrine concerning eternal truths that is clear, consistent with an overall interpretation of his system, and able to perform all the tasks he expects of it.

One way to appreciate the problems being faced is to consider a philosophically natural, but obviously incorrect interpretation. One might take as given simply that eternal truths are true as such and that is why God, in his omniscience, knows them. This is to regard the eternal truths as something like propositions or facts whose truth is somehow independent of God himself. Taking a paradigmatic case, one might say that the proposition from Euclid, "The sum of the interior angles of a triangle is equal to a straight angle" (hereafter, P32) is a fact the truth of which is prior to God's knowing it. This is represented in Figure 15.1.

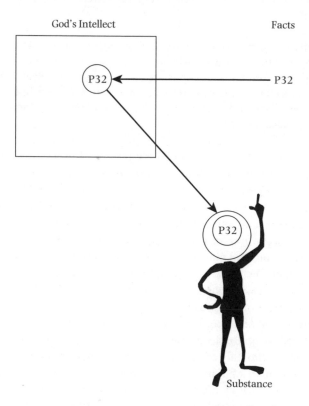

Figure 15.1

This is, to repeat, obviously mistaken as an interpretation of Leibniz. One of the uses of the doctrine is to prove God's existence by insisting that the eternal truths reside in God. This is spoiled if spirits' knowledge of them expresses God's knowledge of something like propositions or facts that reside outside God. It does not help matters to suggest that it is God who, in the first place, makes the eternal truths as creatures because Leibniz joined most thinkers in emphatically rejecting that tenet from Descartes. A correct interpretation must respect the fact that Leibniz was a deep and thoroughgoing nominalist, or idealist, about everything except God and monads. Anything else regarded as having being must have that being traced to these individual substances.

Russell knew this much, of course, and did some more work before indicting Leibniz. Geometrical truths, truths concerning spatial relations, are paradigmatic of eternal truths. Leibniz writes:

> [Space] is a relationship: an order, not only among existents, but also among possibles as though they existed. But its truth and reality are grounded in God, like all eternal truths. (LNE 149)

The idea is that spatial relations obtain among possibly existing things, substances considered as possible (including the actual considered as possible). In one sense, therefore, God is the ground of eternal truths because the concepts of possible objects of relations, *qua* possible, have their being in the divine understanding. This is more generally borne out in many texts, for example in the 1686 "A Specimen of Discoveries About Marvelous Secrets":

> If there were no eternal substance there would be no eternal truths; so this too affords a proof of God, who is the root of possibility, for his mind is the very region of ideas or truths . . . The reason for truths lies in the ideas of things, which are involved in the divine essence itself. (G 7: 311)

This might suggest that there are, as it were, at least two compartments in the divine intellect. One of these contains ideas of all the "things," the possible finite substances. Since the concept of an individual substance is complete in the very strong Leibnizian sense, we can take these concepts to be partitioned into concepts of possible worlds – maximally complete sets of harmonized, compossible substances. A second component of God's intellect might, then, contain knowledge of relations concerning the possibles. This knowledge is "grounded" in the knowledge of the possible existents, so it need not be grounded in (that is, be true *of*) anything outside God. So Russell wrote: "God, according to Leibniz, sees not only individual monads and their various states, but also the relations between monads, and in this consists the reality of relations" (Russell 1900: 178).

Russell proceeds to construct difficulties from the contrast between the ideas in God which constitute the right hand compartment of God's intellect in figure 15.2 and God's knowledge of these ideas. Does this knowledge constitute a third compartment as shown in figure 15.3? Russell says that either answer to this question raises insurmountable difficulties, for reasons that need not concern us here.[4]

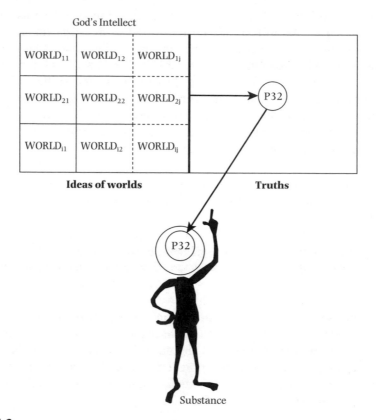

God's Intellect

WORLD$_{11}$	WORLD$_{12}$	WORLD$_{1j}$
WORLD$_{21}$	WORLD$_{22}$	WORLD$_{2j}$
WORLD$_{i1}$	WORLD$_{i2}$	WORLD$_{ij}$

Ideas of worlds   **Truths**

P32

P32

Substance

Figure 15.2

The meager discussion of this difficult issue in the literature remains very nearly where Russell left it. For example, after an incisive discussion, Adams concludes with much care, but without much conviction:

> Such considerations should probably lead Leibniz to the conclusion that the being of necessary truths typically consists in their being recognized or accepted as true by God, though the reason why they are true (and hence accepted) is to be found in their content rather than in the divine acceptance as such. (Adams 1994: 191)

Jolley concludes his discussion in much the same vein, as follows: "Thus Leibniz's remarks to the effect that God is the domain of the eternal truths must ultimately be unpacked in psychological terms; they must be reduced to claims about God's propositional thoughts" (Jolley 1990: 169). Here Jolley is clearly adopting the three-compartment analysis and agreeing with Russell and Adams that this requires (for one thing) a "psychological" interpretation of God's knowledge of the right compartment. This apparently means that God forms (presumably from eternity) affirmative attitudes toward propositions expressing the relations among possibles.

Thus, where Adams refers to the "content" of the ideas in the lower right hand compartment, Jolley refers to God's knowledge of these ideas as "propositional thoughts."

I read these analyses as trying to uphold the three-compartment picture, but without attempting to provide navigation through the various icebergs showing on Russell's radar screen. I sympathize with Adams and Jolley's inclination to think that Russell's considerations are difficulties rather than refutations, but hope to resolve the difficulties by drafting a different picture of how Leibniz was deploying these materials.

The texts lay down two unequivocal constraints on an interpretation. One is that it is in virtue of *our* knowledge of the eternal truths that we express God. The other is that the eternal truths must somehow be grounded by the possibles in God's intellect. The two-compartment analysis is constructed to conform to these constraints. Before introducing Russellian problems with this interpretation it is helpful to notice that it possesses a feature that would have struck Leibniz as highly undesirable. Spirits express God in virtue of their knowledge of the eternal truths, but spirits are finite after all. It would be unseemly if their knowledge of the eternal truths fully equaled God's knowledge in its completeness and perfection. But this is exactly what we have in figure 15.3. It is the proposition (or idea-content of) P32 that both spirits and God know. It is misleading, of course, that I have written P32 in English. That is supposed to be no more than a symbol (in Russell's terminology) for the proposition which is what we and God really understand when we know the truth as opposed to merely mouthing the words. God's knowledge should be more perfect than ours in every respect, and this includes his knowledge of the foundation of the eternal truths.

> When God displays a truth to us, we come to possess the truth which is in his understanding, *for although his ideas are infinitely more perfect and extensive than ours,* they still have the same relationships that ours do. (LNE 397, emphasis added)

It might be noted in defense of figure 15.3 that God knows all the infinitely many eternal truths, while we can actually attain to only some of them. This would provide a weak sense in which God's knowledge is more perfect or extensive, but it is ultimately of no help. We have the capacity to know any eternal truth whatsoever, since (1) whether or not any spirit actually consciously and distinctly thinks a particular eternal truth, we express, usually non-consciously, God's intellect, which contains them all; thus (2) the eternal truths (presumably all of them) are innate in spirits; and (3) any eternal truth is capable of finite demonstration, and therefore is within the grasp of a finite intellect.

The defense is ineffective because these considerations do not bear on the fact that when a spirit does distinctly perceive P32, figure 15.3 has it that it perceives it just as well as God, which is still unseemly. Another weak defense of figure 15.3 might appeal to God's applying his knowledge of the eternal truths to more particulars than spirits can. The two-compartment picture might have it that God "applies" his knowledge of the eternal truths to infinitely many actual and possible instances, while it might be said that we are able, at best, to "apply" truths to finitely many actual instances. This attempted defense fails because it does not show God's knowledge of the eternal truths themselves superior to our own; it merely attributes to God a superior ability to contemplate instances of their application. The point I am making does rely on God's

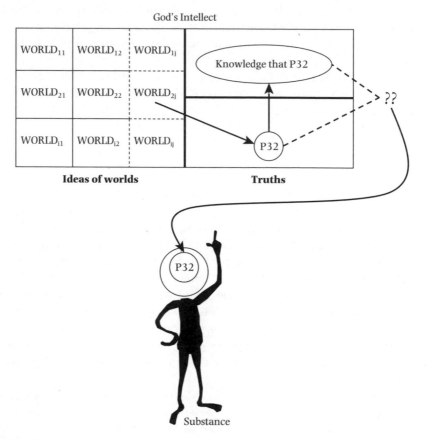

Figure 15.3

superior knowledge of the *foundation* of the eternal truths as opposed to the eternal truths themselves. Again, this distinction will grow in importance as we proceed.

Let's back up and construct a picture according to which God's knowledge is indeed more perfect than spirits'. Recall that one can regard an eternal truth as what Leibniz sometimes calls a "metaphysical" law. Eternal truths are laws governing not only what God creates, but the possibles or essences as well.[5] And note that God knows intuitively and *a priori* every last detail about every aggregate of monads that are phenomenally expressed as triangularly shaped bodies in every world. He also knows every particular thought about triangles that any possible spirit has, etc. In light of all this infinite knowledge, notice that the generalization expressed by P32 does not add anything to God's infinite, finitely unanalyzable knowledge of all the possible worlds.

This suggests that a fitting representation of God's infinite knowledge is fully given by a one-compartment picture.

"Where are the eternal truths?" in figure 15.4, one might ask. To answer this, consider that the possibles in God's intellect ground the truths and in knowing the possibles, God knows them perfectly in infinite detail. Spirits are incapable of this. They

288

God's Intellect = Ideas of Worlds

WORLD$_{11}$	WORLD$_{12}$	WORLD$_{13}$	WORLD$_{14}$	WORLD$_{15}$	WORLD$_{1j}$
WORLD$_{21}$	WORLD$_{22}$	WORLD$_{23}$	WORLD$_{24}$	WORLD$_{25}$	WORLD$_{2j}$
WORLD$_{i1}$	WORLD$_{i2}$	WORLD$_{i3}$	WORLD$_{i4}$	WORLD$_{i5}$	WORLD$_{ij}$

P32

Substance

Figure 15.4

are capable of very distinctly expressing God's particular infinite knowledge by think-ing eternal truths in their general, abstract, finitely demonstrable form. Spirits having a finitized version of God's infinite knowledge means that their intellects are *images* of God's, and not that they contain exact duplicates or miniaturizations of one compart-ment of God's intellect. This is best articulated by saying, with Leibniz, that the *know-ledge* of eternal truths is a feature of the intellects of finite spirits, while the *ground* for this knowledge is in the divine intellect. This ground is the divine ideas themselves. And what God has ideas of are the possibles and the worlds into which they are parti-tioned. In other words, the divine intellect comprises ideas of things upon which the divine will might be exercised and those are ideas of substances, each of which in-volves its worldmates (to borrow an apt term from David Lewis). God's knowledge is therefore perfectly infinite and fully concrete; God's omniscience does not require the aid of abstractions drawn from his perfect knowledge of particulars. These aids are fitted to finite means that spirits deploy for understanding what is infinitely complex. In short, the eternal truths *are* the means by which spirits express the divine know-ledge of all particular possibles.

What might support this interpretation apart from the texts employed in laying it out? There are a number of Leibnizian arguments that favor it over the three-compartment interpretation of figure 15.3. Before examining the arguments, however, I want to forestall one objection to the statement of the view itself. One might object to characterizing the eternal truths as themselves "law-like," "abstract," and "general." Let us consider some contexts in which Leibniz himself thinks of them that way.

> It is also through the knowledge of necessary truths and through their *abstractions* that we are raised to reflective acts, which enable us to think of that which is called "I." (*Monadology* 83)

> And when God displays a truth to us, we come to possess the truth which is in his understanding, for although his ideas are infinitely more perfect and extensive than ours, they still have the same relationships that ours do. (LNE 397)

> So the concept of the sphere in general is incomplete or abstract, that is to say that one considers only the essence of the sphere in general or in theory without regard to the particular circumstances. (G 2: 38)

These straightforward texts are sometimes elaborated.

> As for "eternal truths," it must be understood that fundamentally they are all conditional; they say, in effect, given so and so, such and such is the case. For instance, when I say: "Any figure which has three sides will also have three angles," I am saying nothing more than that given that there is a figure with three sides that same figure will have three angles.
> And lest you should think that it is unnecessary to have recourse to [the Supreme and Universal] Mind, it should be borne in mind that these necessary truths contain the determining reason and *regulating principle* of existent things – the *laws of the universe*, in short.

> Therefore, since these necessary truths are prior to the existence of contingent beings, they must be grounded in the existence of a necessary substance. That is where I find the pattern for the ideas and truths which are engraved in our souls. They are engraved there not in the form of propositions, but rather as sources which, by being employed in particular circumstances, will give rise to actual assertions. (LNE 446–7, emphasis added)

This rich but obscure passage from the *New Essays* can be read as making the following points. The "conditional" character of the eternal truths arises from their being generalized expressions of an infinity of particular items: If we consider triangular array A, then etc. If we consider triangular array B, then etc. And so on *ad infinitum*. Clearly, God knows each of the infinite actual and possible triangular configurations. We cannot do that, but we can express them all through the generalization. The "necessary truths" that are prior to creation are not generalizations in the divine intellect, they are instead the ideas of the possible (including the actual) existents. Recall Russell's emphasizing that the possibles themselves are necessary. It is necessary that *all* the possibles be exactly what they are; no other possibles are possible. These possibles then regulate divine creation functioning like a metaphysical law. God's choice in creation must be drawn from the set of maximal compossible sets of monads. He then wills the best.

This consideration can be extended into a positive argument for the interpretation summarily schematized in figure 15.4. If the eternal truths we understand are "metaphysical" laws covering principles of creation and possible creation, how are we to understand familiar natural laws? Can mundane, natural laws governing phenomena in the actual world fit into Leibniz's theory in the same way we have specified for metaphysical laws? Central texts strongly suggest they do. To explore the connection, we can begin by noting that Leibniz refers to natural laws as being subordinate to what grounds metaphysical laws.

> The extraordinary concourse of God is comprised in what our essence expresses, for this expression extends to everything, but it surpasses the forces of our nature or our distinct expression, which is finite and follows certain subordinate maxims.
> . . . Miracles and the extraordinary concourses of God have this peculiarity, that they cannot be foreseen by the reasoning of any created spirit, however enlightened it might be, because distinct comprehension of the general order surpasses all of them: whereas everything that is called natural depends on less general maxims that creatures can understand. (DM 16)

> Although what creatures conceive is not the measure of God's powers, their conceptivity or power of conceiving is the measure of nature's powers: everything which is in accord with the natural order can be conceived or understood by some creature. (LNE 65)

So spirits are created such that they are able to discover the subordinate laws governing their own world. As Leibniz put it to Arnauld:

> For as there is an infinity of possible worlds, there is also an infinity of laws, some proper to one world, some to others, and each possible individual of any one world contains in its concept the laws of its world. (G 2: 39)

Their finite minds are crafted to understand these finite versions of what God understands about a particular world. Spirits can, consequently, understand mechanics, astronomy, material science, biology, etc., and these provide very distinct understanding of their subject matter. God, in contrast, understands the absolutely complete infinite series of each of the infinitely many substances (including the possible ones, of course). We can put this by saying that God knows the general law of the world. And this most general, infinite understanding is much more than a conjunction of the subordinate laws our sciences can deliver. The subordinate character of our science is shown, for example, by miracles. They appear to us as suspensions, or even violations, of the laws we discover, but God understands their place in the general harmony. This absolutely infinite knowledge cannot be grasped by finite minds, but it is well *expressed* by the natural laws our sciences uncover.

The analogy with the eternal truths turns out to be closer than one might have expected. In each case, it is important to see that the divine intellect contains perfect particular concepts of the substances in each world considered as possible. The scientific laws we understand are hypothetically and not absolutely necessary because some other subordinate laws will govern other possible worlds. So when we very distinctly understand our natural laws, we are not expressing the entire divine intellect as we do when we understand the absolutely necessary eternal truths. We instead abstractly express God's perfect particular knowledge of our world. God, therefore, does not know these subordinate regulations as such. His omniscience does not require it because he knows the entire, infinite law of the series. The subordinate regulations are a proprietary part of the innate equipment of spirits. They provide us with a finitized way of reflectively understanding (as opposed to brutely expressing) the law of the series for the actual, created world.

A different kind of positive argument for figure 15.4 can be introduced by means of a solution to a potential problem. It might initially seem odd that this interpretation has it that there are some items (P32 or the laws of chemistry, for example) that we can come to know but which God, strictly speaking, cannot. It seems we ought to say that since we understand P32 propositionally, God must as well, on pain of his lacking some knowledge we have and failing to be omniscient. The problem is really the same as the one raised in a different context by Frank Jackson's popular fable of a physically "omniscient" being who has no sensation of red. Jackson's point is that many are tempted to say that this being cannot be unqualifiedly omniscient because she does not know what red looks like. From the perspective of an early modern thinker in possession of the distinction between primary and secondary qualities, this issue appears in a different light.

Consider our knowledge of what red is like, or more concretely, "that roses are red." According to Leibniz, this can count as knowledge of an indistinct sort for us in our finite state. It is knowledge to the degree that it expresses more distinct forms of knowledge. More distinct knowledge would include the properties of light, the microstructure of roses, and the operation of our visual system. That might be the end of the analysis for someone like Descartes, but for Leibniz even these forms of scientific knowledge are further analyzable. Ultimately, there are the brute monadic features that result in the phenomena covered by natural law. From our point of view it would require an infinite analysis to reach this perfect understanding, but God has all that knowledge *a priori*. Leibniz's God, therefore, has no need of an imperfect indication of what he knows perfectly. For God to have sensory ideas or "qualia" would be an imperfection in knowledge rather than the reverse.

Similarly, our knowledge of P32 and other eternal truths is our finitized way of understanding part of what God knows perfectly about, not only our worldmates, but also all the possibles. In this sense, we express God's knowledge of those aspects of all the possible worlds. "For the soul is a little world where distinct ideas represent God and confused ones represent the universe" (LNE 109). We can safely conclude that our analysis of Leibniz's treatment of the "God's image" requirement does not in any way impugn God's omniscience. On the contrary, it magnifies the infinite gulf between infinite intellect and finite intellect while sharpening the sense in which spirits are like little divinities.

We have so far supported our reading of the "God's image" requirement by examining how God's intellect is expressed by finite intellects. Yet another positive argument for figure 15.4 and against figure 15.2 and figure 15.3 exploits the interconnection among some different respects in which we are created in God's image. Note that the innately implanted eternal truths come to be apperceived through reflection on particular cases – even sometimes particular cases of sensory experience. We arrive at occurrent appreciation of eternal truths through the psychological processes of abstraction and generalization. These operations require the apperception and reflection that distinguish us from brutes. One main burden of this chapter's argument is that one result of proper abstraction and generalization is eternal truths that are themselves abstract and general. This strikingly brings out the core of Leibniz's objections to Locke on this topic. Locke thought abstractions were ultimately empty unless derived from sensation. For Leibniz, our reflective appreciation of eternal truths is grounded in the divine intellect, while particular occurrent thoughts of eternal truths psychologically result from contemplating written and spoken words and other sensory experiences. Consider again *Monadology* 30: "It is also through the knowledge of necessary truths and through their abstractions that we rise to reflective acts, which enable us to think of that which is called 'I'." Consciously formed generalizations serve as conscious reasons for acting. And it is our ability to reflect on reasons that makes us moral agents specially related to God as subjects, children, and so on.[6]

The psychological processes spirits undergo in the active abstraction of eternal truths (and for that matter, natural laws) is in this way an integral part of the theory basing the "God's image" requirement on the contrast between the structure of infinite and finite intellect. Consider animals, unable to think of "I," non-rational and amoral. This need not prevent intelligent beings from explaining the behavior of brutes with recourse to reasons they reflectively understand – "the dog barked because it was hungry and wanted food." The universal harmony guarantees that they confusedly and passively express their universe. They are, however, unable to express God because they lack the apperception that would enable them to reflect on their phenomena and abstract generalizations from them. Without being able to reflect on maxims and laws, they are irrational and not subject to divine justice. These theoretical interconnections are lost if Leibniz is read as adhering to figure 15.3, in which spirits' expression of eternal truths is simplistically analyzed as cognizing them just as God does.

We now come to the last, and most weighty, positive argument for conceiving the divine intellect and its finite images in monads as summarized in figure 15.4. It is drawn from Leibniz's systematic approach to necessity and contingency. We begin with the problem of contingency and will next work our way back to the conception of divine intellect that we have seen to provide a tidy account of some important connections among eternal truths, expression, and human cognition. For the topic of contingency, it is useful to concentrate on the familiar 1686 texts, but the resulting reading is, as before, general enough to provide a broad understanding of Leibniz's entire mature period. A good place to start is with DM 13 that famously states:

> As the individual notion of each person contains once and for all everything that will ever happen to him, there are to be seen in this the proofs *a priori* or reasons of the truth of every event.

When Leibniz had the section headings of the *Discourse* sent to Arnauld, that astute critic reacted with "fright" to the "more than fatal necessity" that he detected in, for example, DM 13. The irony here is almost amusing, since Leibniz took preemptive measures against exactly this reaction in the unsent body of DM 13 and he rehearses these considerations in his next letter for Arnauld. What he writes, however, does not amount to a sustained argument, but instead appears to be a shotgun blast of various philosophical pellets, some old, some new. Leibniz here combines,

(a)   that reasons for free actions incline without necessitating,
(b)   the distinction between what is certain and what is necessary,
(c)   the distinction between hypothetical and absolute necessity,

and perhaps in elucidation of (c) we find the rest:

(d)   things possible in themselves,
(e)   things following from free decrees of God,
(f)   things following from possible free decrees of God, and
(g)   principles of contingency, existence, and perfection.

An ambitious interpretation of the sort attempted in this chapter means to show why Leibniz took all of (a)–(g) to be expressions of the same underlying treatment. It is, therefore, at odds with more diachronic interpretations of Leibniz's thought. Adams, for example, traces the appearances of (a)–(c) in the Leibnizian corpus, reading them as more or less independent, but mutually consistent attempts to come to grips with freedom and contingency (Adams 1994: 9–46). Sleigh focuses on the same texts emphasized here and arrives at the conclusion that Leibniz's main solution around 1686 revolves around elucidating the distinction between what is essential to a substance and what is "intrinsic" to it (Sleigh 1990: ch. 4).

Let's begin as before with the mathematical examples that come very naturally to both Leibniz and Arnauld. The difficulty arises from Leibniz's saying that everything follows from or is contained in the concept of an individual. What kind of determination comes with this following or containing? Leibniz and Arnauld agree that in mathematical examples the truths that follow from such concepts as sphere, triangle, and the like are absolutely necessary and that this kind of necessity applied to God or creatures would be a wholly unacceptable fatal necessity. Arnauld understandably reads Leibniz as being committed to the mathematical kind of "following" for substances because Leibniz does write that everything follows from the concept of an individual. In this context, Leibniz's strategy must be to break the analogy between the truths that follow (with absolute and fatal necessity) from a mathematical concept and those that follow from an individual concept.

Now, there are in turn two possible strategies for breaking the analogy. One is the strategy that I understand Sleigh to be attributing to Leibniz. The concept of a sphere (as I think both Leibniz and Arnauld see the matter) contains all and only what is essential to spheres. So everything that follows from the concept of sphere is necessary in the sense that it is part of the essence of sphere. But, says Sleigh's Leibniz, the essence of an individual contains less than the concept contains. So the things that follow from the essence are indeed very strictly necessary, but there is much true of an individual that is intrinsic to the individual, but does not in any way follow from its essence. These non-sequiturs then provide a basis for, or at the very least are connected with, freedom and contingency.

The strategy favored here focuses instead on understanding Leibniz's special theory of hypothetical necessity. Let us not begin with Leibniz's definition of hypothetical necessity. If we can first understand how he uses the idea, then we can subsequently see why Leibniz so defines it. Here, then, is the leading idea. Something is hypothetically necessary if it follows from a hypothesis. What are the relevant hypotheses for Leibniz? It is important to attend here to the metaphysics without being distracted by logical matters concerning propositions. If one is careful, it does no harm to say that Samson's existing is necessary on the hypothesis that Adam exists – and Leibniz often does write this way. The hypotheses that matter to hypothetical necessity, however, are not propositions about individuals. Adam's existing is perfectly harmonized with all the other substances that exist; Adam's concept contains once and for all everything that will ever happen to him and all his worldmates. God's creating Adam is merely one aspect of God's creating the world of individuals that includes Adam. Obviously, it won't do to say that God bothers to perform an infinite number of actions when he creates the world; he wills one thing: to create the most perfect.

> God's plans respecting the whole of this universe being interconnected in accordance with his sovereign wisdom, he took no decision about Adam without taking one about everything in any way connected with him. It is not, then, because of the decision taken about Adam, but because of the decision taken at the same time about everything else . . . that God has made up his mind about all human events. (Correspondence with Arnauld, G 2: 48)

Samson's existing, as well as Adam's existing, are necessary on the hypothesis that God creates this world. We can say that their existing follows from the hypothesis that this world exists. In fact, everything contained in the concepts of Adam, Samson, and all the other individual substances (and that is everything) is hypothetically necessary in this way. This can be summarized by saying that Leibniz's notion of hypothetical necessity captures items that follow from the concepts of things that God has created. Since he creates harmoniously, we might as well simplify by saying that the hypothesis is that this world is created. The notion can be generalized to the uncreated possible worlds because God conceives less perfect beings inhabiting less perfect worlds. So items that follow from the concepts of those possible beings are necessary on the hypothesis that God create a possible world containing the possible individual or individuals in question. That is, if we consider the possible divine decree that one of these other worlds exists, everything concerning the individuals in one of those worlds would follow "once and for all" from the hypothesis of that decree considered as possible. Let us see how this construal of hypothetical necessity fits what Leibniz writes. We will then see how this interpretation of (c) fits with (e) and (f).

We first pick up the contrast between substances and mathematical examples. Items that follow from the concept of a sphere are not relative to any hypothesis about what is created. Such items are eternal truths; they would be true no matter what world was created. As we have seen, a spirit's understanding of an eternal truth is a distinct expression of the entire divine intellect, which is the realm of possibles. We are now brought to the official definitions of hypothetical and absolute necessity. In DM 13 (and many other places) Leibniz writes that absolute necessities are such that "the contrary implies contradiction," while in hypothetical necessities, "the contrary implies no contradiction." What do these pronouncements mean? Nowadays many philosophers are inclined to take the notion of contradiction as brute, unanalyzable, and maximally perspicuous and intuitive. Leibniz (and other rationalist philosophers) would not have accepted this way of thinking, requiring instead a metaphysical underpinning even for "logic." Here is an analysis of "the contrary implies no contradiction" to which I think Leibniz subscribed.

> For all truths of the form "X is P," where X is a substance or possible substance, *the contrary implies no contradiction* just in case God understands a world in which "X is P" is false.

Concerning this analysis, we should observe:

1 For all X, everything contained in the concept of X is such that its contrary implies no contradiction. This follows from the *in esse* principle and from Leibniz's denial of trans-world identity. Every X is found in one world only, so in every other world "X is P" is false. The point is that the falsity of "X is P" in the other worlds does not entail any contradiction in those worlds. On the contrary, a world can be defined as a maximal set of compossible substances.
2 From Leibniz's definition it then follows that all truths concerning substances are hypothetically necessary.
3 Since, for example, the mathematical concept of a sphere and everything that follows from it is an eternal truth, God does not understand any worlds in which items following from the concept are false. As we noted above, spirits' understanding of any eternal truths constitutes a distinct expression of *all* the possible worlds. Therefore, the contrary of any truth following from the concept of a sphere does "imply a contradiction."
4 It therefore follows from Leibniz's definition that eternal truths are absolutely necessary.
5 The absolute necessity of eternal truths is thus metaphysically connected with their not being relative to any hypothesis about divine decrees.

By way of summarizing the interpretation to this point, let me emphasize that we have begun by taking as metaphysically fundamental God's understanding of possible substances (organized into possible worlds of course) as depicted in figure 15.4. For any substance X we can, therefore, say that X exists on the hypothesis that God creates X's world. This is called a "hypothesis" because God understands alternative possible worlds that do not include X. And that is definitionally equivalent to saying that for anything following from X's concept "the contrary does not imply a contradiction." In still other words, since God understands worlds such that if they existed, X would not exist, nothing that is actually true of X would be true in those worlds.

Contingent truths are necessary given the hypothesis of a particular world, that is, they are hypothetically necessary. They are not absolutely necessary because the contrary (not the contradictory) is possible; that is, other worlds are possible because God knows them. It suffices to render a hypothetical necessity contingent that nothing – that is, no monad that is in the hypothesized world – is in any of the other worlds (that is, there is no trans-world identity). So, quite literally, the contrary holds in all other worlds. Since, for example, Judas does not exist in any other world, every other world is such that Judas does no betraying in that world. When a truth is absolutely necessary, there is no world such that there is an instantiation of a negative instance of the truth. Furthermore, we have access to these absolutely necessary truths because, unlike contingent truths, they do not require infinite intellects to analyze or know *a priori*. On the contrary, they are shaped to finite intellects, being finitely analyzable into identities. This distinction is closely related to the distinction explained earlier between the abstract, incomplete, and therefore demonstrable truths understood by spirits, and the actually infinite *ground* of these truths in the divine intellect.

An important point in connection with this analysis of contingency is that Leibniz thought it enough to ground metaphysically our freedom that nothing concerning substances is absolutely necessary. In other Leibnizian words, it suffices to ground freedom that there be other possible worlds because this is enough to secure the alternate hypotheses that make things following from one's concept merely *hypothetically* necessary. One potential objection to consider here is that this conception of freedom is too thin – it is not real freedom. But Leibniz does not see his project as postulating a theory to account for uneducated intuitions about what freedom is "really." His project is instead to arrive at an understanding of what freedom must be, given a distinct understanding of metaphysical principles. Another kind of objection would be that textual evidence indicates a thicker, or at least a more thickly textured, notion of freedom. My strategy in replying is to argue that texts seeming to represent either confusion (inscrutable subtlety, or a shotgun approach) are instead simply ways of laying differing emphases on the core position already elaborated. We have seen how Leibniz connects theses (c), (e), (f), and (g) with the underlying theory of spirits' cognition of eternal truths and the structure of the divine intellect. We are now in a position to examine some more important texts that serve to add depth and texture to Leibniz's system.

Leibniz very often says that freedom is connected with alternatives being "possible in their own nature" or "possible in themselves" and similar things. Adams demonstrates that Leibniz relied heavily on this kind of talk right through to the *Theodicy* (Adams 1994: 12–20). That much is clear, but we can now provide a very clear reconstruction of the apparently abstruse notion. God understands possible substances that are not worldmates of Caesar, or what is the same thing, Caesar's crossing the Rubicon is merely hypothetically necessary. Caesar's not crossing the Rubicon is thus possible in itself. Again, this does not mean that God understands world in which *Caesar* does not cross the Rubicon. Nor does it mean that God must understand worlds in which individuals very similar to Caesar cross things very similar to the actual Rubicon. It means only that God understands worlds without Caesar and those definitely do not include Caesar's crossing the Rubicon. This might also be expressed (with some obscurity, it must be admitted) by saying that it is in the nature of *our Caesar* that he possibly not cross the Rubicon. Here "possibly not cross the Rubicon"

297

would mean "actually crossing the Rubicon is not absolutely necessary," or in other words, "actually crossing the Rubicon is merely hypothetically necessary."

It is therefore simply an infelicity of word choice making it seem that Leibniz wants to indicate that God understands a world comprising Caesar and the Rubicon in which the former does not cross the latter. It certainly helps that he is crystal clear in DM 30, the correspondence with Arnauld, and many other places, that when he helps himself to the suggestive counterfactual way of speaking, in full rigor Adam, Caesar, and the rest exist only in this world. There are, perhaps, other worlds in which substances similar to our worldmates behave somewhat differently, but as we have seen, this is not relevant to the matter at hand. For Caesar to be free from an absolute, fatal necessity to cross the Rubicon it suffices that God understands a world in which he does not cross it and any world in which Caesar does not exist (which is all the worlds!) performs this function. This is what it means to say that the "contrary is possible in itself." The present point is that this is exactly equivalent to saying it is hypothetically, and not absolutely, necessary that Caesar cross the Rubicon. The result is that "things possible in their own nature" (or (d) from our list) have been brought under the umbrella of the general theory.

Leibniz realized that hypothetical necessity would be fatal if the hypothesis itself were absolutely necessary. The hypothesis that this world exists is not absolutely necessary because God freely chooses it. There is, then, a sense in which the freedom of substances is parasitic on the freedom of God. Although God knows which world is the best, this knowledge inclines without necessitating, despite the fact that God essentially does the best. Leibniz notices the apparent tension here and commentators have worried much about it. In the divine case as well as the finite, however, the matter can now be simply understood. The freedom of God's choice consists in there being alternatives for him to contemplate. Naturally, these alternatives are possible in themselves, they are harmonized worlds of substances. We should, therefore put great weight on such texts as the following from the 1686 correspondence with Arnauld:

> And if one wanted totally to reject purely possible things, one would be destroying contingency and liberty: for if nothing were possible except what God in fact creates, what God creates would be necessary, and God, wanting to create something, could create nothing but that, without having freedom of choice. (G 2: 55–6)

This explicitly links finite freedom to the divine and yields another way in which monads are god-like.[7] Leibniz's device is to analyze "contingency and liberty," the play of the divine will and intellect, but stressing the structure of the latter. It would, of course, be pointless to object that Leibniz has not shown how it is "really possible" that God create a less perfect world. The real possibility consists in its being understood. The possible worlds are an analysis of possibility, so it is unfair to base an internal objection to Leibniz's procedure on a further unanalyzed notion of possibility. There is, therefore, no inconsistency on this view between the hypothetical necessities in the world and the absolute necessity of the hypothesis, because the contrary of the hypothesis itself "implies no contradiction."[8] This suffices to vouchsafe divine freedom.

Finally, where do the notions of contingency and infinite analysis fit into this picture? It is, again, mostly a matter of emphasis. To see this, note that absolute necessity can be defined in two ways. One is as above, in terms of the opposite involving a contradiction, and again in terms of finite reduction to identity. These characterizations amount to the same thing, because only those matters involving substances require infinite analyses and are contingent.[9] The absolutely necessary eternal truths concern incomplete concepts, and this means that finite demonstrations can be produced. Leibniz switches from emphasizing the possibles to emphasizing the contingent when the context concerns demonstrations or our knowledge of things. Infinite analysis is nicely related to our inability perfectly to predict the future, a familiar psychological mark of our freedom.

It might be helpful at this point to consider the abiding difficulties that Arnauld himself had with Leibniz's account. There are, in particular, two things that Leibniz takes as absolutely fundamental and that Arnauld denies. One is that it makes sense to speak of God's understanding possible worlds. Since Arnauld rejects this (Nelson 1993), he is left with what Leibniz himself would call absolute necessity of this world. The second concerns complete concepts. Arnauld will allow that God, at least understands a complete concept of created individuals, but he will not allow that this complete concept is a Cartesian essence. Almost everything in the complete concept allowed by Arnauld is accidental and so cannot be "intrinsically" connected to the essence. For Leibniz, there is not much point in quibbling over "essential" and "intrinsic."

> I imagine that M. Arnauld has been reluctant to concede [what is stated in DM 13] only because he has considered that the connexion which I support is intrinsic and at the same time necessary, whereas I consider it intrinsic but not at all necessary; for I have by now sufficiently explained that it is based on free acts and decrees. (G 2: 46)[10]

The disagreement with Arnauld comes from his rejecting even intrinsicality while, as Sleigh points out, Leibniz finds it unquestionable. It might be helpful to recognize here that a potential obstacle to accepting the interpretation I am proposing is deep-seated agreement with Arnauld's commitment to a Cartesian theory of essence. Arnauldians will be unwilling to accept Leibniz's structure of possible worlds and his fundamental commitment to superintrinsicality.[11]

The theory of contingency and necessity under discussion has been offered as a kind of evidential support for the interpretation of eternal truths and the "God's image" requirement with which we began. It would not be entirely unfair to object that the theory of contingency is not independent evidence because it depends on attributing to Leibniz the same underlying commitments as the theories of cognition, expression, and eternal truths. It would not make much difference to the basic argument of this chapter if it were to begin with the theory of contingency and then adduce the treatment of the expression of the divine intellect as evidence for it. We might say that aside from its fidelity to the texts, the principal argument for the entire framework is the neat theoretical coherence it brings to issues that might otherwise appear disparate. Whether this consideration is ultimately convincing might well depend on whether or not one expects a coherent, integrated metaphysics from Leibniz.

As a conclusion, the main points argued for in this chapter can now be succinctly summarized. The divine intellect is fully constituted by its knowledge of the actual and possible worlds. Omniscience involves only knowledge of the substances in each world, and not knowledge of logical principles, general laws, geometrical facts, etc. Each world must therefore be fully constituted by its substances. Worlds do not contain "facts," laws, relations, or anything else apart from substances. Finite spirits (e.g., humans) express God's intellect in virtue of their expressing and being able to understand eternal, necessary truths.

These truths are abstract and "incomplete," so they admit of finite demonstration as befits a finite intellect. The absolute, finitely demonstrable necessity of the eternal truths is fully compatible with the underlying contingency that finds its source in the possibles perfectly understood by the divine intellect, and expressed by us with eternal truths. The appropriate notion of contingency is developed from a reading of Leibniz's analysis of what he calls hypothetical necessity.

Notes

1 Not much depends here on the biographical question of when Leibniz arrived at a fully monadic conception of individual substance. I shall use the terms "monad" and "substance" interchangeably.

2 This is in agreement with Jolley's assessment: "In Leibniz's philosophy, [this] doctrine achieves an almost complete ascendancy; it is pushed further perhaps than ever before" (Jolley 1990: 9).

3 It is not relevant here to discriminate among occurrent knowledge, dispositional knowledge, and potential knowledge. Spirits *always* express the eternal truths, even if the expression is indistinct.

4 Russell's evaluation of Leibniz's position as "scandalous" and "confused" can be found in Russell (1900: 178–82).

5 I take it that the "essences" understood by God are one and the same as the possibles. This use of the term suggests one context in which the descriptive term "superessentialism" is appropriate.

6 In arriving at the encapsulation, I benefited from the wide-ranging discussion in Grua (1953: ch. 2).

7 Aside from this volitional resemblance, Leibniz notes that by expressing the whole of creation we have something like power over the other substances, and that in virtue of understanding eternal truths our knowledge is god-like. It is interesting that Descartes says that our volition is the respect in which we most resemble God; his reasons are quite different.

8 This is not to deny that God's freedom can also be understood as connected with the important circumstance that there is no finite demonstration that this world is the best.

9 Note that even the bestness of this world is not an exception because no world contains more than the harmonized substances that constitute it.

10 Here Leibniz obviously means that the connection is intrinsic and hypothetically, rather than absolutely, necessary. So "not at all necessary" means "not absolutely necessary." Notice here, against Sleigh, that intrinsicality is not opposed to essentiality, but it is instead linked to divine freedom in choosing a hypothesis. Any hypothesis intrinsically involves everything in a hypothesized individual and its worldmates.

11 For further discussion of this and related issues, see Nelson (1993).

References and Further Reading

Adams, R. M. (1994). *Leibniz*. New York: Oxford University Press.

Gerhardt, C. J. (ed.) (1875–90) [1965]. *Die philosophischen Schriften von G.W. Leibniz*, 7 vols., reprinted. Hildescheim: Olms.

Grua, G. (1953). *Jurisprudence Universelle et Theodicee selon Leibniz*. Paris: Presses Universitaires de France.

Jolley, N. (1990). *The Light of the Soul*. Oxford: Clarendon Press.

Nelson, A. (1993). Cartesian actualism in the Leibniz–Arnauld correspondence. *Canadian Journal of Philosophy*, 23, 675–94.

Remnant, P., and Bennett, J. (trans. and eds.) (1981). *Leibniz: New Essays on Human Understanding*. Cambridge: Cambridge University Press.

Russell, B. (1900). *A Critical Exposition of the Philosophy of Leibniz*. London: Allen and Unwin.

Sleigh, R. C. (1990). *Leibniz and Arnauld*. New Haven, CT: Yale University Press.

16

Rationalist Moral Philosophy

ANDREW YOUPA

Introduction

Descartes, Spinoza, and Leibniz are best known today for their contributions to metaphysics and epistemology, but they were also deeply interested in moral philosophy and such traditional ethical questions as how one should live and what is the supreme good. In fact, all three treat their proposed solutions to these questions as the fruit of their labor in the more abstract, less practical investigations they undertake. So, if they are metaphysicians first, it is because they maintain that the correct way to philosophize is to begin with what is most fundamental in reality and build up from there, crowning their systems with a recipe, or blueprint, for the good life. Not surprisingly, the proper exercise of one's faculty of knowledge is a key ingredient in the recipe each puts forward. A qualification in Descartes' ethics notwithstanding (to be discussed shortly), the three giants of modern rationalism place as much confidence in reason's unaided power to reveal and lead to the good life as they do in its unaided power to reveal the fundamental order and content of reality.

The overarching structure of the ethical theories put forward by Descartes, Spinoza, and Leibniz is *eudaimonistic*. As moral philosophers, they aim chiefly to discover the most surefire path to true happiness. The word "eudaimonism" comes from the Greek word for happiness, flourishing, or wellbeing. Generally speaking, classical Greek and Hellenistic philosophers take reflection on how to lead a flourishing human life as the starting point of ethical inquiry. That which above all makes a life go well is called the highest good, or *summum bonum*, as it later came to be known in Latin. Thus, central to a eudaimonistic theory is the identification and characterization of a good (or goods) that is (are) necessary, sufficient, or necessary and sufficient for human flourishing.

In line with a prominent school of ethical thought within the eudaimonistic tradition, the rationalists subscribe to *moral perfectionism*. This is the view that the highest good consists in the cultivation and perfection of a characteristic or a set of characteristics that is fundamental to what we are. Such a characteristic in a cultivated state is called a perfection or virtue. Clearly, there can be as many distinct forms of moral perfectionism as there are legitimate candidates for being a fundamental characteristic and as there are combinations of them, but two principal characteristics are the faculty of choice (i.e., the will) and the faculty of knowledge (i.e., the intellect). As might be expected, the rationalists maintain that an essential element of happiness involves the cultivation of one's faculty of knowledge. But it will become apparent in what follows that not only do they differ in interesting ways on the role they assign to the will, emotions, and desires in a flourishing human life, but also regarding the limits of knowledge as a guide for action.

Before looking closely at the perfectionist theories of Descartes, Spinoza, and Leibniz, it will prove helpful to note another sense of the word "perfectionist" that also picks out an important feature of their theories. That is, in addition to subscribing to moral perfectionism, they also subscribe to what may be called *metaphysical perfectionism*. This is perhaps easiest to see by simply looking at some passages where it is expressed in their works. In what is known as the "Geometrical Exposition" of the Second Replies appended to the *Meditations on First Philosophy*, Descartes' sixth axiom is: "There are various degrees of reality or being: a substance has more reality than an accident or a mode; an infinite substance has more reality than a finite substance" (CSM 2: 117). Although the full meaning of this Cartesian axiom cannot be ascertained independent of his views concerning the nature of substances and modes and of the relation between them, for now it is enough to see that he takes it as self-evident that there are degrees of reality, that an infinite substance has more reality than a finite substance, and that a finite substance has more reality than its particular modifications. Similarly, in definition six of Part Two of the *Ethics*, Spinoza says: "By reality and perfection I mean the same thing" (2def.6), and the scholium of proposition 11 of Part Three begins: "We see then that the mind can undergo considerable changes, and can pass now to a greater perfection, now to one of lesser perfection" (3p11s). Since "reality" has the same meaning as "perfection," an individual's mind can undergo increases in reality as well as decreases in reality, indicating that Spinoza shares Descartes' view that reality comes in degrees.

This view is also one that Leibniz clearly accepts. For instance, in the *Monadology* he says: "From this it follows that God is absolutely perfect – perfection being nothing but the magnitude of positive reality considered as such, setting aside the limits or bounds in the things which have it. And here, where there are no limits, that is, in God, perfection is absolutely infinite" (Leibniz 1989: 218). For Leibniz, to say that God's perfection is infinite is equivalent to saying that God's magnitude of positive reality is infinite. And this is so, according to Leibniz, because God has no limits. God's creatures, however, are necessarily limited, which means that they have a finite amount of perfection, or positive reality. In his *Theodicy*, Leibniz explains: "For God could not give the creature all without making of it a God; therefore there must needs be different degrees in the perfection of things, and limitations also of every kind" (Leibniz 1985: 31). Like Descartes and Spinoza, Leibniz is suggesting that things have varying degrees of perfection or reality and holds that the supreme being has the most perfection – indeed, infinite perfection.

It is important to keep the idea of moral perfectionism distinct from the idea of metaphysical perfectionism not only because Descartes, Spinoza, and Leibniz happen to subscribe to both doctrines, but also, and more importantly for our purpose, because in the ethical theories of Spinoza and Leibniz metaphysical perfection is in an important sense the characteristic that is fundamental to what we are and which we therefore ought to cultivate. Thus their ethical theories are perfectionist in two different but connected senses. First, human fulfillment resides in the *perfection* of a fundamental characteristic. Second, the characteristic we ought to perfect is metaphysical *perfection*. This does not mean, however, that metaphysical perfection can and ought to be cultivated in any way that happens to give us the right results. Instead, for Spinoza and Leibniz, perfecting the intellect by increasing one's knowledge is, as we shall see, constitutive of the cultivation of one's metaphysical perfection.

Descartes' Ethics

The last book Descartes published in his lifetime, *The Passions of the Soul* (1649), is a work in psychology and ethics. The psychological theory is developed and presented there in the service of the eudaimonistic ethical goal of providing an account of happiness and the essential elements contained in the happy life. But it is not only eudaimonism that dictates the structure of Descartes' ethics. Also contributing to its structure is his vision of philosophy as a unified system of knowledge. For example, in the preface to the *Principles of Philosophy*, he says:

> Thus the whole of philosophy is like a tree. The roots are metaphysics, the trunk is physics, and the branches emerging from the trunk are all the other sciences, which may be reduced to three principal ones, namely medicine, mechanics, and morals. By "morals" I understand the highest and most perfect moral system, which presupposes a complete knowledge of the other sciences and is the ultimate level of wisdom.
>
> Now just as it is not the roots or the trunk of a tree from which one gathers the fruit, but only the ends of the branches, so the principal benefit of philosophy depends on those parts of it which can only be learnt last of all. (AT 9B 14; CSM 1: 186)

For Descartes, philosophy is a unified system, and it is hierarchically structured with the most important knowledge at the top of the structure. This does not mean that the knowledge beneath the uppermost level is unimportant. On the contrary, the highest knowledge depends on the lower orders of knowledge but not vice versa, and so the former can be acquired only after knowledge at the lower levels has been reached. Metaphysics, physics, and psychology are therefore valuable as the necessary means for reaching the ultimate level of wisdom.

It should therefore not only come as no surprise that his ethical treatise, the *Passions*, is largely devoted to an investigation of human psychology, but also that it was not written until after he had written and published his works on metaphysics and physics – *Meditations on First Philosophy* (1641) and the *Principles of Philosophy* (1644). This is confirmed in a letter from June 1646 in which he writes:

> Of course, I agree . . . that the safest way to find out how we should live is to discover first what we are, what kind of world we live in, and who is the creator of this world . . . I must say in confidence that what little knowledge of physics I have tried to acquire has been a great help to me in establishing sure foundations in moral philosophy. Indeed I have found it easier to reach satisfactory conclusions on this topic than on many others. (AT 4: 441; CSMK 289)

The most reliable method for arriving at moral knowledge, Descartes maintains, is by first acquiring knowledge of human nature, the natural world, and the divine nature. These three preconditions for moral knowledge are what he tries to supply in the *Meditations* and the *Principles*, and it is clear from the above letter that he feels he had some success in reaching moral knowledge on the basis of the secure foundations he had established in those subordinate fields of inquiry.

As we know from his correspondence, Descartes' concentrated reflection on ethics began in the summer of 1645. In July of that year he suggested in a letter to Princess Elizabeth of Bohemia that they read Seneca's *On the Happy Life* together (AT 4: 253; CSMK 256). However, Descartes quickly became dissatisfied with the reading selection due to what he considered insufficient philosophical rigor in the Stoic philosopher's treatment of the subject matter. So he proposed instead to write down his own thoughts on the happy life to share with Elizabeth and receive her feedback. The ethical theory that emerges in his correspondence with the princess is by and large that which is found in a more systematic, though more diluted, form in the *Passions*.

Like Seneca, Descartes' approach in ethical inquiry is eudaimonistic, and he agrees with the ancients, and Seneca in particular, that everyone desires to be happy first and foremost (AT 4: 263; CSMK 257). The question is, what is happiness? Happiness, Descartes suggests, is to have a "perfectly content and satisfied mind" (AT 4: 264; CSMK 257). The happy life is one throughout which a person experiences the pleasure of peace of mind. This does not mean, he points out, that the happy life is the most cheerful one; contentment of mind is not necessarily accompanied by laughter and gaiety, for instance. Rather, he approves of the account of contentment that he takes Epicurus and his school of philosophy to have endorsed: *ataraxia*, which, in Descartes' view, is a stable state of mind untroubled by such emotional disturbances as anxiety and regret (AT 4: 276–7; CSMK 261).

Although his conception of happiness as contentment is Epicurean in character, his conception of what is most important in achieving such contentment has an affinity with Stoicism. Indeed, Descartes' moral philosophy can be viewed in part as a chapter in the early modern revival of Stoicism, which was ignited in the sixteenth century by the neo-Stoic works of Guillaume du Vair (1556–1621) and Justus Lipsius (1547–1606). So it is not just by chance that Descartes' ethics appears to combine elements of Epicureanism and Stoicism; Descartes in fact takes himself to have reconciled the key ethical doctrines of the two Hellenistic schools. In a 1647 letter to Queen Christina, in whose service he later died of pneumonia, he says: "In this way I think I can reconcile the two most opposed and most famous opinions of the ancient philosophers – that of Zeno, who thought virtue and honor the supreme good, and that of Epicurus, who thought the supreme good was contentment, to which he gave the name of pleasure" (AT 5: 83; CSMK 325). Whether or not Descartes successfully reconciles Epicurean and Stoic ethics or merely splices them together at the expense of coherence is something we need to consider after looking at his account of virtue in more detail, but clearly his ethics embodies a conscious attempt on his part to fuse the two.

Like the ancient Stoics, then, Descartes holds that being virtuous is sufficient for having a happy life. Virtue on his view is a highly developed or perfect condition of the will. What this developed condition of the will consists in, he tells Elizabeth, is a "firm and constant resolution to carry out whatever reason recommends without being diverted by . . . passions or appetites" (AT 4: 265; CSMK 257–8). Similarly, to Queen Christina, he writes: "virtue consists only in the resolution and vigor with which we are inclined to do the things we think good" (AT 5: 83; CSMK 325). For Descartes, virtue is a matter of having a firm resolution to do what one judges to be the best thing to do. By "firm resolution" he means a steadfast motivational disposition or habit that is aligned with reason and the all-things-considered judgments issued by reason. A person of perfect virtue is therefore impervious to what his or her passions and desires present in appearance as worth pursuing before, during, and after practical deliberation – that is, after the agent has reached an all-things-considered judgment about what is best to do under the circumstances.

Descartes takes virtue in this sense to be sufficient for contentment because being reliably motivated by reason and its all-things-considered judgments ensures that one will never give oneself any legitimate cause for regret, one of the chief obstacles to happiness. Now, in his correspondence with Elizabeth he adds that, in addition to virtue, wisdom is in a sense necessary for happiness (AT 4: 267; CSMK 258). While virtue is the highly developed or perfect condition of the will, wisdom is the cultivated state of the intellect. Early on in the ethical correspondence with Elizabeth, he treats virtue and wisdom as independent conditions of happiness. He says: "So virtue by itself is sufficient to make us content in this life. But virtue unenlightened by intellect can be false: that is to say, the will and resolution to do well can carry us to evil courses, if we think them good; and in such a case the contentment which virtue brings is not solid" (AT 4: 267; CSMK 258). So virtue as steadfast resolution is sufficient for contentment, but it is not sufficient for making contentment invulnerable. For that, wisdom is required; without correct beliefs, we are susceptible to making incorrect choices, and making an incorrect choice may give rise to feelings of regret. Therefore, for the most solid or invulnerable contentment we can achieve, proper motivation (i.e., virtue) must be conjoined with correct beliefs (i.e., wisdom).

Although not published until the late fall of 1649, a draft of his last work, *The Passions of the Soul*, appears to have been completed in the winter following the summer and fall in which he carried on his correspondence on ethics with Elizabeth (AT 4: 442; CSMK 289). Much of the ethical theory is the same, but a noteworthy difference between the correspondence and that of the *Passions* is that in the latter Descartes treats steadfast resolution and knowledge as two components that make up one central, all-purpose virtue, which he calls *generosity*. Generosity is described as the "key to all the virtues and a general remedy for every disorder of the passions" (AT 11: 454; CSM 1: 388). In addition to being steadfastly motivated by reason, this super virtue involves "knowing that nothing truly belongs to him but this freedom to dispose his volitions, and that he ought to be praised or blamed for no other reason than his using this freedom well or badly" (AT 11: 446; CSMK 384). Descartes is saying that the knowledge that nothing but one's motives are really up to oneself and that moral responsibility concerns nothing other than what motives one allows to move oneself comprises the wisdom that serves as a component of the virtue of generosity.

Knowledge concerning what is truly up to us is one of the most important parts of wisdom, Descartes explains, because it serves as the basis for dignity, for the appropriate amount of respect we owe ourselves and others (AT 11: 445; CSM 1: 384). Every individual deserves the same amount of esteem as anyone else, since the capacity for self-directed and virtuous action is equal in everyone, and there is no other genuine basis for such regard (AT 11: 447; CSM 1: 384).

Although generosity requires perfection of the will as well as perfection of the intellect, in the *Passions* intellectual perfection appears to be a more modest ideal than the one originally presented in the correspondence. Earlier, we saw that he suggests to Elizabeth that achieving invulnerable contentment requires that one never make incorrect choices out of ignorance. But if this were so, true happiness would appear to be completely inaccessible or, at least, inaccessible to all but a very few who have God-like wisdom. Spinoza and Leibniz would certainly not consider this a shortcoming of Descartes' ethics, but Princess Elizabeth appears to have viewed it as such and she seems to have brought it to Descartes' attention (AT 4: 291; CSMK 265). What is more, there is internal pressure to reduce the ideal of intellectual perfection – internal, that is, to Descartes' philosophical system. This comes from his theological voluntarism, his view that all truth and goodness is entirely dependent on God having willed things to be as they are, which holds as much for what are commonly thought of as contingent truths as for necessary, or what he refers to as *eternal*, truths, such as those contained in arithmetic and geometry (AT 2: 138; CSMK 103; AT 5: 159–60; CSMK 343; AT 7: 432; CSM 2: 291). It follows from this that perfection of the human intellect cannot be anything like coming to understand things from God's point of view for, no matter how highly cultivated the human intellect comes to be through the acquisition of knowledge, divine wisdom is different in kind from human wisdom in virtue of the fact that, as far as we are concerned, there is no ultimate reason for things being as they are, or for things being at all, other than God's will. From this it does not follow that intellectual perfection cannot be set as high as inherent limitations permit. It is just that in the end that runs counter to the egalitarian spirit of Descartes' eudaimonism. So the ideal of wisdom is considerably more modest in later correspondence with the princess, and in the *Passions* wisdom in the relevant sense is trimmed down to the two aforementioned items of knowledge concerning what is truly up to us and what alone we deserve praise and blame for.

The question remains, does Descartes succeed in reconciling Stoic and Epicurean ethics insofar as he is able to combine contentment of mind and the virtue of generosity into a consistent eudaimonistic theory? Putting the question that way, it seems that he never gets around to reconciling Zeno and Epicurus but, at best, his Zeno and his Epicurus. Setting that difficulty aside, the doctrines that he feels call for reconciliation are, on the one hand, that virtue is the supreme good, and, on the other, that contentment is the supreme good (AT 5 83; CSMK 325). Descartes' proposed solution is that virtue and contentment, properly understood, go hand in hand: true virtue necessarily accompanies true contentment and true contentment accompanies true virtue. So, in the end, it makes no difference which is said to be desired for the sake of which because, in pursuing either, one is also pursuing the other (AT 4: 275; CSMK 261). To use his analogy, an archery contestant cannot win the prize without aiming at the bull's-eye, and the bull's-eye would not be targeted without the archer seeing that there is a prize for hitting the bull's-eye (AT 4: 277; CSMK 277). The bull's-eye and the prize then are equally deserving of being said to be the contestant's end. Similarly, virtue (i.e., perfection of the will and the intellect) and happiness are inseparable aspects of what each of us is ultimately after. Thus, Descartes concludes that they are equally deserving of being considered our final end.

Spinoza's Ethics

Like Descartes, Spinoza regards philosophy as a unified system of knowledge and, like his predecessor, views moral knowledge as the highest level of wisdom in the sense that it depends on knowledge of the divine nature, the natural world, and human nature and, therefore, can be achieved only after knowledge has been reached in metaphysics, physics, epistemology, and psychology. However, unlike Descartes, Spinoza does not hold that knowledge from these other fields of inquiry is valuable merely as a necessary means for obtaining moral knowledge. Rather, the knowledge in the other fields plays an essential role in the ideal of intellectual perfection which serves as Spinoza's ideal of human nature. So it turns out on Spinoza's view that we must gather the fruit from the roots and trunk of Descartes' tree of philosophy or, more precisely perhaps, that the roots and trunk *are* the fruit. As a consequence, Spinoza's ethics does not share the egalitarian spirit one finds in Descartes'; that is, the eudaimonistic end of true happiness is less egalitarian in the former in the sense of being less readily available to everyone equally. After all, if moral perfection depends on intellectual perfection and if intellectual perfection requires acquisition of knowledge in metaphysics, physics, etc., clearly not everyone is equally well situated for the undertaking. But this is not something Spinoza would necessarily consider a drawback of his theory. For, as he famously says in the final line of his masterpiece the *Ethics*, "All things excellent are as difficult as they are rare" (5p42s).

The greatest happiness awaiting those with the wherewithal to reach it Spinoza calls blessedness (*beatitudo*). "Blessedness," he tells us, "is not the reward of virtue, but virtue itself" (5p42). In order to get a sense of what Spinoza is saying here, it is necessary to take a look at some of the metaphysical, epistemological, and psychological doctrines that serve as the basis for its demonstration and the demonstration of the other ethical theorems in Parts 4 and 5 of the *Ethics*.

In the introduction above I indicated that, like Descartes and Leibniz, Spinoza subscribes to metaphysical perfectionism. This is the view that reality, or perfection, is something that is manifested in different things to different degrees. Each holds that there is only one thing with infinite reality and that that thing is properly called God. Furthermore, each maintains that finite things have a limited amount of reality or perfection. Where Spinoza and Leibniz part company with Descartes is that they take the further step of suggesting that finite things are capable of undergoing increases and decreases in their amount of reality. This is not held by Descartes, but it is nevertheless a natural extension of the doctrine of metaphysical perfectionism.

The power a thing exerts to exist, for Spinoza, is metaphysical perfection (1p11s, 3p11s). God's power, being infinite, implies that God exists necessarily (1p11). The power of a finite thing, such as a particular human being, being limited, means that it exists for an indefinite period of time (3p8). The existence of a finite thing involves an indefinite period of time and not a finite frame of time because a finite thing's existence would never come to an end if it never encountered anything external to itself to bring about its destruction (3p4). Although Spinoza takes this to be self-evident, some light is cast on what is supposed to make it the case by his view that the power that a finite thing exerts to exist is a share of the infinite power of God (3p6p). The object of the power that a finite thing exerts is therefore nothing but its own continued existence. So long as it encounters no resistance, a finite thing will continue exerting its share of God's unlimited power.

This exertion of power to exist Spinoza calls *conatus*, which is translated as *striving* or *endeavor*, and this is the essence of a finite thing (3p7). It is what makes a thing the particular thing that it is. An individual's loss of his or her *conatus*, then, is equivalent to the destruction of the individual.

Spinoza's view that the essence of human nature is striving, or endeavoring, to continue in existence is one of the key doctrines in the foundation of his ethical theory and one he shares with, among others, his contemporary, the English philosopher Thomas Hobbes (1588–1679). Given this common tenet, it is tempting to understand Spinoza's ethics as having been, as it were, cut from the same cloth as Hobbes' That is, it might seem that Spinoza, like Hobbes, takes the foundation of morality to be its utility in prolonging an individual's life, and so whatever is most effective in leading to this end serves as the basis of a moral precept. However, such a reading, I believe, is mistaken. An important difference between the foundations of the ethical theories of the two seventeenth-century naturalists concerns the self to be preserved in self-preservation. For Hobbes, the self to preserve is none other than the one each of us for the most part is already deeply concerned with preserving – the emotional, imaginative, somewhat credulous one we are familiar with in everyday life. In contrast, Spinoza holds that the self to preserve is exclusively the rational self, which on his view is identical with what he calls the intellect or reason (4App4, 5p38s, 5p40c). And this encompasses none of our passions and imaginings, that is, none of our passive emotions and imagistic, sense-based thoughts. As one scholar puts it, at bottom Spinoza adheres to the "primacy of the intellect" (Delahunty 1985: 270).

What the rational, or intellectual, self encompasses will be examined shortly, but first I want to emphasize that this difference in their views of the subject to be preserved is in part what accounts for the un-Hobbesean character of Spinoza's ethics. For instance, it appears to be in the background of the following passage from the appendix to Part 4 of the *Ethics*:

> Therefore it is of the first importance in life to perfect the intellect [*intellectum*], or reason [*rationem*], as far as we can, and the highest happiness or blessedness for mankind consists in this alone . . . So there is no rational life [*vita rationalis*] without understanding [*intelligentia*], and things are good only insofar as they assist a man to enjoy the life of the mind, which is defined by understanding [*intelligentia*]. Those things only do we call evil which hinder a man's capacity to perfect reason [*rationem*] and to enjoy a rational life [*rationali vita*]. (4App4–5)

Here it is being suggested that perfection of the intellect alone is sufficient for happiness, and that the meanings of the terms "good" and "evil" are grounded in nothing but what helps or hinders our achieving such perfection. All our efforts then should be geared toward developing and preserving our rational selves above all else.

309

Apart from any difference there might be in their views of the self to be preserved, it might still be thought that prolonging one's life is the ultimate basis of morality on Spinoza's view as well as Hobbes'. It might seem that the difference, if any, is isolated to Spinoza's somewhat rarefied conception of the sort of life that we are supposed to prolong. What is being said in the passage cited above is perfectly compatible with the view that it is of the first importance to perfect the intellect because it so happens that perfecting the intellect is the most effective means to prolong one's life. In addition, even if the text does not bear this strong Hobbesean reading, it might seem that at the very least Spinoza is committed to the weaker commonsense view that self-preservation in a mundane sense is a necessary condition of perfecting the intellect and, therefore, that it is always permissible for an individual to do whatever it takes to avoid his or her own death.

Although the strong Hobbesean interpretation and the weak commonsense reading have some plausibility, neither is entirely accurate. To see why this is so, we need to take a closer look at Spinoza's ethics.

As we have seen, a human being is an exertion of power to exist, and power to exist is metaphysical perfection, or what is also referred to as *reality* (2def.6). An increase in power is therefore an increase in metaphysical perfection; a decrease constitutes a decrease in perfection (3p11s). Moreover, increases in an individual's power give rise to pleasure or joy (*laetitia*); decreases produce pain or sadness (*tristitia*) (3p11s). The greater an increase in power for an individual as a whole and not just one part at the expense of others, the stronger the pleasure or joy that is generated thereby. Likewise, the greater the decrease, the more pain or sadness produced. Since power is the metaphysical basis for emotions of pleasure and pain, and since they are linked such that increases in overall power give rise to increases in pleasure, while decreases produce increases in pain, states of pleasure and pain gauge changes in levels of perfection (reality). Knowledge of good, Spinoza concludes, is the cognition of emotions of pleasure, while knowledge of evil is cognition of pain (4p8; cf. 4p41).

Good things are good, then, by virtue of contributing to an increase in an individual's overall power. Bad things are those that diminish overall power. This might seem to conflict with the preface to Part 4, where Spinoza explains that by "good" he means "that which we certainly know to be the means for our approaching nearer to the model of human nature that we set before ourselves," and that by "bad" he means "that which we certainly know prevents us from reproducing the said model" (Spinoza 2002: 322). But here "good" and "bad" are simply being defined in moral perfectionist terms – that is, in terms of what does and does not contribute (respectively) to an individual's realization of an ideal of human nature. This is not inconsistent with "good" and "bad" as that which does and does not contribute (respectively) to an increase in an individual's power, because the latter is a substantive conception whereas the former is merely formal. The formal account indicates that the highest good is the realization of the ideal of human nature, while the substantive account reveals that power is what the ideal is an idealization of. Thus the content of the model of human nature is supplied by Spinoza's portrait of the highest realization of power: the free man (4p66s–4p72). The free man just is a representation of an individual who has achieved the utmost amount of power possible. Also, since virtue and power mean the same thing (4def.8), it can also be said that the model of the free man is a representation of an ideally virtuous person.

To say that goodness is whatever increases one's power to exist and badness whatever results in its decrease is not yet a fully substantive account of what is good and bad. It is not yet clear, for instance, whether we should make it our top priority to acquire an arsenal of weapons or something else altogether different. That the latter is the case is suggested by the more substantive but nonetheless incomplete account of the good that we saw earlier in the appendix to Part 4, where he tells us "things are good only insofar as they assist a man to enjoy the life of the mind, which is defined by understanding. Those things only do we call evil which hinder a man's capacity to perfect reason and to enjoy a rational life" (4App5). This account is more informative but not yet fully complete, since it can be legitimately asked whether we should make it our top priority to acquire knowledge of how to acquire and operate an arsenal of weapons or, again, knowledge of something altogether different. That the latter is the case is made clear at 4p28: "The mind's highest good is the knowledge of God, and the mind's highest virtue is to know God." Thus the greatest happiness and greatest virtue (i.e., power) is knowledge of God or, what is the same thing, knowledge of nature (1p29s, 4Preface, 4p4p). From the claim that the greatest happiness and power is knowledge of God-or-Nature, it follows that such knowledge is not pursued for the sake of anything else, which was made explicit in 4p26: "Whatever we endeavor according to reason is nothing else but to understand; and the mind, insofar as it exercises reason, judges nothing else to be to its advantage except what conduces to understanding." Since acquisition of knowledge alone perfects the intellect, knowledge is pursued for its own sake and not for the sake of some further end.

Now we are in a position to see why, for Spinoza, preserving the self is not about prolonging one's life in either its strong Hobbesean sense or its weak commonsense form. The former, recall, treats the rational life as that which is most effective in prolonging one's life. The latter, commonsense reading considers prolonging one's life to be a necessary condition of leading the rational life. However, because, considered as thinking things, reason is definitive of what we are (4p26p, 4p27), any departure from reason and reason's requirements constitutes at least some loss of self. Therefore, it is never the case that it is advantageous to put longevity ahead of rationality. To do so is self-destructive. What is destroyed is one's rational self. This I take it is the basis for the otherwise paradoxical claim made at 4p72: "The free man never acts deceitfully, but always with good faith." Preserving oneself requires nothing but living in accordance with reason, and since reason just is what we fundamentally are, it cannot be overridden by the prospect of prolonging life. So, in the scholium of 4p72, Spinoza says:

> The question may be asked: "What if a man could by deception free himself from imminent danger of death? Would not consideration for the preservation of his own being be decisive in persuading him to deceive?" I reply . . . that if reason urges this, it does so for all men; and thus reason urges men in general to join forces and to have common laws only with deceitful intention; that is, in effect, to have no laws in common at all, which is absurd.

This passage maintains that it is contrary to reason to lie in order to avoid death. Self-preservation, therefore, is not a matter of avoiding death and thereby prolonging

311

one's life. Rather, preserving oneself is a matter of preserving one's intellect. Self-preservation, it turns out, just is rationality-preservation.

The following passage from the *Theological-Political Treatise* provides a nice summary of Spinoza's views on all this:

> All worthy objects of desire can be classified under one of these three general headings:
>
> 1   To know things through their primary causes.
> 2   To subjugate the passions, i.e., to acquire the habit of virtue.
> 3   To live in security and good health.
>
> The means that directly serve for the attainment of the first and second objectives, and can be considered as the proximate and efficient causes, lie within the bounds of human nature itself, so that their acquisition chiefly depends on human power alone, i.e., solely on the laws of human nature . . . But the means that serve for the attainment of security and physical wellbeing lie principally in external circumstances, and are called the gifts of fortune because they mainly depend on the operation of external causes of which we are in ignorance. So in this matter the fool and the wise man have about an equal chance of happiness and unhappiness. (Spinoza 2002: 417–18)

Being wise and virtuous are worthy objects of desire, or goods, that can be achieved through human power without external assistance. Security, wellbeing, and things belonging to the same class are worthy objects of desire, but the problem is that their acquisition does not exclusively depend on human power. In fact, it is largely a matter of fortune, or luck, whether one possesses such goods. As a result, a fool and a wise person have nearly the same chances of achieving happiness where this is understood as security and physical wellbeing. Since the likelihood of a fool and that of a wise person of obtaining happiness in this sense is about equal, it is there-fore implausible that Spinoza commends the ideal of intellectual perfection presented in the *Ethics* for the sake of a happiness that inherently depends on security and phys-ical wellbeing.

In any event, Spinoza holds that intellectual perfection is the key ingredient in the good life, but it would be a mistake to conclude that this requires the complete eradica-tion of the emotive side of our nature. On the contrary, intellectual perfection on Spinoza's view is accompanied with a rich and colorful palette of emotions. The differ-ence between the emotional palette of a fool and that of a wise person is that that of the former is for the most part comprised of passive emotions or, simply, passions, whereas the latter's is for the most part comprised of active emotions (3p58, 3p59). The basis for this distinction between passions and active emotions is Spinoza's distinc-tion between opinion and imagination, on the one hand, and reason and intuition, on the other. So it is to his theory of knowledge that we must now turn.

By *opinion* or *imagination* Spinoza means the ideas or beliefs corresponding with the imagistic contents of sense perception, and such beliefs belong to the lowest grade of knowledge (2p40s2). This inferior grade of knowledge, Spinoza maintains, is the only source of falsity (2p41). The reason is that the ideas of sensory contents are inad-equate (2p24, 2p25), and they are inadequate in virtue of being based on the confused and fragmentary contents of sense perception (2p28, 2p35). What makes the imagistic deliverances of sense perception confused and fragmentary is that they are the products of the causal interaction between an individual's sensory apparatus and external stimuli (2p16). Our sensory apparatus is not perfectly transparent and, as a result, systematic-ally distorts what things are like independent of the way they are perceived (2p16c, 2p25). Therefore, when we take the ideas of our sensory contents at face value, we view things in a fragmentary way in the sense that we fail to understand that such ideas are merely results of causal chains extending into our environment, and that the stimuli composing our environment make up various links in those causal chains (2p35s). This, I take it, is what Spinoza is getting at when he says that our sense-based beliefs "are like conclusions without premises" (2p28p). As we come to learn more about why things appear to us the way they do – say, by means of the science of optics – the less fragmentary and more adequate our knowledge comes to be.

An individual who takes his or her ideas of the contents of sense perception at face value views things in accordance with what Spinoza calls the "common order of nature" (2p29cs). Viewing things in this fragmentary way is infused with arbitrariness, since the order in which things appear to an individual is no indication of the way things are causally ordered in reality, the metaphysical order. The trick is to come to know things in accordance with the metaphysical order, or the "order of the intellect" (2p18s). To do so, it is necessary to ascend to the second and third grades of knowledge, namely, reason and intuition.

The knowledge involved in reason and intuition is necessarily true (2p41). Reason consists of "common notions and adequate ideas of the properties of things" and intuit-ive knowledge "proceeds from an adequate idea of the formal essence of certain attri-butes of God to an adequate knowledge of the essence of things" (2p40s2). Featured in both grades is adequate cognition. Reason contains adequate cognition of the com-mon properties of things, making this knowledge general, whereas intuition involves adequate cognition of the essence of a particular thing or things arrived at through the laws of nature.

Reason on Spinoza's view includes two sets of adequate general ideas. First, com-mon notions are ideas of properties common to all things, from the relatively simple to the relatively complex (2p38). So, for example, common to all physical things is the property of being extended in length, breadth, and depth as well as the property of motion-and-rest (2p13l2p). Second, *adequate ideas of the properties of things* are ideas of properties common to all relatively complex things, such as the human organism and other complex organisms (2p39). The idea of a fixed pattern of motion and rest, for example, is an adequate idea of a property shared by all complex physical entities (2p13l3cdef.). Just as there are properties common to all things considered under the attribute of extension, there are also properties common to all things considered under the attribute of thought (2p7). Interesting suggestions as to what this includes are the laws of logic (as a property common to all relatively simple and complex thinking things) and the laws of psychology (as a property shared by all relatively complex thinking things) (Allison 1975: 110).

The highest grade of knowledge, intuition, is knowledge of a particular thing or things through the infinite series of finite causes (i.e., prior finite conditions) and the finite series of infinite causes (i.e., the laws of nature). This is clearly not some-thing that can ever be fully achieved by a finite mind, but it seems that Spinoza must be committed to the view that some progress in this can be made to a limited extent, for otherwise it would be impossible even to get a taste of the greatest happiness, blessedness.

As rudimentary as this brief overview of Spinoza's epistemology admittedly is, it should suffice for grasping the character of his ideal of intellectual perfection and, specifically, the space for emotion and correct motivation in the good life.

At the heart of Spinoza's moral psychology is the distinction he draws between passions and active emotions. Passions are emotions and desires that result from opinion – the inadequate ideas of the confused and fragmentary contents of sensory perception (3def.3, 3p3, 5p4s). Active emotions and desires, on the other hand, arise from the knowledge arrived at by reason and intuition (3p58, 4p59, 4p61, 5p4s). Active emotions and desires, in other words, are rational. Now, just as someone who takes the deliverances of the senses at face value draws arbitrary causal connections among appearances, so this same individual is arbitrarily assailed by various and often conflicting passions. Passions are arbitrary in the same way sensory contents are: they result from an individual's fortuitous encounters with external stimuli, disconnected from the metaphysical order that reason and intuition reveals (4p4c). Those of us who are dominated by passions, Spinoza tells us, "are in many respects at the mercy of external causes and are tossed about like the waves of the sea when driven by contrary winds, unsure of the outcome and of our fate" (3p59s). An individual who is at the mercy of external causes is governed by his or her passions and is therefore unfree (4 Preface). Hence, Spinoza calls such a person a slave in contradistinction to the free man, the ideal of human nature (4p66s).

A life dominated by passions on Spinoza's view is a life of bondage, but his view is not that all passions are painful. Some are emotions of pleasure. However, in addition to arising from an increase in perfection in one part of an individual independent of the person as a whole, passive emotions of pleasure are transitory and often preceded or followed by painful emotions. For instance, hope, according to Spinoza, is an emotion of pleasure, but it is "inconstant pleasure arising from the idea of a thing future or past, of whose outcome we are in some doubt" (Definitions of the Emotions 12). Not only is hope inconstant, it is also always accompanied by a painful emotion, since "there cannot be hope without fear" (4p47p) and fear is a painful emotion (Definitions of the Emotions 13). So, just as inadequate ideas comprise the lowest grade of knowledge, passive emotions of pleasure constitute the lowest grade of pleasure.

What is more, conflicts among different individuals as well as internal psychological conflicts arise from the transitory and variable nature of passions (4p32, 4p33, 4p44). With respect to the same object, conflicting emotional reactions among different people engender disagreement about the value or disvalue of the object, and such disagreements tend to lead to skepticism and ultimately to unhappiness (1Appendix, 4p35c1). A similar sort of phenomenon can arise within one and the same person who is subject to conflicting passions. At one moment something might meet with strong approval which a short while later meets with strong disapproval, dividing the person against himself and, as a consequence, rendering an individual unhappy. To provide remedies for the passions, the source of interpersonal and psychological conflicts, is one of Spinoza's primary aims.

314

He proposes six therapeutic remedies (5p6, 5p20s). First, he suggests that in simply coming to know why one has the passions one does, one thereby gets an upper-hand on them and, as a result, they cease being passive emotions (5p4). The second proposed remedy involves detaching the affective aspect of a passion from the object of the emotion by coming to see that the object is at best merely part of the total explanation for one's feelings about it (5p2, 5p4s). The third and fourth are based on his view concerning the superior durability of active emotions over passions (5p7, 5p8). The idea is that emotions arising from knowledge are firmly anchored in reality and are therefore much less transitory than passions that come and go with any change in oneself or one's immediate environment (5p9, 5p11). Fifth, by means of repeated cognitive conditioning an individual can come to have different emotional reactions to things that previously had given rise to obsessive or otherwise excessive feelings (5p10, 5p12–14). Spinoza says:

> For example, if anyone sees that he is devoted overmuch to the pursuit of honor, let him reflect on its proper function, and the purpose for which it ought to be pursued, and the means by which it can be attained, and not on its abuse and hollowness and the fickleness of mankind and the like, on which nobody reflects except from a morbid disposition. It is by thoughts like these that the most ambitious especially torment themselves when they despair of attaining the honor that they covet, and in vomiting forth their anger they try to make some show of wisdom. (5p10s)

As this indicates, Spinoza maintains that by focusing one's attention on certain thoughts rather than on others, one is capable of reprogramming oneself so that after a certain point one is less disposed to have certain emotional reactions to a stimulus of a certain type. The sixth and final therapeutic remedy is a matter of subscribing to a strong form of determinism, which Spinoza defends early on in the *Ethics* (1p33). Dubbed *necessitarianism* by scholars, this says that events could have turned out in no other way than the way they have and do. An alternative formulation of this thesis is to say that the actual universe with its actual history is the only possible universe with the only possible history. By viewing things in this light, Spinoza believes that we will be less susceptible to having *passive* emotional reactions to whatever events we observe (5p6).

These six cognitive therapies are meant to serve as ways of empowering whoever takes up any or all of them. As such, they are not techniques for eradicating all emotions, only those that prevent us from achieving true virtue and happiness. Virtue, as we saw earlier, is power, and true power consists in being motivated and guided by reason (3p3, 4p37s1). True happiness, for Spinoza, is blessedness, and this is the emotive aspect of the cognitive condition that is equivalent to the state of having reached a level of complete metaphysical perfection (5p33s, 5p36s). Since power is metaphysical perfection, it follows that blessedness is the emotive aspect of the highest realization of true power. Thus, in the last theorem of the *Ethics*, Spinoza concludes: "Blessedness is not the reward of virtue, but virtue itself" (5p42). Having taken a closer look at Spinoza's ethical theory, it might now seem that this final proposition is somewhat of an overstatement, in that it seems an exaggeration to say that blessedness is identical with virtue. But I take it that what Spinoza is up to is similar to what we saw earlier in Descartes. Recall that Descartes suggests that, because true virtue is necessarily conjoined with true happiness, these are in reality just two aspects of one and the same thing. So each can with equal accuracy be considered our final end. Spinoza, it seems, can be understood as making a similar point: blessedness is virtue itself in the sense that blessedness, the greatest emotion of pleasure, and virtue, the highest realization of power, are essential and inseparable aspects of our final end, the knowledge of God-or-Nature.

Leibniz's Ethics

Like Descartes and Spinoza, Leibniz is a moral perfectionist: he subscribes to the doctrine that true happiness consists in the development and perfection of a characteristic or a set of characteristics fundamental to our nature. Moreover, like Spinoza, Leibniz holds that intellectual perfection is the primary ingredient in the good life and yet that this does not require the complete eradication of the emotive side of our nature. Indeed, he shares Spinoza's view that intellectual perfection is accompanied by motivational perfection because proper motivation results from correct cognition. Leibniz says:

> The Stoics took the passions to be beliefs: thus for them hope was the belief in a future good, and fear the belief in a future evil. But I would rather say that the passions are not contentments or displeasures or beliefs, but endeavors – or rather modifications of *endeavor* – which arise from beliefs or opinions and are accompanied by pleasure or displeasure" (Leibniz 1996: 167; cf. Leibniz 1985: 52)

An emotion, for Leibniz, is a particular state of an individual's endeavor toward metaphysical perfection, and a particular state of this endeavor is the effect of the individual's perceptual or representational states, his or her beliefs or opinions.

Thus the manner in which an individual's endeavor toward perfection is channeled in a particular case depends on the level of distinctness of the individual's perception. Endeavor is channeled actively insofar as an individual's perception is distinct or is becoming more distinct. It is in a passive state to the extent that perception is confused or is becoming more confused. According to Leibniz:

> But if we take "action" to be an endeavor towards perfection, and "passion" to be the opposite, then genuine substances are active only when their perceptions (for I grant perceptions to all of them) are becoming better developed and more distinct, just as they are passive only when their perceptions are becoming more confused. Consequently, in substances which are capable of pleasure and pain every action is a move towards pleasure, every passion a move towards pain. (Leibniz 1996: 210)

An action and active emotion, for Leibniz, results from an increase in the distinctness of perception. An increase in confusion gives rise to passive behavior and passions. Since on his view there are no other types of motivation besides active and passive motivational states, cognition alone is the source of the particular modifications of an individual's endeavor toward metaphysical perfection.

316

Given that Leibniz holds that cognition motivates via the representation of an object in a favorable light, there is no such thing as weakness of will in the sense of choosing and acting against one's better judgment (Leibniz 1996: 185–7). Such a psychological phenomenon is not possible because motivation is a consequence of cognition, which influences the will by presenting its objects under an aspect of goodness. "The will," Leibniz says, "is never prompted to action save by the representation of the good, which prevails over the opposite representations" (Leibniz 1985: 45). It follows that the phenomenon commonly called weakness of will turns out to be a defect in the intellect. Weakness is nothing over and above ignorance or error, and these have their basis in confusion and, ultimately, finitude (i.e., a lack of metaphysical perfection). Distinct perception therefore constitutes our power or "dominion," whereas bondage is a state of being submerged in confusion (Leibniz 1985: 64, 289).

Furthermore, increases in metaphysical perfection cause pleasure and decreases cause pain. Leibniz thus also agrees with Spinoza that awareness of pleasure is a perception of perfection, while awareness of pain is a perception of imperfection. He says: "I believe that fundamentally pleasure is a sense of perfection, and pain a sense of imperfection, each being notable enough for one to become aware of it" (Leibniz 1996: 194; cf. Leibniz 1988: 83). Pleasure is the sense perception or knowledge of perfection and pain is the perception or knowledge of imperfection. This is so because it is perfection that brings about pleasure and imperfection that produces pain in rational creatures.

Pleasures of the senses are merely confused perceptions of perfection (Leibniz 1988: 83). The pleasure taken, for example, in listening to music is a sense pleasure and therefore a confused perception of perfection, but Leibniz takes the pleasure we derive from listening to music to approximate a purely intellectual pleasure. Since pleasures are nothing but perceptions of perfection and these differ in degree on a scale from confusion to distinctness, it follows that pleasures of the senses do not differ in kind from intellectual pleasures. Rather, pleasures of the senses are simply low-grade intellectual pleasures. Ultimately, then, "pleasures of the senses reduce to intellectual pleasures known confusedly" (Leibniz 1989: 212).

So metaphysical perfection and its increase is the source of active emotions, pleasure, and freedom; imperfection and decreases in metaphysical perfection are the source of passions, pain, and a life of bondage. True happiness, according to Leibniz, is nothing other than a lasting state of pleasure (Leibniz 1988: 83; Leibniz 1996: 194). Since pleasure is caused by metaphysical perfection and its increases, and since it is the distinctness of cognition that is responsible for the maintenance and increase of metaphysical perfection, intellectual perfection constitutes Leibniz's ideal of human nature. The highest realization of metaphysical perfection is the highest realization of intellectual perfection. God alone possesses absolute metaphysical perfection, and though finite things enjoy a limited amount of perfection, all of a finite being's efforts are geared toward becoming more like God.

Leibniz defines virtue as "the habit of acting according to wisdom" (Leibniz 1988: 83). Nevertheless, since on his view there is no such thing as weakness of will, wisdom is doing all the work in Leibniz's analysis of virtue. Without the possibility of moral weakness, a habit of acting according to wisdom comes to a habit of being wise, which in turn boils down to simply being wise. A similar consequence follows from the account Leibniz gives of what he takes to be the most important virtue: justice. Justice he defines as the "charity of the wise man" (Leibniz 1988: 171). He describes charity as a habit of loving others and willing their good (Leibniz 1988: 83, 171). Since love, like all emotions, arises from cognition and it is impossible to choose and act against one's better judgment, being just first and foremost requires the acquisition of wisdom. Having acquired wisdom, love and charity necessarily follow.

From all this then it may seem that Leibniz's ethics does not differ significantly from Spinoza's. That, however, would be an oversimplification. There is certainly substantial overlap in their ethical theories. Both, for instance, offer highly intellectualized conceptions of the good life. True happiness wholly depends on virtue, but virtue, they hold, is intellectual perfection; proper motivation being a product of correct cognition. Despite such important similarities, however, there are also deep differences, perhaps the most fundamental of which is their conception of metaphysical perfection. In fact, Leibniz's conception of metaphysical perfection sets his ethics apart from Spinoza's as well as from Descartes' ethics.

All three maintain that reality is manifested in different things to different degrees. Yet Descartes and Spinoza treat metaphysical perfection as a matter of ontological independence and dependence. A thing has more perfection or reality than another if and only if the former is more ontologically independent than the latter. Leibniz, on the other hand, takes a Platonist approach and ties metaphysical perfection to order and harmony. On his view, the more order or harmony manifested in a particular thing, the more metaphysical perfection that thing can be said to possess. So, like Descartes and Spinoza, Leibniz subscribes to metaphysical perfectionism but, unlike them, he treats perfection as a function of metaphysical harmony. In a letter to Christian Wolff (1679–1754), Leibniz explains: "*pleasure* is the sensation of perfection. *Perfection* is the harmony of things, or the state where everything is worthy of being observed, that is, the state of agreement [*consensus*] or identity in variety; you can even say that it is the degree of contemplatibility [*considerabilitas*]. Indeed, order, regularity, and harmony come to the same thing" (Leibniz 1989: 233–4). So, by "harmony," Leibniz means agreement, or unity, in variety. This is a set of circumstances wherein many different things are governed by a general rule, like terrestrial and celestial objects being governed by Newton's law of gravitation. Since the perception of harmony, no matter how confusedly, is inherently pleasurable to some extent, a universe containing the most harmony is potentially the most pleasing for a finite thinking thing. A maximally harmonious world is best in virtue of being the most pleasing to a perfectly rational mind, which is why it can also be described as the most worthy of contemplation.

The perfection-as-harmony doctrine has at least two important consequences for his ethics that sets it apart from the ethical theories of Descartes and Spinoza. First, it provides Leibniz with some philosophical basis for suggesting that there is an afterlife where none of the deeds we perform in this life go unrewarded or unpunished. Order and harmony, he holds, would be vitiated if a good action went unrewarded or a bad action unpunished. Therefore, given that this world is maximally rich in harmony, we can be assured that things are organized such that in the end happiness and unhappiness are perfectly proportioned to merit. This moral order within the universe Leibniz calls the "city of God" (Leibniz 1989: 224), evidencing his indebtedness to St. Augustine.

The idea that true happiness is available only on the supposition that there is an afterlife where pleasure and pain harmonize with merit is an apparent departure from the ethics of Descartes and Spinoza in particular and from eudaimonism generally. Traditionally, a eudaimonistic ethical theory gives an account of the happy life where "life" means the natural life of a human being. This is Descartes' exclusive concern, and although in the second half of Part 5 of the *Ethics* Spinoza reaches some conclusions about a sense in which true happiness can be enjoyed even after the destruction of the body, he clearly does not take any of this to undermine or even diminish the importance of his recipe for achieving happiness during our natural lives (5p41s). Leibniz's account of true happiness, in contrast, extends beyond our natural lives, which makes characterizing him as a eudaimonistic moral philosopher somewhat tenuous. Still, even if Leibniz's ethics does not fit neatly within the eudaimonistic tradition because it is not restricted to the happiness available in our natural lives, consideration must also be given to the fact that what is ordinarily meant by "natural life" undergoes considerable expansion in Leibniz's metaphysics. That is, on Leibniz's view, an individual's so-called natural life is merely the temporary emergence of conscious awareness sandwiched between two long periods of stupor – one prior to and leading up to birth and the other taking place after what is ordinarily but mistakenly regarded an individual's death (Leibniz 1989: 208, 214). This expanded view of life thus strongly mitigates the significance of his apparent departure from his rationalist predecessors in particular and the eudaimonistic tradition as a whole.

Nevertheless, the perfection-as-harmony doctrine does serve as the basis for what Leibniz himself takes to be a key difference between Descartes' and Spinoza's ethics in comparison with his own. This concerns their conception of happiness. From Leibniz's point of view, the happiness analyzed in the ethical theories of Descartes and Spinoza amounts to nothing more than mere patience. Against what he calls the "sect of the new Stoics," Leibniz says:

> If they knew that all things are ordered for the general good and for the particular welfare of those who know how to make use of them, they would not identify happiness with simple patience . . . In fact, these are Spinoza's views, and there are many people to whom Descartes appears to be of the same opinion. Certainly, he made himself very suspect by rejecting the search for final causes, by maintaining that there is no justice nor benevolence, nor even truth, except because God has determined them in an absolute way. (Leibniz 1989: 282)

Here Leibniz complains that the neo-Stoics, among whom he includes Descartes and Spinoza, endorse a second-rate conception of happiness. It is not even real happiness they endorse, but patience, meaning that their ethical theories teach at best only how to calmly bear misfortune. This is the most their ethical theories are capable of offering, he explains, because the metaphysics on which they rest are axiologically neutral in the sense that, for Descartes and Spinoza, the metaphysical order is not designed with any consideration given to the wellbeing of its inhabitants. This latter point is precisely what Leibniz sees as allowing him to claim a superior conception of happiness and, as a consequence, a moral philosophy superior to Descartes' and Spinoza's.

Conclusion

As mentioned at the outset, Descartes, Spinoza, and Leibniz treat their proposed solutions to ethical questions as outgrowths of the results of their more abstract investigations into the fundamental structure and content of reality. Metaphysical inquiry for them is not an end in itself. Instead, it is undertaken for the sake of the practical advantages such knowledge may ultimately bring, that is, for the sake of the light it casts on the path to true happiness. The following from Leibniz nicely encapsulates their shared outlook:

> On the other hand, everything is relevant to our happiness, and so could be included within practical philosophy. As you [Philalethes] know, theology is rightly regarded as a practical science; and jurisprudence, and medicine too, are not less so. So that the study of human happiness or of our well- or ill-being, if it deals adequately with all the ways of reaching the goal which reason sets before itself, will take in everything we know. (Leibniz 1996: 522)

Like Descartes and Spinoza, Leibniz's view is that every branch of knowledge subserves practical philosophy. Metaphysics, in other words, just is metaphysics of morals. Although this vision of philosophy as a system unified under practical philosophy came under attack not long after Leibniz's death in the first half of the eighteenth century and again in the first half of the twentieth century, today's students of the moderns are guilty of an anachronism insofar as we fail to appreciate the interdependence of theory and practice in rationalism.

References and Further Reading

Allison, Henry E. (1975). *Benedict de Spinoza*. Boston, MA: Twayne.

Bidney, David (1940). *The Psychology and Ethics of Spinoza*. New Haven, CT: Yale University Press.

Brown, Gregory (1995). Leibniz's moral philosophy. In Nicholas Jolley (ed.), *The Cambridge Companion to Leibniz*. Cambridge: Cambridge University Press.

Cottingham, John (1998). *Philosophy and the Good Life*. Cambridge: Cambridge University Press.

Curley, Edwin (1979). Spinoza's moral philosophy. In Marjorie Grene (ed.), *Spinoza: A Collection of Critical Essays*. Notre Dame, IN: University of Notre Dame Press.

—— (1988). *Behind the Geometrical Method: A Reading of Spinoza's Ethics*. Princeton, NJ: Princeton University Press.

Delahunty, R. J. (1985). *Spinoza: The Arguments of the Philosophers*. New York: Routledge and Kegan Paul.

Donagan, Alan (1988). *Spinoza*. Chicago: University of Chicago Press.

Garrett, Don (1990). "A free man always acts honestly, not deceptively": Freedom and the good in Spinoza's ethics. In Edwin Curley and Pierre-Francois Moreau (eds.), *Spinoza: Issues and Directions*. Leiden: Brill.

—— (1996). Spinoza's ethical theory. In Don Garrett (ed.), *The Cambridge Companion to Spinoza*. Cambridge: Cambridge University Press.

Gueroult, Martial (1985). *Descartes' Philosophy Interpreted According to the Order of Reasons, Volume II: The Soul and the Body* (Roger Ariew, trans.). Minneapolis: University of Minnesota Press.

Hampshire, Stuart (1983). *Morality and Conflict*. Cambridge, MA: Harvard University Press.

Hostler, John (1975). *Leibniz's Moral Philosophy*. New York: Harper and Row.

Jarrett, Charles (2002). Spinoza on the relativity of good and evil. In Olli Koistinen and John Biro (eds.), *Spinoza: Metaphysical Themes*. Oxford: Oxford University Press.

Leibniz, Gottfried (1985). *Theodicy: Essays on the Goodness of God, the Freedom of Man, and the Origin of Evil* (E. M. Huggard trans., Austin Farrer ed.). La Salle, IL: Open Court.

—— (1988). *Political Writings*, 2nd edn. (Patrick Riley, ed. and trans.). Cambridge: Cambridge University Press.

—— (1989). *G. W. Leibniz: Philosophical Essays* (Roger Ariew and Daniel Garber, trans.). Indianapolis, IN: Hackett.

—— (1996). *New Essays on Human Understanding* (Peter Remnant and Jonathan Bennett, ed. and trans.). Cambridge: Cambridge University Press.

Marshall, John (1998). *Descartes's Moral Theory*. Ithaca, NY: Cornell University Press.

Riley, Patrick (1996). *Leibniz' Universal Jurisprudence: Justice as the Charity of the Wise*. Cambridge, MA: Harvard University Press.

Rutherford, Donald (1995). *Leibniz and the Rational Order of Nature*. Cambridge: Cambridge University Press.

Schneewind, J. B. (1998). *The Invention of Autonomy*. Cambridge: Cambridge University Press.

Shapiro, Lisa (1999). Cartesian generosity. *Acta Philosophica Fennica*, 64.

Spinoza, Baruch (2002). *Spinoza: Collected Works* (Samuel Shirley trans., Michael L. Morgan ed.). Indianapolis, IN: Hackett.

Williston, Byron, and Gombay, André (eds.) (2003). *Passion and Virtue in Descartes*. Amherst, NY: Humanity Books.

Yovel, Yirmiyahu (1999). Transcending mere survival: From *Conatus* to *Conatus Intelligendi*. In Yirmiyahu Yovel (ed.), *Desire and Affect: Spinoza as Psychologist*. New York: Little Room Press.

321

17

Spinoza, Leibniz, and the Rationalist Reconceptions of Imagination

DENNIS L. SEPPER

In chapter 9 of this volume, we saw that imagination was central not just to Descartes' mathematics and physics, but also to his conceptions of method, problem solving, and living a fully human life. Contrary to what might appear from a cursory look at his works, Descartes did not so much reject previous theories of imagination as radicalize them. He did not abandon the old Aristotelian and scholastic dictum that there is no thinking without phantasm or imagining, but instead determined that it was for the most part true – although the "I" recognized in the being of the radical doubter and the God recognized as the existing cause of the doubter and all his ideas ultimately transcend imagining. Analytic geometry and the natural sciences based on it were projections of directed, accurate imagining within a comprehensively imagined space. The human passions and emotions, long considered as alien to reason, were instead fundamental consequences of the embodiment of the willing and perceiving *res cogitans* in a psychophysiological network of nerves, animal spirits, and brain. This network, in its turn, was the basic element of imagination. Imagination was thus embodied reason. Descartes' innovative use of "idea," foundational for all early modern philosophizing, was patterned on an analogy according to which the ideas, the forms of thought of the human mind, were in essence like the products of God's imagination – his phantasia – despite the fact that God, being perfectly incorporeal, has no imagination.

The appropriation of Descartes' philosophy by the next generation of Cartesians brought a shift away from this center of gravity in imagination. The *Port-Royal Logic* of Arnauld and Nicole insisted on the radical differentiation of ideas from images, while Malebranche argued that imagination, however necessary for living and however useful in mathematics and science, was a prime source of human error and even possibly the medium that transmitted original sin. The union of body and soul was, at any rate, merely temporary. In this corporeal world we can rise to the level of seeing ideas in God; in the next life our intellect will not be obscured by the body.

The question of the ontological and epistemological status of ideas and their difference from images was the chief legacy of Cartesianism to the following generations of philosophers. But it is arguable that Descartes' major concern was less the ontological–epistemological status of the image than what the human mind does with and to images: that is, imagination as a fundamental psychological and anthropological operation. Philosophers after Descartes tended to assume that the operations of intellect and imagination were abysally separate, and they understood ideas and images as fixed, even reified entities.

Not all those influenced by Descartes were Cartesians, of course. We call Spinoza and Leibniz rationalists, not Cartesians, for good reason. Yet they, more than the Cartesians and other lesser rationalist philosophers, drew important lessons from Descartes' conception of imagination as embodied reason. If neither understood the imagination quite as comprehensively as he had, each in his way nevertheless privileged major aspects of the French philosopher's conception and thought out more fully the consequences.

Spinoza and the Passionate Imagination

Cornelius Castoriadis has noted a recurrent phenomenon in the history of theories of imagination, beginning with Aristotle. As quickly as a theory illuminates important facets of imagination's functions and character, just as quickly the insights are occulted and recede into a conventionalized and denatured form of the theory. Often enough this begins happening already in the very works in which theorists have shed the brightest light on these things. The history of imagination amounts to a few brilliant lessons followed by their minimization and eclipse. In particular, imagination is rarely allowed to put the ultimate primacy of human rationality in question (Castoriadis 1997: 213–16).

Such an illumination accompanied by eclipse occurs in Benedict (Baruch) Spinoza (1632–77). As with the other great rationalist thinkers, it is an eclipsed and narrow form of imagination that strikes us first and most memorably. Imagination in this narrow sense is problematic and limited. A larger sense becomes evident only when we view this narrow imagination in its specific context, with our minds focused on the ultimate aims of his philosophy and the inheritance from Descartes.

In *Ethics* (composed in the 1660s but published posthumously in 1677), book 2 ("Of the Nature and Origin of the Mind"), proposition 40, scholium 2, Spinoza describes three ways in which "we perceive many things and form universal notions." The first two ways he immediately combines under a single term, *knowledge of the first kind*, which he then uses more or less synonymously with "opinion" and "imagination." The first way in this first kind comes "from individual objects presented to us through the senses in a fragmentary and confused manner without any intellectual order," "from casual experience"; the second way in the first kind comes "from symbols" ("from having heard or read certain words we call things to mind and we form certain ideas of them similar to those through which we imagine things"). The third way of perceiving things and forming universal knowledge he designates *knowledge of the second kind*, or, more simply, *reason*. It comes about "from the fact that we have common notions and adequate ideas of the properties of things." Finally, he anticipates the *knowledge of the third kind*, which is discussed more thoroughly in book 5; it is knowledge by intuition, which "proceeds from the adequate idea of certain of God's attributes to the adequate knowledge of the essence of things."

Imagination in Spinoza is thus more or less synonymous with one of three kinds of knowledge, the kind that comes first but is not best. In comparison to the knowledges

323

by reason and by intuition it has little weight or dignity. It consists of confused and fragmentary experience, perceived either at first hand or by hearsay (words evoke in our minds ideas like those we have previously perceived at first hand). The imagination can safely be discounted as a defective and merely transitional form of human experience that everyone should aim to surpass as quickly as possible.

Indeed, in the main body of that same proposition 40 Spinoza explains that it is by this casual knowledge gathered from the senses that we form "composite and confused images." For example, our constant sensory acquaintance with other human bodies allows us to form a rather vague image of "man." But our ability to combine and perceive images is rapidly overtaxed by their sheer quantity, so it is only understanding essences through reason that will permit us to have clear and distinct ideas of the things that imagination perceives confusedly. What is worse, the life of imagination is essentially passive and reactive; we are constantly led around by the contingent, transient impressions of things. Not the least reason for the randomness of this way of living is that the contingent images evoke in us passions and emotions that are also unstable.

As Spinoza argues in the appendix to book 1 of *Ethics*, the problem of imagination's cognitive weakness infects even religion. Scripture was written by prophets, who are distinguished more by their vivid (and various) imaginations than by their intellect. They expressed in images and words – the first kind of knowledge – what exceeds their higher understanding. This form of expression is adapted to common people, who live by imagination, even to the point of turning religious piety into superstition and confusing the mind with prejudices. At its best, religion can positively affect the imaginations of ordinary people, yet this happens not by inducing understanding but rather by eliciting in them an inclination to obedience that is needed for security and good order.

Like Descartes, Spinoza understands imagination as having a physiological basis. But if that basis induced Descartes to compose rules for the good direction of the human powers that lead to understanding, for Spinoza it appears, at first glance, only to make human cognition more desperate. The notions of the ignorant "are nothing but models of imagining whereby the imagination is affected in various ways." "All this goes to show that everyone's judgment is a function of the disposition of the brain, or rather, that he mistakes for reality the way his imagination is affected" (*Ethics*, bk. 2, pt. 1, appendix). Controversies therefore are not disagreements with respect to truth but with respect to differences in men's brains and bodies. The ignorant do not understand the nature of things but imagine things and mistake their imagining for intellect. What they can easily picture and remember they ascribe to things themselves. What is orderly in images they assume is orderly in things, as though God had imagined things exactly in the way human beings do. Moreover, many things lie beyond the capacity of and confuse imagination because it is so weak.

It seems unlikely, then, that any positive notion of Spinozan imagination can be derived from these considerations. Imagination is understood above all in invidious distinction from reason, and *Ethics* as a whole can be portrayed largely as a doctrine of how one should limit imagination. That itself would be evidence that imagination is *important* for Spinoza, just negatively so. But as with the other rationalists this would be to exaggerate one-sidedly the obvious and to miss what is less apparent yet even more fundamental.

A specific basis for Spinoza's understanding of imagination is laid early in book 2 of *Ethics*. The discussion is governed by what is called his dual-aspect monism. There is only one substance, called God or Nature. This substance is infinite, and its existence is implied by its essence. It has different attributes, each of which expresses the nature of this substance in a limited but nevertheless infinite way; furthermore, each attribute can take on a limitless number of particularizations or modes. Space, for instance, is an attribute that can be articulated into an infinite number of positions; it presents a limitless number of bodies, which can undergo limitless (though rule-governed) changes. Thinking, another divine attribute to which humans have access, is articulated into an infinite number of ideas and their connections. Human beings are not substances but ideas in God, and their being is expressed in the two infinite attributes of which human beings are aware, thinking and extension.

Because God is infinite, and infinite in each of his attributes, it is important to recognize that we misunderstand what human beings are if we assume that they are purely and simply an idea in God associated with a certain body. Properly speaking, *any* finite being, human or not, corresponds to an idea in the mind of God insofar as that idea is affected and caused by an infinite series of ideas (*Ethics*, bk. 2, prop. 9). There is always, in Spinoza, a strict correlation between the order and connection of ideas and the order and connection of causes. And this turns out to be crucial for understanding not just what a human being is but also what imagination is and does.

Propositions 11 through 13 explain that "the actual being of the human mind is basically nothing else but the idea of an individual actually existing thing." Whatever happens in the object of this idea "is bound to be perceived by the human mind. That is to say, if the object of the idea constituting the human mind is a body, nothing can happen in that body without its being perceived by the mind." Proposition 13 states "the object of the idea constituting the human mind is the body – i.e., a definite mode of extension actually existing, and nothing else."

At this point Spinoza introduces a series of axioms and lemmas presenting his physical theory: how individual bodies are composed of parts and how these parts and wholes interact. This very long section of proposition 13 is an extension and correction of Descartes' conception of bodies and the rules governing their motions and collisions (as found in part 2 of his *Principles of Philosophy*). But just as in Descartes, the intellect must understand the laws of matter's divisibility and motion in order to govern the division and motions in the space of imagination so that what we imagine will correspond to what is physically real. Spinoza's version serves rather as the basis for understanding the relation of human mind, human body, and all other bodies. The human body is affected by the actions of external bodies that impinge on it. Since the formal being of the human mind is the body; since the body is composed of parts that are themselves composed of parts; since in God there is the idea of each of these parts; therefore the idea of the human body is composed of the many ideas of these bodily parts. Furthermore, the mind can perceive as many ideas as there are ways in which the body that is its principal object is affected in its parts. Finally, since the effects on the parts of the body involve the interaction of the human body with external bodies, the corresponding ideas involve the natures both of the human body and of the external bodies. This of course means there is no such thing as a purely objective idea:

325

every idea of a physical object reports something about the state of the perceiver's body as well as of the external object.

Spinoza thus sets up a very close correlation between states of the body and ideas in the mind. For human beings, the perception of the body, and of external bodies through the medium of its interaction with them, is purely and simply the primary activity of the mind.

In the scholium to proposition 17 Spinoza announces his definition of images. The proposition itself says that the mind perceives an external body as existing or present to itself when the body is affected in a way that involves the nature of that external body, and this existing presence will continue until the human body undergoes a further change that excludes the existence and presence of the external body. The scholium makes clear that images in the most accurate sense are purely physical affections of the human body; nevertheless, they are affections of body that correspond to mental things, "the ideas of which set forth external bodies as if they were present to us, although they do not represent shapes. And when the mind regards bodies in this way, we shall say that it 'imagines.'" Thus, as in Descartes, we find in Spinoza the distinction between the corporeal image formed in the body and the image-idea in the mind.

If there is a general tendency in the history of thought to explain imagination as an appendage of sensation, Spinoza in effect reverses it. He does not define sensation as independent and original; rather, the verb "imagine" and the corresponding abstract noun "imagination" are conceived as referring to the *power of originally conceiving physical states in the mind*. Whether a body is actually interacting with the human body is less important than the correspondence between a certain state of the human body and the idea that is correspondingly conceived, whether that state is present or past. And so memory, too, in proposition 18, is basically reduced to a function of imagination – in particular, memory amounts to an inclination to repeat sequences of imaginations that have previously been experienced, sequences that correspond to physical sequences of bodily states that the human body has undergone. Thus imagination more generally is the power of mind to conceive the ideas of sequences of events, whether past, present, or anticipated.

It is clear that this power might well operate at random in most life situations, that it could be overtaxed by the flood of contingent events in sense, memory, and fantasy, that it might encourage the formation of poorly defined notions and even superstitions. But there is no necessity that imagination always operate thus. In fact the only way for human beings to reach the second and third kinds of knowledge, reason and intuition, is not by transcending imagination but rather by using it well. For Spinoza, the ultimate goal of human life is to achieve freedom through the guidance of reason. The guidance by reason allows the human being to progress from a merely passive existence, in which the mind simply receives and automatically responds to ideas from its bodily interactions, to a management and control of ideas that proceeds by knowing.

Only God is infinite, so in us this guidance by reason is the activity of an intrinsically finite being. Nevertheless, the task of understanding begins with God conceived as the infinite, existing substance and the ultimate cause of all other things. Though finite beings, we are still able to relate the experience of our bodies and of external bodies to this God. If book 1 of *Ethics* established that God or Nature was the only existing (and infinite) substance, it is in propositions 23–31 of book 2 that Spinoza spells out the process by which human beings can relate body to God. "The mind does not know itself except insofar as it perceives ideas of the affections of the body" (prop. 23); that is, the mind knows itself only insofar as it imagines. We do not, however, have adequate knowledge of the components of the human body, or of any other extended thing. Moreover, "the idea of any affection of the human body does not involve adequate knowledge of the human body" (prop. 27). All these ideas, "insofar as they are related only to the human mind, are not clear and distinct, but confused" (prop. 28). And so "the idea of the idea of any affection of the human body does not involve adequate knowledge of the human mind" (prop. 29).

This is the crisis or turning point of Spinoza's theory of human experience and knowledge. What it implies is that the idea of the ideas of bodily affections – that is, our reflection on the ideas of bodily affections, on image-ideas – cannot by itself yield true knowledge. Therefore, the first kind of knowledge, which takes place by casual experience and symbols or words – and words would seem to be the symbols that correspond to the ideas of ideas – will always be inadequate. Yet in the scholium to proposition 29 Spinoza offers a more promising alternative:

> I say expressly that the mind does not have an adequate knowledge, but only a confused and fragmentary knowledge, of itself, its own body, and external bodies whenever it perceives things from the common order of nature, that is, whenever it is determined externally – namely, by the fortuitous run of circumstances – to regard this or that, and not when it is determined internally, through its regarding several things at the same time, to understand their agreement, their differences, and their opposition. For whenever it is conditioned internally in this or in another way, then it sees things clearly and distinctly, as I shall later show.

In proposition 31 Spinoza expressly turns to God: that is, to the notion that ideas are true insofar as they are explicitly related to God. And that sets the stage for rising above the first kind of knowledge to the second and then the third kinds.

Yet we must recognize that this "rising above" does not leave imagination behind. We rise from falsity, which is due to inadequacy, first to common ideas. Common ideas are elicited by methodically comparing the ideas we have received casually, in contingent imagination. That is, our mind, rather than just receive passively the ideas from bodily states, becomes active, producing and reproducing such image-ideas so that we can discover what is common and, finally, what their essences are by relating them to God. In this process we move from *passive* imagination to *active* imagination.

We have already mentioned the two concepts key for understanding this progress of imagination. First is the idea of ideas of bodily affections (*Ethics*, bk. 2, prop. 20–2). For example, the many image-ideas we have of human beings form, by a more or less passive natural reflection, a vague idea of human being. This is an idea of the ideas of bodily affections. No matter how many images of however many human beings we have experienced, by itself this passive process will not lead to a clear and distinct idea. Yet the mind can take control of this process, turn it from passive to active, and arrive at clear and distinct ideas. Passive imagination thus turns into active imagining according to reason.

327

The second important concept for the progress of imagination is the common ideas. These are the ideas that are in all bodies and in all parts of bodies; because of this omnipresence in bodies they are conceived adequately (that is, *only* adequately, never inadequately; see prop. 38–9). Extension is thus one of the common ideas. Every body and every part of every body fully and adequately has extension. Whether one considers a cube a meter on a side, a billion meters on a side, or a billionth of a meter on a side: extension is fully and adequately presented in each, and therefore the idea of extension is adequately conceived in every space and every representation of space. Thus we see the truth in each cube by perceiving it and simultaneously being aware of its true relation and cause (extension and its modes).

Every sensed or imagined thing is true when we perceive it and are simultaneously aware of extension and the laws of its division and motion as presented in proposition 13 (*Ethics*, bk. 2, prop. 35, schol. 2). Nothing positively existing in such image-ideas can be false. Positivity is grounded in the common ideas or notions, which are the foundation of all human reasoning processes and thus of the second kind of knowledge. What this means is that the second kind of knowledge does not so much surpass imagination as fulfill the positivity of what is contained in imagination. It appears clearly only when the mind actively produces and compares images and is simultaneously mindful of their true relations and causes.

In short, in the second kind of knowledge the mind takes control of the imagination by discovering the ideas of ideas and the common ideas therein and developing an awareness of imagination's positively true content. This begins the progress of the mind toward an understanding of the eternal and infinite essence of God. Since the body is the principal object of the mind, mind cannot make this progress by abstracting itself from the body, but only by seeing all the chains of ideas, the chains of physical causes, and their unity as the expression of God's essence: God's essence expressed in its attributes and the necessity of all the modes of these attributes. This, of course, is the third, highest kind of knowledge. The third kind of knowledge displaces imagination no more than does the second. It in fact further intensifies the positivity of imagination. We imagine, we are simultaneously aware of the laws of the causes and relations of the imagining, and we are simultaneously aware of the unity of the first and the second as kinds of knowledge by seeing it in the substance and causality of God. In a completely unexpected way, even the rationalist Spinoza can agree with his own version of the Aristotelian dictum, "There is no thinking without phantasm."

Yet the "payoff" of Spinoza's conception of imagination is not to be found in book 2 of *Ethics*. The work as a whole is not epistemology but ethics; knowledge must serve life. Although book 2 explains how a human being can take control of his image-ideas by relating them to God, this is a cognitive result rather than the fulfillment of human life. It is in books 3 through 5 that Spinoza presents the substance of his ethics; not coincidentally, he does this by way of extrapolating from and extending book 2's explanation of how the human mind can manage its imagination.

On the surface, books 3 through 5 look like something else, a discussion of the nature and control of the human passions and emotions. If the aim of book 2 was to escape the passivity of the mind by turning passive imagination into an active form, books 3 through 5 aim to escape the passivity of mind with respect to the passions by discovering an analogous form of passional activity. Again we see a parallel in Spinoza to something in Descartes. But if Descartes in the *Passions of the Soul* explained how imagination was strongly related to the passions and therefore could be used to control them, Spinoza is more radical still.

One of the first things to notice is that the term Spinoza uses for "emotion" or "affect" is, in the original Latin, *affectus*. "Image" was defined in book 2 as *affectio* (plural *affectiones*), the affection of the human body that is represented to the mind as idea. Passion or affect, in definition 3 of book 3, is defined as "the affections of the body by which the body's power of activity is increased or diminished, assisted or checked, together with the ideas of these affections." Emotions or affects are, like images, affections of the body – special ones that increase or decrease the body's power to act – plus the ideas of these affections. But of course having in one's mind the idea of an affection of the body is by definition *imagination*. To express it in a formula that is perhaps only a little too simple, emotion is imagination plus a change in the level of the body's power. This change is experienced as feeling, which itself is a kind of image-idea that, like most human images, is by its nature not clear and distinct.

Book 2 explained how to move from passivity to activity with respect to ideas. The key was not (as a facile understanding of rationalism might suggest) to transcend the realm of imagination by thinking pure ideas purely, untouched by imagination. That would be to forget that the human mind has as its proper object the body: first the body to which the mind is attached, and then, by means of that body, all the rest of the bodies in the infinitely extended universe. The first contents of the mind are the ideas that correspond to the affections of matter in its body: the image-ideas. A deepened human knowledge and the freedom it makes possible come on the scene when the human being is no longer subject to the fluctuation of image-ideas as they randomly present themselves to the mind. The human mind has the power to summon image-ideas and to grasp what the arrays and sequences have in common. This begins a process that can rise to the level of understanding all things as caused by God. Again, the aim is not to annul all imagination but rather to have the mind actively engage whatever comes before it: to be active and to be in control. Human freedom is perfected when we use the perfected knowledge of our image-ideas to control our passions, so that we replace the random succession of feelings and emotions with the passions that correspond to the autonomous use of human knowledge. In its turn, this knowledgeable guidance and production of passions leads to the intellectual love of God. This special love is in fact the highest passion human beings can experience, along with the joy – another passion – that we take in it. Like Malebranche, Spinoza locates the fulfillment of human being and knowing in God; but because for Spinoza "God" is "God or Nature," unlike Malebranche he does not leave behind the body and its full engagement in the world.

Where this leaves the conventional "rationalist" interpretation of Spinoza is a question that we shall leave for the future.

Leibniz and the Logic of Imagination

Except for the *Theodicy*, Gottfried Wilhelm Leibniz (1646–1716) published no lengthy opus magnum; apart from the relatively brief *Discourse on Metaphysics* and *Monadology*, he produced no overviews of his philosophy. Thus, his interpreters are immediately faced with the problem that, whatever topic one is investigating, it is necessary to scour a massive number of notes, letters, and occasional writings, composed over four or five decades, in order to glean relevant passages. Only then can serious interpretation begin.

In the case of imagination there is a further complication that has been noted by Robert McRae. In the late 1690s and early 1700s Leibniz wrote a long dialogue, the *New Essays Concerning Human Understanding*, which was intended as a critical response to John Locke's *Essay Concerning Human Understanding*, but not published because of Locke's untimely death in 1704. The fundamental unit in Locke's theory of knowledge is the idea. Similarly to Hobbes, Locke understands ideas in the first instance as the images received by the senses; what the understanding then does is to consider and classify them according to similarities and differences. Put into other words, for Locke, ideas are images, and understanding, the having and manipulating of images, is a form of imagination. It is not surprising, then, to find the rationalist Leibniz criticizing Locke by pointing out "how essential it is to distinguish images from exact ideas, which are composed of definitions" (LNE 137).

At about the same time, however, Leibniz was making a claim (reminiscent of Descartes) in correspondence with the Queen of Prussia: that the mathematical sciences and their exact ideas are products of imagination. McRae suggests that his silence about this in the *New Essays* is "tactical" (McRae 1995: 184). Now it is not unusual, as we have seen, to find in rationalist thinkers a strong contrast between pure ideas and images of sense (LNE 77; see also chapter 9, this volume); nor have we found it unusual that such contrasts often conceal a more subtle doctrine. An indication of the subtler doctrine in Leibniz can be found just a few lines after the representative of Leibniz, Theophilus, contrasts pure ideas and images:

> It is an admirable arrangement on the part of nature that we cannot have abstract thoughts which have no need of something sensible, even if it be merely symbols such as the shapes of letters, or sounds; though there is no necessary connection between such arbitrary symbols and such thoughts. (LNE 77)

This in effect sounds like a Leibnizian affirmation of the old Aristotelian dictum, there is no thinking without phantasm. Before we can interpret these items, we first need to examine the various functions of imagination in Leibniz's thought.

In the correspondence with Queen Sophie Charlotte of Prussia, Leibniz retained the traditional distinction between external senses and internal ones. The external sensibles perceived by the external senses, for instance color, are very familiar to us, but we do not truly understand them; they are clear, though not distinct. But the notions or ideas we attribute to the common sense both appear and are definable – number and shape, for example. The common sense is not sufficient for conceiving these clearly and distinctly and building sciences from them, however. For that, we need "something which the senses cannot provide and which the understanding adds to the senses" (Leibniz 1989: 187). The internal sense that allows us to unite the perceptions of the different external senses, so that we can compare (for example) numbers and shapes in color with the number and shapes involved in touch, is imagination. Imagination contains both the *notions of the particular senses*, which are *clear but confused*, and the *notions of the common sense*, which are *clear and distinct*. And these clear and distinct ideas, subject to imagination, are the objects of the *mathematical sciences*, namely arithmetic and geometry, which are *pure* mathematical sciences, and the objects of these sciences as they are applied to nature, which make up applied mathematics. (Leibniz 1989: 187–8)

In order to produce demonstrative proof rather than just inductive and observational truth, however, sense and imagination need the assistance of intelligence. It deals with what is "only *intelligible*, the *object of the understanding alone*; and such is the object of my thought when I think of myself" (Leibniz 1989: 188). Thinking of a color and considering that one is thinking a color are "two quite different thoughts," then. My recognition of the "I" and of the right of other beings to say "I" as well allows me to conceive substance; and similarly from considering myself I arrive at other metaphysical notions like

cause, effect, action, similarity, etc., and even those of *logic* and *ethics*. Thus it can be said that there is nothing in the understanding that did not come from the senses, except the understanding itself, or that which understands. (Leibniz 1989: 188)

For Leibniz, mathematics, geometry, and universal mathematics "fall under the imagination." They are the "science of imaginable things" or the "science of universal imagination." Universal mathematics deals with "that which falls under the imagination or that which I call the logic of the imagination" (quoted by McRae 1995: 182).

Leibniz subscribed to Descartes' distinction between image and idea in the critique of Locke's concept of idea in the *New Essays*. He inverts the standard empiricist criticism of rationalism: it is not the rationalists who misunderstand things because they talk about the idea as distinct from the image, it is the empiricists who fail to make the necessary distinctions. The specialist who from long experience can perceive in a glance that a displayed figure has ten sides, or that a weight is exactly 99 pounds, has a clear image but very likely a confused idea (LNE 262). A distinct idea would "reveal the nature and properties of the figure or weight."

Moreover, there is no image of the infinite, and it cannot even be put together by assembling parts. Of eternity we have a "comprehensive" or "accurate" idea only because we have a definition of it. False reasoning about infinite things derives from confused ideas, not from a bad image or the lack of one. Locke, for example, had argued that we have a confused idea of atoms because, although we have a clear idea of division, there is no distinct difference between our conceiving the smallest atom of dust ever perceived divided into a *hundred thousand* and conceiving it divided into a *million* parts. Leibniz's Theophilus responds:

This is that same mistake of taking the image for the idea; I am amazed to see them so confounded. The having of an image of something so small is utterly beside the point. Such an image is impossible, given how our bodies are now constituted. If we could have it, it would be pretty much like the images of things which now appear to us as within range of our awareness; but we should have to pay a price, for the present object of our imagination would be lost to us, becoming too large to be imagined. There are no images of size, in itself; and the images of it which we do have depend merely on comparing

331

things with our organs and with other objects. Here the employment of imagination is useless. So what emerges from your latest remarks is that you are expending your ingenuity on creating needless difficulties for yourself by asking for too much. (LNE 263)

Imagination per se does not take account of scale, it merely presents an appearance. If a millionth part of the smallest dust particle is presented to the imagination as though it were macroscopic, one would precisely lose the sense of its being small *in comparison to the realm of ordinary visibility*. That is something that only the intellect can track by *coordinating* various acts of sense, memory, and imagination.

So far we have seen a side of Leibniz's theory of imagination with strong affinities to Descartes' mathematical imagination. But there are two additional aspects that appear, in the one case, to be at odds with the French thinker, and, in the other, to go far beyond him. They are Leibniz's understanding of space, and his theory of a universal language expressing logical structure, called the universal characteristic.

It is well known that Leibniz did not believe that space exists in any absolute sense; rather, it is a "true phenomenon" or appearance that is due to the way in which finite intelligences (like us) perceive the world of really existing entities. To explain this adequately we would need to have an explicit understanding of Leibniz's conception of the universe as consisting of the community of monads arranged into supremely good order by God, who is the infinite monad of all monads. Suffice it to say that if we perceived things as they are in full reality we would see the infinitely dense complexity of all simultaneously coordinated monads, which is a spiritual rather than a physical reality and thus not intrinsically spatial. Monads are also all – except for God – associated with matter, so there must be something true even in our perceptions of the material universe. In the material universe, however, we are not able to perceive anything other than certain gross characteristics of physical things; the microscopic scales are too small for us to perceive, and beyond a certain scale of largeness we no longer notice things (for instance, we have to develop conceptually rather than immediately perceive the spiral structure of the Milky Way galaxy).

Our perception thus works by simplifying the existing relationships in the world. A contemporary analogy might help. We do not notice the blind spot of each retina – the place where there are no light receptors because the optic nerve enters the eyeball there – because the visual system "fills in" the spot according to the appearance of the surrounding visual field.

For Leibniz, something like the filling in of the blind spot happens constantly, but over our *entire* field of vision. A general term for this phenomenon is the *continuum* or *diffusion of the same*. To continue with the example of sight, there is far more information conveyed to the eye than is displayed in the field as we see it. The radiation coming to our eyes from the sky is constantly and almost infinitely varied, yet we see the sky as *uniformly* blue. Our perception "creates" a uniform field populated by discrete objects, even though the field and the objects contain infinite visual complexity.

A related thought is also behind Leibniz's theory of space. Space is not an entity that is simply there and perceived as it is. It is instead a "true phenomenon." (This puts Leibniz at odds with Descartes: for the latter, our ideas of space are innate, built into our being, but they are also true of an objectively existing reality.) This means that space is a non-deceptive appearance of a place within which the fundamental entities (monads) relate to one another in sensory consciousness. It is, in essence, a projection of a relational environment or emplacement. Space is true insofar as it maintains certain fundamental relationships that hold between entities. In particular, it is continuous because our finite human consciousness diffuses or spreads the continuity of appearance indefinitely, between and beyond the objects perceived. This means that space is an ideal phenomenon, one of the most fundamental projections of the action of our imagination.

This doctrine of space is in conformity with Leibniz's foundational conception of the expressivity of the monad-soul: perception is the expression or representation of the many in one, and "our soul expresses more directly (all other things being equal) what pertains to its body, since it is an expression even of the whole universe in a certain sense." Moreover,

> One thing *expresses* another (in my terminology) when there exists a constant and fixed relationship between what can be said of one and of the other. This is the way that a perspectival projection expresses its ground plan. (Quoted in McRae 1976: 20)

If Kant was later critical of the thesis that the structures of visual perception express deep metaphysical truth, he nevertheless was quick to adopt the active creativity of a projective perception in his doctrine of the imaginative synthesis of the manifold of intuition, which produces space and time as objects of intuition that form the basis of mathematics.

Leibniz's theory of the universal characteristic helps make clearer in what sense he thinks the true phenomena of space and appearances can express something about deeper reality. The universal characteristic was the symbolic writing system that Leibniz worked on throughout his life and hoped to develop to the point that it could express, beyond the limits of natural languages, the structural relations of complex truths. As such it is an ancestor of modern symbolic logic. An early brief dialogue he composed (in August 1677) gives some insight into the relationship between this universal characteristic and imagination.

The context of the dialogue, which appears to date from a time when he was reading the work of Hobbes, is the question of where truth and falsity properly reside. Hobbes believed that they belong to speech, not to things, especially since truth depends on definitions, which are arbitrary. Truth and falsity thus depend on the thoughts of the person making the definition. Character B, a proponent of Hobbes, is inclined to say that truth is in things; but when he must admit in response to the objections of A, the representative of Leibniz, that falsity has to be in thought rather than things, he switches hesitantly to the conclusion that truth, too, is in thoughts. In a typically Leibnizian move, A gets B to see that we need to talk about possible propositions rather than just the actually thought ones and that truth and falsity apply to possible propositions/thoughts as much as to actual ones. A thought will be true or false because it is or is not in the nature of possible things, and also in or not in my nature – in or not in my nature to *know* such things. A points out that although there can be thoughts without words, there cannot be thoughts without signs or characters:

> If characters can be applied to reasoning, there must be some complex arrangement, some order which agrees with things, an order, if not in individual words (though that would be better), then at least in their conjunction and inflection. And a corresponding variegated order can avoid the difficulty. For though the characters are arbitrary, their use and connection have something that is not arbitrary, namely, a certain correspondence [*proportio*] between characters and things, and certain relations among different characters expressing the same things. (Leibniz 1989: 271)

Whatever the words or characters one chooses, then, as long as the characters refer to the same elements (or at least as long as one can produce an equivalent of those elements in alternative format), and as long as the structural relationships expressed are the same, it does not matter precisely what characters one uses, for the (possible) truths will remain unchanged.

In the course of the dialogue, A affirms that "the most useful of characters" are those that maintain "a certain similarity" to the object. About figures in geometry he says that they "must be regarded as characters, for a circle drawn on paper is not a true circle, nor is it necessary that it be, but it is sufficient that it be taken by us for a circle" (Leibniz 1989: 271). Thus we see that Leibniz understood the universal characteristic as an extension of what we talked about in connection with Descartes: it is an extended imagination, one that uses images to stand for structures and relations as much as for objects, and then marks those images with symbols that allow a clear, distinct, and manipulable representation of those relations with all their terms and elements.

For Aristotle's "no thinking without phantasm," Leibniz substitutes "no thinking without signs." The signs most conducive to thinking clearly and distinctly are those that image the fixed properties of relations. Thus, insofar as we use an imagined circle to think about the properties of circle, we are no longer simply using a weakened sensation, but instead a schematized appearance that preserves in its resemblances relations that hold in the "true circle." This schematized appearance is not a rational concept, either; it is, to be exact, an image.

Although Leibniz showed no particular interest in Descartes' understanding of passions, we can see that in his pursuit of the expressivity of being Leibniz radicalized implications of Descartes' mathematics and physics. Perhaps not until Charles Sanders Peirce and Ferdinand Saussure (that is, in the late nineteenth and early twentieth centuries), did anyone press further the signitive use, the sign use, of imagination. Logic itself, insofar as it is expressive of sign relations, might be a radical extension of imagination – radical in that it goes to the very *root* of imagination. But that is a question best left for the future.

Wolff and the Scholasticism of Imagination

After Leibniz, European rationalism became progressively more scholastic – that is, it developed, in the setting of university education, into a conventionalized, abstract form. The key figure in this development was Christian Wolff (1679–1754), professor of mathematics and philosophy at Halle and Marburg in Germany.

Wolff wrote many treatises and compendia, in German and in Latin, very few of which have been translated into English. For the purposes of understanding imagination, the most important treatises are *German Metaphysics* (1720), a compact presentation of the full scope of his philosophical thought, and *Empirical Psychology* (1732) and *Rational Psychology* (1734), two of the many Latin treatises he published almost annually from 1728 to 1754 as expansions of the *German Metaphysics*. The presentation in all of them is very tightly organized. They begin with basic concepts and principles, then carefully introduce new phenomena and concepts by closely linking them to what has previously been discussed, where possible by a kind of logical deduction. The account I give here follows the *German Metaphysics* and cites that work by section numbers.

After a first chapter that offers the proof that since we are conscious of ourselves we must exist, and a second that presents the basic principles underlying the being of things and our knowledge of them, the *German Metaphysics* turns in chapter 3 to a study "Of the Soul in General, viz. What We Perceive of It." Wolff says that his aim is "not to show what the soul is, and how changes occur in it [that is, the concerns of rational psychology], but . . . only to tell what we perceive of it through everyday experience" (191). When we attend to the soul we perceive that we are conscious of many things as outside of us. This is called thinking, and so we call the changes in the soul of which we are conscious *thoughts* (194).

Insofar as thoughts are constituted so as to let us know and differentiate what we are thinking, we call them clear (198); distinct thoughts are those we have already determined and can talk about if asked (206). Distinctness is increased the more we discover parts within parts or a greater variety of single parts (208). Clarity and distinctness thus proceed from level to level. When something displays itself to us as a previously unrecognized thing in something known, or as a new variety of a thing already known, the display or showing of that thing is called *clear*. When we subsequently discover parts or variety *within* the new part or variety, the original part or variety is called not just clear but now also distinct (211). What we perceive outside us is bodies, which produce changes in the sense organs of our own bodies; the thoughts that have their basis in these organ changes are called sensations (217–20). Sensations can be clear or obscure. What we have once sensed can be presented (*vorgestellt*) again and again, and this occurs more easily the more distinct the sensation has been. If we consider sight, colors are clear, but they are not distinct, whereas figure, size, and position can be both clear and distinct. I can again present to myself figure, size, and position much more successfully than colors because they are intrinsically more distinct (232). Wolff finally arrives at images proper (which in the *German Metaphysics* he calls *Einbildungen*): they are "the presentations of such things that are not present" (235). The power of the soul to produce these is imagination (*Einbildungs-Kraft*, which hereafter became the standard German term for imagination).

Wolff's account of images is conventional but also rigorously set into the context of sensations and judged according to clarity and distinctness. Images are obscurer than sensations; when I imagine a person I have seen before I can present the figure, size, and position very nicely, but "the colors remain almost entirely absent, and everything becomes nearly black" – though when they appear without the simultaneous operation of the senses, for example as in dreams, these images are much clearer, though never as clear as in sensation itself (237). Images take their origin from the senses by association and similarity. Whenever our senses present us with something "that has something in common with a sensation we had at another time," the latter comes before our minds. When part of the present sensation shares something in common with just a part of a past sensation, then "the entire past one comes forward again." The same holds true of images we have had or produced in the past. Thus images are constantly shifting by virtue of this association and reassociation based on resemblance and part-sharing in sensations and images. In dreams these changes occur by leaps because the successive images are not well grounded in one another. But the imagination involves not just things that we have already thought:

> We can also present to ourselves what we have never sensed before. We experience this in geometry, when we present to ourselves the drawing of a curved line of a kind we have never before seen, also when following this we draw the same line on paper and thereby bring it to sensation for the first time. (241)

This marks a decisive and unanticipated turn in Wolff's presentation. In the following paragraphs he explicates this *productive and inventive* power of imagination. His chief examples are from the arts, which are hardly so much as mentioned by earlier rationalist philosophers. What for Wolff justifies including the arts is the analogy to the imaginative function that was crucial for Descartes, Leibniz, and even Malebranche, its constitution of mathematics. The first "manner" of this imaginative production of what has never been experienced before depends on our ability to divide what we have already experienced into parts, then recompose the parts as we please, to arrive at a composite being like a mermaid, a winged angel, or the gods of the pagans. Wolff calls this "the power of feigning" (*die Kraft zu erdichten*; in the Latin works this becomes *facultas fingendi*). Through it we often produce something that is not literally possible, what he calls an "empty image." This first use of the power is often not under our control, because, as we engage in feigning, the free association of images can carry us far beyond our original intention. This explains "the images of painters, sculptors, and other artists who bring to market wild adventures" and other bizarre creations. But there is a second "manner" of producing things never before seen. In it the imagination "employs the principle of sufficient reason, and brings forth images in which there is truth." Wolff provides three examples: "the image under which a sculptor presents to himself a statue and into which he has brought everything beautiful he has seen in the human species," after engaging in much research and effort; the aforementioned geometrical curve never before seen or drawn; and finally the image of a building "which an architect presents to himself in thoughts according to the rules of the art of building" (242–5).

Wolff goes into detail, both here and even more in the *Empirical Psychology*, about how architects engage in this second manner of imaginative production. First, they gather pictures and plans of already existing buildings, as well as plans for others that have not been constructed. Then, in designing a new building, they examine these pictures one after another, in the same way that "the imagination brings forth, one after another, things that have a relationship to the thing we are thinking about.

336

What pleases them [the architects] they bring together afterward in a new design plan" (246). The role of the principle of sufficient reason – a crucial notion in Leibniz, which states that everything that is or is possible must have reasons or causes sufficient to produce it precisely as it is – is to bring to bear not just the rules that all architects follow but also to give the individual building an "appropriate ground of perfection." When, on the other hand, the architect instead follows the first manner, the manner of feigning with its free association of images, he ends up introducing all sorts of errors and imperfections into the design.

Wolff's discussion here bears some resemblance to theories of artistic production of the late seventeenth and early eighteenth centuries that had been influenced by rationalism. In them, imagination was involved as serving the subordinate function of adorning or decorating the portrayed object in a manner that gives it some distinctiveness and specificity, according to the taste, skill, and experience of the artist (Becq 1984). This of course connects the rationalist period to earlier ones, going all the way back to Greek antiquity, when the purpose of art was above all to present good models according to good proportion (Eco 1986).

Wolff, like Descartes, recognizes that imagination allows itself to be exercised and increased (262–3). In particular he gives as an example the British mathematician John Wallis, who could extract the square root of a 53-digit number in the dark (that is, without the aid of pencil and paper). Again, it is clear that, like Descartes and Leibniz, Wolff (himself a professional mathematician) conceives mathematics as an imaginative function. The distinct use of imagination requires attention: the mind's power that allows for reflection by directing our attention now to one aspect or part of what we imagine, now to another. This enables us to distinguish things more carefully, and noting the similarities and differences of things allows us to achieve the presentations of species and genera, "which one is accustomed to call actual concepts and that are the ground of universal knowledge" (273). The progressive refinement and combination of these ultimately leads to scientific knowing. Immediately after explaining how attention to sensations and images produces concepts, Wolff introduces the faculty of understanding: the power of distinctly presenting what is possible. He points out that, by themselves, the senses and imagination can at most achieve clear presentations; if you bring in the understanding they can be made distinct. Understanding, strictly speaking, has its sufficient reason in the distinction and naming of the presentations of sense and imagination. This conception of understanding that is a methodically controlled work with images is reminiscent of what we find, in various forms, in Descartes, Spinoza, and Leibniz.

But this is the point in Wolff's account where the conventionally understood "rationalist" separation of intellect from sense and imagination begins – a separation that is in fact uncharacteristic of those earlier thinkers. Wolff distinguishes between distinct knowledge by means of pure understanding, and indistinct knowledge with impure understanding. "Understanding is separated from the senses and the imagination whenever we have fully distinct knowledge." In discussing this conclusion he dismisses the claim of "those who pretend the pure understanding is an empty [that is, *contentless*] image of mathematicians"; such people do not understand the difference between pure and impure understanding. But then he immediately concedes that the understanding is *never* entirely pure (282)!

337

The reasons for such distinct indecision become progressively more apparent. Wolff's account of understanding culminates in the making of judgments. Judgments, of course, put two concepts into propositional relationship, and they require conceptual distinctions made in experience that are tracked and registered by distinct signs or words. When we attend to a glowing iron rod we have a concept of it, says Wolff. But to turn that experience into a judgment we need to distinguish the glowing from the iron rod as two separate things, and then at the same time we need to see these two things as joined together. So for a judgment we really need three concepts: the thing or substance, its property, and their being united (289–90). Precisely here Wolff introduces words as a type of sign that tracks such distinctions: "words are nothing but signs of thoughts" (291). Thus, understanding is the power of presenting what is possible in words. Properly speaking, words do not stand for the individual thoughts we have but rather for their kinds, their species and genera. As Wolff examines the different grammatical categories of words he notes in particular that because the imagination presents things clearly but not distinctly it leads to the tendency of human beings to substantialize – we might say "reify" – the properties of things. Thus, for example, the virtues that are proper to the soul are, in allegorical drama, often represented as individual characters.

The discussion of words leads to a further conclusion relevant to imagination. Either we present to ourselves things themselves, or we present them through words or other signs. Signs allow for the exact tracking of things in "figurative knowledge"; it is opposed to "intuiting knowledge," which presents the thing itself or its image (316). The words and signs are class names based on our having already compared and contrasted the various relevant sensations and images; they are the marks of what we have made distinct in our imaginal experience. Thus the figurative kind of knowing, knowing in propositions of natural language or other systems of signs, is distinct; intuitive knowing can be no better than clear.

There is, nevertheless, the danger in figurative knowing of its being contentless or empty. Words really indicate nothing definite or distinct without our remembering that they "indicate a certain thing of which we have had a concept, that is, in remembrance of the intuiting knowledge" (323) – so figurative knowledge based on language does not have by itself any certainty or clarity. Oddly enough, Wolff immediately qualifies this by arguing that it is conceivable that there is a better kind of figurative understanding.

> It is possible that clarity and distinctness can also be brought into figurative knowledge, and that it even can, as it were, place before the eyes what is to be met with in a thing, and through which one distinguishes it from others, in a manner that if, following this, composite signs that are indifferent to the concepts are held up against one another, one can also see from that the relation of the things to one another. (324)

The example Wolff gives of this presentation in signs that can bypass the concepts and directly mirror the relations of the thing is modern algebra. He does immediately acknowledge a problem: there has been so little success in achieving this algebra up until now, and so few people understand what has been done, that this technique of perfect figurative knowledge has hardly been invented yet. He mentions specifically that Leibniz's universal characteristic intended, but did not achieve, this kind of figurative knowledge. Thus Wolff once again makes a strong assertion of the independence of real knowledge from sense and imagination, but then immediately has to qualify and even contradict it.

Progressing toward the ultimate faculty of reason, Wolff advises us to use common experience and the refined experience of deliberate experiments to note and name all the differences in our sensations and in the corresponding changes in our soul, and to "name them with their right names, so that we do not mix imaginings and preformed opinions with experience" (325–6). After showing that experience is expressed in judgment-propositions, and that higher knowledge is a knowledge of these propositions according to the canons of logic, he presents the culminating human faculty of reason, *Vernunft*. Reason allows us to rise to a knowledge that does not even need to take its propositions from experience – though once again we read that most knowledge, including the fundamental knowledge of nature, cannot escape from resorting to experiential propositions. Yet about mathematics he asserts an important difference. "In arithmetic and geometry, and similarly in algebra, we have samples of refined reason [*lautere Vernunft*]: for here all the conclusions proceed from distinct concepts and reasons that are separated from the senses" (382). Presumably, then, they are also separated from imagination. Wolff does not qualify this conclusion, even though it rests uneasily alongside what he has said earlier.

Wolff's method of rational derivation of higher level concepts tends to reify them. They are treated as objects or things rather than signs, which refer to other phenomena. Images are like signs in that they always have a referral, to whatever they are images of. The more concepts are absolutized as existing per se, the easier it is to conceive the life of the mind as taking place in complete abstraction from sense, imagination, and memory.

One thing that Wolff's step-by-step, comprehensive scholasticism established was the possibility of conceiving of a more detailed, scientific study of the senses and imagination as such. That is, his careful analyses led directly to the kind of science of the sensible that we find in Alexander Baumgarten's *Aesthetica*, a book often regarded as the founding work of modern aesthetics. What is ironic is that, at the same time, Wolff tried to raise the intellectual realm beyond the imaginative. He thereby arrived at a conclusion, with wavering certainty, that had never been asserted by the greatest of his rationalist predecessors. Malebranche had, perhaps, prepared the way for this by emphasizing the ultimate, eternal destination of human being, to the detriment of the sensory realm and its imaginative extensions. He did this for religious or theological reasons, however, whereas Wolff, consistent with what he says at the beginning of part 3 of the *German Metaphysics*, seems to be arguing that, just by devoting one's attention to the activities of consciousness, one can see that the intellect leaves imagination and sense behind. But Descartes, Spinoza, and Leibniz had never offered the prospect of a life or even a developed science apart from sense and imagination; rather, the first two had argued for the intelligent direction of a life that could never transcend the sensory and the imaginative, and the first and the last for a mathematics that was intrinsically imaginative. With inconsistent consciousness, and perhaps even with bad conscience, Wolff offers an attitude toward imagination that we associate with rationalism but that his predecessors never did, except perhaps at the very ultimate limit of human insight – a place where, at any rate, one does not stay for very long, because it cannot support human life.

Conclusion

Except for Leibniz's theory of *conatus* (inclination or effort; see Engell 1981; Kearney 1988), few students of the history of imagination have found anything of interest in rationalist thinkers. There are likely two principal reasons for this. One is that, coming after the great Idealist and Romantic reconception, even hyperinflation, of imagination, they expect that theories of imagination will either be embedded in an outdated metaphysics or be of interest only to aesthetics. That until the early eighteenth century it was a nearly universal belief that imagination was an essential and even inescapable companion to cognition, whatever one's metaphysics, and that the great rationalist thinkers understood and explained mathematics as an essential function of imagination – these things seem to have escaped later thinkers and historians. In addition, the expectation that rationalism means intellectualism and therefore a purely *a priori* kind of knowledge that completely transcends sense and imagination – an expectation compounded by the modern prejudice that mathematics is primarily a rational, rather than an imaginative, activity – has doubtless further obscured the ability of later readers to recognize the meaning of the relevant rationalist texts.

Misreading rationalist imagination leads to misreading later philosophy as well. In particular, in light of the great rationalists' understanding of imagination, Kant seems in several respects far less revolutionary than he is portrayed in conventional historiography. One of his most original notions, the synthesis of the manifold of sense into the intuitable frameworks of space and time (and arguably also, in the first, 1781 edition of the *Critique of Pure Reason*, the synthesis of the categories), is due to imagination. But a more careful comparison with Descartes and Leibniz's understanding of space makes his originality harder to define. The imaginative space in which Descartes' analytic geometry operates mixes physical and metaphysical considerations in a way that Kant regards as inadmissible. Once the question turns to whether the real world of actually existing things is extended in the same way as it shows in appearance, the phenomenal realm becomes inextricably mixed with the noumenal. Yet the fact is that Descartes conceived of space as projected, divided, and moved by human imagination (embodied reason) according to rules recognized by intellect. This brings Descartes much closer to Kant. Something similar is true of Leibniz's understanding of space as true imaginative phenomenon. Although to Kant this notion is objectionable insofar as it expresses real relations of monads, it seems as in Kant to result from a synthetic imaginative process that decisively shapes the act of sensory perception.

If one turns one's historical attention to Idealism and Romanticism, one could easily conceive Fichte and Schelling as extending the conceptual initiatives of the great rationalists, particularly the projective inventiveness of rationalist mathematics and the association and even derivation of emotion (by way of drive) from imagination. Fichte's ruthless pursuit of the logical structuring of appearance into all the nooks and crannies of consciousness seems to be especially compatible with the approaches of Spinoza and Wolff. Historical work that could account for these things would shed light on the question of why and how the nineteenth century largely lost track of the cognitive use of imagination in favor of purely aesthetic and artistic uses. We might then even be able to appreciate more deeply the "linguistic turn" that progressively emerged from Descartes, Leibniz, and Wolff's reflections on how signs emerge from and reflect images and thus bear the capability of imaginatively expressing the complex structures of things.

Of course, past philosophers and historians were hampered in their understanding rationalist imagination by objective factors. Descartes and Leibniz in particular were more expansive about imagination in letters, notes, and drafts than in the works that came to be considered canonical, and some of those writings were essentially unknown until the early twentieth century. Although once we have sharpened our awareness for all the evidence and traces of imagination we can easily discover how central it was to the rationalist thinkers, the historical fact is that the imagination and its functions entered into conceptual eclipse after Romanticism. The Romantics pitted rationality against emotion, intellect against imagination, science against art, whereas the rationalist thinkers had built bridges between them and understood them in progressive interrelationship. If we do not notice these things, we can have no sense of what the various psychological powers and functions – not just imagination – meant to the rationalists.

In the wake of what is now more than a century of strong philosophical and psychological prejudice against "psychologism," perhaps we have lost sight of the delicacy of thinking and conceptuality necessary for understanding and even describing conscious human experience. The rationalists, empiricists, and idealists of the seventeenth and eighteenth centuries were not shy about these things; and the rationalists had, at the very least, a strong sense of the positivity of the relationship between body and mind while at the same time a sophisticated appreciation of the network of correspondences between the different levels of consciousness. It is not at all certain that twenty-first century psychology, neuroscience, and philosophy have yet achieved a comparable sophistication.

The conventional understanding of rationalism has obscured our ability to see its true history. A Western tendency to subordinate, overshadow, even supplant imagination by reason was effective here (see Castoriadis 1987: 160–1). Imagination receded in apparent importance, for reasons incidental to its real importance in human life: in human making, acting, and knowing. Whether that conventional understanding of rationalism has also obscured our ability to understand things themselves must await future determination. But it is at least possible that one or several of the rationalist thinkers knew what they were doing when they wrote about imagination and therefore have something to teach us about experiencing and understanding it.

"There is no thinking without imagining"; "there is no thinking without signs"; "there is no mathematics without directed imagination"; "emotion is inchoate imagination": these are some of the principles concerning imagination that the rationalists explored and justified. Even if all such slogans need to be qualified or corrected, even if each must be differently inflected for each of the thinkers, they point toward a profound experience of a commonplace but hardly negligible human power that has always been subject to being both under- and overrated. And, at the very least, they

341

more faithfully express the nature of rationalist imagination than the formulas later thinkers and scholars have put in their place.

References and Further Reading

Baumgarten, A. (1750). *Aesthetica* [Aesthetics]. Frankfurt.

Becq, A. (1984). *Genèse de l'esthétique française moderne: De la raison classique a l'imagination créatrice, 1680–1814* [Genesis of modern French aesthetics: From classical reason to creative imagination, 1680–1814]. Pisa: Pacini.

Brann, E. T. H. (1991). *The World of the Imagination: Sum and Substance*. Savage, MD: Rowman and Littlefield.

Castoriadis, C. (1987). *The Imaginary Institution of Society* (K. Blamey, trans.). Cambridge, MA: MIT Press.

—— (1997). *A World in Fragments: Writings on Politics, Society, Psychoanalysis, and the Imagination* (D. A. Curtis, trans.). Stanford, CA: Stanford University Press.

Eco, U. (1986). *Art and Beauty in the Middle Ages*. New Haven, CT: Yale University Press.

Engell, J. (1981). *The Creative Imagination: Enlightenment to Romanticism*. Cambridge, MA: Harvard University Press.

Kant, I. (1996). *The Critique of Pure Reason* (W. S. Pluhar, trans.). Indianapolis, IN: Hackett.

Kearney, R. (1988). *The Wake of Imagination: Toward a Postmodern Culture*. Minneapolis: University of Minnesota Press.

Leibniz, G. W. (1981). *New Essays on Human Understanding* (P. Remnant and J. Bennett, trans.). Cambridge: Cambridge University Press.

—— (1989). *Philosophical Essays* (R. Ariew and D. Garber, trans.). Indianapolis, IN: Hackett.

Locke, J. (1975). *An Essay Concerning Human Understanding* (P. H. Nidditch, ed.). Oxford: Clarendon Press.

McCracken, C. J. (1983). *Malebranche and British Philosophy*. Oxford: Clarendon Press.

McRae, R. (1976). *Leibniz: Perception, Apperception, and Thought*. Toronto: University of Toronto Press.

—— (1995). The theory of knowledge. In N. Jolley (ed.), *The Cambridge Companion to Leibniz* (pp. 176–98). Cambridge: Cambridge University Press.

Negri, A. (1991). *The Savage Anomaly: The Power of Spinoza's Metaphysics and Politics* (M. Hardt trans.). Minneapolis: University of Minnesota Press.

Sallis, J. (2000). *Force of Imagination: The Sense of the Elemental*. Bloomington: Indiana University Press.

Spinoza, B. (2002). *The Complete Works* (S. Shirley, trans.). Indianapolis, IN: Hackett.

Wolff, C. (1969) [1732]. *Psychologia empirica* [Empirical psychology] (J. École ed.). In Christian Wolff, *Gesammelte Werke*, div. 2, vol. 5 (J. École et al. eds.). Hildesheim: Georg Olms.

—— (1972) [1734]. *Psychologia rationalis* [Rational psychology]. In Christian Wolff, *Gesammelte Werke*, div. 2, vol. 6 (J. École et al. eds.). Hildesheim: Georg Olms.

—— (1983) [1720]. *Vernünfftige Gedancken von Gott, der Welt und der Seele des Menschen, auch allen Dingen überhaupt* [Rational thoughts about God, the world, and the soul of man, also about all things; known as *German Metaphysics*] (C. A. Corr ed.). In Christian Wolff, *Gesammelte Werke*, div. 1, vol. 2 (J. École et al. eds.). Hildesheim: Georg Olms.

18

Kant and the Two Dogmas of Rationalism

HENRY E. ALLISON

Philip Kitcher (1981) suggested that Kant came close to writing "Two Dogmas of Empiricism." Although I do not intend to challenge this intriguing suggestion, I shall attempt to take the matter in the opposite direction and propose that with at least equal justification Kant may be thought to have come close to producing a work entitled "Two Dogmas of Rationalism." In fact, in many ways the *Critique of Pure Reason* is just such a work. Or so I shall argue.

The discussion is divided into five parts. In the first, I specify the two dogmas and attempt both to explain their inherent plausibility and to provide a preliminary sketch of Kant's reaction to them. The remaining parts are devoted to a consideration of four domains in which these dogmas are at work and the Kantian critique of them is carried out: the nature of human cognition; the distinction between analytic and synthetic judgments; the nature of space and time; and the ideality of appearances. Far from being isolated topics, we shall see that they are intimately related to one another.

I

The first and best known of these dogmas is often referred to as the "predicate-in-notion principle" or some close variant thereof. It states that in every true proposition the predicate is contained in the concept of the subject. The second does not come with a familiar name and I shall call it the "reducibility principle." It maintains that sensible knowledge acquired through experience is reducible [in principle] to the intellectual variety, which is supposedly attained through the pure understanding independently of any appeal to experience. Although each of these dogmas is associated directly with Leibniz, who was clearly the most important representative of the rationalist tradition for Kant, they actually have a broader scope and may be viewed as underlying assumptions of the project of classical rationalism.

But before proceeding with the analysis of these dogmas and the Kantian critique of them, there are two points to be noted. First, they reciprocally entail one another. If one assumes the predicate-in-notion principle, then one is thereby committed to the reducibility principle and vice versa. Second, they are mirror images of Quine's more famous dogmas, namely, the analytic–synthetic distinction and what Quine terms "reductionism," which he initially characterizes as "the belief that each meaningful statement is equivalent to some logical construct upon terms which refer to immediate experience" (Quine 1963: 20).

In considering the first of these dogmas, it is important to realize that, however strange the predicate-in-notion principle may seem to us today, it has an inherent plausibility, which was exploited by its rationalist proponents. In fact, for Leibniz, it is a simple consequence of a consideration of the nature of truth and it underlies the well-known rationalist dictum that "whatever I clearly and distinctly perceive about a thing is true or is assertable of the thing in question" (Leibniz 1989a: 26). As Leibniz famously put it, "It is common to every true affirmative proposition, universal and particular, necessary or contingent, that the predicate is in the subject, that is, that the notion of the predicate is somehow contained in the notion of the subject" (Leibniz 1989b: 95).

Here, as elsewhere when dealing with this topic, Leibniz is effectively asking: inasmuch as a true proposition is, by definition, one which correctly affirms (or denies) a predicate of a subject, what could its truth consist in other than its predicate being included in (or, in the case of negative propositions, excluded from) the notion or concept of the subject? To Leibniz, at least, this seemed to be virtually axiomatic.

Nevertheless this seemingly innocent "axiom" has a number of not so innocent implications, which Leibniz exploits in constructing his philosophical system. First and foremost, if everything truly predicable of x is contained in the concept of x, then for every x there must correspond a complete concept containing everything truly predicable of it. Moreover, since finite beings like ourselves obviously do not possess such concepts, at least not of individual things, it follows that we must regard them as possessed by God.

As is well known, Leibniz uses this principle to distinguish between necessary and contingent truths. The former are those in which the containment of the predicate in the concept of the subject can be ascertained by a finite process of analysis (either immediately or by deduction from evident axioms), whereas the latter are those in which this is not possible, because an infinite analysis would be required to uncover the predicate in the concept of the subject. The former pertain to the domain of "eternal truths," which features, but is not limited to, those of mathematics; the latter pertain to what Leibniz calls "truths of fact." It is not that one cannot determine a simple truth of fact, say that I (Henry Allison) am currently sitting before my computer, without providing an infinite analysis; it is rather that one cannot fully understand the grounds of this truth (its sufficient reason) apart from possessing the complete concept of Henry Allison. Consequently, it is in this sense that our sensible cognition, such as the example cited above, must be viewed as reducible in principle (though not by us) to the intellectual or purely conceptual variety, which is just the second dogma.

Expressed in Kantian terms, this means that all true propositions are analytic, even though only a small subset of these (truths of reason) can be shown to be such, because we lack the requisite capacity for an infinite analysis. Clearly, if this is true, then the analytic–synthetic distinction must either be rejected outright or viewed as a variable one, which is entirely a function of one's level of cognition or, what amounts to same thing, of the "adequacy" of one's ideas. In other words, what is synthetic for some might be analytic for others, who possess a more adequate concept of the subject, and it necessarily is so for God. In that case, however, the distinction appears to lose much of its philosophical bite.

Consequently, it is no coincidence that precisely this objection was raised against Kant by his Leibnizian opponents (see Allison 1973: 36–46). Indeed, since Kant uses this distinction as one of his major weapons in his attack on traditional metaphysics, of which the Leibnizian is a prominent example, they had good reasons for doing so. For, seen from their point of view, Kant's distinction rests upon a problematic assumption of its own, which is the converse of the Leibnizian, namely, not everything that pertains to *x* (that may be truly predicated of it) is contained in the concept of *x*. In fact, when looked at from a Leibnizian or, more generally, a rationalist point of view, this Kantian assumption seems highly paradoxical. For what could conceivably ground the truth of the predication of some property of *x*, other than its somehow being already contained in *x*'s complete concept?

It is precisely at this point that the battle lines between rationalism and the critical philosophy are to be drawn. Kant's answer to this question is simple and, from his point of view, obvious; namely, that such predication is made possible through an appeal to the intuition of *x*. Rationalism could hardly accept this response, however, since it rests on the assumption of a difference in kind (not merely degree) between intellectual concepts and sensory intuitions. And to accept this would require rationalism to abandon its second dogma.

Kant's retort to this is his so-called "Copernican revolution." In order to appreciate this, however, we must revisit briefly the rationalist position, against the backdrop of which the Kantian revolution is to be understood. As we have seen, essential to this position, and to the conception of truth on which it is based, is the notion of the complete concept of an individual. By its very nature, such a concept must be infinitely complex, since it encompasses everything truly predicable of the individual, including its relations to other individuals and ultimately to the universe as a whole. Although rationalism denies that we (or any finite being) actually have such concepts, it tacitly assumes the legitimacy of what we might term the "concept of a complete concept" as an idea that is to be approached asymptotically, if never fully attained. Moreover, since it thereby appeals to a concept accessible only to God in its analysis of human cognition, rationalism may be appropriately described as committed to a theocentric paradigm (see Allison 2004: ch. 2).

By contrast, Kant's Copernican revolution may be viewed as a turn to an explicitly anthropocentric model of cognition, a "paradigm shift" if you will. It is not, however, merely a shift to the human understanding (or human nature) as the first object of philosophical reflection. That is the standpoint of classical empiricism, which for Kant is equally "pre-Copernican." It is rather something much more radical and counter-intuitive, namely, the assumption that the human understanding is itself somehow the source of the normative principles on which our cognition is based. Indeed, this is the true significance of Kant's famous "experiment": "Let us once try whether we do not get farther with the problems of metaphysics by assuming that the objects must conform to our cognition" (Kant 1998: 110). To suggest that objects conform to our cognition is not to imply that the human mind somehow creates its world *ex nihilo*; it is rather to advance the epistemological thesis that objects must conform to the (subjective) conditions through which alone they can become objects for us. Elsewhere, I have termed the latter "epistemic conditions" (Allison 2004: chs. 1, 2).

For present purposes, however, the essential point is that for Kant, God's knowledge is not a norm against which the human variety is to be measured and found wanting, but a problematic concept through a contrast with which it is to be understood. Expressed in Kantian terms, this conception of cognition serves a "critical" rather than a "dogmatic" function: it frees us from one picture of cognition (the theocentric) in order to enable us better to appreciate another (the anthropocentric or Copernican). Moreover, it is only against this backdrop that we can begin to understand not merely Kant's critique of rationalism but also the "critical" project as a whole.

II

Since the kind of cognition that pertains to the anthropocentric paradigm is discursive, I call Kant's claim that our cognition is of this sort the "discursivity thesis." To say that our cognition is discursive is to say that it is based on concepts; but since concepts require some already given data to be brought under them, discursive cognition is to be understood as consisting in the application of concepts to sensory intuition, which is the sole source of the requisite data. Thus, such cognition, at least as Kant conceives it, assumes an ineliminable duality or distinction in kind between its sources or conditions. As Kant puts it at the very beginning of the Transcendental Analytic:

> Our cognition arises from two fundamental sources in the mind, the first of which is the reception of representations (the receptivity of impressions), the second the faculty for cognizing an object by means of these representations (spontaneity of concepts); through the former an object is given to us, through the latter it is thought (in relation to that representation (as a mere determination of the mind). Intuition and concepts therefore constitute the elements of all our cognition, so that neither concepts without intuition corresponding to them in some way nor intuition without a concept can yield a cognition. (Kant 1998: 193)

As this passage indicates, what makes intuitions and concepts irreducible to one another is that the former are connected with the receptivity of the senses and the latter with the spontaneity of the understanding. Accordingly, all our intuitions, including the pure or *a priori* variety, are sensible in nature. And since without the contribution of sensibility there would simply be nothing to be thought through concepts, sensibility makes an absolutely indispensable contribution to human cognition. It is equally important, however, to keep in mind that sensory intuition is merely a necessary and not also a sufficient condition of discursive cognition. As its name suggests, the latter also requires concepts through which the intuitively given content can be thought. According to Kant's oft-cited formula:

> Thoughts without content are empty, intuitions without concepts are blind. It is thus just as necessary to make the mind's concepts sensible (i.e., to add an object to them in

intuition) as it is to make its intuitions understandable (i.e., to bring them under concepts). (Kant 1998: 193–4)

As a first step in understanding this doctrine, we must become clear about the nature of the two elements (concepts and intuitions) required for discursive cognition. But since this is a complex issue, about which there remains a good deal of controversy in the literature, I can here attempt to provide merely a greatly simplified account (for a fuller treatment, see Allison 2004: ch. 4).

In his *Logic*, Kant defines an intuition simply as a "singular representation" (*repraesentatio singularis*) (Kant 1992: 589). He repeats this in the *Critique*, adding that it is "immediately related to the object" (*bezieht sich unmittelbar auf den Gegenstand*) (Kant 1998: 399). Thus, a Kantian intuition has two defining properties – singularity and immediacy – which turn out to be inseparable. What a Kantian intuition does is to present particulars to the mind and, for reasons that should become clear shortly, it can do so only if it presents these particulars "directly" or "immediately," that is, without the mediation of a concept. Moreover, it must be kept in mind that this is intended to apply to the "genus" intuition, which itself contains two radically distinct species: the sensible and the intellectual. The former is characterized as "sensible" because it requires an "affection" by some object; the latter is termed "intellectual" because it consists in the spontaneous excogitation of an object, without any sensory input. Although *our* intuition is necessarily of the former sort and is the only kind with which we are acquainted, Kant thought the division important for at least two reasons: first, it helps to distinguish his view from that of Leibniz and other rationalists; second, it indicates that the characterization of our intuition as sensible is informative, which, in turn, is necessary for appreciating the discursive nature of our cognition.

Correlatively, in his *Logic* Kant characterizes a concept (as opposed to an intuition) as "a universal representation, or a representation of what is common to several objects, hence a representation insofar as it can be contained in various ones." Consequently, it is redundant to speak of universal or common concepts, as if concepts could be divided into universal, particular, and singular. "Concepts themselves," Kant remarks, "cannot be so divided, but only their use" (Kant 1992: 589). In the parallel account in the *Critique*, Kant notes that a concept, in contrast to an intuition, refers to its object "mediately by means of a mark [*eines Merkmals*] which can be common to several things" (Kant 1998: 399). In other words, because of its generality, a concept can refer to an object only by means of features that are also predicable of other objects falling under the same concept. Thus, unlike a Leibnizian complete concept, a Kantian concept, no matter how complex, can never refer uniquely to a particular object. That is why intuition is required to acquaint the mind with particulars, thereby determining whether or not the concept has an application.

Since a concept is a collection of marks (or "partial representations"), which are themselves concepts, every concept may be viewed as a collection of concepts. For example, the concept of gold is that of a yellow, malleable metal that is soluble in *aqua regia* etc., each of which is itself a concept potentially applicable to other things beside those composed of gold. Kant does not, however, understand such a collection of marks in the manner of Berkeley and Hume, as merely the product of frequent experience,

347

joined together in the mind by principles of association and brought under a general term. Instead, he considers concepts as rules for the unification in thought (not the imagination) of these marks. Accordingly, to have the concept of gold is to have the thought of these (and other) marks as linked together conceptually. This is not to say that being a yellow metal somehow entails being soluble in *aqua regia*. The point is rather that if something is thought to be gold it must also be thought as containing properties corresponding to its marks, that is, as metal, yellow, malleable, and soluble in *aqua regia*, etc.

This presupposes what has been aptly termed the "fixity" of concepts (Beck 1967: 237), and we shall see below that it provides the key to understanding the Kantian view of analyticity. But we first need to explore somewhat more fully the nature and function of concepts in general, which requires understanding their connection with judgment. In fact, the fundamental unit of discursive thought for Kant is the judgment, not the concept. Discursive thinking, for Kant, just is judging and the latter consists in the subsumption of sensory data provided by intuition under concepts stemming from the understanding. Thus, while there can be no judging without concepts, it also follows that "the understanding can make no other use of its concepts than that of judging by means of them" (Kant 1998: 205).

In the same context, Kant also remarks that "Concepts . . . serve as predicates of possible judgments" (Kant 1998: 205). Although the point is crucial, it can be easily misunderstood. In characterizing concepts in this way, Kant is not limiting their function to that of being logical or grammatical predicates. For example, in Kant's paradigmatic example of a judgment, "All bodies are divisible" (which, incidentally, is analytic for him), both concepts function as predicates in the judgment. Since the subject concept, "body," provides the initial content for the judgment, it may be said to stand in a more direct, though still not immediate, relation to the object, because no concept can do that. Thus, the judgment affirms that the x's (the data given in the intuition to which the concept is applied) also fall under the broader concept "divisibility." This analysis enables Kant to claim:

> All judgments are . . . functions of unity among our representations, since instead of an immediate representation a higher one, which comprehends this and other representations under itself, is used for cognition of an object, and many possible cognitions are thereby drawn together into one. (Kant 1998: 205)

Setting aside obscurities in Kant's account of judgment, it might appear that his discursivity thesis, which is completely intertwined with the conception of judgment, is not particularly newsworthy or controversial. Indeed, it has been viewed by present-day philosophers in much the same way as the predicate-in-notion principle was regarded by Leibniz and his fellow rationalists. Typical of this approach is Strawson, for whom the discursivity thesis reduces to the inescapable necessity in any thinking about experience or empirical knowledge to assume a "duality of general concepts, on the one hand, and particular instances of general concepts on the other" (Strawson 1966: 20).

Although this may be correct as far as it goes, to leave matters here is to ignore the revolutionary nature of Kant's thesis. In order to understand this, however, it is necessary to view this thesis in its historical context as challenging both rationalism and empiricism. The challenge to empiricism is obvious and need not be pursued further here. Since the empiricists (with the partial exception of Locke) tended to view ideas as particular images, they really had no place for anything like a Kantian concept and the discursive view of cognition it entails. But the challenge to the rationalists clearly calls for some comment, since they typically did not deny conceptual representation as such and were as opposed as Kant to the "picture theory" of the empiricists.

The issue is a subtle one and once again I cannot here pretend to give it the attention it deserves (for a fuller discussion, see Allison 2004: ch. 2). The main point is that, even though the rationalists did not altogether reject conceptual representation and the discursive model of cognition it entails, they did tend to regard it as inferior to direct intuitive cognition. This is perhaps clearest in the case of Spinoza, who famously distinguished between *ratio*, which is just discursive cognition, and what he terms *scientia intuitiva*, which supposedly acquaints us directly with the essence of individual things, rather than indirectly by means of concepts applicable to a number of things (common notions) (Spinoza 1985: 477–8). In Malebranche, Spinozistic intuition becomes the capacity to see all things in God; while in Leibniz, Spinoza's distinction between *ratio* and *scientia intuitiva* reappears as the contrast between "blind" or "symbolic" and "intuitive" knowledge. Moreover, though both may be adequate, only the latter is "absolutely perfect," which might be glossed as "fully adequate" (Leibniz 1989a: 25).

In fact, the point is already evident from rationalism's characteristic tendency to elevate the idea, with its normative properties of clarity, distinctness, and adequacy, over the judgment as the basic epistemic unit. Once the idea is given such a status, the first dogma of rationalism becomes unavoidable and anything like Kant's discursivity thesis is a non-starter.

From the Kantian standpoint, perhaps the most important feature of rationalism's approach to conceptual representation and discursivity is its ambiguous view of the epistemic function of sensory intuition. Rationalists tend to deny any essential cognitive role for such intuition. Although it is generally acknowledged that some sensory input is required to set the mind's cognitive machinery in motion, it is also claimed that this is merely a consequence of our finitude and does not conflict with the core doctrine that sensory cognition is the lowest and least adequate kind and ought to be replaced by more adequate modes of cognition to the extent possible. At the same time, however, by considering cognition in this way, rationalism shows itself committed to the thesis that the senses of themselves do yield some cognition, albeit of the lowest grade. Moreover, here again, rationalism comes into conflict with Kant's discursivity thesis, since the latter affirms that without the contribution of the understanding there could be no cognition at all, not even the highly inadequate kind assumed by the rationalists.

Finally, it must be emphasized that rationalism's ambiguous treatment of the sensory component of human cognition is no mere accident or failure to recognize the obvious. It is rather a direct consequence of its commitment to a theocentric paradigm. That is why, from Kant's point of view, nothing less than a Copernican revolution is required in order to recognize the essentially discursive nature of human cognition and the indispensable but limited role therein of sensibility.

349

III

Since present-day discussions of the analytic–synthetic distinction, the most influential of which is clearly Quine's, tend to focus on the concept of analyticity and the notorious difficulties involved in giving it an acceptable definition or characterization, it is not surprising that Kant's critics concentrate on his manifestly inadequate account of analytic judgments in the Introduction to the *Critique*. As we all know, Kant there describes such judgments in two supposedly equivalent ways: (1) those in which "the predicate B belongs to the subject A as something that is (covertly) contained in this concept A"; (2) as "those in which the connection of the predicate is thought through identity" (Kant 1998: 141). For reasons that I shall not rehearse here, these formulations have met with almost universal disapproval from Kant's time to the present. Equally important, though less often noted, they give the false impression that synthetic judgments are to be regarded virtually as an afterthought, since they appear to be defined in essentially negative terms as those that are not analytic. And from this point of view, which is that of those who, like Quine, understand the analytic–synthetic distinction in empiricist terms, this effectively means that synthetic judgments as such are seen as relatively unproblematic, with the whole problem being with those that are supposedly both synthetic and *a priori*.

Although the centrality of the problem of synthetic *a priori* judgments to the critical project can hardly be gainsaid and will be touched upon below, this approach to Kant's analytic–synthetic distinction is seriously misleading for at least two reasons. First, it ignores the fundamentally anti-rationalistic orientation of the distinction itself, that is, it fails to recognize its significance as an essential ingredient in the Kantian critique of the first dogma of rationalism. As we have seen, this dogma poses a challenge to the possibility of synthetic judgments in general, at least insofar as they are thought to be more than provisionally or relatively synthetic, not merely to those that are supposedly *a priori*. Second, it neglects the close connection between the analytic–synthetic distinction and Kant's discursivity thesis or, what amounts to the same thing, his account of judgment. The distinction, after all, is claimed to be between different species of judgment (not statements, propositions, or the like). Accordingly, if we are to understand the distinction between these two species, it is necessary to keep in mind their common genus: the judgment.

Obvious as it may seem, the latter point is generally neglected, perhaps because of the casual way in which Kant introduces the distinction in the Introduction to the *Critique* and the corresponding portion of the *Prolegomena*, neither of which makes any reference to the nature of judgment as such. Nevertheless, this may easily be explained by their location in the texts prior to any discussion of the topic. Like many philosophers, Kant was frequently confronted with the problem of not being able to say everything that needed to be said on a topic at once. Thus, his initial presentation of many important distinctions tends to have a provisional character and often needs to be reinterpreted in light of subsequent treatments of the subject. The distinction between analytic and synthetic judgments is no exception.

Fortunately, elsewhere Kant does indicate, if not fully explain, the connection between the analytic–synthetic distinction and his underlying theory of judgment.

Perhaps the most helpful of these is his brief discussion of the matter in the published version of his *Logic*, where the distinction between the two species of judgment is drawn in terms of a contrast between a formal and a material extension of knowledge (Kant 1992: 606–7).

Analytic judgments are there said to provide a formal extension of knowledge by clarifying or explicating what is already contained in a given concept. This involves the uncovering of implications of which one may not have been previously aware, but which are derivable by strictly logical means from this concept, which once again is regarded as fully determinate or "fixed." Kant takes "All bodies are extended" as an example of an analytic judgment, which he renders schematically as "To everything x to which the concept of body $(a + b)$ belongs, belongs also extension (b)" (Kant 1992: 607). This shows that in analytic judgments the predicate (b) is related to the object (x) by virtue of the fact that it is already contained (as a mark) in its concept (the logical subject). Analytic judgments are, therefore, "about" an object; they have a logical subject and, as Kant's example shows, they may also have a real one or object. Nevertheless, since the truth or falsity of the judgment is determined merely by analyzing the concept of the subject, the reference to the object becomes otiose (see Beck 1967: 230).

In his polemic with Eberhard, who pressed him on the matter from a Leibnizian point of view, Kant supplements this account by introducing what amounts to a distinction between immediately and mediately analytic judgments. "All bodies are extended" is immediately analytic, because "extension" (together with "figure," "impenetrability," etc.) is a mark of the concept "body." By contrast, "All bodies are divisible" is only mediately analytic because "divisibility" is not itself part of the concept (logical essence) of body, but rather of one of its constituent marks (extension). In other words, it is a mark of a mark. Despite the fact that this implies that the judgment rests on an inference and in that sense extends our knowledge, Kant insists that this does not amount to a difference in kind, since in both cases the predicate is derived from the concept of the subject by a finite process of analysis.

This should suffice to show that Kant's conception of analyticity is of a piece with the discursivity thesis. As the preceding account indicates, both rest upon the conception of a concept as a set of marks (themselves concepts), which are thought together in an "analytic unity," and which can serve as a ground for the cognition of objects. These marks collectively constitute the intension of a concept. One concept is contained in another, just in case it is either a mark of the concept or a mark of one of its marks. In either case, it is subordinated to the concept in which it serves as a mark, which is precisely the relation that is brought out in an (affirmative) analytic judgment. Thus, unlike most contemporary conceptions of analyticity, Kant's is thoroughly intensional.

A synthetic judgment, by contrast, extends our knowledge in a "material" sense. Kant's example is "All bodies have attraction," which he renders schematically as "To everything, to which the concept of body $(a + b)$ belongs, belongs also attraction (c)" (Kant 1992: 607). Like its analytic counterpart, this judgment asserts a connection between the predicate (c) and the object (x), which is thought through the concept $(a + b)$. But, unlike the latter, it asserts this independently of any connection between the predicate and the concept of body. To be sure, in the judgment the predicate is connected with this concept; but the connection is grounded in, and mediated by, the reference of both to an intuition of the object. Consequently, the judgment extends our knowledge of x (in this case, of all x's) by providing a determination or property of x that is not already contained in its concept. This is what is meant by a "material extension."

Looked at from this point of view, the problem is to explain how a material extension is possible at all, whether it be *a priori* or *a posteriori*. And since this is precisely what is denied by rationalism's first dogma, Kant's account of the possibility of such judgments may be viewed as his response to the challenge posed by that dogma. But, even though this effectively transforms the notorious problem of the synthetic *a priori* into a special case of a more general problem rather than a freestanding one, synthetic *a priori* judgments present difficulties of their own, which call for some comment.

Within the Kantian framework, what is distinctive about such judgments is that they require both pure concepts and pure intuitions. It is obvious that they require pure concepts as predicates and *some* corresponding intuition. Without the former they could make no claim to universality and necessity (the criteria of the *a priori*), and without the latter they would not be synthetic. Consequently, the question is why an empirical intuition does not suffice and a pure one is required. Indeed, the further question arises whether something like the latter is even possible. Certainly, Kant's predecessors, rationalist and empiricist alike, had no place for such a hybrid conception. Moreover, Kant himself poses the problem in a particularly sharp form when he asks, "How is it possible to intuit something *a priori*?" (Kant 2002a: 78). This is a problem that arises only for intuitions (not concepts), since it suggests that something could be given in intuition prior to and independently of our experiential encounter with it, that is to say, *a priori*.

I shall return to the latter question in the next section, in connection with a consideration of Kant's views on space and time, which, as pure forms of sensibility, are alleged to be the sources of the required pure intuitions. Before doing so, however, I shall address the first and lesser of these questions. In brief, the answer is that a merely empirical intuition does not suffice for a synthetic *a priori* judgment because of its particularity. As the representation of a particular individual, an empirical intuition cannot exhibit intuitively the universality thought in the concept. To cite a familiar mathematical example: as synthetic, the judgment that the sum of the interior angles of a triangle is equal to two right angles must be grounded in an intuition of a triangle, while as *a priori* it cannot be grounded in the intuition of any particular triangle. Its possibility thus rests upon there being some non-empirical or pure intuition of something like "triangularity as such," that is, a singular representation that nonetheless can "attain the generality of the concept, which makes this valid for all triangles, right or acute etc." (Kant 1998: 273). The problem is somewhat more complex in the case of judgments involving pure, as opposed to mathematical, concepts, because these cannot be directly exhibited in intuition. For example, we cannot just "see" or perceive a cause, though we can *judge* that certain occurrences are such. As I have argued elsewhere, however, Kant's solution to this problem is to assign such a role to the transcendental schema (Allison 2004: ch. 8).

IV

Kant's account of space and time is, among other things, a direct assault on rationalism's second dogma. Without explicit reference to Leibniz, Kant initially characterizes the latter's position as the view that space and time are "only determinations or relations of things, yet ones that would pertain to them even if they were not intuited." This is contrasted with Kant's own view that they are "relations that only attach to the form of intuition alone, and thus to the subjective constitution of our mind, without which these predicates could not be ascribed to anything at all" (Kant 1998: 157).

Kant here expresses his partial agreement with Leibniz. They are one in rejecting the Newtonian absolutistic theory in favor of a relational one, but they differ radically in the understanding of the nature and function of the relations involved. As Kant makes clear, the issue between them turns on the connection of these relations to the "subjective constitution of our mind," which he here equates with its form or manner of our sensible intuiting. By contrast, for Leibniz, at least as Kant reads him, human sensibility and its subjective conditions have nothing to do with the true nature of space and time, though, as we shall see below, they do play a major role in explaining why we think about them in the way that we do.

In order to understand Kant's critique of the Leibnizian view (I shall limit the discussion to space), it is necessary to take a brief look at the latter. Here the chief text is Leibniz's correspondence with Clarke, which contains his fullest discussion of the matter and was closely studied by Kant, as indeed it was by most eighteenth-century philosophers. Although Leibniz's main concern was to criticize the Newtonian absolutistic theory rather than to spell out or to defend his own view, under pressure from Clarke he was led to do both, particularly in his fifth and final letter. Space, as Leibniz there construes it, is nothing but the order of coexisting phenomena and in light of this he attempts to explain why we nonetheless naturally tend to think of it in the Newtonian (and perhaps commonsensical) manner as something more than such an order.

Since Leibniz viewed the latter as a fiction (and a theologically dangerous one at that), it is perhaps not totally surprising that his account seems almost Humean at points. Basically, his claim is that space viewed as something more than an order is a kind of imaginative gloss, which results from our inability to perceive distinctly minute differences between the relations of the situation of things, which is itself a consequence of the limitation of our senses. This inability, Leibniz further argues in a proto-Humean fashion, leads to a confounding of resemblance or agreement with numerical identity. On this basis, he then contends that the notion of an absolute space, which somehow subsists apart from the order of things in it, is a "mere ideal thing," meaning thereby a fiction (Leibniz 1956: 69–72). Thus, though the "true," that is, adequate, representation of space as an order of coexisting things is purely intellectual, the one that we actually have contains a sensory component, which reflects the limits of our conceptual capacities.

This is diametrically opposed to the Kantian view, according to which space serves as a condition of the representation of such an order rather than as a sensibly distorted or confused product thereof. Later in the Aesthetic and elsewhere, Kant expresses his

353

disagreement by claiming that the Leibnizians falsify the concept of sensibility and of appearance by "considering the distinction between sensibility and the intellectual as merely logical" (Kant 1998: 186). "Logical," as Kant here understands it, means a difference in degree (clearness and distinctness) rather than a difference in kind, which he terms "transcendental." Thus, the claim that the Leibnizians "falsify" the concepts of appearance and sensibility, which are strictly correlative for both Leibniz and Kant, is equivalent to the claim that they regard what is, in fact, a difference in kind between two radically distinct species of cognition (the sensible and the intellectual) as if it were merely a matter of degree. Once again, this is the second dogma of rationalism, which, as already noted, is entailed by the first.

Kant's basic strategy is to turn the tables on Leibniz. Rather than being derived from some kind of prespatial ordering, conceivable by the intellect alone, which, due to the unavoidable limits of our senses, is mistaken for something more, the representation of space is now seen as a subjective condition of the cognition of the very order from which Leibniz claims it is acquired. Kant further argues that this representation stands in an ineliminable relation to human sensibility, which blocks the kind of reduction or, if one prefers, "logicification" of space that is affirmed by the Leibnizians.

In the Kantian lexicon, this dual thesis amounts to the claim that the representation of space is both *a priori* and intuitive (with the same applying, *mutatis mutandis*, to time). After establishing this to his own satisfaction in what in the second edition is called the "Metaphysical exposition of this concept" (Kant 1998: 174), Kant proceeds to argue in the "Transcendental exposition of the concept of space" (Kant 1998: 176) that this alone is able to account for the synthetic *a priori* status of geometry, a thesis that a Leibnizian rationalist must deny, since it runs directly counter to the first dogma.

This is Kant's notorious "argument from geometry," which has come under intense criticism ever since the discovery of non-Euclidean geometries, if not before. Fortunately, for present purposes, this immense issue may be ignored, since Kant viewed his account of geometry as an application or confirmation of the result already attained in the "Metaphysical exposition" rather than as an independent argument. Although Kant is committed by his account of the conditions of the possibility of synthetic *a priori* judgments in general to the view that if geometry is to be regarded as both synthetic and *a priori* it must rest on a pure intuition of space, this is merely a necessary and not also a sufficient condition of the possibility of geometry so conceived. Accordingly, I shall here consider the argument of the "Metaphysical exposition" in its own terms, bracketing the issue of the adequacy of Kant's views on geometry.

This argument is composed of four sub-arguments. The first two attempt to show that the representation of space is *a priori* rather than empirical and the second two that it is an intuition rather than a concept. In essence, the apriority arguments contend that the representation of space must be regarded as *a priori*, since it serves as a condition of the experience of any spatial ordering of things and, therefore, cannot, on pain of circularity, be regarded as derived from such an experience. Although this certainly cuts against the Leibnizian view, it also applies to any broadly empiricistic account of the matter. Nevertheless, taken by itself, it seems perfectly compatible with the possibility that the representation of space is an *a priori concept* (an innate idea), which, as such, has nothing essentially to do with human sensibility. Consequently, we must look to the intuition arguments to establish the connection with sensibility that is necessary in order to refute the Leibnizian view. Indeed, if the representation of space were a concept, the second dogma of rationalism would hold.

Assuming his underlying discursivity thesis, according to which concept and intuition constitute the two elements of human cognition, Kant in effect argues by elimination. Since space cannot be the former it must be the latter, that is, the representation of an individual that is somehow immediately present to the mind, prior to and independently of any act of conceptualization. It is not that we cannot form concepts of space (clearly, we can and do), but rather that any such concepts presuppose a prior intuition. Thus, the original representation of space must be an intuition.

Although Kant provides two distinct arguments for this thesis, one from the singularity of space (we can represent to ourselves only a single space of which all particular spaces are delimited parts) and the other from its infinity or limitlessness, I shall here consider these together, since they turn on essentially the same point, namely, Kant's view of a concept as a general representation. We have seen that a concept, so understood, is composed of marks (partial representations), which are themselves concepts and which can serve in turn as marks of other concepts. In other words, every concept, *qua* concept, has both an intension and an extension. The former is constituted by the marks of which it is composed and the latter by the concepts falling under it of which it serves as a mark. In a later terminology, one might say that the former determines the sense of a concept and the latter its reference.

Given this, Kant has little difficulty in showing that the representation of space possesses neither of the defining features of a concept, though, as a singular representation, it does fit the definition of an intuition. First, unlike the relation between a concept and its marks, we cannot think of this single space as a product of its parts (particular spaces). On the contrary, unlike the relation between a concept and the marks of which it is composed, that is, its intension, the parts of space presuppose the whole and can be thought as parts only in relation to it. Second, these parts are thought as in space rather than as falling under it, as they would if space were a concept and they constituted its extension.

It is in the context of his conclusions from the analysis of the representation of space as both pure (*a priori*) and intuitive that Kant explicitly addresses the problem of the possibility of an *a priori* intuition posed above. His solution is that such an intuition is possible only "if it contains nothing else except the form of sensibility, which in me as subject precedes all actual impressions through which I am affected by objects" (Kant 2002a: 79). In other words, the only thing that could conceivably be intuited *a priori* by discursive cognizers such as ourselves is the form or manner in which the sensory data for the thought of objects are given to us in empirical intuition. As devoid of sensation (the "matter" of empirical intuition) such a form would be *a priori*, while as pertaining to intuition rather than to thought it would belong to sensibility. And since the representation of space has been shown to be a pure intuition, it follows that the content of this intuition (what is actually intuited *a priori* through it) is merely a subjective form under which objects are given to us in empirical intuition.

Kant concludes from this that though "empirically real" (applicable to everything encountered in human experience), space is nonetheless "transcendentally ideal," that is, a nonentity insofar as one abstracts from the subjective conditions of human

355

sensibility and considers it as either a property or relation of things as they are in themselves. And since Leibniz is committed to the latter alternative, it follows that his view is incorrect.

It might seem that a Leibnizian could attempt to evade the force of this argument by challenging the discursivity thesis on which it is based. For if Kant's sharp concept–intuition distinction be denied, one can hardly argue in the Kantian manner that the representation of space must be intuitive simply because it is not conceptual. In fact, the denial of the discursivity thesis might be thought to open up conceptual space for the possibility that our representation of space is a kind of intellectual intuition, albeit one that must remain confused for finite beings such as ourselves. It is not so easy to argue in this way, however, since, as we have seen, it would involve a host of questionable epistemological and metaphysical assumptions of its own, not the least of which is a commitment to the two dogmas.

V

Although Kant had already characterized space and time as transcendentally ideal in the Aesthetic, he only gets around to defining transcendental idealism itself in the Dialectic. He does so in two places, only one of which is retained in the second edition. In the one that is retained, Kant depicts this idealism as the doctrine that "all objects of an experience possible for us, are nothing but appearances, i.e., mere representations, which, as they are represented, as extended beings or series of alterations, have outside our thoughts no existence grounded in itself." This is contrasted with what Kant terms "transcendental realism," which is charged with making "these modifications of our sensibility into things subsisting in themselves, and hence makes mere representations into things in themselves" (Kant 1998: 511).

As Kant here describes these two forms of transcendentalism, they appear to encompass the entire philosophical landscape. One either regards the objects of possible human experience as appearances or one does not, in which case they are viewed as things in themselves. Moreover, if this is true, it clearly follows that transcendental realism must be understood in a very broad sense as including all other philosophical positions, many of which are not generally regarded as forms of realism. In fact, as I have argued at length elsewhere, transcendental realism may be viewed as the flip side of the theocentric paradigm (Allison 2004: ch. 2). In other words, it is to be understood as a kind of metaphilosophical stance from which the problem of human knowledge is considered, rather than as a distinct metaphysical or epistemological position.

If this is correct it follows that transcendental realism's opposite, transcendental idealism, is likewise to be considered in this way, that is, as a metaphilosophical stance, rather than, as it usually is taken to be, a distinctive metaphysical doctrine. Moreover, so considered, it may be seen as a correlate of the anthropocentric paradigm, which is the product of Kant's Copernican revolution.

In order to appreciate what is at stake here, it is essential to recognize that the very idea of a Copernican revolution, as described above, brings with it an idealistic commitment of a sort, inasmuch as it regards the human mind (with its sensible and intellectual conditions) as the source of the norms and principles through which what counts as "objective" is determined by and for cognizers such as ourselves. Since these conditions which prominently include the sensible conditions through which objects are given in intuition (space and time), it follows that we can cognize objects only as they appear to us under these conditions, not as they may be in themselves independently of them. And, as we have already seen, Kant's position here differs *in toto* from the rationalist's with its theocentric paradigm, which assumes that the cognitive task is to apprehend truths that hold independently of any conditions or principles of the human mind, that is, to come as close as possible to the God's-eye view of things from which alone the truth is fully accessible. Indeed, we have seen that precisely such a view underlies the Leibnizian reduction of the sensible to the intellectual. Although this is not a reduction that we can perform, it is one that the theocentric paradigm requires us to assume is performed by God.

The essentially methodological nature of Kant's idealism becomes more apparent when one examines the key distinction between appearances and things in themselves on which it is based. To begin with, "things in themselves" is to be understood as elliptical for "things as they are in themselves" or, more precisely, "things considered as they are in themselves" (see Prauss 1974. 13–23). In other words, the Kantian distinction is between two ways of considering things, that is, the very objects of our experience, in a reflection on the conditions of their cognition (transcendental reflection) rather than between two ontologically distinct kinds of thing. And since, lacking a capacity for an intellectual intuition, sensibility and understanding are the only cognitive tools by means of which these things can be considered, it follows that to consider them independently of their relation to human sensibility and its *a priori* conditions just is to consider them as putative objects of some "pure understanding," which is not ours. Once again, this is to adopt the theocentric paradigm. Moreover, this also explains why Kant insists that we can think things as they are in themselves, even though we cannot cognize them as such.

Before proceeding further, it must also be noted that, in spite of the daunting theological terms in which transcendental realism's conception of the cognitive task has been expressed, it is the picture implicitly adhered to by common sense, which naturally assumes that the proper object of cognition is a reality existing *an sich*. Anything short of this simply does not count as knowledge, or, if it is regarded as such, it can be only knowledge of how things seem to us rather than of how they really are. At one place in the *Critique* Kant refers to this assumption as the "common but fallacious presupposition of the absolute reality of appearance" (Kant 1998: 535), while at another he characterizes it as the "common prejudice" (Kant 1998: 664). Under either description, the rationalist view is closer to common sense than the Kantian.

Nevertheless, it may still seem odd for Kant to charge rationalism, particularly the Leibnizian variety, with affirming the absolute reality of appearance, thereby effectively regarding the spatiotemporal objects of human experience as if they were things in themselves. Since Kant's main objection against Leibnizian rationalism is that it systematically denies a positive cognitive role for sensibility, and since it is precisely because of the ineliminable role of the latter that Kant thinks that we are acquainted merely with things as they appear rather than as they are in themselves, it might seem more appropriate for Kant to charge such rationalism with simply denying the reality of appearances rather than with conflating them with things in themselves. Consider, for example, the following passage from Leibniz, which is typical of his thought on the matter:

> If Bodies are phenomena and judged in accordance with how they appear to us, they will not be real since they will appear differently to different people. And so the reality of bodies, of space, of motion, and of time seems to consist in the fact that they are phenomena of God, that is, the object of his knowledge by intuition [*scientia visionis*]. And the distinction between the appearance bodies have with respect to us and with respect to God, is, in a certain way, like that between a drawing in perspective and a ground plan. For there are different drawings in perspective, depending upon the position of the viewer, while a ground plan or geometrical representation is unique. Indeed, God sees things exactly as they are in accordance with geometrical truth, although he also knows how everything appears to everything else, and so he eminently contains in himself all other appearances. (Leibniz 1989c: 199)

This passage provides a nice illustration of how Kant appropriated Leibnizian terminology, while giving it a radically different sense. For both thinkers, bodies in space and time are "mere phenomena," and space and time themselves are regarded as "ideal." From the Kantian point of view, the difference is that bodies are not "phenomena of God," since there is no such thing, and space and time are transcendentally ideal. In other words, looked at from the framework of the anthropocentric paradigm, the latter are forms of human sensibility, which partially define the conditions and limits of possible experience for beings like ourselves, rather than regrettable, though unavoidable, sources of the limitations of our cognition. For the same reason, Kant would reject the favorite Leibnizian metaphor of a perspective. It is not that we perceive the same world that God does, albeit from a limited perspective or point of view, it is rather that we perceive our own world, that of possible experience, which is governed and limited by the conditions of our cognition.

This does not mean, however, that our world is, ontologically speaking, less than "really real," since there is no other. What it means instead is that the traditional idea of a God's-eye view of things (a "view from nowhere") is to be understood as a limiting concept, helping to define the conditions and limits of our cognition, rather than as a goal to be approached asymptotically. In fact, the reason why such a limitation is necessary is that the human understanding, as a faculty of thought, has a natural tendency to extend itself beyond its proper sphere, which is limited by our forms of sensibility. Thus, like the Cartesian will, the reach of the Kantian understanding exceeds its grasp. Moreover, for Kant, the clearest example of this in modern philosophy is the Leibnizian monadology and the two dogmas on which it is based.

References and Further Reading

Allison, H. E. (1973). *The Kant–Eberhard Controversy*. Baltimore, MD: Johns Hopkins University Press.
—— (2004). *Kant's Transcendental Idealism*, new enlarged edn. New Haven, CT: Yale University Press.

Beck, L. W. (1967). Can Kant's synthetic judgments be made analytic? In Moltke S. Gram (ed.), *Kant: Disputed Questions*. Chicago: Quadrangle Books.

Kant, I. (1992). *Lectures on Logic* (Michael Young trans. and ed.). Cambridge Edition of the Works of Immanuel Kant. Cambridge: Cambridge University Press.

—— (1998). *Critique of Pure Reason* (Paul Guyer and Allen Wood trans.). Cambridge Edition of the Works of Immanuel Kant. Cambridge: Cambridge University Press.

—— (2002a). *Prolegomena to any Future Metaphysics: Theoretical Philosophy after 1781* (Henry E. Allison and Peter Heath eds., Gary Hatfield trans.). Cambridge Edition of the Works of Immanuel Kant. Cambridge: Cambridge University Press.

—— (2002b). *On a discovery whereby any new critique of pure reason is to be made superfluous by an older one: Theoretical Philosophy after 1781* (Henry E. Allison trans.). Cambridge Edition of the Works of Immanuel Kant. Cambridge: Cambridge University Press.

Kitcher, P. (1981). How Kant almost wrote "Two Dogmas of Empiricism" (and why he didn't). *Philosophical Topics*, 12, 217–49.

Leibniz, G. W. (1956). *The Leibniz–Clarke Correspondence* (H. G. Alexander ed.). Manchester: Manchester University Press.

—— (1989a). Meditations on knowledge, truth, and ideas. In Roger Ariew and Daniel Garber (eds. and trans.), *Philosophical Essays* (pp. 23–7). Indianapolis, IN: Hackett.

—— (1989b). On freedom. In Roger Ariew and Daniel Garber (eds. and trans.), *Philosophical Essays* (pp. 94–8). Indianapolis, IN: Hackett.

—— (1989c). Notes for letter to Des Bosses, February 5, 1712. In Roger Ariew and Daniel Garber (eds. and trans.), *Philosophical Essays* (pp. 199–200). Indianapolis, IN: Hackett.

Prauss, G. (1974). *Kant und das Problem der Dinge an sich*. Bonn: Bouvier.

Quine, W. V. O. (1963). *From a Logical Point of View*. New York: Harper and Row.

Spinoza, B. de (1985). *Ethics*. In Edwin Curley (ed. and trans.), *The Collected Works of Spinoza*. Princeton, NJ: Princeton University Press.

Strawson, P. F. (1966). *The Bounds of Sense: An Essay on Kant's Critique of Pure Reason*. London: Methuen.

Part IV

RATIONALIST THEMES IN CONTEMPORARY PHILOSOPHY

19

Rationalism in the Phenomenological Tradition

DAVID WOODRUFF SMITH

The Emergence of Phenomenology Amid Varieties of Rationalism

Rationalism and empiricism are typically glossed as opposing theories of knowledge. For rationalism, knowledge is founded in reason; for empiricism, knowledge is founded in sense perception. Yet the rationalist impulse is felt in different areas of philosophy, and it is felt differently in different epochs (see chapter 1).

Plato's metaphysics focused on the ideal forms (*eidos*, *logos*) in which all concrete things participate. Our knowledge or appreciation of the forms, witnessed in Plato's dialogues, is approached through Socratic dialectic. In the next generation Aristotle furthered Platonic rationalism by codifying logic (for the first time in human history), both canonizing the discipline and crafting his theory of syllogism. Yet Aristotle also sought a metaphysics of forms that placed them in matter in the natural world. This naturalism invited the turn to empirical methods in the formation of knowledge, though this empiricist impulse remained restrained until the beginnings of modern science in Galileo and Newton.

With the dawn of modern science, Descartes' epistemology fashioned the rationalism we associate with the seventeenth century, followed by Leibniz, Malebranche, and Spinoza. For Descartes, knowledge is developed through the practice of reason very much as in mathematical proof or demonstration. In the pure light of reason, over the course of Descartes' *Meditations on First Philosophy* (1641), we see the steps of inference that lead from the *cogito* (I think, therefore I am) ultimately to the metaphysics of mind–body dualism. In Descartes' hands, then, rationalism defines epistemology but in practice grounds his metaphysics. So too the other great early modern rationalists produced magnificent systems of metaphysics, in Leibniz's monadology and Spinoza's monism. The light of reason leads thus through reflection into insight about the fundamental nature of reality. Thus, early modern rationalism moved through epistemology to metaphysics. Soon, modern empiricism arrived in opposition. For Locke, Berkeley, and Hume, knowledge begins with sensory perception; all our ideas of things begin or are formed from ideas of sense. And empiricist epistemology led into idealist metaphysics. For Berkeley, material objects are but bundles of ideas, ultimately sensory ideas; for Hume, they may as well be mere impressions (we cannot be sure of anything else); for Locke, the things themselves lie beneath our ideas but are we know not what.

Immanuel Kant's critique of pure reason (in his magnum opus of that title, 1781/ 1789) sought in effect a synthesis of rationalist and empiricist epistemology. For Kant, knowledge of things is constituted in the mind's synthesis of sensation and concepts. The faculty of sensibility registers the empiricist foundation of knowledge, and the faculty of understanding (guided by the 12 basic categories of the understanding, or categories of concepts) registers the rationalist foundation of knowledge. So, for Kant, pure reason operates on pure sensation, albeit in ways we cannot be directly aware of, ways innate in the operation of our mind. Kant's quasi- or neo-rationalism, however, withdraws from ultimate metaphysics. For, Kant holds, we cannot know things as they are in themselves, dubbed noumena; we can know only things as they appear in our experience, that is, as formed by concepts of the understanding, concepts that impose form on the world of phenomena, or things-as-they-appear.

In the early nineteenth century Bernard Bolzano reacted against Kantian philosophy, reviving elements of Platonic rationalism in the province of logic, in a logical form of epistemology. Thus we find a logical–rationalist impulse in Bolzano's *Wissenschaftslehre*, or *Theory of Science* (1837). For Bolzano, every science or body of knowledge – every systematic theory – is structured as a deductive system of ideal propositions in themselves, or *Sätze an sich*. Where Kant eschewed the thing in itself, claiming that we know only the *Vorstellung*, a representation-of-the-thing, Bolzano charted a careful distinction between subjective ideas (*Vorstellungen*) and objective ideas, or ideas in themselves (*Vorstellungen an sich*). Subjective ideas are concrete events in our minds, what the empiricists called ideas; whereas objective ideas are, as it were, ideal forms of subjective ideas. Thus, when you think "P" and I think "P," you experience your act of thinking and I experience my act of thinking, yet we both think the same proposition in itself, "P." Ideal propositions are the domain of logic, and their existence is similar to that of Platonic forms: the heart of ancient rationalism.

Bolzano's conception of logic and its place in science was echoed a century later in W. V. O. Quine's conception of knowledge – especially scientific knowledge – as a web of belief. (See Quine, 1995, configuring his work over prior decades, and Quine and Ullian 1978.) Quine was a naturalistic philosopher looking to modern science as our best kind of knowledge. Where science begins with sensory stimulus and observation, our theories themselves are structured by logic and mathematics. In Quine's metaphor, a theory is a web of belief wherein observations lie at the periphery of the web and there tie most directly to the world, while logic and mathematics lie at the center of the web and are used to structure our knowledge claims that ultimately explain (to the best of our ability) our observations. Quine's theory of knowledge followed his rejection of Rudolf Carnap's experiment with logical empiricism in *The Logical Structure of the World* (1928) (see chapter 20, this volume). In the present context, we may see Quine's epistemology as empiricist on the role of observation in knowledge formation, but rationalist on the role of logic and mathematics in science. Unlike Bolzano, Quine rejected abstract entities such as ideal propositions. But, like Bolzano, Quine counted logical truths – defined in terms of logical form alone (the Bolzano–Quine criterion of the logical) – as central to the structure of knowledge of the world around us. Moreover, Quine stressed that observations which do not fit with the rest of the structured web of theory may be revised or rejected, while the logic and mathematics of the theory are the most resistant to revision. In this way Quine's epistemology is rationalist – logic plays a central role in knowledge – even though sensory observation is the starting place of knowledge.

At the beginning of the twentieth century, in his *Logical Investigations* (1900–1), Edmund Husserl took up all the above issues, in a philosophical system comprising views on epistemology, ontology, logic, and – something new – phenomenology. Husserl laid out a complex theory of knowledge beginning with Bolzano's conception of logic. Amid the development of that theory lay Husserl's articulation of the new discipline of phenomenology. As we shall see, phenomenology involves a type of reflection on experience, beginning, as it were, with observation of our own consciousness. This method of self-observation is not a kind of sensory observation, but *qua* observation it brings an extended empiricist impulse into phenomenology. And yet, in Husserl's definitive account of the discipline, phenomenology studies ideal forms or meanings in our experience, as logic studies ideal meanings in our deductive theories. Here is the rationalist impulse at the heart of phenomenology.

Perhaps that impulse explains why phenomenology has been so difficult for analytic philosophers to understand. As Alan Nelson notes (chapter 1, this volume), the rationalist finds that insight – into ideal forms, etc. – comes only through the practice of a regimen that requires special training. We do not simply open our eyes and "see" ideal forms or meanings or logical truths, as Plato, Descartes, and Husserl sought to grasp the ideal. We see trees and tables by opening our eyes and looking around. But "seeing" ideal forms or meanings or truths requires a subtle practice that gradually leads to insight. Logic, with its own discipline, has been part of the training of analytic philosophers for a century now, and logic-trained philosophers have highly developed "intuitions" about which forms of inference are valid – even if they reject Platonistic ontologies of ideal meanings. However, phenomenology has not been part of the training of most analytic philosophers. Meanwhile, phenomenology, with its own discipline, has been central to the training of many continental philosophers, who have a highly developed sensibility regarding forms of experience and the role of everyday language therein.

Let us turn, then, to an account of phenomenology, with an eye to the rationalist – and empiricist – elements in phenomenology.

Phenomenology in Brief

The phenomenological tradition developed over the first half of the twentieth century, in the philosophies of Husserl, Martin Heidegger, Maurice Merleau-Ponty, Jean-Paul Sartre, and many others. The tradition remains vibrant today. But we may distinguish the phenomenological movement – a historical cultural tradition – from the discipline of phenomenology, which is a part of philosophy alongside ethics, logic, metaphysics or ontology, epistemology, political theory, etc. For present purposes we focus largely on the work of Husserl, in whom a strong strain of rationalism is manifest. (For a discerning overview of the continental tradition of phenomenology, its methods and results, see Moran 2000. For a detailed account of the Husserlian theory of intentionality, the basis of phenomenology in Husserl's hands, and its relation to logical or semantic theory, see Smith and McIntyre 1982.)

The discipline of phenomenology came into its own in the work of Husserl, in the wake of the historic debates between rationalism and empiricism that defined early modern philosophy. Husserl's conception of phenomenology grew out of Franz Brentano's conception of descriptive as opposed to genetic psychology, in *Psychology from an Empirical Standpoint* (1874). Genetic psychology seeks the causes of psychological phenomena, whereas descriptive psychology analyses the basic types of mental phenomena and their intrinsic structure: perception, judgment, emotion, etc. While Brentano admired the empiricists, his primary concern was the nature of mind rather than the nature of knowledge. As his title implies, his task was to chart the terrain of psychology, which began to separate itself from philosophy in his hands, and he cast psychology in an empiricist mold. After all, the empiricists Locke and Hume had analyzed different types of "ideas" or "impressions," and Locke developed the very notion of "consciousness," bringing that term of art to full prominence. Thus, Brentano sought to distinguish mental from physical phenomena, proposing that the distinguishing feature of mental phenomena – acts of consciousness – is their being "directed" toward something. In Husserl's gloss, consciousness is a consciousness *of* something. That property of consciousness, its being "of" or "directed" toward something, Husserl called *intentionality*.

Building on Brentano, Husserl defined phenomenology as the science of the essence of consciousness (*Ideas* I: sect. 34). Over the course of nearly four decades, Husserl analyzed in detail various structures of perception, judgment, consciousness of space, consciousness of time, experience of things in nature, awareness of one's own body, empathic experience of other persons, and more. With Brentano, Husserl held that the central feature of an act of consciousness – whether perception or judgment or whatever – is its intentionality. But Husserl diverged from Brentano in a way that is crucial to the present discussion. Husserl was trained initially as a mathematician, and he looked to mathematical logic (emerging in his day) along with Bolzano's theory of logic, while conceiving phenomenology. Accordingly, Husserl integrated psychological theory with logical theory. If you will, psychology gave phenomenology its empirical or indeed empiricist base, while logic gave phenomenology its logical or indeed rationalist base. For phenomenology, the central problem is not the foundation of knowledge, but the essential structure of consciousness – from which the nature of knowledge emerges.

Husserl's *Logical Investigations* began with a long critique of "psychologism" in nineteenth-century logic. This critique occupied most of the original first volume of the *Investigations*, called "Prolegomena to Pure Logic." In the empiricist tradition, John Stuart Mill had presented logic as a study of how we happen to think and reason, leaving logical validity a contingent empirical feature of how we happen to draw inferences. Husserl argued at length against this philosophy of logic. Citing Bolzano as his hero, Husserl held that "pure logic" is concerned not with how people happen to think and reason, but with ideal forms of meaning. A valid deduction or implication is a relationship among ideal propositions in themselves. What makes it valid has nothing to do with the contingencies of human existence, but lies in the ideal deductive relations among propositions in themselves. Given this objective philosophy of logic, what has logic to do with human knowledge? What has logic to do with consciousness, with our unfolding experience, an empirical matter of how the human mind happens to work – among other things, in the production of knowledge? How does phenomenology, in Husserl's hands, take shape around a philosophy of logic? That is a central part of the story that unfolds in the *Logical Investigations*, and therein lies the rationalist impulse in phenomenology.

Phenomenologists after Husserl took an existential turn toward the concrete contingencies of human experience. Heidegger stressed the everydayness of human existence, wherein our familiar forms of comportment are defined by cultural practices beyond our awareness. Sartre stressed our radical freedom in concrete historical situations, such as the French faced under Nazi German occupation in World War II. Of direct relevance to the present study, however, is Merleau-Ponty's phenomenology of perception. For Merleau-Ponty developed an explicit critique of both empiricism and rationalism, arguing from principles of Gestalt psychology that consciousness is essentially structured around one's own "living body." This analysis seems a far cry from rationalism. Yet Merleau-Ponty's phenomenology retains much of Husserl's basic results. We consider Merleau-Ponty's critique of rationalism, accordingly, at the end of this chapter.

From Logic to Phenomenology

The course of argument in Husserl's *Logical Investigations* runs for nearly 1,000 pages, including the Prolegomena and six Investigations. In that long narrative Husserl develops a theory of logic, a theory of language, a theory of universals, a theory of parts, a theory of parts of meanings, a theory of intentionality, and finally a theory of knowledge. Husserl defines phenomenology in terms of his theory of intentionality and applies this to produce a theory of knowledge. Remarkably, all this is tied together in a unified philosophical system of which phenomenology is a part (see Smith 2003).

In the Prolegomena, Husserl develops his conception of "pure logic" as the theory of theory: logic concerns ideal *meanings*, especially propositions and their deductive relations within a given deductive axiomatic theory consisting of a unified body of propositions about some domain. In the First Investigation, Husserl moved on to an account of language. Logic itself concerns ideal propositions and their relations within theories. But we express meanings – concepts and propositions – in speech and writing. These meanings are ideal contents of thought and experience. We share the same content when we think the same thought or proposition. And the function of language (among other things) is typically to convey to another person a meaning expressed by the words we utter, and so to share that meaning with others through language. But what are these ideal meanings that we share in language? Husserl proposes that meanings are ideal species of thought expressed in language. What then are ideal species in general?

In the Second Investigation, Husserl turns to the traditional theory of universals. *Species* are shared by their instances and are in that sense ideal entities. Thus, two red apples share the species Red; the apples are concrete things, the species Red is ideal. One species stands over two, indeed many, individuals: the one over the many. Here is a variant on Plato's ontology of forms or *eidos*. Later, in *Ideas* I, Husserl calls ideal species or *eidos* simply essences (*Wesen*), or what things are. Husserl does not rest,

367

however, with this broadly Platonistic theory of species. He incorporates an Aristotelian element, with a novel twist, in a theory of part and whole.

In the Third Investigation, Husserl develops an intricate ontology of *parts* and wholes. He distinguished two kinds of part. An independent part can exist without the whole to which it belongs, but a dependent part cannot exist apart from the whole of which it is a part. For instance, a red bicycle has a front wheel: the wheel is an independent part of the bicycle (it can be removed), but the red of this bicycle is a dependent part of the bicycle, as this particular red could not exist apart from the bicycle. (If the cycle were repainted with blue paint, its blue would be a dependent part of the bicycle, but its prior red would have been destroyed rather than removed like a wheel.) Here is a variant on Aristotle's ontology: for Aristotle, a quality such as this red is a particularized universal that exists "in" an object and could not exist apart from it. Husserl calls independent parts "pieces" and dependent parts "moments." Thus, the bicycle is an individual, its wheel is a *piece* of the bicycle, and its particular redness is a *moment* of the bicycle.

In the Fourth Investigation, Husserl develops a theory of *grammar*, in the form of a theory of the parts of ideal meanings, including the ways that concepts are combined to form propositions. As the sentence "Grass is green" is formed from the subject term "grass" and the predicate term "green," so the ideal proposition "Grass is green" – the meaning expressed by that sentence – is formed from the individual concept "grass" and the predicate concept "green." The subject concept "grass" is an independent part of the proposition, while the predicate concept "green" is a dependent part of the proposition. Here Husserl applies the theory of parts to ideal meanings – a striking application of part-whole theory, but resonant with traditional grammar where we speak of the parts of a sentence.

In the Fifth Investigation, Husserl lays the foundation for phenomenology. Here he develops a theory of the *intentionality* of consciousness. Fundamentally, he distinguishes act, content, and object of consciousness. An *act* or experience of seeing a tree, for instance, is a concrete experience, a part of one's stream of experiences. This act is a consciousness *of* the tree, if such tree exists, and the tree is the *object* of the act. But the act is directed toward the tree by way of a certain intentional *content*, say, "that oak tree on the hill." Content and object must be distinguished because the same object can be presented in different ways in different acts of consciousness; for instance, I might see the object instead as "the tree under which I once read Proust." Intentional contents are what we variously call ideas, images, concepts, thoughts, or propositions, etc. These are the entities Husserl calls ideal meanings. For Husserl, then, intentionality consists in the relation among act, content, and object of consciousness: an act is intentionally directed via a content toward an object (if such object exists). Husserl propounds what we might call a semantic theory of intentionality: an act is directed toward a particular object if and only if the act's content or meaning prescribes (presents, represents, intends) that particular object – alternatively, that object satisfies the act's content.

Now, phenomenology is basically the study of the various forms of intentionality we find in our experience, in perception, thought, imagination, desire, etc. Accordingly, Husserl's new science of phenomenology is articulated in terms of the complex philosophical theory he develops through the Prolegomena and the first five Investigations.

Thus, Husserl proposes, the intentional content of an act of consciousness is its *intentional essence*: its ideal species *qua* intentional experience, the species that defines its form of intentionality. In other terms, the content of an act or experience is an ideal *meaning*. It has a structure, with whatever component meanings are parts of it, either dependent or independent parts, as the case may be. So the content of an experience is a *structured ideal meaning* that can be shared by other acts. Such meanings can be expressed in language, at least in the case of discursive thoughts (such as "Grass is green"). The logical or grammatical structure and deductive implications of meanings can be studied in pure logic. Phenomenology, then, focuses on the meanings that are contents of acts of consciousness, meanings whose structure is broadly logical. When he wrote the *Logical Investigations*, he identified meanings with act species (as above). After further reflection, in *Ideas* I, he saw them as a new type of ideal entities: not ideal species, but ideal meanings (*Sinn*), which he then called *noemata* (reviving a term Aristotle used for what is known). Of course, ideal meanings – including propositions and theories (deductive systems of propositions) – are the domain of pure logic. But with phenomenology we see, according to Husserl, where meanings enter our experience: they are the intentional contents of acts of consciousness. In this way phenomenology is more basic than logic, in Husserl's overall philosophy. This position would be his emphasis in the late work, *Formal and Transcendental Logic* (1929). Nonetheless, phenomenology studies ideal meanings found in our experience.

In the Sixth Investigation, the last of the *Logical Investigations*, Husserl finally turns to the theory of knowledge per se. Here *logos* and *episteme*, reason and knowledge, come together in a way that joins elements of Platonic and Cartesian rationalisms. Where Husserl began the *Investigations* with a logical theory of theory, he closes with a phenomenological theory of knowledge. What makes a system of propositions count as a *theory* is how they hang together by deductive relations: a matter of logic. What makes a theory count, further, as *knowledge* is how its propositions are supported by evidence, by evident experience: a matter of phenomenology.

A Phenomenological Theory of Knowledge

Husserl's theory of knowledge is outlined in the Sixth of the *Logical Investigations* (a book-length treatise). The key notion is that of "intuition" (*Anschauung*, literally 'looking-at'). Husserl holds that knowledge is founded always in some form of intuition. *Intuition* is defined as the type of experience in which an object is presented with *evidence*, that is, the experience is a self-evident presentation of its object, so that the object is posited as existing and the evidence for so positing the object is already a feature of that experience itself. Simply put, the experience is an *intuitive* or *evident* intentional presentation of the object. What is this character of intuitiveness?

Consider a mundane example: it is one thing to *think* that grass is green; it is quite another thing to *see* green grass, or to *see* that this grass is green. The difference is phenomenological. For the experience of seeing something green, or seeing that this grass is green, is evident or intuitive: the experience has the phenomenological character of evidence or intuitiveness. But that character is lacking in an experience of merely thinking that grass is green. We appreciate the phenomenological character of evidence or intuitiveness by observing this contrast, reflecting on our own experience of the difference.

Husserl's theory of intuition takes its place within his wider theory of intentionality, the basis of his conception of phenomenology. Accordingly, the character of intuitiveness takes its place within his account of intentional content. Specifically, Husserl divides the intentional content of an act or experience into two basic components. The "matter" of the act specifies "what" the act intends, the object *as* intended, while the "quality" specifies the "way" in which that is intended. For instance, if I think that Plato was Greek, the matter of my act is the proposition that Plato was Greek (as opposed, say, to the proposition that Plato was Persian), and the quality of my act is the character of thinking (as opposed, say, to wishing). Now, the character of intuitiveness is a part of the quality of an experience, as opposed to its matter. Seeing something is thus an evident experience, while merely thinking something is not an evident experience. That is to say, for Husserl, the *quality* of seeing carries the specific character of intuitiveness: seeing is a form of intuition.

In Husserl's analysis, knowledge is grounded in the *phenomenological* character of intuitiveness, a feature of certain acts of consciousness. When we turn to scientific knowledge, however, we find knowledge distributed more widely than in any discrete act of intuition. (Recall Bolzano's "theory of science," which so impressed Husserl.) Scientific knowledge takes the form of a proper theory, ideally an axiomatic deductive system of propositions about a particular domain or subject matter. Further, such knowledge is based in intuition, that is, in particular intuitive acts of consciousness. A science – a body of scientific knowledge – is distributed, then, over a system of propositions supported by evidence gathered in particular acts of intuition. So it does not consist simply in what can be known in a single act of intuitive judgment about something, as where I know that this object is a tree because I see that it is a tree. Indeed, most of our scientific knowledge is grounded in a historical tradition that includes the work of many people gathering observations, reasoning, developing intricate mathematical models, etc. Thus, our knowledge, say, in physics ranges from Galileo's observations of the moons of Jupiter, to Newton's mathematical theory of gravity, to Einstein's theory of relativity, and so on. Husserl emphasized this historically developed form of knowledge in his posthumous work *The Crisis of European Sciences and Transcendental Phenomenology* (1935–8).

In the Husserlian theory of knowledge so far sketched, we see a typical form of empiricism: knowledge of nature is founded in sensory perception, which counts as intuition because it has the character of self-evidence. The term "intuition" was already used by Kant, for whom knowledge was founded in a synthesis of sensations organized by concepts so as to form "intuition." This Kantian view is echoed in Husserl's account of perception in *Ideas* I (sect. 84). In Husserl's developed theory of perception, an act of (say) visual perception is a whole incorporating two moments (dependent parts) called *hyle* and *noesis*. (*Hyle* is the Greek term for "matter," *noesis* for "knowing.") The hyletic part of a perception consists in the preconceptualized sensory activity, and the noetic part of the perception consists in the interpretive or meaning-giving activity in the experience. The meaning "given" in the experience is the ideal intentional content of the act, which Husserl calls its *noema* (the Greek for "what is known"). What I experience as seeing that tree, then, is the whole act formed by the fusion of these sensory and meaning-giving parts – I am not aware of any separate sensory and noetic activities; indeed, they are inseparable from each other as dependent parts of the experience. Now, in perception, there is already a conceptual or logical element in the ideal meaning that serves as its content. So here we find a rationalist element in the structure of perception, which, in empiricist style, is the foundation of knowledge of physical objects.

So far we have focused on sensory perception (say, seeing a tree) as a type of intuition. But on Husserl's analysis, there are other types of intuition, including intuition of essences and intuition of meanings, to which we turn shortly. Over the course of his many writings, Husserl recognized several remarkably different types of intuition: (1) sensory intuition of physical objects – what we call perception, in seeing, hearing, touching, smelling, tasting, and also kinesthetic awareness of one's bodily movement; (2) eidetic intuition of essences; (3) logical intuition of the logical forms of propositions and their entailments; (4) categorial intuition of the ontological forms of states of affairs, forms that combine individuals and proporties; (5) transcendental-phenomenological intuition of intentional contents, or noemata; (6) mathematical intuition of mathematical entities such as numbers, sets, etc. What qualifies these different types of experience as intuition is an appropriate character of evidence in each. Husserl's most explicit account of various types and strengths of "evidence" in experience appears in his later work, *Cartesian Meditations* (1929).

Where the *Logical Investigations* begins with a conception of "pure logic," it ends (800 pages later) with what Husserl calls a "phenomenological theory of knowledge." What makes his theory of knowledge *phenomenological* is the analysis of the structures of evidence and intentionality in intuition. He calls intuition "seeing," generalizing the sense of the term beyond seeing with our eyes – a familiar idiom when speaking about insight as opposed to sight per se. Husserl's doctrine of "seeing essences" (*Wesenschau*) was criticized by empiricist philosophers such as Moritz Schlick, a founding figure of the Vienna Circle of logical positivists. Interestingly, Husserl would later declare, "We are the real positivists" (*Ideas* I). What Husserl meant, we may infer, was that the proper core of positivism ought to be observation in the wider sense of "intuition," though the classical positivists, like the classical empiricists before them, recognized only sensory perception as the observational base of knowledge. The doctrine of "seeing" ideal essences or ideal meanings echoes the ideals of classical rationalists. Characteristic of Husserl's philosophical vision, Husserl's theory of knowledge thus seeks to incorporate, correct, and extend elements of both rationalism and empiricism.

Intuition of Essences

Husserl's doctrine of *Wesenschau*, or seeing essences, incorporates and updates both of the core notions of traditional rationalisms: Plato's notion of ideal forms, and Descartes' notion of insight achieved by the light of reason. Husserl's doctrine has been poorly understood, usually by parody, as if we are to "see" features of an essence by peering into the Platonic heavens with a kind of intellectual telescope. A more careful study of Husserl's doctrine brings it down to earth amid rather familiar practices – even if the method of *Wesenschau* requires practice and must be developed by a regime of

371

intellectual training. (For a sympathetic contemporary study of Husserl's method and its import for *a priori* knowledge, see Kasmier (2003), in which Husserl's method is favored over recent accounts of "intuition" by various analytic philosophers.)

For Husserl, we saw, *essences* are what philosophers since Aristotle have called universals: what we may call properties of things, including kinds, qualities, and relations. In *Logical Investigations* Husserl spoke of ideal species or universals, but in *Ideas* I he preferred to speak of essences, *Wesen*, what things are. Concrete individuals have or instantiate essences, and different individuals can have the same essence – which is why essences are called universals, as one essence covers many individuals. For example, two red balls each have the essence Red – and the essence Ball. Where these two individuals each exist at a certain time and place, the essence they share cannot be said to exist at either of their locations. In that sense, Husserl says, individuals are *real*, or spatiotemporal entities, while essences are *ideal*, or non-spatial, non-temporal entities. In Husserl's ontology, an essence is instantiated in an individual insofar as an instance of the essence is a moment, or dependent part, of the individual: this red in this ball is a moment of the ball and an instance of the ideal species Red; but while this red is in the ball, the essence Red is not literally *in* the ball. (See the Third Investigation of the *Logical Investigations*.)

What philosophers have long found problematic about essences is precisely their ideal status. Where are they? If they are not located in the spatiotemporal world of nature in which we live, how do we know that they exist? How indeed can we know anything at all about them? Husserl tackles the problem head-on. He proposes an explicit method for grasping or "seeing" an essence (*eidos*), a method he calls *eidetic variation*. (The method is discussed in *Logical Investigations* and again in *Ideas* I.)

In order to grasp an essence, we conceive, in phantasy or imagination, a number of individuals that are prospective instances of the essence. We imagine various properties these individuals might have. Gradually, we come to "see" that the essence involves having certain properties but not others. In this way we come to appreciate the nature of the essence. For example, we consider, say, a variety of balls that we consider red. Yellow and blue balls are discounted. We imagine a shade between fire-engine red and purple. If the shade is far enough from the bluish red of purple and close enough to the intense red of a fire engine (in the traditional color used in the United States), we count that shade as red. We thereby come to appreciate the essence Red. Or consider this table. We imagine it having a spherical top surface: no, that would not be a table – it may be an interesting sculpture, but it will not do as a table. We imagine it without legs: no, that would not be a table. We imagine it with not four, but six legs: yes, that would be a table. We imagine it with one leg, a pedestal base: yes, that would still be a table, not the usual sort but a table nonetheless. In this way we come to appreciate or "see" the essence Table. Thus we "vary" our conception of the *eidos*, judging when a prospective individual does or does not have the essence.

This method of "eidetic variation" sounds esoteric at first. Yet, despite its new name, the method is a development of classical philosophical practice. Aristotle emphasized the differences among distinct *categories* of things: individuals, species, qualities, etc. In the Prolegomena of the *Logical Investigations*, Husserl proposed to distinguish categories not only for language (grammatical categories), but also for meanings (conceptual categories), and also for objects in the world (ontological categories). As grammar distinguishes nouns and predicates, so ontology distinguishes individuals and essences. Husserl then defines *formal* ontology as the theory of different forms or categories of objects in the world. In a categorical ontology, it is a mistake – a category mistake – to think that essences must have location in space-time: individuals have spatiotemporal location, but essences are a fundamentally different type of thing. Indeed, in everyday life and language we treat individuals and their properties differently. Accordingly, we may see this table with our eyes, but its essence Table we come to "see" rather by appreciating what makes it count as a table – its having a flat, level top and its having legs that support its top. We consider this table, a concrete individual, by casting our eyes upon it from different spatial perspectives. But we consider its essence, Table-hood, by reflecting on the differences in properties among things that we judge to be tables and things we judge not to be tables. This type of reflection is not unfamiliar.

In Husserl's account of eidetic variation analytic philosophers should recognize a form of "conceptual analysis." Analytic philosophers often use thought experiments to test, in conceptual imagination, the necessary and sufficient conditions, say, for something's being a table. The method is to test our concept of being a table. The difference in Husserl's account is that he further specifies that the object of analysis – studied through conceptual variation – is the essence Table, the objective entity (the universal) represented by our familiar concept "table." We direct our thought toward this essence, the property of being a table, *through* our varying conceptions of the essence.

The method of eidetic variation is to be practiced in *imagination*. We conceive or imagine individuals, and in imagination we vary their properties until we have a good idea of what makes them qualify as having a certain essence. We thereby come to grasp – or "see" – that essence. But what if the essence is not a familiar everyday kind such as Red or Table, but, say, an unfamiliar kind found in nature? Take the Chinese ginkgo tree, the species biologists call Gingko biloba. Husserl presumably was unfamiliar with this species; there were none in his garden in Freiburg. Given his range of experience, he could not conceive of this kind of tree, he could not vary its prospective properties in his imagination, and he could not, therefore, grasp the essence of that species by practicing eidetic variation. Indeed, Husserl could not, through the exercise of his imagination, come to appreciate the biochemical properties of the Gingko biloba leaf, which we today are told increases blood flow in the human brain. And even today we cannot through our imagination discern the molecular structure of the chemical in the Gingko leaf that has this power over our brains. Evidently, then, there are limits to the efficacy of eidetic variation as a method for grasping essences.

Or take a case closer to Husserl's heart (as a former mathematician). We all have some familiarity with numbers, as we all learned to count early in childhood. Mathematicians, however, have developed an axiomatic theory of the natural (whole) numbers: 1, 2, 3, . . . etc. Prime numbers are defined as those divisible only by themselves and the number 1. Hence, we contemplate the essence Prime Number. But mathematicians ask whether there is a largest prime number. We suspect not, but we await proof. It seems, then, that we cannot fully grasp the essence Prime Number by varying the properties of numbers in our imagination. Again, we encounter limits on the method of eidetic variation.

These cases make it clear that the method of eidetic variation itself must rest on a practice of getting to know about individuals having the essence at hand. In everyday life we have acquired a background knowledge of tables and on that basis we can practice eidetic variation on the essence Table. In order to practice eidetic variation on the essence Gingko biloba or Prime Number, however, we must develop some background of knowledge about things having these essences: the first by learning from botanists and biochemists, the second by learning from mathematicians. We should recognize, however, that there will be aspects of a given essence that lie beyond our present range of knowledge. Tables we know well, numbers fairly well, but the chemistry of the gingko tree and the nature of "dark matter" lie beyond our current powers of well-grounded imagination.

We practice variations on this method in developing our understanding of what things are, things like tables known by going down to the kitchen, or things like gingko trees known by exploring the biosphere, or things like numbers known by exploring mathematics. When we consider such examples of the practice Husserl called eidetic variation, we gradually recognize it as a familiar part of our traditional modes of knowledge formation. In fact, Husserl has begun a phenomenological description of that practice.

Intuition of Meanings

The discipline of phenomenology proceeds, in effect, through eidetic variation on the structure of intentionality. In the Fifth of the *Logical Investigations*, Husserl considers varying examples of intentional experiences. He argues, by way of examples, that every intentional act of consciousness has a content that is distinct from its object. Thus, every intentional experience is directed toward some putative object. But sometimes, as in thinking of Santa Claus or of the Golden Mountain, there does not exist such an object; still, the act has a content, which as it were aims the act in such a direction. Hence, we must distinguish an act's content from its object. Furthermore, in two acts we may think of the same object in different ways: we may think of Napoleon as "the victor at Jena" or as "the vanquished at Waterloo," whence the same object is presented through two distinct contents. Again, we see that we must distinguish an act's content from its object. These thought experiments are exercises in eidetic variation on the essence of consciousness, the ideal form Intentionality, whereby we come to "see" the role of content in the structure of intentionality.

In the Fifth Investigation, Husserl simply identified the content of an act with its "intentional essence": the essence that defines the way the act is directed, its ideal species of intentional consciousness, its ideal form of intentionality. Thus, the essence of my thinking of Napoleon (in a certain way) is the form Thinking-of-the-victor-at-Jena. On further reflection, however, in *Ideas* I, Husserl concluded that intentional contents – meanings or noemata – are a distinct and fundamental type of ideal entity, different in principle from essences or species. Husserl does not explain his change of mind. Perhaps he came to "see" meanings and essences differently, that is, he came to see that *their* essences differ. Eidetic variation, after all, can be applied to any type of entity: to essences themselves, to meanings, to numbers, or to tables or trees. We might well observe, in this regard, that it is the role of essences to be *instantiated* by particular individuals, but it is the role of meanings to *represent* particular individuals.

The concept or meaning "the victor at Jena" represents Napoleon; but the essence The-victor-at-Jena is instantiated by Napoleon.

If meanings are a type of ideal entities distinct from species or essences, they are – as Bolzano, Husserl, and Frege urged – not something tied to spatiotemporal location. Here we have a Platonistic ontology of meanings (*Sinn*, *Satz*). But if meanings are not found among things around us in the spatiotemporal natural world, then how can we know anything about them? In *Ideas* I, Husserl proposed an explicit method for grasping meanings or noemata. This method he called "bracketing" or *epoché*.

Consider an act of consciousness in which I see "that oak tree on the hill." In this experience my consciousness is directed toward an object, a certain tree. In the method of phenomenological bracketing, I bracket the question of the existence of the object and thereby turn my attention away from the object itself and toward the way in which it appears or is presented in my experience. The object *as* presented or "meant" Husserl calls the (noematic) sense (*Sinn*) of the experience. This meaning embodies the way I experience the object, the way the object is "intended" in my act of consciousness. As Husserl says, the tree itself, the thing in nature, can burn away, but the sense it has for me in this experience is not something that can burn away – the meaning is an ideal entity. (Husserl also uses the ancient Greek term *epoché*, meaning to abstain from belief, from positing the existence of the object so meant.)

This method of bracketing is designed, then, to turn our attention from the *object* of an experience to the ideal content or *meaning* entertained in the experience. Here we find a specific element of rationalism at the heart of phenomenology. Husserl always bemoaned the fact that his successors did not properly understand this basic methodology of phenomenology. His critics seemed to think that Husserl was rejecting the external world – along the lines of a Berkeley, who reduced material objects to ideas, or at least a Hume, who in his skeptical phase withdrew belief in material objects and rested secure only with our ideas or impressions of material things. Now, Berkeley and Hume were two of the three classical empiricists. But Husserl, while much impressed with both Hume and Berkeley, insisted on the core of "pure logic" in phenomenology. For Husserl, phenomenology proper resists all manner of "psychologism," which would reduce meaning to what happens to occur in our minds. No, meanings are, for Husserl, ideal entities. And we must approach them in a method appropriate to them: in their role in intentionality, as contents of acts of consciousness. As phenomenology emerges in Husserl's practice, then, we find a distinctly rationalist feature: we come to "see" ideal meanings only through the practice of a particular method. Here is a new type of intuition, the *intuition of meanings*.

Husserl thus proposes a discrete method for the practice of phenomenology, a method for phenomenological reflection. We are to *reflect* on our own experience, from a first-person perspective. But it is not as if we can each put up a periscope and peer around inside our own mind, looking at different types of experience and observing their ideal meanings. Instead, we must learn to turn our attention away from the normal focus of our consciousness, and toward the ideal content of our consciousness. In this way we come to "see" ideal meaning.

Logicians may recognize in Husserl's notion of bracketing a form of "semantic ascent." For Quine, we understand the force of a linguistic expression by "ascent" from its intended referent to the expression itself, whose logical force we understand by studying the language rather than the objects we use the expression to talk about. Similarly, for Husserl, we understand a form of experience by "ascent" from the object of such an experience to the content or meaning we use to present that object to ourselves in consciousness.

A Phenomenological Critique of Empiricism and Rationalism

Husserl's new science of phenomenology took European philosophy by storm. Soon, however, three emerging phenomenologists set out their own conceptions of phenomenology that turned sharply away from the logico-rationalist foundation laid by Husserl. Heidegger stressed the role of historically formed cultural practices in defining the meaning (*Sinn*) we find in our familiar everyday forms of "comportment" (*Verhalten*), reconfiguring Husserl's "logocentric" conception of intentionality (to co-opt a term popularized by a later revisionist phenomenologist). Sartre stressed the role of radical freedom in human consciousness, focusing on the experience of "engaged" action in concrete historical situations, a far cry from Husserl's lofty logic-minded phenomenology. But it remained for Merleau-Ponty to address the issues of rationalism as we have pursued it in the theory and practice of phenomenology.

Merleau-Ponty's *Phenomenology of Perception* (1945) adopts and adapts Husserl's basic phenomenological notions, emphasizing the "meaning" and "horizon" of experience. Husserl often used perception, especially visual perception, as a paradigm of consciousness. Merleau-Ponty takes perception to be not only a paradigm of intentional experience, but also the proper foundation of all our experience. This motif might seem to turn phenomenology away from rationalism and firmly toward empiricism. Yet Merleau-Ponty launched his conception of phenomenology with an explicit critique of both empiricism and rationalism, or "intellectualism" as he put it.

Empiricism was wrong to claim that fundamentally we see sensory qualities such as red; typically, we see something like "this woolly red of the carpet." Indeed, what is difficult is to "say what we see." Yet rationalism, or intellectualism, was wrong to claim that fundamentally we see ideal (pure, mathematical) forms such as circles or squares. Drawing Gestalt psychology into phenomenology, Merleau-Ponty assays that what we see is normally a *figure* against a *ground*: I see that oak tree on the hillside – not a patch of brown and green, not an oak-tree shape, nor simply a free-floating oak tree. Moreover, in Merleau-Ponty's analysis, what I see is configured in relation to *my own body*: not this body as articulated by physiology, but this body as I know it in walking and looking around the tree – what Husserl called a "living body" (*Leib*), this living body that I am. In Merleau-Ponty's famous observation, "The theory of the body is already a theory of perception." Thus, the "phenomenal field" – the field of things I am given in perception – is structured in relation to my body as embodied subject. Indeed, on Merleau-Ponty's analysis, the *cogito* (Descartes' pronouncement, "I think, therefore I am") reveals not a purely mental subject "I," but an embodied subject "I." According to Merleau-Ponty, then, phenomenology avoids the mistakes of both empiricism and rationalism, and sets off in a new direction, studying the more complex meaning things have in our lived experience oriented in relation to our own living body.

Aron Gurwitsch – both influencing and influenced by Merleau-Ponty – developed in closer detail a phenomenological theory of the "field of consciousness" (see Gurwitsch 1964). Having worked in a Gestalt psychology laboratory, Gurwitsch extended Husserl's analysis of the "horizon" of experience, specifying an articulate structure in the field of vision, and of consciousness generally. When I see that oak tree on the hillside, my *field* of consciousness is structured into three parts: the *theme* is the oak tree, as perceived, that which is the focus of my consciousness; the *thematic field* includes the "relevant" background features of hillside surroundings; and the *marginal field* includes my body and bodily movement as I approach the tree, my stream of experiences (in which this perception takes place), and the wider world around me – things of which I am only marginally aware and which are not relevant to this experience but are part of the wider *meaning* of my experience in seeing that tree on this occasion. The intentional structure of the experience is defined by this wider structure of meaning, whose form defines the field of consciousness.

This structural analysis of the "field" of conscious experience seems richly concrete, bound to our earthly human existence with two eyes two inches apart, two hands with opposable thumbs, two hinged legs, and so on – all very far from the lofty ideal structures posited by Husserl in his meta-theory of phenomenology. Yet both Gurwitsch and Merleau-Ponty stressed the *meaning* and correlative horizon of meaning in our experience. If we abstract this structure of meaning in itself, articulating the formal structure of our consciousness and its typical context, we find a "logic" of situated, embodied, active consciousness (cf. Smith 2004).

The rationalist impulse in phenomenology, then, moves us toward the "formal" structures of experience: intentionality, the form of space and time as experienced, even the form of the phenomenal field itself. At the same time, the empiricist – even existentialist – impulse in phenomenology moves us toward the "material" structures of experience: which colors and sounds we sense, which eyes and hands we move, which passions move us – even the passion for the ideal.

References and Further Reading

Bolzano, Bernard (1972) [1837]. *Theory of Science: Attempt at a Detailed and in the main Novel Exposition of Logic With Constant Attention to Earlier Authors* (selections) (Rolf George ed. and trans.). Berkeley: University of California Press.

Brentano, Franz (1995) [1874]. *Psychology from an Empirical Standpoint* (Antos C. Rancurello, D. B. Terrell, and Linda L. McAlister trans.). New York: Routledge.

Carnap, Rudolf (2003) [1928]. *The Logical Structure of the World and Pseudoproblems in Philosophy*. Chicago: Open Court. German original, *Der Logische Aufbau der Welt*.

Gurwitsch, Aron (1964). *The Field of Consciousness*. Pittsburgh, PA: Duquesne University Press. Original French version 1957, from manuscript of 1953.

Husserl, Edmund (1969) [1913]. *Ideas [pertaining to a Pure Phenomenology and a Phenomenological Philosophy, First Book]: General Introduction to Pure Phenomenology* (W. R. Boyce Gibson trans.). London: George Allen and Unwin; New York: Humanities Press. First English edition, 1931. Called *Ideas* I. Alternative translation (1991) *Ideas pertaining to a Pure Phenomenology and a Phenomenological Philosophy, First Book: General Introduction to Pure Phenomenology* (Fred Kersten trans.). Boston, MA: Kluwer Academic Publishers.

—— (1969) [1929]. *Formal and Transcendental Logic* (Dorion Cairns trans.). The Hague: Martinus Nijhoff. Now from Kluwer Academic Publishers, Boston, MA.

—— (1969) [1931/1929]. *Cartesian Meditations* (Dorion Cairns trans.). The Hague: Martinus Nijhoff. Now from Kluwer Academic Publishers, Boston, MA. Original German manuscript 1929. First published in French translation 1931. First published in German 1950.

—— (1970) [1935–8]. *The Crisis of European Sciences and Transcendental Phenomenology* (David Carr, trans.). Evanston, IL: Northwestern University Press. Called the *Crisis*.

—— (2001) [1900–1]. *Logical Investigations*, Vols. 1–2 (J. N. Findlay trans., Dermot Moran ed. and revd.). New York: Routledge. From the revised second edition, 1913, 1921. Abridged version (2001) *The Shorter Logical Investigations* (Dermot Moran ed.). New York: Routledge.

Kasmier, David (2003). Husserl's theory of *a priori* knowledge: A response to the failure of contemporary rationalism. Doctoral dissertation, University of Southern California. Available from University Microfilms, Ann Arbor, MI.

Merleau-Ponty, Maurice (1996) [1945]. *Phenomenology of Perception* (Colin Smith trans.). New York: Routledge.

Moran, Dermot (2000). *Introduction to Phenomenology*. New York: Routledge.

Quine, W. V. O. (1995). *From Stimulus to Science*. Cambridge, MA: Harvard University Press.

Quine, W. V. O., and Ullian, J. S. (1978). *The Web of Belief*. New York: Random House.

Smith, David Woodruff (2003). Edmund Husserl: *Logical Investigations* (1900–1901): From logic through ontology to phenomenology. In Jorge J. E. Gracia, Gregory M. Reichberg, and Bernard N. Schumacher (eds.), *The Classics of Western Philosophy: A Reader's Guide* (pp. 423–39). Oxford: Blackwell.

—— (2004). The structure of context and context-awareness. In Lester Embree (ed.), *Gurwitsch's Relevancy for Cognitive Science*. Boston, MA: Kluwer Academic Publishers.

Smith, David Woodruff, and McIntyre, Ronald (1982). *Husserl and Intentionality: A Study of Mind, Meaning, and Language*. Boston, MA: D. Reidel. Now Kluwer Academic Publishers.

20

Rationalist Elements of Twentieth-Century Analytic Philosophy

PAUL LIVINGSTON

The history of the analytic tradition in twentieth-century philosophy has often been recounted as the story of a failed empiricism, but actually it is methods tracing back to the modern tradition of rationalism that have most enduringly determined its practice and continue to define it today. The variety of analytic, explanatory, and interpretive methods that have made up the analytic tradition have shared a central and abiding concern with the investigation of the logical and conceptual structure of language as a means of understanding the metaphysical structure of the world. Historically, this concern descends directly from Leibnizian rationalism, although the program it suggests was articulated and developed, much more fully than Leibniz himself could have imagined, through the new tools of logical analysis developed by Russell, Wittgenstein, and the philosophers of the Vienna Circle at the beginning of the twentieth century.

In this chapter, I survey rationalist elements in the articulation and development of analytic philosophy. I argue that the significance of these elements has been under-appreciated in historical retrospection, and that their identification can give us a new source of insight into the character of the analytic tradition as a whole. This is so, not only because rationalist ideas played a decisive and under-appreciated role in the *origins* of analytic philosophy, but also because essentially rationalist methods have continued to support the practice of analytic philosophy throughout its development, giving it, far more than the empiricist goals that these methods have sometimes served, the specific unity of a tradition grounded throughout its history in a particular conception of the nature of philosophical inquiry.

Although the explicit repudiation of various forms and assumptions of empiricism has been a central theme of the tradition since the 1950s, the rationalist elements of analytic philosophy have seldom been subject to critical scrutiny either from within or without the tradition. Partly because of this lack of scrutiny, the rationalist elements of the project of analytic philosophy have continued to exert a decisive influence on its results, long after its most ambitious empiricist claims were repudiated and purged. By identifying the rationalist elements in the development of analytic philosophy, indeed, we can begin to correct a standard view of this development that misportrays the character of its deepest theoretical motivations. On this standard view, the history of analytic philosophy so far has been a two-stage affair, consisting first in the articulation of an ambitious program of foundationalist epistemological analysis by Russell,

Wittgenstein, and the philosophers of the Vienna Circle, and second in the more critical phase begun by the historically decisive repudiation of that program by Quine, Sellars, and late Wittgenstein. Because the successful arguments of the postpositivist repudiators mostly attacked the foundationalist notion of an uninterpreted "given" element in experience at the basis of knowledge – a notion central to empiricism both in its early modern and contemporary forms – the standard interpretation has usually seen the positive project to which they responded as a variety of empiricism, essentially a linguistically inflected descendent of the empiricist epistemology of Locke, Berkeley, and Hume. But, I argue here, the project of Russell, Wittgenstein, and the Vienna Circle was as much rationalist as empiricist, and actually derived from rationalism rather than empiricism its most innovative claims and enduring methods. Appreciation of these elements yields a substantially different picture of the large-scale history of the analytic tradition, a picture that reveals rather than conceals the methodological continuity of the tradition through both its positivist and postpositivist phases. On the improved view, the mid-century critique of the original project embodied not so much a decisive repudiation as a relatively superficial amendment of its most significant methodological assumptions, and the contemporary philosophers who celebrate the critique actually carry further the most significant elements of the project they claim to replace.

I

It is well known that what would become the analytic tradition began with Russell and Moore's rejection of the then-dominant philosophy of Hegelian idealism and their subsequent development of an anti-idealist program of linguistic or logical analysis as the basis of a fundamentally new kind of philosophy. The new program drew its central inspiration from the logical concepts and symbolism that had been developed over the second half of the nineteenth century, and its first applications were applications of these new logical tools to derive epistemological and metaphysical results at variance with the idealist picture. Over the first decade of the twentieth century, Russell began to articulate an atomist ontology, according to which the world is composed of logically distinct and separable items which Russell called propositions. Whereas the idealists had argued for the existence and ultimate unity of an absolute reality, to which all propositions can only approach imperfectly, Russell's atomism insisted that individual propositions about particular things and properties can have *complete* truth despite concerning only part of the universe.

Despite the terminology, Russell did not initially conceive of propositions as linguistic entities; but his application of the new logic developed by Frege to the problem of the logical foundation of mathematics soon led him in the direction of an increasingly linguistic program of analysis. Initially, the logical analysis of a proposition had simply been the elucidation of its metaphysical component structure; but drawing on Frege's innovations and suggestions, Russell soon saw that logical analysis, if seen as *linguistic* analysis, could have substantial metaphysical consequences as well. Ordinary language, Frege had suggested, often has a superficial grammatical form that hides its deep logical or conceptual structure, leading us in philosophy to propound distinctions where there are none and to misunderstand the real conditions for the meaningfulness of our sentences. Logical analysis, then, has the task of revealing the genuine, underlying logical form of propositions, over against our tendency to misunderstand it. Thus, for instance, the Russellian theory of descriptions showed that sentences apparently naming fictional or non-existent objects – for instance, "the current king of France" – could be analyzed as involving concealed definite descriptions, and thereby shown not to call for metaphysically puzzling "non-existent entities." The linguistic analysis shows that logic allows a sparer and more austere metaphysics than had previously been thought, paving the way for the replacement or elimination of many or most of the profligate and problematic entities demanded by traditional philosophical systems.

The linguistic analysis program thereby defined had straightforward epistemological consequences as well. Essential to epistemological analysis, according to Russell, was the idea of logical construction: given a set of simple elements or objects at the basis of knowledge, more complicated objects of knowledge could be analyzed as constructions definable in terms of the simple objects and their logical combinations. Given the theory of descriptions and other analytical innovations, it was reasonable to suppose, the concepts and entities of scientific knowledge could be revealed as logical constructions from the simple elements of experience, what Russell called sense data. This constructional project could, Russell supposed, show the genuine epistemological status of scientific knowledge claims by isolating the portion of their meaning that traced to direct empirical knowledge of sense data, what Russell called "knowledge by acquaintance."[1] A completed logical analysis of a knowledge claim could thus distinguish its empirical from its logical components, separating the elements of its structure that are actually given in immediate experience from those superadded by linguistic categories and concepts. In this way, the logical analysis of a knowledge claim shows its real empirical content by identifying the simple experiences which would verify it, the experiences which an investigator must have in order to assert the claim's truth. From this root in the practice of logical analysis grew the doctrine of verificationism, according to which the meaning of any empirically meaningful proposition is the method of experientially verifying it, and the decisive suggestion, already implicit in Russell's method of analysis, that the doctrine could be used to purge science of metaphysical claims unconnected to any possibility of verification.

By around 1914, then, Russell's rejection of idealism had led to a recognizably empiricist program of epistemological analysis; but it is noteworthy that much earlier in his development, Russell had originally developed the central idea behind this program – that insights from logic could be used to elucidate the metaphysical structure of the world – under the determinative influence of the rationalist Leibniz. Russell's book on Leibniz, written following a series of lectures he delivered in 1900, was his first primarily philosophical work. Its central interpretive claim – that Leibniz had derived most of his metaphysics from the logical claim that all propositions have, essentially, a subject-predicate form – stood as a model for the kind of logically based metaphysical analysis that Russell had begun to think he himself could provide, by applying a new logical theory of relations that went substantially beyond the subject-predicate logic of Leibniz's day. Thus, although Russell's interpretation criticized Leibniz for the inadequacy of his particular logical assumptions, he took the

381

logical determination of Leibniz's metaphysics as a methodological model for his own developing conception of philosophy as analysis. He began his exposition of Leibniz's philosophy with a declaration of his allegiance to this conception:

> That all sound philosophy should begin with an analysis of propositions, is a truth too evident, perhaps, to demand a proof. That Leibniz's philosophy began with such an analysis, is less evident, but seems no less true. (Russell 1992: 8)

Leibniz's example would soon inspire Russell in the invention of a style of analysis that has characterized analytic philosophy throughout its development, whereby formal analysis of the logical structure of language yields philosophically significant insight into the metaphysical structure of reality.

To understand Russell's developing conception of analysis, though, it is helpful to examine in detail its roots in his critique of Leibniz's metaphysics. According to Russell, the most significant failing of Leibniz's metaphysics, and the one that led most directly to the contradictions of his system, was its failure to account for the nature of relations. Historically, it is significant (though hardly surprising) that Russell located Leibniz's largest failing here, for it was on its handling of the nature of relations that Russell would soon most directly criticize the dominant idealist tradition. Doubtless, he already saw substantial continuities between Leibniz's rationalist metaphysics and the holistic metaphysics of Bradley and McTaggert's idealism, and indeed he already saw both as arising from a widely shared but ultimately incorrect logical assumption.[2] The assumption was that of the subject-predicate form of all propositions; beginning with it, Russell averred in the Leibniz book, could only issue in a theory of relations that construes them as ultimately unreal, as both Leibniz and the metaphysics of idealism were inclined to do (Russell 1992: sect. 10). For the underlying assumption of the subject-predicate form of all propositions led Leibniz to suppose that the entire truth of an apparently relational proposition (such as "the oak is taller than the elm" or "seven is greater than five") must consist in its attribution of a predicate to a particular subject, rather than in its referring to an actually existing relation. This, in turn, led directly to the doctrine of substances as sempiternally existing bearers of properties, complete in that each substance reflects within itself each of what would otherwise be called its relations to other substances (Russell 1992: sects. 8, 10). This much Russell saw as common ground for both Leibniz and the metaphysics of absolute idealism, which formulated the same conclusion as the doctrine of the "internality" of all relations. With the doctrine of substance in place, it was simply the further assumption of a plurality of substances, which Leibniz made but the absolute idealists did not, that marked his doctrine off from theirs and produced its particular contradictions:

Thus Leibniz is forced, in order to maintain the subject-predicate doctrine, to the Kantian theory that relations, though veritable, are the work of the mind:

> In the belief that propositions must, in the last analysis, have a subject and a predicate, Leibniz does not differ either from his predecessors or from his successors. Any philosophy which uses either substance or the Absolute will be found, on inspection, to depend upon this belief. Kant's belief in an unknowable thing-in-itself was largely due to the same theory. It cannot be denied, therefore, that the doctrine is important. Philosophers have

differed, not so much in respect of belief in its truth, as in respect of their consistency in carrying it out. In this latter respect, Leibniz deserves credit. But his assumption of a plurality of substances made the denial of relations particularly difficult, and involved him in all the paradoxes of the preestablished harmony. (Russell 1992: 15)

Sharing with Leibniz the assumption of the subject-predicate form of logic and accordingly arriving at essentially the same doctrine of substance, the idealists diverged from him, according to Russell, only in that they thought there could be only one substance, a unified, all-encompassing absolute; whereas Leibniz's belief in the plurality of substance, given the shared assumption, led him instead to the doctrine of monads and to its most problematic implication, the theory of the preestablished harmony. In the rest of the book, Russell diagnosed the implausibilies of Leibniz's theories of continuity, number, space, and time. In each case, he thought, the contradictions and paradoxes of Leibniz's theory arose directly from his denial of real relations. Ultimately, Russell argued, Leibniz's assumption of the reality of the external world produced, when combined with the denial of real relations, a central inconsistency that vitiated the whole philosophy of monadism. The idealists, by contrast, maintained the same denial of the reality of relations but denied the existence of a mind-independent reality, producing a system that, for all its other failings, was at least a consistent whole.

Since Russell thought that Leibniz's central failing traced to the logical assumption of subject-predicate form, it is not surprising that he recommended its replacement with a substantially different picture of the logical form of the proposition. On the suggested picture, the proposition consists of both simple objects and metaphysically real relations in articulated combination; the subject-predicate form is to be understood as a special case of relational form, rather than the converse (Russell 1992: 15). Russell did not yet have the logical tools necessary to make this suggestion rigorous; he would encounter Peano's axiomatization of arithmetic, which derived from Frege's new logic and nineteenth-century developments in what would become set theory, only months after the Leibniz book. But already he insisted that only a genuinely relational logic could give an adequate characterization of the structure of mathematical propositions, for instance propositions asserting equality, inequality, and number. The new logical methods of Frege and Peano would soon lead Russell, in fact, to envision the possibility of reducing mathematics completely to logic and set theory by showing the entities and operations of mathematics to be logical constructions from sets.

But the most important and enduring result of Russell's early encounter with Leibniz was not the reduction of mathematics that Russell undertook in *The Principles of Mathematics* and *Principia Mathematica*, but rather the conception of philosophical method that he drew from Leibniz's system. On this conception of philosophical method, logic is not just a special theory of the structure of thought or a symbolic system for the rigorization of proofs and chains of reasoning, but a substantial source of philosophical insight in its own right. The underlying logical structure that characterizes meaningful language has immediate metaphysical and ontological implications; for this reason, the logical analysis of propositions – which Russell saw as the obvious beginning of philosophical theory – can be expected to solve traditional philosophical problems and elucidate the metaphysical structure of the world. Russell sought to make explicit

383

in his own philosophy what had been only implicit in Leibniz's, the straightforward derivation of claims about the large-scale metaphysical structure of the world from an understanding of the logical structure of the proposition. In so doing, he defined an essentially rationalist method of analysis that would characterize analytic philosophy through the next several decades of its development.

II

Russell's early analysis of Leibniz played a decisive role, therefore, in suggesting a philosophical method whereby analysis of the logical structure of language would yield decisive results in epistemology and metaphysics. But it was Russell's student Wittgenstein who would present the method in its purest form, in the terse and precisely written *Tractatus Logico-Philosophicus*. In the *Tractatus*, Wittgenstein sought to fix the bounds of meaningful language by elucidating the nature of the logical conditions for its possibility. At the center of its account of meaning is the idea of a kind of structure – what Wittgenstein called "logical form" – that is shared between meaningful propositions and the worldly states of affairs they are about (*Tractatus* 2.18, 2.2). According to the *Tractatus'* "picture theory" of meaning, a sentence pictures a fact or state of affairs by mirroring its form; names in the sentence correspond to objects in the world, and the formal or structural relations among names in the written or spoken sentence mirror the relations that the objects stand in to compose a fact (3, 3.14, 3.21). By sharing logical form with an actual or possible state of affairs, then, each logically well-articulated sentence has a particular, determinate meaning; and this suggests that the *analysis* of a meaningful sentence in ordinary language, by showing their actual logical form, can display its actual meaning by showing which fact it corresponds to. Writing an ordinary language sentence in a perspicuous, logical notation shows the actual structure in virtue of which it has meaning, over against the superficial form given it by the grammar of a particular language (3.25, 3.323–3.325). This, in turn, distinguishes those ordinary language sentences which have a genuine meaning from those which do not; and the standard statements of traditional philosophical problems, Wittgenstein thought, could now be exposed as meaningless, artifacts of the misunderstanding of the logic of our language that arises when we take its overt grammar, rather than its deep logical structure, to sort sense from nonsense.

His articulation of the picture theory led Wittgenstein to argue for a metaphysics according to which the world is composed of the totality of actually obtaining facts within the "logical space" of all possible states of affairs (1–1.13). He understood the facts themselves as objects standing in relations, complexes whose logical structure would be mirrored by the relational structure of names in sentences about them (2.0121). Accordingly, he argued for the existence of a class of logically simple and eternally existing particular objects whose possibilities of combination into states of affairs made for all actual and possible states of affairs (2.0123, 2.02, 2.0271, 2.03). The argument for this, moving from the formal requirements for the possibility of meaning to a concrete and general metaphysical result, exhibits particularly clearly the formal method of argument that Russell had developed under the influence of Leibniz.

The core of the argument is given at *Tractatus* 2.021 and the following remarks:

> 2.021 Objects make up the substance of the world. That is why they cannot be composite.
> 2.0211 If the world had no substance, then whether a proposition had sense would depend on whether another proposition was true.
> 2.0212 In that case we could not sketch out any picture of the world (true or false).

The implication of 2.0212 expresses a demand that Wittgenstein consistently places on the theory of meaning he develops in the *Tractatus*: that it explain the possibility of a proposition's having meaning or sense, its possibility of saying something that is true or false (see also 3.23 and the remarks that follow it). The demand is the basis for much of the *Tractatus'* analysis of meaning, and it allows for a familiar type of transcendental argument which Wittgenstein relies on a great deal to derive semantic as well as metaphysical and ontological conclusions. The argument typically begins with the claim that the possibility of meaningful language demands that certain general logical conditions be satisfied, both by our linguistic systems and by the worldly objects and states of affairs to which they refer. Since meaningful language is possible, we can conclude that these conditions are indeed satisfied. This kind of argument allows the derivation of the shared structure of language and the world simply from reasoning about the preconditions for the possibility and determinacy of sense. The argument for the existence of simples exhibits this structure particularly clearly. It has the form of a two-stage *modus tollens*: if the substance of the world were not simple, non-composite objects, then whether a proposition had sense would depend on whether another proposition were true. But in that case, propositions would not, in general, have any determinate sense at all, and the linguistic drawing of a true or false picture of the world would be impossible. Drawing such a picture is, however, possible; so (contraposing twice) we must conclude that the world is, indeed, composed of simple objects.

The argument, thus reconstructed, has two steps, each of which depends on Wittgenstein's particular understanding of the nature of logical analysis and each of which involves moving from claims about the logical structure of meaningful language to the logical structure of the world.[3] A fully analyzed sentence contains only names, organized in various logical relations; given this, the argument for simples concerns the relationship of these names to the entities to which they refer (3.2–3.202). It claims that they cannot refer to entities that are composite; the logical names revealed by a completed analysis must refer to entities that are mereologically simple. For if such a name referred to a composite, then a proposition involving the name could be false in either of two ways. It could be false because what it claims of the composite is false, or it could be false because the composite fails to exist (that is, because the simpler entities which would make it up, were the proposition true, fail to be arranged in the right way or at all). If the proposition were false in the second way, then its falsity would amount to the falsity of a second, simpler proposition – the one asserting the existence of the composite. So if the possibility of falsity of the second type could not be ruled out, then the truth of even a completely analyzed proposition might depend on the truth of a logically simpler proposition; there would be no requirement or expectation that the complete logical analysis of a proposition would exhibit the conditions for its truth.

If the world were not composed of simple objects, then there would be no general expectation that logical analysis of propositions into simple names and their logical analysis could clarify the structure of propositions. Wittgenstein's argument for simples, however, goes further than simply insisting on the possibility of instructive analysis; for it claims that, if the world were not composed of simples, not only logical analysis but also sense would be impossible. We have seen already that the denial of atomism makes the sense of even completely analyzed propositions dependent on the truth of other propositions. But why should this dependence, if it obtained, vitiate the possibility of any proposition's having sense at all? The reason for the additional requirement traces to Wittgenstein's additional claims, elsewhere in the *Tractatus*, about the nature of meaning and the determinacy of sense. For a proposition to have meaning, he argues, is for it to show how things are *if* it is true; and a meaningful proposition must be able to show this *no matter how* the world actually is. A meaningful proposition must be true or false in any possibility whatsoever; but if its having sense depended on the obtaining of contingent facts, then there would be some possible situations – the situations in which those facts did not obtain – in which it was neither true nor false (because senseless). In particular, in the second situation considered in the last paragraph, a logically simple proposition would lack sense if the composite to which one of its simple names referred failed to exist; the sense of such a proposition would then depend on the truth of another proposition, which is only contingent. Thus, the requirement that sense be determinate across all possible situations itself demands that logically simple names not refer to complexes. They must, instead, refer to simple objects which are not made up of other objects. Moreover, the simple objects must be sempiternal and changeless; for only in this way can the determinacy of sense, across all possible situations and at all times, be ensured.

Considered as an instructive example of one of the argumentative methods that defined analytic philosophy at its origin, Wittgenstein's argument for the existence of simples is noteworthy in several respects. In its style and conclusion it resembles quite closely the flawed argument for monadism that Russell found in Leibniz; the difference is that Wittgenstein's argument, unlike Leibniz's (as Russell reconstructs it), departs not from the logical assumption of subject-predicate form but from that of relationally structured language with a logical form capable of mirroring the logical and relational structure of entities in the world. Because of his avoidance of the assumption of subject-predicate form, Wittgenstein's argument need not conclude, as Leibniz's had to, that all relations are internal to atoms; and because of this, Wittgenstein's argument avoids, as well, the obscurities of the doctrine of preestablished harmony. But the simples demanded by Wittgenstein's argument resemble Leibniz's monads in being simple, eternal, and necessary constituents of the world; and Wittgenstein's recognition of the kinship between his simples and those required by early modern rationalist systems is shown by his retention of the term "substance" to describe them. And most significantly, the method of argument that Wittgenstein employs to establish the metaphysical existence of simples is essentially the same one that Russell found in Leibniz and that he himself adopted in his own ontological and epistemological theory. The method begins, as we have seen, with the elucidation of logical requirements for the possibility of a proposition's meaningfulness; in this case, the requirement is that the sense of a meaningful proposition must be determinate across all possible worlds and at all times.

It then derives from these logical requirements for the possibility of sense, general metaphysical claims about the structure of the world and its constituents, claims which must hold true if the logical requirements are to be fulfilled. In this way, insight into the logical structure of language, when conjoined with reasoning about the logical pre-conditions for the possibility of meaning, issues in substantial ontological conclusions that are authorized by nothing more controversial or demanding than logic itself. The method of logical or conceptual analysis, although it operates purely on linguistic material, can accordingly yield substantial and general philosophical results with logical necessity and certainty. The conundrums and perplexities of traditional philosophical problems can be shown to result from their misunderstanding of the underlying logic of language, and the new methods of logic allow their swift replacement.

In view of the subsequent history of analytic philosophy and its usual interpreta-tion, it is particularly significant that Wittgenstein's argument makes no mention of an empirical or experiential basis for meaningful propositions or knowledge claims. It is no part of Wittgenstein's concern to argue that the simples which he shows to exist are simple elements of experience or sense data, and no part of his argument depends on the suggestion that they are. Indeed, Wittgenstein in the *Tractatus* is generally unconcerned with epistemology; it is likely that, at this stage at least, he thought epistemology akin to psychology in being irrelevant to logical analysis.[4] The simples for which Wittgenstein argues are necessary for the meaningfulness of any proposi-tion, but it is notorious that he gives no general characterization of their nature. In this quietism about the nature of simples Wittgenstein certainly diverged from Russell, who consistently held, during and after the period of his greatest contact with Wittgenstein, that at least some simples are sense data, and may have believed that properties and logical objects are also simples. The doctrine of sense data, we have seen, came to play an important role in Russell's hopes for an epistemologically illumi-nating reconstruction of scientific knowledge claims. But the structure of Wittgenstein's argument shows that the atomism that Russell and Wittgenstein shared does not at all depend on assumptions about the nature of experience or its relation to knowledge, and that it can be established by the purely logical method of reasoning that Russell himself recommended and that Wittgenstein applied. The method of logical analysis itself, though it could be applied to epistemology given the assumption that at least some simples are sense data, does not demand any particular epistemological claim or reasoning in order to yield substantial metaphysical conclusions about the structure of the world. In the context of the influential project of the *Tractatus*, then, Wittgenstein's argument shows clearly that the epistemological commitments of the method of logi-cal analysis are by no means as deep as has usually been thought. The method itself has no need for such commitments in order to secure metaphysical insight; and the empiricist assumption of the reducibility of all knowledge to propositions concerning immediate experience is, accordingly, no essential part of its proper concern.

III

In the late 1920s and early 1930s, the philosophers of the Vienna Circle sought to develop Russell's constructional method, in conjunction with the analytical practices developed by Frege and Wittgenstein, into a far-ranging program of "scientific philosophy" that put reconstructive epistemology at the center of its concerns. With the epistemological structure of scientific knowledge clarified through the new logical tools now available, they reasoned, traditional philosophical confusions and problems could be eliminated in favor of a new method whose logical basis would put it on the secure path of an apodictic science. The program of the Vienna Circle has often, subsequently, been understood as a foundationalist empiricism; for the reconstructive epistemologies initially propounded by its most prominent members, Schlick and Carnap, placed subjective, elementary experiences at the epistemological basis of scientific knowledge, and sought the reduction of the meaning of scientific propositions to their basis in experience. But actually this element of foundationalist empiricism was the first element of the Circle's program to be abandoned, and its repudiation in the early 1930s left in place the significant rationalist elements that had informed the program from its beginning. In the Circle's protocol sentence debate of 1932–5, the sociologist Neurath successfully challenged Schlick and Carnap's assumption of a basis of scientific claims in immediate, subjective experience, eventually convincing Carnap of the universality of a "physical language" concerning only public, objective entities and events, and of the necessity that the epistemologically basic sentences of science be expressible in this language. After the protocol sentence debate, analytic philosophers would increasingly reject the Circle's foundationalist project and its empiricist hope of finding a basis for knowledge in immediate experience. But the essentially rationalist conception of philosophical method that the Circle developed from the suggestions of Russell and Wittgenstein would remain characteristic of the projects of analytic philosophy long after this historically decisive rejection.

An essentially rationalist understanding of philosophical method is already prominent in Carnap's first masterpiece, the influential *Der Logische Aufbau der Welt*. Written from 1922 to 1925, just before the beginning of Carnap's involvement with the Circle, the *Aufbau* embodies a particularly clear and historically significant development of the project of scientific philosophy that initially united the Circle. Its aim is to show the possibility of a clarificatory epistemology of scientific knowledge that reveals all scientific claims and concepts as logical constructions from simpler, epistemologically more fundamental entities, and indeed to actually begin this constructional project by showing how objective claims about entities and events in space and time can be constructed from a basis of immediate, elementary experiences (*Aufbau*, sects. 1, 2, 67, 78). Because the logical constructions that Carnap carries out in the *Aufbau* take immediately given elementary experiences as their basis, attempting to show the ultimate reducibility of all scientific claims to claims involving only such experiences and a single, basic relation of similarity among them, the *Aufbau* has often been interpreted as suggesting a foundationalist empiricism. But more recently, commentators have begun to question this usual way of interpreting the *Aufbau*, emphasizing the Kantian and rationalist ideas that actually influenced Carnap's project more deeply and enduringly (see, especially, Friedman 1987, 1999). The construction of objective claims from a basis in immediate, subjective experience, these commentators have pointed out, was intended by Carnap as only one possible example of the more general program of construction theory that it is the main goal of the *Aufbau* to defend; in fact, Carnap explicitly suggests the possibility of other, non-experiential bases for a reconstruction of scientific knowledge, including the physicalist basis that he would later endorse (*Aufbau*, sects. 59, 62).

To understand Carnap's project, it is also important to note what he took to be its most significant logical innovation: the development of a theory of relations that made possible the definition of all scientific concepts and objects from a stock of basic objects and a single, fundamental relation among them. Given Frege's logic of relations, Carnap reasoned, scientific claims could be understood as *structural definite descriptions*, purely relational statements whose terms are "implicitly defined" by their place in the total relational web of scientific knowledge, rather than ostensively or by example (*Aufbau*, sects. 71–3). The method of implicit definition that Carnap employed had originally been discovered by Hilbert in his influential axiomatization of geometry (Hilbert 1962). Rather than defining the basic terms of geometry (such as "point," "line," and "plane") by reference to actual examples of drawn figures, Hilbert's system begins with a set of axioms asserting the holding of various relations among the bearers of these basic terms. In this way, the basic terms are implicitly defined simply as the bearers of all the relations asserted by the axioms. The resulting system yields all the theorems of geometry by structural means alone, without ever having to refer to an actual figure or perception. Similarly, Carnap reasoned, constructional theory could "structuralize" the terms and concepts of science by defining them in terms of their relational positions within the total web of knowledge. Within the context of the particular version of constructional theory that he worked out in the *Aufbau*, indeed, Carnap considered the possibility of structuralization essential to showing how claims about immediate, subjective experience could provide the basis for the objective propositions of science:

> Now, the fundamental thesis of construction theory (cf. sect. 4), which we will attempt to demonstrate in the following investigation, asserts that fundamentally there is only one object domain and that each scientific statement is about the objects in this domain. Thus, it becomes unnecessary to indicate for each statement the object domain, and the result is that *each scientific statement can in principle be so transformed that it is nothing but a structure statement*. But the transformation is not only possible, it is imperative. For science wants to speak about what is objective, and whatever does not belong to the structure but to the material (i.e., anything that can be pointed out in a concrete ostensive definition) is, in the final analysis, subjective. One can easily see that physics is almost altogether desubjectivized, since almost all physical concepts have been transformed into purely structural concepts . . . From the point of view of construction theory, this state of affairs is to be described in the following way. The series of experiences is different for each subject. If we want to achieve, in spite of this, agreement in the names for the entities which are constructed on the basis of these experiences, then this cannot be done by reference to the completely divergent content, but only through the formal description of the structure of these entities. (*Aufbau*, sect. 16)

Immediate experiences and their relations are ultimately, Carnap thought, subjective in character; if they were to provide the basis of objective scientific knowledge, they could only do so insofar as all scientific knowledge claims are structuralized relational descriptions. Structuralization was the essential precondition, not only for the intersubjective intelligibility of scientific claims, but even for their meaningfulness; for only structural or structuralizable propositions could express claims with the generality

389

characteristic of scientific propositions. The relations in virtue of which scientific terms are implicitly defined could themselves, Carnap thought, be reduced to purely logical ones, together with the single, extensionally given relation of similarity among elementary experiences; accordingly, the reduction of objective scientific claims to the basis in immediate experience would not be a straightforward reduction of objects to objects, but a logical, definitional reduction of relations to relations.

Carnap perceived that the relational theory developed in the *Aufbau* and its method of using logical means to structuralize factual propositions were already anticipated by modern rationalism:

> The fundamental concepts of the theory of relations are found as far back as Leibniz' ideas of a *mathesis universalis* and of an *ars combinatoria*. The application of the theory of relations to the formulation of a constructional system is closely related to Leibniz' idea of a *characteristica universalis* and of a *scientia generalis*. (*Aufbau*, sect. 3)

The idea of a *mathesis universalis* or "universal character" to which Carnap alludes figures in some of Leibniz's earliest writings, in which he suggests the possibility of developing a universal language by associating characteristic numbers with the simple notions that are the basis for all linguistic terms and categories. The development of such a language, Leibniz thought, could vastly improve human reasoning by giving it a unified mathematical calculus by means of which all arguments and conclusions could be evaluated:

> Once the characteristic numbers of most notions are determined, the human race will have a new kind of tool, a tool that will increase the power of the mind much more than optical lenses helped our eyes, a tool that will be as far superior to microscopes or telescopes as reason is to vision. The compass never provided navigators with anything more useful than what this North Star would give us for swimming the sea of experiments . . . Moreover, who could doubt that reasoning will finally be correct, when it is everywhere as clear and certain as arithmetic has been up until now. (Leibniz 1989: 8)

With the development of the universal characteristic, Leibniz argued, both empirical and *a priori* reasoning could proceed according to a method whose results would be as certain and indisputable as the results of mathematics. Of course, it was just this kind of universal method of reasoning which analytic philosophers beginning with Frege saw in the new logic he had developed. Given the new logic, the method of logical analysis, akin to Leibniz's proposed method of identifying the simplest notions from which all others are constructed, could put reasoning in mathematics and science alike on a secure path of certainty. But the most significant implication of Leibniz's idea for Carnap's project was its suggestion of a universal logical form shared by all significant, objective propositions, the characterization of which would show the real content of any such proposition over against our superficial tendency to misunderstand it. Just as Leibniz had thought that the content of any proposition could be expressed by the association of characteristic numbers with its simple notions, Carnap's structuralism held that the content of any objective proposition amounts to its place in a system of relations ultimately reducible to the simple structural relations of logic.

390

And as for Leibniz, the essential precondition of this reduction was a logical under-standing of the nature of linguistic meaning, an understanding that would allow logical analysis to clarify the meaning of scientific and ordinary propositions alike by resolving them into their logical components. For Carnap, Leibniz's suggestion of a universal characteristic was, doubtless, centuries ahead of its time; accordingly, it was little surprise that Leibniz lacked the logical details necessary to develop it into a usable method. But with the new logical tools available to him and the structuralism about meaning that they suggested, Carnap now thought he could implement the very project that had inspired Leibniz two and a half centuries earlier.

In the early 1930s, discussion in the Vienna Circle's weekly meetings turned to the question of the logical status of the basic observation statements or "protocol sentences" thought to comprise the empirical foundation of science. Despite substanti-ally sharing Carnap's structuralist view of the nature of objective meaning, Neurath attacked Carnap's assumption that the protocol sentences must be records of imme-diate, private, subjective experience (Neurath 1932, 1934). Neurath argued that all meaningful scientific propositions, including those that are most empirically funda-mental, must be expressible in the single, unified language of physics. The doctrine of protocol sentences as experiential reports that Carnap and Schlick shared, Neurath complained, could give no account of the truth of such sentences. For according to the doctrine, protocol sentences must be true in virtue of their correspondence with private, ineffable experience; but Carnap and Schlick could give no account of the relation of comparison between experience and language that would be necessary to explain this. According to Neurath's physicalism, by contrast, protocol sentences are not subjective, first-personal reports of immediate experience, but rather perfectly objective reports of an observer's having made a particular observation, recording, or measurement at a particular time. Nowhere in scientific reasoning is there any need for comparison of linguistic with extra-linguistic or subjective items; the truth of objective claims is to be evaluated only in terms of their rational relations to other objective claims, including the physicalistically reconstructed protocol sentences.

By 1932, Neurath had convinced Carnap to repudiate his former view in favor of a version of the physicalist view of protocol sentences, on the ground that only the universality of physicalist language could ensure the unity of scientific knowledge as a single, comprehensive framework (Carnap 1934a, 1987). Carnap's conversion to physicalism demanded that he abandon any hope of the sort of epistemological con-struction of scientific objectivity from the subjectivity of immediate experience that he had sketched in the *Aufbau*; but it is significant that he nevertheless still envisioned a successor project of analysis that continues in the vein of the *Aufbau*'s structuralist theory of meaning. Carnap outlined the successor project in *The Logical Syntax of Lan-guage*, written in 1934. The project of *Syntax* departed from the notion, which Carnap derived from Tarski and Godel's work on the metalogical representation of logical symbolism, that the formal or logical structure of a particular, conventionally struc-tured language could be represented within that language itself. Given this possibility, Carnap thought, the logical rules of scientific language could be treated as purely conventional stipulations, allowing for an unending variety of possible languages for science, among which only pragmatic considerations should decide. The role of philo-sophical analysis, then, was to clarify the conventional logical structure of the language

391

scientists use and to facilitate the articulation of new languages that might be better able to satisfy natural explanatory demands.

Carnap now rejected, therefore, his earlier project of explaining the logical structure of (what he had taken to be) the *single* language of science, and along with this he rejected the epistemological project of defining the empirical basis of that language. But even within the context of his newly anti-empiricist conventionalism, Carnap's new view of logical analysis preserved the structuralist account of meaning that had provided the basis of the *Aufbau* program. As on the earlier program, the content of a proposition can be identified with its place in the total relational pattern of inferences that characterizes the logic of the language. Though Carnap now thought of this relational pattern as established by conventional stipulations, he continued to hold that the analysis of a proposition displays its formal or structural character, and that a complete analysis of a proposition results in its complete structuralization. The idea of the universality of logical structure that Carnap had drawn from Leibniz's suggestion of the universal characteristic continued to support his structuralist theory of meaning, and the doctrine of physicalism that Carnap drew from Neurath added to this support by establishing the possibility of a language whose purely structural characterizations could unify science into a single, comprehensive framework of unified explanation.

Neurath's historically decisive attack on the *Aufbau* project, then, had the effect of thoroughly and permanently repudiating its empiricist epistemic foundationalism; but it left wholly intact the rationalist motivation of Carnap's understanding of analysis and the structuralist theory of meaning that supported it. In its criticism of empiricist foundationalism, in fact, Neurath's attack significantly anticipated, both in general and in detail, the Quinean, Sellarsian, and Wittgensteinian criticisms of the Vienna Circle's project that would characterize mid-century analytic philosophy and seemingly usher in a new, postpositivist phase of the tradition. But like these mid-century critiques, Neurath's criticism of the empiricist *claims* of Carnap and Schlick's project left largely in place the originally definitive investigative *methods* of analytic philosophy, methods that, as we have seen, developed primarily from rationalist roots. We have seen that, despite his later development of the empiricist doctrine of sense data, it was the rationalist influence of Leibniz that first suggested to Russell his conception of philosophical analysis, and we have seen that Wittgenstein's understanding of the nature of analysis, and the doctrine of meaning that it suggested, contained no admixture of empiricism at all. Carnap's structuralist theory of meaning preserved and extended the methodological assumptions that Wittgenstein and Russell had shared, according to which the meaning of a proposition is shown by an analysis of its underlying logical form. Long after the mid-century purging of the empiricist elements of analytical epistemology, versions of this conception of philosophical insight would continue to characterize the aims and constrain the results of the various investigative projects grouped under the heading of "analytic philosophy."

IV

It is usual to see the history of analytic philosophy in the twentieth century as having consisted of two distinct but internally interrelated historical phases. The first phase, according to the usual picture, was characterized by the formulation of a strong and ambitious program of epistemologically foundationalist analysis, by means of which scientific and ordinary propositions would be analyzed cleanly into two components, one empirical and experiential and the other conceptual. The project would thereby reveal the empirical foundations of knowledge in the immediacy of uninterpreted experience; and the conceptual component of knowledge could then be treated as purely a matter of conventional stipulations and patterns of linguistic use. According to the usual picture, the second phase of analytic philosophy began with the decisive repudiation by Quine, Sellars, and Wittgenstein of this original project. Quine's influential "Two Dogmas of Empiricism" showed the untenability of the distinction, presupposed by the proponents of the original project, between analytic truths, true in virtue of concepts and logic alone, and synthetic ones, true in virtue of experience. At about the same time, Sellars' manifesto "Empiricism and the Philosophy of Mind" polemicized against the conception of experience as representing a "Given," uninterpreted contribution to knowledge that had been basic to hopes for foundationalist epistemology; and Wittgenstein's complicated and elusive *Philosophical Investigations* seemed to show the possibility of an alternative account of linguistic meaning as linguistic use that owed nothing to the verificationism of analytic philosophy's first phase. These three prominent critiques, along with less prominent ones that anticipated or imitated them, are often seen as marking a decisive change in the methods and practices of analytic philosophy.

The standard picture has well served the purposes of retrospective accounting for analytic theorists concerned to portray their own projects as radical breaks with the legacy of the Vienna Circle; but actually it is a poor fit to the historical record, if that record is considered from a position of philosophical sensitivity to the deep methodological characteristics and tendencies of the analytic tradition. Appreciation of the rationalist origins of the methods of analysis that defined the tradition can help us to remedy the usual picture, checking its generalizations by situating it in a larger and more instructive philosophical context. For like Neurath's original criticism of Carnap's epistemic foundationalism, the mid-century critiques of what was supposed to be the univocal project of existing analytic philosophy almost universally focused on the specifically *empiricist* elements of that project. They issued in a historically decisive repudiation of those elements, effectively ending philosophers' hopes of using the method of analysis to produce an epistemological reconstruction of the relationship of experience to knowledge. But because they focused on the empiricist applications rather than the rationalist sources of the method of analysis, they left largely unscathed the methodological and semantic assumptions that had continuously determined the scope and character of analytic projects. As a result, a basically rationalist understanding of the logical nature of philosophical insight and a correlative structuralism about meaning remained the background of projects in analytic philosophy *even when* these projects seemed to wholly replace their analytical antecedents and *even when* philosophers impressed with the success of the mid-century critiques became reluctant to characterize their practice as anything like "logical analysis." Instead of developing into a farther-ranging critique of the fundamental methodological assumptions of analytic philosophy, the mid-century critiques led to an increasing reluctance on the part of analytic philosophers to discuss the methodological background of their practice. With the rationalist determinants of the methodology of analytic philosophy, early and late, clearly in view, historical retrospection can begin to remedy this reluctance, equipping analytic philosophers with a fuller understanding of the philosophical bases and implications of their own practice.

To understand the enduring methodological determinants of the practice of analytic philosophy in greater detail, it is helpful to see specifically how one of the most important mid-century critiques of the original analytical projects of Russell, Wittgenstein, and Carnap actually preserved the most important theoretical motivations of these projects even as it appeared thoroughly to repudiate them. In "Two Dogmas of Empiricism," Quine construed Carnap's *Aufbau* as exemplifying a logically inflected empiricism, and argued that this empiricism depended on two unsupported dogmas. The first, and more historically significant, was the dogma of the analytic/synthetic distinction, which distinguishes analytic propositions true "in virtue of meanings" alone from synthetic propositions grounded, at least in part, in matters of empirical fact. Quine objected that there is no tolerably clear or univocal criterion of analyticity, and accordingly that scientific propositions cannot be sorted by analysis, as the logical empiricists had supposed, into separable empirical and conceptual components. The second dogma that Quine held to have been essential to Carnap's empiricism was the dogma of reductionism, or "the belief that each meaningful statement is equivalent to some logical construct upon terms which refer to immediate experience" (Quine 1951: 20). The two dogmas were intimately related, Quine thought, in that empiricism could only construe synthetic statements as those true in virtue of their confirmatory experiences; thus, the attack on the analytic/synthetic distinction sufficed, if successful, to demolish reductionism and its empiricist constructional project. But as we saw in the last section, Carnap had already abandoned the empiricist project and the dogma that Quine called reductionism two decades earlier, under the pressure of Neurath's physicalism. Though based on the rejection of the analytic/synthetic distinction rather than the assumption of physicalism, Quine's attack on Carnap's supposed empiricism focused on the very same doctrine of reducibility to experience that Neurath had criticized in his own attack two decades earlier. In so doing, it stopped short of questioning the elements of Carnap's program that had been most important, even at the time of the *Aufbau*, to Carnap himself: the theory of relational definite descriptions and the structuralist conception of meaning that he had defended as an offspring of the Leibnizian idea of the universality of logic.

But it is Quine's positive suggestion of a reconstructed theory of knowledge, purged of the two dogmas, that exhibits most clearly the continued influence of the rationalist methodology of the project common to Russell, Wittgenstein, and Carnap on Quine's own understanding of philosophical method. When he first introduces his suggestion for a replacement to reductionism, in fact, Quine explicitly refers to the physicalism that Carnap had first suggested in the *Aufbau* as a possible alternative to empiricist reduction and later endorsed under the influence of Neurath:

> The dogma of reductionism survives in the supposition that each statement, taken in isolation from its fellows, can admit of confirmation or information at all. My counter-suggestion, issuing essentially from Carnap's doctrine of the physical world in the *Aufbau*,

is that our statements about the external world face the tribunal of sense experience not individually but only as a corporate body. (Quine 1951: 38)

Quine's positive suggestion for a reconstructed theory of knowledge, further elaborated in the final section of "Two Dogmas," would prove immensely influential for the development of postwar analytic semantics and epistemology. On the suggestion, the totality of knowledge has the structure, not of a founded edifice, but of a rationally interconnected web. Experience influences the shape of the web overall, but only by impinging upon it at its outer boundaries; given any new experience or experimental result, there is always a variety of possible ways in which the total web can be reshaped to accommodate it. The dichotomy between analytic and synthetic truths is replaced by a more gradual and variegated continuum between propositions that are relatively closer to empirical confirmation, and hence more likely to be revised given a recalcitrant experience, and those that are farther away and less likely to be revised; but there is no proposition that is totally immune from possible revision under the constraint of experience.

Quine's holistic picture of empirical confirmation, therefore, suggested to him the untenability of any foundationalist program of analysis designed to analyze scientific propositions into the separate empirical and conceptual components of their meaning. But although he would not endorse foundationalist programs of analysis, Quine's own semantic holism was derived not so much from the rejection of Carnap's deeper methodological and semantic assumptions as from the inheritance of them. Like Carnap, Quine understands the semantic content of a proposition as a matter of its place in a comprehensive, rationally interconnected web. As for Carnap (and Russell and Wittgenstein before him), this structuralism about meaning also suggests a program of philosophical investigation on which an understanding of the logical structure or form of propositions allows the clarification of their meaning for metaphysical and epistemological purposes. Over the years succeeding "Two Dogmas," Quine would develop the picture of knowledge first sketched there into a spare ontology derived from reflection on the metaphysical implications of first-order logic and a "naturalized" epistemology that followed Neurath in treating the philosophical theory of knowledge as a straightforward component of natural science rather than a tribunal for it.

Throughout the development of his philosophical method, though, Quine retained a basic structuralism about meaning and continued to look to the structure of logic as the main source of philosophical insight. Quine (1960) suggested that the imagined scenario of "radical translation" could clarify the large-scale logical structure of language. In radical translation, an interpreter attempts to understand the language of a foreign nation or tribe, given only the gestures and reports of its members. Reflection on the variety and structure of the interpretations possible, Quine reasoned, would show us how to understand the logical categories and distinctions present in our own language; the thought experiment yielded, in fact, several surprising semantic results, including the result that the intentional language with which we ordinarily describe mental states and propositional attitudes could be eliminated without violence to our ability to state the facts about the world. Both in its sources and its results, then, the thought experiment of radical translation figured as a fundamental component of a

395

view of philosophical method on which understanding of the large-scale structure of language yields substantial metaphysical results. In the extended applications of the radical translation scenario that have since been developed and defended by Quine's followers Davidson and Dennett, much the same conception of philosophical method – a conception of logically and semantically based insight into the structure of the world that Davidson has described as "metaphysics in the mirror of meaning" – has continued to the present day.

Nor was Quine's new method, and the methods that his students derived from it, atypical in its retention of the originally rationalist idea of using reflection on the logical structure of meaningful language to secure philosophical insight. By the 1960s, most analytic philosophers had realized the untenability of the atomism of the classical style of analysis, which had sought to analyze propositions *individually*; instead, they turned to practices of analysis and investigation aimed at clarifying the semantic structure of the language as a whole, in its pragmatic context of its embedding in our ordinary concerns and practices. Though the practitioners of "ordinary language philosophy" and "descriptive metaphysics" often characterized the semantic and pragmatic interrelations among linguistic propositions as matters of "grammar" rather than logic, the underlying picture of content as the position of a proposition in a structural, rationally articulated web of linguistic relations remained much the same. In the 1970s and 1980s, under the influence of Quine's naturalistic picture of philosophy, these practices of explicitly linguistic and conceptual analysis would largely cede to more scientifically minded metaphysical projects; but even these projects continued to look to logic as the essential source of philosophical insight, continuing to derive from reflection on the logical structure of scientific explanation claims about the metaphysical structure of the world.

With the rationalist influences on the enduring method of analytic philosophy clearly understood, we can begin to understand the methodological continuity of the tradition as a whole, allowing a deeper, more comprehensive, and more philosophically suggestive view of its history. For decades, the picture of analytic philosophy that sees the repudiation of empiricism as the central event of its history has rendered inaccessible any clear understanding of the rationalist conception of analytic practice that determined its origin and have characterized it in all of its forms. The standard picture has even convinced some leading historians of the analytic tradition that it no longer *has* any particular method or anything more than sociological unity.[5] Appreciation of the rationalist elements of analytic philosophy, however, allows us to identify the basic rationalist faith that has sustained the tradition at *each* of its moments and in *all* of its most significant theoretical ambitions. After more than a hundred years of the practice of analytic philosophy, the interpretive task of understanding this practice by situating it with respect to its philosophical antecedents and anticipating its possible philosophical descendents has scarcely begun. The identification of the determinative rationalist influences on the methods of analytic philosophy, I have argued, provides an important first step towards the completion of this task, suggesting the existence of a fundamental and philosophically significant set of methodological assumptions at its core. But the further development of methodological reflection on the history and legacy of analytic philosophy can, no doubt, hardly avoid involving historical interpretation in deeper and more radical reflections.

Notes

1   Russell had not always held that only sense data can be known by acquaintance; indeed, the earlier form of his logical atomism had construed Platonic universals and the so-called "logical constants" – the real-world representatives of the logical operations of negation, disjunction, and conjunction – as possible objects of acquaintance.
2   For a trenchant and detailed account (which I partly follow here) of Russell's reaction to Leibniz against the backdrop of his rejection of absolute idealism, see Hylton (1990).
3   My account of the argument partially follows the reconstruction given by Anscombe (1959: 48–9).
4   This is suggested by *Tractatus* 4.1121; additionally, it was essentially on this basis that Wittgenstein convinced Russell to abandon work on a projected *Theory of Knowledge*.
5   This is the view, for instance, of Rorty (1979), who derives it directly from his celebration of the Quinean repudiation of the analytic/synthetic distinction:

> If there are no intuitions into which to resolve concepts (in the manner of the *Aufbau*), nor any internal relations among concepts to make possible "grammatical discoveries" (in the manner of "Oxford philosophy"), then indeed it is hard to imagine what an "analysis" might be. Wisely, few analytic philosophers any longer try to explain what it is to offer an analysis . . . The present lack of metaphilosophical reflection within the analytic movement is, I think, symptomatic of the sociological fact that analytic philosophy is now, in several countries, the entrenched school of thought. Thus in these countries anything done by philosophers who employ a certain style, or mention certain topics, counts (*ex officiis suis*, so to speak) as continuing the work begun by Russell and Carnap. Once a radical movement takes over the establishment against which it revolted, there is less need for methodological self-consciousness, self-criticism, or a sense of location in dialectical space or historical time.
>
>   I do not think that there any longer exists anything identifiable as "analytic philosophy" except in some such stylistic or sociological way. (Rorty 1979: 172)

If the present analysis is correct, of course, Rorty's account, over-impressed with the import-ance of the Quinean critique, simply misses the methodological unity that continues to underlie the "stylistic" and "sociological" unity of the tradition; and the kind of methodolo-gical reflection for which Rorty sees no need could actually bring the tradition to a new level and kind of philosophical self-understanding.

References and Further Reading

Anscombe, G. E. M. (1959). *An Introduction to Wittgenstein's Tractatus*, 2nd revd. edn. New York: Harper.

Carnap, R. (1934a). *The Logical Syntax of Language*. London: Kegan Paul.

—— (1934b) [1932]. The physicalist language as the universal language of science. *Erkenntnis*, 2, 432–65. Trans. by Max Black as *The Unity of Science*. London: Kegan Paul.

—— (1967) [1928]. *The Logical Structure of the World* (Rolf A. George, trans.). Berkeley: University of California Press.

—— (1987) [1932]. On protocol sentences. *Nous*, 21, 457–70.

Friedman, M. (1987). Carnap's *Aufbau* reconsidered. *Nous*, 21 (4), 521–45.

—— (1999). *Reconsidering Logical Positivism*. Cambridge: Cambridge University Press.

Hilbert, D. (1962) [1899]. *The Foundations of Geometry* (E. J. Townshend trans.). Chicago: Open Court.

Hylton, P. (1990). *Russell, Idealism, and the Emergence of Analytic Philosophy*. Oxford: Clarendon Press.

Leibniz, G. W. (1989) [1679]. Preface to a universal characteristic. In R. Ariew and D. Garber (eds.), *Philosophical Essays*. Indianapolis, IN: Hackett.

Neurath, O. (1932). Protocol sentences. Reprinted in A. J. Ayer (ed.) (1959) *Logical Positivism* (pp. 199–208). New York: Free Press.

—— (1934). Radical physicalism and the "real world." Reprinted in Robert S. Cohen and Marie Neurath (eds.), *Philosophical Papers, 1913–1946* (pp. 100–14). Vienna Circle collection, vol. 16. Dordrecht: Reidel.

Quine, W. V. O. (1951). Two dogmas of empiricism. *Philosophical Review*, 60, 20–43.

—— (1960). *Word and Object*. Cambridge, MA: MIT Press.

Rorty, R. (1979). *Philosophy and the Mirror of Nature*. Princeton, NJ: Princeton University Press.

Russell, B. (1992) [1900]. *A Critical Exposition of the Philosophy of Leibniz*. London: Routledge.

Wittgenstein, L. (1961) [1921]. *Tractatus Logico-Philosophicus* (D. F. Pears and B. F. McGuinness trans.). London: Routledge.

21

Proust and the Rationalist Conception of the Self

ALAN NELSON

Introduction

Modern philosophical theorizing about the self has been greatly concerned with the problem of personal identity. Under the pressure of the philosopher's analysis, the self assumes the fragility of an eggshell. And should the shell be shattered into fleeting, transitory "mental states" it seems doubtful that the philosophers can put it together again. Descartes, the great rationalist champion of the mind, drew attention to this problem by noting:

> The time of a life can be divided into innumerable parts, each one of which in no way depends on the others. (AT 7: 48–9)

On the basis of this enormously influential passage, Descartes and subsequent rationalists are usually interpreted as conceiving time atomistically, as a discontinuous quantity. And if the "time of a life" spans atoms of discontinuous time, it would seem that the life itself is similarly fragmented.

In this chapter, I shall advance a different interpretation which stresses the unity and simplicity of the self. The problem for rationalists, therefore, is not the construction of self from temporal fragments. The rationalist must instead explain the phenomenology of diversity, change, and temporal division. One crucial insight for the development of this interpretation was unavailable to the great rationalists of the seventeenth century, but is very clearly expressed in Marcel Proust's masterpiece *A la recherche du temps perdu* (*Remembrance of Things Past*). I conclude with some observations on what this circumstance shows about the relationship between philosophy as expressed in theoretical treatises and philosophy as expressed in art.

I

It is perhaps Descartes' influence that is mainly responsible for modern philosophy's fascination with the problem of the self. Descartes' sharp, "real" distinction between the mind and the body insinuated that what is most important to the self is the mind, the thinking thing. But what is a purely thinking thing? After noting in the *Meditations* that he exists, Descartes shows us what is meant by examples. He is a thing that doubts, understands, affirms, wills, imagines, remembers, and senses. Naturally, he has all these thoughts serially, and this leads him to wonder whether it is "one and the same I" who has all the thoughts. Descartes cannot take the question completely seriously, but the question is dismissed without much explanation. "The fact that it is I who am doubting and understanding and willing is so evident that I see no way of making it any clearer" (AT 7: 28).

Later in the *Meditations*, Descartes seems to make matters worse by simultaneously drawing our attention to the structure of the self and the nature of time: "The time of a life can be divided into innumerable parts, each one of which in no way depends on the others" (AT 7: 48–9). This idea of radical fragmention is more colorfully, if less radically, discussed by Locke in his famous case of the prince's soul occupying the body of a cobbler, which prefigures popular "switched brain" science-fictional thought experiments.

The conception of self as subject to temporal fragmentation thus gave direction to much subsequent philosophy. When Descartes proclaimed "I think, therefore I am" and then "I am a thinking thing" or "I am my thinking" he believed himself to be drawing attention to the manifest simplicity and knowability of the self. Our opening observation about time has, however, often made Descartes' proclamations about self seem to ring hollow. Hume's assessment is canonical:

> If any impression gives rise to the idea of self, that impression must continue invariably the same, thro' the whole course of our lives; since self is supposed to exist after that manner. But there is no impression constant and invariable. Pain and pleasure, grief and joy, passions and sensations succeed each other, and never all exist at the same time . . . I may venture to affirm of the rest of mankind, that they are nothing but a bundle or collection of different perceptions, which succeed each other with an inconceivable rapidity, and are in a perpetual flux and movement. (Hume 1988: 251)

Hume argued further that we must not suppose that the self is a unified substratum to which our impressions "have reference," for it is impossible that we form an idea of the self.

> For my part when I enter most intimately into what I call *myself*, I always stumble on some particular perception or other, of heat or cold, light or shade, love or hatred, pain or pleasure. (Hume 1988: 252)

Kant, greatly impressed and greatly appalled by Hume's arguments, placed the problem of self at the center of his critical philosophy. He concluded that Hume was right to deny that we have straightforward knowledge of our self, but that "transcendental unity of apperception" was a precondition of experience. The unity of apperception, that is, the unity of a temporal series of apperceptions, makes use of obscure transcendental glue to defragment Hume's impressions.

Instead of further unraveling the historical thread, let us return to Descartes and begin afresh. We have rehearsed how Descartes' apparently unwarranted "I am, I exist" takes on the aspect of a blunder in light of the implications of his own observation about the nature of time. If we begin by granting unconditional primacy to time's atomic nature, we will always be left with the task of the king's horses and men: putting things back together in the medium of time. The nature of time is, therefore, crucial to both formulations and solutions of problems of the self. As we shall see, this point was seen more clearly by Proust than by some large figures in the philosophical pantheon.

The evidence that belief in the self is threatened by temporal fragmentation is almost entirely based on the texts quoted above: the treatment of the *cogito* in the Second Meditation and the premise concerning the nature of time in the proof of God's existence in the Third Meditation. Far more important for understanding Descartes' thought on these matters is the material found in his *Principles of Philosophy*, written after the *Meditations* and intended as a textbook treatment of his philosophy. Here we find a technical distinction between substances and their attributes. Descartes terms that which is unchanging in a substance an "attribute" (*Principles* 1: 56). He elucidates this by noting that since God is eternal and unchanging, he has no modes, but only attributes.

> And in the case of created things, that which always remains unmodified – for example, existence or duration in a thing which exists and endures – should not be called a quality or mode but an attribute. (*Principles* 1: 56)

This suggests a close connection with attributes and substances' essences, which a substance can never be without. Descartes marks this by terming a substance's essence its "principal attribute" (*Principles* 1: 53). Since a substance has various attributes (existence and duration have already been mentioned), what is the relationship between the principal attribute of a substance and all the other attributes? The answer is that there is no difference or "distinction" between the attributes of a substance in the substance itself. They are distinguished only in the thought of a mind regarding a substance now this way and now that.

> A rational distinction is between a substance and some attribute of that substance without which the substance is unintelligible; alternatively, it is a distinction between two such attributes of a single substance . . . For example, since a substance cannot cease to endure without also ceasing to be, the distinction between the substance and its duration is merely rational. (*Principles* 1: 62)

Descartes here expresses the doctrine that the attributes, including the essence or principal attribute, are identical one with another and identical with the substance of which they are attributes (for an explanation of this doctrine and some of its consequences, see Nolan 1997). The passage continues as follows:

> Thought and extension can be regarded as constituting the natures of intelligent substance and corporeal substance; they must then be considered as nothing else but thinking substance itself and extended substance itself – that is, as mind and body . . . we have some difficulty in abstracting the notion of substance from the notions of thought and extension, since the distinction between these notions and the notion of substance itself is merely a rational distinction. (*Principles* 1: 63)

401

So the essence of a thinking thing, namely thought itself, is in no way separate from the thinking thing. This has a number of striking implications, two of which are of utmost importance in connection with the problem of the fragmentation of the self.

Descartes does not hold that the self is a general something or *I think* underlying all our thoughts. In these texts, he is rejecting the theory that a substance is a substrate that supports a series of changes. A self, a thinking thing, is only rationally or conceptually distinguished from thought, its principal attribute. Thought *is* the thinking thing. Given Descartes' famous commitment to our being fully aware of everything in our thought (ruling out the sub- or unconscious), it follows that the self simply is whatever it is thinking. So Hume was entirely wrong to search in his thought for a separate impression of a substrate if he meant to be criticizing Descartes in particular. Kant was similarly wrong in the Paralogisms to suppose that the "rational psychologist" is committed to a mere, abstract, empty ego.[1] This means that Descartes and like minded rationalists are not supposing there is a substratum or a transcendental self to serve as metaphysical glue for a temporal mist of atomized individual thoughts. But this still leaves an apparent problem about defragmenting thoughts; it only removes from discussion a certain way of formulating the problem and Kant's unsatisfactory solution to it. A satisfactory rationalist solution must be found in the nature of time itself.

Descartes' technical terminology in the *Principles* marks an important additional clarification. 'Time,' as the term is typically used, Descartes tells us, is simply a measure of change; thus, "when time is distinguished from duration taken in the general sense and called the measure of movement, it is simply a mode of thought" (*Principles* 1: 57). So if we are to find a sense of 'time' that signifies more than something produced in our thought (a mere mode of thought, or way of thinking), we must not distinguish it from duration. This does not help until we get a fix on what is meant by 'duration.' As we have seen above, duration is only rationally distinct from substance: "Since a substance cannot cease to endure without also ceasing to be, the distinction between a substance and its duration is merely a rational one" (*Principles* 1: 62). Duration, therefore, is intrinsic to the self and is not a feature it has in consequence of its being operated upon by Time conceived as some kind of separate force or being.

How do we conceive substance as enduring? In the special case of God, the infinite being, the term 'eternal' applies because God is perfectly simple and immutable. In the case of finite beings like selves, conceiving something as enduring is to conceive it as diverse, as having many modes. And since thinkers are aware of everything in their thought, diverse modes of thought require us to conceive them as if spread over their duration.

> Thought and extension may also be taken as modes of a substance, insofar as one and the same mind is capable of having many different thoughts . . . The distinction between thought or extension and the substance will then be a modal one. (*Principles* 1: 64)

This means that when we regard thought as diverse, we can proceed to isolate the features constituting that diversity – its modes. So Descartes' identification of the self and its thought (because they are only rationally distinct) is here elaborated. (For further discussion of the interpretation of *Principles* 1: 64, see Sowaal 2001: ch. 4.) For convenience of expression, let us take it that the self's durational diversity is measured by time.[2] The elaborated doctrine becomes: *a temporal interval of a self is identical with its thought over that interval.* Keeping in mind the absence of subconscious thought, this emphasizes the futility of Hume and Kant's attempts to provide *internal* criticisms of Descartes (supposing that is what they were up to).

Nevertheless, all is not entirely well with the theory of the self. The problem is not to construct a self from prior atomistic experiences. Descartes' philosophy does not require the constitution of selves from perceptions which are essentially "in a perpetual flux and movement" as Hume put it. Rationalist considerations urge the fundamental unity of the self. The problem, therefore, is to explain the *appearance* of temporal fragmentation that Hume so vividly describes. And it requires an explanation of the phenomenology of fragmentation, even if the critics of rationalism grossly exaggerate the pervasiveness of such experiences.

This stands on its head the traditional problem of self under discussion. The rationalist needs to reconcile the simplicity and unity of the self with the durational diversity of its thought. We have no texts in which Descartes faced this problem directly, but subsequent rationalists did face it. Leibniz, for example, in what is probably his most famous work, the *Monadology*, begins by stressing the unity of thinking things, the "monads."

> 1. The Monad, which we shall discuss here, is nothing but a simple substance that enters into composites – simple, that is, without parts . . .
> 3. But where there are no parts, neither extension, nor shape, nor divisibility is possible. These monads are the true atoms of nature. (AG 213)

But if monads are to differ one from another, and to experience change, then there must somehow be modes and diversity in each monad. This brings Leibniz to what, on the surface, appears to be a paradox:

> 13. This diversity must involve a multitude in the unity or in the simple. (AG 214)

He then moves to an announcement of the resolution of the apparent paradox through his theory of perception.[3]

> 14. The passing state which involves and represents a multitude in the unity or in the simple substance is nothing other than what one calls perception . . .
> 16. We ourselves experience a multitude in a simple substance when we find that the least thought we ourselves apperceive involves variety in its object. (AG 214–15)

Leibniz plainly thought that the *Monadology*'s theory of perception involving universal expression and preestablished harmony solved the problem. Leibniz is also more explicit than Descartes in affirming the ideality of time, so he too is unable to appeal to the device of an independent Time to account for the diversity constituting the duration of the self (e.g., see Leibniz's *Fifth Letter to Clarke*, AG 337–43). Whether or not Leibniz eventually solves the rationalist problem of self, he certainly states it with great force.

403

II

Keeping in mind the treatment of the self in the early modern rationalists, it becomes possible to appreciate Proust's advancement of that sort of theory. It helps to note first the acuity with which he grasps the problem. He displays sensitivity to the experience of evanescence to which the examined self is susceptible. Such experience seems foreign to Marcel as a child, but Swann as a suffering lover can, at least in retrospect, express Humean fragmentation with great intensity.[4]

> For what we suppose to be our love or our jealousy is never a single, continuous and indivisible passion. It is composed of an infinity of successive loves, of different jealousies, each of which is ephemeral, although by their uninterrupted multiplicity they give us the impression of continuity, the illusion of unity. (Proust 1981, 1: 404)

In a nice twist, Marcel eventually comes to qualify the ephemerality of mental "states": it is their evanescing that is merely an "impression." A love, a jealousy, a "sensory impression" is indeed ephemeral, but it is nevertheless subject to recovery by the characteristic Proustian involuntary memory. As we shall see, it is ultimately the "illusion of unity" noted by Swann that is itself illusory. To put the point directly, the Proustian self is intrinsically very much a unity.

The crucial theoretical device in Proust's theory of self is his analysis of the phenomenon of involuntary memory.[5] This familiar though infrequent experience, perhaps most famously typified in Marcel's tasting of the tea-soaked madeleine, involves a present impression (only rarely a visual impression) evoking strongly a past impression. The recovery of the past impression can require some excavation, though a recalcitrant memory must be approached obliquely. Involuntary memory is related to *deja vu*, but it must result in the recovery of a very specific past impression and not a vague sense of "having encountered this before."

The involuntariness of these memories involves a number of interrelated, but separable points:

1 One cannot successfully attempt to produce them. Their appearance is entirely fortuitous and literally "against one's will."
2 Voluntary memory, in contrast, requires the active participation of one's conscious mental faculties. This means that these memories are partly shaped by the operation of the mental processes brought to bear. The intellect, for example, abstracts from a past impression all the contiguous (to use Hume's term) past impressions that originally framed it. Insofar as the past impression's character depended on its mental surroundings, the voluntary memory consequently falsifies it. There is also positive falsification, as the memory is nested in current contiguous impressions. The differences among impressions

> derive probably from the following cause: the slightest word that we have said, the most insignificant action that we have performed at any one epoch of our life was surrounded by, and colored by the reflection of, things which logically had no connexion with it and which later have been separated from it by our intellect. (Proust 1981, 3: 902)

3   Involuntary memory, continuing the contrast, contains no contribution from the present mental faculties. It results, therefore, in a pure replication of the past impression as it was.

The characterization of involuntary memory so far is mostly within the bounds of (slightly speculative) psychological observation. Proust extends these points into a bold thesis of theoretical philosophy. He proposes that the involuntary memory is identical with the past experience, or more precisely that there is something in the two experiences that is identical. This common essence, in a sense to be further specified, is thus *extra-temporal*.

> The truth surely was that the being within me which had enjoyed these impressions had enjoyed them because they had in them something that was common to a day long past and to the present, because in some way they were extra-temporal, and this being made its appearance only when, through one of these identifications of the present with the past, it was likely to find itself in the one and only medium in which it could exist and enjoy the essence of things, that is to say: outside time. (Proust 1981, 3: 904)

The choice of the term *essence* to designate what is identically present to thought in an experience and the later involuntary memory of it is obviously rationalistic. Descartes, for example, famously insisted that the essences created by God are themselves "eternal truths" – truths whose duration is a unity unfragmented by time. Descartes is notoriously obscure in this regard, but Spinoza – the third member of the great early modern rationalist triumvirate – makes achieving understanding of eternity central to his philosophy. (Needless to say, it is debatable whether or not Spinoza succeeds in being less obscure than Descartes). For Spinoza, roughly speaking, the first step to our acquiring an understanding of eternity is finding what is common in things. This "essence," Spinoza maintains, transcends the particular things in which we find the commonality (see *Ethics*, Pt. 2, Props. 37, 38). Proust further characterizes the essences revealed in involuntary memory in a Spinozistic vein:

> A moment of the past, did I say? Was it not perhaps very much more: something that, common both to the past and to the present, is much more essential than either of them? So often in the course of my life, reality had disappointed me because the instant when my senses perceived it my imagination, which was the only organ that I possessed for the enjoyment of beauty, could not apply itself to it, in virtue of that ineluctable law which ordains that we can only imagine what is absent. (Proust 1981, 3: 905)

For Proust then, as for Spinoza, there are two realities to consider. There is first the idea that our experiencing identically the same essence at different times reveals the profound unity of the self. The transitory selves discovered by Locke, Hume, and Swann in love are revealed to be the illusory constructions of voluntary memory. Part of the power and joy we feel in involuntary memories (the power and joy so well described by Proust) comes from their revelation of the identity of the self through time – or better, the self's identity outside time. "Outside time" means simply eternally; the self is revealed to us *sub specie aeternitatis*, as Spinoza taught in the *Ethics*:

405

It is the nature of reason to perceive things *sub specie aeternitatis*. (Pt. 2, Prop. 44, Corollary 2)

Insofar as the mind conceives things in accordance with the dictate of reason, it is equally affected whether the idea be of a thing that is future, past, or present. (Pt. 4, Prop. 62)

Nevertheless we sense and experience that we are eternal. For the mind senses those things that it conceives in the intellect no less than those it has in the memory . . . Although, therefore, we do not remember existing before the body, we nevertheless sense that our mind, insofar as it involves the essence of the body *sub specie aeternitatis*, is eternal and that the existence it has cannot be defined by time. (Pt. 5, Prop. 23 Scholium)

Our mind, insofar as it knows itself and the body *sub specie aeternitatis* necessarily has knowledge of God, and knows itself to exist in God and to be conceived through God. (Pt. 5, Prop. 30)

As the Demonstration of this Proposition continues: "Eternity is the very essence of God . . . Therefore to conceive things *sub specie aeternitatis* is to conceive things insofar as . . . they involve existence through the essence of God." And Proust can finally conclude with Spinoza that conceiving "things," ourselves in particular, "through the essence of God" is to conceive it adequately, as it is in reality.

Descartes, Leibniz, and Spinoza seem to have proceeded from the fundamental assumption of the self's unity to confidently supposing that the trained intellect could enforce a linear narrative unity on the apparent fragmentation resulting from the self's diversity of thoughts. They are classical rationalists. Proust, a twentieth-century modernist in the literary rather than philosophical sense of the term, cannot share that supreme confidence in the power of the pure intellect. The faculty of pure intellect is allied with the falsifying, fragmenting mechanism of voluntary memory. The Proustian redemption of the self from temporal fragmentation, therefore, can be undertaken only in light of the fortuitous deliverances of involuntary memory. The reality of the self reveals itself not in the production of treatises based on intellectual meditation, but instead in the creation of autobiography. Marcel's work based on his life, the subject and object of Proust's novel, is no linear narrative. Whatever formal structure the story of Marcel's life has is not reflective of the self's essential unity. The structure is imposed on experience by the creative force of self-narration. To exercise this creative force is to appreciate the beauty and importance of life. And it can make the self-narrator feel, if not like a creating God, at least like a Giant.[6] The final sentence of the eighth and final volume of Proust's novel reads:

But at least, if strength were granted me for long enough to accomplish my work, I should not fail, even if the results were to make them resemble monsters, to describe men first and foremost as occupying a place, a very considerable place compared with the restricted one which is allotted to them in space, a place on the contrary prolonged past measure – for simultaneously, like giants plunged into the years, they touch epochs that are immensely far apart, separated by the slow accretion of many, many days – in the dimension of Time. (Proust 1981, 3: 1107)

Notes

I have slightly altered some of the translations cited in this chapter.

1   The least object of perception (for example, even pleasure or displeasure), if added to the universal representation of self-consciousness, would at once transform rational psychology into empirical psychology (Kant 1933: A343/B401). Descartes' categories cut across the ones with which Kant saddles him. Descartes would separate the self-awareness of all thought from the metaphysical knowledge that the self is a substance in his technical sense.

2   That is, it is compared with "great and uniform motions" like the rotation of the earth (*Principles* 1: 57). Compare Proust: "Each individual therefore . . . was a measure of duration for me, in virtue of the revolutions which like some heavenly body he had accomplished not only on his own axis but also around other bodies, in virtue, above all, of the successive positions which he had occupied in relation to myself" (Proust 1981, 3: 1087).

3   By "perception" Leibniz means "thought," what a monad is or does. Of course, Leibniz's use of the term is not the same as Descartes'. For example, Leibnizian perception encompasses the subconscious.

4   I follow the convention of using the name "Marcel" to refer to the narrator of the novel. The anti-rationalist philosopher encourages us to grossly exaggerate the pervasiveness of experiences of fragmentation. One should resist this by keeping in mind that the fragments typically (though not invariably) take form only in moods of theoretical detachment from lived experience.

5   I have benefited here from the treatment in Beckett (1970), which is still in many ways the most insightful philosophical treatment of Proust available.

6   Leibniz wrote in article 83 of the *Monadology*: "Minds are images of the divinity itself, or of the *author* of nature . . . each mind being like a little divinity in its own realm" (AG 223, emphasis added).

References and Further Reading

Beckett, S. (1970) [1957]. *Proust*. New York: Grove Press.

Gebhardt, C. (ed.) (1925). *Spinoza Opera, Vol. 2*. Heidelberg: Carl Winter.

Gueroult, M. (1953). *Descartes selon l'ordre des raisons*, 2 vols. Paris: Montaigne.

Hume, D. (1988) [1739–40]. *A Treatise of Human Nature* (L. A. Selby-Bigge and P. H. Nidditch eds.). Oxford: Oxford University Press.

Kant, I. (1933) [1787]. *Immanuel Kant's Critique of Pure Reason* (N. K. Smith trans.). London: Macmillan.

Leibniz, G. W. (1989). *Philosophical Essays* (R. Ariew and D. Garber ed. and trans.). Indianapolis, IN: Hackett.

Nelson, A. (1997). Descartes' ontology of thought. *Topoi*, 16, 163–78.

Nolan, L. (1997). Nominalism and reductionism in Descartes' theory of attributes. *Topoi*, 16, 129–40.

Proust, M. (1981) [1913–27]. *Remembrance of Things Past*, 3 vols. (C. K. Moncreiff, T. Kilmartin, and A. Mayor trans.). New York: Random House.

Sowaal, A. (2001). Individuation and motion in Descartes' ontology of body. PhD dissertation, Department of Philosophy, University of California-Irvine.

22

Rationalism in Science

DAVID STUMP

If rationalism is to be defined, in part, as the belief that at least some of our knowledge of the world is gained by pure reason alone, prior to experience, then science, as the main example of human knowledge, should be a focus of discussion in philosophical debates over rationalism. Although the traditional characterization of modern philosophy as a debate between the British empiricists and the continental rationalists that was superseded by Kant has been widely acknowledged to be problematic for various reasons, recovering the scientific influences on modern philosophers will be the key to discussion here. Descartes and Leibniz were scientists as much as they were philosophers, and Locke explicitly claimed to be representing scientists. Hobbes, Berkeley, and Kant, who, unlike Descartes and Leibniz, are classified purely as philosophers, also engaged in scientific studies, albeit with mixed success. Furthermore, in both the early modern and in later periods, scientists such as Newton, Boyle, Herschel, Helmholtz, Duhem, Mach, Poincaré, and Einstein all wrote on philosophical topics. To a great extent, the philosophical debate between rationalism and empiricism took place within science.

The fact that the philosophical debate over rationalism and empiricism followed in the wake of the establishment of modern science does not seem accidental. The new science was taken to be the best, if not the only way, to discover the true nature of the world, most significantly expressed in laws of nature in mathematical form. Perhaps some claims of the newness of modern science and of its overwhelming superiority to scholasticism are simply overstated rhetoric, but nevertheless, both sides of the philosophical debate over rationalism and empiricism embraced modern science. Since the distinctive trait of modern science is taken to be its combination of experiment and the application of reason, especially mathematics, to the study of nature, it may seem paradoxical that the philosophical debates over rationalism and empiricism should arise, given that modern science could be viewed as the ideal compromise between rationalism and empiricism. In fact, the roles of reason and the senses in knowledge and in the formation of ideas are at stake in the philosophical debates over rationalism and empiricism precisely because of the inconsistent claims made about their roles in the new science. These debates can be seen as having been born out of the methodological reflections on the relative roles of experiment and reason in creating the success of the new science.

The rationalist claims that some part of scientific knowledge about the physical world is *a priori* – known through reason or intellectual intuition – while the empiricist claims that knowledge about things in the world can only be obtained through experience. Both sides accept the ability of the mind to formulate and to understand representations of nature and acknowledge the role of perceptual knowledge in science and in everyday experience, but empiricists claim that reason is limited to what Hume calls the "relations of ideas," that is, the defining of one term by means of another, or the discovery of the logical consequences of propositions (*Enquiry* IV). It is important to note that a rationalist need not be committed to *a priori* knowledge of the existence of anything, nor of the properties of any individual object, but rather only to general claims about the nature of things in the world. For example, a rationalist might claim that geometry expresses the real nature of space and the things in it, so any triangle (or even something that approximates to a triangle) in nature must have certain characteristics that we can discover *a priori*. Once we know that a triangle is a three-sided figure, we can use pure reason to show that the sum of the three angles of any triangle must be equal to two right angles (Descartes 1984: 45; AT 64). Rational intuition is claimed to tell us how the world must be, since the general principles and laws that the rationalist claims to discover are not contingent facts.

The burden of proof for the rationalist is explaining what rational intuition is and why we should think that it will reliably tell us something about the world. A consideration of thought experiments that purport to give an *a priori* justification of claims about the physical world will be part of the basis of this discussion. Even if thought experiments seem to lead to reliable knowledge about the world, the rationalist cause also carries the burden of explaining the overthrow by later science of various principles that were claimed to be *a priori*, necessary, and known with certainty. A consideration of some of the philosophical response to the development of non-Euclidean geometries will be the basis of this discussion. The burden of proof for the empiricist in this argument, especially after Kant, is to show how science can exist without any *a priori* knowledge. While Kant limited reason and acknowledged that experience is the main source of scientific knowledge, he also argued that there is a residual element of *a priori* synthetic knowledge, what we might now call the theoretical elements of a science, that cannot be eliminated. For example, Kant argued mathematics is both *a priori* and synthetic, that is, it tells us more than Hume's relations of ideas convey. Since mathematics is clearly central to science, it becomes a major stumbling block to the empiricist claim that there is no *a priori* element in science. This suggests that a good way to investigate rationalism in science is to ask whether there are some elements of science that are intractably *a priori*. Mathematics, a few fundamental principles or laws of nature, and other theoretical elements of science seem to be good candidates for *a priori* knowledge for which the empiricist will need to provide an account. Thus, the focus of this chapter will be on a few illustrative examples of potentially *a priori* sources of knowledge in science: thought experiments, mathematics, and theory in science.

The New Experimental Science as a Challenge to Intuition

Although it is still a matter of controversy among historians of science, many now say that there is much more continuity between early modern science and medieval scholasticism than the standard histories of the scientific revolution allow (Barker and Ariew 1991; Duhem 1980; Martin 1991; Lindberg and Westman 1990; Freeland and Corones 2000). The question of continuity is important here because the distinguishing mark of modern science is often taken to be its empirical nature, despite the fact that, as much as anyone, Descartes and Leibniz, the exemplary scientific rationalists, defined themselves in opposition to scholasticism and in favor of the new science (e.g., see Garber 1992, 1995). Consider Bertolt Brecht's *Life of Galileo*, a surprisingly influential history of the scientific revolution that is more fun and perhaps only slightly more fictitious than some of the standard histories of science. Brecht's Galileo disproves Aristotle's theory of why ice floats by performing a simple experiment, while the characters of the mathematician and the philosopher refuse to look at the moons of Jupiter through the telescope, insisting that *a priori* argument alone settles the question of their existence (Brecht 1967: 63, 32). Empirical evidence proves that *a priori* methods are bankrupt.

Of course, there are far more nuanced ways for advocates of modern science to make the case that the scientific revolution marked a radical break from scholasticism. Interpretation of the complex and comprehensive works of figures such as Galileo, Descartes, Newton, and Leibniz in simple terms is difficult. As noted above, the development of modern science is often viewed as the unification of mathematical methods and experimental methods, embodied especially well in figures such as Galileo and Newton. Advocates of this position seem to claim that rationalists do not take the role of experimental science seriously enough, or indeed think that actually conducting an experiment is superfluous. In the concluding section of the first study in the famous *Harvard Case Histories in Experimental Science*, James Bryant Conant remarks:

> The development of experimental science in the seventeenth century was the consequence of the combination of deductive reasoning with the cut-and-try type of experimentation. Two great figures of this period who contributed to the study of pneumatics symbolize the two traditions whose combination produced modern science. Blaise Pascal was primarily a mathematician, Robert Boyle primarily an experimentalist . . . In Pascal's treatise on hydrostatics and his work on pneumatics it is hard to tell whether or not most of the so-called experiments were ever performed. They may well have been intended rather as pedagogic devices – as demonstrations that the reader performs in his imagination in order better to understand the principles expounded . . .
>
> Boyle in one of his discussions of hydrostatics (1666) gently pokes fun at Pascal for having written of experiments that appeared impossible of execution . . . As an example of some of the things that Pascal described that strained one's credulity, Boyle refers to an experiment in which a man sits 20 feet under water and places against his thigh a tube that extends above the surface of the water. (Conant 1957: 59–60)

In contrast to Pascal, Boyle set the standard for reporting complete results of experiments, even when they seemed irrelevant and especially when they were negative. He was also meticulous about providing detail so that experiments could be reproduced, though the air pumps that he had built were beyond the technical resources of all but a few elite centers of scientific research. In the history of science, whole areas of inquiry and knowledge sometimes depend on the invention of a new piece of equipment to investigate nature. Boyle claimed that facts were exhibited in the air pump, but the experiments were very difficult to carry out. It took two strong men "divers hours" to evacuate the chamber, it constantly leaked, and phenomena were open to multiple interpretations (Conant 1957: 9). Granting that proper empirical investigation leads reliably to scientific knowledge, we can consider here whether thought experiments can also lead reliably to such knowledge.

Advocates of thought experiment sometimes claim that a successful thought experiment provides us with genuine knowledge about the physical world by pure reason alone. This has been called the "paradox of thought experiment" by Horowitz and Massey (1991) and has also been recognized as a rationalist position (e.g., Sorensen 1992). As an antidote to Brecht, and to utilize a scientific thought experiment that most commentators take to be convincing, we can consider Galileo's refutation of Aristotle's law of free fall, not by dropping balls off of the Tower of Pisa, but rather by an argument that appears in *Discourse on Two New Sciences* (Galilei 1974: 66ff.). According to Aristotle, heavier objects fall faster than lighter objects. Galileo asks us to consider what will happen to the rate of fall of a heavier and a lighter object if they are combined in various ways, assuming that objects do indeed fall in accordance with Aristotle's law. Consider putting the smaller object directly on top of the larger one before dropping them. If the objects fall in accordance with Aristotle's law, they should separate and each fall at the speed at which they would have fallen if they were never in contact. If the heavier object is put on top, however, it will push down on the slower, smaller object, which in turn will act as a brake on the larger one. The resulting speed will be in between that of the two objects falling separately. If the objects are connected, we can also imagine non-uniform results. If the connection is a flexible chain, for example, the heavier object should fall faster at first, but then experience drag from the slower-moving object chained to it. On the other hand, if there is a rigid connection between the two objects, we might want to say that they together form a new heavier object that will fall even faster. However, this situation is hardly different from the case where the heavier object is simply pushing down on the lighter one, without being connected at all. We have arrived at the apparently contradictory result that the combination of two objects will sometimes fall faster than the heavier of the original two alone, and sometimes fall slower. Galileo concludes that the way to avoid this result is to give up Aristotle's law. Indeed, he says that the natural conclusion to draw from this thought experiment is that free fall always occurs at the same rate, no matter what the weight of the object. If Galileo's argument is correct, free fall must be independent of weight, so (if we replace the term "weight" with "mass") it would seem that the modern law of free fall is not empirical at all. Furthermore, the law of free fall would be necessary in a very strong sense because, if Galileo is right, it is the only possible law of free fall. Contrast this law of nature to another law of nature that governs the behavior of physical bodies: light travels at 186,000 miles per second and we discovered that speed empirically. It seems natural to say that we might have discovered that the speed of light was much faster or much slower.

One response that the empiricist might make to thought experiments is to claim, like Mach, that thought experiments do not by themselves lead to knowledge about the world – even successful thought experiments must be repeated physically. While thought experiments might be useful as guides to research, pedagogy, etc., they are in a strict sense superfluous (Sorensen 1992: 61–2). John Norton (1991) clarified this line of response by defending the view that thought experiments are arguments (cf. Bishop 1999). In the philosophical debate between rationalists and empiricists, both sides accept that genuine knowledge can be logically deduced from known premises. Therefore, if the premises of a thought experiment are already known empirically, they are unproblematic; if not, the advocate of the thought experiment must be claiming that there can be a non-empirical source of knowledge about the physical world. Whether the empiricist can be convincing would seem to depend on whether or not all thought experiments can be seen as arguments, and that it is possible to obtain the information resulting from the thought experiment in some empirical way.

Another response that the empiricist might make is to simply deny that the thought experiment leads to the given conclusion. For example, Alexandre Koyré's analysis of Galileo's thought experiment focuses on the issue of whether the connected bodies form a new unitary object or not. According to Koyré, Galileo has not derived a contradiction from Aristotle's law of free fall, but rather has given one case where there is a new single object that falls faster than the original heavier object and another case where there are two separate objects that fall slower than the original heavier object (Koyré 1968: 51). The question of whether or not a connection between the original two objects makes it into a new unitary one is vexing. Perhaps we can agree that the connection must be rigid, but how rigid? What if the distance between the two objects was great? There is at least some ambiguity about what to call a single object here, but perhaps not a contradiction, as Galileo claimed.

Dijksterhuis (1986: 327) rejects Stevin's purported proof of the law of the inclined plane in a very similar manner. Stevin's argument depends on the assumption that perpetual motion is not possible, even in an idealized, frictionless system. Since Stevin has not justified his claim that perpetual motion is impossible in an idealized system, Dijksterhuis refused to accept the validity of the argument. If an empiricist can show that the thought experiment does not lead to the given conclusion, then there is no risk of thought experiments being used to show that rationalism is true. Faulty arguments do not show that thought experiments can lead to genuine knowledge of the physical world.

Geometry and Intuition

As noted above, both rationalists and empiricists accept argument as a source of genuine knowledge; that is, it can be logically deduced from known premises. However, rationalists claim that some fundamental principles or laws of nature can be known *a priori* by intellectual intuition, while empiricists claim that such principles must either be definitions in disguise, like Hume's relations of ideas, or else they must be justified empirically. Intellectual intuition is understood as a kind of "grasping" by which we recognize the truth of a proposition or understand the meaning of an idea. Descartes spoke of the "natural light" by which we could understand "clear and distinct ideas" and recognize their certainty. Propositions known by intellectual intuition are said to be "self-evident," that is, needing neither logical demonstration nor evidence gained from sense experience. As such, they are taken to express necessity and to be known with certainty, but not all claims of *a priori* knowledge seem certain and many have been shown to be false by later developments in science (Hahn 1933). This hardly makes *a priori* claims look like candidates for reliable knowledge. Equally as problematic for the rationalist as changes in supposedly certain and obvious principles, however, is the fact that the rationalist cannot explain such a principle or convince someone who does not understand it.

Kant tried to correct the use of reason in science by limiting its scope. Kantian critical philosophy does not go beyond what it can legitimately prove. Many traditional philosophical issues are ruled out of court as unanswerable and many others are left to empirical science to settle. Despite the limits that Kant set out and despite the fact that Kant was deeply engaged with the Newtonian exact sciences of his time and even produced some original scientific work, Kantian philosophy was also proven wrong by later advances in science. The fall of Euclidean geometry from its place in Kant's philosophy is perhaps the most famous case of a former bit of necessary and certain knowledge that became merely one of several alternatives that are perhaps not true at all. Kant argued that Euclidean geometry is a true description of space (space as a phenomenon, not as noumena) and that knowledge of space and, hence, knowledge of Euclidean geometry, was a necessary precondition for the possibility of any science at all. Kant had argued that our knowledge of Euclidean geometry is thus both *a priori* and synthetic, and it is also certain because alternatives to Euclidean geometry are impossible. To make a long story far too short, mathematicians first showed that alternatives to Euclidean geometry were possible and physicists (especially Einstein) next showed that the actual structure of space was not Euclidean.

Euclidean geometry has zero curvature, there is exactly one parallel to a given line through a point outside that line, and the sum of the interior angles of a triangle is equal to 180 degrees. Bolyai-Lobachevskii geometry has negative curvature, there is more than one parallel to a given line through a point outside that line, and the sum of the interior angles of a triangle is less than 180 degrees (how much less depends on curvature). Riemannian geometry has positive curvature, there are no parallel lines, and the sum of the interior angles of a triangle is greater than 180 degrees (how much greater depends on curvature). Riemann went even further and developed general coordinate systems that can describe spaces of variable curvature. After the acceptance of non-Euclidean geometries around 1870, Helmholtz directly challenged Kant's view of geometry (Helmholtz 1977a, 1977b; Nowak 1989).

Not all was lost for defenders of Kant, however. Even though Kant seemed to say that only Euclidean geometry was possible, he could not have meant that other geometries were logically inconsistent. One of the criteria that Kant put forward as a definition of an "analytic" statement is that its negation leads to a contradiction. If alternatives to Euclidean geometry were contradictory, they would have to be analytic in Kant's terms. But Kant thought that both geometry and arithmetic were synthetic, that is, they are not merely built up from explicit definitions, but also require intuition in a quite specific sense. Intuition is what allows us to construct figures and objects in our minds. Thus, the neo-Kantian of the early twentieth century could maintain part of Kant's claims about intuition that leads to *a priori* knowledge of the world, despite the mathematical challenge (Renouvier 1889, 1892).

Of course, the situation changed dramatically with Einstein's General Theory of Relativity, in which space (more precisely, space-time) has no fixed structure at all

413

independent of the matter and energy distributed in it. The geometry of space is determined empirically, not *a priori*, and far from being necessary, Euclidean geometry is not even true. It is, of course, approximately true of small regions of space-time and good enough for engineering, but so are all of the alternative metric geometries. Einstein's General Theory of Relativity had a tremendous impact on Schlick, Carnap, and Reichenbach, the great founders of philosophy of science as we know it today. All three wrote philosophical interpretations of Einstein's Theory of Relativity in the 1920s and 1930s, and developed their strictly empiricist philosophy in response to the new physics (Carnap 1922; Schlick 1920; Reichenbach 1965, 1969).

Prior to the development of the General Theory of Relativity, Henri Poincaré had extended Kant's strategy of giving up one kind of *a priori* knowledge while maintaining others, arguing that while arithmetic follows from a synthetic and *a priori* intuition of the concept of whole number and of the principle of mathematical induction, our intuition of the metric properties of bodies is completely empty. The issue to consider here is how Poincaré came to view geometry and arithmetic so differently and whether or not there can be a consistent criterion for accepting rational intuition in one area of knowledge while rejecting it in others. Poincaré's basic position on the role of intuition in geometry is developed in an 1889 article on logic and intuition, and is repeated in several places in his works (Poincaré 1889). Like Mach, he accepts the role of intuitive arguments in pedagogy and in scientific discovery, in addition to its special synthetic *a priori* role in the epistemology of arithmetic. Poincaré also recognizes the increasing demand for rigor in mathematics. Crucial to this rigor is the idea that we must ferret out all of our implicit assumptions, replacing them with explicit definition and strict proof. For geometry especially, this work culminates in Hilbert's *Foundations of Geometry*, and in a review of this work, Poincaré agrees that rigor demands avoiding all appeals to intuition:

> Is the list of axioms complete, or have we let escape some that we apply unconsciously? This is what we need to know. To find this out, we have one and only one criterion. We must investigate whether or not the geometry is a logical consequence of the explicitly stated axioms; that is to say, if these axioms, entrusted to a reasoning machine, could produce the entire series of geometric propositions. If they can, we will be certain that we have not forgotten anything, because our machine cannot function except according to the rules of logic by which it was constructed. It does not know of this vague instinct that we call intuition. (Poincaré 1902c: 269)[1]

Poincaré argues that geometry concerns only the properties that are common to all of the alternative metric geometries. Since projective geometry studies the properties of figures that are invariant under a group of projective transformations, groups alone are fundamental:

> The different ways in which a cube can be superposed upon itself, and the different ways in which the roots of a certain equation may be interchanged, constitutes two isomorphic groups. They differ in matter only. The mathematician should regard this difference as superficial, and he should no more distinguish between these two groups than he should between a cube of glass and a cube of metal . . . What we call geometry is nothing but the

study of formal properties of a certain continuous group; so we may say, space is a group. (Poincaré 1898: 40, 41)

Poincaré's central argument for the elimination of metric intuition from geometry is that geometric objects can be stipulatively defined from more fundamental objects. In his early work, groups play this role, since all of the metric properties of geometries can be expressed in the theory of continuous groups (Poincaré 1889: 129). Thus, part of what had seemed to be *a priori* knowledge to Kantians can be seen to be "empty," as empiricists suggested.

There is a strong tradition in nineteenth-century mathematics of interpreting unknown (or seemingly impossible) objects as combinations of known simples. This tradition goes back at least to Hamilton's geometric interpretation of complex numbers, and continued in Beltrami and Klein's early treatment of non-Euclidean geometries. Poincaré follows tradition; however, there are limits to this process, and a synthetic *a priori* element must be maintained in science, according to Poincaré. Thus, groups maintain their status as innate concepts that are known *a priori* (Poincaré 1889; Picard 1901), and our knowledge of arithmetic depends essentially on the principle of mathematical induction and on the concept of number taken to be a synthetic *a priori* element of science. Indeed, distancing himself from the "global conventionalism" of Elouard Le Roy, Poincaré distinguishes three elements of science – *a priori*, conventional, and empirical:

> Here are three truths: (1) The principle of mathematical induction; (2) Euclid's postulate; (3) the physical law according to which phosphorus melts at 44° (cited by M. Le Roy). These are said to be three disguised definitions: the first, that of the whole number; the second, that of the straight line; the third, that of phosphorus. I grant it for the second; I do not admit it for the other two. I must explain the reason for this apparent inconsistency. First, we have seen that a definition is acceptable only on condition that it implies no contradiction. We have shown likewise that for the first definition this demonstration is impossible; on the other hand, we have just recalled that for the second Hilbert has given a complete proof. As to the third, evidently it implies no contradiction. Does this mean that the definition guarantees, as it should, the existence of the object defined? We are here no longer in the mathematical sciences, but in the physical, and the word existence has no longer the same meaning. It no longer signifies absence of contradiction; it means objective existence. (Poincaré 1920: 185–6; 1913: 468)

Metric primitives can be explicitly defined in terms of more basic primitives and a complete proof of the consistency of the metric geometries can be given formally. However, in reply to logicism and formalism, Poincaré argues that it is impossible to prove the consistency of arithmetic without using mathematical induction or its equivalent (Poincaré 1902a, 1920). Therefore, while one can eliminate metric geometry by taking all of geometry to really concern numbers plus some group theoretic or topological primitives that are non-metric, one cannot eliminate arithmetic and our intuitive knowledge of mathematical induction. In a second argument presented on the following page, Poincaré repeats his claim that geometric (i.e., metric) terms can be "defined away," while arithmetical ones cannot, arguing that whole number and the principle of mathematical induction have equivalent definitions, but only in virtue of a synthetic *a priori* judgment, not on the basis of an explicit stipulative definition (Poincaré 1920: 188–9; 1913: 469–70).

After reading Hilbert's *Foundations of Geometry*, Poincaré extended his strategy of eliminating primitive terms in geometry. In a review of Hilbert (Poincaré 1902b) and even more explicitly in the nomination that he wrote for the awarding of the third Lobachevskii prize to Hilbert (Poincaré 1904), Poincaré argues that Lie's work contains an artificial limit: the study of continuous groups. Hilbert shows how to move beyond this limit and thus overcome the idea that "group" is a primitive concept. However, this simply moves the intuitive element back to a more abstract level, from projective geometry to topology. Referring to Hilbert's second group of axioms – the axioms of order – Poincaré says:

> The axioms of order are presented as dependant on projective axioms, and they would not have any meaning if one did not allow the latter, since one would not know what three points in a straight line is. And yet, there is a peculiar geometry which is purely qualitative and which is absolutely independent of projective geometry, that does not presuppose as known either the notion of a straight nor that of a plane but only the notions of line and surface; it is what one calls topology. (Poincaré 1904: 8)

How are we to understand Poincaré's arguments that metric geometry is a formal, non-intuitive science, when at the same time he defends intuition in arithmetic? First, Poincaré's arguments for formalism in geometry and against formalism in arithmetic both seem remarkably question begging. His view that we have no geometric intuition seems to be equivalent to his acceptance of the consistency of non-Euclidean geometries and his rejection of formalization of arithmetic seems to depend on his belief that the principle of mathematical induction or its equivalent is fundamental to arithmetic in a way that metric was not fundamental to geometry.

Given what Poincaré says about the meaning of primitive terms in geometry, it is unclear how we can know in advance what an arithmetical system is. Negating the parallel postulate obviously changed the metric properties of geometry – indeed, the very idea of what a straight line is. Nevertheless, non-Euclidean geometries were accepted. It seems compelling to say that we need mathematical induction to show that arithmetic is consistent and that everyone accepts consistency as a requirement. However, the consistency of Bolyai-Lobachevskii was only gained by removing metric properties from what counts as geometry. Why could not the same argument be made in arithmetic?

A second problem for Poincaré and for rationalists generally is how to maintain a distinction between acceptable and unacceptable forms of intuition. For example, what do we say about the axioms of topology? Or the continuum? We could say (a) that there is no geometric intuition, and that "analytic geometry" is fundamentally arithmetical, rather than geometric. This interpretation fits the early passages quoted above. Or, we could say (b) that there is a limited form of geometric intuition, the analytical or qualitative part. This second interpretation fits the later passages that I have cited and also Poincaré's remarks on the intuition of the continuum and his rejection of the arithmetization of the continuum (see Folina 1992: ch. 6). Under both interpretations, however, Poincaré still has to claim that some intuition is completely bankrupt, while other intuition is *a priori* knowledge in a classically rationalist sense and thus true and certain. Under interpretation (a), Poincaré can at least argue that while geometric intuitions are problematic, arithmetic intuitions are not. Under (b), the problem is amplified, since Poincaré must say that some geometric intuitions are reliable, while other kinds of geometric intuition are not. A single neat classification of intuitions would be preferable.

One of the most promising ways to understand Poincaré's rejection of some forms of intuition while maintaining other forms as necessary is to see his view as stemming from a distinction between intellectual and sensual intuition.[2] The neo-Kantians of the end of the nineteenth century had given up Kant's intuition as a form of sensibility, but left a conceptual intuition of the categories of the understanding in place. Poincaré seems to be firmly in this tradition, since he maintains that we can create geometry without any representations at all:

> The words, point, straight, and plane themselves should not cause any visual representation. They could arbitrarily designate objects of any nature, provided that one can establish a correspondence between these objects such that for all systems of two objects called points there corresponds one, and only one, of the objects called straights . . . The reasoning ought to be able, according to [Hilbert], to lead to purely mechanical rules, and to do geometry, it is sufficient to apply strictly the rules to the axioms, without knowing what they mean. One will in this way be able to construct all of geometry, I would not exactly say without understanding it at all, since one grasps the logical connection of the propositions, but at least without seeing anything. One could give the axioms to a reasoning machine, for example the logical piano of Stanley Jevons, and one would see all of geometry come out. (Poincaré 1904: 6–7)

Thus, Poincaré firmly rejects intuition as a visual representation of geometric objects. However, he claims that we need some conceptual intuition in order to understand mathematics, if only to understand what is explicitly in the axioms. Presumably, the reason why Poincaré would reject the idea that Jevons' logical piano could understand geometry is that it does not have the necessary *a priori* intuition of topology and arithmetic needed to do so.

A third and final problem with all Kantian and post-Kantian arguments for rationalism is that they are mostly negative: rationalists are only able to tell us that intuition leading to synthetic *a priori* knowledge is necessary to understand mathematics and science. Any attempt by Poincaré to argue that the mind has special intuitive capacities must be suspect, because he definitely changed his view on what is taken as primitive and intuitive. Originally, geometry is nothing but a group, but later it is even less than that. Poincaré's change of mind does not inspire confidence in intuition or in claims about what can and cannot be known intuitively. Will he now say that it is a topological concept that preexists in the mind? On the contrary, Poincaré even says that some topological properties of space are conventional, as well as intuitive and necessary; in particular, that the number of dimensions of space is conventional. However, he may be excused for such inconsistent views in this case, since the topological invariance of dimension was not completely understood at the time. The first proof was given by Brouwer in Dutch in 1911, one year before Poincaré's death (see Johnson 1979, 1981).

417

The Mathematical Tradition and Theoretical Science

It would certainly be uncontroversial to say that advances in mathematics were repeatedly responsible for tremendous progress in science. Archimedes solved practical experimental problems with Euclidean geometry, Descartes' invention of analytic geometry allowed him to invent a new physics as well, and Newton and Leibniz dramatically extended the mathematical methods available for science with their co-discovery of the calculus. In the nineteenth century, Gauss, Riemann, and many others made major contributions to extend the mathematical tools of physics. Fisher did the same for biology in the twentieth century and, of course, there are more such examples. The success of mathematics once again puts the burden of proof on the empiricist, who must explain why mathematics works. As before, the empiricist is left with the strategy of either arguing that mathematics is "formal" and does not tell us anything about the world, or instead that it is empirical, but the burden of proof seems even higher than it was in the case of thought experiments, since the use of mathematics cannot be eliminated from science (Field 1980; Sober 1999).

It seems ironic that the development of Newtonian mechanics is frequently described as a competition between English experimentalism and French analysis, thus echoing in a scientific context the traditional British empiricist vs. continental rationalist account of the philosophical debate. The development of Leibniz's version of the calculus by French mathematicians such as Pierre-Simon de Laplace and Joseph Lagrange put French mathematics far ahead of English mathematics. The subsequent applications of analytical methods not only to classical Newtonian mechanics but also to thermodynamics, by Fourier, electromagnetism by Ampère, and light by Fresnel, were extraordinarily successful. Poincaré, who is often said to be the last in this line of French mathematical physicists, expresses the traditional divide between the British and continental scientific styles, but finds that the debate between those who see science as *a priori* and those who see it is as experimental can be resolved by understanding some elements of science as hypothetical:

> The English teach mechanics as an experimental science; on the Continent it is taught always more or less as a deductive and *a priori* science. The English are right, no doubt . . . the difficulty is largely due to the fact that treatises on mechanics do not clearly distinguish between what is experiment, what is mathematical reasoning, what is convention, and what is hypothesis. (Poincaré 1982: 89)

We would likely now say that a highly mathematical science is "theoretical" instead of *a priori*, which is indicative of the extent to which rationalism has been out of favor. Of course, even with this change in terminology it would be an overstatement to say that the French success at analysis led to their total neglect of empirical science. For example, Ivor Grattan-Guinness (1984) has noted how much emphasis the French put on engineering. On the other side of the Channel, it seems impossible to justify calling Newton an empiricist, even if he did say, famously, that he will "frame no hypotheses." Indeed, many have argued that the most philosophically appealing aspect of Newton's methodology was his resistance to the extremes of empiricism and rationalism (Stein 1990), expressed in the recognition of a need for both analysis and synthesis and for empirical experimentation (Hankins 1985: 20).

From Aristotle onwards, an analytic and synthetic method was distinguished in natural philosophy. One can either start from first principles and show how phenomena can be explained by them, or one can start with phenomena and infer fundamental laws of nature. Modern science adopted a hypothetical method, justifying the first principles or the existence of theoretical entities solely by their empirical adequacy. Thus, the only test for the truth of a hypothetical law of nature or the existence of a theoretical entity is whether or not a theory is consistent with observation. According to this contemporary view, there is never a need for *a priori* rational justification in science. Hypotheses are first adopted provisionally without evidence, and subsequently either accepted or rejected on the basis of empirical evidence. The hypothetical method that Poincaré mentions became the mainstream in late nineteenth- and early twentieth-century philosophy of science and in science itself, generally at the expense of rationalism, since the theoretical elements of a scientific theory might be understood without any appeal to rational intuition.

As noted at the beginning of this chapter, conflicting philosophical interpretations of the methodology of modern science can be seen as precipitating the rationalist–empiricist debate. Even with substantial agreement that rationalism in science was dead, a philosophical debate ensued over what follows from the evidence for hypotheses that we obtain empirically. So called "scientific realists" believe that we can legitimately claim to know that theoretical entities exist and that scientific theories are true, while "empiricists" or "instrumentalists" believe that theoretical entities are convenient fictions and that scientific theories are empirically adequate, but not true (or known to be true). Although "empiricist" has become the preferred name for the philosophical position that I am describing here, and "instrumentalism" is associated with a view that has been widely repudiated, I will use the term "instrumentalist," since both scientific realists and instrumentalists are very likely to be empiricists in the sense of the debate between rationalists and empiricists at issue in this volume. Indeed, scientific realism and instrumentalism can each be seen as a rejection of rationalism in science by means of showing that the success of science can be explained entirely by reference to what is learned empirically. While scientific realists claim that when we have the appropriate evidence, empirical data give us a legitimate claim to knowledge, even if that knowledge is indirect, instrumentalists claim that theoretical claims in science are never validated, empirically or by any other means. Both realists and instrumentalists consider the former *a priori* elements of scientific knowledge to be theoretical. Realists claim to show that all scientific knowledge is empirical, despite the existence of theoretical elements in science for which there can be no direct empirical evidence. Instrumentalists claim that empirical methods should strictly limit claims of scientific knowledge to phenomena and that theoretical elements are dispensable. The overwhelming majority of both scientific realists and instrumentalists reject rationalism, seeing no need for *a priori* synthetic claims in the sciences.

The theoretical aspects of science have not been so easy to dismiss, however. Indeed, major figures in twentieth-century science, starting with Einstein, are known for their theoretical work in science. While documenting the development of theoretical science, especially in Germany, Jungnickel and McCormmach (1986) emphasize how recent our current conception of theoretical science really is and what a major part of science it has become. Stephen Toulmin's *The Return to Cosmology* (1982) does not claim that theoretical science is new, but it does make a strong argument that there is far more theoretical work in science now than before and that science must include elements that are theoretical or even speculative. One striking feature of twentieth-century philosophy of science is the extent to which the topics that it took up are precisely those that had been considered *a priori* knowledge by Kant, such as geometry, space and time, causality, and the principles violated by quantum mechanics. While philosophers are not required to conclude that theoretical science is evidence for rationalism, its centrality does show that much of science is not empirical in any straightforward sense. Indeed, although synthetic *a priori* knowledge was officially rejected by the Vienna Circle in the 1929 manifesto (see Neurath and Cohen 1974), statements about the former Kantian *a priori* have often been given a special role, either as conventions, or as the hard core of scientific theories. Quine's critique of the analytic–synthetic distinction was supposed to replace the notion of any special status for what was formerly considered to be *a priori* with a thoroughgoing empirical holism, but several authors have questioned Quine's result (Creath 1991; Friedman 2001; Stein 1992; Richardson 1997). Going beyond mere critique of Quine's empiricism, some have even advocated a return to a form of rationalism, giving some element of our knowledge a special *a priori* status (De Pierris 1992; Friedman 2001).

The development of non-Euclidean geometries and especially of the General Theory of Relativity made a profound impact on philosophy of science in the early twentieth century by showing philosophers that the most fundamental aspects of physical theory could change. Geometry, space and time, causality, and the fundamental principles of physical theories were still seen to have a special role, even if Kant's rationalism was rejected. Mach and Poincaré took such elements of science to be conventions, a matter of free choice, regardless of what experiment says. Slightly different versions of conventionalism were developed by C. I. Lewis, Victor Lentzen, Arthur Pap, and Russell Norwood Hanson. Ian Hacking (1992) has advocated something similar to conventionalism with his notion of "styles of reasoning." Many of these treatments of *a priori* knowledge share the idea that what Kant took to be necessary can and indeed has changed through the development of scientific theories.

Conceptual change of this sort is what many postpositivist philosophers of science, such as Kuhn, Toulmin, Laudan, and Shapere, saw as a fundamentally important aspect of science. Indeed, Kuhn (1990) eventually (and tentatively) picked up the idea of a conventional treatment of synthetic *a priori* knowledge as an explication of his views. The idea that there are revisable conventions at the heart of science was already well developed prior to logical positivism, continued in logical positivism itself, and was maintained even in postpositivist philosophy of science. While Quine admits that some elements of empirical theory are much less likely to be revised than others, he underestimates the asymmetric relations between the "hard core" and the "periphery." It is not just that the "periphery" is more likely to be revised than the "hard core," but rather that the statements of the "periphery" cannot even be stated, let alone tested, without the "hard core" functioning in the Kantian sense as a necessary precondition. It is possible that fundamental elements of science will be *a priori* in a functional sense, given that they must be chosen prior to proceeding with any theoretical or empirical work, and that these elements can be justified neither by rational intuition, nor by empirical test (Stump 2003). If they remain untestable empirically, and cannot be justified by rational intuition, there will be a component of scientific theory that falls outside of the range of the options provided by traditional philosophical rationalism and empiricism.

Notes

1   The "reasoning machine" to which Poincaré refers is Stanley Jevons' "logical piano," the logic of which is equivalent to Venn diagrams. Jevons demonstrated his machine in 1866 (Jevons, 1869: 59–60; 1958: 170ff.). The machine was conceived as a "logical abacus," a set of blocks representing subject, predicate, and middle terms. With the addition of levers to move the blocks, Jevons developed a sort of logical adding machine (see Gardner 1982: ch. 5).

2   Michael Detlefsen suggested such a distinction in his talk at the 1994 Poincaré Congress in Nancy, France. If the distinction can be maintained, we can credit Poincaré with having at least one clear way of distinguishing acceptable and unacceptable uses of intuition.

References and Further Reading

Barker, Peter, and Ariew, Roger (eds.) (1991). *Revolution and Continuity: Essays in the History and Philosophy of Early Modern Science*. Washington, DC: Catholic University of America Press.

Bishop, Michael A. (1999). Why thought experiments are not arguments. *Philosophy of Science*, 66 (4), 534–41.

Brecht, Bertolt (1967). *The Life of Galileo*. London: Methuen.

Brown, James Robert (1991a). *The Laboratory of the Mind: Thought Experiments in the Natural Sciences*. London: Routledge.

—— (1991b). Thought experiments: A Platonic account. In T. Horowitz and G. J. Massey (eds.), *Thought Experiments in Science and Philosophy*. Savage, MD: Rowman and Littlefield.

Carnap, Rudolf (1922). *Der Raum. Ein Beitrag zur Wissenschaftslehre, Kant-Studien Erganzungshelf No. 56*. Berlin: Reuther and Reichard.

Conant, James Bryant (ed.) (1957) [1948]. *Harvard Case Histories in Experimental Science, Vol. 2*. Cambridge, MA: Harvard University Press.

Creath, Richard (1991). Every dogma has its day. *Erkenntnis*, 35, 347–89.

De Pierris, Graciela (1992). The constitutive *a priori*. In P. Hanson and B. Hunter (eds.), *Return of the a priori*. Calgary: University of Calgary Press.

Descartes, René (1984) [1641]. *Meditations on First Philosophy*. In J. Cottingham, R. Stoothoff, and D. Murdoch (eds. and trans.), *The Philosophical Writings of Descartes*. New York: Cambridge University Press.

Dijksterhuis, E. J. (1986). *The Mechanization of the World Picture*. Oxford: Oxford University Press.

Duhem, Pierre M. M. (1980). *The Evolution of Mechanics* (G. é. Oravas ed.). Alphen aan de Rijn: Sijthoff and Noordhoff.

Field, Hartry (1980). *Science Without Numbers: A Defense of Nominalism*. Princeton, NJ: Princeton University Press.

Folina, Janet (1992). *Poincaré and the Philosophy of Mathematics*. London: Macmillan.

Freeland, Guy, and Corones, Anthony (eds.) (2000). *1543 and All That: Image and Word, Change and Continuity in the Proto-Scientific Revolution*. Boston, MA: Kluwer.

Friedman, Michael (1992). *Kant and the Exact Sciences*. Cambridge, MA: Harvard University Press.

—— (2001). *Dynamics of Reason: The 1999 Kant Lectures at Stanford University*. Stanford, CA: CSLI Publications.

Galilei, Galileo (1974). *Two New Sciences* (S. Drake trans.). Madison: University of Wisconsin Press.

Garber, Daniel (1992). Descartes' metaphysical physics. In D. L. Hull (ed.), *Science and Its Conceptual Foundations*. Chicago: University of Chicago Press.

—— (1995). Leibniz: Physics and philosophy. In N. Jolley (ed.), *The Cambridge Companion to Leibniz*. Cambridge: Cambridge University Press.

Gardner, Martin (1982). *Logic Machines and Diagrams*. Chicago: University of Chicago Press.

Grattan-Guinness, Ivor (1984). Work for the workers: Advances in engineering mechanics and instruction in France 1808–1803. *Annals of Science*, 41, 1–33.

—— (1990). *Convolution in French Mathematics, 1800–1840: From the Calculus and Mechanics to Mathematical Analysis and Mathematical Physics*. Boston, MA: Birkhauser Verlag.

Hacking, Ian (1992). "Style" for historians and philosophers. *Studies in History and Philosophy of Science*, 23, 1–20.

Hahn, Hans (1933). The crisis in intuition. In B. McGuinness (ed.), *Empiricism, Logic and Mathematics*. Dordrecht: Reidel.

Hankins, Thomas L. (1985). *Science and the Enlightenment*. Cambridge: Cambridge University Press.

Hanson, N. R. (1958). *Patterns of Discovery*. Cambridge: Cambridge University Press.

Hanson, Philip, and Hunter, Bruce (eds.) (1992). *Return of the a priori: Canadian Journal of Philosophy Supplementary Volume 18*. Calgary: University of Calgary Press.

Helmholtz, Herman (1977a) [1868]. On the facts underlying geometry. In P. Hertz and M. Schlick (eds.), *Epistemological Writings*. Dordrecht: Reidel.

—— (1977b) [1870]. On the origin and significance of the axioms of geometry. In P. Hertz and M. Schlick (eds.), *Epistemological Writings*. Dordrecht: Reidel.

Hilbert, David (1971) [1899]. *Foundations of Geometry* (L. Unger trans.). La Salle: Open Court.

Horowitz, Tamara, and Massey, Gerald J. (eds.) (1991). *Thought Experiments in Science and Philosophy*. Savage, MD: Rowman and Littlefield.

Hume, David (1966). *Enquiries Concerning the Human Understanding and Concerning the Principles of Morals*, 2nd edn. Oxford: Clarendon Press.

Jesseph, Douglas Michael (1993). *Berkeley's Philosophy of Mathematics*. Chicago: University of Chicago Press.

—— (1996). Hobbes and the method of natural science. In T. Sorell (ed.), *The Cambridge Companion to Hobbes*. New York: Cambridge University Press.

—— (1999). *Squaring the Circle: The War between Hobbes and Wallis*. Chicago: University of Chicago Press.

Jevons, W. Stanley (1869). *The Substitution of Similars, the True Principle of Reasoning*. London: Macmillan.

—— (1958) [1874]. *The Principles of Science: A Treatise on Logic and the Scientific Method*. London: Macmillan.

Johnson, Dale M. (1979, 1981). The problem of the invariance of dimension in the growth of modern topology. *Archive for History of Exact Sciences*, 20, 97–188.

Jungnickel, Christa, and McCormmach, Russell (1986). *Intellectual Mastery of Nature: Theoretical Physics from Ohm to Einstein*, 2 vols. Chicago: University of Chicago Press.

Koyré, Alexandre (1968). *Metaphysics and Measurement: Essays in Scientific Revolution*. Cambridge, MA: Harvard University Press.

Kuhn, Thomas S. (1977). A function for thought experiments. In *The Essential Tension: Selected Studies in Scientific Tradition and Change*. Chicago: University of Chicago Press.

—— (1990). Dubbing and redubbing: The vulnerability of rigid designation. In C. W. Savage (ed.), *Scientific Theories*. Minneapolis: University of Minnesota Press.

Laudan, Larry (1977). *Progress and Its Problems: Towards a Theory of Scientific Growth*. Berkeley: University of California Press.

Lenzen, Victor (1937). Experience and convention in physical theory. *Erkenntnis*, 7, 257–67.

Lewis, Clarence Irving (1923). Pragmatic conception of the *a priori*. *Journal of Philosophy*, 20.

—— (1970) [1941]. Logical positivism and pragmatism. In J. D. Goheen and J. L. J. Mothershead (eds.), *Collected Papers of Clarence Irving Lewis*. Stanford, CA: Stanford University Press.

Lindberg, David C., and Westman, Robert S. (eds.) (1990). *Reappraisals of the Scientific Revolution*. New York: Cambridge University Press.

Mach, Ernst (1901). *The Science of Mechanics: A Critical and Historical Account of its Development* (T. J. McCormack trans.). Chicago: Open Court.

Mancosu, Paolo (1996). *Philosophy of Mathematics and Mathematical Practice in the Seventeenth Century*. New York: Oxford University Press.

Martin, R. Niall D. (1991). *Pierre Duhem: Philosophy and History in the Work of a Believing Physicist*. La Salle, IL: Open Court.

Neurath, Marie, and Cohen, Robert S. (eds.) (1974). *Empiricism and Sociology*. Dordrecht: Reidel.

Norton, John (1991). Thought experiments in Einstein's work. In T. Horowitz and G. J. Massey (eds.), *Thought Experiments in Science and Philosophy*. Savage, MD: Rowman and Littlefield

Nowak, Gregory (1989). Riemann's *Habilitationsvortrag* and the synthetic *a priori* status of geometry. In D. E. Rowe and J. McCleary (eds.), *The History of Modern Mathematics, Vol. 1: Ideas and Their Reception*. Boston, MA: Academic Press.

Pap, Arthur (1946). *The a priori in Physical Theory*. New York: King's Crown.

Picard, Émile (1901). Introduction générale. In *Exposition universelle internationale de 1900 à Paris: Rapport du jury international*. Paris: Imprimerie Nationale.

Poincaré, Henri (1889). La Logique et l'intuition dans la science mathématique et dans l'enseignement. *L'Enseignment mathématique*, 1, 157–62.

—— (1898). On the foundations of geometry. *Monist*, 9, 1–43.

—— (1902a). Du Role de l'intuition et de la logique en mathématique. *International Congress of Mathematicians, Proceedings*, 115–30.

—— (1902b). Les Fondements de la géométrie (essay review of Hilbert, 1899). *Bulletin des sciences mathématiques, 2e série*, 26, 249–72.

—— (1902c). Sur la valeur objective de la science. *Revue de métaphysique et de morale*, 10, 263–93.

—— (1904). *Rapport sur les travaux de M. Hilbert, professeur à l'Université de Goettingen, présentés au troisième concours du prix Lobatchefsky*. Kasan: Imperial University Press.

—— (1920) [1908]. *Science et méthode*. Paris: Flammarion.

—— (1982) [1913]. *The Foundations of Science: Science and Hypothesis, The Value of Science, Science and Method*. Lanham, MD: University Press of America.

Quine, Willard Van Orman (1953). Two dogmas of empiricism. In *From a Logical Point of View*. Cambridge, MA: Harvard University Press.

Reichenbach, Hans (1958). *Philosophy of Space and Time*. New York: Dover.

—— (1965). *The Theory of Relativity and a priori Knowledge*. Berkeley: University of California Press.

—— (1969). *Axiomatization of the Theory of Relativity* (M. Reichenbach trans.). Berkeley: University of California Press.

Renouvier, C. (1889). La Philosophie de la règle et du compas, ou des jugements synthétique à priori dans la géométrie élémentaire. *La Critique philosophique* (n.s.), 5 (2), 337–48.

—— (1892). La Philosophie de la règle et du compas, théorie logique du jugement dans ses applications aux idées géométrique et à la méthode des géomètres. *L'Année philosophique*, 2 (deuxième année 1891), 1–66.

Richardson, Alan (1997). Two dogmas about logical empiricism: Carnap and Quine on logic, epistemology, and empiricism. *Philosophical Topics*, 25 (2), 145–68.

Schlick, Moritz (1920). *Space and Time in Contemporary Physics: An Introduction to the Theory of Relativity and Gravitation.* New York: Oxford University Press.

Sober, Elliott (1999). Mathematics and indispensability. *Philosophical Review,* 102 (1), 35–57.

—— (2000). Quine's two dogmas. *Proceedings of the Aristotelian Society,* suppl. vol. 74, 237–80.

Sorensen, Roy A. (1992). *Thought Experiments.* New York: Oxford University Press.

Stein, Howard (1990). On Locke, "the Great Huygenius, and the incomparable Mr. Newton." In R. I. G. Hughes (ed.), *Philosophical Perspectives on Newtonian Science.* Cambridge, MA: MIT Press.

—— (1992). Was Carnap entirely wrong, after all? *Synthese,* 93, 275–95.

Stöltzner, Michael (2003). The principle of least action as the logical empiricist's shibboleth. *Studies in History and Philosophy of Science Part B: Studies in History and Philosophy of Modern Physics,* 34, 285–318.

Stump, David (2003). Defending conventions as functional *a priori* knowledge. *Philosophy of Science,* 70 (5), 1149–60.

Toulmin, Stephen (1961). *Foresight and Understanding: An Enquiry into the Aims of Science.* Bloomington: Indiana University Press.

—— (1982). *The Return to Cosmology.* Berkeley: University of California Press.

23

Rational Decision Making: Descriptive, Prescriptive, or Explanatory?

JONATHAN MICHAEL KAPLAN

Introduction: Rational Decisions as an Ideal

To what extent is human behavior best thought of as emerging from "rational" decisions? Our answer to this question will obviously depend upon (1) our view of rationality and rational behavior – what, for example, we take to be exemplars of rational behavior – as well as (2) our view of decisions – what, for example, we take to constitute making a decision. In this chapter, the focus will be on a very specific view of the rationality of decision making, that given by rational choice theory (RCT). Here, agents are rational (roughly) if they act to maximize their expected payoffs, given their preferences and beliefs about the world. This description is ambiguous between two related positions: first, that agents are rational if their decisions are made in the way that RCT recommends (agents use, perhaps unconsciously, a formal system like RCT to make their decisions), and second, that agents are rational if the decisions they make *agree* with those that RCT *would* recommend (however they come to those decisions). A related question is to what extent the kinds of assumptions and technical reasoning used in RCT are generally applicable to the kinds of decisions people face – that is, even if people don't make rational decisions in the sense just described, would they be better off if they did? Is our failure to act in accordance with the recommendations of RCT a weakness (albeit perhaps an unavoidable weakness) on our part? The first question is about the *descriptive* strength of RCT as a model of human behavior more generally; the second question is about the *prescriptive* strength of RCT as a guide to human behavior.

Here, I argue that RCT provides neither a strong model of human behavior nor a valuable guide to how we should act. It is, in other words, neither a descriptively useful nor normatively valuable guide to much of our lives. There are, I argue, large and important areas of our lives that are not appropriately modeled by RCT (nor *a fortiori* by economic rationality or other traditional decision theoretic tools), and where the expansion of these systems of description and explanation of our actions should be actively resisted: neither the *descriptive* element of RCT nor the *prescriptive* elements should be accepted in these areas. In many of these arenas, I will suggest, our actions have, on the face of it, nothing to do with decisions at all, let alone "rational" decisions of the sort described by these models. For this reason, I will suggest that even the use of the apparatus and language of decision theory and economic models of rationality to *explain* our actions in these areas of our lives is inappropriate.

The argument presented here has several distinct but related threads. Perhaps least controversially, I argue that the methodological practices and ontological assumptions of those programs that attempt to make most aspects of (at least voluntary) human behavior out to be the result of rational decisions are respectively of questionable value and implausible – we have good evidence that at least many of the key assumptions are false in practice. But even if this weren't the case, I argue that the expansion of the decision theoretic/economic rationality paradigm to describe broad areas of our lives blurs distinctions about the different ways we have of dealing with different aspects of our lives (different sorts of problems, questions, etc.) that ought to remain distinct; this encourages us to misrepresent important differences as insignificant, and can result in important details about the way we live our lives being hidden from us. The paradigm further implies that we retain a sort of control over our lives that, at least in many of the areas I wish to focus on, is at best improbable. This is problematic insofar as the expansion of the paradigm into these areas might cause us to view our own (and other people's) successes and failures as emerging from personal choices and powers in a way that is unrealistic and therefore unfair (and therefore likely to lead to morally problematic reasoning and actions). In some areas, indeed, the expansion should be resisted because it is grossly offensive – the description of us making decisions in a decision theoretic way makes us out to be the sort of people we shouldn't want to be. If taken too seriously, it may in fact result in us becoming the sorts of people we don't (or shouldn't) want to become (Frank, Gilovich, and Regan 1993, 1996).

Rational Decision Making?

In many cases, the idea that we are making decisions, and that we aim for these decisions to be rational, seems obvious to us. We often think of particular kinds of events in our lives as forcing us to make decisions; generally, these are times when there is a break in the continuity of our lives, when, for example, we graduate from school, lose a job, get divorced, meet someone new, etc. In these kinds of cases, where because of a break in continuity a decision is thrust upon us, there is a tradition of actively worrying over these sorts of decisions – making an active attempt to find the right decision.

The reason we actively worry in these kinds of cases seems fairly straightforward: we live in a culture that assumes that individuals have the power to make decisions that control their lives, and hence that the basic shape of most people's lives (how successful they are, for example) is the result of the decisions they make. This can be seen clearly in the huge numbers of self-help books that are perennially on the lists of bestsellers in the US, for example, and more seriously in discussions surrounding welfare "reform" in the US (see also Sen 1997: 750ff.). The idea that people's lives are controlled primarily by the decisions they make as individuals has a very long history in the US (see, for example, Tocqueville 1990, 2: sect. 2, "Individualism") and, more recently, such views on individual responsibility have been explicitly defended by writers such as Herrnstein (Wilson and Herrnstein 1985; Herrnstein and Murray 1994) and Posner (1981, 1992; Philipson and Posner 1993).

426

Given the assumption that it is the major decisions in our lives that form the basic shape of our lives, we are lead rather naturally to worrying about getting those major decisions "right" (Davis and Douglas 1976; Meichenbaum et al. 1989). Examples of such major decisions would for many people include, at various points in their lives, such things as choosing schools, changing jobs, major purchases such as houses and cars, moving long distances, and the like. In order to ensure we get these kinds of decisions right, the tradition has it, we should spend time mulling over them, weighing the various options, talking with friends or other informed sources (e.g., job counselors, therapists) about them, perhaps even going so far as to make physical lists of the pros and cons (see Kumboltz and Vosvick 1996 on career choice).

Given the active consideration of several different choices, and the concern over what possibilities each different choice might engender, the move towards more formal methods of dealing with these decisions is an obvious one. Decision theory, for example, provides a formal framework for thinking through decisions, and is supposed to aid in making "high quality" decisions. So, for example, particular kinds of possible outcomes can be ranked according to how much they are valued (or disvalued), and probabilities can be assigned to particular outcomes given particular courses of action (decisions). One can draw decision trees (see panel 23.1) to represent the decision, and there are computer programs that are supposed to make some aspects of the process automatic (quick web-searchers reveal literally hundreds of such programs commercially available).

What I've described so far is the process of moving from the belief that where there is the chance to do well and the chance to do poorly in the world, it is our decisions which drive this difference, coupled with the obvious concern about making "good" rather than "poor" decisions, towards some fairly well-defined system the aim of which is to aid people in making "good" decisions – decisions that will tend, on average, to result in those outcomes considered "good." In part, this move is supposed to be descriptive of what we actually do, and in part this move is supposed to be a normative claim about the way we should act if we wish to achieve certain sorts of results in our lives.

---

1 A Decision Tree

Take as an example a student who has a major exam in the morning that they wish to pass, but has been invited out for a night drinking. Thinking about the possible outcomes, the student realizes that there are only four kinds of outcomes that matter to them, and that they can rank these easily. They would most prefer to go drinking *and* to pass the exam. They would, however, rather pass the exam than go drinking, but they would rather go drinking and fail the exam than stay home and study but fail anyway. They believe, however, that staying home and studying for the exam will increase their chances of passing the exam.

After some thought, they come to believe that the difference in value to them between passing the exam and drinking, and passing the exam and studying, is much smaller than the difference between *failing* the exam and drinking *or* failing the exam and studying. And they come to believe that the difference between failing

427

the exam and drinking and failing the exam and studying is about as small as the difference between passing the exam and studying and failing the exam and studying. After more reflection, they come to the following consistent assignment of values:

Passing and drinking: 100 utils
Passing and studying: 80 utils
Failing and drinking: 20 utils
Failing and studying: 0 utils

And, after some thought, they come to believe that if they study their chances of passing the exam would be excellent (about 90 percent), whereas if they go out drinking their chances of passing would be much lower (about 50 percent). Given this, their decision can be represented by the following decision tree:

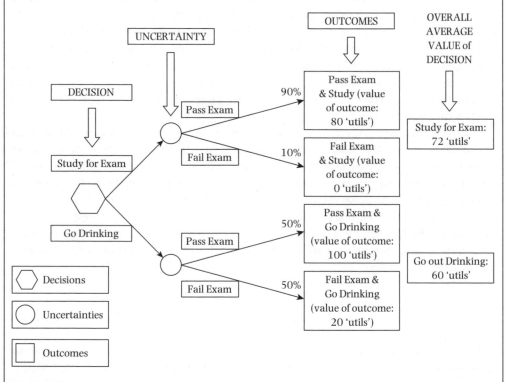

Figure 23.1

Given this, the correct decision is obvious. Consider, however, what would happen if the student in question was less confident of the probabilities that they would pass the exam, and/or less confident of their preference rankings. Finding out to what extent the "correct" decision is sensitive to changes in the probability estimates or the preference rankings is referred to as performing a "sensitivity analysis." Such an analysis would reveal that the above "correct" decision is sensitive to relatively small changes in either or both.

Part of the appeal of RCT, then, is its relationship to preexisting concerns about those kinds of decisions that many people already actively worry about. The temptation to see our decision-making process in these cases as "rational" and as aiming (successfully?) at making "high quality" decisions that will tend towards "good" outcomes is part of our desire to see ourselves as in control of the major aspects of our lives. But, of course, it isn't only the major aspects of our lives we think of ourselves as in control of, and some authors have claimed that RCT (and the related formal/mathematical structures) apply equally well to *all* the decisions that we make. Increasingly broad arenas are seen as analyzable in terms of formal decision theoretic reasoning, both in terms of the description of the behaviors and in the normative claim that the "best" behaviors would follow the recommendations arising out of the formalized process (Posner 1981, 1992; Philipson and Posner 1993; Becker 1981, 1996; Becker and Becker 1997; Holtzman and Kornman 1992; Patrick and Erickson 1993). Note that this approach is also that taken by most basic (micro) economic texts (e.g., Mansfield 1975; Asimakopulos 1978; Peterson 1980; Varian 1993).

But is every decision best analyzed in terms of RCT? And what counts as a decision in this context? Many (micro) economists construe what counts as a decision in this context quite broadly – on this view, everything from our buying our morning cup of coffee, to how we spend an afternoon, to whom we marry, is a decision undertaken in an attempt to maximize the satisfaction of our preferences; that is, a decision made out of rational self-interest. Here, any (broadly voluntary) action is assumed to be the result of our acting to satisfy our preferences given our beliefs about the world – hence, our actions are all the result of our making decisions the aim of which is to forward our rational self-interest, and RCT, it is argued, is the best model. But, of course, it is obvious that we don't make lists, call friends for advice, assign numbers, or run sophisticated computer programs every time we buy coffee, choose an ice-cream flavor, lie in the sun with a book, or accept a dinner invitation.

This would seem a major blow for the descriptive side of the theory, at least. Of course, supporters of RCT as an unifying account of human behavior have an answer to the problem – these are still decisions that we make, but, in general, we do the calculations roughly and more or less unconsciously in the vast majority of the cases where those things we are "deciding" upon aren't very significant or where the "decisions" are "obvious" and we've thought of them before. In part, the issue is one of marginal returns; there is a cost to spending time and energy thinking about decisions (assigning numbers, working through calculations, etc.), and the possible gains in most minor decisions we face are too small to warrant sophisticated decision-making techniques, where their use would be more costly than the likely gains they might make possible. In the case of significant but "obvious" decisions, we act rationally, but do so in a way that we don't notice *as* rational. Philipson and Posner write:

"Rational choice" in economic analysis need not be conscious, deliberative, cool, or informed . . . When the obtaining or absorbing of information is costly, an uninformed choice . . . may still be expected-utility-maximizing . . . And while many choices are habitual rather than deliberated, they may have become habitual *because* they are such obviously good choices. (Philipson and Posner 1993: 8)

429

But what this decision theoretic view of human behavior must defend is the thesis that our "decisions" (which can, on this reading, include habitual actions), even in the most trivial cases, approximate to some degree or other both to the processes of the paradigmatic technical cases, and the sorts of results/ranking those techniques would result in were they used. While, in most cases, the "decisions" are relatively unimportant or totally obvious, and the processes are done wholly unconsciously (and the calculations are correspondingly rough), the theory claims that if we are to achieve any sort of success in our lives at all (if we are to engage in any successful means–ends reasoning and actions), somewhere in our heads must lurk the shadow of the sophisticated processes. In short, the descriptive side demands that decision-making processes be "in our heads" somewhere. Normatively, the quality of the decisions we make is given by the results we would have obtained had we gone through the process (good decisions are *like* those we *would* have obtained had we done the work, bad decisions are *unlike* them).

This can be seen quite clearly in microeconomics textbook discussions of consumer choice. So, for example, Peterson, after a discussion of the concept of marginal utility in consumer choice in his *Principles of Economics*, writes:

> Your reaction to the preceding discussion on marginal utility is likely to be, at best, one of incomplete acceptance. Certainly, you might argue, no one takes the time to think of the utils he obtains from consuming an item, much less writing them down and dividing by price. You are right . . . Rather the main value of marginal utility is to give you a framework for thinking about your purchases . . . In fact, most wise shoppers are already using the idea of marginal utility without realizing it. (Peterson 1980: 21)

According to Peterson, descriptively, the actions of "most wise shoppers" are really explained by the theory of consumer choice; normatively, if you want to get the most out of life (both the best value for your money, and the wisest use of your time and other resources), your actions *should* be in line with (and therefore explained by) the predictions of the model (Peterson 1980: 3).

The decision theoretic view of human behavior (often expressly associated with economic rationality) takes the *consistency* of human behavior with the decision theoretic interpretation as good evidence that people's decisions reflect the decision process they describe, consciously or unconsciously. Posner, again, is quite explicit about this: where economic analysis is "illuminating" we are, he argues, justified in the assumption that people are acting "rationality" (see Posner 1981: 2; Philipson and Posner 1993: 6–7). When is such an analysis illuminating? When we are able to explain the observed behaviors by reference to such an analysis; in other words, when an analysis can be made that is consistent with observed behaviors. For all the talk of predictive ability, the limitations of microeconomic theory to deal rigorously with "consumer" preferences (e.g., see Sen 1977) severely limits the expected accuracy of any predictive abilities; "retrodiction" is generally the best that can be hoped for. The problem here is that in order to predict the behavior of individual consumers we would need to know all their relevant preferences and beliefs about the world. But it is very difficult to discover these preferences and beliefs about the world, or to test empirically those beliefs and preferences that the individuals in question have "revealed" through their previous actions (e.g., Tversky and Kahneman 1974, 1981; Kahneman, Slovic, and Tversky 1982; see also Sen 1997, esp. 747ff. and n.5). The upshot is that while it is usually possible to understand people as acting more or less in accord with what would be expected given the assumption that their actions were motivated by rational self-interest if we assign to them the appropriate set of preferences and beliefs, the only way we can discover the appropriate set of preferences and beliefs *just is* to assume that their actions are so motivated.

Thus the result we are left with is that our actions in the world can be understood on these models as the result of our making rational decisions to act in certain ways – decisions that aim to maximize our expected outcomes. Even where these decisions are not made in any obviously deeply reflective way (indeed, even when we do not notice them as decisions at all), our behavior can be understood in such a way that the unconscious decisions and decision-making processes are strongly *equivalent* to the decisions and the process we would have used *had* we made the decision in a self-reflective way. Insofar as the actions we take are not equivalent to those that RCT would suggest as the "best" decisions, we are, on this view, acting irrationally.

Assumptions and Difficulties: Preferences, Outcome Spaces, and Probabilities in the World

The question of how fair this description of our decision making is to our actual practices in the world is usually passed over in near-silence. In the next section, I will suggest that alternative accounts of human behavior that do not focus on our attempting to make "rational decisions" in order to satisfy preexisting preferences can provide a far more satisfying (if less unified) account of many of the kinds of actions we take in the world. But before exploring alternative accounts of human behavior, it is worth pausing to summarize some of the assumptions and the difficulties with these assumptions regarding people's preferences and beliefs that are built into RCT, and indeed, into the view that most human actions are best viewed as the result of decisions that aim at particular kinds of outcomes.

The most obvious assumptions are those relating to preferences. For RCT to apply, it must be assumed that we have preferences for particular kinds of outcomes, and that our preferences for these different outcomes are commensurable and well ordered (see panel 2). That is, given any set of possible outcomes, we have to be able to *rank* the desirability of these outcomes in a consistent way. The claim that our preferences can be ranked in this way – that in fact our actions reveal preferences that are already ranked in this way – is often taken to be uncontroversial.

These assumptions are at their clearest in basic microeconomic texts; while the examples tend to be put in terms of consumer behavior, keep in mind that in these contexts "consumer behavior" is interpreted quite broadly and encompasses more or less all voluntary actions. In the introduction of *A Course in Microeconomic Theory* (1990), Krebs states the "actor chooses from some specified set of options, selecting the option that maximizes some objective function," that is, that "consumers have *preferences* that are represented by a *utility function*, and they choose in a way that maximizes their utility subject to a *budget constraint*" (Krebs 1990: 4, emphasis in original).

431

2 The Assumptions of RCT

RCT assumes that our preferences for outcomes obey the following conditions:

1 Ordering axiom

Preferences for outcomes exist and are transitive, that is:

For any two possible outcomes A and B, either A is preferred to B, or B is preferred to A, or A and B are equally preferred. Further, for any three outcomes A, B, and C, if A is preferred to B, and B is preferred to C, then A is preferred to C.

2 Independence axiom

Preferences for a risky prospect are independent of whether it has one stage or two, that is:

if L_1 is:

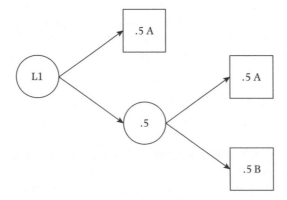

Figure 23.2

and L_2 is:

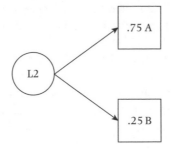

Figure 23.3

Then $L_1 = L_2$

3 Standard gamble

There is a continuity of preferences, such that for any three outcomes A, B, and C, such that A is preferred to B, and B is preferred to C, there exists a likelihood n such that the agent is neutral between a certainty of outcome B and the gamble of a n chance of A versus a $(1 - n)$ chance of C.

432

That is, there is some *n* such that agent is neutral between the choice represented in the following decision tree:

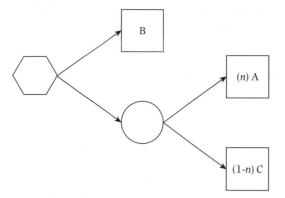

Figure 23.4

Also, given the use of notions of probability in this formulation, these notions must be interpreted as obeying at least the first four axioms of probability theory. There follows a set theoretic approach to these, with an interpretation.

If we define:

P(x): Probability function on x
S: outcome space – a set of mutually exclusive and exhaustive outcomes
F: a field of subsets of S
P (A | B): probability of A given that B
P (A $\cup$ B): probability of A *or* B
(A $\wedge$ B): intersection of the fields A and B

Then:

1. $1 \geq P(A) \geq 0$ for all A in S
Each outcome considered in the outcome space has probability of between zero and certainty.

2. $P(S) = 1$
There are no possible outcomes that are not part of the outcome space.

3. $P(A \cup B) = P(A) + P(B)$ if $(A \wedge B) = 0$
The probability of one of two outcomes occurring is equal to the sum of the probability of each of their occurrences, *if* the probability of *both* occurring is zero.

4. $P (A | B) = P (A \wedge B) / P(B)$, where $P(B) \neq 0$
The probability of A's occurring given that B occurs is equal to the probability of their both occurring, divided by the probability of B's occurrence, where the probability of B's occurring is not equal to zero.

Unless individual preferences for outcomes obey the above assumptions and the axioms of probability, RCT cannot guarantee the availability of a decision (or set of decisions) that maximizes the average preference satisfaction. That is, unless the above are satisfied, the person in question will lack a set of consistent preferences that can be used in the attempt to maximize the satisfaction of those preferences.

Krebs goes on to note that while consumers may not think in these terms, the models presuppose "that consumers act *as if* this is what they do" and that this leads to "*testable restrictions* of the models" used, in that some behaviors, if observed, would be inconsistent with the models; those models that "are not falsified by our observations" are "good positive models" (Krebs 1990: 4). Although Krebs is in fact somewhat skeptical about the robustness of these traditional models, he explicitly notes the way in which treating actions as if they revealed consistent underlying preferences can then permit the determination of preferences that are consistent with observed behaviors, at least in the short term (Krebs 1990: 42ff.). Asimakopulos, summarizing a chapter on consumer behavior, writes that in the analysis presented, the consumer

> was assumed to be rational and to act on the basis of tastes that . . . change only slowly over time . . . The consumer was assumed to be very knowledgeable about the technical characteristics of the goods he was purchasing. The utility he expected to get from these goods was in fact what he obtained from them. (Asimakopulos 1978: 133)

After noting that this leaves out many problems that a realistic analysis might have to account for, Asimakopulos notes "the predictions obtained from such a theory do seem to have general applicability" (Asimakopulos 1978: 133). Again, consistency between observed behaviors (changes in purchasing patterns, etc.) and the model that treats people as consumers making decisions in order to maximize their expected outcome is taken to be good evidence that the model is descriptively and explanatorily useful.

Blight and Shafto note that consumers are rational in the "very limited sense" that they "will seek to maximize utility" and that therefore the assumption is that they will apportion their resources "between competing economic goods in such a way that the highest possible level of utility is achieved" (Blight and Shafto 1989: 63, 64). While they note that consumers fail to maximize their possible enjoyment of any *particular* good, this is to be explained by the constraint of their not having unlimited resources (Blight and Shafto 1989: 63).

Varian explicitly defines utility as a description of preferences that are revealed through "choice behavior" (Varian 1993: 54–5), and argues that consumer preferences "are stable over the time period" through which we are likely to observe them making choices (Varian 1993: 118). Further, Varian claims consumer behavior can be best explained by attempts to "maximize utility"; where consumers are failing to maximize some particular resources used as a proxy for "utility" it is likely, Varian suggests, that the proxy is simply inadequate in this case. For example, if individuals in some case are failing to maximize their expected returns in a risky investment, they perhaps have different preferences for risk-taking behavior, and so they can be seen as in fact maximizing their overall utility (which is a function of the expected monetary return on the investment and the thrill or lack thereof they get from the risk) (Varian 1993: ch. 12).

But this view of preferences is problematic, and indeed, it is not shared even among all decision analysts. Holtzman, a decision analyst of the so-called "Stanford school," argues it is common for preferences to be actively created during decisions; on this view, part of what makes some decisions hard for us is that we lack coherent preferences.

In Holtzman's view, this argues for an approach to decision analysis which recognizes that the decision-making process will be "creative" and ought to aim at generating "insight" rather than "answers" (Holtzman and Kornman 1992: 848–9). In cases where we are *not* engaged in a decision analysis undertaken to deal with a difficult decision, however, there is no reason to assume that these lacks in our preferences will be *felt*; we could live our whole lives and never form certain kinds of preferences at all. To develop an example from Holtzman and Kornman (1992), most of us are fortunate enough that we do not have to choose between teeth that are relatively easy to care for but not particularly attractive by Western standards, and teeth that are harder to care for but relatively attractive; and, not having had to make that choice nor even having had to think about it, it is likely that most of us do not have any well-formed preferences between these options. Even in places where we have *some* preferences, there may yet not be any coherent or consistent preferences. But unless something occurs that forces us to try to organize our preferences, we would have a hard time finding this out. That is, if there comes a time when we are faced with a particular set of options, we can form preferences, but the assumption that these preferences preexisted our having to make the choice and were simply waiting to be *discovered* is unfounded. Indeed, it is worth noting that even if we assume that such preferences exist, uncovering and interpreting them in ways that make them out to be reasonably consistent is difficult at best (see Froberg and Kane 1989a–d on the difficulties with determining preferences with respect to medical conditions; in the general case the challenge seems more – rather than less – severe).

Even if we grant that preferences exist independently of the decisions they are involved in, the assumption that these preferences will be stable over reasonably long periods of time should strike us as a poor one. Froberg and Kane (1989b) cite research which suggests that people's preferences for particular health-states often change fairly radically in relatively short periods of time; there is no reason to think that this problem is unique to medical contexts. It seems obvious that part of the cause of these changes in our preferences are the very decisions that we make – when decisions change the situations we find ourselves in, our preferences will tend to change in response to these new situations. But, of course, these changes are not predictable, nor modelable, on any decision theoretic model. Perhaps psychology would be a better place to look, but then, psychology's *predictive* ability is not generally considered impressive, either.

A closely related problem involves not our ability to generate consistent preference rankings, but rather our ability to "properly" partition the outcome space – that is, our ability to figure out what might follow from our decisions, and which of the possible outcomes are relevantly similar to each other and which are relevantly different. In some situations, this isn't a problem at all, largely because the situations have been actively created to avoid that problem – most games of chance are of this sort. So when we play roulette, the relevant outcomes *vis-à-vis* our decisions are clear: if we bet on "black," say, the relevant outcomes are that the ball lands on a black number, or it lands in play but not on a black number, or, very rarely, the ball fails to land in play (e.g., it leaves the table or otherwise fails to land properly). No other outcomes matter – unless, that is, we are playing at a table with either a "Surrender" or "En Prison" rule, in which case the ball landing on 0′ or 00′ has different consequences for us than

435

its landing on red. Similarly, if we bet on a particular number, the relevant outcomes are that the ball lands on that number, or that it lands in play but on some other number, or (very rarely) that it fails to land in play. But it doesn't matter, for example, what the orientation of the ball is when it lands (indeed, roulette balls tend to be made so that the orientation is wholly cryptic), or how the ball spun (or failed to spin) on its own axis while rolling around the table. Assuming we wish to win, then, the relevant partitions of the possible outcome space as well as our preferences between these possible outcomes are clear – if, say, we bet on black, if the ball lands in play on a black number, that is our preferred outcome, and the orientation of the ball, its spin, etc., are all irrelevant.

However, if rational decision making is to explain our actions in everyday situations, then we must be able to partition the outcome space into appropriately similar and dissimilar outcomes more generally. But what, for example, are the appropriately similar and dissimilar possible outcomes when we are deciding whether or not to invite an attractive person out for a cup of coffee – simply their accepting or refusing? Or their accepting and our enjoying it or not? Or our having a future with them or not? Or . . . ? We *might* consider any one of these distinctions relevant, or any of a huge number of other possibilities. After all, while, when we invited them out for coffee we might have been thinking that we might be interested in having sex with them at some point, whether our eventually having sex with them is a preferred outcome will depend critically on any number of factors we likely haven't yet considered: are they married and hiding the fact? Are they reasonably emotionally healthy? Are their preferences *vis-à-vis* relationships like our own? And so on.

If we really wish to make *rational* decisions in the decision theoretic sense, in cases like this we must be able to partition the possible outcomes into classes of relevantly similar outcomes given our preferences. Indeed, if we wish to use the tools of RCT, the need to maintain mathematical tractability in decision theoretic reasoning demands that the outcomes considered be of (at most) several different sorts (see Skyrms 1990 and references therein). But certainly our ways of interacting with the world are very complex, and superficially similar situations can have quite different meanings for us. Any attempt, then, to create a well-defined outcome space will force us to group various sorts of outcomes together; there is, though, in general, no way of telling what outcomes will mean the same thing to us, and so no way to tell in advance *which* outcomes can be sensibly grouped together. That is to say, there is no telling which groupings will hide differences, and which perhaps create non-existent ones.

Again, this problem doesn't emerge in those situations that were explicitly created around probabilities, such as games of chance. In these cases, which outcomes can be grouped together (that is, which differences make a difference) are obvious – as in the roulette case, it is built into the situation, just because *we* built it there. But in the more general case of actions taken in the course of our daily lives, what the possible outcomes are, and which matter to us and why, will not be so clear.

Similarly, in the case of roulette, we can assign reasonable probabilities to the partitions in the outcome space, and given enough time, even test the reliability of the probabilities we've assigned. This, it should be fairly obvious, is not the case in our hypothetical coffee date. What, in this case, is the probability that we will have a happy long-term relationship with this person if we ask them out for coffee? What is the probability that we'll have a relatively satisfying "fling" with them that ends well? Recall that in order to use the techniques of RCT to make the "right" decision, or for RCT to *explain* our behavior in terms of rational decisions (however these are in fact made), we must not only be able to partition the outcome space into relevantly similar outcomes given our preferences, but we also have to be able to assign probabilities to each of those sets of outcomes (see panel 2). It seems clear that this task will be, at best, very difficult and the results correspondingly unreliable in the general case.

None of this should be taken as claiming that we don't sometimes talk as if general events in our lives are more or less likely – obviously, we do. But it would be a mistake to take this sort of talk for a well-defined claim about the state of the world. Most of our actions do not involve outcomes determined by, for example, fair coins, and to think that the sort of "clean" probabilities engendered by our *creation* of game-theoretic situations (gambling, etc.) already preexist in the sorts of complex situations we find ourselves in general is nothing more than a prejudice for a modelable world (on the creation of probability and the situations that make sense of them, see Hacking 1975).

These problems are not primarily epistemological in nature. That is, these problems do not emerge from our just not knowing enough about what kinds of things might happen or our just having not thought hard enough about what kinds of outcomes we would prefer. Rather, the idea that preexisting our making a decision, there exists a well-defined outcome space, within which exists our reactions to various different sorts of outcomes, relies on a view of the world's ontology that is, at the very least, questionable. Dupré, for example, has argued persuasively that nature is basically *disunified*; attacking the notion of a preexisting well-defined outcome space that can be assigned preexisting, well-defined probabilities is an obvious application of his general thesis regarding the disunified nature of causation and the lack of causal completeness in the world (Dupré 1993: esp. chs. 8, 9). That is, there is no good reason to think that there are well-defined possible outcomes and associated probabilities that exist independently of our actual actions in the world.

Even if we reject the strong ontological claim suggested above, the basic problem remains. Insofar as different kinds of outcomes can engender different ways of dealing with the world (again, often in unpredictable ways), how do we consider the relevant outcome space may *change* based on what actually happens? Even if, in some sense, the "outcome space" (the possible outcomes) does not change, what outcomes we consider relevantly similar or dissimilar can obviously change, and hence our partition of the outcome space will not in general be stable through either the "decisions" we are making or through events in our lives more generally. If nothing else, our interpretation of the outcome space and the partitions of it is going to be subject to such things as framing biases, and our assignment of probabilities will be subject to such problems as people's general insensitivity to the predictability (or lack thereof) of features of the world (both of these difficulties are noted by Tversky and Kahneman 1974, among others).

The upshot of this is that the application of RCT to broad areas of our lives, either as a descriptive account of how we actually make decisions or as a normative account of how we ought to make decisions, demands that we accept a number of assumptions. Aside from the more obvious assumptions about the existence, stability, and consistency of our preferences (see panel 2), RCT makes assumptions about the relationship between our actions and outcomes in the world, about the probabilities that attach to outcomes given actions on our parts, and about our ability to properly partition the outcome space and assign probabilities to the relevant partitions. None of these assumptions is particularly well justified, and their implausibility should be reason enough to be suspicious of the claim that RCT is a good model of human behavior in general. In the next section, the plausibility of the *goals* of RCT will be challenged – even if the above difficulties with the assumptions necessary for RCT to work are addressed, there are still good reasons to suspect that a rational account of human behavior of the sort RCT attempts to provide would be less valuable than has sometimes been implied.

Before moving on, however, it is worth noting that the assumptions necessary for RCT to gain traction have been criticized even with respect to *traditional* market behavior, such as the decisions undertaken by those people in stock markets, currency markets, or commodities markets. While it is sometimes assumed that any irrational acts taken by individual actors in such markets will tend to cancel each other out, this assumption has not proved to be empirically well founded, and RCT and economic rationality fail to provide good predictive or descriptive models even in traditional market arenas. Thaler's recent work acknowledges these sorts of difficulties, and calls for microeconomic analyses in traditional market arenas (e.g., stock market and commodities market behavior) to take explicit account of the fact that people act in ways which are not fully rational and hence not fully captured by models that assume rational decision making (Thaler 2000 and references therein). In his programmatic "From Homo Economicus to Homo Sapiens," Thaler argues for taking proper account of a number of different kinds of confounding factors in microeconomic modeling, including the sorts of biases to which Tversky et al. have drawn attention (see Kahneman, Slovic, and Tversky 1982; Bell, Raiffa, and Tversky 1988), the recognition that not all economic actors will act in their rational best interests, the recognition that human cognition is complex and that these complexities need to be taken account of in any theory which attempts to model human behavior, and the recognition that "emotional" reasons for acting can be powerful but hard to model using theories that assume agents to be motivated by rational self-interest. Thaler argues that some of this work has in fact already been done, and that some of the better models of stock market behavior, for example, take account of at least some of the factors these difficulties point towards (Thaler 2000: 136). By testing particular hypotheses about why agents perform the actions they actually perform, including hypotheses that make at least some of the agents out to be performing actions that are in some deep sense non-rational from the perspective of economic rationality, Thaler argues that one can sometimes determine the actual "mix" of rational and non-rational actors, and the ways in which the non-rational actors actually make decisions, and from there begin to develop more reasonable (and hence more predictively accurate) models of economic (and more general) behavior.

Tellingly, Thaler claims that the reason economic models could not begin to include such information until recently is that economists lacked both the conceptual and empirical tools for incorporating such complex information into their models, and indeed for *determining* the empirical results themselves (Thaler 2000: 140). Advances over the last few decades, Thaler suggests, have made it possible to build models of human behavior which use empirically grounded assessments of the actual reasons that particular agents perform particular actions, albeit with great difficulty. Part of the difficulty, Thaler argues, is the incorporation of the empirical results into the models, but part of it remains simply determining those results (Thaler 2000: 140). As we will see below, however difficult it is to model *economic* behavior by assuming that our reasons are all of one type and that they in fact guide our actions, the situation for the case of more general behavior is much worse.

Reasons without Decisions

Holtzman, arguing for the Stanford school of decision analysis, claims the goal of any decision analysis should be to generate "the insight necessary for action" on the part of the person making the decision (Holtzman and Kornman 1992). For Holtzman, a good decision analysis helps the agent decide what to do in part by forcing the agent to reconsider what they want to get out of the situation they find themselves in. This might mean actively creating preferences that didn't exist before, reevaluating what one wants in life, what kind of person one wants to be, and what sorts of things one thinks one ought to want (see Sen 1977). The kinds of decision analyses that Holtzman recommends, therefore, do not resemble solving a preexisting problem (uncovering preexisting preferences for and assigning probabilities to various possible outcomes) but, rather, involve the co-creation of the problem to be solved and its solution by cycling through multiple iterations of the decision process until the agent making the decision is "comfortable" with taking a particular course of action. That is, rather than trying to find some preexisting "right" answer, Holtzman argues that a decision analysis should attempt to make decision makers comfortable enough with a particular view of their situation and related decision to *act*, that is, to irrevocably commit resources to a particular course of action. Traditional decision analyses often fail to generate the insight that makes this commitment possible, Holtzman argues, because without the creative aspects of the appraisal cycle (where the decision maker critiques the models developed by the decision analyst based on the decision maker's inputs) "most of the inconsistencies and lack of initial focus that made the decision difficult in the first place" will remain represented in the decision analysis (Holtzman and Kornman 1992: 848).

Notice, however, that this approach to decision analysis is at odds with the traditional understanding of rational decision making, and it cannot (even in principle) be considered a good *descriptive* model for our everyday actions. This approach to decisions can *only* be normative, and it is normative in a different sense than are traditional understandings of rational decision making. There is not, in Holtzman's approach, a uniquely best decision for the agent to make – different ways of going through the decision process will tend to produce different understandings of the situation the agents find themselves in and hence can result in their developing different preferences and desires, and committing to different courses of action.

Where this approach is descriptively relevant to our everyday actions is not in explaining why we perform certain actions rather than others, but rather to the explanations we give for the actions that we perform. One of the major goals of Holtzman's approach is to make the decision maker *confident* in the action they take; this confidence emerges because they have found, in the decision-making process, what they come to see as good reasons for taking one course of action rather than another. This view hints at another way of thinking about reasons for acting more generally: the reasons we give to ourselves and others are not primarily causal explanations for why we acted – they are not about *deciding* what to do. Rather, the reasons we give for our actions are more often about having confidence in what we have done. That is, insofar as we are forced to have arguments (to give reasons) for why we do or did one thing rather than another (and, of course, most of the time we don't have to), these arguments are meant to *justify* why we do what we do, both publicly and to ourselves.

So, at least for much of the time, our reasons for acting are meant to be justificatory rather than action guiding. Our "reasons" for the "decision" we make, whether contemplated in advance of the decision or after the fact, are meant to help us wrap our actions in a narrative that will make sense of our lives to ourselves and to others around us. A closely related phenomenon, the search for good *ex post rationalizations*, is well known (but under-analyzed) in economics; for example, there is evidence that the vast majority of people who closely scrutinize advertisements have recently already *purchased* the item in question. The best explanation for this is that these people are searching for reasons to support the decision that they have already made (Varoufakis 1998 110). Reasons for acting, then, are often primarily *inventions* meant to lend support for actions we've already taken, and are emphatically not any sort of deep grounding for the way we will live our lives, for those actions our lives are made of.

On the view that I am suggesting here, it is our actions in the world themselves that are primary, and our reflections and discourse about them should often be thought of more as ways of rationalizing and explaining them than as ways of actually "making decisions." On this interpretation, for the most part, what we do is not the result of some internal decision-making processes which mirror (more or less accurately) some technical decision theoretic reasoning, but rather the result of (and, simultaneously, the reason for) our being enmeshed in rich, complex social lives.

We do not, in other words, unconsciously or otherwise, go through any formalizable decision process when we choose ice-cream flavors, accept dinner invitations, or look for a parking space. Even if we sometimes get into (rather silly) arguments about "the best" flavor of ice-cream or whether we ought to have asked someone out on a date, the reasons we give in these arguments likely have little or nothing to do with traditional concepts of rational decision making (or instrumental rationality), and indeed, may not have had much – if anything – to do with why (in a causal sense) we ordered that ice-cream flavor or proposed that date.

But what of those cases where we do actively deliberate before taking actions? In most cases where there are clear alternatives facing us, and where we have some reason to think that our preferences are well established, the "correct" action given our preferences tends to either be trivially obvious or entirely opaque. This point is made forcefully by Brockway:

> Difficult decisions usually are difficult because they are close, and close decisions tend to be close because there is not much to choose among the alternative possibilities. In such situations, it doesn't make much difference which way the ball bounces. Really important

decisions, on the other hand, decisions that do make a difference, are often blindingly obvious. (Brockway 1992: 89)

While Brockway was criticizing high CEO salaries, his point is more generally applicable. Where good reasons can be given for many different courses of actions, often any of these courses of action will be defensible; while which action one takes might "matter" in some sense, that sense may not be one in which maximizing the satisfaction of preferences plays a role. After all, since good decisions can have bad outcomes, and bad decisions good outcomes, judging the quality of the decision from the outcome is difficult at best, and a poor outcome does not automatically lead to considering the decision poor. In choosing, for example, between various "good" (but different) jobs, which job one takes may well "matter" in some sense, but the choice of any of them could be defended *whatever* ends up happening. Rational choice theory will be unhelpful in illuminating *either* the "blindingly obvious" sorts of decisions *or* those that are close – in the first case because the "decisions" need no illumination and in the latter case because the theory could be used to support (and hence to explain) any of a number of decisions – the supposed "illumination" in this case is entirely illusionary. (Note that in panel 1, changing the assumptions about the probabilities of passing the exams by as little as 10 percent can result in the "best" decision changing.)

This points towards a general problem for the view of human action as guided primarily by rational decisions (decisions undertaken to maximize the satisfaction of preferences). Many of the problems with the assumptions necessary for RCT to apply don't apply in the case of gambling, where, it was noted, we decided which outcomes mattered and which didn't, and where probabilities can be calculated in fairly straightforward ways. And indeed, in the case of gambling with the intent of winning, game theory is of course a nearly ideal tool. But even here we should remember that most people who gamble *don't* gamble to win (very few people, for example, restrict themselves to playing blackjack carefully and counting cards). Often, when we gamble, while we hope to win, we in fact fully expect to lose – and this is a reasonable expectation. It is worth recalling here Wittgenstein's comment to Pattisson regarding roulette: after staring at the roulette table in thought for some minutes, Wittgenstein is reported to have blurted: "I don't see how you can win!" (quoted in Monk 1990: 360). Indeed, roulette *is* structured so that there is no winning strategy available to the players. Of course, there is an account for our playing roulette despite there being no winning strategy that is *consistent* with our decision to gamble being the result of a rational calculation – such apparently "irrational" gambling behavior can be explained in terms of economic rationality by claiming that the "fun" of gambling outweighs the cost (Skousen and Taylor 1997: 44). On this view, using the technical apparatus of game theory to try to "beat the house" (which would involve avoiding roulette) would actually have too high a cost (in terms of utility) for most people. A *similar* calculation to the too technical and boring one we would use if we were tying to beat the house explains why we gamble in terms of the fun of gambling outweighing the likely cost in money. While this story is consistent with the observed behavior, it should be clear that the consistency is of a particularly easy to achieve sort, and shouldn't count for much.

If reasons for acting are more often about justifying particular courses of action rather than deciding on them, the ability of RCT and decision theoretic approaches to

441

human behavior to find stories *consistent* with our actions is unsurprising, as is the failure of these approaches to make reasonably powerful predictions – that is, to generate meaningful (and testable) restrictions on human behavior. If the assumptions required for RCT to be generally applicable actually applied, and the facts assumed to exist (e.g., preference rankings for sets of outcomes, etc.) could be accurately determined, then of course RCT could be used to generate such predictions. But, as we have seen, the assumptions are difficult to justify, and even if the facts assumed to exist did in fact exist, they are difficult (if not impossible) to accurately determine in practice. Indeed, as we have seen, some approaches to decision analysis admit these failures, and embrace the decision analysis process not as a way of *discovering* what we ought to do given our preferences and beliefs about the world, but rather as a way of *inventing* those preferences and beliefs and hence our being able to *justify* a particular course of action (to ourselves and others). This strikes me as not only a reasonable approach to formal decision analysis, but also the only reasonable approach to understanding the kinds of informal "decisions" such programs as RCT attribute to us.

What Kinds of Reasons? The Failure of RCT as a Unifying Principle

RCT, then, does not provide a *causal* account of our actions, nor is an account of actions in terms of their consistency with RCT *explanatory* in any robust sense. However, our ability to come up with *reasons* for our actions – both after the fact and before we take those actions – suggests another view of the relationship between RCT and our actions, namely that RCT can be seen as descriptive of the *kind* of reasons for our actions that we should find compelling. On this view, the consistency of RCT with our actions is not the issue – as we have seen, it is trivially easy to come up with an account of our actions that is consistent with RCT. Rather, it is the *reasons* that we give for acting that must be compatible with RCT if our actions are rational; our account of why we acted ought to be, on this view, an account in terms of our actions following from a rational decision.

As suggested above, it seems likely that most of the reasons we give for our actions are not explanatory in a causal sense, but rather provide satisfying accounts of our behavior; they provide, in other words, a narrative structure to what we have done and what we are going to do. If we think of the stories we tell about our reasons for individual actions as *first order* narratives (narratives about actions), then we can think of the view of RCT suggested above as providing a *metanarrative* – a narrative account of the narrative accounts of why we acted. That is, RCT provides us with a story about why we ought to give particular kinds of reasons rather than others. Being "rational" on this view is about being able to give reasons for our actions that are compatible with RCT.

At this point, the temptation of RCT as a unifying principle should be clear: RCT provides us with a simple end-point to any question about why we did something – that is, that we decided to do it based on some sort of (perhaps entirely unconscious) decision-theoretic game-theory oriented approach to achieving some ends or other. All of our actions, on this view, can be explained in the same way, and our successes and failures in the world are made out to follow from our decisions in a straightforward way. When we fail, we can blame poor luck (an unlikely probability actually came up, as they are wont to do on occasion), poor judgment (we thought some possibility was unlikely, whereas it was actually nearly certain; we thought some outcome would make us happy, whereas actually we find there are unexpected aspects of it we hate), hasty decisions, etc. Our successes and failures emerge from the same kinds of reasons, and we can tell the same kinds of stories about them both.

Before criticizing this view of RCT, it is worth reiterating what it is not. On the view being considered here, RCT does not provide a *causal* account of human behavior – we should not expect to find that people actually go through some process that is like decision theoretic reasoning when making decisions. On this view of RCT, the key assumptions are not supposed to be true in any grand ontological sense; rather, it is the assumptions about our ability to tell stories that make those assumptions out to be true. So, for example, the assumption that our preferences are consistent is not an assumption about the independent existence of discoverable consistent preferences; rather, it is simply to say that we can assume that if we work hard enough, we can tell a story about a set of consistent preferences that will make sense of the actions we have taken or are going to take. So, on this view, RCT ought not even to attempt to provide *predictive* ability. Rather, RCT is simply a view about what kind of reasons we ought to give (what kind of narratives we ought to tell) for the actions we undertake in our lives.

Even this rather weak form of RCT is deeply problematic. Many authors have suggested that the attempt to explain all of human behavior, even all of human "economic" behavior, through the single lens of utility-maximizing rational decision making, is doomed to failure – not because stories consistent with RCT can't be told, but because such stories are inadequate to account for the complex nature of our lives. That is, the attempt to use RCT as a metanarrative will fail not because it is impossible to tell first-order narratives that are consistent with RCT, but because using *only* stories of that sort will be unsatisfying. Our lives are too complex, and our reasons of too many different sorts, for stories in terms of rational decision making to work (be satisfying) all the time. (For one of the classic statements of this objection, see Sen (1977); Varoufakis (1998) provides more recent articulations of such objections.)

Sen, for example, argues that social commitments and moral imperatives cannot be successfully reduced to a single utility function, nor can conventional rule following (Sen 1997: 748; see also Sen 1999: 76–7; 1977). Further, these are all *different* kinds of reasons and cases, and cannot be reduced to each other, nor to a more "fundamental" desire or reason. A person with "no use for these distinctions between quite different concepts . . . must be a bit of a fool" (Sen 1977: 102), no matter how successful they are at local utility maximization, or, for that matter, telling stories about their behavior in terms of utility maximization. Sen's later work suggests that a theory which attempts to make every individual action out to have the same causal structure (rational deliberation, either conscious or unconscious) or overall end (utility maximization) should, likewise, seem a bit foolish (Sen 1997, 1999). What the underlying causal pathways are that result in particular kinds of behaviors seems, on Sen's analysis, to be an empirical matter, albeit one that is difficult to determine

443

satisfactorily given contemporary empirical and conceptual tools (Sen 1999: 261–81; 1997: 748–50).

What we *can* say, however, is that human actions do not occur in a void. Our lives are filled with constraints upon the choices we make, and even constraints upon what areas of our lives are subject to rational deliberation at all (Sen 1997: esp. 747–51). Sometimes we may find ourselves in positions where the only options we can accept, for one reason or another, fail to be utility maximizing (Sen 1997; 1999: 261–81). While we might be able to tell a story consistent with RCT in these kinds of cases, doing so will *hide* from us our "real" reasons for acting, and fail to help us determine them. Again, it would be foolish (or insane) to claim that we *never* make decisions to act with particular aims in mind, or that *none* of our habitual actions were originally undertaken because they are useful to us in one way or another. But our ability to undertake "utility-maximizing" actions in the world is so constrained by our need to live at least marginally coherent lives within rich and complex social systems that the latter represents a far more important and interesting place to look for explanations of our behavior than the former (Sen 1999: 8–10, 199–203, 263–81). And these explanations will not, obviously, be of any one kind, or indeed, any few kinds. Rather, they are likely to be at least as diverse as the explanations we use to explain our actions in everyday life (few of which, of course, involve explicit references to utility maximization). Of course, as Sen (1977) notes, we cannot use stories that are consistent with RCT to provide us with insight into what kind of people we want to be – what we want to desire and what we want to be committed to.

As noted above, Thaler (2000) has argued that it is impossible to generate good predictive or even descriptive accounts of simple market behavior if we assume there is only one kind of reason – the kind given by RCT – for the actions of agents in traditional markets. Rather, if we are to have any hope of generating theories that will permit some prediction (or even reasonable explanatory accounts) of market behavior, we will have to take account of those kinds of reasons that are incompatible with making our actions in the world out to be compatible with RCT. Again, while stories consistent with RCT can always be told, many of these stories will be, in some important sense, *false* – they will be poor analyses of why we did certain things, and will hence fail to provide insight into why we act.

The Failures of RCT and Rethinking Rationality

So far, then, we have seen that theories that make our actions out to be the result of decisions that we have undertaken given particular kinds of ends we wish to achieve fail descriptively because for the most part we do not in fact make decisions to act in that way, as we fail to have the requisite kinds of preexisting preferences. Normatively, such theories fail to describe the way we *should* act for much the same kinds of reasons – our preferences and reasons are not of the right sort for RCT to apply. Nor can such theories provide an adequate account of the kinds of *stories* about our reasons for acting that we tell (descriptively) or ought to tell (normatively) because our reasons for acting (even in traditional market situations, but especially more broadly) are of too many different sorts. These are serious failures, and they ought to make us rethink not only the literal application of RCT to most of the actions in our lives, but also our reliance on more metaphorical talk about our making decisions and our having particular kinds of reasons for actions in these cases.

If we accept the description of our behavior that makes it out to be heavily constrained by social expectations, daily practices, and the need to maintain a coherency with other parts of our lives, it is clear that we don't in fact make as many decisions as the RCT paradigm would imply. While Peterson (1980: 3), for example, writes that "managing just a modest income for a family requires thousands of economics decisions each year," this seems both to understate the number of the decisions RCT attributes to us (why not a decision for every product we purchase or fail to purchase? Or more?) and overstate the frequency of (self-conscious, action-guiding) economic decision making we really engage in. This kind of analysis of our making decisions that guide our actions towards desired outcomes should be viewed with deep suspicion in all but the most rare and specific of instances (gambling to make money, dealing with certain sorts of commodities narrowly understood, etc.). The use of these stories about economic rationality and utility maximization to give those actions in the world that make up the majority of our lives any sort of overarching order, while perhaps tempting, in the end presents us with a task both hopeless and offensive. Most of the actions in the world that we care about cannot be accounted for by these theories, and the merest attempt to do so with those actions in the world involving the people we most care about should strike us as distasteful in the extreme. We neither treat the people we care about from a perspective which would allow the use of such systems, nor should we (for similar criticisms in the context of moral reasoning, see Walker 1997; Addelson 1994; Held 1987). There are times (e.g., when we are dealing with friends, lovers, etc.) when answering some question about why we did something with something as simple and blunt as "because that person is my friend" should simply end the line of questioning, where our ideas of friendship and love should be thought of as prior to any decision theoretic narratives we could tell, let alone might be tempted to tell (cf. Sen 1997: 759ff.).

It might be thought that this rejection of the stories involving decisions would leave something of a void. For, in one natural way of talking, we do indeed *choose* which flavor of ice-cream to buy, which movie to see and with whom, and the like. But the fact that we talk this way says nothing at all about the way that the putative "choices" are made, and to think that they are made by some sort of deep consideration of the alternatives reads far too much into our language and our actions. If the language of choice is read as a description of what we do, including our ways of talking about our plans and pasts, rather than what we think (rather, that is, than as something in the head), the void of course vanishes, for we obviously continue to do much the same things but under, perhaps, a slightly different description.

More importantly, though, perhaps what is missing can be replaced with other narratives that make better sense of our experience. We are not, after all, in the sort of control of our lives that the economic paradigms imply. To greater or lesser extents, our lives are not of our own making in the sense that they would have to be for the sorts of issues regarding decisions and answers demanded by economic theory to matter (see MacIntyre1997: 213). This realized, it should be obvious that most of what we do, we do for reasons that are in part social, in part idiosyncratic, but in any event have nothing much to do with our considered judgments of hypothetical probabilities and mythical alternatives (and a good thing too, given how *bad* our estimates of probabilities and ways of considering alternatives turn out to be in practice). While there are no doubt some kinds of "reasons" (historical reasons, reasons related to the relationship of these to other actions, social reasons about going along with things, etc.) why these actions rather than others are undertaken, they will not be *rational* in any meaningful way. Any sort of rationalization (any kind of "rational reconstruction") meant to account for these sorts of actions will be hopeless (for a similar critique in the context of anthropology, see Wittgenstein 1979).

Now, this sort of view might be thought to be too forgiving of people who make "bad decisions," whose lives are not going as they (or any sane person) would wish. And indeed, by not acknowledging as wide or as important an arena for decisions, by radically narrowing the scope of actions that are to be thought of as amenable to discussion in decision-theoretic terms, this view demands that most of our actions in our lives be thought of in terms less blameworthy (or for that matter, praiseworthy) from a decision theoretic perspective. But, of course, in rejecting the decision theoretic paradigm, we reject the notion that it is the only story available to assign blame and praise, and indeed, we deny that narratives of blame and praise should, in general, even be of that form. If you think that it is often the case that actions are primary and that reasons are after-the-fact stories, you are going to be less impressed with reasons for actions in any event, and your language of condemnation is not going to be limited to those that involve reasoning. The ability to tell narratives of blame (and praise) would not be lost, but (some of) the narratives we tell would perhaps be changed, and fewer would be converted into a form amenable to discussion in terms of decision theoretic or economic models.

More importantly, though, giving up the idea that our actions in the world are driven by decisions we make in order to attempt to satisfy our preferences will change what we view as sensible ways of attempting to modify or influence people's actions and behaviors on the social level. Abandoning those models of human behavior, one is also forced to reject the view that the way to affect actions in the world is to influence the decisions made about what to do, and that the way to do this is to manipulate the information the decisions are made under. That is, one cannot successfully influence action by changing some hypothetical "payoff matrix" if no such thing exists, if nothing like that is guiding action in the first place. Simply making certain kinds of actions unattractive is unlikely to change outcomes if the actions already were unattractive, but were undertaken without the kind of "deep" consideration of alternatives that would have made other kinds of actions live possibilities.

Indeed, the "systems" approach to understanding and preventing industrial accidents, for example, is successful because – rather than primarily attaching blame and punishment to mistakes (changing the "payoff matrix") – it attempts to prevent certain kinds of situations from arising (Petersen 1996). That is, the systems approach to accident prevention attempts to make certain kinds of actions undoable (or very difficult to perform) rather than unattractive. While directly applying the lessons of the systems approach to error management in industrial contexts to moral issues (and especially to social and political issues) may be unpalatable in the extreme, perhaps some aspects of the basic idea can be usefully pushed into these arenas. For example, it seems likely that programs aimed at "reforming" welfare by creating punitive situations for actions society disapproves of (having additional children, not actively looking for work, etc.) are unlikely to succeed, at least if they are not combined with approaches that aim to change patterns of behavior more directly (e.g., by encouraging the creation of certain sorts of social networks rather than others).

Even worse, systems that worked by simply changing the "payoff matrix" would be morally problematic even if they did succeed in changing people's actions. That is, even if such programs succeeded, their success would demand treating people from a perspective we should reject, and their success would point towards the creation of a class of people that think in a way that makes them unlikely to be good members of society. As Frank's work implies, learning to think in terms of economic rationality and rational choice theory creates disincentives towards socially responsible behavior (it creates people that tend to be less cooperative, more selfish, etc.) (Frank, Gilovich, and Regan 1993, 1996). It would therefore be unfortunate if an attempt to fix one social problem relied on creating people who thought in ways that made them unlikely to be good members of society more generally.

Fortunately, as we have seen, narratives that are compatible with decision theoretic reasoning or models of economic rationality are not the only sort we can tell, either as individuals or as a culture. We have not lost the ability to talk about other sorts of reasons for actions, to create and tell stories that don't involve our conscious or unconscious plottings regarding decision theoretic considerations (Rorty 1982; Nussbaum 1990). If we accept a pluralistic view of our actions in the world and the kinds of explanations that might best make sense of them, we must accept that different sorts of answers will be required for explaining these different sorts of actions. Insofar as there are reasons for what we do at all (and often there are not), these reasons are wildly varied, of very different sorts entirely. And there is no more reason to think that there is a single kind of explanation for these explanations than that our different actions will require the same sort of explanation. There is, in other words, no one kind of reason, no single strategy, that could explain all of what we do.

Does this mean we are irrational? If we accept the view of rationality given by RCT, then of course, accepting that most of what we do is compatible with RCT only in the most anemic of ways implies that much of what we do we do not do for "rational" reasons, and that most of our actions are therefore not rational. But, of course, if being rational is primarily about having reasons *of an appropriate* kind for the actions we take – being able to defend those actions to ourselves and others – then our failure to act according to RCT both descriptively and normatively is no more a failure to be rational than is our failure to *always* act out of love or friendship or anger or any other human motivation. How rational we are depends not on whether we have succeeded in maximizing the satisfaction of our preferences given the state of the world, but rather on a much more complex set of holistic and partially social judgments. These would include judgments not only about how we've tried to achieve what we want and how successful we've been at satisfying our desires, but also (*pace* Hume) how well we can defend our desires themselves and how coherent our lives are, all given the particular social constraints we find ourselves acting within.

This kind of rationality will likely be impossible to define precisely, nor will it always be clear whether, on this kind of view of rationality, someone is rational or not. And of course, on this view, what counts as rational behavior (what counts as being rational) will no doubt shift and change with the particular social milieu. But that is exactly the kind of complexity we must learn to embrace if our explorations of the reasons for human actions, and what it means to be a rational person, are to be fruitful.

References and Further Reading

Addelson, K. P. (1994). *Moral Passages: Toward a Collectivist Moral Theory.* New York: Routledge.

Asimakopulos, A. (1978). *An Introduction to Economic Theory: Microeconomics.* New York: Oxford University Press.

Baier, A. C. (1995). *Moral Prejudices: Essays on Ethics.* Cambridge, MA: Harvard University Press.

Becker, G. S. (1981). *A Treatise on the Family.* Cambridge, MA: Harvard University Press.

—— (1996). *Accounting for Tastes.* Cambridge, MA: Harvard University Press.

Becker, G. S., and Becker, G. N. (1997). *The Economics of Life.* Boston, MA: McGraw-Hill.

Bell, D. E., Raiffa, H., and Tversky, A. (1988). *Decision Making.* Cambridge: Cambridge University Press.

Blight, D., and Shafto, T. (1989). *Microeconomics.* London: Hutchinson.

Brockway, G. P. (1992). *The End of Economic Man.* New York: W. W. Norton.

Davis, R. B., and Douglas, J. (1976). Environment, habit, self-concept, and approach pathology. *Journal of Children's Mathematical Behavior,* summer, supplement 1, 229–65.

Dupré, J. (1993). *The Disorder of Things.* Cambridge, MA: Harvard University Press.

Frank, R. H., Gilovich, T. D., and Regan, D. T. (1993). Does studying economics inhibit cooperation? *Journal of Economic Perspectives,* 7 (2), 159–71.

—— (1996). Do economists make bad citizens? *Journal of Economic Perspectives,* 10 (1), 187–92.

Froberg, D. G., and Kane, K. L. (1989a). Methodology for measuring health-state preferences – I: Measurement strategies. *Journal of Clinical Epidemiology,* 42, 345–54.

—— (1989b). Methodology for measuring health-state preferences – II: Scaling methods. *Journal of Clinical Epidemiology,* 42, 459–71.

—— (1989c). Methodology for measuring health-state preferences – III: Population and context effects. *Journal of Clinical Epidemiology,* 42, 585–92.

—— (1989d). Methodology for measuring health-state preferences – IV: Progress and a research agenda. *Journal of Clinical Epidemiology,* 42, 675–85.

Hacking, I. (1975). *The Emergence of Probability.* Cambridge: Cambridge University Press.

Held, V. (1987). Non-contractual society: A feminist view. In M. Hanen and K. Nielsen (eds.), *Science, Morality and Feminist Theory.* Calgary: University of Calgary Press.

Herrnstein, R. J., and Murray, C. (1994). *The Bell Curve.* New York: Free Press.

Holtzman, S., and Kornman, K. S. (1992). Decision analysis for periodontal therapy. *Journal of Dental Education,* 56 (12), 844–62.

Kahneman, D., Slovic, P., and Tversky, A. (1982). *Judgment Under Uncertainty: Heuristics and Biases.* Cambridge: Cambridge University Press.

Krebs, D. M. (1990). *A Course in Microeconomic Theory.* Princeton, NJ: Princeton University Press.

Kumboltz, J. D., and Vosvick, M. A. (1996). Career assessment and the Career Beliefs Inventory. *Journal of Career Assessment,* 4 (4), 345–61.

MacIntyre, A. (1997). *After Virtue: A Study in Moral Theory,* 2nd edn. Notre Dame, IN: University of Notre Dame Press.

Mansfield, E. (1975). *Microeconomics: Theory and Applications.* New York: W. W. Norton.

Meichenbaum, D., et al. (1989). *Exploring Choices: The Psychology of Adjustment*. Glenview, IL: Scott, Foresman.

Monk, R. (1990). *Ludwig Wittgenstein: The Duty of Genius*. New York: Penguin Books.

Nussbaum, M. C. (1990). *Love's Knowledge*. New York: Oxford University Press.

Patrick, D. L., and Erickson, P. (1993). *Health Status and Health Policy*. New York: Oxford University Press.

Petersen, D. (1996). *Human Error Reduction and Safety Management*, 3rd edn. New York: Van Nostrand Reinhold.

Peterson, W. L. (1980). *Principles of Economics: Micro*. Homewood, IL: Richard D. Irwin.

Philipson, T. J., and Posner, R. A. (1993). *Private Choices and Public Health*. Cambridge, MA: Harvard University Press.

Posner, R. A. (1981). *The Economics of Justice*. Cambridge, MA: Harvard University Press.

—— (1992). *Sex and Reason*. Cambridge, MA: Harvard University Press.

Rorty, R. (1982). *Consequences of Pragmatism*. Minneapolis: University of Minnesota Press.

Sen, A. K. (1977). Rational fools: A critique of the behavioural foundations of economic theory. *Philosophy and Public Affairs*, 6 (4), 317–44. Reprinted in Hahn and Hollis (eds.), *Philosophy and Economic Theory*. Oxford: Oxford University Press.

—— (1997). Maximization and the act of choice. *Econometrica*, 65 (4), 745–79.

—— (1999). *Development as Freedom*. New York: Alfred A. Knopf.

Shafir, E., and Tversky, A. (1992). Thinking through uncertainty: Nonconsequential reasoning and choice. *Cognitive Psychology*, 449–74.

Skousen, M., and Taylor, K. C. (1997). *Puzzles and Paradoxes in Economics*. Brookfield, CT: Edward Elgar.

Skyrms, B. (1990). *The Dynamics of Rational Deliberation*. Cambridge, MA: Harvard University Press.

Thaler, R. H. (2000). From homo economicus to homo sapiens. *Journal of Economic Perspectives*, 14 (1), 133–41.

Tocqueville, A. (1990) [1835, 1840]. *Democracy in America*, 2 vols. (H. Reeve, F. Bowen, and L. Walther, eds.). New York: Vintage.

Tversky, A., and Kahneman, D. (1974). Judgement under uncertainty: Heuristics and biases. *Science*, 185, 1124–31.

—— (1981). The framing of decisions and the psychology of choice. *Science*, 211, 453–8.

Varian, H. R. (1993). *Intermediate Microeconomics: A Modern Approach*, 3rd edn. New York: W. W. Norton.

Varoufakis, Y. (1998). *Foundations of Economics: A Beginner's Companion*. New York: Routledge.

Walker, M. U. (1997). *Moral Understandings: A Feminist Study in Ethics*. New York: Routledge.

Wilson, J. Q., and Herrnstein, R. J. (1985). *Crime and Human Nature*. New York: Simon and Schuster.

Wittgenstein, L. (1979). *Remarks on Frazer's Golden Bough*. Atlantic Highlands, NJ: Humanities Press International.

24

What is a Feminist to do with Rational Choice?

MARIAM THALOS

Around me bags of skin are draped over chairs, and stuffed into pieces of cloth; they shift and protrude in unexpected ways ... two dark spots near the top of them swivel restlessly back and forth. A hole beneath the spots fills with food and from it comes a stream of noises. (Gopnik and Meltzoff 1997: 31)

Introduction

Plato and Descartes, each in his own way, bequeathed to us a certain two-edged legacy: a methodology of withdrawal from all the influences of an unpredictable world of purportedly deceptive and corrupting *appearances*, in pursuit of *first principles* for every major intellectual and moral enterprise. Now familiar under the label of rationalism, this methodology commends a swift retreat to the safe haven of Reason, as the only worthy shore and soil for all that is reliable, good, and worthy of affirmation. Reason in this tradition is conceived, not as an aspect of physical or embodied functioning – a facet of so-called cognition, whose exploits include the processing of numerous varieties of sensory stimuli. It is conceived, rather, in terms that contrast with such functioning. In this tradition, Reason is a realm unto itself, a realm of both inquiry and value. Rationalism treats the world of experience as a realm of bondage, where one is subject to forces one can neither know straightforwardly nor control; starkly contrasting with the life of the mind as a realm of freedom, wherein everything is transparently known and where the human being – and being human – really comes into its own. The rationalist therefore diagnoses a tension between what we see and experience, on the one hand, and on the other hand what things – including ourselves – really are, fundamentally, in a truer realm. Furthermore, the rationalist bids us, like the prophets, retreat from the world of superficial appearances, nevermore to return to that unworthy place out of which Reason calls us. The true human realm is a *transcendental* realm. To the rationalist, consequently, theories of human agency and moral behavior in terms of principles of reason and reasoning are quite natural, because to the rationalist there is nothing more central to being human than founding action upon Reason.

To be sure, appeals to Reason for purposes of moral or political theory are attractive: this route keeps us having to appeal to authorities, especially divine authorities, for moral and political imperatives. From the beginning, Western moral philosophy has appealed to a deliberative human nature as grounding the dictates of morality. Reason, as the refrain goes, calls us out of a "state of nature" into a state of civilization. Reason, acting among us, is the agent that transforms our formerly grisly lives, famously "nasty, brutish and short" and tantamount to a condition of war of all against all. Hobbes and Locke, no more and no less than the scores of our own contemporaries wearing contractarian badges, appealed to the transformative powers of reason (and more recently also discourse).

Some feminist moral philosophers have recently joined the ranks of those who appreciate the force of these appeals for the purposes of moral and political philosophy. Some feminists – for example, Jean Hampton (1993) – are attracted to contractarian approaches. Other feminists (see, for example, a number of papers in Brennan 2002) extract philosophical resources from certain rationalist, and specifically Kantian, frameworks – resources that enable them to articulate feminist criticisms of contemporary culture; we thus have our rationalist heritage to thank for the concepts of objectification and commodification. And yet other feminists (perhaps most prominently, Martha Nussbaum) appeal to conceptions of human capacities rooted in Reason to secure an account of human flourishing for the sake of feminist goals. "I take it to be feminism's position," writes Louise Antony, "that women under patriarchy are systematically *dehumanized* – treated in ways that prevent or impede the full development of the *human* capacities" (Antony 1998: 85).

The "realms of Reason" approach to "matters distinctively human" springs out of a conception of philosophical inquiry – or at any rate the *philosophical* part of philosophical inquiry – as an armchair business (*a priori*, in technical jargon) concerned with topics to which there is no routine scientific access. This conception of philosophy owes us an account of why the methodology has any validity. The answer typically ready to hand is that philosophy deals with concepts and first principles, and that there is no other form of direct access to these things. The trouble with this rationale is, of course, that it is difficult to support in light of controversies that swirl – with good reasons – around issues of articulating just what concepts and first principles are, how they originate, and how they make contact with objects and realities that antecede them. The concepts and guiding principles in play at any given time and place stand *de facto* in important relations to the culture that cultivates and maintains them. Furthermore it is no small matter to justify the directions taken by a theoretical enterprise that purports to deal in a proprietary fashion with certain special concepts and principles of guidance, against a background of common knowledge of the checkered history that certain of those concepts (e.g., reason and human nature) have enjoyed, how certain factions have fought over control of them, and how they have played a role in social and intellectual history.

The retreat to reason therefore faces the problem of having to justify the use of the instruments (concepts, rules of argumentation, and principles of guidance) that reason respects and puts into motion. When it comes out – as eventually it does – that the social arrangements to which we have in this vale of tears become acculturated, and that subsequently appear natural to us, are to some extent arbitrary, because they are home-grown (or, as they now say, *constructed*) – indeed, negotiated through power struggles that could have turned out differently – it is often also contended that not only social arrangements, but also concepts, principles of guidance, and strategies of argumentation are the result of power struggles: those referring to persons of differ-ent genders, races, sexual orientations, and classes, to name just some of the most controversial.[1] And so, continues the thought, these things appear appropriate in the exercise of reason, when they do, simply because they maintain existing social arrangements. And therefore, when we – on the outside – judge existing power arrangements undesirable, we ought to retreat to another realm – a realm of escape from these things, a realm where freedom and equality are possible. But retreat whither? And what resources shall we find there? Can reason itself, as such, shorn of tainted concepts and principles – and which ones are not? – be a site of genuine refuge? Is not the language and discourse of reason too closely associated with the corridors of power? And so what could the "realm of freedom" be for a liberationist seeking escape from routine exercises of power, and specifically for the feminist who despises disenfran-chisement of women on grounds that they purportedly fail the test of Reason?

Two related strategies have been tried. The first retains the transcendental concep-tion of Reason as withdrawal to a separate sphere, but enlarges the community of the reason-capable: membership in the club of those who exercise Reason becomes inclu-sive of women, mothers, the underclasses, aboriginals, and non-Europeans of every sort. The society of scholars who advance this strategy is centered upon Harvard: John Rawls, Robert Nozick, and Christine Korsgaard. The difficulties with articulation of this strategy lie in the production of criteria for demarcating between reasoners and non-reasoners – for there are obvious difficulties in extending membership to humans formerly excepted from full enjoyment of a deliberative nature: children, immatures, and individuals lacking or deviating from normal cognition (not to mention ailing relatives) are not obviously full-fledged members of the Reason club. There can be no transcendental analysis of the qualifying physical markers or phenotypical manifesta-tions of reasoners: armchair analysis cannot separate between them on the ground. And there is also the question of how to make sense of the idea that there are duties that reason-capable entities owe to those that are not.

The second strategy seeks to naturalize or reform the notion of reason, so that it refers to embodied cognition. The phenomenologists are perhaps best known for this style of analysis (see chapter 19). Mainstream philosophers who draw upon this strat-egy are Michael Bratman and John Doris. While this is a commendable strategy, its champions continue to adhere largely to aprioristic methods of analysis for much of their treatment. In particular, they rely upon aprioristic methodologies for answering such questions as: "What is practical reasoning good for?" "How are practical reason-ing and moral reasoning related?" Champions of this strategy therefore continue to adhere to the conception of philosophy as a kind of service industry to transcendental philosophy, but still operating out of the armchair. Thus the strategy is shorn of its natural roots – roots that should reach into the soil of aposterioristic analysis.

A third strategy – and the one I shall be commending – insists that retreat from so-called "appearances" is unworthy and does a disservice to human life as we experience it. We must defeat the forces against which we struggle for liberation within the one and only arena of reality there is; for if this realm of tears is not worth fighting for, what's the point of joining the battle? Retreat is therefore unthinkable. So, just as reason, conceived in the bare and disembodied sense old-style rationalists insisted upon, is no foundation for a science of the contingent world that presents itself to our senses, neither can it serve as the foundation for an understanding of ourselves, as we truly and deeply are. We humans, in our fullest humanity, are palpable, and so knowable to ourselves and to one another in the realm of the palpable, without the aid of refugee camps. There are no places of retreat, but also no need for them. This is an empiricist credo. And to my mind it is the only one worthy of a liberationist.

The epigraph to this chapter is extracted from a contemporary rationalistic manifesto, circa 1997. Its authors are intimating that our knowledge of what is distinctively human – namely, human minds – cannot be channeled directly through our senses: ordinary perceptual categories are inappropriate for systematizing knowledge about minds and agent. And so, since children become competent reasoners about the mental, they must come by this knowledge some other way. The plain fact is that we never, ever, not in our wildest dreams, experience other people as the passage suggests. The description in this passage is *supposed* to strike us as preposterous. The authors' position is that we find the passage preposterous because we have a "theory of mind module" – essentially an organ, or sub-organ of our brains, that autonomously manages our affairs when it comes to dealing with minds. (Roughly, a module is a domain-specific, relatively autonomous piece of functional architecture, subject to a paced and distinctively arranged developmental sequence, and more susceptible to specific and characteristic forms of impairment.[2] A module simply develops in due time – *ex nihilo*, as it were; its functioning cannot be left up to a general learning process – for, as the argument goes, the contents and outputs cannot be secured through training upon multiple observations of the empirical world.)

But to my mind, the right explanation of the fact that we find the passage preposterous is that the so-called "realm of freedom" in which we experience other people as sources of behavior, as agents or sources of behavior rather than as patients only, is the world of experience itself, to which we are exquisitely attuned. All necessary cues signaling the fact that other organisms enjoy varieties of cognition are out there in the world. Minds are (among other things) tracking devices; tracking devices coordinate upon certain features of the world; and this reality – that minds track – is itself trackable by other tracking devices. And trainable upon this reality we are, provided we do not suffer cognitive deficits such as autism. The appropriate response to the rationalist contention that experience is impoverished, is therefore utter disbelief: "You've got to be kidding!" This is the empiricist manifesto, for which I shall not be mounting a full defense, but which I shall instead be applying. The proof of the pudding will be in the eating.

My plan in this chapter is as follows. I shall begin with a certain theory – specifically, rational choice theory – that purports to treat in a proprietary fashion with normative questions about how to proceed with making choices. The theory is founded upon axioms that have the status of first principles, although there are some disputations as to which of a variety of possible such axioms should be adopted. This arena of inquiry fails to overlap with arenas of philosophical inquiry on the subject of so-called "practical reason": there is very little interaction between investigators in the different spheres. I shall be asking the philosophical question of what a normative theory of decision – such as rational choice theory – is good for. This is a question rarely raised explicitly in philosophical terms, even among philosophers. The philosophical investigations in this chapter will focus on that question. The mode of inquiry is empiricist. The investigations will result in articulation of a distinctively empiricist conception of the practical enterprise and the role of intellection in it, and a proposal in answer to the question of what rational choice theory is good for. It will turn out that it has feminist uses.

Rational Choice

Rational choice theory (RCT) presents the appearance of being a framework within which to answer the question: What is the correct principle upon which to model one's practical decision making? The theory of expected utility (EU) is one such principle or model.[3] What the RCT framework does is make it possible to separate theoretical treatment of value (what is or should be sought, valued, or prioritized) from theoretical treatment of the means of realization of what is valued. And EU takes advantage of this opportunity for separation, to remain silent on the first question, while offering (in answer to the second) the familiar risk-weighted cost-benefit analysis. Here is how.

Suppose I have a choice between doing A and doing B. Suppose also that there are two possible states of nature r and s, which will affect the outcome of my chosen course of action in different ways. Suppose, finally, that between r and s I am unremediably uncertain as to which will occur. Then my choice between A and B is a choice between two packages of potential outcomes. Suppose that if r is the case and I do A, then $Q_{A,r}$ occurs; and that if r is the case and I do B, then $Q_{B,r}$ occurs; and so on. To choose between A and B, I shall be weighing up the merits and demerits of $Q_{A,r}$ and $Q_{A,s}$ taken as a certain package, against those of $Q_{B,r}$ and $Q_{B,s}$ taken as an alternative package. We can think of these packages as the prospects attaching to single actions. They are "vectors" of different possible outcomes, for example $<Q_{A,r}, Q_{A,s}>$ and $<Q_{B,r}, Q_{B,s}>$, and it is not known which of the potential "loci" of a given prospect will materialize if the prospect is chosen. The vectors span full rows in the "matrices" that constitute our decision problems.

(If it weren't for uncertainty, decision would presumably be much simpler. These simpler cases of decision require purely *instrumental* reasoning, we might say. In such cases we'd simply choose the prospect that offered the best outcome. But since a preponderance of our deliberations takes place under uncertainty, we require a framework for handling that uncertainty. Once this is in place, we can maintain the idea that instrumental reasoning now directs us to choose the best *prospect*. This directive instructs us to rank prospects as wholes. And arranging for such rankings is rather more theoretical work than arranging for a ranking of simple outcomes – the work of a theory of rational decision. One way of working this out is EU theory.)

The premise of such a theory as EU is that there is something deeper and more fundamental to mounting a choice than organizing, along a particular scale, a ranking of prospect wholes. In other words, that justification of any given choice must appeal to rankings of items that are themselves more fundamental to our preferences than packages of prospects. If there is to be sensible deliberation at all – deliberation over prospects that proceeds at least part way through reasoning and analysis, and not entirely viscerally – there must be a level of preferences ranging over a field of more fundamental commodities and more atomic goods, which justifies or at least explains our preferences for the outcomes, $Q_{A,r}$, $Q_{B,s}$ and so on, in which the goods are enjoyed, and which in turn justify or at least explain our ranking of prospect wholes. This idea is the true cornerstone on which modern decision theory is founded.[4] It is the doctrine that whatever is sought for its own sake must be located entirely in the outcome in which it is enjoyed, as a proprietary property of it.

But what exactly is something like EU seeking to model? What is the subject matter, or that domain of the universe, that it is attempting to mirror or cast some light upon? I think this is a critical question. The name of RCT reveals that it is engaged in modeling something entitled to the name of "*rational* choice." But what is that? Do we actually see it on the ground? And when we do – assuming of course we do – do we recognize it for what it is? And if so, how so? These are non-trivial questions. Answering them amounts to answering the question of what is RCT good for, and in a way that no one to my knowledge has done satisfyingly thus far.

One natural and familiar way with this question proposes that RCT is one of possibly many ways of giving some specificity to the idea that the name of "rational choice" signifies choice of the right means to your ends, as Bertrand Russell used to say; rational choice has nothing whatever to do with the choice of ends themselves. So RCT comes out as a purely instrumental conception of practical reason. RCT is engaged in modeling rational choice, when rational choice is deployed purely instrumentally – which is to say it is modeling proper exercise of reason in *pursuit* of ends, while exercising maximum restraint in criticizing the ends to which the instruments are put.

Conceived this way, RCT says that the "realm of freedom" is strictly a calculus (or, perhaps, a menu of calculi) for determining which, of a predefined set of prospects, best advances a predefined set of aims. Nowhere in it is there evaluation of ends. Naturally there will be feminist concerns with such a proposal. Indeed it is of some substantial (and especially feminist) concern that the discipline studying practical reasoning should *not* waive the right to participate in theoretical evaluation of *all* the ingredients that go into producing action. If it turns out that the discipline that studies practical reasoning cannot engage in criticizing ends at all, then where *will* we find a discipline that engages in criticizing ends on practical grounds?

RCT's straightforwardly computational way of conceptualizing practical reasoning – and instrumental reasoning generally – has certain failings. True, its aspirations are low, and so it has come in for some commendation by those who do not wish to venture too far into the realm of Reason, with a capital R. It has thus been seen as something of an empiricist halfway house. But once we appreciate the fact that an individual's choice of ends is shaped in many hundreds and thousands of ways by their special circumstances, their local upbringing, and their society more broadly, it becomes more and more clear that leaving those matters outside the so-called realm of freedom leaves out too much. It would therefore appear that once we venture, even ever so slightly, into the realm of criticism, we end up having to venture much farther than modesty would dictate.

It might therefore seem to someone (as perhaps it did to Hume) that there can be no criticism of someone's ends on practical grounds – that one has to occupy higher ground (*moral* ground) from which subsequently to criticize such things. This would seem to be a good reason to adopt the rationalists' distinction between a realm of

455

bondage and a realm of freedom, and subsequently to divide (as Kant did) the realm of freedom into two: one that is concerned with hypothetical (purely instrumental) reasoning, and a second sub-realm that is concerned with categorical (moral) reasoning, where evaluation of ends has pride of place. Categorical reasoning supplies and occupies a transcendental perspective – a perspective that rises above how things are with us, here on the ground, and passes judgment from a self-conscious height upon what we ought to be doing or valuing or what-have-you. Categorical reasoning enjoys a much higher status than that enjoyed by the practical perspective envisioned by Russell (and perhaps also by Hume), which is much more like that lesser status enjoyed by a financial consultant on your payroll, whose job in your cognitive economy is simply to identify for you the best route to objectives that – as far as *that* hired gun is concerned – are completely non-negotiable.

But surely the doctrine that no criticism of ends can be made from a purely instrumental, purely hypothetical perspective requires some defense. It cannot be simply a matter of legislation that evaluation of ends can be made only from within a perspective that withdraws to a rarified height. The remainder of this chapter will be devoted to arguing that criticism of ends does not require the sort of transcendental perspective envisioned by either Hume or Kant, or any of their followers. And it is much more congenial to feminist reservations about the transcendental. It offers a different vision of being grounded than does the rationalist conception.

Moral Philosophy

Moral philosophy has, at least since Kant, viewed moral questions as a subspecies of practical questions, because they deal with the question of "what shall we do?" under a special aspect: namely, "what does *morality* require us to do?" I propose this is a misdiagnosis of the matter.

What is practical reasoning, and what is it to engage in practical deliberation? These questions are, on their face, metaphysical in character: they are after characterization, in metaphysical terms, of that something, *if* there is something, as yet unknown how to conceive of it, that goes *before* archetypes of action, securing or preparing the way for those behaviors that are paragons of practical success. For the name of "reasoning" juxtaposed with "practical" signals a regulative conception. It signals commendation of certain performances, in comparison with certain others. And so a certain, traditionally empiricist strategy of answering the questions here posed suggests itself as highly eligible: why not approach the question by, first, identifying unimpeachable paradigms of action deserving of admiration on practical grounds; second, extracting an account of agency from them; and then, third, giving the same kind of attention to their precursors *if* there are any. This was Aristotle's approach, and it led him – *not* to an account of principle-guided action, as the Kantians have now got in the space where one wants a general account of agency – but to an account of character-guided agency. Character is an embodied thing, or at least something requiring training into the organisms that manifest it.

However, Aristotle's approach has not been the standard since the modern era. Today's prominent conceptions of practical reasoning and engagement in it – Christine

Korsgaard's, or J. David Velleman's, or Michael Bratman's – are thoroughly procedural, algorithmic, and furthermore, intellectual: practical deliberation, as conceived today, is a process of intellection or cogitation, the application of a rule or algorithm in advance of action, concerning what to do in a select and often high-minded space of choice situations. There's nothing organic about it. Furthermore, such extant accounts as offer us a linking of practical reasoning to agency, proceed in a very counter-empirical fashion as well (Korsgaard 1996a, b; Velleman 2001): no empirical studies of agents are performed or surveyed; instead, intuitions are mined for philosophical treasure.

R. Jay Wallace opens his entry "Practical Reason" in the *Stanford Encyclopedia of Philosophy* as follows: "Practical reason is the general human capacity for resolving, through reflection, the question of what one is to do." This opening sentence is in no way marked as something that has been or even can be challenged, and certainly not open to empirical examination. But, pray tell, how does Wallace know that choice issues are to be resolved *through reflection?* Ironically, this definition of practical reason appears in the very same paragraph as this passage:

> There are questions about how deliberation can succeed in being practical in its issue. What do we need to assume – both about agents and about the processes of reasoning they engage in – to make sense of the fact that deliberative reflection can directly give rise to action? Can we do justice to this dimension of practical reason while preserving the idea that practical deliberation is genuinely a form of reasoning? (Wallace 2003)

The point I'm trying to make is that if one simply *assumes* at the outset that issues of choice are solved through reflection, then one has created for oneself a problem – truly an artifact of one's methodology – the problem of showing how reflection can give rise to action. If deliberation comes first, as a matter of principle, by what *further* principle does deliberation result in action? The speculation that agentive choice is founded upon deliberation results in the doctrine that human behavior is totally and completely different from that of animals, unrelated to it even. But is this right?

Let's move from the realm of speculation to the realm of observation – to science. The exercise will take us on a journey whose destination is articulation of a distinctively empiricist conception of practical reason. Two important conclusions will also emerge: (1) the conception so arrived at is rightly deserving of the name of an instrumental conception, but *without* being such as to forbid criticism of chosen ends; (2) this conception is very remote from RCT as we have known and grown to love it. Still, the conception we are left with is suggestive of what RCT can be a theory of.

Science of Human Behavior

Social psychology since the 1960s and 1970s has demonstrated nothing if not that human judgment and behavior are enormously sensitive to – indeed, profoundly shaped and contoured by – the presence of other people, who those people are in our social economy, and what they are doing and saying. For example, it should come as old news that people take cues from the behavior of others when taking stock of their circumstances (their "interpretations" of what they see are dependent upon how they see other people as interpreting the situation), that the influence of women is subordinate to the influence of men (over both men and women), that men and women exert influence in different ways, and that their group behavior is different, among many other things. (Differences in group behavior between American men and American women are especially fascinating, but not the subject of this chapter.) What's more, people's behaviors vary quite predictably with circumstance: circumstance – and sometimes rather trivial circumstance – shapes behavior in ways unrecognized in common or folk psychology. (Nisbett and Ross, 1991, is one of the best treatments of a range of such facts. A more recent but also more contentious treatment is Doris 2002.)

On the very cutting edge of this research is the work of social psychologist Richard Nisbett and his many collaborators (Nisbett 2003). They are demonstrating in a wide range of studies how culture impacts how we judge, and even how we perceive. They are showing that differences in culture between East and West result in – and indeed are sustained by – differences in cognition. Importantly, they are demonstrating that there is nothing universal about the Western ways of categorizing objects, or engaging in debate over the worthiness of a hypothesis, in spite of the fact that Western categories and methods of intellectual engagement are more conducive to the production of good science.

What is perhaps less well known is that an individual's behavior is also shaped by their level – and type – of attention to themselves, a factor often discussed in the field of social psychology as self-focus. For example, it is well known that the presence of a simple mirror enhances task performance. (Subjects are given, for example, a foreign-language text copying task; when there's a mirror or camera in the room subjects produce better copies than when there's not. Interestingly, a similar effect can be produced by giving the subject a minority status in a group: subjects with minority status perform better on neutral tasks than subjects who are not in the minority.) Why does attention to self produce better task performance? The standard answer among social psychologists is that self-focus produces better self-evaluation of one's performance: it triggers on-line self-assessment.

A word of caution: the effects of self-focus are not simply that a personal standard of excellence comes into play when self-focus is brought to bear. It is rather that self-focus produces the application of *some* standard (or other) of assessment – and there are many forms of assessment that can be triggered by a mirror or a camera – and that this triggering has a profound effect on the control of behavior. So what is crucial is not that self-focus brings a proprietary standard (the "agent's avowals") into play (although it can do this) but, rather, that it triggers an evaluative form of executive control. (Which standard will be triggered by self-focus, of the many that might be available to an agent, is at this point in time unknown.) In summary: self-focus is a way of triggering a standard of evaluation, and can be such that subjects are not aware of this triggering. (For more on this, see the many interesting essays in Wegner and Vallacher (1980). And compare the role of self-focus in the account of executive control offered by Philip David Zelazo and his co-workers.)

That behavior has many such sources is not necessarily a good thing – though neither is it in itself a bad thing. (Indeed, one should view the mirror as a very helpful – and extremely inexpensive – behavioral program for improving school performance, for example.) A theory of the regulation of executive function would (among other things) delineate cases where self-focus is good for performance from cases where it is not. And this is what an empiricist account of practical reason can be good for: articulating the principles that apply to regulation of executive function. This is enormously relevant to an account of practical reason. And if it turns out that mirrors yield better task performance, then a theory that tells you to put one in every room where practical endeavors take place is in no way a theory of how to perform better through *reflection* (with apologies for the pun), *contra* the definition Wallace offers. I think it's a theory *vis-à-vis* the practical, all the same.

I therefore want to express these now well-worn results of social psychology as follows: self-focus is a means of putting or shifting executive function into an evaluative mode. And that this mode of operation in which executive function is functioning evaluatively, is quite different from other modes of its operation. For example, it is quite different from modes in which executive function is being exercised only passively or in a semi-automated or caretaker mode; this is a mode in which the executive is not intervening but simply monitoring an automated (or over-learned) task in a permissive manner. And furthermore I want to insist that the exercise of executive function – whether in an evaluative or caretaker mode – is what practical reason amounts to.

Now for a crucial philosophical point: executive function is just a function. It's not a principle of action: it is thoroughly contentless, and especially *vis-à-vis what* we should do. It is the container, subject to being filled in any way an agent likes, or simply any way whatever (whether the agent in question likes it or not). Here now is more on what executive function is.

In articulating the nature of executive function, I will be following a lead discernible in an article by psychologists Robert J. Sternberg and Louise Spear-Swerling (1998). There they are lobbying for what they refer to as a "new construct" in psychology, one whose measurement will be a better predictor of success in life. They suggest calling it personal navigation (PN), and note that in both fiction and true life we are familiar with the idea: it is present in the notion of life as a voyage. I like the name. And I will be lobbying for the same thing, in a distinctively philosophical way: I am lobbying for philosophical conversations in which we conceptualize practical reasoning as an exercise in navigation. While I take certain cues from Sternberg and Spear-Swerling, my articulation of the notion is in service of a distinctively philosophical project: I want to articulate a purely practical, counter-intellectual conception of the practical enterprise. Here goes.

It is quite well documented that some people experience serious difficulties in early childhood, but nonetheless enjoy enviable success in adult life. Other youngsters enjoy spectacular achievement in early childhood – often as a result of opportunities provided by parents – but then proceed to snatch failure out of the jaws of success. One tempting conclusion is that there are no reliable predictors whatever of success – that it's all a matter of chance. But if there is anything at all in the idea that the successful person possesses traits that enable success, one is obliged to say something, however rough, about what the sorts of trait in question might be like. I want to do just that. The analysis I am proposing is aimed at making sense of a trait that could function as such a predictor; it is not so much a study of successful individuals, as it is a study of what such individuals *might* be like: I'm now engaging in model construction,

459

empiricist style. Whether successful individuals are indeed as I'm modeling them is a matter for further empirical research to decide. But we make progress one step at a time. (First there is hypothesis; testing comes afterwards.)

Consider a trait that enables an agent to exercise control over his or her voyage through life. Such a trait might be implicated in the formulation of certain kinds of goals, plans, and beliefs. Not just any goals, plans, and beliefs, but specifically those that are involved in finding a direction in life, maintaining that direction (whether actively or passively), changing direction when appropriate, moving at such a speed as befits the circumstances and with an eye towards guarding against general fatigue *vis-à-vis* the overarching goal, using navigational aids when they are available, overcoming obstacles that prove easily surmountable, avoiding those that may not be. Now, the concept of direction is itself deserving of some analysis, but I shan't provide such a thing here, as there is enough to do. I shall simply take it for our purposes that a life direction is a goal in the most macroscopic sense. Sternberg and Spear-Swerling talk about self-understanding in this connection, as well as the importance of fit between abilities, interests, personality characteristics, and goals in the attainment of success. And they strenuously resist the equation of the form of self-understanding that is at the heart of their would-be PN with a range of currently measurable intellectual functions ("constructs," as psychologists have it), such as planning capacities, general intelligence, and even emotional intelligence. All these other functions, as Sternberg and Spear-Swerling argue, are much too intellectual for the purposes of navigation: they have much more to do with know-that than know-how; and PN is nothing if not pure know-how.

Now this conception admits of criticism of ends. The grounds for criticism, on this instrumental conception, are contentions to the effect that the chosen ends do not fit with the resources at the agent's disposal. And these are fitting grounds for an instrumental conception, and quite different from grounds that moral rebukes can appeal to. What's more, some of this sort of thing can sound distinctively feminist: to someone who has chosen to devote her life to sustaining her husband, a feminist criticism is that she should choose ends more fitting to the capacities she has, because she would otherwise be unhappy. And this has a distinctively instrumental ring, as contrasted with a moral one.

Back to Moral Philosophy

We now have a counter-rationalist – let's call it empiricist – conception of practical reason. Can we, like the rationalists, think of moral reasoning as a species of this? In other words, is moral reasoning a special instance or form of PN? I think not. Here is why.

The idea that moral reasoning is a species of practical reasoning rests on (among other things) a presumption that morality is a personal affair – in other words, that moral imperatives are directed at individual persons in the first instance. And this, consequently, leads to the doctrine that political and legal philosophies have to be built upon moral theories in some way – that political and legal theories are founded upon certain principles that appeal to an independent moral realm. These doctrines are grounded in instincts deeply rooted in armchair methodologies, because from the armchair all questions of what I should do have the ring of personal rather than political questions. And this is the dogma of the armchair. Indeed, it is in the very nature of the armchair – the armchair's inferior grain.

We have here performed an articulation of a conception of personal navigation that bypasses the armchair. Might we not have a companion conception of moral and political realms that similarly bypass it? I think we can. We seek an articulation of the relationship between moral and practical realms, in which the latter is *not* more fundamental. It will turn out to be the conception on which communities also enjoy ontological status as targets of moral and political imperatives.

Traditionally, title to equal moral, social, or political standing, in philosophy, rests on something shared in the community of moral agents. Elsewhere (Thalos 2002), I argued that findings in the cognitive and clinical sciences, particularly the sciences of functional deficit, should incline us to the conclusion that there is no such thing as a *universal* human nature – at least not when it comes to behavior or even to a structure for controlling behavior. I argued also that this conclusion is no less forthcoming from the findings in evolutionary science. I won't repeat the arguments here; I will simply take the conclusion as a premise.

This premise causes problems for those moral philosophies that insist upon moral claims and moral standings resting upon certain (shared) cognitive capacities or features, as for example Kantian theories do. (Perhaps it is to give voice to the idea that the "ought" implies the "can," and possibly also to the idea that justice is between equals.) These moral philosophies contrast, on this matter, to those that conceive of moral standing as resting upon simple membership in a community that pools or utilizes a certain range of resources to some advantage, or simply upon relations of relatedness. Such theories, which include all varieties of consequentialism, do not require the presupposition of universals, and so are not troubled by the non-existence of universals. The trouble caused is especially acute for views of the moral or political that seek to ground the title to certain (moral or political) privileges or standings upon hypothetical agreements (or equivalents thereof) entered into by numerous parties, on the basis of some (possibly hypothetical) exercise of reason, under a veil of ignorance, or some such. For the question naturally arises: what do they look like who enter into such contracts? To achieve its results, the contractarian methodology strips away, or abstracts away from, a range of phenotypic specifics. This procedure is sure to strip individuals of some particular feature that is relevant to *their* governing of *their* behavior. For according to the premise we are now taking for granted, human agency is very different from the romantic, rationalistic image to which contractarian theories appeal: human behavior is sensitive to a very large number of factors specific to one's own genetic endowment.

The solution, to my mind, is to say that moral and political imperatives are not addressed to individuals in the first instance, in virtue of a feature that settles the matter of their candidacy as targets of such directives. These imperatives are addressed to communities, in virtue of the fact that they exist. For their existence necessitates mechanisms of conflict resolution – whether conflict actually arises or not. The existence of communities necessitates norms by which systemic possibilities of conflict must be regulated. (There are parallel imperatives involving conflict resolution among the

461

subsystems of an individual organism – imperatives with which all biological organisms must comply or perish.) This is a fact well known to systems theorists.

The idea that moral and political imperatives are corporate in character taps a deeply feminist instinct. And so now, how are conflicts to be regulated? There is a very compelling framework for representing and thinking through the nature of conflict: rational choice theory.

Rational Choice, Finally

RCT is a framework for calculating something out. It is an intellectual exercise. But I've been saying that the practical enterprise, on the ground, is decisively *not* an intellectual exercise. I've been going on about the fact that intellection is precisely what the practical is to be *contrasted* with. So what is the RCT good for? Is it good for anything at all?

I think it's good for a great deal. RCT has two (linked) features that mark it as distinct from PN. First, it is entirely transparent – and rendered so partly by the fact (discussed at the outset) that RCT separates the treatment of value from the treatment of choice among valued things in concrete circumstances, so as to allow disputations on each to proceed independently of one another. And so, far from foreclosing disputation on what is of value, it allows disputation of that question to proceed independently of disputation about how to achieve high-priority items, once identified. (Of course, the framework assumption is that these two dimensions of the choice process can be separated; and it is indeed a substantive assumption, but this is not now the place to worry about it.) Second, RCT is available to everybody, and indeed can be applied by one person in behalf of another. So we have the means of taking everybody's perspective, when we try. (But, of course, we have to try.)

Both these features derive from the fact that RCT is top-to-bottom formulaic and universally available. These features suit it very well as a contrast with what is *not* formulaic and *not* available to everybody: PN. PN is exclusively an individual's resource, where by contrast RCT can be a collective's resource. And in an especially felicitous way: as an instrument for making decisions or crafting policy impacting a heterogeneous group, it is a way of securing transparency and objectivity. And so RCT can be to the community what PN can only be to an individual. RCT can be a community's means of navigation, provided there is a culture that legitimates its use in public settings. (Its legitimacy must be forged in the culture that puts it into action: this does not simply happen *ex nihilo*.) Its presence there fills a void: for there can be much less in the way of organic PN for collectivities (or at least, it seems to me, plausible to suppose). And so if you, as an individual, think (as I do) that RCT as a public policy can be desirable, you must work to make its legitimacy a reality, by advocating for it in your community.

Against Orthodoxy

The point of view we have thus far sketched strains mightily against orthodoxy when it comes to the topic of the nature of the practical. We have thus far marked a strong distinction between collective navigation and individual navigation, stressing the ineffability of the personal, and emphasizing the contrasting nature of that thing deserving of the name of collective navigation. We began at ground level, thereby allowing for the possibility of ineffability – and indeed found a need to postulate it at the organismic level. But then proceeding upwards we found space for the algorithmic or formulaic form of decision, as something quite distinct from the ineffable form one finds (or, more modestly, might find upon empirical inquiry) at the individual level. The orthodoxy against which this strains is Bayesian decision analysis, the mainstream of decision analysis. This mainstream simply assumes from the outset the propositional/algorithmic paradigms as central to the analysis of practical agency. Additionally, Bayesian analyses aim at treating cooperative endeavors, defined as ones in which exists a potential for enforceable agreements among the atomic individuals who enter into them, as they treat non-cooperative endeavors, which admit of no such agreements. And so Bayesians aim at representing collective decision making as a species of individual decision making, not as something different in kind. The goal is manifestly reductive, guided by the idea that the regime of the cooperative does not deserve a separate category of its own. It is to assimilate what may be called *collective rationality*, the process whereby coordination of action is achieved, to what may be called *individual rationality*, the process of achieving action as an (undistributed) individual. The general colonizing move is to handle the overt process of deliberations as a series of strategic bargaining steps, in a competitive game played out among the members of the coalition, within the boundaries of the larger game. The bargaining game is itself viewed as governed by independent rules of interaction among multiple players, and therefore clearly *not* as something which someone can undergo purely as a single, unified psyche. Under the Bayesian proposal, it thus becomes *impossible* to view the coordinative process (which we familiarly refer to as deliberation) as a means of bringing into being a single, multi-member decision-making body aiming at collective goals. Instead, deliberation with others comes to be viewed exclusively as a means for each participating individual to reach an individual end, within a purely competitive framework. This is, for example, a goal of Harsanyi and Selten's (1988) monumental work on equilibrium selection, although as they themselves acknowledge, the goal is never reached.

The point I'm making now is that what Bayesians have thought is good enough for collectivities, because it's good for individuals, isn't always good for individuals at all. I have elsewhere argued that the reductive approach (that simply assumes at the outset a formulaic version of decision making for individuals) understates the human organism's non-logical – and indeed very organic – resources, and in so doing willfully fails to treat with proper respect her capacity for forming *true* alliances. Human beings, like almost all organisms that provide for their young, have a capacity for bonding. This capacity goes above and beyond the capacity for personal navigation. It is something that transcends the personal. The thesis that humans have the capacity to transcend a personal, individual perspective is the only form of transcendentalism worthy of the name.

And so I commend RCT to feminists, particularly in cultures that value transparent decision making, equality, and collaboration. Seize it as an instrument for building coalitions and consensus. It can work to the powerful advantage of feminist goals. More importantly, nothing is gained in forswearing its use.

463

I will close the section by displaying an application of RCT in service of a goal all feminists can endorse – an application for which we have the United Nations to thank, in the form of an agency called UNICEF. The United Nations' Children's Fund was founded to protect children around the world. One of their top five priorities today, under that broader mission, is the education of girls. UNICEF adopted in April 2004 the goal of gender equality in education. UNICEF's aim now is to get more girls into school, to ensure that they stay in school, and that they are equipped with the basic tools they need to succeed in later life. The stated reasons for these goals are not purely feminist or egalitarian (though some of them are). The UN also notes that education of girls is the *single most important correlate* of economic development, improved public health, and poverty reduction in today's world. This reality is described on their website as the "biggest lesson in history." And so UNICEF presents itself as having performed something of a very rough cost-benefit analysis of educating girls, showing that education of girls very efficiently advances a number of important values. These values are cast as collective goals – goals that certain collectivities, and individuals in their capacities as members of these collectivities, are expected to endorse. UNICEF is trying to build a coalition behind its priority of educating girls. Feminists can be brought on board with UNICEF on grounds of equal rights for girls. Others can be brought on board in the name of economic development, or improved public health, or world poverty reduction. Some will climb aboard in the name of *all* those things. Educating girls is good for a lot of things. And by building a coalition around consensus based upon a pool of valued ends, we – as a collectivity, conceiving of ourselves as complying with an imperative directed at collectivities and sub-collectivities to which we severally belong – can improve the lives of women around the globe.

Public and Private

Feminists have traditionally been critical of the distinction between public and private, between the personal and the political, as independent and non-intersecting spheres. Indeed, a famous feminist slogan is that the personal is political. Ironically, the conceptions of navigation articulated here – with its strong contrasting of personal and collective forms – promise to serve feminist aims. We have identified at least two conceptions of navigation, one appropriate at the individual organism level of analysis, and another appropriate for collectivities. Once these are independently articulated – in other words, articulated from an empiricist stance, that does not stand off the ground – we can proceed to ask what implications this might have for moral and political theory. Right away a natural proposal suggests itself: imperatives (moral, political, or what have you) are directed toward entities with navigational powers. This leaves entirely open the question of whether there are relations of dependence among practical imperatives, moral imperatives, and political ones. And so within this framework, no reductive relationship between classes of imperatives is necessitated. Moreover, within this framework it's more natural to think of political imperatives as directed in the first instance at collectivities, instead of indirectly to collectivities through individuals. Rather than having to postulate dependence relations, from a transcendental position, among the different varieties of imperatives, it becomes open to us to examine the ways in which the different varieties of imperatives interact.

So it becomes possible to inquire – rather than simply to postulate – whether practical imperatives, thought of in the first instance as personal, interact with imperatives directed at collectivities. In other words, it becomes possible to raise, as an open question, the issue of whether corporate and private spheres are related. And once the question is regarded as genuinely open, it becomes possible to explore – indeed, it seems more fitting to seek – answers that spring from an empiricist methodology. How to do that?

Empiricist methods are the most eligible methods for answering questions like: what is such-and-such a function good for? Under what conditions does it produce such-and-such desirable outcomes? It is once again time for conjectures – which are subject, as always, to refutation by careful observations.

I conjecture that PN utilizes fast and frugal heuristics that are occasionally infelicitous (and more infelicitous in our present age than they would have been under the conditions in which they first evolved). And so it will probably turn out that rational choice produces better results when considerably more is at stake and there is more time to devote to the decision. And so it will turn out that there is a parallel with theoretical reasoning – reasoning about how matters stand in the world. Here is what I mean.

Organisms like ourselves have evolved fast and frugal *theoretical* heuristics – for example, heuristics for computing the relative size and shape of an object in the visual field. But some of these heuristics are subject to errors of various kinds, and even prone to persistent illusions. In the face of this fact, we require more reliable means of ascertaining the facts of relative size and shape, when enough is at stake. (Hence, various methods of scientific inquiry, as well as a receptivity to correction, at least on the appropriate occasions.) In parallel fashion, organisms like ourselves have evolved fast and frugal *practical* heuristics for navigating in life – for example, some of us subscribe to "Avoid long-term commitment." Some of these heuristics lead to unhappiness, or underachievement, or simply to reduced forms of life. In the face of this fact, we require more reliable means of making decisions, particularly when there is enough at stake. (Hence, RCT.) But the more reliable means are also less cost-effective, for there is typically a trade-off between economy and accuracy.

Those who agitate for accuracy, always and everywhere, as do the rationalists, have left economy quite far behind. In agitating for high intellectual solutions to all decision problems, rationalists are asking us to take discursive reasoning to choice situations most economically handled in other ways – ways for which we have evolution itself to thank. For the transcendentalists have no means of separating among cases. Nor do they have means of applying considerations of economy. And yet, for practical purposes, what considerations could be so important as to trump all considerations of economy in every case? No retreat to reason alone can profit us so well as empiricist methods when it comes to matters to which economy is relevant. And cases of decision fall under this category of matters. And for this reason, we must conclude that transcendental methods of inquiry are blind to central realities that underlie the exercise of practical intelligence, and its relations to the moral and political.

465

Notes

1 Shapin and Schaffer (1985) propose that this is true also of contemporary scientific methodology.
2 The doctrine of "massive modularity," as now it is called, is characteristic of the highly controversial research program now going under the label of Evolutionary Psychology. Peter Carruthers (2004) offers a recent defense of the doctrine, which is countered in Woodward and Cowie (2004).
3 Jean Hampton held a rather different – and less complimentary – opinion of EU. She thought that it is a theory divided against itself, and so can model nothing. She wrote: "While it [EU] is supposed to permit our preferences over actions to be partly a function of attitudes toward risk, one of its central axioms requires that our preferences over actions be *purely* a function of our preferences over consequences" (Hampton 1994: 235). The point is simply that, whereas EU is prepared to render judgments utilizing any utilities you please to specify, whether you care about consequences only, or care also about the states in which you enjoy them, it nonetheless demands that your utilities for outcomes be state-independent at *some* level. According to Hampton, EU requests that, at some level, your preferences be purely over the outcomes, rather than also over the conditions in which the outcomes come out. These restrictions concern the *metaphysics* of your preferences, rather than their content. I am prepared to countenance that, while there is some tension, it is not so bad as a contradiction.
4 Jean Hampton, offering this very point as a criticism of the atomizing move, says succinctly: "While it [EU theory] is supposed to permit our preferences over actions to be partly a function of attitudes toward risk, one of its central axioms requires that our preferences over actions be *purely* a function of our preferences over consequences" (Hampton 1994: 235).

References and Further Reading

Antony, L. (1998). "Human nature" and its role in feminist theory. In J. Kourany (ed.), *Philosophy in a Feminist Voice* (pp. 63–91). Princeton, NJ: Princeton University Press.
Bratman, M. (1989). *Intentions, Plans and Practical Reason*. New York: Cambridge University Press.
Brennan, S. (ed.) (2002). *Feminist Moral Philosophy. Canadian Journal of Philosophy*, supplementary volume 28.
Carruthers, P. (2004). The mind is a system of modules shaped by natural selection. In C. Hitchcock (ed.), *Contemporary Debates in the Philosophy of Science* (pp. 293–311). Oxford: Blackwell.
Doris, J. (2002). *Lack of Character*. New York: Cambridge University Press.
Gopnik, A., and Meltzoff, A. (1997). *Words, Thoughts and Things*. Cambridge, MA: MIT Press.
Hampton, J. (1993). Feminist contractarianism. In L. Antony and C. Witt (eds.), *A Mind of One's Own: Feminist Essays on Reason and Objectivity*. Boulder, CO: Westview Press.
—— (1994). The failure of expected-utility theory as a theory of reason. *Economics and Philosophy*, 10, 195–242.
Harsanyi, J., and Selten, R. (1988). *A General Theory of Equilibrium Selection in Games*. Cambridge, MA: MIT Press.
Korsgaard, C. (1996a). *The Sources of Normativity*. New York: Cambridge University Press.
—— (1996b). *Creating the Kingdom of Ends*. New York: Cambridge University Press.
Nisbett, R. (2003). *Geography of Thought*. New York: Free Press.
Nisbett, R., and Ross, R. (1991). *The Person and the Situation*. Philadelphia, PA: Temple University Press.

Shapin, S., and Schaffer, S. (1995). *Leviathan and the Air Pump.* Princeton, NJ: Princeton University Press.

Sternberg, R. J., and Spear-Swerling, L. (1998). Personal navigation. In M. Ferrari and R. Sternberg (eds.), *Self-Awareness: Its Nature and Development* (pp. 219–45). New York: Guilford Press.

Thalos, M. (2002). From human nature to moral philosophy. *Canadian Journal of Philosophy,* supplementary volume 28, 85–128.

Velleman, J. D. (2001). *The Possibility of Practical Reason.* New York: Oxford University Press.

Wallace, R. J. (2003). Practical reason. In E. N. Zalta (ed.), *The Stanford Encyclopedia of Philosophy* (winter 2003 edition), forthcoming URL: www.plato.stanford.edu/archives/win2003/entries/practical-reason/.

Wegner, D., and Vallacher, R. (eds.) (1980). *The Self in Social Psychology.* New York: Oxford University Press.

Woodward, J., and Cowie, F. (2004). The mind is not (just) a system of modules shaped (just) by natural selection. In C. Hitchcock (ed.), *Contemporary Debates in the Philosophy of Science* (pp. 312–34). Oxford: Blackwell.

Zelazo, P. D. (1996). Towards a characterization of minimal consciousness. *New Ideas in Psychology,* 14, 63–80.

Zelazo, P. D., and Muller, U. (2002). Executive function in typical and atypical development. In U. Goswami (ed.), *Blackwell Handbook of Childhood Cognitive Development.* Oxford: Blackwell.

Zelazo, P. D., Carter, A., Reznick, J. S., and Frye, D. (1997). Early development of executive function: A problem-solving framework. *Review of General Psychology,* 1, 198–226.

25

Rationalism in the Philosophy of Donald Davidson

RICHARD N. MANNING

Introduction

W. V. O. Quine's attack on the intelligibility of the distinction between analytic and synthetic truths – the distinction between claims made true entirely by the meanings of the words used to express them and those made true by the course of experience – is surely among the most significant events of twentieth-century philosophy. Quine's attack is generally taken to lead to a holism according to which our beliefs face the tribunal of experience as one corporate body. But if this is right, the idea of *a priori* truths, claims that are true independently of the course of experience and thus obtaining necessarily, is bankrupt. It is a central tenet of rationalism that some truths, indeed substantial truths about the world and not the mere meanings of our terms, are *a priori*. Thus we may well ask: "Can there be a post-Quinean rationalism?"

Rationalism clearly does survive after Quine, for example in the nativist views about language and meaning of Noam Chomsky and his followers. But Chomsky does not operate in a post-Quinean climate, in the sense I intend. For his nativism amounts to a rejection of Quine's arguments against analytic truth. However, Donald Davidson is an avowed Quinean in rejecting the analytic/synthetic distinction. He is not alone in this; two other notable philosophers who do so are Quine himself, of course, and Richard Rorty. But whereas Quine tends either to eliminate or deflate subjects of traditional philosophical interest, or to naturalize them into grist for the empirical sciences, and Rorty scorns the very project of giving philosophical accounts of these or pretty much any other phenomena, Davidson instantiates thoroughly the traditional conception of the philosopher as offering a synoptic and explanatory vision of how the various basic elements of the world and concepts which enable us to think about them relate to one another. For this reason, Davidson's work provides us with a promising example from which to learn what may survive of rationalism in a post-Quinean but nonetheless traditionally philosophical enterprise.

My plan will be as follows. I shall first discuss more fully how Quine's attack on the analytic/synthetic distinction seems to undercut the possibility of rationalism. I shall then discuss a pair of theses central to Davidson's thinking, and indeed central, according to Davidson, to all thinking. I shall argue that these principles are, for Davidson, warranted *a priori*, as constituting intelligible domains of discourse and inquiry. So characterized, Davidson's commitments may seem to place his views more properly with the transcendentalist Kant than with the classical rationalists whom Kant opposed. But, I shall argue, this appearance is misleading. As to the constitutive character of their *a priori* principles, Kant and the classical rationalists were not really divided; and where their divide is deep, Davidson is on the rationalist side of the schism. This, I shall try to show, makes him better able than the transcendentalist to claim that his *a priori* principles give us substantial knowledge of a substantial world. I should say at the start that my aim here is not to defend or criticize Davidson's views, but simply to display the way and extent to which they exemplify a post-Quinean but genuine rationalism.

Rationalism and the Analytic/Synthetic Distinction

Quine (1953) framed his attack on the analytic/synthetic distinction as an attack on a dogma of empiricism. He further claimed that a second dogma of empiricism, reductionism, falls with the first, since any putative definitions reducing theoretical expressions in a language to purely observational terms would have to be analytic. But in attacking empiricism it is clear that Quine did not mean to plump for its traditional rationalist alternative instead. Rather, he takes his attack to undermine the very framework that supports each term of the opposition. This might not be obvious. For while the classical rationalists and the classical and positivist empiricists both accepted the analytic/synthetic distinction, their disagreement concerned a putative distinction among synthetic truths. Empiricists hold that all such truths are contingent and empirical, depending for their truth on the course of experience, while rationalists hold that some are *a priori*: necessarily true regardless of the course and content of experience. But Quine's attack is directed at the analytic side of the distinction, purporting to show that we cannot make sense of the idea of sentences made true merely by the meanings of our words. Thus the synthetic side of the distinction might seem untouched, and with it the debate between rationalists and empiricists over whether any of the non-analytic truths (i.e., any of all the truths) are *a priori*.

Indeed, Quine's graded and pragmatic recasting of the analytic/synthetic distinction as one between those sentences we are less and more likely to give up, respectively, in the face of "recalcitrant experience" (Quine 1953: 43–4),[1] may seem to allow us to make good a distinction between sentences whose epistemic status depends upon experience, and those whose status does not. A claim whose probability of being revised in the light of recalcitrant experience is 0 would seem to owe none of its epistemic status to experience; and given Quine's arguments, such claims would have to be substantial and not analytic. The rationalist, then, would be one who holds that some claims are unrevisable.[2] But Quine would certainly not allow this way of reformulating the notion of the substantial *a priori*. For he takes his argument to have done in, not just analyticity, but any notion of necessary truth. Quine argues that none of the concepts and distinctions in terms of which we might explicate analyticity – truth by definition, by linguistic or semantic rules, through synonymy, necessary truth – is both independently intelligible and sufficiently clear to make sense of the others; the attempt to explicate analyticity in such terms "has the form, figuratively speaking, of a closed curve in space" (Quine 1953: 30). In including the idea of necessary truth within the too-tightly inter-defined circle of notions, Quine thus intends to call this idea into doubt as well. For Quine, the revisability of claims comes in degrees from 0 to 1 *exclusive*. No claim is unrevisable in the light of experience, hence none could count as knowable independently of the course of experience. Quine thus adopts a holism in which our beliefs face experience as a corporate body, any one of whose members is subject to termination. Such a holism is plainly inconsistent with the possibility of *a priori* truth upon which rationalism depends.

But there is room to maneuver here for the rationalist who nonetheless accepts the argument against analyticity.[3] She can start by realizing that Quine's immediate dialectical targets were Carnap and the other Vienna School positivists, to whom the idea of synthetic *a priori* knowledge was already dead, killed off, they thought, by non-Euclidian geometry and in virtue of their peculiar, epistemologized reading of the early Wittgenstein on necessity, sense, and nonsense. For them, necessity just was reducibility to tautology by analysis. Not surprisingly, then, the sense of necessity Quine discusses and dismisses is one that is tightly tied to analyticity. This tight link is explicit in Quine's argument, in which the "adverb 'necessarily' . . . is so construed as to yield truth *when and only when applied to an analytic statement*" (Quine 1953: 29, emphasis added). It would be odd indeed if this narrowly tailored sense of necessity were the same one invoked in the rationalist claim that there are substantial *a priori* synthetic truths. But what other sort of necessity might there be? Let us look to Davidson for an answer.

A priori Principles I: Davidson on Causation and the Mental

According to Davidson, events related as cause and effect necessarily fall under strict laws (e.g., Davidson 1980b, 1980c, 1980d, 1980e, 1995). More precisely, if *c* causes *e*, then there are descriptions C of *c* and E of *e* such that "if C, then E" instantiates a strict law. Typically termed the "principle of the nomological character of causation," I shall, for brevity's sake, call it the "laws/cause thesis." Davidson, in light of his agreement with Quine concerning the A/S distinction, would certainly agree that the laws/cause thesis is not analytic; indeed, he abjures altogether any claims to have given, with this thesis or anywhere else, an *analysis* of causation. But he also holds that "the thesis cannot be established empirically (1995: 264).

Nor, evidently, can it be refuted empirically. Davidson has consistently declined to revise or relax his strict nomological conception of causation in the face of challenges offered to it on the basis of the pretty well undisputed fact that the generalizations to which, not just psychology, but biology and even chemistry, appeal are typically if not invariably laden with *ceteris paribus* clauses and provisos, and are otherwise limited in scope. Yet such paradigmatic sciences purport to provide causal explanations by appeal to such generalizations. If this does not count as evidence against the laws/cause thesis, then it is hard to see what sort of *a posteriori* evidence could. But according to Davidson, it does not. Indeed, Davidson quotes with approval Henry Margenau's remark that "physics can never inform us of a failure of the causality principle" (Davidson 1995: 277).

To see further why the laws/cause thesis "must be in some sense *a priori*" (Davidson 1995: 264), note that according to Davidson, "Hume was wrong in supposing we never directly perceive that one event has caused another" (Davidson 1995: 269). Indeed, despite the laws/cause thesis, we can judge that two events are related causally even when we are in ignorance of any description of them under which they instantiate a law; generally we will not know any such description. Given this, we surely cannot justify the claim that there is such a law, hence that a given relation is causal, by means of inductive evidence from observed causal interactions. Yet still, "we have reason to believe the singular statement only insofar as we have reason to believe there is such a law" (Davidson 1980c: 160). Since the reason to believe there is such a law cannot derive from the perception of the event alone, it must arise from an independent knowledge that causal relations are necessarily nomological. That is, it must arise from the *a priori* knowledge of the cause/laws thesis.

The *a priori* considerations Davidson offers for this thesis rely on the claims that causal relations involve changes, and that whether a situation involves a change is relative to the predicates used to describe it. To recur to Nelson Goodman's (1965) familiar example, an object's appropriately timed shift from blue to green is a change relative to the color predicates "blue" and "green," but not relative to the predicates "bleen" and "grue." Put another way, "green" projects relative to "blue," but not relative to "grue," in the sense that they enter together into valid inductions. Thus an emerald's being observed to be green licenses an inductive inference to the generalization that all emeralds are green rather than blue, but not an inductive inference that all emeralds are green rather than grue. Relative to the latter hypothesis, an emerald's shifting from green to blue does not count as a change; relative to the former, it does. The idea of a real change, then, is the idea of an event whose antecedent and consequent conditions are correctly describable by predicates that enter together into valid generalizations. But this idea of mutually projectible predicates just is the idea of predicates that figure in law-like statements. Thus commitment to the idea that changes are real events susceptible of causal explanation itself entails a commitment to the idea of such changes may be captured in statements which instantiate strict laws. Moreover, since the notion of a law is essentially linguistic – it is statements that are law-like or not – a commitment to singular causal statements either in commonsense vocabulary or in a vocabulary of the special sciences entails a commitment to the in-principle availability of a vocabulary of mutually projectible predicates which would allow the formulation of strict laws and true singular causal statements which would instantiate them.

This commitment does not reflect an empirical fact, but one knowable only *a priori*. "Nature," Davidson says, "doesn't care what we call a change, so we decide what counts as a change on the basis of what we want to explain, and what we think available as an explanation. In deciding what counts as a change, we also decide what generalizations to count as law-like" (Davidson 1995: 273). The important point for our purposes is that the justification of the cause/laws thesis is a fully *a priori* matter. The thesis is required to make a kind of discourse – namely, causal explanatory discourse – intelligible. This discourse is, at the ideal limit, physics,[4] for on Davidson's view, "our concept of a physical object is the concept of an object whose changes are governed by laws" (Davidson 1995: 274). Thus adherence to the *a priori* laws/cause thesis is constitutive of physical and causal talk, understanding, and phenomena.

471

Davidson holds the principle of the constitutive rationality of the mental. Mental states are characterized by both inter- and intra-attitudinal holism. An agent's having a belief with a given content depends upon her having other beliefs related to it. One cannot believe that a ketch is a yawl without believing both to be boats, for example. Moreover, "all the attitudes ... depend upon belief to give their contents substance ... we would not want to go to the opera unless we thought we would enjoy it (or that someone else wants us to be there, etc.)." Moreover, since "intentions and actions follow from, and require, practical reasoning," and practical reasoning "requires the collusion" of values and cognitive judgments, intentional actions "are also caught up in the web of evaluative attitudes and practical knowledge" (Davidson 2004b: 16).

This essential rationality of the mental arises from the role mental talk plays in the interpretation of the speech and behavior of others and ourselves. The basic mental categories of belief, desire, and intention have their home in the project of understanding certain of the movements of certain beings as actions. Actions by their very nature are undertaken for reasons, which make rational sense of the actions they are cited to explain by revealing a kind of normative propriety of so acting in the light of what the agent in question both desires and believes. That a given behavior is an intentional action and not a mere movement generally entails that its producer desired to bring it about, that she believed that she could do so by certain means, and that she intended so to do. What action it is depends on the contents of the belief and desires that rationally explain it. Davidson offers this pithy example: "If I pay my bill by writing a check, it is necessarily the case that I wrote the check because I wanted to pay my bill and believed that by writing the check I would be paying my bill" (Davidson 2004c: 122) (note that the entire conditional ought to fall within the scope of the modal operator).

Davidson's idea here is that we lose grip on the very possibility and point of giving any determinant content to beliefs, desires, and actions if they are not rationally related to one another. What grounds might there be for saying that a person going downstairs is off to fetch the dinner wine if, for example, we know they believe that the wine is upstairs, or if we know they want beer with dinner? And, supposing they do go fetch the wine, what ground could there be for saying that they desired to fetch the beer, unless we also hold that they believed that the wine they fetched is after all beer? The contents of the mental states it makes sense to ascribe to agents in order to explain their actions depend upon their interrelating holistically so as to render the overall pattern of their mental states and actions roughly rational, that is, roughly so that they meet normative standards according to which their actions are appropriate in light of their beliefs and desires. Grounds for changing the characterization of any one of the elements is grounds for adjusting the characterization of the others. And absent a connection of this norm-satisfying sort between an action and the reasons for which it was undertaken, grounds for characterizing any of the events involved in mentalistic vocabulary at all are lost.

The understanding of behaviors as actions grounded in reasons thus requires the construction of an explanation constrained by norms of rationality. As Davidson says, "the normative, holistic ... elements of psychological concepts cannot be eliminated without radically changing the subject" (Davidson 2004c: 122–3) – without, that is to say, our ceasing to speak or think of the mental. Just as the very nature of our concepts of cause and effect depends for its application upon the idea that the events that we take to be changes conform to an order or pattern in which the latter follow the former as a matter of nomological necessity, so too our concepts of belief, desire, and action depend for their application upon the idea of an order or pattern in which the last is consequent upon the first two as a matter of normative propriety in the light of reason. Adherence to the principle of the rationality of the mental is constitutive of mental talk, understanding, and phenomena.

Constitutive Principles and Classical Rationalism

Note that the principles I have discussed, and the arguments Davidson offers for them, are transcendental in character, in that they seek to articulate the conditions of the possibility of certain kinds of phenomena. The classical rationalists, Descartes, Spinoza, and Leibniz, are not typically understood as offering transcendental grounds for their epistemic principles. Rather, they are most often viewed as grounding all knowledge in some form or other of rational insight into the necessary structure and being of things. Descartes speaks of the light of reason, and of a faculty of clear and distinct perception by which we know our own existence and nature, God's nature and existence, and matter's nature. He attempts, it is true, to certify the epistemic bona fides of this faculty, but the arguments are plainly and famously circular, relying upon the insights of the very faculty whose trustworthiness they are supposed to demonstrate. In part against Descartes' circular efforts to certify the epistemic adequacy of clear and distinct perception, Spinoza more forthrightly claims that truth is its own standard (Spinoza 1985: 479–80; E2P43n), and seeks no more than self-evidence to reflection as warrant for his axioms, from which it follows by reason itself that infinite substance must exist. And Leibniz claims that his reasoning is founded on two principles: that of non-contradiction, and that of sufficient reason, where the latter either is or entails the principle that whatever happens is for the best. The latter, in some writings, seems derived from the moral perfection of God, but in others, the reverse is true: the existence and moral perfection of God is inferred from the principle of sufficient reason and the fact that there is something rather than nothing (see Leibniz 1998b: 262). The legitimacy of this inference to an existence claim and the principle on which it is based is not further grounded in anything; it is apparently self-evident to reason. In each case, a substantial claim about what exists in the real order – self, substance, God – and about the nature of these things, is based on inference from principles whose truth is taken as self-evident.

In contrast, Davidson's principles speak to the conditions of possibility of certain kinds of phenomena, namely those answering to our notions of the physical and mental. Kant is the figure most closely and clearly associated with the articulation of *a priori* conditions on the possibility of phenomena. That is the point of his famous Copernican turn, in which we transfer our attention from things in themselves to things as they must appear to us, given the structure of our cognitive faculties. Kant of course held that there is synthetic *a priori* knowledge. In this, he is a rationalist. But Kant, unlike the classical rationalists, thematized the synthetic *a priori* as such, finding its ground problematic. In his transcendentalist attempt to account for the possibility of this kind of knowledge, Kant takes himself precisely to have overcome the dogmatism of rationalism, and indeed to have overcome the opposition between rationalism and empiricism altogether. Despite his acceptance of the idea of substantial *a priori* knowledge, it would, therefore, be misleading simply to categorize Kant as a rationalist of the classical stripe. So, given the typical view of the difference between classical rationalist *a priori* insight and Kantian *a priori* constitutive principles, the constitutive character of Davidson's own *a priori* principles might suggest that he is better classed with Kantian transcendentalism than with classical rationalism.

However, we should resist the suggestion, as the standard view of the rationalists I have just rehearsed is on this point seriously misleading. In the *Principles of Philosophy*, Descartes sets out what he claims to be the clear and distinct, hence indubitable, foundations of his physical science. These do not follow merely from the nature of extension as the sole attribute of body, but from certain principles concerning the nature of the divine creator. In Descartes' official view, these principles follow from the eternal perfection of God, which must perforce be expressed in a changeless consistency in the created world (Descartes 1985: 240ff.). The principles include basic physical conservation laws as well as the basic laws of mechanics. Now of course these laws turn out not to be indubitable – indeed, they are not even true, as Leibniz's observation-based demonstration that the fundamental quantity Descartes took to be conserved – motion, measured as a function of size and speed – is clearly not (Leibniz 1998a: 69ff.). This principle, then, while it may not have been based on any experience, is confuted by it. But this interesting fact sheds light on, rather than obscures, what is of importance. What it shows is something about the actual work that *a priori* rational principles are supposed to do philosophically. For why did Descartes take this precise quantity to be conserved? Descartes was eager to secure the epistemological bona fides of the new science founded by Galileo and himself, in which the book of nature, in the Italian's phrase, is written in the language of mathematics. To be a mathematical science, realized Descartes, physics required some conserved quantities. The mathematical techniques available to him – those of analytic geometry – enable calculations based on the measurement of dimensions and speeds of objects; thus they could in principle handle physical description under the assumption that quantity of motion as a function of these is conserved. The claim that matter essentially is extension, a claim also allegedly available to mere rational insight, wards off the threat that matter might have features that cannot be represented in and subdued by the analytic geometry. The law also circumscribed the power of mind to influence body, prohibiting the former from being conceived in a way that permits its operations on the latter to alter the conserved quantity; to the extent those operations seem to do so, the effect is only apparent, in reality compensated for by some other correlative but unnoticed consequence. Thus Descartes' conservation laws and other allegedly pure *a priori* rational principles operate to constitute a domain over which our modes of understanding – here mathematical – can operate. In this sense, even though Descartes gives no transcendental argument or deduction for his basic principles of nature, they are transcendental – they provide the constitutive conditions for the possibility of understanding the world. It then becomes the work of actual natural science to bring the phenomena into accord with these principles, to the greatest extent possible. These constitutive conditions are thus ideals as well.

Leibniz had the calculus, which gave him descriptive techniques unavailable to Descartes. In essence, Descartes had been unable to represent instantaneous rates of change, hence accelerations. Leibniz could, and this enabled him to describe, hence to see as real, rather than as merely apparent or anomalous, the differential effects of objects that are identical in their extension and motion. But why would the effects of objects of exactly the same shape, size, and motion be different? Here Leibniz saw need for a further kind of explanatory principle. To understand phenomena, to bring them to order, we need to assume there is a sufficient reason for everything's being as it is rather than some other way. Assuming that there is a reason for a thing's being as it is cannot help make it intelligible if we allow that the reason might be poor or the means by which that reason is implemented ill-suited to the task. The principle of sufficient reason, to be of any help, must be or imply the principle of the best. So in order to render the phenomena subject to our understanding, we must see them as products, not just of a perfect power, but also of a perfect power with a perfect will, operating with perfect knowledge. This exoteric formulation puts the point theologically; but esoterically, the principles stem not so much from the demands of God, as from inquiry's own demand that the book of nature be written in a language we can read. Conformity to the principle of reason becomes then the mark of the bona fide natural phenomenon. Apparent failures so to conform signal, not phenomena that are not for the best, but phenomena we have not understood, or which are not even well grounded appearances. Nature as an intelligible domain, as a possible object of inquiry, discourse, and understanding, can appear only insofar as we subject it to that condition.

Thus Descartes and Leibniz in fact concern themselves more with the project of determining the constitutive principles of domains of discourse and inquiry than they did with focusing the lens of intuitive insight on reality itself.[5] The deep difference between them and Kant lies elsewhere. And in respect of this difference, I shall urge, Davidson is with the classical rationalists against Kant. Moreover, it is for this reason that Davidson's *a priori* principles can be seen to represent a claim to substantial knowledge.

Interlude: Cartesianism about the physical, Leibnizianism about the mental, and Spinozism about their relation

Before diving into these deep waters, I want to take a little time to explore some comparatively shallow, but also comparatively substantive, affinities between Davidson and the classical rationalists. Davidson is, to a first approximation, a Cartesian about the physical. For Descartes, the physical world is a closed system, in the sense that nothing outside of it can add or subtract anything relevant to its physical description. It is *necessarily* closed, in that we can know this *a priori*: a physical system is, for him, a system subject to a kind of complete mathematical description. For this reason, we can know *a priori* that whatever influence the non-physical (e.g., the mental) has on the world must not alter the quantities represented in the complete mathematical description that constitutes the physical. All of this characterizes Davidson's views as well. The physical domain for him is *necessarily* closed, else it could not be described by the strict laws to whose in-principle formulability we are committed through our practices of causal explanation, and through our commitment to the notions of physical objects and real change. Indeed, the closure of the physical and the laws/cause thesis amount to the same thing, given that physical vocabulary just is the vocabulary in which strict laws governing events can be formulated. Moreover, we can know from this that even if (even though) the mental influences the physical, that influence does not violate closure. This operates as a constraint, for Davidson, as for Descartes, on how we must conceive the mental.

A further affinity between Descartes and Davidson on the nature of the physical can be seen in their contrast with Leibniz. For Leibniz, but not for Descartes, the physical may be grasped through final causes, and is, indeed, a domain ordered according to purpose. Thus we can know not only that nature is governed by laws, but also that these laws are, as an instantiation of perfect reason, maximally beautiful, in producing the greatest variety of effects by the most economical means possible. Descartes does not deny that God had purposes in his creation, or the moral perfection, hence beauty, thereof. But he does deny that our physical theorizing should be guided by these facts, since we cannot possibly understand God's purposes or what moral perfection entails, and since thinking otherwise led the scholastics wrong at nearly every turn. Hence the yield of our physical descriptions – the complete mathematical description of the world – need not be constrained by the requirements of beauty, elegance, or similar properties that would characterize a morally perfect creation. Any physics we actually devise will be simple purely in virtue of the fact that we can understand it, and our understanding is limited. But this does not follow from the *a priori* constraints proper to the idea of the physical itself. Davidson is again like Descartes here: there is no hint in Davidson of the idea that the vocabulary and laws of a final physics need be elegant, simple, economical, or in any way beautiful. They must simply be exceptionless. He does not deny our cognitive need for simplicity in our theorizing, nor do I know of any place where he expressly denies (or affirms, as Kant does) that our scientific thinking is generally informed by the principle of sufficient reason; after all, we want not just explanation, but explanations with explanatory and predictive power for us. But the elegance and tractability these practical constraints produce in our scientific theories is likely to keep them from being physical theories proper. Thus Davidson says "the more precise and general our laws are, the less likely it is that we will be in a position to employ them in predicting the outcomes of ordinary actions or the weather" (Davidson 1995: 276). What we call a change will depend on our practical interests, but insofar as we formulate generalities that allow useful predictions with respect to these changes, they will not be statements of physical laws. Where our theorizing has no practical aim whatever, we can "in principle . . . seek laws that have no exceptions" (Davidson 1995: 276). But there is no guarantee that we can find them, and no guarantee that their formulation would be simple, or even possible in practice, as it is possible in principle. For Leibniz, the physical world is literally made for our understanding; in Descartes and Davidson, it is not.

Descartes recognized the mental as a *sui generis* domain marked by reason, which is in principle not a possible property of extension. Beyond this, he had little positive to say about reason. His main concern was to delimit the mental from the physical in a way that made possible a mathematical description of the latter. But Descartes' recognition of the *sui generis* rational character of the mental has been largely ignored in the tradition that is his legacy, which has instead tended to treat the mental as some kind of non-physical domain nonetheless subject to mechanistic laws like those that govern the physical. This is the most general version of the sort of category mistake of which Ryle (1949) accuses post-Cartesian thinking. Davidson does not make this mistake. Indeed, his views of the mind and of mental phenomena have more in common with Leibniz's account of the physical than they do with the views bequeathed to us in Descartes' legacy. Leibniz, as we saw, thought that the physical world must be a prod-uct of a perfect rational will and power, and he thought our thinking about it must necessarily reflect this. The creation, then, is and must be seen as a product of agency. Thus, upon seeing a phenomenon, we can assume that the creator wanted to bring it about, believed that by acting on a particular conception of the means to do this, and that he acted on that conception. If we come across a phenomenon we do not or cannot see as the product of a knowing, rational will, this reflects either a limitation of our understanding, rather than a failure of perfection in the agent, or that the phenomenon was mere illusion, rather than an incomprehensible surd. This strategy applies the model for interpreting the significance of intentional action to phenom-ena generally, excepting that in the case of the perfect creator, the assumptions of maximal rationality, intelligence, and benevolence of intention are guaranteed by his divine nature. Davidson is not a theist, nor, as we saw, does he think the world is in general created on a rational plan; phenomena are not generally meaningful. There is no echo in physical theory of the rationality and coherence of phenomena characterizable in vocabulary suitable to agency and action. But the criteria used for interpreting those phenomena that are meaningful – actions, including linguistic actions – are similar to those Leibniz exploits in interpreting creation as a whole. But since Davidson, unlike Leibniz, does not make the intentional the model for the nat-ural, our inability to understand a given phenomenon as rational need not signal either a limit in us or that the phenomenon is mere illusion; it might signal that the phenomenon was real but meaningless, or less than fully meaningful. Irrationality in nature is impossible for Leibniz, given the perfection of the creator. Perfect rationality is an ideal that must be actualized in nature. Irrationality in agency is not impossible for Davidson, but it cannot be the rule, and requires extraordinary explanation. In this sense, Davidson is, to a first approximation, a Leibnizian in his thinking about the mental.

Recall that Descartes' views about the physical allowed him to hold that the mental interacts with the physical. So long as it does not alter the quantity of motion, the closure of the physical will not be violated. But as we saw, given developments of physical theory, this was an unstable position. Given the demands of closure, some other view of the relation of the mental to the physical is required. Spinoza proposed one. Rather than taking mind and body to be distinct substances, Spinoza treated them as distinct attributes of a single substance. An attribute is that "which intellect perceives of a substance as constituting its essence" (Spinoza 1985: 408; E1DIV). We think of substance through its attributes, then. So to ascribe ideas to substance is to perceive it as thinking, and to ascribe extension to it is to perceive it as body. In this sense, mind and body are just different ways of describing the same thing. Modifica-tions of substance are conceived under one or the other attribute, so an idea is a modification conceived under the attribute thought, and a motion is a modification conceived under the attribute extension. Ideas, that is, modifications conceived under the attribute thought, are token identical to bodies, that is, to modifications conceived under the attribute extension.

Davidson, too, sees the relationship of mental to physical events as one of token identity. This follows from the two principles we have seen, together with the claim that the mental is causal. The laws/cause thesis states that any events that figure in causal relations will have a physical description. The principle of the rationality of the mental, on Davidson's view, entails that the mental is anomalous: mental descriptions of events cannot figure in strict laws. Davidson argued for the claim that the mental is anomalous in various ways at various times, but the fundamental reason the mental is anomalous stems from its constitutive rationality. Since the mental description of the beliefs and desires pair that figure in mental generalizations must successfully rationalize an action to which it is antecedent, that description cannot in general be stated in advance of and independently from knowledge of that action. Strict laws, on the other hand, allow us "to tell in advance whether the condition holds" (Davidson 1980b: 233). Thus strict laws and their instantiations cannot contain mental description. Yet if the events referred to by such descriptions are to be causal, the same events must be describable in such a way that they do figure in strict laws (i.e., in physical vocabulary). Thus a conclusion strikingly like Spinoza's own: the very same events that are mental must also be physical.

This similarity has often been noticed, and indeed Davidson himself has pointed it out. But it would be unwise to overemphasize it, for there are serious differences. For one thing, Spinoza is a panpsychist, while Davidson holds only that some physical events, namely, those with descriptions under which they play a role in action explanation, are mental. Moreover, for Davidson, causal statements are extensional: the truth-value does not depend upon how the events it refers to are described; thus it can be true to say that a belief, for example, caused a bodily motion. Spinoza, on the other hand, given his views of the relation between causation and conception and his view that conception is always under an attribute, denies that there can be cross-attribute causation. Thus the truth of causal statements is not extensional; it depends upon how the modifications it refers to are described. The reason we take it that our ideas can cause bodily movements is that we conceive the modifications that are respectively a cause and an effect under two different attributes. This much Davidson agrees with. But for Davidson the resultant causal judgment may be true, and for Spinoza it cannot be. Another crucial difference is that Spinoza does not see the mental as rationally constituted. His parallelism precludes the sort of view Davidson holds, in which the nomological character of the physical coexists with the anomalous domain of the mental. In fact, Spinoza's accounts of psychological phenomena are just as mechanistic in nature as are his accounts of physical phenomena. The similarity between Davidson and Spinoza pretty well ends with the dual aspect token identity doctrine.

Classical Rationalism or Kantian Transcendentalism?

We have seen that, in Davidson's philosophy, the *a priori* survives the death of analyticity by taking the form of constitutive principles that make domains of discourse and phenomena intelligible. This, I have argued, does not suffice to ally him more with Kantian transcendentalism than with classical rationalism. As a final preliminary to a discussion of the deep difference between the classical rationalists and Kant, I should address briefly an issue that seems to, and may in fact, divide Davidson from both. The classical rationalists and Kant are commonly viewed as epistemological foundationalists, who hold that our knowledge of the world rests entirely upon a basis whose secure epistemic status is both entirely independent of that which rests upon it and entirely responsible for the epistemic status thereof. Davidson, however, rejects all species of foundationalism, including, explicitly, rationalistic (Davidson 2004b: 17). Whether the epistemological positions of the classical rationalists and Kant are in fact foundationalist according to this familiar picture, and exactly how to conceive the various grounding relations that may exist between *a priori* constitutive principles, perceptual reports, and theoretical empirical judgments are interesting and very complex questions that would take us well beyond the bounds of this chapter. For present purposes, I want simply to point out that, however the classical rationalists and Kant may see the matter, the constitutive *a priori* principles I have identified in Davidson's philosophy need not be conceived as foundations in any traditional or pernicious sense. Davidson's objections to foundationalism are focused on the ideas that our knowledge "depends upon indubitable beliefs, or upon something given to the mind which is impervious to doubt, [or] that the contents of our beliefs may be in principle independent of what lies outside of us" (Davidson 2004b: 17). But the claim that his principles are *a priori* requires no such ideas. First, we need not take them to be certain or indubitable in the way such foundations, both rationalist and empiricist, purport to be; dubitability and necessity are mutually consistent. Second, we may accept that these principles merit their epistemic status in virtue of the way they cohere with and help to make intelligible our further beliefs and practices, including empirical practices involving perceptual judgment. Indeed, constitutive principles, since they serve to constitute domains of inquiry and phenomena, could claim no degree of warrant whatsoever independently of the intelligibility and objectivity of the discourses and phenomena they help constitute. Thus their justification is in a sense a matter of their coherence with our other beliefs, just as Davidson's coherentism (see Davidson 1986: 310) would have it. This does not mean that such principles are justified *a posteriori*, on the basis of the content of experience. They are justified independently of experience, not in the sense that experience or other knowledge is irrelevant to their epistemic status, but in the sense of being warranted in the light of any and all possible experience or knowledge that might be revealed in the discourse and phenomena underwritten and enabled by these very principles. The classical rationalists and Kant, in their own ways, may or may not have been foundationalists in the sense Davidson rejects; but rationalism, understood as a commitment to substantial *a priori* knowledge, does not require such foundationalism.

Let us return to our main thread. To see where classical rationalism and Kantian transcendentalism differ deeply, consider the possibility of a skeptical challenge to the idea that Davidson's constitutive principles genuinely represent substantial *a priori* truths. A skeptic might concede, on the basis of Davidson's arguments, that if there are any causal relations in the world, then they are describable in a way that instantiates a law, and that if there are any physical objects in the world, then they are subject to generation, alteration, and destruction according to laws. But she may deny that this gives us any reason to suppose that there are in the world about which we think any relations or objects genuinely answering to those concepts. Perhaps events are in fact related only "shmausally," according to non-strict quasi-regularities; and perhaps objects are merely "shmysical," their doings, undoings, and shmanges governed only by shmlaws. Similarly, she might agree that any phenomena answering to our mental concept must conform to the constitutive rationality of the mental. But she might deny that this gives us grounds for supposing that anything in the world conforms to those concepts. Perhaps there are only shmeliefs, shmesires, and shmactions. The same sort of skeptical challenge can of course be formulated in connection with the classical rationalist *a priori* and Kantian transcendental *a priori* principles. What deeply divides Kant and the classical rationalists is their respective postures towards this kind of challenge. In my view, it is here that we can see how Davidson's thinking is more rationalistic than it is Kantian.

Kant's entire critical project may be seen as a response to the sort of skeptical worry I have just articulated. Kant sought, in his Copernican turn, to defend the possibility of knowledge of reality by restricting the legitimate scope of our knowledge claims to the world insofar as it conforms to the conditions of our cognition. Transcendentally, that is, independently of the conditions of our possible cognition, the world we know is idea, not real. It has no transcendent being whatever. Empirically, that is, considered in terms of the conditions of our cognition, it is fully real. The response to the skeptic here is that we can know that our *a priori* principles have application to the world to which we refer them because that world just is the world insofar as it conforms to the conditions on the possibility of our knowledge. According to Kant, classical rationalists – "dogmatic rationalists," he would call them[6] – are transcendental realists: they believe that objects considered independently of the conditions of our cognition have the same sort of being, are real and real in the same way, as they are when considered in terms of the conditions of our cognition. This is not so much an express claim rationalists make or an article of faith, as it is an implicit confidence revealed in their comportment towards philosophical inquiry. Because of this, they do not see the skeptic's challenge, or feel it as genuine. Therein, for Kant, lies their dogmatism.

It is very hard to see Kant's strategy of securing our empirical knowledge as successful without conceiving empirical reality as some sort of *product* of our own power cognitive faculties – without, that is, seeing empirical realism as a kind of idealism in spite of itself, and its constitutive principles as principles of construction. And while there is much in Kant to support this kind of reading, there is no hint of it anywhere in Davidson. Throughout both the Aesthetic and the Analytic of the *Critique of Pure Reason*, Kant emphasizes the role played by the *a priori* forms of intuition and the synthetic operations of the understanding in shaping the matter given in sensibility into contents of experience suitable for the application of our basic concepts. All experience of the world must be in time, and time is an *a priori* form of intuition, into which we place the unsynthesized matter of sensory impressions. Experience of an outer world must be spatial, but space too is a form of intuition lying *a priori* in the mind. It is "in us," he says (A 370). The very being of objects, however ephemeral, as unified bearers of distinct properties, seems to result from our own activity. "The combination (conjunction) of a manifold in general can never come to us through the senses" (B 129). Synthesis is combination, and "we can represent nothing as combined in the object without having previously combined it ourselves . . . Combination is . . . not given through objects but can be executed only by the subject itself" (B 129–30). This essential synthesis "is an act of the spontaneity of the power of representation, and, since one must call the latter understanding, in distinction from sensibility, all combination . . . is an action of the understanding" (B 129–30). The very objects that appear in experience and of which we judge, then, are products of the activity of our cognitive faculty of understanding.

The idea that the world of which we think is a product of our cognitive apparatus may leave no room for doubt that it conforms to our thinking, but it certainly leaves room for doubt that it is real in the sense required to answer the skeptic's challenge satisfactorily. For it compromises the independence of the world, by compromising the idea central to objectivity and exploited by the skeptic, that, at least for the most part, the world is as it is independently of what we happen to think about it. A world we construct by our cognitive faculties lacks this independence; it is ideal, not real.

The threat of idealism clearly exercised Kant himself long after the publication of the first *Critique*. The second edition's massively reworked "Transcendental Deduction of the pure concepts of the understanding" may be seen as an attempt to avoid the problem, and the Refutation of Idealism added to the second edition, and expressing an entirely new line of thought, is directed squarely at it. As Guyer (1987) documents, Kant continued to rework the argument of the refutation until well after the publication of the second edition. He cannot have thought the charge of idealism entirely idle. What is crucial to note here is that the threat represents a challenge to the idea that our constitutive *a priori* knowledge is substantial, in the sense of being knowledge of reality, and consequently of making intelligible real domains of inquiry and discourse. The threat arises in Kant as a result of his apparent constructivist response to the skeptic's challenge that the world about which we think may not be one to which our *a priori* constitutive principles apply. But there is no hint of such a constructivism in Davidson. This suggests that his posture towards that challenge is rather different.

But is it like that of the classical rationalist? To better understand their posture *vis-à-vis* this sort of skeptical challenge, it is important to realize that the pair of options Kant articulates in his diagnosis and solution of the same doubts, transcendental realism and transcendental idealism, were not really present as such to the rationalists. The idea that woke Kant from his own rationalistic dogmatic slumbers and motivated transcendental idealism was one he shared, rather, with the empiricists. This is the idea that our encounter with the world – the world with which we interact – is mediated epistemically by sensible representations before the mind, of which we are immediately aware and of whose content we can be certain, but to whose content our own modes of cognition make an ineliminable contribution.

To see the interdependence of transcendental idealism and representationalism, consider Kant's diagnosis of how transcendental idealism inevitably succumbs to a skeptical empirical idealism. The transcendental realist regards "outer appearances (if their reality is conceded) as things in themselves, which would exist independently of us and our sensibility and thus would also be outside us according to pure concepts of the understanding" (A 369). The transcendental realist, however, is forced into empirical idealism, on Kant's view, since he finds that "all our representations of sense are insufficient to make their reality certain." He must then suppose that knowledge of the reality of things must owe its epistemic status to representations of sense. And again, transcendental realists fall into the embarrassment of empirical idealism, because "even with our best consciousness of our representation of these things, it is obviously far from certain that if the representation exists, then the object corresponding to it would exist" (A 371). Here too, entitlement to claim the reality of things outside us is essentially mediated by consciousness of representations.

Thus the idea that our access to the empirical objects of which we think is essentially through sensible representations is crucial to the claim that transcendental realism cannot avoid empirical idealism. But for this claim, there is no need to make Kant's move to transcendental idealism, and to the problematic constructivism according to which empirical objects owe their reality to the constitutive operation of our cognitive faculties. But if we reject the representationalism according to which sensory representation is the essential epistemic medium through which our thinking about the world proceeds, then the basis for the slippage between our thoughts of how objects are and how they are in themselves vanishes.

The Refutation of (Transcendental) Idealism

Davidson rejects such representationalism. For him, sensibility in the form of sensory representations given transparently to the mind plays no essential epistemic role in our thinking. He does not deny that sensation exists; rather he denies that it has or could have any force to ground our empirical beliefs. According to Davidson, "the relation between a sensation and a belief cannot be logical, since sensations are not beliefs or other propositional attitudes" (Davidson 1986: 311). Similarly, he says that sensation that engenders belief cannot literally be construed as information, since "the notion of information . . . applies in a non-metaphorical way only to the engendered beliefs" (Davidson 1986: 311). The emphasis on propositional attitudes here is a bit unfortunate, for surely logically structured entities other than propositional attitudes or their objects can have logical relations to beliefs, and constitute information. So the general point is better put by saying that sensations cannot bear logical relations to beliefs because they have no logical structure (see Manning 2003: 361–2). Be that as it may, on Davidson's view, the relation between sensation and belief is causal, rather than logical or epistemic. "Sensations cause beliefs and in this sense the basis or ground for beliefs. But a causal explanation of a belief does not show how or why the belief in question is justified" (Davidson 1986: 311). "Of course there are causal intermediaries. What we must guard against are epistemic intermediaries" (Davidson 1986: 312).

In significant part, the tendency to feel that the epistemic credentials of our claims to knowledge must be based on sensory episodes stems from the peculiar certainty apparently possessed by first-person reports of our own mental states. Kant himself takes it as a signal virtue of transcendental idealism that it allows us to have empirical knowledge "without going beyond mere self-consciousness and assuming more than the certainty of representations in me" (A 370). Descartes is often also cited as having insisted that all empirical knowledge must depend upon our perfect knowledge of the contents of our own minds. But there is a crucial difference. Descartes thought that specifically sensory consciousness was so confused, so unclear and indistinct, as barely to count as real. Our clear and distinct ideas are not sensory. This does not, for him, debar empirical knowledge, as it does for the empiricists and Kant. Knowledge of the empirical world, he thinks, indeed, knowledge of the whole of physical nature, can be based on our clear and distinct perception of *a priori* principles. Davidson does not deny that we have an epistemic authority over the contents of our own minds that we lack with respect to the contents of the world and other people's minds. But his diagnosis of this fact does not depend upon positing objects, sensory or other, as transparently present to our minds. Instead, first-person authority stems from the fact that interpreting someone as acting, hence as having beliefs and desires, and in the case of linguistic actions, as meaning something by their words, essentially depends upon our presuming that they know what they think and mean. Though an agent may in any particular case be mistaken about what she believes (or means by her words), "what is impossible is that she should be wrong most of the time." Absent a presumption of self-knowledge, "there would be nothing for an interpreter to interpret" (Davidson 2001b: 38). But this presumption does not require us to posit mental contents, sensory or otherwise, as objects with which they are acquainted in some more perfect way than they are with the objects of empirical belief.

Absent the idea that our judgments about the world must be epistemically grounded in sensory representations, it is hard to feel the pressure that leads from transcendental realism to empirical idealism. For if sensory representation is not a lens through which alone our cognition of empirical objects is possible, then the threat that that lens provides only a distorted view of what lies beyond is idle. This way of putting the point draws attention to another related way in which Davidson has rejected the Kantian posture. For it highlights the idea shared by empiricists and Kant alike that that with which we are immediately in touch in our thought and experience is some joint product resulting from the schematizing operations of our cognitive capacities on some utterly unschematized (not to say utterly unstructured) content.[7] Davidson rejects this idea, too, as ultimately unintelligible. In his much discussed "On the Very Idea of a Conceptual Scheme" (1984b), Davidson argues that it makes no sense to talk of a scheme as set over against content unless it makes sense to say that there might in principle be alternative ways to schematize the same content. But he denies that we can make sense of such alternatives. This argument proceeds by way of an identification (quite controversial) of schemes with languages. Since what can be said in one of a pair of inter-translatable languages can be said in the other, genuinely alternative schemes would be languages that are not inter-translatable. Yet, according to Davidson, we cannot have any basis for taking something to be a language unless we can find much truth in it, and this requires that we be able to translate it into our own language, to interpret it as expressing things we can express in our language. Thus, "given the underlying methodology of interpretation, we could not be in a position to judge that others had concepts or beliefs radically different from our own" (Davidson 1984b: 197). So there can be no evidence that something is a language that isn't also evidence that its speakers' scheme is not significantly different from ours. The upshot is that we cannot make good sense of the idea that there is some content which is, as it were, neutral between our own way of conceptualizing it and other possible ways. But if we are not, in our thinking, schematizing some unschematized content, then it surely cannot be that the way the world appears to us in our thinking is the product of our thinking it. It cannot be that our thoughts, if true, are true only because the world that makes them true was made by us. There would be no sense to the claim that the constitutive principles of our thinking are in fact principles of construction.

What we are in touch with in our thinking, for Davidson, is neither some sensory given on which our thoughts must be based, nor some product of our own devise for them to be about. But without either of these two possibilities to exploit, it is hard to see how the skeptic can motivate a doubt as to the applicability of our constitutive *a priori* principles to an objective world. The rejection of schemes and epistemic intermediaries is, according to Davidson, "an unmediated touch with the familiar objects whose antics make our sentences and opinions true or false" (Davidson 1984b: 198). Unmediated touch without construction: this is realism of a rationalist kind, without the presuppositions that give a point to calling it transcendental.

Rationalism Full-Blown

Throughout this chapter I have spoken of rationalism largely in terms of its commitment to the existence of substantial *a priori* truth. But full-blown rationalism is committed to more than this. It is committed to the view that all of our knowledge of the world, whatever its source, depends ultimately for its epistemic status upon this *a priori* knowledge. Davidson agrees.

A third *a priori* principle, the principle of the radical interpretability of content, flows from the rationality of the mental. According to this principle, the contents of agents' beliefs and desires, and the semantic contents of their words, are those contents they would be ascribed in the course of radical interpretation. This principle ensures that the mental states of believing and desiring ascribed to agents actually satisfy the condition laid down by the principle of the constitutive rationality of the mental. A detailed discussion of Davidson's account of radical interpretation and its consequences for epistemology and metaphysics would be out of place here. But I want to expose enough of it to reveal just how full-blown Davidson's rationalism is. Radically interpreting a speaker involves coming to understand her propositional attitudes, thus coming to understand her as rational, and coming to understand her language as well (see Davidson 1984c, 1984d). This cannot be done without applying the methodological principle of charity, according to which the sentences held true by a speaker are to be treated as in fact true when possible. Hence the principle of the radical interpretability of content ensures not just that speakers are rational, but that they are in the main correct about the world.[8] For this reason, coming to understand a language from the standpoint of radical interpretation is part and parcel of learning about the world. We come to knowledge of the world through a grasp of language and we come to this through the application of a conception of the mental essentially in accord with the constitutive principle of rationality. One cannot be a knower independently of language mastery, and language mastery is a matter of radical interpretability, in that language masters are both radically interpretable and capable of such interpretation themselves. But what can interpret and be interpreted is, *a priori*, in conformity with the constitutive rationality of the mental. The application of the principle is an *a priori* condition on all knowing.

We saw above that Davidson treats sensory experience as a merely causal and not epistemic intermediary between world and thought. Nonetheless, while the causes of belief do not justify them, "causality plays an indispensable role in determining the content of what we say and believe" (Davidson 1986: 317). Radical interpretation must begin with the ascription of meaning to occasion sentences – sentences to which a speaker's assent comes and goes with changes in the passing scene – and of contents to the beliefs such assent manifests. There is no choice but to interpret such sentences "according to the events and objects in the world that cause them to be held true" (Davidson 1986: 317). In Davidson's later writings, this theme takes center stage. The very possibility of thought depends upon speaker and interpreter triangulating to determine the common cause of their thoughts. "Without sharing of reactions to common stimuli, thought and speech would have no particular content – that is, no content at all. It takes two points of view to give location to the cause of a thought, and thus to define its content" (Davidson 2001c: 212). Moreover, unless these causal identifications are in the main correct, interpretation will fail, and so will our understanding and claims to knowledge. But as we saw above, one can have reason to accept a singular causal statement only if one knows that there is a description of it which instantiates a strict law; such knowledge rests on *a priori* knowledge of the laws/cause thesis.

Thus Davidson puts our knowledge of the two principles at the core of the possibility of our grasp of language. But our grasp of language just is our way of knowing the world. Language is, in his terms, "the organ of propositional perception" (Davidson 1997). Thus there can be no knowledge apart from our grasp and implementation, however implicit, of these *a priori* truths. I began by citing Quine's rejection of the analytic/synthetic distinction as apparently undercutting the possibility of rationalism. The irony is that this same rejection paved the way to the recognition that there is no distinction to be made between coming to understand a language and coming to know the world, the very recognition in the light of which Davidson's *a priori* constitutive principles can be seen to lie at the base of all of our knowledge.

Notes

1   Quine's views disentitle him to the use of the term "experience" in anything like a traditional sense. Only beliefs, on his view, can conflict with one another in a way that motivates revision of the web, and the only thing that marks a belief as "experiential," that locates it toward the periphery of the metaphorical web of belief, is its relatively high probability of being revised in the light of conflict with other beliefs. This, for Quine, is entirely a psychological matter, and certainly does not depend logically upon whether a belief is, for example, inferential or cognitively spontaneous, or accompanied or occasioned by some sensory episode, or anything of the like. Hence the scare quotes in my text.

2   I omit here any discussion of logical truths, for Quine's holism does not even permit him to give these a special epistemic or modal status. Supposing that logical truths do have special epistemic status, say, in virtue of their being tautologies, hence empty of content, the rationalist would be one who holds that there are unrevisable non-logical truths.

3   In a recent discussion of the *a priori* in post-Quinean philosophy, Michael Friedman points out that the undifferentiated holism Quine adopts is neither mandatory nor in conformity

with actual epistemic practice as revealed in the history of science. Some elements of our web of belief display an asymmetric dependence upon others, in the sense that the latter constitute the former as intelligible. However, Friedman evidently accepts Quine's idea that no claims are wholly unrevisable, and hence accepts only a relativized *a priori*. But there is no hint in Davidson that the constitutive principles he adopts represent optional ways of thinking, non-necessary, however deep.

4 That the laws of such a final physics might be ultimately and irreducibly probabilistic does not, Davidson argues, compromise the laws/cause thesis. In brief, the probabilities themselves, which operate over states precisely defined, admit of no exceptions.

5 For a reading of the developments in rationalism leading to Kant as an increasing self-awareness of the extent to which reason, under the idea of the "mathematical," gives its own laws to the phenomena thereby constituting them as intelligible, see Heidegger (1967).

6 Kant typically has Leibniz and Leibnizians in mind; the case of Descartes is trickier. But in light of the blatant circularity of Descartes' efforts to certify the principle of clear and distinct perception, it is plausible that those efforts are for appearances only, designed rhetorically to persuade readers of a skeptical bent.

7 It is by no means trivial to capture exactly how one should conceive the respective roles of scheme and content in the Kantian framework. This in large measure owes to an ambiguity in Kant's use of the term "intuition," which he sometimes uses to refer to sheer, utterly unsynthesized sensible givens, and sometimes to refer to synthesized proto-conceptual representations suitable for judgment. For a penetrating discussion of Kant's two senses of intuition and his need for them, see Sellars (1968). McDowell (1998) offers a reading of Kant intended, in part, to absolve him of this charge of equivocation, as well as the charge of constructivist idealism, by denying that sheer, non-conceptual content plays any role whatever in Kant's account of experience and judgment. This is simply too hard to square with Kant's text, and moreover seems to turn transcendental idealism into the utterly bland idea that we cannot cognize the being of objects independently of their meeting the conditions of our cognition, an idea with which the most dogmatic rationalist could agree. McDowell shares with Davidson the anti-representationalism that I argue undercuts the motivation to invoke the spicier sense of transcendental idealism, but it seems wrong to me to impose it on Kant.

8 In a perceived appreciation of the extent of Davidson' rationalism, Thomas Nagel (1999) points out the *a priori* character of Davidson's anti-skeptical arguments, amusingly contrasting Descartes' "je pense, donc je suis" with Davidson's own, much stronger "je pense, donc je sais." Without actually rejecting Davidson's view, Nagel says "it is absolutely amazing that there should be an *a priori* argument which proves that *this* set of propositions, which I believe . . . is largely true" (Nagel 1999: 202). Davidson, in response, points out that the proof is not entirely *a priori*, since the "Je suis" is not *a priori*, and "since it depends on the fact that I have just the beliefs I do" (Davidson 1999: 209). Nonetheless, the ground for supposing one does have the beliefs one has essentially involves our ability to interpret ourselves, and this depends upon our grasp and application of *a priori* principles.

References and Further Reading

Davidson, D. (1980a). *Essays on Actions and Events*. Oxford: Clarendon Press.
—— (1980b). Psychology as philosophy. In Davidson (1980a), pp. 229–39.
—— (1980c). Causal relations. In Davidson (1980a), pp. 149–62.
—— (1980d). Actions, reasons and causes. In Davidson (1980a), pp. 3–19.
—— (1980e). Mental events. In Davidson (1980a), pp. 207–27.

—— (1984a). *Essays on Truth and Interpretation*. Oxford: Clarendon Press.

—— (1984b). On the very idea of a conceptual scheme. In Davidson (1984a), pp. 183–98.

—— (1984c). Radical interpretation. In Davidson (1984a), pp. 125–39.

—— (1984d). Belief and the basis of meaning. In Davidson (1984a), pp. 141–54.

—— (1986). A coherence theory of truth and knowledge. In E. Lepore (ed.), *Truth and Interpretation: Perspectives on the Philosophy of Donald Davidson* (pp. 307–19). Oxford: Blackwell.

—— (1995). Laws and cause. *Dialectica*, 48, 263–79.

—— (1997). Seeing through language. In J. Preston (ed.), *Thought and Language* (pp. 15–27). Cambridge: Cambridge University Press.

—— (1999). Reply to Nagel. In L. E. Hahn (ed.), *The Philosophy of Donald Davidson* (pp. 207–8). La Salle, IL: Open Court.

—— (2001a). *Subjective, Intersubjective, Objective*. Oxford: Clarendon Press.

—— (2001b). Knowing one's own mind. In Davidson (2001a), pp. 15–38.

—— (2001c). Three varieties of knowledge. In Davidson (2001a), pp. 205–20.

—— (2004a). *Problems of Rationality*. Oxford: Clarendon Press.

—— (2004b). The problem of objectivity. In Davidson (2004a), pp. 3–18.

—— (2004c). Could there be a science of rationality? In Davidson (2004a), pp. 117–34.

Descartes, R. (1985). *Principles of Philosophy*. In J. Cottingham, R. Stoothoff, and D. Murdoch (eds. and trans.), *The Philosophical Writings of Descartes*. Cambridge: Cambridge University Press.

Friedman, M. (2000). Transcendental philosophy and *a priori* knowledge. In P. Boghossian and C. Peacocke (eds.), *New Essays on the a priori* (pp. 367–83). Oxford: Clarendon Press.

Goodman, N. (1965). *Fact, Fiction and Forecast*. Indianapolis, IN: Bobbs-Merrill.

Guyer, P. (1987). *Kant and the Claims of Knowledge*. Cambridge: Cambridge University Press.

Heidegger, M. (1967). *What Is A Thing?* Chicago: Henry Regnery.

Kant, I. (1997). *Critique of Pure Reason*. Cambridge: Cambridge University Press.

Leibniz, G. (1998a). *Discourse on Method*. In R. S. Woolhouse and R. Francks (trans. and eds.), *G. W. Leibniz: Philosophical Texts* (pp. 54–89). Oxford: Oxford University Press.

—— (1998b). Principles of Nature and Grace. In R. S. Woolhouse and R. Francks (trans. and eds.), *G. W. Leibniz: Philosophical Texts* (pp. 258–66). Oxford: Oxford University Press.

McDowell, J. (1998). Having the world in view: Kant, Sellars, and intentionality. *Journal of Philosophy*, 95, 9.

Manning, R. (2003). Interpretation, reasons, and facts. *Inquiry*, 46, 346–76.

Nagel, T. (1999). Davidson's new *cogito*. In L. E. Hahn (ed.), *The Philosophy of Donald Davidson* (pp. 194–206). La Salle, IL: Open Court.

Quine, W. V. O. (1953). Two dogmas of empiricism. In *From a Logical Point of View* (pp. 20–46). Cambridge, MA: Harvard University Press.

Ryle, G. (1949). *The Concept of Mind*. London: Hutchinson.

Sellars, W. (1968). *Science and Metaphysics: Variation on Kantian Themes*. London: Routledge and Kegan Paul.

Spinoza, B. (1985). *Ethics*. In E. Curley (trans.), *The Collected Works of Spinoza, Vol. 1*. Princeton, NJ: Princeton University Press.

Index